The Nature and Scope of Individual Rights

The Nature and Scope of Individual Rights

Emerging Debates in Constitutional Law

Robin D. Barnes

Carolina Academic Press
Durham, North Carolina

Library of Congress Cataloging in Publication Data

Barnes, Robin D.
The Nature and scope of individual rights : emerging debates in constitutional law / by Robin D. Barnes.
p. cm.
Includes bibliographical references and index.
ISBN 10: 0-89089-106-0 ISBN 13: 978-0-89089-106-3 (alk. paper)
1. Constitutional law--United States--Philosophy. 2. Civil rights--United States. I. Title.

KF4550.B275 2007
342.7308'5--dc22

2007018551

Carolina Academic Press
700 Kent Street
Durham, NC 27701
Telephone (919) 489-7486
Fax (919) 493-5668
www.cap-press.com

Printed in the United States of America

To Denise and Muhammad—
for their courage and honor

Table of Contents

Dedication v

Table of Cases xi

Acknowledgments xiii

Introduction xv

Excerpts from United States Constitution xvii

Part One
Pillars of the Fundamental Rights Debate

Chapter One Guiding Principles of the Great Social Compact 5

The Revolutionary Spirit—Necessity of Dissolving Political Bands 6
Impact of the Declaration of Independence 11

Chapter Two Justifying Rules of Law & Monitoring Legal Institutions 19

Judicial Independence 20
Reason & the Rule of Law 22
Reason in Legal Academia 26
Critique of Legal Education 27
Regulating Members of the Bench 30
The Role of the Chief Justice 33

Chapter Three Autonomy, Bodily Integrity & Our Right to Die 43

Organ Donation 45
Gametes, Concepti & Reproductive Organs 51
Persistent Vegetative States & Assisted Suicide 55
Additional Commentary on the Suicide Debate 70

Chapter Four State Interests in Matters of Life & Death 73

Capital Punishment 73
U.S. Military Conscription 80
Abortion on Demand & Emergency Contraception 88

Part Two
Unitary Families, Alternative Families & the Limits of Personal Liberty

Chapter Five Construing Sovereign Rights of Unitary Families 97

The Realm of Personal Liberty 97
Interests of Unwed Fathers & Couples 107
Statutory Rape & Controversial Cases 121

Chapter Six Post-Modern Notions of Love Without Limits 137

Evolving Theories of Social Freedom 137
Free Love Grows Up 141
Polyamory, Polygamy & Multi-Parent Families 148

Chapter Seven Sexual Offenses: Consent Implied & Denied under Criminal Statutes 161

Evolution of Marital (Acquaintance) Rape Law 161
The Early Role of Consent in Conjugal Rights Theory 161
Incest, Recovered Memories & Child Sexual Abuse 173
Incest Defined in Two State Statutes 177
Family Nudity 179
What We Remember—Recovered Memories of Incest 180
Child Protection, Technology & the First Amendment 186
Murder, Attempted Murder & Animal Rights 192

Part Three
Claiming Individual Rights under a System of Group Privileges & Immunities

Chapter Eight The Racial Divide & American Identity 203

The Nation's Legacy of Group Rights [& Wrongs] 203
Nazis, Race & International Public Relations 215
Apartheid in the Courthouses 217
Race-Conscious Policies & Practices 219

Chapter Nine Sexual Orientation, Gender Identity & DNA 243

Transexuality, Intersexuality & Bisexuality 244
Discrimination Based on Sexual Orientation 251
Early Impact of Sexual Predator Registration Laws 261
Revisiting Marriage As a Fundamental Right 281

Chapter Ten Gendered Roles & Questions of Equality under the Law 293

Noble & Benign Roles 293
Women in the Military 304
Nuances of Gender Discrimination 312
Understanding Domesticity 317

Part Four
Information Privacy & the Role of Lawyers in the 21st Century

Chapter Eleven Civil Liberties, National Security & USA PATRIOT Act 325

Post-9/11 Privacy in the Workplace 330

Effects of Data Mining 336

One Nation under Surveillance 340

SMART Security 344

Chapter Twelve Legal Training & Responsibilities in the New Empire 349

Lawyers for Enron & the Catholic Church 349

Government Lawyers in the News 354

Future Role of Lawyers 362

Global Access to Justice 363

Imagine a Just World 367

Conclusion 373

Notes 375

Index 391

Table of Cases

Allen v. Farrow, 197 AD2d 327, 61 1 NYS2d 859 (1994), 381
Atkins v. Virginia, 536 U.S. 304 (2002), 79
Baehr v. Lewin, 74 Haw. 530 (1993), 385
Booth v. Maryland, 482 U.S. 496 (1987), 77, 379
Bowers v. Hardwick, 478 U.S. 186 (1986), 254, 273, 275, 385
Bradwell v. Illinois, 83 U.S. 130 (1872), 293, 385
Brown v. Board of Education of Topeka, Kansas, 347 U.S. 483 (1954),30, 206, 209
Carey v. Population Services International, 431 US 678 (1977), 120, 256
Clay, aka Ali v. United States, 403 U.S. 698 (1971), 83
Cruzan v. Missouri Department of Health, 497 U.S. 261 (1990), 55
Doe v. Kamehameha Schools, 441 F.3d 1029 (9th Cir. 2006), 219, 384
Dred Scott v. Sanford, 60 U.S. (19 How.) 393, 198, 208
Einstadt v. Baird, 405 US 438 (1972), 380
Frontiero v. Richardson, 411 U.S. 677 (1973), 385
Gay Alliance of Students v. Matthews, 544 F.2d 162 (4 th Cir. 1976), 250
Hecht v. Superior Court, 20 Cal Rptr 2d 275 (1993), 51, 115
Goodridge v. Dept. of Public Health, 798 N.E.2d 941 (Mass. 2003), 286
Griswold v. Connecticut, 381 US 479 (1965), 43, 120, 255+256, 378
Hollenbaugh v. Carnegie Free Library, 439 U.S. 1052 (1978), 116, 380
Johnson v. Johnson, 701 F.Supp 1363 (Ill. D. 1988), 183, 221, 381
Lawrence v. Texas, 123 S.Ct. 2472 (2003), 155, 243, 273, 385
Lee v. Oregon, 869 F.Supp. 1491(Or. D. 1994), 65
Lochner v. State of New York, 198 US 45 (1905), 89, 137, 302
Loving v. Commonwealth of Virginia, 388 U.S. 1 (1967), 102, 107, 289
Maynard v. Hill, 125 US 190 (1888), 104, 107
McClesky v. Kemp, 481 US 279 (1987), 75
Meyer v. State of Nebraska, 262 U.S. 390 (1923), 97
Michael H. et al. v. Gerald D., 491 U.S. 110 (1989), 108
Michael M. v. Superior Court of Sonoma, 450 U.S. 464 (1981), 380
Minor v. Happersett, 88 U.S. 162 (1874), 385
Moore v. City of East Cleveland, 431 US 494 (1977), 137
Morton v. Mancari, 417 U.S. 535 (1974), 221
Muller v. Oregon, 208 U.S. 412 (1908), 385
Murray v. State, 202 Miss. 849 (1948), 218
NAACP v. Alabama, 357 U.S. 449 (1958), 216
NAACP v. Hunt, NAACP v. Hunt, 891 F.2d 1555 (11th Cir.1990),, 239
Pierce v. Society of Sisters, 268 U.S. 510 (1925),, 256, 380
Planned Parenthood v. Casey, 505 U.S. 833 (1992), 43, 60, 67, 91, 378
Poe v. Ulman, 367 US 497 (1961), 376, 380

Prince v. Massachusetts, 321 US 158 (1944), 256
Riley v. Garrett, 133 SE2d 367 (1963), 258
Rich v. Secretary of the Army, 735 F.2d 1220, 1228 (10th. Cir.1984), 250
Roe v. Wade, 410 U.S. 113 (1973), 88, 91, 255+256
Romer v. Evans, 517 U.S. 620 (1996), 251, 385
Roper v. Simmons, 543 U.S. 551 (2005), 80, 379
Rostker v. Goldberg, 453 U.S. 57 (1981), 385
Rowland v. Mad River Local School District, 105 S.Ct. 1373 (1985), 247
Skinner v. State of Oklahoma, 316 US 535 (1942), 100
South Carolina v. Gathers, 109 S. Ct. 2207 (1989), 77, 379
Stanford v. Kentucky, 492 U.S. 361 (1989), 79
Stanley v. Georgia, 394 US 557 (1969), 255, 257
Thompson v. Aldredge, 200 S. E. 799 (1939)., 258
Troxel v. Granville, 99-138) 530 U.S. 57 (2000), 381
United States v. Seeger, 380 US 163 (1965), 84
United States v. Virginia, 518 U.S. 515 (1996), 308, 385
Vacco v. Quill, 521 U.S. 793 (1997), 73, 378
Washington v. Davis, 426 U.S. 229 (1976), 227, 236, 239+240
Washington v. Glucksberg, 521 U.S. 702 (1977), 59
Woody Allen v. Mia Farrow, 197 A.D.2d 327 (Sup. Ct. N.Y. 1994), 173
Zablocki v. Redhail, 434 U.S. 374 (1978), 380

Acknowledgments

This book developed as a result of teaching numerous advanced constitutional law courses to students eager to understand the policies driving laws that govern privacy and individual rights. I wish to honor all of the great legal and political theorists, philosophers, journalists, and poets whose work served to prod me toward greater substantive coverage of the most controversial subjects in the book. Some have passed away, while others (whether on speaking tours or chained to their computers) seem to be changing interpretive paradigms and rearranging the terms of debate throughout the world. In particular, I'd like to thank Lani Guinier, Kathryn Abrams, Pierre J. Schlag and Patricia Joyce Williams.

To every author who said yes to my request to reprint edited excerpts of their published work for this edition, I send a special note of appreciation and acknowledgement. Your willingness to share the fruits of your own hard work and commitment have enabled me to assemble a vivid, albeit complex, portrayal of American law and policy.

Over the years, students have read and commented upon several earlier versions of this text to my amusement and delight. Numerous research assistants have tinkered with the chapters, indices or tables of cases, and gathered permission to reprint forms from the far corners of the earth, on top of countless other small tasks that contributed to the finished project. I offer heartfelt thanks to each. I also wish to thank my administrative assistant, the University of Connecticut, and production managers at Carolina Academic Press for their generous support and patience.

Introduction

Constitutional law is an enormous field, and casebooks devoted to the entire field often sacrifice depth for coverage. Unlike traditional material on civil or political rights, this casebook is about emerging debates in the areas of life that have been deemed a matter of personal, autonomous choice. Designed for use in upper-level seminars, the material leads students to the core of the fundamental rights debate. With an intense focus upon issues pertaining to substantive due process, information privacy, and their impact on social and political freedom, ordered liberty is shown to be a vital founding principle.

Many find the study of personal liberties to be complex and exciting. Where else do we passionately discuss concepts like justice and neutrality with a straight face? Within this paradox is one overriding pedagogical reality: whereas there may be a broad range of choice in how to approach substantive areas of law, ignoring them because they generate controversy is no longer an option. Few subjects provide as much grist for the analytic mill as the study of individual rights. These topics stimulate heated dialogue that transcends the limits of critical legal reasoning on multiple levels; I appreciate the long-cherished notions of academic freedom that make this possible.

This book describes the institutions where lawyers are trained and where justice is meted out as it summarizes historic and contemporary critiques of legal institutions. The comparison renders a bird's eye view of the social and political theories that encourage us to think of the United States as the greatest and oldest living democracy. The text illustrates the extent to which we've formulated laws and legal remedies that are consistent with our highest ideals of liberty, autonomy, and governance for the general welfare.

In areas specific to individual rights, the text highlights notable trends in judicial reasoning. Key issues surrounding the rights of terminally ill patients have emerged with the general transfer of decision-making power from families to the state. Re-emergence of the death penalty, victims' advocates, conscientious and other objections to military conscription, technologies affecting the abortion debate, and use of affirmative defenses for marital rape illustrate interesting developments in the area of consent.

Exploring the Court's most recent patterns of regulating intimate relations suggests a shift toward redefining the limits of familial privacy and the concept of fundamental liberty in the areas of marriage and procreation. Transformation of the social order, linked to evolving scrutiny of the marital contract, demonstrates that the role of marriage as a social institution is changing course. With that reality, we find a re-emergence of early theories rejecting traditional monogamous relationships.

The absence of a coherent linkage between actual legislation and a corresponding state interest raises clear obstacles to gender neutrality and justice in the criminal prosecution of many statutory rape cases. Trends related to those charged with crimes ranging from incest and trafficking in child pornography, to the mandatory reporting of movement and location of convicted sex offenders present additional areas where the law operates without an obvious correlation between means and ends.

The legacy of group rights established at the nation's founding is documented in its historical context by examining the social and legal doctrines that developed throughout the 20th century. This legacy is the primary obstacle to full recognition of the rights of individuals today. Significant developments in constitutional doctrine can be traced to meaningful attempts to transform what should have rightfully begun as a contractual or employment relationship, rather than a *property right* at the nation's founding, into a contractual or labor relation among equals.

Developments in the law and science related to gay, lesbian, bi-sexual, and transgendered people are viewed in light of congressional actions that attempt to neutralize their social impact. The historical defense of gender roles is featured as less interesting in theory, than for its impact as a subtext in debates about modern family life.

Restraints on civil liberties since September 11, 2001, and the passage of the USA PATRIOT Act are discussed in relation to congressional activity leading up to its passage. Changes in foreign and domestic surveillance policies, aided by new telecommunications technology and practices, have wholly altered the debate surrounding privacy rights, rendering much of our traditional privacy law obsolete.

Examining individual rights within analytic paradigms that are rarely embraced by American jurists provides an exceptional opportunity to evaluate intricate connections between law and social scientific theory, and their nascent influence on global public policy initiatives. Re-shaping the role of lawyers and the nature of their legal training have become central to developing the complex range of domestic policies and practices necessary for a coherent response to imminent demands for global standards and compliance in areas involving individual rights and liberties.

CONSTITUTION
OF THE UNITED STATES OF AMERICA

Select Passages

PREAMBLE

We the People of the United States, in Order to form a more perfect Union, establish Justice, insure domestic Tranquility, provide for the common defence, promote the general Welfare, and secure the Blessings of Liberty to ourselves and our Posterity, do ordain and establish this Constitution of the United States of America.

ARTICLE I

Section 2

[3] Representatives and direct Taxes shall be apportioned among the several States which may be included within this Union, according to their respective Numbers, which shall be determined by adding to the whole Number of free Persons, including those bound to Service for a Term of Years, and excluding Indians not taxed, three fifths of all other Persons.

Section 8

[1] The Congress shall have Power To lay and collect Taxes, Duties, Imposts and Excises, to pay the Debts and provide for the common Defence and general Welfare of the United States; but all Duties, Imposts and Excises shall be uniform throughout the United States.

[15] To provide for calling forth the Militia to execute the Laws of the Union, suppress Insurrections and repel Invasions.

[16] To provide for organizing, arming, and disciplining, the Militia, and for governing such Part of them as may be employed in the Service of the United States, reserving to the States respectively, the Appointment of the Officers, and the Authority of training the Militia according to the discipline prescribed by Congress.

Section 9

[1] The Migration or Importation of such Persons as any of the States now existing shall think proper to admit, shall not be prohibited by the Congress prior to the Year one thousand eight hundred and eight, but a Tax or duty may be imposed on such Importation, not exceeding ten dollars for each Person.

ARTICLE IV

Section 1

Full Faith and Credit shall be given in each State to the public Acts, Records, and judicial Proceedings of every other State. And the Congress may by general laws prescribe the Manner in which such Acts, Records and Proceedings shall be proved, and the Effect thereof.

Section 2

[1] The citizens of each State shall be entitled to all Privileges and Immunities of Citizens in the several States.

[2] A person charged in any State with Treason, Felony, or other Crime, who shall flee from Justice, and be found in another State, shall on Demand of the executive Authority of the State from which he fled, be delivered up, to be removed to the State having Jurisdiction of the Crime.

[3] No Person held to Service or Labour in one State, under the Laws thereof, escaping into another, shall, in Consequence of any Law or Regulation therein, be discharged from such Service or Labour, but shall be delivered up on Claim of the Party to whom such Service or Labour may be due.

Section 3

[1] New States may be admitted by the Congress into this Union; but no new State shall be formed or erected within the Jurisdiction of any other State; nor any State be formed by the Junction of two or more States, or Parts of States, without the consent of the Legislatures of the States concerned as well as of the Congress.

[2] The Congress shall have Power to dispose of and make all needful Rules and Regulations respecting the Territory or other Property belonging to the United States: and nothing in this Constitution shall be so construed as to Prejudice any Claims of the United States, or of any particular State.

AMENDMENT I [1791]

Congress shall make no law respecting an establishment of religion, or prohibiting the free exercise thereof; or abridging the freedom of speech, or of the press; or the right of the people peaceably to assemble, and to petition for redress of grievances.

AMENDMENT II [1791]

A well regulated Militia, being necessary to the security of a free State, the right of the people to keep and bear Arms, shall not be infringed.

AMENDMENT III [1791]

No Soldier shall, in time of peace be quartered in any house, without the consent of the Owner, nor in time of war, but in a manner to be prescribed by law.

AMENDMENT IV [1791]

The right of the people to be secure in their persons, houses, papers, and effects, against unreasonable searches and seizures, shall not be violated, and no Warrants shall issue, but upon probable cause, supported by Oath or affirmation, and particularly describing the place to be searched, and the persons or things to be seized.

AMENDMENT IX [1791]

The enumeration in the Constitution, of certain rights, shall not be construed to deny or disparage others retained by the people.

AMENDMENT X [1791]

The powers not delegated to the United States by the Constitution, nor prohibited by it to the States, are reserved to the States respectively, or to the people.

AMENDMENT XIII [1865]

Section I

Neither slavery nor involuntary servitude, except as a punishment for crime whereof the party shall have been duly convicted, shall exist within the United Sates, or any place subject to their jurisdiction.

Section 2

Congress shall have power to enforce this article by appropriate legislation.

AMENDMENT XIV [1868]

Section 1

All persons born or naturalized in the United States, and subject to the jurisdiction thereof, are citizens of the United States and of the State wherein they reside. No State shall make or enforce any law which shall abridge the privileges or immunities of citizens of the United States; nor shall any State deprive any person of life, liberty, or property, without due process of law; nor deny to any person within its jurisdiction the equal protection of the laws.

Section 2

Representatives shall be apportioned among the several States according to their respective numbers, counting the whole number of persons in each State, excluding Indians not taxed. But when the right to vote at any election for the choice of electors for President and Vice President of the United States, Representatives in Congress, the Executive and Judicial officers of a State, or the members of the Legislature thereof, is denied to any of the male inhabitants of such State, being twenty-one years of age, and citizens of the United States, or in any way abridged, except for participation in rebellion, or other crime, the basis of representation therein shall be reduced in the proportion which the number of such male citizens shall bear to the whole number of male citizens twenty-one years of age in such State.

AMENDMENT XV [1870]

Section 1

The right of citizens of the United States to vote shall not be denied or abridged by the United States or by any State on account of race, color, or previous condition of servitude.

Section 2

Congress shall have power to enforce this article by appropriate legislation.

AMENDMENT XIX [1920]

Section 1

The right of citizens of the United States to vote shall not be denied or abridged by the United States or by any State on account of sex.

Section 2

Congress shall have power to enforce this article by appropriate legislation.

The Nature and Scope of Individual Rights

Part One

Pillars of the Fundamental Rights Debate

Supreme Court work leads the Justice to develop a view of the Constitution as a whole. My own view is likely similar to that of others insofar as I see the document as creating a coherent framework for a certain kind of government. Described generally, that government is democratic; it avoids concentration of too much power in too few hands; it protects personal liberty; it insists that the law respect each individual equally; and it acts only upon the basis of law itself.[1]

Justice Stephen Breyer, ACTIVE LIBERTY

Chapter One

Guiding Principles of the Great Social Compact

Graduate study of constitutional democracy begins with its theoretical foundations. The student of law must also examine the dynamics of legal institutions in order to observe how rules are put into practice. The practical realities of law reflect the nature of legal training, the actual work that lawyers do, the reach of judicial power, and authority of legislative bodies. There is value in understanding the intricate framework within which they all interact. According to James Madison, at the nation's founding, the goal was to contrive the "interior structure of government so that its several constituent parts may be the means of keeping each other in their proper places,"[2] counteracting "ambition because government itself is the greatest of all reflections on human nature."[3] Ultimately, the American ideal presupposes an impartial and independent judicial process that guards the core values upon which the entire system rests.

The study of law is an ongoing lesson in history, tradition, and sociology. The lessons are cumulative insofar as changes in the law are incremental, rather than sweeping. Its evolution is structured by near-universal adherence to and respect for legal precedent. Judicial opinions proceed from a series of interrelated discussions around the scope of the law and its application to earlier, similar fact patterns. They note changes in legislative priorities and refer to evolving standards of fairness and decency. They build upon what has already been established and accepted, under a system of stare decisis.[4]

According to the late Justice Cardozo, in THE NATURE OF THE JUDICIAL PROCESS, "the judicial branch is not a super legislature, but a group of ordinary men looking for the means to a socially desired end. Those who believed in the role of stare decisis, think that clear articulation of abiding principles would leave matters of justice less vulnerable to manipulation."[5]

Most would agree that when a legal system functions well there is a tangible connection between justice and neutrality. The concluding theme of the Pledge of Allegiance to the U.S. flag promises "liberty and justice for all."[6] The U.S. Constitution guarantees, by various amendments, the rights of the individual to due process, equal protection, freedom of conscience, and security in their person and property. A core of fundamental rights is thought to be indispensable to the prosperity of citizens of free nations.[7]

Freedom from unwarranted governmental intrusion, while pursuing widely approved personal and political objectives, remains central to our understanding of civil rights. The right to vote—*THE* symbol of representative democracy—was first denied to women even though they were citizens of the United States. When it was later granted with the passage of the Nineteenth Amendment, a woman's right to vote was properly defined as a civil right. Autonomy to engage in a broad range of activities, consume products and services, and pursue that which satisfies in the personal and intimate realm animates popular understanding of civil liberties. Under most state legislation, the right to marry interracially was first denied to the majority of Americans. When the Supreme Court overturned such laws, the right to marry the partner of choice was commonly understood as a civil liberty.

Conceptually, rights and liberties are often presented interchangeably. However, history demonstrates that they have traveled along different roads of constitutional analysis. The right to vote is seen as a fundamental right that carries substantial provisions for its enforcement. The right to marry on the other hand—never mentioned in the Constitution—is subject to various "state interests." The very nature of a course that examines "Individual Rights" is to explore the means by which those interests are justified, articulated, and ultimately balanced in the courts and legislatures.

For Your Consideration

It has often been noted that the challenge of democratic governance is not necessarily in enabling government officials to control the governed (they manage), but in obliging them to control themselves. If true, then which branch of government is likely to remain most responsive to matters of social justice? How should we evaluate the theory that "an act of legislature contrary to the great first principles of the social compact" is not a law that one need obey?[8] How do we fashion a judiciary that remains cognizant of and responsive to the just application of guiding principles? If the judicial dilemma is one of commanding respect for the rule of law, is there a way to measure whether there is sufficient consensus among the citizenry around the "guidance" to be found in these first principles?

It is said that in order to understand a nation you must begin with its history, and the story of the United States of America, as it is typically told, begins with its founding documents.

The Revolutionary Spirit—Necessity of Dissolving Political Bands

When in the course of human events, it becomes necessary ...

Britain began its slave trade in Africa in the 1500s.[9] In subsequent years, development of plantation colonies in the Americas increased the need for cheap labor. Plantation owners turned to the International slave trade that began in the mid-1400s. [10] Between 1650 and 1900, historians estimate that between ten and twenty-eight million Africans were forcibly removed from central and western Africa.[11]

By the mid-1600s, colonist had fully embraced the idea of lifetime servitude for Blacks. Late 17th Century law required those who would free slaves to transport them out of the United States. Free Blacks created two problems for southern slaveholders. First, they exposed racial myths surrounding industry and aptitude. Prosperous Blacks undermined the social justification for slavery and, as a result, were often driven from their land. Next, there was fear of retribution. Slave revolts leading to Black Independence in the Caribbean created such widespread fear, that free Blacks were deemed a threat to national security.[12] Thus, the assembly of large numbers of Blacks (particularly slaves) was prohibited.

Black labor in the form of human property was the source of colonial wealth for hundreds of years.[13] Noting the prosperity, the British government sought to build its revenue through a series of legislative acts. Collection was difficult due to widespread corruption. Tax commissioners rarely set foot in the colonies and most traders paid a fraction (if any) of the taxes due. Customs officers were also traders who smuggled by rule rather than exception.[14] In response, the British Parliament passed the 1764 Sugar Act to halt colonists' participation in the triangular trade, where molasses was shipped from the West Indies to New England and distilled into rum, then exchanged in Africa for captured slaves whom traders loaded onto ships and transported to the colonies.[15] The Sugar Act precluded colonists from procuring quality molasses at a discount rate from the French islands and infuriated traders. In a rage of anti-government rhetoric that ignited the American Revolution, radical thinkers argued that England sought to enslave White men through the passage of the Sugar Act, because it sharply decreased the profits for Rhode Island. Their legendary statements of political principle equated the status of colonial Whites to that of a slave. For example, the 1775 Declaration of the Causes and Necessity of Taking Up Arms, written by Thomas Jefferson, begins by asking:

> Is it possible for men who exercise their reason to believe that the Divine author of our existence intended a part of the human race to hold an absolute power in and an unbounded authority over others? We are of one mind, determined to die free men rather than to live as slaves.[16]

Colonists were ridiculed in England. Blatant hypocrisy overshadowed their protests with an irony of tragic proportions. Their insistence that Blacks remain slaves gave American slavery its bifurcated meaning: for Blacks it meant a lifetime of involuntary servitude under brutal and inhumane working conditions, without benefit and comfort of family ties. Although dehumanizing for both races, it was elevated to an act of treason punishable by death for Blacks to escape slavery and attempt to live free. For Whites, any law or enactment that limited their economic freedom or reduced the value of their property was likened to enslavement.

Although the downfall of the Roman Empire was presented as evidence that pure republican governments were doomed from the start, those who signed the Declaration of Independence were not persuaded as they pursued a theory of natural or inherent rights of mankind.[17] As revised by Thomas Jefferson, in June of 1776, the Declaration of Independence is *THE* modern symbol of American liberty.

Jefferson summarized a popular philosophy couched in "self-evident truths" that were followed by a long list of accusations against the King of England, which were used to justify breaking ties with the country. The Declaration is rightfully recognized for its boldness. In the face of what he characterized as abuse by his government, Jefferson simply declared war. He begins by invoking history, necessity, nature, and God, then moves to the central tenet: that men are created equal and endowed with unalienable rights to life, liberty, and to pursue happiness.

Jefferson's original draft included a moving list of indictments charging the King with waging war upon the innocent, and imposing taxes without representation, followed by a peculiar attack on slavery. The Declaration as finally adopted fails to mention slavery. The original draft was presented on July second, and widely debated in the Continental Congress. The revised draft was adopted on July fourth, 1776, after striking only one provision: Jefferson's invective against the international slave trade.

> He has waged a cruel war against human nature, violating sacred rights of life and liberty in the persons of a distant people who never offended him, captivating and carrying them into slavery in another hemisphere or to incur miserable death in their transportation thither. Determined to keep an open market where MEN should be bought and sold.[18]

Europeans mocked Jefferson's piercing silence around the continuation of slavery in the colonies; life-long enslavement began in his own state of Virginia. In 1705, the Virginia Assembly cast votes declaring that: "All servants imported and brought into this country, by sea or land ... shall be ... slaves, and as such be here bought and sold notwithstanding a conversion to Christianity." It was then known, and modern history has since documented the fact that Jefferson owned many slaves, including one Sally Hemmings whom he inherited from his father-in-law's estate, also known to be the half-sister of Jefferson's wife, Martha. Following Martha's death, Jefferson took Hemmings as his common law wife and fathered many children whom he freed in his will.[19] Jefferson's personal notes acknowledge, "the clause reprobating the enslaving of the inhabitants of Africa, was struck in compliance to South Carolina and Georgia. Our Northern brethren too felt a little tender for they had been pretty considerable carriers of slaves."[20]

An essay by Stephen E. Lucas, entitled **The Stylistic Artistry of the Declaration of Independence**, [21] describes what he considers to be the extraordinary merits of the Declaration as political prose. "Its literary qualities and rhetorical power contain the secret of its design and method for convincing "a 'candid world' that the American colonies were justified in seeking to establish themselves as an independent nation."[22] Without explicit reference to the British-American conflict Jefferson's prose rendered revolution justifiable and meritorious:

> We hold these truths to be self-evident, that all men are created equal, that they are endowed by their Creator with certain unalienable Rights, that among these are Life, Liberty and the pursuit of Happiness. That to secure these rights, Governments are instituted among Men, deriving their just powers from the consent of the governed. That whenever any Form of Government becomes destructive of these ends, it is the Right of the People to alter or to abolish it, and to institute new Government, laying its foundation on such principles and organizing its powers in such form, as to them shall seem most likely to effect their Safety and Happiness. Prudence, indeed, will dictate that Governments long established should not be changed for light and transient causes; and accordingly all experience hath shown that mankind are more disposed to suffer, while evils are sufferable, than to right themselves by abolishing the forms to which they are accustomed. But when a long train of abuses and usurpations, pursuing invariably the same Object evinces a design to reduce them under absolute Despotism, it is their right, it is their duty, to throw off such Government, and to provide new Guards for their future security.

According to Lucas, Thomas Jefferson was a "diligent student of rhythm, accent, timing, and cadence in discourse."

> The preamble has a powerful sense of structural unity. This is achieved partly by the latent chronological progression of thought, in which the reader is moved from the creation of mankind, to the institution of government, to the throwing off of government when it fails to protect the people's unalienable rights, to the creation of new government that will better secure the people's safety and happiness. This dramatic scenario, with its first act implicitly set in the Garden of Eden

(where man was "created equal"), may, for some readers, have contained mythic overtones of humanity's fall from divine grace. At the very least, it gives an almost archetypal quality to the ideas of the preamble and continues the notion, broached in the introduction, that the American Revolution is a major development in "the course of human events." [23]

Relevant Edited Excerpts
Reprinted with permission

The indictment of George III, which Samuel Adams called his catalogue of crimes, began with a single transitional sentence immediately following the preamble:

> Such has been the patient sufferance of these Colonies; and such is now the necessity which constrains them to alter their former Systems of Government.
>
> The history of the present King of Great Britain is a history of repeated injuries and usurpations, all having in direct object the establishment of an absolute Tyranny over these states.
>
> The bill of particulars lists twenty-eight specific grievances. Lucas writes that:
>
> Steady, laborious piling up of "facts" without comment takes on the character of a legal indictment, while the repetition of "He has" slows the movement of the text, draws attention to the accumulation of grievances, and accentuates George III's role as the prime conspirator against American liberty. Although scholars often downplay the war grievances as "the weakest part of the Declaration," they were vital to its rhetorical strategy. They came last partly because they were the most recent of George III's "abuses and usurpations," but also because they constituted the ultimate proof of his plan to reduce the colonies under "absolute despotism." The first twenty-two grievances describe the king's acts with such temperate verbs as "refused," "called together," "dissolved," "endeavored," "made," "erected," "kept," and "affected," the war grievances use emotionally charged verbs such as "plundered," "ravaged," "burnt," and "destroyed," to support the accusation that George III was spreading "death, desolation and tyranny ...
>
> John Lind composed the most sustained British response to the Declaration. He used 110 pages to answer the charges set forth by the Continental Congress in fewer than two-dozen sentences. Although Lind deftly exposed many of the charges to be flimsy at best, his detailed and complex rebuttal did not stand a chance against the Declaration as a propaganda document. Nor has Lind's work fared much better since 1776. While the Declaration continues to command an international audience and has created an indelible popular image of George III as a tyrant, Lind's tract remains a piece of arcana, buried in the dustheap of history.

The Declaration follows the attack on George III by noting that the colonies had also appealed in vain to the people of Great Britain:

> Nor have we been wanting in attentions to our British brethren. We have warned them from time to time of attempts by their legislature to extend an unwarrantable jurisdiction over us. We have reminded them of the circumstances of our emigration and settlement here. We have appealed to their native justice and magnanimity, and we have conjured them by the ties of our common kindred to disavow these usurpations, which would inevitably interrupt our connections and correspondence. They too have been deaf to the voice of justice and of consanguinity. We must, therefore, acquiesce in the necessity, which de-

nounces our Separation, and hold them, as we hold the rest of mankind, Enemies in War, in Peace Friends. This is one of the most artfully written sections of the Declaration.

The British brethren section essentially finished the case for independence. Congress had set forth the conditions that justified revolution and had shown, as best it could, that those conditions existed in Great Britain's thirteen North American colonies. All that remained was for Congress to conclude the Declaration:

> We, therefore, the Representatives of the United States of America, in General Congress, Assembled, appealing to the Supreme Judge of the world for the rectitude of our intentions, do, in the Name, and by Authority of the good People of these Colonies, solemnly publish and declare, That these United Colonies are, and of Right ought to be Free and Independent States; that they are Absolved from all Allegiance to the British Crown, and that all political connection between them and the State of Great Britain, is and ought to be totally dissolved; and that as Free and Independent States, they have full Power to levy War, conclude Peace, contract Alliances, establish Commerce, and to do all other Acts and Things which Independent States may of right do. And for the support of this Declaration, with a firm reliance on the protection of divine Providence, we mutually pledge to each other our Lives, our Fortunes and our sacred Honor.

This final section of the Declaration is highly formulaic and has attracted attention primarily because of its closing sentence. Carl Becker deemed this sentence "perfection itself":

> It is true (assuming that men value life more than property, which is doubtful) that the statement violates the rhetorical rule of climax; but it was a sure sense that made Jefferson place "lives" first and "fortunes" second. How much weaker if he had written "our fortunes, our lives, and our sacred honor"! Or suppose him to have used the word "property" instead of "fortunes"! Or suppose him to have omitted "sacred"! Consider the effect of omitting any of the words, such as the last two "ours"—"our lives, fortunes, and sacred honor." No, the sentence can hardly be improved.

"Lives and fortunes" was one of the most hackneyed phrases of eighteenth-century Anglo-American political discourse. Colonial writers had used it with numbing regularity throughout the dispute with England (along with other stock phrases such as "liberties and estates" and "life, liberty, and property"). Its appearance in the Declaration can hardly be taken as a measure of Jefferson's felicity of expression.

What marks Jefferson's "happy talent for composition" in this case is the coupling of "our sacred Honor" with "our Lives" and "our Fortunes" to create the eloquent trilogy that closes the Declaration. The concept of honor (and its cognates fame and glory) exerted a powerful hold on the eighteenth-century mind. Writers of all kinds—philosophers, preachers, politicians, playwrights, poets—repeatedly speculated about the sources of honor and how to achieve it. Virtually every educated man in England or America was schooled in the classical maxim. As coined in Cato, and widely admired on both sides of the Atlantic: "Better to die ten thousand deaths/Than wound my honour." The cult of honor was so strong that in English judicial proceedings verdicts were not rendered "upon oath, like ordinary juryman, but upon his honor."

By pledging "our sacred Honor" in support of the Declaration, Congress made a particularly solemn vow. The pledge also carried a latent message that the revolutionaries, contrary to the claims of their detractors, were men of honor whose motives and actions could not only withstand the closest scrutiny by contemporary persons of quality and merit but would also deserve the approbation of posterity.

The final sentence completes a crucial metamorphosis in the text. Although the Declaration begins in an impersonal, even philosophical voice, it gradually becomes a kind of drama, with its tensions expressed more and more in personal terms, it sustains an almost perfect synthesis of style, form, and content. Its solemn and dignified tone, its graceful and unhurried cadence, its symmetry, energy, and confidence, its combination of logical structure and dramatic appeal, its adroit use of nuance and implication all contribute to its rhetorical power. And all help to explain why the Declaration remains one of the handful of American political documents that, in addition to meeting the immediate needs of the moment, continues to enjoy a lustrous literary reputation.[24]

Impact of the Declaration of Independence

Countless American leaders have adopted the language of the Declaration as a means of commanding the attention of the men who have governed this nation.

Seneca Falls Resolution 1848[25]

When, in the course of human events, it becomes necessary for one portion of the family of man to assume among the people of the earth a position different from that which they have hitherto occupied, but one to which the laws of nature and of nature's God entitle them, a decent respect to the opinions of mankind required that they should declare the causes that impel them to such a course.

We hold these truths to be self-evident: that all men and women are created equal, that they are endowed by their creator with certain inalienable rights, that among these are life, liberty, and the pursuit of happiness. That to secure these rights governments are instituted, deriving their just powers from the consent of the governed. Whenever any form of government becomes destructive of these ends, it is the right of those who suffer from it to refuse allegiance to it, and to insist upon the institution of a new government, laying its foundation on such principles, and organizing its powers in such form, as to them shall seem most likely to effect their safety and happiness....

The history of mankind is a history repeated injuries and usurpations on the part of man toward woman, having in direct object the establishment of an absolute tyranny over her.

To prove this, let facts be submitted to a candid world.

He has never permitted her to exercise her inalienable right to the elective franchise.

He has compelled her to submit to laws in the formation of which she had no voice.

He has withheld from her rights that are given to the most ignorant and degraded men—both natives and foreigners.

He has made her, if married, in the eye of the law civilly dead.

He has taken from her all right in property, even to the wage she earns.

He has monopolized nearly all the profitable employment and from those she is permitted to follow she receives a scanty remuneration. He closes against her all the avenues to wealth and distinction that he leaves open to himself, permitting her to teach neither theology, medicine nor law.

He has denied her the facilities for obtaining a thorough education, all colleges being closed against her.

He has endeavored in every way that he could to destroy her confidence in her own power, to lessen her self-respect, and to make her willing to lead a dependent and abject life.

Now in view of this entire disenfranchisement, of one-half the people of this country, their social and religious degradation—in view of the unjust laws mentioned above, and because women do feel themselves aggrieved, oppressed and fraudulently deprived of their most sacred rights, we insist that they have immediate admission to all the rights and privileges which belong to them as citizens of the United States.

Susan B. Anthony Elizabeth Cady Stanton

Throughout the past one hundred fifteen years, millions of children have pledged allegiance to the flag and the "Republic for which it stands, One Nation, Under God, Indivisible, with Liberty and Justice for all."[26] Famous Americans are fond of declaring that these elements of freedom form the core of our national identity.

Relatively few political figures have actually advanced national debate on questions of freedom and equality. Some are widely known while others are virtually ignored in textbooks that describe the historic periods where they exerted the greatest influence. For example, Victoria C. Woodhull, an outspoken Women's Rights advocate and late 19th century Presidential candidate, believed that freedom was intricately related to truth. In a speech entitled: ***Principles of Social Freedom***, delivered in Steinway Hall on Nov. 20, 1871, she expressed the following.

And the Truth Shall Make You Free[27]

Victoria C. Woodhull

Relevant Edited Excerpts

Religious freedom does, in a measure, exist in this country, but not yet perfectly; that is to say, a person is not entirely independent of public opinion regarding matters of conscience.

The necessary corollary to Religious and Political freedom is Social freedom, which is the third term of the trinity; that is to say, if Religious and Political freedom exist, perfected, Social freedom is at that very moment guaranteed as the fruit of that condition.

So Be It:

Resolved, That the basis of order is freedom from bondage....

Resolved, That freedom is a principle, and the woman's movement means no less than the complete social as well as the political enfranchisement of mankind.

Resolved, That the evils, sufferings and disabilities of women, as well as of men, are social still more than they are political, and that a statement of woman's rights which ignores the rights of self-ownership as the first of all rights is insufficient to meet the demand, and is ceasing to enlist the enthusiasm and even the common interest of the most intelligent portion of the community.

Resolved, That the principle of freedom is one principle, and not a collection of many different and unrelated principles; that there is not at bottom one principle of freedom of conscience as in Protestantism, and another principle of freedom from slavery as in Abolitionism, another of freedom of locomotion as in our dispensing in America with the passport system of Europe, another of the freedom of the press as in Great Britain and America, and still another of social freedom at large; but that freedom is one and indivisible.

Now, is there anything so terrible in the language of these resolutions as to threaten the foundations of society? They assert that every individual has a better right to herself or himself than any other person can have. No living soul, who does not desire to have control over or ownership in another person, can have any valid objection to anything expressed in these resolutions.

Our government is based upon the proposition that: All men and women are born free and equal and entitled to certain inalienable rights. We who demand social freedom simply ask that the government of this country be administered in accord with the spirit of this proposition. Nothing more, nothing less.

It means that every person who comes into the world of outward existence is of equal right as an individual, and is free as an individual, and that he or she is entitled to pursue happiness in whatever direction he or she may choose.

The world has come up to the present time through the outworking of religious, political, philosophical and scientific principles, and we have arrived where the very foundation of all that has been must be analyzed and understood—the relation of the sexes.

To love is a right higher than Constitutions or laws. It is a right which Constitutions and laws can neither give nor take, and with which they have nothing whatever to do, since in its very nature it is forever independent of both Constitutions and laws, love exists—and comes and goes—in spite of them. Governments might just as well assume to determine how people shall exercise their right to think or to say that they shall not think at all, as to assume to determine that they shall not love, or how they may love, or that they shall love.

The proper sphere of government in regard to the relations of the sexes, is to enact such laws as in the present conditions of society are necessary to protect each individual in the free exercise of his or her right to love, and also to protect each individual from the forced interference of every other person, that would

> compel him or her to submit to any action which is against their wish and will. When the law does this, it fulfills its duty. If it does not afford this protection, or worse, if it sanctions this interference with the rights of an individual, then it is an infamous law a form of despotism; and tyranny forms no part of the guarantee of, or the right to, individual freedom.
>
> I think it will be generally conceded that without love there should be no marriage. In the constitution of things nothing can be more certain. This basic fact is fatal to the theory of marriage for life: since if love is what determines marriage, so, also, should it determine its continuance.
>
> If it be primarily right of men and women to take on the marriage relation of their own free will and accord, so, too, does it remain their right to determine how long it shall continue and when it shall cease. But under the law, in order to be respectable, people comply; thousands comply therewith, while in their hearts they protest against it as an unwarrantable interference and proscription of their rights.
>
> Marriage laws that would be consistent with the theory of individual rights would be such as would regulate these relations only as much as they regulate all other associations of people. Individuals should only be obliged to file marriage articles, containing whatever provisions may be agreed upon, as to their personal rights, rights of property, of children, or whatever else they may deem proper for them to agree upon. And whatever these articles might be, they should in all cases be equally entitled to public respect and protection. Should separation afterward come, nothing more should be required than the simple filing of counter articles.
>
> There are hundreds of lawyers who subsist by inventing schemes by which people may obtain divorces, and the people desiring divorces resort to all sorts of tricks and crimes to get them. And all this exists because there are laws that would compel the oneness of those to whom unity is beyond the realm of possibility.
>
> There are another class of persons who, while virtually divorced, endeavor to maintain a respectable position in society, by agreeing to disagree, each following his and her individual ways, behind the cloak of legal marriage. Thus there are hundreds of men and women who to external appearances are husband and wife, but in reality are husband or wife to quite different persons.

Woodhull ran for President on a platform that promoted discourse favoring women's independence with a message so threatening to the social order of her time that she spent a month in jail during the election. As a vocal proponent of a Movement that claimed for women the same social freedoms that men typically reserve for themselves, she has been labeled scandalous, radical and notorious, but she had an undeniably simple approach to gender equality: if it's good for the goose.[28]

Woodhull's message was received with about as much equanimity as many present day feminist scholars.

Charles Johnson notes that conservative critics of feminism paint feminist demands in terms of liberal claims for equity (for example, unequal pay) and caricature those demands as women wanting to become like men—"the women's own desires, the particularities of women's lives, the needs of the family, and anything else that gets in the way be damned." Progressive critics of feminism portray feminist demands in terms of "radical opposition to sexual harassment, prostitution, pornography, and sexualized denigration of women, and caricature those demands as little more than kill-joy Puritanism."

> Catharine MacKinnon has argued that this double-bind may simply be the result of the male Right and the male Left's inability to see any issue except on men's terms, and so mistake feminist opposition to the Right as liberalism and feminist opposition to the Left as reaction. Consider, for example, how she illustrates her points of agreement, and conflict, with liberalism and conservatism—and draws out the vital importance of understanding feminism on its own terms, on women's terms instead of men's terms—in Not by Law Alone.

Catherine MacKinnon has devoted a career to demonstrating how "the "group" called women has a collective social history of disempowerment, exploitation, and subordination extending to the present. Social treatment as a woman ... refers to a "diverse material reality of meanings and practices such that to be a woman is not yet a way of being human."[29]

Altogether, Jefferson's battle against tyranny, Anthony's fight against fraudulent deprivation, Woodhull's quest for social and religious freedom, and MacKinnon's declaration of human rights abuse are all represented in the now-famous remarks of Dr. Martin Luther King, Jr. King, a martyred civil rights activist and follower of Indian philosopher/activist Mahatma Gandhi, spread a message of non-violent resistance to government brutality. His advocacy of peaceful protests against denial of basic human freedom has secured a unique place for him in American history.

I Have a Dream[30]

Dr. Martin Luther King, Jr.

Relevant Excerpts

Delivered on the steps of the Lincoln Memorial on August 28, 1963.

> Five score years ago, a great American, in whose symbolic shadow we [now] stand signed the Emancipation Proclamation. This momentous decree came as a great beacon of hope to millions of Negro slaves who had been seared in the flames of withering injustice. It came as a joyous daybreak to end the long night of captivity. But one hundred years later, we must face the tragic fact that the Negro is still not free.
>
> One hundred years later, the life of the Negro is still sadly crippled by the manacles of segregation and the chains of discrimination. One hundred years later, the Negro lives on a lonely island of poverty in the midst of a vast ocean of material prosperity. One hundred years later, the Negro is still languishing in the corners of American society and finds himself an exile in his own land.
>
> So we have come here today to dramatize an appalling condition. In a sense we have come to our nation's capital to cash a check. When the architects of our republic wrote the magnificent words of the Constitution and the Declaration of Independence, they were signing a promissory note to which every American was to fall heir.
>
> This note was a promise that all men would be guaranteed the inalienable rights of life, liberty, and the pursuit of happiness. It is obvious today that America has defaulted on this promissory note insofar as her citizens of color

are concerned. Instead of honoring this sacred obligation, America has given the Negro people a bad check which has come back marked "insufficient funds." But we refuse to believe that the bank of justice is bankrupt. We refuse to believe that there are insufficient funds in the great vaults of opportunity of this nation.

Let us not wallow in the valley of despair. I say to you today, my friends, that in spite of the difficulties and frustrations of the moment, I still have a dream. It is a dream deeply rooted in the American dream.

I have a dream that one day this nation will rise up and live out the true meaning of its creed: "We hold these truths to be self-evident: that all men are created equal." I have a dream that one day on the red hills of Georgia the sons of former slaves and the sons of former slave-owners will be able to sit down together at a table of brotherhood. I have a dream that one day even the state of Mississippi, a desert state, sweltering with the heat of injustice and oppression, will be transformed into an oasis of freedom and justice. I have a dream that my four children will one day live in a nation where they will not be judged by the color of their skin but by the content of their character. I have a dream today.

I have a dream that one day the state of Alabama, whose governor's lips are presently dripping with the words of interposition and nullification, will be transformed into a situation where little Black boys and Black girls will be able to join hands with little White boys and White girls and walk together as sisters and brothers. I have a dream today.

I have a dream that one day every valley shall be exalted, every hill and mountain shall be made low, the rough places will be made plain, and the crooked places will be made straight, and the glory of the Lord shall be revealed, and all flesh shall see it together. This is our hope. This is the faith with which I return to the South. With this faith we will be able to hew out of the mountain of despair a stone of hope. With this faith we will be able to transform the jangling discords of our nation into a beautiful symphony of brotherhood. With this faith we will be able to work together, to pray together, to struggle together, to go to jail together, to stand up for freedom together, knowing that we will be free one day.

This will be the day when all of God's children will be able to sing with a new meaning, "My country, 'tis of thee, sweet land of liberty, of thee I sing. Land where my fathers died, land of the pilgrim's pride, from every mountainside, let freedom ring." And if America is to be a great nation, this must become true.

So let freedom ring from the prodigious hilltops of New Hampshire. Let freedom ring from the mighty mountains of New York. Let freedom ring from the heightening Alleghenies of Pennsylvania! Let freedom ring from the snowcapped Rockies of Colorado! Let freedom ring from the curvaceous peaks of California! But not only that; let freedom ring from Stone Mountain of Georgia! Let freedom ring from Lookout Mountain of Tennessee! Let freedom ring from every hill and every molehill of Mississippi. From every mountainside, let freedom ring.

When we let freedom ring, when we let it ring from every village and every hamlet, from every state and every city, we will be able to speed up that day when all of God's children, Black men and White men, Jews and Gentiles, Protestants and Catholics, will be able to join hands and sing in the words of the old Negro spiritual, "Free at last! Free at last! Thank God Almighty, we are free at last!"

As key figures in national debates surrounding when, where and for whom the freedom bell rings, it is interesting to note that nearly all clear articulations of freedom and liberty warn of abuse of governmental power. Consider the remarks of the late Justice Douglas:

> One of the earmarks of the totalitarian understanding of society is that it seeks to make all subcommunities—family, school, business, press, church—completely subject to control by the State. The State then is not one vital institution among others: a policeman, a referee, and a source of initiative for the common good.
>
> Instead, it seeks to be coextensive with family and school, press, business community, and the Church, so that all of these component interest groups are, in principle, reduced to organs and agencies of the State. In a democratic political order, this megatherian concept is expressly rejected as out of accord with the democratic understanding of social good, and with the actual make-up of the human community.[31]

Woodhull and King, without benefit of either race or gender affinity with the ruling elite, endured abuse of state power and were forced to wear the badges and suffer incidents of slavery. Restraints upon their social and political activities extended to members of the classes for whom they struggled. Both reference the founding theories, guiding principles, and quintessential spirit of the great social compact. Their critics charged them with miscomprehending the nature of representative democracy. Invariably, the late Brazilian educational theorist, Paulo Freire, characterizes freedom as the legacy to which we are joint heirs.[32] There is but one democracy and one way to be free. Freedom does not submit with long-suffering patience while injustice runs amok. The ordination of human freedom, according to Jefferson, rests upon the belief that the "Divine author of our existence never intended one part of the human race to hold an absolute power in and an unbounded authority over others." In its inevitable historic trajectory, the spirit of freedom and courage gave rise to the militant organizing of the 1960s.

The Black Panther Party For Self-Defense created a Ten Point Program that hinged upon economic freedom, self-determination, full employment, reparations, fair housing, education, healthcare, an end to war, police brutality, and the release of political detainees being held in the United States.[33] Their written plan concluded with these now famous words: When, in the course of human events, it becomes necessary for one people to dissolve the political bonds [with those evincing] a design to reduce them under absolute despotism, it is their right, [nay] their duty, to throw off such government, and to provide new guards for their future security.

For Your Consideration

How would you define Freedom? Explain the nature of the liberty guaranteed in our great social compact, the liberty that defines us insofar as we've taken on the obligation of leading the "free world."

Throughout history, ruling elites have characterized proponents of universal freedom as radical and dangerous. These Movements were viewed as a considerable threat to the established order. My methods for exploring the nature and scope of individual rights throughout this book will bring us back to the brand of freedom they championed in order to examine why some conceptions of freedom are still considered radical to this very day.

Chapter Two

Justifying Rules of Law & Monitoring Legal Institutions

> That life is complicated is a fact of great analytic importance. Law too often seeks to avoid this truth by making up its own breed of narrower, simpler, but hypnotically powerful rhetorical truths. Acknowledging, challenging, playing with these as rhetorical gestures is, it seems to me, necessary for any conception of justice. [O]ne of the most important results of reconceptualizing from "objective truth" to rhetorical event will be more nuanced sense of legal and social responsibility.[1]
>
> Patricia J. Williams, ALCHEMY OF RACE AND RIGHTS

Is it possible to achieve the ideal we know as the 'rule of law:' to govern a nation by laws rather than men? "It is an ideal that is closely associated with whatever measure of legitimacy any particular system might be able to claim."[2]

Is it rational to assume that there are two sides to every legal issue merely because we have licensed attorneys arguing on both sides? The debate about the efficacy and fairness of the adversarial model itself has intensified in the last decade. According to Chris Gus Kanios, at the Center for Guerrilla Law:

> Far too often we have romanticized the ability of the adversarial system to protect against injustice. The odds are virtually always in favor of parties who have the resources to wage legal battles and who enjoy the biases of the legal system. Even when individual rights can be vindicated, underlying societal conditions are rarely transformed. A landowner, for example, might continue to act in selfish, disrespectful ways, despite being forced to rescind an unfair eviction in one isolated incident. Instead of being an arena to protect the less powerful from abuses of the powerful, the legal system often helps perpetuate the existing power imbalances, leaving the [perpetrators] to continue their harmful practices.[3]

Kanios speaks to judicial processes that impact individual legal rights and meaningful enforcement against well-connected parties.

Judicial Independence

Independent Courts: How Important Are They?[4]

Ed O'Brien

Relevant Edited Excerpts

ABA Commission on Separation of Powers Report 1997

Making vs. Interpreting Law

[Recent] debate centers around "judicial activism," a term applied by some when they see "judges becoming legislators" and getting involved in "making law," rather than just enforcing and interpreting it. These detractors complain that for the last 40 years the courts have told police what to do when they arrest defendants, made parents send their children to certain schools, "discovered" a right to abortion and even decided the results of a Presidential election. They see these actions as over-reaching and inappropriate.

Many legal experts, however, believe courts need to step in to protect minorities and preserve the rights protected in the Constitution and the Bill of Rights. They point to decisions that voided racial discrimination, established privacy rights, and protected free speech as examples in which crucial freedoms, neglected by other branches of government, were upheld by the judicial branch. This school of legal opinion says that the country might have had to wait for years before lawmakers acted in such areas. Stating the position of this side of the debate is Professor Erwin Chemerinsky, who has said, "I am unsure of what exactly judicial activism means ... My sense is that it is a label that conservatives use to attack the decisions that they do not like." He points out that in recent years most of the "activism" in the judicial arena has been by conservative justices who now form a majority on the U.S. Supreme Court.

While criticism on the activism issue, along with many others, is still alive, few if any federal judges have actually been impeached. The real danger of such debates, says the ABA, is not the actual removal of individual judges but that judges feel restrained from ruling in ways that go against the majority for fear of being put though impeachment proceedings.

The Selection of Judges

Perhaps the greatest impact on judicial independence is derived from the methods by which judges are selected. The U.S. system is best known by the federal method of judge selection, wherein the President nominates all federal judges for a life term and they are confirmed or rejected by a vote of the U.S. Senate.

Though the federal process gains more prominence in the media, most jurists in the United States are state judges. There are more than 30,000 judges in the 50 states, 87 percent of whom—in 39 states—must face voters regularly in some type of popular election.8 The election structure differs among the states, though most judges are elected in nonpartisan contests, meaning that they do not run under the banner of one political party. Many judges, however, must obtain the endorsement a political party, garner favor from party leaders, raise campaign contributions from individuals, law firms and corporations and take positions in campaigns. Organizations such as the American Bar Association have criticized this process, saying it undermines the independence of judges. Recently, a report by the Committee for Economic Development (CED) concluded, "elective systems tend to undermine the independence and impartiality of the judiciary" and called on leaders to "take actions to initiate reforms that would eliminate judicial selection by election."

The problems with election of judges seem obvious. If judges have to raise money, how can we expect them to be totally independent and impartial when campaign contributors come before them at trial? Even when judges honestly put aside biases, the appearance of favoritism remains. Meanwhile, campaign costs are rapidly rising, with television ads putting some judicial campaigns over the million-dollar mark.

Foreign commentators and jurists, who often express admiration of the independence of our judiciary and the life-terms of federal judges, are often shocked when they hear about the system of electing state judges. Judge V. Robert Payant of the National Judicial College writes that a judge from Russia, where some judges are appointed for life terms, felt that appointed jurists "have a much better chance at judicial independence than the poor American judges who are facing an [elective] system."

The most popular alternative to straight elections is known as the "Missouri Plan," which was first outlined the 1870s and then gained support in the 20th century, at a time when reformers felt the election of judges diminished the difference between judges and other elected officials. Under the Missouri Plan, a nominating commission comprising lawyers and laypersons, often chaired by a respected judge, would propose the names of potential judges. The commission in some cases has the power to name the judges outright; in others, it sends a name or names to the governor of the state, who makes the final selection. The system, often referred to as "merit selection," is supported by many who believe it results in a much higher caliber of judge than elections or straight appointments by a governor, who may appoint political cronies or campaign contributors.

Another aspect of the Missouri Plan that has been widely adopted is that of "retention elections." Generally this means that, after a certain term of years, the name of a judge who was initially appointed through a nominating commission or another type of merit selection is placed on the ballot. The voters then vote "Yes " or "No" to retain or not retain this judge for another term. The advantage of this system is that the judge does not have to run against another candidate. Yet the retention system does not eliminate all the dynamics of judicial elections—candidates might still have to take positions and seek campaign contributions.

Though it appears that most legal scholars, judges, bar association leaders and officials of many other organizations support abolishing judicial elections, these same experts predict that it will difficult to change this system. In its 2002 report the CED predicted that eliminating judicial selection by election "will not come quickly." Professor Roy Schotland of Georgetown Law Center, commenting on the CED report, writes, "For the 96 years of major efforts to replace contestable elections for the bench, not a singe state has eliminated elections." To some extent, the reasons for this lie in Americans' love of democracy. In the 19th century, the prevalent concern of most citizens was holding judges directly accountable to the public's will. Today, there are other reasons that may prevent the elimination of judicial elections, including the fact that it is in interest of political parties to field candidates for as many offices as possible. More electoral races mean greater interest in elections in general and more offices parties can use to reward loyal party workers or financial contributors.

Conclusion

So where does all this leave our country on the issue independence of the judiciary? First, it is important to note that public confidence in the courts has been declining. Polls uniformly confirm this. In a 1995 survey by U.S. News and World Report, only eight percent of respondents had a great deal of confidence in the judicial system, while 46 percent said they had some confidence and 45 percent said they had no confidence at all. One factor influencing these statistics is publicity. The most sensational and most atypical cases are often the most publicized and tend to show the courts in a negative light. Socio-economics also influence confidence in the judiciary; polls often reflect the fact that poor people, members of minority groups and other disadvantaged Americans are the most alienated from the courts. One NAACP lawyer said, "There are sectors of the public I cannot discuss the judicial system and the judiciary with any more and convince them that they should have faith in it, they should view it as impartial ... We have lost poor people, at least in the area that I work. It is beyond the reach because what they see is anything but impartial and anything but fair."

Why is the issue of judiciary independence of such concern to the legal, business and academic communities? Perhaps because without independent courts, we might not be able to restrain a President who has gone too far, void a state law requiring the segregation of schools, or hold police accountable. As Senator Sam Ervin Jr. of Watergate fame said more than 30 years ago, judicial independence is "perhaps the most essential characteristic of a free society."

In February 2007, Paris Hilton sped down Sunset Boulevard without her headlights close to midnight, on a suspended license, in the middle of a 36-month probation resulting from her DUI arrest the previous September. Two traffic stops and failure to enroll in a mandated alcohol education program landed Hilton back in court. On May 4, 2007, she was ordered to report to a women's jail in suburban Lynwood by June 5th to serve a 45 day sentence or face 90 days behind bars: no work release, furloughs, alternative to incarceration, or electronic monitoring. Judge Michael T. Sauer determined that "there's no doubt she knew her license had been suspended," and she continued to drive in violation of the terms of her probation in an alcohol-related reckless driving case. The petition to FREE PARIS WHITNEY HILTON notes that Nick Nolte, Mel Gibson, Tracy Morgan, Wynonna Judd, Busta Rhymes and Eve "never did a day in jail after their initial arrests for drunk driving/DUI /DWI charges." When asked about the petition, California Governor Arnold Schwarzenegger reportedly told Associated Press that he had better things to think about.[5]

Reason & the Rule of Law

Analyzing the nuances of social and legal responsibility in the realm of individual rights requires knowledge of judicial interpretative process. The parties are before the Court, all evidence is in, relevant legislation has been dissected at multiple appellate stages: What does the Constitution now require? How do justices approach the social, economic, and moral issues that are influenced by rulings issued from the bench? "They choose between rules (e.g., contributory vs. comparative negligence); they choose between interpretations (e.g., broad vs. narrow readings of a statute or a precedent); and —when the law's commands seem to conflict with their notion of a just outcome—they choose between giving in and pressing on in search of a plausible argument to the contrary."[6]

In a book entitled THE METAPHYSICAL CLUB, Louis Menand defines various types of legal reasoning, which are all supported by a brand of theory:

> A legal theory that stresses the logical consistency of judicial opinions is called formalist; a theory that emphasizes their social consequences is called utilitarian; a theory that regards them as reflections of the circumstances in which they were written is called historicist. The problem with all such theories is that they single out one aspect of the law as the essential aspect. [L]aw has no essential aspect.[7]

Supreme Court Justice Stephen Breyer might disagree. He suggests that there is widespread consensus as to the Constitution's primary role in preserving democratic objectives.

> People have a right to an active and constant participation in collective power. [As such] courts should take great account of the constitution's democratic nature when interpreting both constitutional and statutory texts. Interpretation of legal text should yield better law. Law that helps a community of individuals to democratically find practical solutions to important contemporary social problems, the practical consequences of which are important in relation to their value for constitutional purposes.[8]

There is no dearth of critiques of legal reasoning.[9] Standard analytic models are used to define its characteristics, flaws, virtues, and inconsistencies. Some critiques are more widely discussed and acknowledged than others.

Law and Politics[10]

David Kairys

> Legal reasoning, of course, is what students learn in law school, and it purports to provide a basis for decision making in particular cases that is separate from politics, social theory, or particular values. Decisions are made on a legal basis rather than on the basis of social, political, moral, or religious perspectives.
>
> Legal reasoning, particularly as it is taught in law schools, has two branches: doctrinal analysis and policy analysis. Doctrinal analysis is supposedly the "hard stuff" of logically analyzing rules and principles and arriving at a required, particular result. When those rules or principles do not lead to a particular result, courts, lawyers, and law teachers resort to policy analysis to fill the void.
>
> With regard to doctrinal analysis, there is an element of criticism going on in the typical law-school class since judicial decisions are not taken necessarily, or even usually, to mean what they say. Instead, they are interpreted to mean more or other than that. There are thought to be some discernible underlying rules, and the traditional law school class often consists of a search for these "real," underlying rules and principles. The professor moves from person to person until someone seems to identify the principle that the teacher thinks explains a particular decision or series of decisions. Then the class moves on to something else.

If there seems to be no rule or principle, nothing that unifies a line of decisions over a period of time, then you start talking about policy. Usually, there is no bench mark signaling a class to move into policy analysis, but after awhile the move becomes apparent. Then the class discusses values, but in a very particular way. Values are usually discussed in a way that assumes their validity, though values vary among all of us. Often it is assumed that all or most people hold these values and that society has democratically adopted them, but almost nothing of any substance seems to have that kind of consensus, and democracy does not seem to have anything to do with the choice of values.

If the values or the interests conflict, then the class shifts into third gear and balances. In this balancing mode, one purports to step back and say that one value or one interest, or some combination of them, leads one way, and another bundle leads the other way. By being objective and fair, and applying expertise as a lawyer, one reaches the correct, required conclusion.

The message in all three of these analytical modes, explicitly or implicitly, is that if you are fair, reasonably competent, neutral, and unbiased, the process will produce a legally required, socially optimal, correct result.

The starting point of critical theory is that legal reasoning does not provide concrete, real answers to particular legal or social problems. Legal reasoning is not a method or process that leads reasonable, competent, and fair-minded people to particular results in particular cases.

Law and legal reasoning involve a body of knowledge that can be passed from person to person, and a language that differs from everyday language. It even includes a unique system of manners. Several years ago, after I had been practicing for a while, a lawyer opposing me was handling his first case. He began to ask a question that I did not want the jury to hear, and I did what a lawyer usually does in that situation: I objected. He turned to me with a glare and said, "Let me finish the question!" I felt bad for a moment; this lawyer was personally offended. He considered it rude that I did not let him finish his question before I raised an objection to it. And in normal social conversation, of course, he would be right. If you are talking to people at a bar and in the middle of someone's sentence you say, "I object to that," people would think you were an idiot. You might even get some beer poured over your head. There is a very different set of manners in the legal world, however, and they are very aggressive to say the least.

The law is also a culture. After you have practiced for a while, you quickly discover that there is a particular bar that public defenders go to after work and to have lunch, which is different from the place where the district attorneys gather. Because law offices are so hierarchically structured, it is also common that, for example, there be one bar for the most important district attorneys and another for the troops. These places might be juice bars, or they could be alcohol bars. The choice may have nothing to do with drinking or with the quality of the food. But each group has its own place, and at these places an entire culture exists: people talk law and tell war stories in a language that is really unintelligible and annoying to non-lawyers, particularly to lawyers' spouses. It is very irritating to spouses and the source of tension and problems in many lawyers' families. Spouses commonly wonder why it seems so appealing to the people who do it.

The law is all these things: it is a culture, a language, and a body of knowledge. What it provides though, in terms of actually deciding cases, is a variety of stylized rationalizations that a judge may freely choose from. These rationalizations go every which way. And the choice of any one or any combination of them bestows legitimacy within the legal system as an explanation for why one is ruling this way or that way. But there is nothing within the law that determines which rationalization a judge should choose in particular situations, and this lack of a legally required result is systematically obscured in law classes, legal discourse, and popular conceptions of the law.

Pierre Schlag's recent book, **THE ENCHANTMENT OF REASON**, issues a direct challenge to American legal thinkers. It offers a comprehensive analysis of the parameters of legal reasoning. He begins by asking, "Why is reason so important to law? Why do jurists and legal thinkers consider it important to rationalize law—to show that it is rational and to cast law in the image of reason?"[11] Chapter Two of this influential work explores the answer.

Faith in the Power of Reason[12]

Pierre Schlag

In 1995, the dean of the Yale Law School, Anthony Kronman, was interviewed on the state of his institution. The occasion for his interview must have been pleasing: a U.S. News and World Report poll had just ranked the Yale Law School first in the nation.

It had not always been thus: At the turn of the century, The [Yale] Law School was for all practical purposes moribund. Its student body was small; its dean, Henry Wade Rogers, a recent appointee to the Second Circuit Court of Appeals, was a part-time teacher who did not want to retire, and its faculty, but for two members, were thoroughly undistinguished, if not better described as unknown.

But this was 1995 and things were different. Commenting on the ethos of his institution, Dean Kronman professed that what unified the Yale Law School was "a faith in the power of reason."

Now, it is well known that law school deans are tragic figures who must routinely say outlandish things in public about the virtues of their own institutions. Still, it is of some interest to take note that what was chosen to praise the Yale Law School at its moment of triumph was a series of conundrums: what unifies the law school is faith in the power of reason.

Far from disputing Dean Kronman's characterization, I will be arguing that he is absolutely correct—and, surely, not just about the Yale Law School. What unifies American law schools is indeed, a series of conundrums: it is faith in the power of reason. What allows these conundrums to unify American law schools is that they are not recognized as such. This nonrecognition, in turn, is exactly what faith in the power of reason produces.

...

The idea that all problems, issues and dilemmas are subject to "reasoned analysis," without fully exploring the *element of subjectivity*, means that an orientation toward, and reverance for, what is presented, looks and sounds like reasoned analysis is put into place, even before reason is called upon to do its work.[13]

Reason in Legal Academia

The veneration of reason in legal academia can be traced to ancient Greece. The Hellenic concept of logos describes the action through which human reason expresses its character. It rests upon commitment to dialectical engagement: the process of reasoning together through critical inquiry and openness to truth. Socrates, an ancient Greek philosopher long revered as "The Father of Virtue," is renown among moral philosophers and remains high on the list of those martyred in the service of free speech and democracy. Plato remains Socrates' most famous pupil. Plato's most famous student was Aristotle, who is known to have exclaimed that "law is reason, free from passion."[14] Long enamored with such theories, law professors are famous (even infamous in rare cases) for their use of the Socratic Method (dialectical inquiry) as a pedagogical tool. So, who was this famous father? His legendary influence captured the imagination of the men who founded this nation, which is amazing given his negative views on democracy.[15]

Interestingly, less than 30 years ago a journalist claimed to have uncovered a much-overlooked fact about the Trial of Socrates. A New York reporter asked retired journalist I.F. Stone, in 1979, what he could have possibly discovered about a trial that the wire services covered 2,378 years ago?[16] Stone quickly clarified that obsession with the Trial of Socrates was not his alone.

> The Athens of Socrates' time has gone down in history as the very place where democracy and freedom of speech were born. Yet that city put Socrates, its most famous philosopher, to death. Presumably this was because it citizens did not like what he was teaching. Yet he had been teaching there all his life, unmolested. Why did they wait until he was 70, and had only a few years to live, before executing him?[17]

Stone needed to know how so blatant a violation of free speech could occur in a city that prided itself on freedom of inquiry and expression. According to the indictment, Socrates violated the law by refusing to revere the Gods of the city, introducing other divinities, and corrupting the youth (by undermining their faith in democracy). At trial, the evidence against him boiled down to one terrifying influence: Critias. He was the bloodiest dictator Athens had ever known, a pupil of Socrates at one time, and a cousin of Plato. The prosecution's case rested upon the assertion that the philosopher's antidemocratic teachings produced a string of pro-Spartan dictators who staged two of Athen's bloodiest revolutions. Although they only ruled for about eight months, the entire nation remained on heightened terror alert. In less than a year roughly 1,500 Athenians were executed and more than ten percent of the population was banished. When they seized power, they either murdered or drove from the city all members of the Democratic Party. Socrates was neither exiled with the democrats or forced to flee with moderate oppositionists, nor did he suffer at the hands of the tyrants. Throughout the reign-of-terror Socrates never once denounced their immorality and lawlessness. When they were eventually overthrown, Socrates remained in the city, as he had from the beginning. Once democracy was finally restored, Socrates continued teaching that government should be left to experts, renouncing popular debate and vote in the assembly.

Perhaps fearing another overthrow, Socrates was indicted and brought to trial where a 510-man jury voted to convict him by a narrow margin. When asked to contemplate what his punishment should be, Socrates used the opportunity to underscore that he neither apologized for his failure to condemn the terrorists, nor defended himself on the grounds that he lacked mens rea (criminal intent). Instead, he proposed that he be honored in the town square. The vote to put him to death was larger than the vote to convict.

Far from teaching anything extraordinary about free speech, it appears that Socrates was, in fact, convicted not for what he said, but for his moral failures. His failures were most evident by what he didn't say. Could this be defined as reasonable error? Declaring the trial a great illustration that speech has its costs, that with freedom comes responsibility, or that the market place of ideas must yield to national security interests in the midst of coup d'état, is theoretically uninteresting. There is no denying the political currency of post-modern theories on the genesis, natural history and purpose of individual liberty. According to Charles Sykes, in THE END OF PRIVACY, "the literature of the last 200 years is a chronicle of what it meant to discover the power and the freedom to be [left] alone."[18] If he's correct, then we may finally be reaching the land of virtue!

Critique of Legal Education

If the study of individual rights invites inquiry into the means by which state interests are justified and balanced by judges and legislators, then it should come as no surprise that the inquiry has extended beyond interplay between the branches of government and theories of dead legal philosophers and toward key components of legal education. That a figure like Socrates has been memorialized in the ivory towers of legal education and training is part of a familiar historic pattern. As a tribute to his so-called genius, law professors use a modified version of the Socratic Method as a standard pedagogical tool.

The dialectical method requires: 1) group participation based upon equal status among its members; 2) development of general consensus around core ideas and values; 3) dialogue that promotes critical reflection; and 4) a framework for connecting the elements. However, one writer observed that in many law schools, the Socratic Method looks more like education by interrogation. It has been characterized as dehumanizing and destructive of positive pedagocial values. Even in its most harmless state, it rewards only neutral, rational explanation in ways that demean arguments for social justice.[19] Under such circumstances, reason, we are told, retains organic immunity from political infection. Yet the propensity of jurists, lawyers and academics to conceal errors of reason was entirely foreseeable. For example, Circuit Judge Wilkinson takes a pragmatic view stating that: "The law's faith in reason must represent something more. Reasoning is a proxy for other values and preferences: order over chaos, evolution over revolution, thought over passion, prolonged argumentation over precipitate action. These, I would argue, are values the federal judiciary should respect ... because the process of change has been constitutionally established."[20]

Pierre Schlag would respect another set of values, those that meet real people at the heart of their lived experiences:

> "There are enough dislocations and disruptions within normative legal thought and within our social order that we can actually begin to recognize that normative legal thought is not as it represents itself to be: its main significance is inscription of a false social aesthetic; its politics are seriously out of date; [and] its contributions to the construction of social and legal reality are ambivalent at best...."[21]

Professor Lucinda Finley would add that:

> "Law is a language of power, a particularly authoritative discourse. Law can pronounce definitively what something is or is not and how a situation or event is to be understood."[22] The concepts, categories, terms, and reasoning organize lawful practices and constructs meanings. Legal language does more than express thoughts. It reinforces certain worldviews and [retains] the "power to silence alternative meanings—to suppress other stories."[23]

Two leading organizations appear united in their edicts around the goals of legal education. The Association of American Law Schools joins with the American Bar Association's Commission on Professionalism in concluding that the highest standards of ethics and professionalism should be adhered to within law schools since it provides the students' first exposure to the profession and professors inevitably serve as important role models.[24] Much of what has been written raises significant questions about the methods employed to train new lawyers. Two observations seem particularly relevant to the goals of preparing lawyers to preserve rights deemed fundamental, the first relates to institutional climate and the other surrounds the nature of justice.

According to Gary Wetlaufer:

> Those who have been around the law for an extended period of time may describe the condition of legal discourse in different terms, but many of us still find it unsatisfactory. We hear a great many arguments in which it seems that people ought to be convincing one another but, in fact, are not. We see arguments that fail to persuade, disagreements that never end, and, all too often, partisans who neither understand nor respect their adversary's positions. It is sometimes as if there were so many ships passing in the night. On any given ship, there might be conversations in which issues are joined and problems are solved, but as between those ships there is barely any communication worthy of the name.[25]

Additional critiques concern efforts to reintroduce notions of justice and accountability. Patricia Williams and Pierre Schlag are supported in their views that human nature must be accounted for against the relative dangers involved in our predisposition of reverence toward hypnotically powerful rhetorical truths about what law is and how it works. These issues are timeless. Critical insight is threatening to traditional legal understanding because it challenges our "moral and existential commitment to authority and obedience." If critical scholars are right, "there is simply no way that obedience to the commands contained in the disembodied meanings of law [compilation of "words" or "texts"] is an even possible mode of life, much less a good one."[26]

At the nation's founding, John Adams spoke passionately about issues of justice and neutrality in an essay where he issued this warning:

> Scarcely any two writers, much less nations, agree in using words in the same sense. Such a latitude, it is true, allows a scope for politicians to speculate, and to deceive the people....
>
> The union of the people, in any principle, rule or system is thus rendered impossible because superstition, prejudice, habit and passions are so differently at-

tached to words, that you can scarcely make any nation understand itself. The nature of mankind [is] one thing, and the reason of mankind another: and the first has the same relation to the last as the whole to a part: the passions and appetites are parts of human nature, as well as reason and the moral sense. In the institution of government, it must be remembered that although reason ought always to govern individuals, it certainly never did since the Fall, and never will til the Millennium, and human nature must be taken as it is, as it has been, and will be.[27]

Law school Deans, as chief administrators, set the tone under which institutional objectives are articulated and realized. They share responsibility for the climate of the institution along with the faculty in separate but equal measure. Consider the following letter to alums, in which one Dean has demonstrated that he understands the fullness of that responsibility. The full text of a letter he wrote upon assuming the Deanship is republished here with his permission.[28]

Dear Graduates and Friends of Yale Law School,

By the time you read this, I will have taken office as the fifteenth dean of Yale Law School. The task feels daunting, but the assignment seems straightforward: making sure that the greatest law school of the 20th century becomes an even greater law school in the 21st century. To do so, we must stay true to our values and traditions, while at the same time changing to meet four key challenges:

First, globalization: Many law schools have waved the globalization banner, but no law school has truly asked and answered the question: "What does it mean to have a genuinely global curriculum, faculty, student body, and programs in the 21st century?" At Yale Law School, we have already integrated an international perspective into many of our core courses. We also have a huge array of internationally focused programs, ranging from the Schell Center on International Human Rights, to the Corporate Law Center, to the Middle East Legal Studies Seminar, to the China Law Center, to our Global Constitutionalism conference. But what is the best way for us to build upon these strengths to create a modern law school that is explicitly global in its focus? Please join us at this year's alumni weekend, when we will ask together: How should a Yale Law School Education Address Global Legal Issues?

Second, speaking to the profession: Our graduates change the world every day. They rank among the leaders of the judiciary, academia, private practice, and public service. Yet the myth lingers that Yale is primarily a school of theory. Our students will face the challenges and demands of a global private and public practice. How can we better train our students to meet the professional responsibilities and regulatory frameworks of a transnational legal profession? What are the best ways for us to bring our unparalleled academic and clinical faculty together with our alumni to do so?

Third, calling our students to public service: Yale Law School has uniquely served the public interest and created lawyers who have most shaped the public interest. My deanship will reaffirm our longstanding commitment to public service. Don't we, the most privileged in our educational fortunes, have a duty to serve the least privileged? How can we ensure that each of our students devotes significant energy toward serving some conception of the public interest as he or she sees it?

> Fourth, and finally, renewing the faculty: We have the world's greatest law faculty, but it needs renewal. How can we diversify and rejuvenate our faculty, to ensure that our faculty is even better twenty years from now?
>
> Globalization, the profession, public service, renewal: these have been my own life's commitments. I see my job as simple: keeping Yale Law School a community of commitment to world-class scholarship, professional excellence, and service for the greater good. In law, there are many committed individuals; there are all too many unfocused communities. But Yale Law School has always been—and under my deanship must always be—a community that is committed to both humanity and excellence, both theory and practice, both talent and passion.
>
> On the fiftieth anniversary of Brown vs. Board of Education, it moves me deeply to think that America's greatest law school has chosen its dean based not on the color of his skin, but on the content of his commitments. It was more than forty years ago that my parents first came to Yale Law School as visiting lecturers. When I walked into the Law School for the first time, I thought—as I thought this morning and as I think every morning—that Yale Law School is the most impressive and humane institution of which I have ever been a part. I promise you that I will do everything in my power to keep it that way. I am hugely excited about the future, and I thank you for joining me in building this community of commitment together.

Respectfully,
Harold Hongju Koh

The Association of American Law Schools has characterized the guardianship of civil liberties as a clear priority in the preparation of students for the practice of law. Responsibility for preparing students to promote justice is deemed a socio-legal responsibility as well as an ethical obligation for law professors, who are typically members of two professions with a duty to comply with the requirements and standards of both.

Regulating Members of the Bench

Members of the bench are held to the highest level of accountability. Canons of Judicial Conduct require judges in every jurisdiction to uphold the integrity and independence of the judiciary, avoid improper behavior, shun the appearance of impropriety, perform the duties of judicial office with impartiality and diligence, limit extra-judicial activities to those specifically designed to improve the law, legal system, or administration of justice, to do so in a manner that minimizes the risk of conflict with judicial obligations, and refrain from inappropriate political activity. The overtures explain why, for example, the preamble of the Canons for the Commonwealth of Virginia reads:

> Our legal system is based on the principle that an independent, fair and competent judiciary will interpret and apply the laws that govern us. The role of the judiciary is central to American concepts of justice and the rule of law. Intrinsic to all sections of these Canons are the precepts that judges, individually and collec-

tively, must respect and honor the judicial office as a public trust and strive to enhance and maintain confidence in our legal system. The judge is an arbiter of facts and law for the resolution of disputes and a highly visible symbol of government under the rule of law.[29]

The Wooing of Our Judges[30]

Judge Abner Mikva
New York Times OP-ED

Reprinted with permission

In a lifetime as a judge, lawyer and lawmaker, I can safely say I've encountered few judges guilty of outright dishonesty. Even when I started practicing law in Chicago in the bad old days, the number of crooked judges was small. But that is not what people believed then or believe now.

That is why so much is built into our judicial system—from the Black robe and "all rise" custom to lifetime tenure for federal judges—to help foster the notion of judicial integrity. It all becomes meaningless, however, when private interests are allowed to wine and dine judges at fancy resorts under the pretext of "educating" them. Between 1992 and 1998, according to a report from the Community Rights Counsel, a nonprofit public-interest law firm, more than 230 federal judges took one or more trips each to resort locations for legal seminars paid for by corporations and foundations that have an interest in federal litigation on environmental topics.

In the seminars devoted to so-called environmental education, judges listened to speakers whose overwhelming message was that regulation should be limited—that the free market should be relied upon to protect the environment, for example, or that the "takings" clause of the Constitution should be interpreted to prohibit rules against development in environmentally sensitive places.

Judges who attended the seminars wrote 10 of the most important rulings of the 1990s curbing federal environmental protections, including one that struck down habitat protection provisions of the Endangered Species Act and another that invalidated regulations on soot and smog. In six of these cases, according to the report, the judge attended one of the seminars while the case was pending before the court. And, the report reveals, many judges failed to disclose required information about these seminars on their financial disclosure forms.

If an actual party to a case took the judge to a resort, all expenses paid, shortly before the case was heard, the judge and the host would be perceived to be acting improperly even if all they discussed was their grandchildren. The conduct is no less reprehensible when an interest group substitutes for the party to the case.

Of course it may be a coincidence that none of the seminars financed by private interests take place in Chicago in January or in Atlanta in July. It may be a coincidence that the judges who attend usually come down on the same side of important policy questions as those who financed the meetings. It may even be a coincidence that environmentalists are seldom invited to speak. But surely any citizen who reads about judges attending fancy meetings under questionable sponsorship will have well-founded doubts about their objectivity.

I know one federal judge who has been on a dozen trips sponsored by the three most prominent special interest seminar groups. I remember at least two occasions where judges on judicial panels where I also served took positions where they had heard advocated at seminars sponsored by groups with particular interest in the litigation.

The federal judiciary has a Federal Judicial Center that provides educational seminars for judges on a wide range of legal topics. Since it uses taxpayer funds and answers to Congress, the program locales are not exotic, but the presentations are balanced.

Unfortunately, the United States Judicial Conference, the governing body for all federal judges has punted on the propriety of privately funded seminars, advising that judges assess their appropriateness "case by case."

Short of requiring judges to stick to federally sponsored seminars, the government could, at least, require that whenever a judge attends any professional seminar, the government must pay his or her way. Then citizens might begin to ask questions about what they were paying for, and whether it was really likely to promote judicial fairness.

For Your Consideration

ABC News Reported the following on Jan. 23, 2006:

> At the historic swearing-in of John Roberts as the 17th Chief Justice of the United States last September, every member of the Supreme Court, except Antonin Scalia, was in attendance. ABC News has learned that Scalia instead was on the tennis court at one of the country's top resorts, the Ritz-Carlton hotel in Bachelor Gulch, Colo., during a trip to a legal seminar sponsored by the Federalist Society.
>
> Not only did Scalia's absence appear to be a snub of the new Chief Justice, but according to some legal ethics experts, it also raised questions about the propriety of what critics call judicial junkets.
>
> "It's unfortunate of course that what kept him from the swearing-in was an activity that is itself of dubious ethical propriety," said Stephen Gillers, a New York University law professor, who is a recognized scholar on legal ethics. Scalia spent two nights at the luxury resort lecturing at the legal seminar where ABC News also found him on the tennis court, heading out for a fly-fishing expedition, and socializing with members of the Federalist Society, the conservative activist group that paid for the expenses of his trip. At a press conference, almost two weeks later, Scalia was not inclined to tell reporters his whereabouts during Roberts' swearing-in. "I was out of town with a commitment that I could not break, and that's what the public information office told you," he said. It "doesn't matter what it was. It was a commitment that I couldn't break," Scalia continued when questioned further. According to the event's invitation, obtained by ABC News, the Federalist Society promised members who attended the seminar an exclusive and "rare opportunity to spend time, both socially and intellectually" with Scalia. One night at the resort, Scalia attended a cocktail reception, sponsored in part by the same lobbying and law firm where convicted lobbyist Jack Abramoff once worked.[31]

Nancy Benac, Washington reporter for the Associated Press, wrote an article "**Scalia Begins Third Decade on Court**" on September 29, 2006. The article states that his 20-

year "anniversary on the court came and went quietly this week, [he] was passed over by President Bush in favor of Roberts for the position of chief justice when William Rehnquist died a year ago. Scalia told reporters at the time, "I'm not even sure I wanted it, to tell you the truth," saying the chief justice's administrative duties would have taken time from his thinking and writing."[32]

One of the least polled questions of the hour was not whether he wanted the job, but whether he possessed the necessary qualifications. Keep in mind that from all reports there appear to be few political/philosophical distinctions between Scalia and the new Chief Justice John Roberts. Interestingly, the testimony of Yale Law Professor Judith Resnik on the appointment of John Roberts before the Senate Judiciary Committee sheds light on the job and the man.[33]

The Role of the Chief Justice

Statement of Judith Resnik

Prepared for the Committee on the Judiciary
of the United States Senate
John G. Roberts, Jr. of Maryland
To Be Chief Justice of the United States
Submitted September 9, 2005

Relevant Edited Excerpts

THE OPPORTUNITIES PRESENTED BY THE CONFIRMATION PROCESS

The consideration of a nominee to the Supreme Court is a unique occasion in American political life—in part because it is a rare event and in part because the Supreme Court plays a central role in our nation. This hearing, convened by virtue of the Constitution's decision to locate the authority for selection of life-tenured federal judges in the two political branches of government, invites open discussion of the American legal system, of the purposes and scope of constitutional rights, and of the obligations and responsibilities of public and private actors under the rule of law.

While focused on a particular nominee, each hearing is a testament to this constitutional democracy's deep commitments to justice under the rule of law. Each hearing is also a moment to focus not only on the many accomplishments of the person under consideration but also on why we care about courts, what the constitutional creation of life-tenured judgeships entails, and what purposes are served by judicial independence.

These propositions are all the more important when a person is nominated to be the Chief Justice of the United States. The Chief Justice is the "symbol of the Court." Personifies "the rule of law in our society; by speaking for the aspirations and beliefs of America as a Nation."

As I will detail below, given the evolution of the role of the Chief Justice, the person holding that office wears many hats. [The] Chief Justice serves as: the senior jurist of nine rendering decisions on America's highest court, America's symbol of justice, chief executive officer of the entire federal judicial system, the spokesperson and agenda-setter for the Third Branch of government, the Chief Justice has enormous discretionary powers.

In recent years, with some difficult confirmation hearings, the process has been criticized as too contentious. Under-appreciated by these critics are the purposes for and the history of disagreements over nominations. Controversy about individuals to serve as jurists is both a longstanding feature of American politics and fairly reflective of the role that law itself plays in American politics. Conflict is not a recent artifact of televised Senate hearings. From 1795 through the twentieth century to the debates during the last several years, participants have used individual nominations to make arguments about what they hope United States law is and will be.

Since this country's founding, the institution of the federal courts has been recognized as a means of shaping the rights of the people and the powers of the national and state governments. Americans have understood that the legal philosophies, the party affiliations, and the ideological commitments of individuals serving as federal judges affect the content of legal doctrine. Then, as now, people in the United States have disagreed about the scope of national powers and about the desirability of an expansive role for federal adjudication. One of the many ways in which those debates occur is through the prism of discussing a given individual's record and qualifications to serve as a life-tenured jurist.

Not only is debate about the nomination of John Roberts constitutionally appropriate and consistent with longstanding practices, it provides an opportunity for all Americans to reflect on our aspirations for this nation and for the role of government in our lives. This is a "constitutional moment," and one we should proudly use to demonstrate our commitment to the panoply of American constitutional values. Now is the time to celebrate the protection of individual liberties and rights in a system in which independent jurists provide justice under the rule of law.

The confirmation process itself has also served, repeatedly, as a means of developing or clarifying legal norms. At hearings in the eighteenth century, conflicts emerged about the Jay Treaty. During the nineteenth century, debate was had on issues relating to railroads and unions. During the twentieth century, hearings addressed the constitutional rights of women and men of all colors, as questions of racial and gender equality came to the fore. Now, in the twenty-first century, the topics include rights to sexual privacy, to reproductive choice, religion and the public sphere, the legally appropriate responses to threats of terrorism, and the scope of Executive and congressional powers. Through discussions about individual nominees, certain of these issues will be identified as powerfully divisive and others as so settled as to not even appear to have "political" implications.

When attitudes are widely shared, they are not perceived as constituting an "ideology." Only when norms and values are contested do we think of a set of questions as touching on ideology.

What are the questions and the issues that should be at the center of these hearings? One cannot answer the question of whether this particular person is the right individual to be both the symbolic and the actual leader of America's great federal judiciary without asking: What are the symbolic and the actual purposes of the courts that he would lead? Why do we care so passionately about courts?

This nominee's attitudes toward adjudication and the role of the Third Branch matter so much because an intense struggle is underway about the role of courts.

Many in this nation (as well as around the world) celebrate courts as central to the well-being of an economically sound democracy. A robust judiciary enables stability, predictability, and security because both institutional and individual actors understand that their grievances will be heard in regular processes that are transparent, rule-based, and precedent bound. Further, courts offer opportunities for independent and impartial third parties to assess the validity of claims. Moreover, courts in democracies serve as deliberate checks on majoritarian power by constraining inappropriate exercises of executive, congressional, and more generally, of sovereign authority. Courts are an especially critical resource for the less powerful who, through adjudication, are given the opportunity to get a fair hearing even when they lack the resources to lobby Congress or to obtain attention from the media.

I urge Senators to learn more about what this nominee believes courts are for, about who should have access to them and for what claims, and about how he understands the role judges should play in checking the power of government, in interpreting constitutional and statutory rights, and in holding accountable those responsible for injury. These words may be abstract, but the principles that they reflect are not. During the last two hundred years, the Congress, the Executive, and the federal judiciary, working in concert and encouraged by many private organizations, have done a remarkable job in creating a substantial, important federal judicial system. Through hundreds of different statutes, Congress has repeatedly turned to the federal courts by vesting authority in the judiciary to enforce new rights aimed at safeguarding consumers, at protecting the environment, and at ensuring fair treatment of all people.

To serve the American populace, Congress has also endowed the federal judiciary with significant resources. The import of the nation's constitutional commitment to judicial independence and authority can be seen in the more than 750 federal courthouse facilities at which the 1200 life-tenured jurists and the hundreds of magistrate and bankruptcy judges (aided by 30,000 in staff) work in response to the 350,000 civil and criminal cases and 1.6 million bankruptcy petitions filed annually. More profoundly, the evidence of the importance of the American commitment to courts can be found in the faith Americans have placed in the federal judiciary—to listen to their claims and adjudicate them fairly, to insist on the human dignity of all persons and recognize their equality before the law, to acknowledge the challenge of enabling equal access in a world of disputants with very unequal resources, and to restrain undue exercises of power.

The nomination of a person to serve as the Chief Justice of the United States is thus a critical occasion upon which to insist on the promotion of a culture that cherishes judging, respects individual judgments when rendered after deliberation, obliges judges to take responsibility for their decisions through explanation and publication, and appreciates judges for protecting constitutional liberties and rights. To do so, we need a Chief Justice committed to a judiciary that is an independent and vibrant branch of government. We need a Chief Justice prepared to serve as the advocate for access to justice.

THE ROLE OF THE CHIEF JUSTICE OF THE UNITED STATES

Today, some 2000 life-tenured and non-life tenured judges work in the hundreds of facilities around the United States that deals annually with the thousands of filings at the trial level and the 60,000 appeals. No longer solo actors, judges are linked together through the Administrative Office (AO) of the United States Courts, created in 1939, and they are supported with educational programs and research provided by the Federal Judicial Center (FJC), chartered in 1967. Their central headquarters is in one of Washington's major new buildings, named after Justice Thurgood Marshall and located across from Union Station. The day-to-day management of the entire judicial enterprise and its $5.4 billion budget falls to the Director of the AO.

But it is the Chief Justice of the United States who has the power to appoint and to remove the Director of the AO, who serves as the permanent chair of the Board of the Federal Judicial Center, who presides at the meetings of the Judicial Conference, who (upon consultation with others) selects the 250 people who sit on the twenty-four committees of the Judicial Conference, and who gives annual addresses to the nation about the administration of justice.

As may be familiar to those who work on the Hill but less obvious to the American public, the judiciary functions in many respects like an administrative agency, seeking to equip itself with the resources needed to provide the service—adjudication—that the Constitution and Congress requires. Further, during the last half century, the federal courts have also become an educational institution teaching judges about how to do their job, a research center on the administration of justice, and an agenda-setting organization—articulating future goals and plans. In addition to an Executive Committee, the Conference's committees cover topics that range from technology to criminal justice. The Conference opines on legislation from security and court construction to proposed new civil and criminal jurisdiction for the federal courts. The Chief Justice is the presiding officer of this entire apparatus and has the ability, through a host of discretionary judgments, to shape the institutional decisions of "the federal courts."

Under the leadership of the Chief Justice, the Judicial Conference may decide to offer its views on pending legislation even though, if enacted, judges may be required to preside on cases calling the legality of a particular provision into question. For example, in the early 1990s, when an initial version of the Violence Against Women Act (VAWA) was introduced, the Judicial Conference created an Ad Hoc Committee on Gender-Based Violence. Appointed by the Chief Justice, the Committee studied the proposed statute, which included that a new civil rights remedy be made available in federal court to victims of violence. The judiciary's Ad Hoc Committee recommended opposition—which became official federal judicial policy as reported by the Chief Justice in the early 1990s.

After the proposed legislation was modified (in part in response to the concerns raised by judges) and its scope narrowed, the Conference took no position on the propriety of enacting the civil rights remedy but supported other aspects of the legislation including educational efforts. In 1994, at the behest of some forty state attorneys general and many others, Congress enacted the Violence Against Women Act, including its provision of federal jurisdiction (supplemental to that available in state courts) giving civil remedies to victims of gender-motivated violence. Thereafter, and again exercising his discretionary authority, the Chief Justice continued his criticism of VAWA. In 1998, the Chief Justice commented in a speech before the American Law Institute that the legislation raised grave problems of federalism. He cited VAWA (as well as other recent statutes) as inappropriate expansions of federal jurisdiction. In his view, "traditional principles of federalism that have guided this country throughout its existence" should have relegated these issues to state court. In 2000, the Chief Justice wrote the majority opinion that ruled, five to four, that Congress lacked the power under the Commerce Clause to confer that form of jurisdiction on the federal courts.

In addition to guiding the Judicial Conference, which adopts formal policy through voting, the Chief Justice has an independent platform from which to speak.

In the 1980s, Warren Burger initiated another practice—providing annual "state of the judiciary" speeches that are released to the nation. Chief Justice Rehnquist followed suit, beginning each new year by setting out agendas and themes. In that capacity, Chief Justice Rehnquist regularly spoke about the values of judicial independence. Upon occasion, he criticized the Congress or the Executive for engaging in behavior that, he believed, suggested that the coordinate branches of government did not sufficiently appreciate the centrality of an independent judiciary to a thriving democracy.

Yet another aspect of the powers of the Chief Justice is important: He has the authority to select individual judges to serve on specific courts. Rather than using a system of random assignment (for example, staffing a court by assigning sitting judges whose names are drawn by lot), Congress has endowed the Chief Justice with the power to pick individual judges to sit on specialized tribunals. Chief Justice Rehnquist made "over fifty such special court appointments, filling more federal judicial seats than did every individual United States President before Ulysses S. Grant."

In sum, the Chief Justice is not only the symbolic leader of the federal judiciary. He also has a number of specific powers and a good deal of practical authority. He is the most powerful person in the entire federal judicial apparatus. Time and again, individual Chief Justices have proven to be the judiciary's most effective lobbyist, the judiciary's most visible spokesperson, and the nation's most important judicial leader.

Such a repertoire of powers is stunning—and anomalous—for a democracy. That role entails authority significantly different from that of either other judges or justices who sit on courts. Judges on appellate courts work collectively; they must persuade others of the correctness of their views in order to prevail. Both constitutional and common law traditions mandate openness in courts. Most decisions are explained by reasons that are available to public scrutiny and then revisited as new cases arise. In contrast, the administrative powers of the Chief Justice are neither officially shared nor constrained by obligations of accounting.

Further, these many grants of power contrast sharply with the authority of other executive officials. Presidents have term limits. Heads of independent agencies generally do as well. Currently, however, the Chief Justice has life-time consolidated authority over the administration of both the Supreme Court and the lower federal courts and does not have legal obligations to share that power with other jurists nor to explain the decisions made.

Given the current configuration of authority, however, too much power is at stake for the office to change hands without intensive inquiry—detailed below.

THE HARD QUESTIONS AT THE HEART OF THESE HEARINGS

To be confirmed to serve as the Chief Justice of the United States, a nominee should demonstrate a prior commitment to advancing a positive role for the judiciary and a longstanding appreciation of the contributions that a robust judiciary makes to American law. Because no person is entitled to a judgeship, a nominee needs to establish that he or she is the appropriate person for the particular position in the offing.

I limited my consideration to decisions made by Judge Roberts on the D.C. Circuit, to memoranda that he authored when, as a policymaking lawyer serving between 1981 and 1986 for the Reagan Administration, he gave advice on whether the government ought to take particular positions. I also reviewed published essays and transcripts of commentary in radio interviews. Unlike his work as a retained lawyer in private practice (upon which I do not rely), Judge Roberts' positions in government gave him many occasions to make his own views plain. Further, since joining the federal bench in 2003, Judge Roberts has written about fifty opinions, including dissents, and he has sat on many more panels. Thus, a good deal of information is available.

I regret to report that, at least on this record, Judge Roberts has not regularly expressed enthusiasm for adjudication or for ready access by members of the public to the federal courts. In the hundreds of pages that I have reviewed, I have not found sustained discussion of why courts are institutions to be treasured or about how courts are necessary to enable individuals or groups to bring claims of right into the public sphere for decision.

Instead, when given an occasion to opine on why courts should remain accessible, on why the Department of Justice should lend its hand to help needy Americans get into court, on why judges should be available to respond to claims for redress, on why a range of remedies should be available, and on why the Constitution's vision of equal protection and due process protected through adjudication should embrace us all, **the nominee has generally argued against the use of courts.** Further, Judge Roberts has been solicitous of the power of the Executive Branch, often at the expense of individual rights and judicial review. Because the record available in advance of these hearings provides little assurance that this person is the one to be charged with protecting judicial independence and the values of judging and because his nomination for this position was an abrupt change of course, I urge the Senate to **undertake a thorough review of the many instances in which Judge Roberts advocated narrowing access to justice and then to consider how those judgments would affect or forecast his work, were he confirmed as Chief Justice, the symbolic center of America's courts.**

A few examples of the positions he advocated or the decisions he rendered explain the concerns. Return first to my analysis of the complex structure of the Constitution, with interdependent branches. Rather than approaching separation of powers as a vibrant principle of American constitutional law that enables nuanced, interactive dialogues among the branches, Judge Roberts has described separation of powers as a "zero-sum game," with actions of one branch coming at the "expense of the other branches."

In practice, in that "zero-sum game," Judge Roberts has often sided with one player: the Executive. The powerful illustration is *Hamdan v. Rumsfeld*, issued in July of this year. Judge Roberts joined the judgment, written by Judge Raymond Randolph of the D.C. Circuit, that gives enormous latitude to the President to label individuals "enemy combatants" and that bar such persons from access to life-tenured judges to adjudicate their claims. Indeed, the decision concludes that violations of the Geneva Convention—the 1949 agreement governing the treatment of war prisoners to which the United States is a party—are not "judicially enforceable." If this decision stands, then the President has the judicially-unreviewable power to consign individuals to such tribunals, which lack one of America's great contributions to world political thought: the insistence that truly independent jurists have the power to sit in judgment of the Executive.

Further Roberts found the idea of giving the Chief Justice the ability to assign sitting judges to the new court a problem for the President. As he explained:

> the new court will assuredly not represent the President's judicial philosophy—and will have the authority to reverse decisions from courts to which the President has been able to make several appointments that do reflect his judicial philosophy. Under the committee proposal a Carter-appointed judge (there definitely will have to be some on the new court) could write a nationally-binding opinion reversing an opinion by Bork, Winter, Posner, or Scalia—something that cannot happen now.

In other words, sitting judges—whether nominated by a President of either party—were not viewed, once in office, as independent jurists but rather expected to "reflect" the President's positions.

Other memoranda also show a deep commitment to Executive power. As an attorney-advisor in the White House, Mr. Roberts worried that a resolution in "Opposition to Torture" was "mildly objectionable" because it could affect "the Executive's conduct of foreign relations;" he also noted (referring to a point made by the Department of State) that the resolution was not at odds with the current policy. In another memorandum, Mr. Roberts commented that a bill to permit the President to "declare an immigration emergency" under certain criteria and then to have the power to "prohibit vessels from traveling to designated areas" is a "broad grant of emergency powers" but not "too broad" given the experience of efforts by Cubans who had been jailed in Cuba to escape to the United States. And yet other memoranda follow the leitmotif of opposition to ready access to the federal courts.

These examples are but some of many instances in which the written record shows a person devoted to the authority of the Executive Branch and of the states at the expense of individual access to courts. While Judge Roberts has often complained about too much access to or too many remedies from courts, he has said little about the need for courts. Not readily available from the many memoranda and opinions is an affirmative vision that the federal courts play a vital role in delivering justice to individuals, in safeguarding their rights, in protecting their human dignity, and in making government transparent, accountable, and responsive to the people.

The Chief Justice of the United States is a leader of all Americans. The person who occupies that office must embody the principle of judicial independence and should proudly assert the unique contributions courts make to the American polity. Given the information available to date, the question is whether the deep skepticism about the role of courts and the ready license to the President—lacing Judge Roberts' written work—will give way, were he confirmed to serve as the Chief Justice. Whether he meets the qualifications for the Chief Justiceship is a judgment reserved for each Senator who must discharge the constitutional obligation of deciding whether to consent to this nomination.

For Your Consideration

Given the information contained in Resnik's testimony, how would you respond to Judge Mivka's piece?

Excerpts from an article by Douglas Kendall demonstrate the severity of the issue four years later:[34]

> This Article, detailing how corporations and special interests lobby the federal judiciary through gifts of expense-paid trips to private seminars, should be utterly unnecessary. Over the past twenty years, the issue has been subject to extensive discussion and criticism. Numerous studies already detail the serious conflicts of interest and perceptions of impropriety that can arise when judges attend private trips. Members of Congress have spoken out against the trips and introduced legislation to ban them altogether. Ethics experts, judges, public interest groups, and more than thirty editorial boards have strongly criticized these programs.
>
> Despite this outcry by policy makers and opinion leaders, the judicial bureaucracy has remained steadfastly unwilling to address the problems these trips can pose. This inexplicable resistance to reform makes necessary this new study: ***Nothing for Free: How Private Judicial Seminars Are Undermining Environmental Protections and Breaking the Public's Trust.*** Conducted by the Community Rights Counsel in July 2000, *Nothing for Free* provides the first comprehensive look at the private educational trips offered to and accepted by federal judges. It details how the "marketplace of privately funded judicial education is overwhelmingly dominated by pro-market, anti-regulatory seminars offering a single and unchallenged line of reasoning in areas of law with many competing views." *Nothing for Free* also chronicles a remarkable and disturbing correlation between seminar attendance and rulings that were hostile to environmental, health, and safety protections. Finally, it explains in detail why existing ethical guidelines were inadequate to stem the conflicts of interest and appearance problems that result from these trips. This Article provides the most devastating evidence yet uncovered of the profound impact that private judicial trips are having on public confidence in the judiciary.

* * * *

Pierre Schlag has explored the path that leads to our ignorance of, if not apathy toward, such behavior on the part of federal judges. His book yields an important insight into the effects of indiscriminately accepting the notion that rules and their meaningful enforcement are the natural consequence of reasoned analysis. He provides an unprecedented look into the base assumptions that we import into our thinking and language about law:

> Among the precepts associated with the rule of law are the notions that the making of specific laws must have been guided by principles that are open, stable, clear, and general. Similarly, fair procedures, notice, and impartial arbiters must have been used in applying the law. Both Courts and other agencies of the government must have been subject to these requirements. Reason is thus an essential aspect of the rule of law. It is the mechanism by which emotions, interests, and force are supposedly kept in check. In legal analysis, anytime that reason is perceived to break down, the rule of law is immediately threatened.
>
> This fear of losing reason is a fear of loss of control. This is in part why the prospect of reason running out is such a dread moment. In the understanding of legal actors, once reason is no longer in control of the decisions of an official decision-maker, arbitrariness, emotion, self-interest, politics, power, and force take over the legal machinery. From the perspective of the rule-of-law ideal, the exhaustion of reason is tantamount to an admission that legal actors do not know what they are doing—that law is, in a word, lawless.
>
> Such a realization, when it occurs, is injurious to the professional and moral self-image of legal thinkers and actors. This point is easy to appreciate if one can imagine the legal machinery just as it is, but stripped of any pretense to being ruled by reason and the rule of law. What emerges in this picture is a legal system stripped of legitimacy.[35]

* * * *

Identify the various social phenomena that might converge to create a strong relationship between democracy, justice and legitimacy in government action. How plausible are your suggestions? How do they relate to the following inquiry? **Daron Acemoglu, Charles P. Kindleberger Professor of Applied Economics at MIT**, applied the Coase Theorem to politics to address the following questions in an article written for the Journal of Comparative Economics.[36]

> *Do societies choose inefficient policies and institutions because of differences in the beliefs and ideologies of their peoples or leaders?*
>
> Or, *are inefficiencies in politics and economics the outcome of social and distributional conflicts?*
>
> This paper discusses these various approaches to political economy, and develops the argument that there are strong empirical and theoretical grounds for believing that inefficient policies and institutions are prevalent, and that they are chosen because they serve the interests of politicians or social groups holding political power, at the expense of the society at large.
>
> At the center of the theoretical case are the commitment problems inherent in politics: parties holding political power cannot make commitments to bind their future actions because there is no outside agency with the coercive capacity to enforce such arrangements.

Chapter Three

Autonomy, Bodily Integrity & Our Right to Die

Conceptually, ordered liberty is an experiment in which men and women would enjoy equality of rights and opportunities in the pursuit of happiness and in service to the common good. The "pursuit of happiness" epitomizes a citizen's freedom to choose among mutually accessible paths toward self-realization as the hallmark of a free society. The individual's sovereign autonomy is exercised through private ownership, decision-making authority and freedom of conscious choice. The realm of constitutional privacy is that sphere of influence in the life of the individual that the law safeguards against outside interference. Individual Rights theory explores the boundaries of that sphere, i.e., the extent to which the individual actually feels empowered to exercise free choice.

Retired Supreme Court Justice Sandra Day O'Connor observed in *Planned Parenthood v. Casey* that the liberty interests related to bodily integrity, individual sovereignty, and informed consent are necessary to shield the most intimate and personal choices a person may make in a lifetime.[1] Personal dignity and autonomy have been characterized as central to the liberty protected mainly by the Fourteenth Amendment. Summarizing what's at stake she concluded that, "the heart of liberty is the right to define one's own concept of existence, of meaning of the universe, and of the mystery of human life."[2]

In June of 1965, the Court ruled in *Griswold v. Connecticut* that the legislature lacked a compelling interest in limiting the privacy rights of married couples. [3] Laws prohibiting their use of contraception and the physician's right to disseminate information about safe and effective means for preventing pregnancy were held to violate substantive due process as an infringement upon their fundamental rights. The Court reiterated that specific guarantees in the Bill of Rights form clusters or penumbras of rights that give life and substance to the principles articulated in specific provisions. Under modern constitutional analysis, the written guarantees have been interpreted as creating zones of privacy, which were evident and sustained under law since before the nation's founding. Those found in the Bill of Rights (first ten amendments) apply to State governments through incorporation under the Fourteenth Amendment.[4] Enacted in 1868, as part of trilogy of amendments intended to eliminate the vestiges of slavery, the provisions are straightforward and apply to: All persons born or naturalized in the United States, subject to its jurisdiction, all citizens of the United States and of the State wherein they reside. The Amendment forbids the State from three categories of action:

Making or enforcing any law that abridges the privileges or immunities of citizens;

Depriving any person of life, liberty, or property, without due process of law;

Denying any person equal protection of the laws;

Section Two addresses issues of taxation and representation and gave Black men the right to vote for the first time in U.S. History.

> Representatives shall be apportioned among the several States according to their respective numbers, counting the whole number of persons in each State, excluding Indians not taxed. But when the right to vote at any election for the choice of electors for President and Vice President of the United States, Representatives in Congress, the Executive and Judicial officers of a State, or the members of the Legislature thereof, is denied to any of the male inhabitants of such State, being twenty-one years of age, and citizens of the United States, or in any way abridged, except for participation in rebellion, or other crime, the basis of representation therein shall be reduced in the proportion which the number of such male citizens shall bear to the whole number of male citizens twenty-one years of age in such State.

The Fourteenth Amendment commands a central place in American Constitutional History because it not only limits the reach of State power, it requires equal protection for all citizens and warrants equal access to the privileges and immunities of citizenship. Take marital privacy for example, while it has been recognized for centuries the historical failure to extend privacy rights to unmarried partners originated in religious doctrine. Thus, "history" remains an insufficient justification for denying unmarried partners equal protection of the law. Reliance upon tradition in the realm of fundamental rights often manifests a peculiar disregard of the historical purpose of the Fourteenth Amendment: elimination of social caste. Divisions spawned by the abused associated with second-class citizenship led this nation to Civil War.

The pledge of liberty, justice and equality for all formed the basis of reunification. Strengthening the wall of separation between Church and State has been an equally important development in placing tradition in a more appropriately neutral space. In identifying the cluster of rights around which privacy has traditionally been protected, the Supreme Court Justices in *Griswold* recognized five provisions:

> *The right of association contained in the penumbra of rights guaranteed by the First Amendment.*
>
> *The Third Amendment's prohibition against the quartering of soldiers in any house during times of peace without the owner's consent.*
>
> *The Fourth Amendment guarantee of the right of the people to be secure in their persons, houses, papers, and effects, against unreasonable searches and seizures.*
>
> *The Fifth Amendment protection against self-incrimination for those accused of crimes, protecting information known to a citizen, that his "government may not force him to surrender to his detriment."*
>
> *The Ninth Amendment reservation; "enumeration in the Constitution, of certain rights, shall not be construed to deny or disparage others retained by the people."*

The *Griswold* Court found constitutional privacy to be a specific grant of protection against all governmental invasions declaring that the principles laid down affect the very essence of constitutional liberty and security, "reaching farther than the case [now] before the court."

> They apply to all invasions on the part of the government and its employees of the sanctity of a man's home and the privacies of life. It is not the breaking of his doors, and the rummaging of his drawers, that constitutes the essence of the offence; but it is the invasion of his indefeasible right of personal security, personal liberty and private property.... [5]

The primary goal for students of constitutional law is to critically evaluate the State's interest in regulating private choices. At what point is the government justified in limiting individual freedom because of the potential long-term effects of their choices upon the social order? This chapter examines individual authority over the body: anatomical gifting, rules concerning medical invasion and interventions, disposition of human biological cells and tissues, and policies that impact our understanding of the so-called right to die.

Organ Donation

Revised Uniform Anatomical Gift Act (2006)[6]

> As of January 2006 there were over 92,000 individuals on the waiting list for organ transplantation, and the list keeps growing. It is estimated that approximately 5,000 individuals join the waiting list each year.
>
> The lack of organs results from the lack of organ donors. For example, according to the Scientific Registry of Transplant Recipients in 2005 when there were about 90,000 people on the organ transplant waiting list, there were 13,091 individuals who died under the age of 70 using cardiac and brain death criteria and who were eligible to be organ donors. Of these, only 58% or 7,593 were actual donors who provided just over 23,000 organs. Living donors, primarily of kidneys, contributed about 6,800 more organs. Between them about 28,000 organs were transplanted into patients on the waiting list in 2005. The 2005 data on cadaveric organ donors suggests there were 5,498 individuals who died that year that could have been donors who weren't and that had they been organ donors there would have been approximately 17,000 additional organs potentially available for transplantation.

SECTION 4. WHO MAY MAKE AN ANATOMICAL GIFT

An anatomical gift of a donor's body or part may be made during the life of the donor for the purpose of transplantation, therapy, research, or education by:

The donor, if the donor is an adult or if the donor is a minor and is:

Emancipated; or

Authorized under state law to apply for a driver's license because the donor is at least [insert the youngest age at which an individual may apply for any type of driver's license] years of age;

An agent of the donor, unless the power of attorney for health care or other record prohibits the agent from making an anatomical gift;

A parent of the donor, if the donor is an unemancipated minor; or

The donor's guardian

SECTION 7. REFUSAL TO MAKE ANATOMICAL GIFT

An individual may refuse to make an anatomical gift of the individual's body or part by:

A record signed by:

The individual; or

Another individual acting at the direction of the individual if the individual is physically unable to sign;

The individual's will, whether or not the will is admitted to probate or invalidated after the individual's death; or

Any form of communication made by the individual during the individual's terminal illness or injury addressed to at least two adults, at least one of whom is a disinterested witness.

A record signed must:

Be witnessed by at least two adults, at least one of whom is a disinterested witness, who have signed at the request of the individual; and State that it has been signed and witnessed as provided above.

An individual who has made a refusal may amend or revoke the refusal:

In the manner provided for making a refusal; or

By subsequently making an anatomical gift inconsistent with the refusal; or

By destroying or canceling the record evidencing the refusal, or the portion of the record used to make the refusal, with the intent to revoke the refusal.

In the absence of an express, contrary indication by the individual set forth in the refusal, an individual's unrevoked refusal to make an anatomical gift of the individual's body or part bars all other persons from making an anatomical gift of the individual's body or part.

As recommended by the National Conference of Commissioners on Uniform State Laws, this model law is presented as the most efficient means for regulating anatomical gifting. Individual state legislatures would have to pass this law or some version of it before it becomes effective in their jurisdiction. However, the Commissioners recommend using the guidance provided in the following way.

> Many states have related laws that should not be repealed but should remain in effect, such as: donor registry provisions; donor awareness programs; Transplant Councils; and licensing provisions for procurement organizations and health care providers. The state may also have regulatory and other law that applies to the subject matter of this [act] that should remain in place. However, it is highly desirable that the core provisions of the [act] be uniform among states as there is very little time available to timely prepare, possibly transport across state lines, and transplant life-saving organs, let alone assess and comply with significant variations of state law.[7]

Anatomical gifting guidelines are consistent with fundamental rights analysis. The assurances that individuals may refuse to gift are a response to global developments in the area of organ transplants. In harmony with those developments, here's one proposal for change in the United States that was expressly rejected by Uniform Commissioners in 2006.

Organ Donation as National Service[8]

Linda C. Fentiman

Edited Relevant Excerpts
Reprinted with permission

America's organ transplantation system is in crisis. At a time when transplant survival rates are at an all-time high, with more than ninety percent of kidney transplant recipients alive two years after transplant, the waiting list for organs grows longer every day. Today, there are more than 26,000 individuals on a waiting list to receive a kidney, more than 2,900 persons waiting for a heart transplant, and a total of 35,000 individuals waiting for one or more vital organs. Since 1988, more than 10,000 people have died while on a waiting list, while thousands more never even made it to a list.

Twenty-five years from now, the tragedy of death due to the lack of an organ transplant may seem like ancient history. Artificial organs and tissues, fetal tissue transplantation, gene insertion technology, improved drug treatments, and xenografts may develop to the point that organ transplantation will no longer be the preferred treatment for many otherwise fatal illnesses. Alternatively, the scarcity of economic resources to provide for Americans' health may grow so severe that only the very wealthy will be able to afford organ transplantation or other expensive forms of medical care.

At the moment, we are at the point in history known as "meanwhile." With organ transplantation holding out the only hope of survival for some persons, and for many others, the only hope of a good quality of life, there is tremendous pressure on medical and governmental policymakers to reform the present organ transplantation system to be more effective and fair in saving lives. Academics, physicians, and government officials writing from many perspectives have criticized the present organ transplantation system, both for failing to adequately tap the potential pool of transplantable organs and for failing to allocate the organs that are available on a more equitable basis.

A 1993 study of UNOS [The United Network for Organ Sharing] criticized the organization for its failure to allocate strictly on the basis of medical criteria. The fortuity of being on the right transplant center's list when an organ becomes available seemed to be a big factor for those responsible for coordinating transplantation services. The study attributed part of the problem to poor oversight by the Department of Health. Critics have noted that wealthy foreigners are somehow able to receive organs which are not available to American citizens and permanent resident aliens.

In addition, a number of recent studies have documented significant disparities between the rate at which White and Black Americans receive organs for transplant and the amount of time they must wait. In part, these disparities are attributable to unequal distribution of human leukocyte antigens (HLAs) among different racial groups. These antigens are what trigger a "rejection" response when the body rejects a non-genetically identical organ. HLA matching has been important in selecting the most suitable organ recipient. The difference in HLA tissue antigens in persons of various races has been offered to explain the disparity in transplantation statistics. However, reliance on HLA tissue matching as a major factor in organ allocation has been challenged on both scientific and ethical grounds.

In response to these and other concerns the House of Representatives passed a bill requiring the Department of Health and Human Services to immediately promulgate regulations to replace the voluntary guidelines that now govern UNOS and organ transplantation centers. This law mandated the development of a single list of organ recipients for each organ procurement organization, with allocation to be made on the basis of strictly medical criteria. American citizens and permanent resident aliens would receive absolute priority over foreign nationals in the allocation of organs for transplant. And finally, the law would diversify the membership of UNOS and other organ provider organizations to include more "citizen," and less institutional, representatives.

If these bills were to be reenacted by the new Congress, they would be insufficient to save thousands of Americans who die each year while awaiting a transplant. Since the late 1960s, when the development of immuno-suppressive drugs made possible the receipt of an organ from a nongenetically related donor, academics and public policymakers have collaborated to develop mechanisms to encourage the donation of organs and tissues for transplant but have achieved only limited success.

The Uniform Anatomical Gift Act has been adopted by every state and the District of Columbia, to make it easy to volunteer to donate organs at the time of death. Sixty-two percent of Americans say they would like to donate their organs upon death, and an even larger percentage are willing to donate the organs of a loved one. However, donor cards have had only minimal impact on increasing the supply of organs and tissue for donation.

The problems are as follows:

Almost all American physicians and nurses refuse to go forward with retrieving organs for transplant without the consent of the dead donor's next of kin, despite the U.A.G.A.'s explicit provisions protecting those who rely on a donor card from legal liability.

Health care providers are reluctant to approach grieving families with a request for organ donation, resulting in a loss of many opportunities for organ donation. A number of factors have been offered to explain this reluctance, including a lack of education or cultural sensitivity on the part of health care workers, a concern about the appearance of overreaching with a bereaved family, fear of legal liability, and the health care professional's own discomfort with death.

In response to the organ shortage under a system of voluntary organ donation, in 1986 Congress enacted "Routine Inquiry" legislation, mandating those receiving Medicare or Medicaid reimbursement to establish protocols under which all families of dead or dying potential organ donors will be asked to consider donating the organs of their loved one. Despite this and similar laws which have been enacted by more than thirty states, organ donation has remained static over the last several years, and in some localities, has actually declined.

Thus, it is time to consider an alternative approach to organ procurement and allocation—one that relies on presumed consent to organ donation, combined with incentives which recognize the communal basis of the obligation to donate one's organs after death.

Providing numerous opportunities for "opting out" of donation in order to promote individual autonomy and providing economic and eleemosynary incentives for persons who actually contribute their organs after death would remedy the shortage. Mere mention of the words "presumed consent" and "compensated donation" may raise ethical eyebrows. However, a system of presumed consent to compensated organ donation should be considered as a rational response to the present organ shortage. We must view organ donation as an act of community service, and support it in the way that we currently encourage service in a volunteer military or the Peace Corps, with the provision of subsidized education, health, and other benefits to those who serve.

Under my proposed statute, all mentally competent individuals over the age of eighteen would be presumed to have consented to the retrieval of their organs at the time of death. Medical personnel could then begin the process of preparing a deceased individual's body for organ transplantation without waiting to find a donor card or the next of kin, which would enhance the viability of organs for transplant. Physicians would no longer need to confront a grieving family with the need to make a quick decision about organ donation because that decision would be out of the family's hands. Presumed consent eliminates conflicts of interest over whether an individual's organs are being harvested for transplant to another patient at the same hospital.

Several European countries, notably Austria, Belgium, and the former Yugoslavia, as well as Israel, New Zealand, Singapore, Tunisia, and more than twenty states, have presumed consent system for the donation of specific organs, most often the cornea and the pituitary gland. This has resulted in the restoration of sight to more than one-half million people, with only infrequent challenges.

Yet proposals for presumed consent to organ donation could be attacked as "un-American," unsuited to a nation in which respect for individual autonomy and self-determination are at the pinnacle of the collective value system, and in which appeals to fears of creeping Big Brotherhood are often successful.

The statute I propose provides six separate occasions on which an objection to organ donation could be made. These are: when obtaining or renewing a driver's license; on filing an income tax return; when applying for welfare disability or other governmental benefits; on every visit to a hospital or doctor's office, when a health care provider explicitly requests a patient to consider donating her organs, and when executing a living will or health care proxy document. Each person's objections to presumed donation would be recorded in a national computerized registry, which would be updated on a daily basis, and would be protected by appropriate back-up systems to prevent losing any objections. Thus, respect for individual dignity and autonomy would be ensured.

Others might object that permitting compensation of any kind for the donation of organs and tissues is dehumanizing and that the proposed statute provides unseemly incentives for the poor to lose the last vestiges of their humanity through the violation of their corpse. But one must recognize that our society already grants the poor numerous opportunities to compromise their humanity and to risk their health based on monetary concerns. Among the examples that leap to mind are prostitution and other selling of their labor at relatively high wages in high-risk, low-prestige jobs, inability of the poor to buy safer cars, or afford comprehensive health insurance for themselves and their families.

Further, under the current organ transplantation system, everyone profits except the organ donors: the transplant surgeons receive ego gratification, prestige, and money for their labor on the transplant team; the transplant center and its workers gain both an enhanced reputation and income; the nonprofit organ procurement organization maintains its raison d'etre—the business of organ procurement and allocation; and, of course, the organ recipient receives the gift of life itself. It is, frankly, hard to understand why even the offer of compensation for the donation of an organ will suddenly transform the vast American organ transplantation enterprise from an exalted and altruistic endeavor into a tawdry and venal business deal, the medical equivalent of haggling with a street vendor.

In addition, if a poor (or a wealthy) person might choose to donate his or her organs after death in exchange for a decent burial, payment for medical treatment prior to death, priority in receiving an organ transplant should the donor need one, a college tuition voucher for his or her children or grandchildren, or a gift to a favorite charity, it would be paternalistic interference of the worst sort to deny the donor the ability to make that rational trade-off. Since the National Organ and Tissue Research and Transplantation Board would establish maximum, uniform compensation for organ donation, all persons would be treated equally, both in deciding to opt "in" or "out" of the presumed consent system and in their receipt of compensation for the gift of life.

Finally, such a statute achieves important communal goals because the statute treats organs and tissues as community resources, which are made available to medically appropriate candidates within that community. The statute states a preference that organs be offered first to a recipient from the donor's community. While allocation of scarce resources such as organs should generally be made in accordance with medical, not social, criteria, a blind insistence on absolute medical equity will cause other important goals to be overlooked, including increasing the organ supply by providing incentives to donate. Thus, for example, to the extent that young, urban African-Americans or other persons of color are likely to suffer an accidental or violent death and become a potential organ donor, a system of presumed consent, compensated donation, and preference for local use of organs will make more organs available to those communities which are presently not receiving an appropriate share. The proposed model statute recognizes that organ donation is a powerful act of virtue. By relying on presumed consent and compensated donation and by giving a preference to local organ recipients, the model statute encourages persons to act on their altruistic impulses and makes it possible to save more lives through organ donation.

All organs and tissues retrieved in the United States, whether they are to be used for transplantation or research, would be retrieved and allocated in accordance with uniform federal laws. The National Organ and Tissue Research and Transplantation Board (NOTRTB), an independent federal agency would be created under the authority of the Secretary of Health and Human Services. The Board would have authority to promulgate regulations to govern all aspects of organ and tissue procurement and distribution, in accordance with the mandate of such a statute.

For Your Consideration

Are states authorized to include the opt-out provisions in Fentiman's proposal in their individual jurisdictions based upon the theory that they are legislating for the general welfare by saving a certain number of lives each year?

How would you decide the outcome of a case where a patient sues a hospital for using an organ removed during surgery for research that led to commercial gain without obtaining her consent? Is your answer consistent with the view that recognizable body parts, human tissue, anatomical remains, and related waste are to be disposed of according to regulations from the State Health Department?

How would you describe the State's interest in invalidating a will provision where the deceased left instructions that she be buried in a red Ferrari wearing a baby-blue nightgown? (It *happened.*)[9]

The law establishes the right of a competent person to make anatomical gifts. In some instances, the gifts are viewed as a form of personal property, in others they fall into an interim category, imbued with characteristics that impact upon the individual's fundamental rights, with interesting gender-related implications.

Within relevant medical guidelines, gametes and concepti are uniformly disposed of at the sole discretion of their donor. Plaintiffs in the following case requested state intervention in order to seize decision-making authority.

Gametes, Concepti & Reproductive Organs

Hecht v. Superior Court

20 Cal. Rptr. 2d 275, 1993

BACKGROUND

At the age of 48, William E. Kane took his own life on October 30, 1991, in a Las Vegas hotel. For about five years prior to his death, he had been living with petitioner, thirty-eight-year-old Deborah E. Hecht. Two college-age children survived Kane.

Kane deposited 15 vials of his sperm in an account at a California sperm bank just prior to his death. Specimen Storage and Release Agreements provided that upon his death the bank would store or release the specimens to the executor of the estate, to Deborah Ellen Hecht or her physician, Dr. Kathryn Moyer.

Kane executed a will that named Hecht as executor of the estate, and bequeathed the sperm stored with any sperm bank or similar facility for storage to Deborah Ellen Hecht. Elsewhere he stated: It being my intention that samples of my sperm will be stored at a sperm bank for the use of Deborah Ellen Hecht, should she so desire, it is my wish that, should [Hecht] become impregnated with my sperm, before or after my death, authorizing her to disregard the wishes expressed in a prior paragraph pertaining to disposition of decedent's diplomas and framed mementoes, to the extent that she wished to preserve any or all of my mementoes and diplomas and the like for their future child or children.

The will also bequeathed Hecht a home in Monterey County and an adjoining seven-and-one-half-acre parcel of unimproved land to his two adult children. He gave the residue of the estate to Hecht, stating that his children were financially secure and he therefore left them nothing more than the land.

Hecht held title to various other assets. Pursuant to an agreement, Hecht had in her possession and was to keep as her sole and separate property the sum of $80,000, an automobile, and some items of household furniture.

An October 21, 1991, letter signed by Kane and addressed to his children stated in part:

I address this to my children, because, although I have only two, Everett and Katy, it may be that Deborah will decide—as I hope she will—to have a child by me after my death. I've been assiduously generating frozen sperm samples for that eventuality. If she does, then this letter is for my posthumous offspring, as well, with the thought that I have loved you in my dreams, even though I never got to see you born. If you are receiving this letter, it means that I am dead—whether by my own hand or that of another makes very little difference. I feel that my time has come; and I wanted to leave you with something more than a dead enigma that was your father. I am inordinately proud of who I have been—what I made of me. I'm so proud of that that I would rather take my own life now than be ground into a mediocre existence by my enemies—who, because of my mistakes and bravado have gained the power to finish me.

After several pages of childhood memories and family history, the letter stated:

> So why am I checking out now? Basically, betrayal, over and over again, has made me tired. I've picked up some heavyweight enemies along the way—ranging from the Kellys of the world, to crazies with guns, to insurance companies, to the lawyers that have sucked me dry.... I don't want to die as a tired, perhaps defeated and bitter old man. I'd rather end it like I have lived it—on my time, when and where I will, and while my life is still an object of self-sculpture—a personal creation with which I am still proud. In truth, death for me is not the opposite of life; it is a form of life's punctuation.

Kane committed suicide on October 30, 1991, in Las Vegas, Nevada.

On December 3, 1991, the two children William Kane, Jr., and Katharine Kane each filed separate will contests.

The plaintiffs ???contended argued??? that:

1. Hecht was responsible for Kane's death having aided his mission and because she failed to provide help to a seriously depressed man.

2. It would inflict great stress upon them knowing that they had siblings born into such a dysfunctional circumstances.

3. It would be void as against public policy to allow a single woman to conceive and raise a child under these circumstances.

The Executor of the estate asked the court for instructions: he was faced with the choice to either destroy the frozen sperm, distribute it to Hecht, include the after-born children as heirs to the estate, and/or hold off administrating the estate pending conception and birth.

Following oral arguments on the petition, the judge said: "Obviously we are all agreed that we are forging new frontiers because science has run ahead of common law. And we have got to have some sort of appellate decision telling us what rights are in these uncharted territories." He then ordered that the sperm be destroyed.

When Hecht's counsel asked for the legal basis of the ruling, the judge (with unusual candor) replied:

It really does not matter, does it? If I am right, I am right and if I am wrong, I am wrong. This is something that is going to have to be decided by the appellate courts. Let's get a decision.

The law provides in pertinent part:

Notwithstanding any other provision of law, recognizable anatomical parts, human tissues, anatomical human remains, or infectious waste following conclusion of scientific use shall be disposed of by interment, incineration, or any other method determined by the state department to protect the public health and safety.

The appellate court reversed the lower court order and distributed the sperm to Hecht, announcing that the decedent's interest in his frozen sperm vials, even if not governed by the general law of personal property, occupies "an interim category that entitles them to special respect because of their potential for human life." The court went on to discuss the nature of those rights.

NATURE OF RIGHTS IN SEMEN

The present legal position toward property rights in the human body is unsettled and reflects no consistent philosophy or approach. Until recently, the common law either refused to recognize a property right in human bodies or recognized only a quasi-property right....

The laws governing such things as human tissues, transplantable organs, blood, fetuses, pituitary glands, corneal tissue, and dead bodies deal with human biological materials as objects sui generis, regulating their disposition to achieve policy goals rather than abandoning them to the general law of personal property. It is these specialized statutes, not the law of conversion, to which courts ordinarily should and do look for guidance on the disposition of human biological materials." One commentator recently noted that although some sperm banks operate as commercial enterprises, they are virtually free from state licensing and other regulation.

Various state statutes modeled after the Uniform Parentage Act address the issue of the legal relationship between the sperm donor and the child born by artificial insemination. However, "[n]one of the statutes on artificial insemination indicate who owns the sperm donation, but sperm banks generally require those donors who are to be anonymous to sign a written waiver of any rights to the deposit and any paternity claims to children born from it. In return, the sperm bank guarantees the donor's anonymity.

Thus, according to the contract between the parties, the donor no longer 'owns' the sperm. Men who use sperm banks to store their sperm for their own future use, however, do own their donation(s) of sperm and are required to pay for its maintenance and its later withdrawal. Upon notice of the death of the donor, however, many storage agreements authorize the sperm bank to dispose of the deposit. Requests from the widow of the donor to be inseminated with the sperm, as a matter of practice, are denied absent express instructions in the donor's will or a court order.

The American Fertility Society, in its ethical statement on in vitro fertilization, has written that "It is understood that the gametes and concepti are the property of the donors. The donors therefore have the right to decide at their sole discretion the disposition of these items, provided they are within medical and ethical guidelines. Today, under federal law and all state statutory law except Louisiana, embryos [created by in vitro fertilization] do not possess rights or have legal status.

The court found persuasive a report of the Ethics Committee of The American Fertility Society, which identified three major ethical positions that have been articulated in the debate over preembryo status.

At one extreme is the view that the preembryo is a human subject after fertilization, which requires that it be accorded the rights of a person.

> The opposite extreme is the view that the preembryo has a status no different from any other human tissue.
>
> A third view, one that is most widely held—takes an intermediate position between the other two. It holds that the preembryo deserves respect greater than that accorded to human tissue but not the respect accorded to actual persons. The preembryo is due greater respect than other human tissue because of its potential to become a person and because of its symbolic meaning for many people. Yet, it should not be treated as a person, because it has not yet developed the features of personhood, is not yet established, and may never realize its biologic potential.

For Your Consideration

How many public policy issues are presented in the *Hecht* case?

How do they relate to individual rights?

The *Hecht* decision rested upon the nature of the interest being conveyed. The donor of an anatomical gift that has the potential to become human life is accorded great deference under medical and constitutional guidelines. What is the legal effect of such deferential treatment?

BBC News reported in January 2007, that parents of a nine-year-old named Ashley have administered hormone doses to limit her height and weight, and opted for surgery to block breast growth and to remove her uterus and appendix.[10] Ashley has static encephalopathy, a rare brain condition that will cap Ashley's mental ability to that of a three-month-old baby who will never walk or talk.

Ashley's parents and the medical ethics board approving the surgery offered three justifications: quality of life, comfort, and safety.

The surgery would improve the quality of life for the entire family. If Ashley remains small she is more easily transported, rather than confined to a bed, bathed and involved in family activities, all of which promote her physical and mental well-being.

Surgery avoids the discomfort associated with womanhood. According to her parents, "Ashley has no need for her uterus since she will not be bearing children, … she will not experience the menstrual cycle or the bleeding and discomfort commonly associated with it." The removal of her breast buds was carried out primarily so she would not experience discomfort when lying down.

Citing fears of abuse, Ashley's parents stated that their decision to remove her uterus and breasts was also done to promote her safety, on the theory is that it would help to avoid sexual abuse and the possibility of pregnancy.

Criticism of the treatment has been unrelenting. George Dvorsky, a member of the Board of Directors for the Institute for Ethics and Emerging Technologies responded by noting that:

> "If the concern has something to do with the girl's dignity being violated, then I have to protest by arguing that the girl lacks the cognitive capacity to experience any sense of indignity. "The oestrogen treatment is not what is grotesque here. Rather, it is the prospect of having a full-grown and fertile woman endowed with the mind of a baby."[11]

"Ashley's parents wrote in their blog: 'A fundamental and universal misconception about the treatment is that it is intended to convenience the caregiver.' "But Agnes Fletcher of the UK's Disability Rights Commission said it was 'unnecessary medical treatment to deal with what is essentially a social problem', referring to 'the poverty and lack of support' faced by families with disabled children."[12]

Where does the difficulty arise, when making arguments that center on the convenience of the caregiver?

Would a pregnancy and birth impact the emotional and psychological well-being of her parents as much as the physical well-being of Ashley?

How likely is it that an individual prone to molesting someone like Ashley would be deterred by height or weight?

How many of the issues presented in the case seem more like the social problems identified by the Disability Rights Commissioner?

Hypothetically, if her parents had requested court permission to terminate Ashley's life, on the theory that the mental capability of a three month old is tantamount to a vegetative state, would denial trigger an equal protection issue?

How would you characterize the interest of the state in regulating in this area?

Assume that as a result of her parents filing the petition to terminate her life, a Court decided that making Ashley a ward of the state would be in her best interest. Would the state be able to do all of the things that the parents did in the original scenario for all of the same reasons? Are state agencies criticized for routinely taking the same preventative measures?

Sixteen years ago, the Court gave some guidance on such questions in *Cruzan*.

Persistent Vegetative States & Assisted Suicide

Cruzan v. Missouri Department of Health[13]

Facts: Petitioner Nancy Cruzan is incompetent, having sustained severe injuries in an automobile accident, and now lies in a Missouri state hospital in what is referred to as a persistent vegetative state. The State is bearing the cost of her care. Hospital employees refused, without court approval, to honor the request of Cruzan's parents, co-petitioners here, to terminate her artificial nutrition and hydration, since that would result in death. A state trial court authorized the termination, finding that a person in Cruzan's condition has a fundamental right under the State and Federal Constitutions to direct or refuse the withdrawal of death-prolonging procedures, and that Cruzan's expression to a former housemate that she would not wish to continue her life if sick or injured unless she could live at least halfway normally was enough to establish that she would not wish to continue in this manner.

Petitioners are Cruzan's parents suing on their behalf and on behalf of their daughter. They have requested a court order directing the withdrawal of their daughter's artificial feeding and hydration equipment. The appellate court denied their petition holding that petitioners lacked authority to effectuate the request because there was no clear and convincing evidence of the daughter's desire to have life-sustaining treatment withdrawn. The United States Supreme Court affirmed.

The Court affirmed the judgment stating that the U.S. Constitution does not require the State to repose judgment on matters concerning the right to refuse treatment with anyone but the patient herself.

> No right is held more sacred, or is more carefully guarded, by the common law, than the right of every individual to the possession and control of his own person, free from all restraint or interference of others, unless by clear and unquestionable authority of law. This notion of bodily integrity has been embodied in the requirement that informed consent is generally required for medical treatment. Every human being of adult years and sound mind has a right to determine what shall be done with his own body; and a surgeon who performs an operation without his patient's consent commits an assault, for which he is liable in damages. The informed consent doctrine has become firmly entrenched in American tort law. The logical corollary of the doctrine of informed consent is that the patient generally possesses the right not to consent, that is, to refuse treatment.

Statements by the Court in Cruzan:

> It is assumed that a competent person would have a constitutionally protected right to refuse lifesaving hydration and nutrition. This does not mean that an incompetent person should possess the same right, since such a person is unable to make an informed and voluntary choice to exercise that right.
>
> Missouri has in effect recognized that under certain circumstances a surrogate may act for the patient in electing to withdraw hydration and nutrition and thus cause death, it has established a procedural safeguard to assure that the surrogate's action conforms as best it may to the wishes expressed by the patient while competent.
>
> It is permissible for Missouri, in its proceedings, to apply a clear and convincing evidence standard, which is an appropriate standard when the individual interests at stake are particularly important.
>
> Missouri has a general interest in the protection and preservation of human life, as well as other, more particular interests, at stake. It may legitimately seek to safeguard the personal element of an individual's choice between life and death.
>
> The State is also entitled to guard against potential abuses by surrogates who may not act to protect the patient.
>
> The State may also properly decline to make judgments about the "quality" of a particular individual's life and simply assert an unqualified interest in the preservation of human life to be weighed against the constitutionally protected interests of the individual.
>
> Due Process does not require a State to accept the "substituted judgment" of close family members in the absence of substantial proof that their views reflect the patient's.
>
> Nancy Cruzan's parents would surely be qualified to exercise such a right of "substituted judgment" were it required by the Constitution.

Justices in dissent

As many as 10,000 patients are being maintained in persistent vegetative states in the United States, and the number is expected to increase significantly in the near future. Technology developed over the past 20 or so years is often capable of resuscitating people after they have stopped breathing or their hearts have stopped beating. Some of those people are brought fully back to life. Two decades ago, those who were not and could not swallow and digest food, died. Intravenous solutions could not provide sufficient calories to maintain people for more than a short time. Today, various forms of artificial feeding have been developed that are able to keep people metabolically alive for years, even decades.

JUSTICE STEVENS, dissenting.

Our Constitution is born of the proposition that all legitimate governments must secure the equal right of every person to "Life, Liberty, and the pursuit of Happiness." In the ordinary case we quite naturally assume that these three ends are compatible, mutually enhancing, and perhaps even coincident.

The Court would make an exception here. It permits the State's abstract, undifferentiated interest in the preservation of life to overwhelm the best interests of Nancy Beth Cruzan, interests which would, according to an undisputed finding, be served by allowing her guardians to exercise her constitutional right to discontinue medical treatment. Ironically, the Court reaches this conclusion despite endorsing three significant propositions that should save it from any such dilemma. First, a competent individual's decision to refuse life-sustaining medical procedures is an aspect of liberty protected by the Due Process Clause of the Fourteenth Amendment.

The Constitution requires the State to care for Nancy Cruzan's life in a way that gives appropriate respect to her own best interests. This case is the first in which we consider whether, and how, the Constitution protects the liberty of seriously ill patients to be free from life-sustaining medical treatment. So put, the question is both general and profound. We need not, however, resolve the question in the abstract. Our responsibility as judges both enables and compels us to treat the problem as it is illuminated by the facts of the controversy before us.

The most important of those facts are these: "Clear and convincing evidence" established that Nancy Cruzan is "oblivious to her environment except for reflexive responses to sound and perhaps to painful stimuli"; that "she has no cognitive or reflexive ability to swallow food or water"; that "she will never recover" these abilities; and that her "cerebral cortical atrophy is irreversible, permanent, progressive and ongoing." Recovery and consciousness are impossible; the highest cognitive brain function that can be hoped for is a grimace in "recognition of ordinarily painful stimuli" or an "apparent response to sound."

After thus evaluating Nancy Cruzan's medical condition, the trial judge next examined how the interests of third parties would be affected if Nancy's parents were allowed to withdraw the gastrostomy tube that had been implanted in their daughter. His findings make it clear that the parents' request had no economic motivation, and that granting their request would neither adversely affect any innocent third parties nor breach the ethical standards of the medical profession. He then considered, and rejected, a religious objection to his decision, and explained why he concluded that the constitutional "right to liberty" outweighed the general public policy on which the State relied.

According to the President's Commission for the Study of Ethical Problems in Medicine and Biomedical and Behavioral Research:

> Just as recent years have seen alterations in the underlying causes of death, the places where people die have also changed. For most of recorded history, deaths (of natural causes) usually occurred in the home.

Everyone knew about death first hand; there was nothing unfamiliar or even queer about the phenomenon. People seem to have known a lot more about the process itself than is the case today. The "deathbed" was a real place, and the dying person usually knew where he was and when it was time to assemble the family and call for the priest.'

Even when people did get admitted to a medical care institution, those whose conditions proved incurable were discharged to the care of their families. This was not only because the health care system could no longer be helpful, but also because alcohol and opiates (the only drugs available to ease pain and suffering) were available without a prescription. Institutional care was reserved for the poor or those without family support; hospitals often aimed more at saving patients' souls than at providing medical care.

As medicine has been able to do more for dying patients, their care has increasingly been delivered in institutional settings. By 1949, institutions were the sites of 50% of all deaths; by 1958, the figure was 61%; and by 1977, over 70%. Perhaps 80% of all deaths in the United States now occur in hospitals and long-term care institutions, such as nursing homes. The change in where very ill patients are treated permits health care professionals to marshal the instruments of scientific medicine more effectively. But people who are dying may well find such a setting alienating and unsupportive.

Ultimate questions that might once have been dealt with in intimacy by a family and its physician have now become the concern of institutions. When the institution is a State hospital, as it is in this case, the government itself becomes involved. Dying nonetheless remains a part of "the life that characteristically has its place in the home." The "integrity of that life is something so fundamental that it has been found to draw to its protection the principles of more than one explicitly granted Constitutional right," and our decisions have demarcated a "private realm of family life which the State cannot enter."

The Cruzan family's continuing concern provides a concrete reminder that Nancy Cruzan's interests did not disappear with her vitality or her consciousness. However commendable may be the State's interest in human life, it cannot pursue that interest by appropriating Nancy Cruzan's life as a symbol for its own purposes. Lives do not exist in abstraction from persons, and to pretend otherwise is not to honor but to desecrate the State's responsibility for protecting life. A State that seeks to demonstrate its commitment to life may do so by aiding those who are actively struggling for life and health.

I respectfully dissent.

For Your Consideration

Terri Schindler Schiavo suffered severe brain damage in 1990 following a heart attack. The brain damage left her in a persistent vegetative state, dependent upon a feeding tube for nutrients and fluids. Terri was awarded a substantial malpractice settlement for the improperly diagnosed potassium deficiency that led to the heart attack and collapse that damaged her brain. Nearly all of the settlement was spent on rehabilitation attempts to which she never responded. Her husband Michael Schiavo sought for years to remove the feeding tube and allow Terri to die. He prevailed at the trial level and the Second Circuit Court of Appeals affirmed the trial court's ruling, permitting him to remove the feeding tube. On October 20, 2003, the Florida Legislature passed bill 35E, which empowered Governor Jeb Bush to issue executive order 03-201, which he did the following day, requiring doctors to reinsert the feeding tube and provide continued medical care.

Is there a meaningful difference between brain death, cessation of breathing in the absence of artificial respiration, and the inability to eat without tubular feeding and hydration?

The Supreme Court has long recognized cessation of brain functions as justification for removal of life support. Terri's brain functioned at a very low level where she was unable to eat or communicate. The controversy was initiated by her parents, who made a videotape claiming to show that she was able to make eye contact and respond in primitive ways to outside stimulus. The Schiavo case (parents against husband) sparked a controversial right-to-die debate engulfing the media, talk radio, courts, Congress, and the White House. The feeding tube was eventually removed and Shiavo died of dehydration. Autopsy results showed a brain at half its normal size when she died, on March 31, 2005.[14]

Public opinion polls consistently show that a majority of Americans agree her feeding tube should have been removed. Ethical concerns abound. Most people have considered the implications of artificial support for aging parents and family members. Nearly sixty percent surveyed in 1998 said they worry about the emotional burdens related to end-of-life decisions. The majority of Americans believe that decision-making authority should repose in the spouse when such cases arise. Thirty percent have already had to make such decisions. Surveys find that the majority of Americans also support assisted suicide.

According to Dr. Timothy Vacco, "we should consider the option of assisted suicide, in a limited, well regulated manner for one who is in pain, for whom there is no treatment or medication that will blunt their suffering."[15] Those who oppose such assistance believe in divine appointment. Those who support these measures contend that only a patient, according to personal beliefs, should determine the level of pain to be endured and how their final days are to be lived, as a matter of human dignity.

Washington V. Glucksberg[16]

> It has always been a crime to assist a suicide in the State of Washington. The State's present law makes "promoting a suicide attempt" a felony, and provides: "A person is guilty of [that crime] when he knowingly causes or aids another person to attempt suicide."
>
> Respondents, four Washington physicians who occasionally treat terminally ill, suffering patients, declare that they would assist these patients in ending their lives if not for the State's assisted-suicide ban. They, along with three gravely ill plaintiffs who have since died and a nonprofit organization that counsels people considering physician-assisted suicide, filed this suit against petitioners, the State and its Attorney General, seeking a declaration that the ban is, on its face, unconstitutional. They assert a liberty interest protected by the Fourteenth Amend-

ment's Due Process Clause which extends to a personal choice by a mentally competent, terminally ill adult to commit physician-assisted suicide.

Relying primarily on *Planned Parenthood v. Casey,* the Federal District Court agreed, concluding that Washington's assisted-suicide ban is unconstitutional because it places an undue burden on the exercise of that constitutionally protected liberty interest. The en banc Ninth Circuit affirmed.

Various descriptions of the interest at stake include:

A right to "determine the time and manner of one's death," the "right to die," a "liberty to choose how to die," a right to "control of one's final days," "the right to choose a humane, dignified death," and "the liberty to shape death...."

Statutes prohibit aiding another person to attempt suicide. Thus, the question before the Court is more properly characterized as whether the "liberty" specially protected by the Due Process Clause includes a right to commit suicide which itself includes a right to assistance in doing so. Like the decision of whether or not to have an abortion, the decision surrounding how and when to die is one of 'the most intimate and personal choices a person may make in a lifetime,' a choice 'central to personal dignity and autonomy.

An examination of our Nation's history, legal traditions, and practices demonstrates that Anglo-American common law has punished or otherwise disapproved of assisting suicide for over 700 years; that rendering such assistance is still a crime in almost every State; that such prohibitions have never contained exceptions for those who were near death; that the prohibitions have in recent years been reexamined and, for the most part, reaffirmed in a number of States; and that the President recently signed the Federal Assisted Suicide Funding Restriction Act of 1997, which prohibits the use of federal funds in support of physician-assisted suicide

Held: Washington's prohibition against "causing" or "aiding" a suicide does not violate the Due Process Clause.

Vacco v. Quill[17]

January 1997

Opinion of the Court:

On their faces, neither New York's ban on assisting suicide nor its statutes permitting patients to refuse medical treatment treat anyone differently than anyone else or draw any distinctions between persons. Everyone, regardless of physical condition, is entitled, if competent, to refuse unwanted lifesaving medical treatment; no one is permitted to assist a suicide. Generally speaking, laws that apply evenhandedly to all "unquestionably comply" with the Equal Protection Clause.

The Court of Appeals, however, concluded that some terminally ill people—those who are on life-support systems—are treated differently than those who are not, in that the former may "hasten death" by ending treatment, but the latter may not "hasten death" through physician-assisted suicide. This conclusion depends on the submission that ending or refusing lifesaving medical treatment "is nothing more nor less than assisted suicide."

Unlike the Court of Appeals, we think the distinction between assisting suicide and withdrawing life-sustaining treatment, a distinction widely recognized and endorsed in the medical profession and in our legal traditions, is both important and logical; it is certainly rational. The distinction comports with fundamental legal principles of causation and intent. First, when a patient refuses life-sustaining medical treatment, he dies from an underlying fatal disease or pathology; but if a patient ingests lethal medication prescribed by a physician, he is killed by that medication.

Similarly, the overwhelming majority of state legislatures have drawn a clear line between assisting suicide and withdrawing or permitting the refusal of unwanted lifesaving medical treatment by prohibiting the former and permitting the latter. And "nearly all states expressly disapprove of suicide and assisted suicide either in statutes dealing with durable powers of attorney in health-care situations, or in 'living will' statutes." Thus, even as the States move to protect and promote patients' dignity at the end of life, they remain opposed to physician-assisted suicide.

The judgment of the Court of Appeals is reversed.

It is so ordered.

Justice O'Connor in Concurrence

Every one of us at some point may be affected by our own or a family member's terminal illness. There is no reason to think the democratic process will not strike the proper balance between the interests of terminally ill, mentally competent individuals who would seek to end their suffering and the State's interests in protecting those who might seek to end life mistakenly or under pressure. As the Court recognizes, States are presently undertaking extensive and serious evaluation of physician-assisted suicide and other related issues.

In sum, there is no need to address the question whether suffering patients have a constitutionally cognizable interest in obtaining relief from the suffering that they may experience in the last days of their lives. There is no dispute that dying patients in Washington and New York can obtain palliative care, even when doing so would hasten their deaths. The difficulty in defining terminal illness and the risk that a dying patient's request for assistance in ending his or her life might not be truly voluntary justifies the prohibitions we uphold here.

JUSTICE STEVENS, concurring in the judgments.

The Court ends its opinion with the important observation that our holding today is fully consistent with a continuation of the vigorous debate about the "morality, legality, and practicality of physician-assisted suicide" in a democratic society. I write separately to make it clear that there is also room for further debate about the limits that the Constitution places on the power of the States to punish the practice. The morality, legality, and practicality of capital punishment have been the subject of debate for many years. In 1976, this Court upheld the constitutionality in Georgia, Florida and Texas. In those cases we concluded that a State does have the power to place a lesser value on some lives than on others; there is no absolute requirement that a State treat all human life as having an equal right to preservation. State legislatures had sufficiently narrowed the category of lives that the State could terminate, and had enacted special procedures to ensure that the defendant belonged in that limited category. In later cases coming to us from each of those States, however, we found that some applications of the statutes were unconstitutional. Today, the Court decides that Washington's statute prohibiting assisted suicide is not invalid "on its face," that is to say, in all or most cases in which it might be applied. That holding, however, does not foreclose the possibility that some applications of the statute might well be invalid.

The Oregon Death with Dignity Act[18]

"Informed decision" means a decision by a qualified patient, to request and obtain a prescription to end his or her life in a humane and dignified manner, that is based on an appreciation of the relevant facts and after being fully informed by the attending physician of:

(a) his or her medical diagnosis;

(b) his or her prognosis;

(c) potential risks associated with taking the medication to be prescribed;

(d) probable result of taking the medication to be prescribed;

(e) feasible alternatives, i.e. comfort care, hospice care and pain control.

"Qualified patient" means a capable adult who is a resident of Oregon and has satisfied the requirements of this Act in order to obtain a prescription for medication to end his or her life in a humane and dignified manner.

"Terminal disease" means an incurable and irreversible disease that has been medically confirmed and will, within reasonable medical judgment, produce death within six (6) months.

An adult who is capable, is a resident of Oregon, and has been determined by the attending physician and consulting physician to be suffering from a terminal disease, and who has voluntarily expressed his or her wish to die, may make a written request for medication for the purpose of ending his or her life in a humane and dignified manner in accordance with this Act.

FORM OF THE WRITTEN REQUEST

(1) A valid request for medication under this Act shall be signed and dated by the patient and witnessed by at least two individuals who, attest their knowledge and belief that the patient is capable of acting voluntarily.

(2) One of the witnesses shall be a person who is not:

A relative, an heir, owner or employee of a health care facility, the patient's attending physician or person disqualified by rules of the Department of Human Resources.

ATTENDING PHYSICIAN RESPONSIBILITIES

The attending physician shall:

(1) Make the initial determination of whether a patient has a terminal disease, is capable, and has made the request voluntarily;

(2) Inform the patient of:

(a) his or her medical diagnosis;

(b) his or her prognosis;

(c) risks associated with the medication;

(d) probable result of taking the medication;

(e) feasible alternatives like hospice care and pain control.

(3) Refer the patient to a consulting physician for medical confirmation of the diagnosis, and for a determination that the patient is capable and acting voluntarily;

(4) Refer the patient for counseling if appropriate pursuant to Section 3.03;

(5) Request that the patient notify next of kin;

(6) Inform the patient that he or she has an opportunity to rescind the request at any time and in any manner, and offer the patient an opportunity to rescind at the end of the 15-day waiting period;

(7) Verify, immediately prior to writing the prescription for medication under this Act, that the patient is making an informed decision;

(8) Fulfill the medical record documentation requirements;

(9) Ensure that all appropriate steps are carried out in accordance with this Act prior to writing a prescription for medication to enable a qualified patient to end his or her life in a humane and dignified manner.

CONSULTING PHYSICIAN CONFIRMATION

Before a patient is qualified under this Act, a consulting physician shall examine the patient and his or her relevant medical records and confirm, in writing, the attending physician's diagnosis that the patient is suffering from a terminal disease, and verify that the patient is capable, is acting voluntarily and has made an informed decision.

COUNSELING REFERRAL

If in the opinion of the attending physician or the consulting physician a patient may be suffering from a psychiatric or psychological disorder, or depression causing impaired judgment, either physician shall refer the patient for counseling. No medication to end a patient's life in a humane and dignified manner shall be prescribed until the person performing the counseling determines that the patient is not suffering from a psychiatric or psychological disorder, or depression causing impaired judgment.

INFORMED DECISION

No person shall receive a prescription for medication to end his or her life in a humane and dignified manner unless he or she has made an informed decision. Immediately prior to writing a prescription for medication under this Act, the attending physician shall verify that the patient is making an informed decision.

FAMILY NOTIFICATION

The attending physician shall ask the patient to notify next of kin of his or her request for medication pursuant to this Act. A patient who declines or is unable to notify next of kin shall not have his or her request denied for that reason.

WRITTEN AND ORAL REQUESTS

In order to receive a prescription for medication to end his or her life in a humane and dignified manner, a qualified patient shall have made an oral request and a written request, and reiterate the oral request to his or her attending physician no less than fifteen (15) days after making the initial oral request. At the time the qualified patient makes his or her second oral request, the attending physician shall offer the patient an opportunity to rescind the request.

RIGHT TO RESCIND REQUEST

A patient may rescind his or her request at any time and in any manner without regard to his or her mental state. No prescription for medication under this Act may be written without the attending physician offering the qualified patient an opportunity to rescind the request.

WAITING PERIODS

No less than fifteen (15) days shall elapse between the patient's initial oral request and the writing of a prescription under this Act. No less than 48 hours shall elapse between the patient's written request and the writing of a prescription under this Act.

MEDICAL RECORD DOCUMENTATION REQUIREMENTS

The following shall be documented or filed in the patient's medical record:

(1) All oral requests by a patient for medication to end his or her life in a humane and dignified manner;

(2) All written requests by a patient for medication to end his or her life in a humane and dignified manner;

(3) The attending physician's diagnosis and prognosis, determination that the patient is capable, acting voluntarily and has made an informed decision;

(4) The consulting physician's diagnosis and prognosis, and verification that the patient is capable, acting voluntarily and has made an informed decision;

(5) A report of the outcome and determinations made during counseling, if performed;

(6) The attending physician's offer to the patient to rescind his or her request at the time of the patient's second oral request;

(7) A note by the attending physician indicating that all requirements under this Act have been met and indicating the steps taken to carry out the request, including a notation of the medication prescribed.

RESIDENCY REQUIREMENT

Only requests made by Oregon residents, under this Act, shall be granted.

REPORTING REQUIREMENTS

(1) The Health Division shall annually review a sample of records maintained pursuant to this Act.

(2) The Health Division shall make rules to facilitate the collection of information regarding compliance with this Act. The information collected shall not be a public record and may not be made available for inspection by the public.

(3) The Health Division shall generate and make available to the public an annual statistical report of information collected.

"Before we try assisted suicide, Mrs. Rose, let's give the aspirin a chance."

Lee v. Oregon

869 F. Supp. 1491, December 27, 1994

Michael R. Hogan, UNITED STATES DISTRICT JUDGE

OPINION

Before the court is Measure 16, passed by Oregon voters on November 8, 1994. This law, for the first time in the history of this country, authorizes physician-assisted suicide for the terminally ill. The law invokes profound questions of constitutional dimension. The narrow issue presented at this juncture is whether those questions justify a brief delay in the implementation of this law. For the reasons set forth below, I find that the balancing of the important factors in this case merits a postponement of the implementation of the legislation until the constitutional concerns are fully heard and analyzed, which will be scheduled as soon as practicable.

Plaintiffs are two physicians, four terminally ill or potentially terminally ill patients, a residential care facility and individual operators of residential care facilities.

Plaintiffs claim Measure 16 violates the Equal Protection and Due Process Clauses of the Fourteenth Amendment, the First Amendment rights of freedom to exercise religion and to associate, and the Americans with Disabilities Act.

Defendants argue that plaintiffs are not entitled to a preliminary injunction because they lack standing. A threshold question in every federal case is whether a plaintiff has sufficiently alleged a "case or controversy" within Article III of the United States Constitution. A plaintiff invoking federal court jurisdiction must establish, at an irreducible constitutional minimum that: (1) they have suffered an "injury in fact" or an invasion of a legally-protected interest which is concrete and particularized and "actual or imminent," (2) there is a causal connection between the injury and the challenged conduct, and (3) it must be likely that the injury will be "redressed by a favorable decision." The United States Supreme Court has recognized that "imminence" is an elastic concept, but one that must be limited so that an alleged injury is not too speculative.

Plaintiff's have terminal illnesses and all claim that they would not choose assisted suicide while exercising sound judgment. Their claims is that they may, at some future time, request physician assisted suicide due to undue influence caused by judgment-impairing depression, or other inappropriate influence.

Equal Protection

Plaintiffs allege that Measure 16 violates the rights of the terminally ill to equal protection under the law. Under Oregon law, a person may be convicted of manslaughter in the second degree for intentionally causing or aiding another to commit suicide.

The Equal Protection Clause of the Fourteenth Amendment states that no state shall "deny to any person within its jurisdiction the equal protection of the laws." This means that all persons similarly situated should be treated alike. "The general rule is that legislation is presumed to be valid and will be sustained if the classification drawn by the statute is rationally related to a legitimate state interest."

The state has identified its interests in Measure 16 as preventing continued pain and suffering of competent terminally ill patients and support of Oregon voters' rights to participate in the democratic process. However, "pain and suffering" is not contained in the terms of Measure 16.

The classification of "terminally ill" patient is suspect if, as plaintiffs claim:

a. Physicians often misdiagnose terminal illness

b. A physician's prognosis of six months to live is often fallible.

c. Would reasoned medical judgment include a patient who can live a normal life span with medication (diabetics) but not without it?

If persons with terminal disease are disabled under Americans With Disabilities Act, does this mean they are a suspect class?

Must Measure 16 serve a compelling state interest, and does it?

Does Measure 16 "deny" terminally ill patients the protections of Oregon's criminal and civil commitment statutes or does it give them the benefit of opting out of coverage under those laws?

Plaintiffs allege that Measure 16 unconstitutionally deprives persons who have the disability of a terminal disease of protections for their right to live.

It violates plaintiffs' liberty interests because it does not sufficiently guarantee that the choice to end life will be both informed and voluntary.

The concept of "liberty" has been well-articulated in the plurality opinion in *Planned Parenthood v. Casey*: Our law affords constitutional protection to personal decisions relating to marriage, procreation, contraception, family relationships, child rearing, and education.... These matters, involving the most intimate and personal choices a person may make in a lifetime, choices central to personal dignity and autonomy, are central to the liberty protected by the Fourteenth Amendment. At the heart of liberty is the right to define one's own concept of existence, of meaning, of the universe, and of the mystery of human life. Beliefs about these matters could not define the attributes of personhood were they formed under compulsion of the State.

Measure 16 provides that an attending physician shall ask a patient to notify next of kin of the request for a lethal dosage of medication but the request cannot be denied if the patient declines or is unable to notify. Should family or guardian notification be required, when possible, because it may be significant:

(a) in diagnosing the severity of a patient's depression?

(b) in providing emotional support that may be lacking and lead the patient to decide to live?

(c) in assisting a trained professional to determine whether the patient is being unduly influenced?

Are safeguards required so that a terminally ill, judgment-impaired or unduly influenced patient is not allowed to take a lethal dosage, even if they received the lethal dosage when they were competent?

Are there sufficient safeguards so that terminally ill patients are making an informed choice? Is it necessary for an independent third party, i.e., a probate or other court, to oversee decision for and implementation of an assisted death request?

First Amendment

Plaintiffs allege that certain provisions of Measure 16 require complicity of physicians and health care providers that is contrary to plaintiffs' religious and moral convictions and violates the Free Exercise Clause and freedom of association protections of the First Amendment and the Religious Freedom Restoration Act.

Plaintiffs contend that the following aspects of Measure 16 infringe on their freedom of association and freedom to exercise their religious beliefs:

1. Measure 16 requires health care providers to transfer records at a patient's request if a facility is unwilling to comply with the patient's wishes.

2. Oregon's "informed consent" law requires physicians to discuss available treatment options with patients. "As a result, Plaintiffs will be required to advise patients of their right to assisted suicide."

3. The federal Patient Self-Determination Act, 42 U.S.C. requires health care facilities to inform patients of their rights under state law. "As a result, medical care facilities will be required in Oregon to advise patients of their right to assisted suicide and to appoint a witness to witness written requests for assisted suicide."

4. Measure 16 prohibits facilities from denying staff privileges to or otherwise disciplining physicians who choose to honor a patient's request for medication.

Defendants contend that plaintiffs' discussion of religious freedom is "largely irrelevant" because "no one denies that freedom of association and the free exercise of religion are protected by the First Amendment."

If a health care provider or physician is required to perform acts to facilitate or accommodate a request for assisted suicide and based on sincerely held religious convictions, reasonably believes that their participation constitutes "complicity" in the suicide, there is a serious question regarding an infringement on religious beliefs against such conduct.

A preliminary injunction in this case results in the maintenance of the status quo for a limited period of time to thoroughly consider the constitutionality of Measure 16. Although the status quo will be regarded as a hardship by some terminally ill patients who want the "option" of physician assisted suicide to be immediately available, the public interest in protecting vulnerable citizens from the irreparable harm of death is greater.

Surely, the first assisted suicide law in this country deserves a considered, thoughtful constitutional analysis.

Justices Uphold Oregon Assisted-Suicide Law in a Blow to Administration; Ruling Paves Way for Other States to Follow Suit[19]

Charles Lane
Washington Post

The U.S. Supreme Court upheld Oregon's law on physician-assisted suicide yesterday, ruling that the Justice Department may not punish doctors who help terminally ill patients end their lives.

By a vote of 6 to 3, the court ruled that Attorney General John D. Ashcroft exceeded his legal authority in 2001 when he threatened to prohibit doctors from prescribing federally controlled drugs if they authorized lethal doses of the medications under the Oregon Death With Dignity Act.

The ruling struck down one of the administration's signature policies regarding what President Bush calls the "culture of life" and lifts the last legal cloud over the state's law, which is unique in the nation. It also frees other states to follow in Oregon's footsteps, unless Congress acts to the contrary.

It is unclear how many states would join Oregon; assisted-suicide initiatives have not fared well in recent years. Still, coming a year after efforts by Republicans in Congress to block the removal of a feeding tube from Terri Schiavo, and after Chief Justice John G. Roberts Jr., and Supreme Court nominee Samuel A. Alito Jr., faced questions from the Senate about their views on end-of-life issues, the court's decision could energize the political debate. Roberts dissented from the ruling, joined by Justices Antonin Scalia and Clarence Thomas.

Conservatives reacted angrily to the ruling. Jay Sekulow, chief counsel of the American Center for Law and Justice, a nonprofit litigation group founded by Pat Robertson, called it "a disturbing and dangerous decision that can only lessen the value of protecting human life."

But Sen. Ron Wyden (D-Ore.) called it "a significant victory for Oregon's voters," who twice approved the Death With Dignity Act in statewide referendums.

Assisting suicide is a crime in 44 states, including Maryland, as well as the District. It is a civil offense in Virginia. In three states—North Carolina, Utah and Wyoming—the law neither prohibits nor permits assisted suicide. Ohio's Supreme Court has decriminalized assisted suicide.

State referendums supporting assisted suicide have failed in California, Maine, Michigan and Washington. A bill failed in Maryland in 1995 and 1996. A measure modeled on Oregon's passed two committees in the California Assembly last year but then fizzled from lack of support. An author of the bill, Assemblywoman Patty Berg (D), said she was "very optimistic" that the ruling would help prospects for the bill this year.

The Supreme Court was aware of the strong feelings on both sides—and portrayed itself as above them.

Although frequently described as a "right to die" case, *Gonzales v. Oregon*, No. 04-623, was not, strictly speaking, about the constitutional right to end one's own life. The court has already ruled, in 1997, that there is no such right and did not revisit that holding yesterday.

Instead, Justice Anthony M. Kennedy noted in the majority opinion that the question was whether Ashcroft acted in accordance with the Controlled Substances Act when he issued an "interpretive rule" in 2001, declaring that assisting suicide is not a "legitimate medical purpose" for which federally regulated drugs may lawfully be prescribed. Ashcroft's successor, Alberto R. Gonzales, has continued the policy.

Kennedy acknowledged that the case was partly a product of the national debate over end-of-life issues but noted that the "resolution requires an inquiry familiar to the courts: interpreting a federal statute to determine whether Executive action is authorized by, or otherwise consistent with, the enactment." The answer, Kennedy wrote, is no: Recasting the issue as involving the states' right to regulate medical practice rather than a patient's right to die, he concluded that Ashcroft had made an overly broad interpretation of the 35-year-old federal Controlled Substances Act (CSA). Kennedy wrote that the law was meant to stop drug abuse and drug trafficking, not to replace the states' traditional role in deciding what state-licensed doctors may and may not do within state borders.

> "The Government, in the end, maintains that the prescription requirement [of the CSA] delegates to a single Executive officer the power to effect a radical shift of authority from the states to the Federal Government to define general standards of medical practice in every locality," Kennedy wrote. "The text and structure of the CSA show that Congress did not have this far-reaching intent to alter the federal-state balance and the congressional role in maintaining it."

Kennedy was joined by Justices John Paul Stevens, Sandra Day O'Connor, David H. Souter, Ruth Bader Ginsburg and Stephen G. Breyer.

In dissent, Scalia argued that Ashcroft had acted well within his legal powers. "If the term legitimate medical purpose has any meaning, it surely excludes the prescription of drugs to produce death," Scalia wrote. He was joined by Roberts—dissenting for the first time on the court—and Thomas. Thomas wrote separately to argue that the court's ruling was inconsistent with its opinion last year upholding a federal override of a California law legalizing the medical use of marijuana.

> The Oregon Death With Dignity Act was adopted by the state's voters in 1994. It permits doctors to prescribe, but not administer, a lethal dose to a terminally ill patient who requests it, provided that the patient is mentally competent.
>
> State voters rejected a challenge to the law in 1997; two efforts to override it in Congress, supported by Ashcroft when he was a senator, failed. President Bill Clinton's attorney general, Janet Reno, declined to act against the law.
>
> From 1997 to 2004, 208 people ended their lives by physician-assisted suicide in Oregon. After Ashcroft issued his declaration as attorney general, a federal district court in Oregon upheld the law, as did the San Francisco-based U.S. Court of Appeals for the 9th Circuit. The Bush administration appealed to the Supreme Court, which agreed last year to take the case.

For Your Consideration

Is the rationale for restricting rights of suicide to the terminally ill, despite its limited deterrent effect, sufficient under equal protection standards?

From a public policy perspective, are the roles of doctors who assist suicide and those who seek to prescribe marijuana for medically approved purposes substantially the same or different?

Additional Commentary on the Suicide Debate

Edited Excerpts From the Stanford Encyclopedia of Philosophy[20]

> Attaching criminal penalties to suicide attempts are futile if the endeavor is successful, and fails to address the nature of the social offense when it's not. Talk about a philosophical maelstrom. Even Socrates inquired about the nature of suicide. Describing and explaining human action, and identifying the necessary conditions that correlate with common understanding and use of the term is especially difficult. The term is fraught with negative emotional connotations that import moral judgments about deliberately ending life. It stirs lofty declarations about the scope of social duty and nature of consent.
>
> Even in the face of great emotional and physical suffering, some claim that society as a whole must reaffirm its commitment to preserve life whenever feasible. Diluting the firm obligations of medical personnel to protect and extend human life would severely undermine the public's faith in the health care profession and encourage American doctors to play God. This line of reasoning remains unsupported by the limited number of available studies.
>
> Suicide research is firmly entrenched in the established scientific paradigm, where fixation on prediction and control is part of the central framework. Students of psychiatry, psychology, public health, and sociology investigate suicide in universities. Research is usually quantitative in character, mining data through random experimental designs.
>
> Theories about suicide often fail to divorce questions about whether an act was suicide from whether we admire the choice. Most contend that Hitler's death was

clearly a suicide, but Socrates' and Jesus' were not. Suicide still carries a strongly negative subtext. There is a greater willingness to categorize self-killings intended to avoid retribution as suicides, than self-killings intended to benefit others. How do we assess suicide bombings in the Middle East and other parts of the world? Some go so far as to deny the possibility that an act of self-killing motivated by altruism can count as suicide. Is a purely descriptive account of suicide even possible? If we conclude that suicide is any self-caused death, how would we classify individuals who know the certain health risks associated with smoking and rock climbing, but participate and die as a result?

One causally responsible for his own death by taking Tylenol laced with cyanide is not suicidal in the mere act of taking pain relievers. Yet, there are self-caused deaths that are not suicides, but result in death and remain suicidal in nature because the act was accomplished through an agent. Arranging the circumstances of her death, a terminally ill patient requests that another inject her with lethal tranquilizers. The deceased, while not the immediate cause of death, bears moral responsibility for initiating the sequence of events with intent to die. The sequence can only be explained with reference to her beliefs and desires.

Some would take away that choice and impose others. The argument goes that since health-care professionals routinely overlook patients' preferences, they often die in immense pain after extensive suffering. Physicians intent on keeping patients alive, fail to treat depression or recognize other life-crises. If the patient's right to control the treatment is a paramount value, then we should enforce a patient's bill of rights rather than authorizing physician-related suicides.

It is important to examine public policy in the context of how a phenomenon occurs: suicide is an individual outcome that takes place in a social context. Inevitably, our approach to studying suicide narrows in on the psychological dimensions, as if totally divorced from the social and spiritual circumstance that makes up the life of the individual.

Thus, does weighing the importance of life require the government to also permit people to experience a humane death? Wherever possible, empowering individuals who are near death or in unbearable pain to determine the time and circumstances to end their lives, with medical assistance is the best of all possible choices. Patients have a right to refuse or withdraw life-support measures. Seeking a physician's assistance in effectuating death seems an equally valid method for honoring human dignity. Sociologists and others who work in the area of cultural psychiatry are particularly concerned with the socially situated nature of suicide, turning their attention to the historically and culturally embedded risks for suicide. These types of investigations raise important questions about the way we construct the problem of suicide, as well as the way in which we plan broad-based prevention programs, none of which need involve the courts.

Suicide is morally permissible whether or not it appears rational or prudent. Attempts by the State or the medical profession to interfere with suicidal behavior are essentially coercive. Why pathologize what is nothing more than one option among many? The right to suicide is a right of noninterference. There is no "duty to live," which the State has an interest in reinforcing. We own our bodies, and our relationship to our bodies is like that of our relationship to other items over which we enjoy personal property rights. The right to suicide follows from a deeper right to self-determination, to shape the circumstances of our lives. As presented in the "death with dignity" movement, the right to suicide is presented as the natural corollary of the right to live.

Chapter Four

State Interests in Matters of Life & Death

During the heat of the debate about reproductive rights in the late 1970s, I stood next to a young man wearing a T-Shirt with CHOOSE LIFE emblazoned across the front. We worked with several others that year, in a summer youth program, finishing an outdoor project that left plenty of room for random discussion. Later, as we sat under a tree, I inquired about the shirt.

> *My Question*: Do you oppose a woman's right to choose?
>
> *His Answer*: No, I advocate life in relation to: pregnant women, the terminally ill, I would abolish the death penalty, end all wars—choose life.

In *Vacco v. Quill*, Justice Stephens made an interesting observation about the government's valuation of life in capital cases:

> A State that has authorized the death penalty has thereby concluded that the sanctity of human life does not require that it always be preserved. There are [presumably] situations in which an interest in hastening death is legitimate.[1]

Capital Punishment

State Power to Order Death of Its Citizens

Sand in the Machine[2]
Ed Lazarus

> Justice Arthur Goldberg, was a deeply religious man and consistently liberal jurist who considered the death penalty morally offensive. He argued that the Eighth Amendment "must draw its meaning from the evolving standards of decency that mark the progress of a maturing society," and condemned the death penalty as unconstitutionally "barbaric and inhumane." The vast majority of "civilized nations," he observed, "had abolished capital punishment," and the worldwide trend was "unmistakenly in the direction of abolition. He admonished fellow justices to consider that the "Court has traditionally guided rather than followed public opinion in the process of articulating and establishing progressively civilized standards of decency."
>
> Goldberg couldn't get the four votes needed to grant cert. in any of the pending capital cases. This failure, however, which the Justice seems to have anticipated, did not stop him from expressing publicly his desire to see the Court look at the death penalty more closely; he issued a number of dissents. Significantly, Gold-

berg carried two other Justices with him. Brennan and Douglas both signed on to his dissenting statement.

Dissents from denials of cert. send a signal to the legal community. They declare that an issue has caught the attention of at least one Justice, who feels strongly enough about the matter to issue a rare public comment effectively inviting other litigants to raise it again. For three Justices—one short of the number capable of forcing the whole Court to hear an issue—to join in a dissent from denial was tantamount to taking out a classified ad seeking new cases.

Coming at the dawn of the era of "public interest" law, Goldberg's dissents found an avid readership among the burgeoning ranks of young, ambitious, liberal-minded lawyers seeking to deploy their skills in the cause of social justice.

Working at a frenzied pace and with an almost religious zeal, [they] set out to prove that death penalty sentencing violated the Fourteenth Amendment's Equal Protection Clause, which, as one of the amendment's leading sponsors had stated, "prohibits the hanging of a Black man for a crime for which the White man is not to be hanged." As a starting point, the LDF lawyers focused on cases in which Black men had received the death penalty for raping White women—the crime for which evidence of racial bias in sentencing seemed most graphic. To lay the groundwork for a legal claim, they hired a respected criminologist, University of Pennsylvania sociologist Marvin Wolfgang, to conduct a statistical analysis of racial patterns in death sentences for rape.

In April 1966, Professor Wolfgang finished his rape sentencing study. Of 119 convicted rapists executed in twelve southern states between 1945 and 1965, Wolfgang found that 110 were black. And after attempting to control for other factors that might account for this apparent gross disproportion, Wolfgang concluded that "in less than one time in a thousand could these [racial] associations have occurred by the operation of chance."

The Legal Defense Fund defended Whites as well as Blacks in the forty-two jurisdictions that still maintained the death penalty. The idea was to create a de facto death penalty moratorium, to stop every execution both for its own sake and to build up a backlog of prisoners on death row.

As Michael Meltsner explained, "The politics of abolition boiled down to this: for each year the United States went without executions, the more hollow would ring the claims that the American people could not do without them; the longer death-row inmates waited, the greater their numbers, the more difficult it would be for the courts to permit the first execution." This was psychological as well as legal warfare. In every capital case that eventually came before the Court, the LDF wanted the specter of a potential bloodbath, the sudden lifting of hundreds of stays of execution, to be firmly implanted in the Justices' minds. The group was betting that no judge and no court would choose to play God en masse.

Accordingly, LDF lawyers orchestrated a nationwide network of death penalty defenders. They developed a "Last Aid Kit," a collection of draft briefs, motions, and habeas petitions that local counsel all across the country could use to apply for stays of execution. They organized friendly lawyers and scholars to help with the campaign and obtained a million-dollar Ford Foundation grant to fund their effort.

The campaign succeeded. Nineteen sixty-eight was one of the most violent years this country has known. Thousands of American soldiers and tens of thousands

> of Vietnamese died in an increasingly unpopular war. Student demonstrators torched draft cards and occupied college campuses. Richard Daley's police busted heads at the Democratic Convention in Chicago. Assassins killed Robert Kennedy and Martin Luther King. Then, the cities burned. Amid this tornado of wrath, for the first year in the country's history, not a single person was executed for a crime.
>
> A majority of the Justices seemed to express their own serious doubts about the penalty.
>
> The war seemed all but won.

In what was widely regarded as the last major broadside attack on the death penalty, in 1987, the justices split five to four in *McCleskey v. Kemp*,[3] holding that statistics showing that Blacks who murder Whites are four times more likely to receive the death penalty than Whites who kill Blacks, did not prove racial bias in the imposition of capital punishment.

In the years since, there have been numerous laws revising the death penalty. Questions of justice and neutrality continue to frame the debate as we collect more data and yet discover few changes in the profiles of those who are typically put to death in this nation.

The execution process raises many of the same questions and dilemmas that surround assisted suicide. Issues of mental competency arise in all cases involving the mentally retarded, and even those initially found competent to stand trial are rendered less so in the post-conviction, pre-execution phase of incarceration. Death row inmates sometimes volunteer to die, relinquishing their constitutional right to appeal, in order to escape prison conditions. The prolonged isolation, coupled with inhumane and degrading treatment that is standard for those awaiting execution, has been characterized as 'death row syndrome.' The essential question is whether the trauma attending the period of isolation between conviction and execution for the average death row prisoner is the functional equivalent of psychological torture, implicating the Eighth Amendment prohibition against cruel and unusual punishment.[4]

The strongest objections to capital punishment relate to unchecked prosecutorial discretion, both in the conviction and sentencing phases.[5] For example, jury pools are often purged of those likely to question prosecutors' motives or maintain a presumption of innocence, or to oppose the death penalty altogether. The process known as "death-qualifying" is a juror screening mechanism that eliminates jurors who might "upset" a capital verdict. In the past it was called scrupling. Potential jurors who oppose execution as retribution, consistent with their religious beliefs, are identified as conscientious objectors to the death penalty. While the Constitution promises the accused a right to a jury of their peers, and the general policy is that an accused is innocent until the state proves guilt beyond a reasonable doubt, death-qualifying creates a bias against those who accept the presumption of innocence. Proponents of the procedure argue that without such discretion, nearly every jury would likely include someone who would veto a death verdict, and essentially render void the capital punishment statutes of thirty-one jurisdictions. Another objection is a consequence of the first. A Columbia University study revealed that more than two-thirds of death penalty sentences are overturned on appeal. According to the late Justice Harlan, "to identify before the fact those characteristics of criminal homicides and their perpetrators which call for the death penalty, and to express those characteristics in language which can be fairly understood and applied by the sentencing authority, appear to be tasks which are beyond present human ability."[6]

"I couldn't agree more—but, then again, I hate even non-lethal injections."

Through technological advances, thousands of inmates have recently been exonerated following long prison stays. As a result, average citizens are also losing confidence in the integrity and fairness with which capital punishment is administered. Across the nation, States are studying the issue in the face of growing calls for moratoria and/or automatic DNA testing for the condemned. Scholar Donald S. Connery, known for his work entitled "History of Miscarriages of Justice" warns that:

> With honorable exceptions, our politicians, police agencies, prosecutors and judges have been slow to learn the lessons of the DNA revolution that has rocked the criminal justice system during the last 15 years. The errors, corruption and racism have always been known ... it was just that people preferred to believe that wrongful imprisonments are rare, and only the truly guilty get a ticket to death row. In fact, that national error rate for mistaken convictions is far higher than even the experts suspected. With more than two million Americans in prison or jail at any one time, the number accused or convicted for crimes they did not commit is in the tens of thousands. If airlines operated this way two to five planes would crash for every hundred taking off. Thanks to DNA we are now forced to confront the ugly reality of a system rampant with faulty eyewitness testimony, false confessions, junk science, jailhouse snitches, inept lawyers, police perjury,

> win-at-any-cost prosecutors, and judges too comfortable with the idea that appeals of jury verdicts are about technicalities, not the possibility of innocence.[7]

Many scholars believe that the problem demonstrtes dysfunction in the office of the prosecutor. Legislative oversight is needed to overhaul institutional culture. Rogue police and prosecutors are plentiful, and most dangerous when operating in rogue departments mired in the corrupt policies and practices that Connery documents.[8] Widespread bias in criminal charging and sentencing must be addressed head-on. State penal laws typically allow prosecutors the option of seeking the death penalty for:

murder of a public safety or correctional officer

murder for pecuniary gain

murder committed during the course of a felony

murder by a defendant with a previous conviction for intentional murder

murder while under a life sentence

murder committed during a kidnapping

illegal sale of cocaine, methadone or heroin to a person who then dies murder during first-degree sexual assault

multiple murders

As a matter of human rights, lack of public accountability for the increasing number of innocent people sitting on death row is a blight upon the nation's honor. Former "Republican Governor George W. Bush presided over more executions (152) than any governor in American history during his reign in Texas. Illinois Governor George Ryan learned that half the people in Illinois that had been sent to death row were wrongly convicted in a series of Chicago Tribune exposés and investigations conducted by Northwestern University's law and journalism schools."[9] Connery notes:

> I have seen the heartbreak, and sometimes the mental breakdown, of parents, children, wives, husbands, brothers and sisters of men and women doomed by our deeply flawed criminal justice system to spend years or decades behind prison walls for crimes they did not commit. I have met and befriended at least two dozen death-row convicts—beginning with Kirk Bloodsworth in Maryland, the first prisoner to be saved by DNA—who were lucky enough to have their innocence proved before it was too late.[10]

In fact, the law seems to be moving in the other direction, reaching a point of tension between the surviving relatives of the victim and the needs of society at large. Prosecutors use community advocates to justify their practices by demanding a formal role for victims of crime in capital cases. One particularly controversial maneuver involved the introductiom of victim-impact statements during sentencing in capital cases, where relatives would describe the impact of the victim's murder on surviving family members. In 1987, by a five-to-four vote in *Booth v. Maryland,* the Court disapproved of the use of victim-impact statements. [11] Justice Powell, the author of the Court's opinion, cast the deciding vote. When he retired at the end of the 1987 term, there was speculation that his replacement, Justice Anthony Kennedy, would tip the balance on the Court toward reconsidering and upholding victim-impact statements. But in 1989, Justice White, who dissented in *Booth*, switched sides in *South Carolina v. Gathers* joining a slim majority that again disallowed the use of victim-impact statements.[12]

With the tide of public opinion turning away from the death penalty, down to 66% in favor from 78% in the last decade, some claim that capital penalty advocates have not fairly represented the wishes of the majority of victims' families.

Murder Victims' Families for Reconciliation (MVFR)

MVFR is an organization of people, all of whom have lost loved ones to violence, who are convening with academics, legal professionals, social workers, theologians, abolitionists and victims' advocates to talk about how to support victims' needs without resort to violence. Having struggled with issues of blame and forgiveness, MVFR members are proponents of restorative justice models and opponents of the death penalty as part of their mission of breaking the cycle of violence and revenge.[13]

Dignity Denied: New Report Reveals Bias against Surviving Family Members Who Oppose the Death Penalty[14]

A new report released today paints a startling picture of systemic bias and discrimination by those who serve victims against surviving family members who, contrary to popular stereotype, oppose the death penalty. "Too often, family members who oppose the death penalty are silenced, marginalized, and abandoned, even by the people who are theoretically charged with helping them," Cushing said. There are three primary ways victims who oppose the death penalty face discrimination:

Denial of the right to speak and be heard.

Denial of the right to information. Often, when prosecutors learn that a surviving family member opposes the death penalty for the perpetrator, that person will be denied information about upcoming hearings, court dates or other important information about the case. "Sometimes this denial is made explicit, as when members of a district attorney's office warn families that if they advocate against the death penalty the office will no longer communicate with them.

Denial of the right to assistance and advocacy. "Dignity Denied" challenges lawmakers, recommending that victims' rights laws should be amended to ban discrimination based upon a victim's position on the death penalty; victims' services should be administered independently, not as part of the prosecutor's office; and leaders in the victims' services community should develop protocols for serving victims' families who oppose the death penalty.

Summary of Roper v. Simmons[15]

October 13, 2004

By a vote of 5–4, the U.S. Supreme Court on March 1, 2005, held that the Eighth and Fourteenth Amendments forbid the execution of offenders who were under the age of 18 when their crimes were committed.

Justice Kennedy, writing for the majority (Kennedy, Breyer, Ginsburg, Souter, and Stevens, JJ.) stated:

> When a juvenile offender commits a heinous crime, the State can exact forfeiture of some of the most basic liberties, but the State cannot extinguish his life and his potential to attain a mature understanding of his own humanity.

The Court reaffirmed the necessity of referring to "the evolving standards of decency that mark the progress of a maturing society" to determine which punishments are so disproportionate as to be cruel and unusual.

Reliance on *Atkins*: The Court outlined the similarities between its analysis of the constitutionality of executing juvenile offenders and the constitutionality of executing the mentally retarded. Prior to 2002, the Court had refused to categorically exempt mentally retarded persons from capital punishment. *Penry v. Lynaugh*, 492 U.S. 302 (1989). However, in *Atkins v. Virginia*, 536 U.S. 304 (2002), the Court held that standards of decency had evolved in the 13 years since *Penry* and that a national consensus had formed against such executions, demonstrating that the execution of the mentally retarded is cruel and unusual punishment. Contrary to *Stanford v. Kentucky*, 492 U.S. 361 (1989), that the execution of 16- and 17-year-old offenders was not constitutionally barred. The Court now concludes that since *Stanford*, a national consensus has formed against the execution of juvenile offenders, and the practice violates society's "evolving standards of decency." The Court overruled its decision in *Stanford*, thereby setting the minimum age for eligibility for the death penalty at 18.

The Court explained that the primary criterion for determining whether a particular punishment violates society's evolving standards of decency is objective evidence of a national consensus as expressed by legislative enactments and jury practices. The majority opinion found significant that 30 states prohibit the juvenile death penalty, including 12 that have rejected the death penalty altogether.

When ruling that juvenile offenders cannot with reliability be classified as among the worst offenders, the Court found significant that juveniles are vulnerable to influence, and susceptible to immature and irresponsible behavior. In light of juveniles' diminished culpability, neither retribution nor deterrence provides adequate justification for imposing the death penalty.

Justice Kennedy, writing for the majority, said:

> Retribution is not proportional if the law's most severe penalty is imposed on one whose culpability or blameworthiness is diminished, to a substantial degree, by reason of youth and immaturity.[16]

International Confirmation: The Court further noted that that the execution of juvenile offenders violated several international treaties, including the United Nations Convention on the Rights of the Child and the International Covenant on Civil and Political Rights and stated that the overwhelming weight of international opinion against the juvenile death penalty provides confirmation for the Court's own conclusion that the death penalty is disproportional punishment for offenders under 18.

Justice Stevens wrote a concurring opinion, joined by Justice Ginsburg, stating:

> Perhaps even more important than our specific holding today is our reaffirmation of the basic principle that informs the Court's interpretation of the Eighth Amendment. If the meaning of that Amendment had been frozen when it was

> originally drafted, it would impose no impediment to the execution of 7-year-old children today.[17]

The Court's ruling in *Roper v. Simmons* affects 72 juvenile offenders in 12 states.

For Your Consideration

Some arguments against the death penalty are largely utilitarian. For example, Connery argues that:

> Just by having a death penalty, candidates for execution receive a wonderful post-conviction gift. They receive something far nicer than a sentence to permanent confinement in noisy, suffocating, high-walled-razor-wired institutions packed with dangerous convicts and surly guards. We give them celebrity instead of obscurity: a safer place in prison, an automatic appeal and top-drawer public defenders fighting to keep them alive. We give them power to play on our emotions, win headlines, and force the State to spend enormous sums during years of legal wrangling, arguing endlessly about what he "deserves." With every capital verdict, all you can do as a citizen is brace yourself for years of expensive nonsense.[18]

Throughout the history of the Supreme Court's capital punishment debate, only Justices Brennan and Marshall address the normative question in maintaining that capital punishment is unconstitutional due to its severity, finality, excessiveness, and denial of human dignity. Capital punishment has been abolished in all 15 countries of the European Union.[19] Capital sentencing is diametrically opposed to many international standards of human rights, and held to be inconsistent with fundamental principles of democratic society. Abolition of the death penalty is a condition for membership.

Jurors who reject capital punishment on moral or religious grounds are called conscientious objectors. Citizens opposed to serving in the armed forces, where one is required to bear arms, kill, or train others to kill, consistent with their moral or religious principles, are also known as conscientious objectors. Successful claims are rare, and usually result in exemption from combat service through placement in non-combative units or details.

U.S. Military Conscription

The United States abandoned military conscription in 1973. However, the Selective Service system remains as a formal registration process, should the need for conscription arise. All males are required to register with Selective Service within 30 days of their 18th birthday. Failure to register is unlawful for citizens, alien residents, and illegal aliens between the ages of 18 and 25, with penalties of up to five years in jail and fines of up to $250,000. Despite these penalties, government records indicate that from 1980 through 1990, there were only 20 indictments. By 1986, public trials were generating a decline in registration. As an alternate method of encouraging registration, federal and state legislators passed laws conditioning eligibility for financial aid, federal grants and loans, and certain government benefits to registration for selective service. During the last draft by lottery, 2.8 million out of 24 million were called to war. Local draft boards classify registrants, according to the United States Code Title 32, Chapter XVI, Sec. 1630.2, into the following categories:

Class 1-A: Available for unrestricted military service

Class 1-A-0: Conscientious objector available for noncombatant military service only.

Class 1-C: Member of the Armed Forces of the United States, the National Oceanic and Atmospheric Administration or the Public Health Service.

Class 1-D-D: Deferment for certain members of a reserve component or student taking military training.

Class 1-D-E: Exemption of certain members of a reserve component or student taking military training.

Class 1-H: Registrant not subject to processing for induction.

Class 1-O: Conscientious objector to all military service. A registrant must establish to the satisfaction of the board that his request for exemption from combatant and noncombatant military training and service in the Armed Forces is based upon moral, ethical or religious beliefs which play a significant role in his life and that his objection to participation in war is not confined to a particular war.

Class 1-O-S: Conscientious objector to all military service.

Class 1-W: Conscientious objector ordered to perform alternative service.

Class 2-D: Registrant deferred because of study preparing for the ministry.

Class 3-A: Registrant deferred because of hardship to dependents.

Class 3-A-S: Registrant deferred because of hardship to dependents (separated).

Class 4-A: Registrant who has completed military service.

Class 4-B: Official deferred by law.

Class 4-C: Alien or dual national.

Class 4-D: Minister of religion.

Class 4-F: Registrant not acceptable for military service. To be eligible for Class 4-F, a registrant must have been found not qualified for service in the Armed Forces by a Military Entrance Processing Station (MEPS) under the established physical, mental, or moral standards. The standards of physical fitness that would be used in a future draft remain undefined. It should be remembered that obesity is more common among young Americans than in other NATO countries that retain conscription. Openly admitted homosexuals are not allowed to serve in the American military.

Class 4-G: Registrant exempted from service because of the death of his parent or sibling while serving in the Armed Forces or whose parent or sibling is in a captured or missing in action status.

Class 4-T: Treaty alien.

Class 4-W: Registrant who has completed alternative service in lieu of induction.

Class 4-A-A: Registrant who has performed military service for a foreign nation.

Longstanding Views of the Catholic Church

A statement issued by the Conference of Catholic Churches described questions of registration and conscription for military service as part of the broader political-moral decision-making process of citizens related to war and peace in the nuclear age. The church's support of the right of selective conscientious objection (SCO) is based upon a moral conclusion that it declares can be validly derived from the classical moral teachings of Just-War theory.[20]

> We call in season and out of season for the international community to turn from war and to do the works of peace. The primary obligation of the nuclear age is to banish resort to force from the daily affairs of nations and peoples.
>
> The moral right of the state to use force is severely limited both in terms of the reasons for which force is employed and the means to be used. While acknowledging the duty of the state to defend society and its correlative right to use force in certain circumstances, we also affirm the Catholic teaching that the state's decision to use force should always be morally scrutinized by citizens asked to support the decision or to participate in war.
>
> We are opposed to any reinstitution of military conscription except in the case of a national defense emergency.

Conscience and War[21]

By David Chandler

> The law does not recognize your right to object to a specific war, but you are a conscientious objector nonetheless. "Conscientious objector" is not something you apply to become on the basis of what is permitted by law. It is a declaration that you will not fight and that your objection is on the basis of your conscience. People have taken this stand throughout history in all nations and in all wars. Those who refuse to fight for reasons of conscience are sometimes persecuted, sometimes imprisoned, or executed (even in US history). Occasionally nations recognize the right to refuse to fight, but the laws cannot define the limits of conscience.
>
> The right to follow ones conscience is a fundamental human right. The sanctity of the individual and the individual conscience is the foundation of all our freedoms. Freedom of speech, freedom of religion, freedom of assembly, all follow from the freedom of the individual to judge for himself or herself what is right and wrong, what is wise and what is foolish. Individual conscience is not infallible, but any political system that forces people to violate their conscience is surely worse: it is totalitarian.
>
> If your conscience tells you that you cannot fight in a specific war for specific reasons, then you owe it to your conscience not to join, or allow yourself to be drafted into, a military machine in which you are not given the freedom to make that judgment. True, your alternate service might take the form of a prison term, but you would be in good company. There have been many prisoners of conscience throughout history and throughout the world today. If we believe that the United States should be a leader in respecting human rights, we must struggle to expand the legal definition of conscientious objector to include all those who truly seek to follow their conscience.

Clay, aka Ali v. United States

403 U.S. 698
June 28, 1971, Decided

Facts: Petitioner Muhammad Ali applied to his local draft board for conscientious objector classification. The State Appeal Board tentatively classified him as eligible for unrestricted military service and referred his file to the Department of Justice for an advisory recommendation, in accordance with then-applicable procedures.

The FBI then conducted an "inquiry" as required by the statute, interviewing some 35 persons, including members of the petitioner's family and many of his friends, neighbors, and business and religious associates.

There followed a hearing on "the character and good faith of Ali's objections" before a hearing officer appointed by the Department. The hearing officer, a retired judge of many years' experience, heard testimony from the petitioner's mother and father, from one of his attorneys, from a minister of his religion, and from the petitioner himself. He also had the benefit of a full report from the FBI. On the basis of this record the hearing officer concluded that the registrant was sincere in his objection on religious grounds to participation in war in any form, and he recommended that the conscientious objector claim be sustained.

The Justice Department, in response to the State Appeal Board's referral for an advisory recommendation, concluded, contrary to a hearing officer's recommendation, that petitioner's claim should be denied, and wrote that board that petitioner did not meet any of the three basic tests for conscientious objector status. Upon receipt of this letter of advice, the Board denied the petitioner's claim without a statement of reasons. Petitioner refused to report for induction, for which he was thereafter tried and convicted for willful refusal to submit to induction into the Armed Forces. The Court of Appeals affirmed.

In order to qualify for classification as a conscientious objector, a registrant must satisfy three basic tests. He must show that he is conscientiously opposed to war in any form.

He must show that this opposition is based upon religious training and belief, as the term has been construed in our decisions. And he must show that this objection is sincere. In applying these tests, the Selective Service System must be concerned with the registrant as an individual, not with its own interpretation of the dogma of the religious sect, if any, to which he may belong.

In asking us to affirm the judgment of conviction, the Government argues that there was a "basis in fact," for holding that the petitioner is not opposed to "war in any form," but is only selectively opposed to certain wars. Counsel for the petitioner, needless to say, takes the opposite position. The issue is one that need not be resolved in this case. For we have concluded that even if the Government's position on this question is correct, the conviction before us must still be set aside for another quite independent reason.

The petitioner's criminal conviction stemmed from the Selective Service System's denial of his appeal seeking conscientious objector status. That denial, for which no reasons were ever given, was, as we have said, based on a recommendation of the Department of Justice, overruling its hearing officer and advising the Appeal Board that it "finds that the registrant's conscientious-objector claim is not sustained and recommends to your Board that he be not [so] classified." This finding was contained in a long letter of explanation, from which it is evident that Selective Service officials were led to believe that the Department had found that the petitioner had failed to satisfy each of the three basic tests for qualification as a conscientious objector.

In this Court the Government has rightly conceded the invalidity of two of the grounds for denial of petitioner's claim given in its letter to the Appeal Board, but argues that there was factual support for the third ground.

As to the requirement that a registrant must be opposed to war in any form, the Department letter said that the petitioner's expressed beliefs "do not appear to preclude military service in any form, but rather are limited to military service in the Armed Forces of the United States.... These constitute only objections to certain types of war in certain circumstances, rather than a general scruple against participation in war in any form. However, only a general scruple against participation in war in any form can support an exemption as a conscientious objector under the Act.

As to the requirement that a registrant's opposition must be based upon religious training and belief, the Department letter said: "It seems clear that the teachings of the Nation of Islam preclude fighting for the United States not because of objections to participation in war in any form but rather because of political and racial objections to policies of the United States as interpreted by Elijah Muhammad.... It is therefore our conclusion that registrant's claimed objections to participation in war insofar as they are based upon the teachings of the Nation of Islam, rest on grounds which primarily are political and racial."

As to the requirement that a registrant's opposition to war must be sincere, that part of the letter began by stating "the registrant has not consistently manifested his conscientious-objector claim. Such a course of overt manifestations is requisite to establishing a subjective state of mind and belief." There followed several paragraphs reciting the timing and circumstances of the petitioner's conscientious objector claim, and a concluding paragraph seeming to state a rule of law—that "a registrant has not shown overt manifestations sufficient to establish his subjective belief where, as here, his conscientious-objector claim was not asserted until military service became imminent.

In this Court the Government has now fully conceded that the petitioner's beliefs are based upon "religious training and belief." "There is no dispute that petitioner's professed beliefs were founded on basic tenets of the Muslim religion, as he understood them, and derived in substantial part from his devotion to Allah as the Supreme Being. Thus, under this Court's decision in *United States v. Seeger*, 380 U.S. 163, his claim unquestionably was within the 'religious training and belief' clause of the exemption provision." This concession by the government is clearly correct. For the record shows that the petitioner's beliefs are founded on tenets of the Muslim religion as he understands them. They are surely no less religiously based than those of the three registrants before this Court in *Seeger*.

The Government in this Court has also made clear that it no longer questions the sincerity of the petitioner's beliefs. This concession is also correct. The Department hearing officer—the only person at the administrative appeal level who carefully examined the petitioner and other witnesses in person and who had the benefit of the full FBI file—found "that the registrant is sincere in his objection." The Department of Justice was wrong in advising the Board in terms of a purported rule of law that it should disregard this finding simply because of the circumstances and timing of the petitioner's claim.

Since the Appeal Board gave no reasons for its denial of the petitioner's claim, there is absolutely no way of knowing upon which of the three grounds offered in the Department's letter it relied. Yet the Government now acknowledges that two of those grounds were not valid. And, the Government's concession aside, it is indisputably clear, for the reasons stated, that the Department was simply wrong as a matter of law in advising that the petitioner's beliefs were not religiously based and were not sincerely held.

This case, therefore, falls squarely within the four corners of this Court's decision in *Sicurella*. There, as here, the Court was asked to hold that an error in an advice letter prepared by the Department of Justice did not require reversal of a criminal conviction because there was a ground on which the Appeal Board might properly have denied a conscientious objector classification. This Court refused to consider the proffered alternative ground:

We feel that this error of law by the Department, to which the Appeal Board might naturally look for guidance on such questions, must vitiate the entire proceedings at least where it is not clear that the Board relied on some legitimate ground. Here, where it is impossible to determine on exactly which grounds the Appeal Board decided, the integrity of the Selective Service System demands, at least, that the Government not recommend illegal grounds. There is an impressive body of lower court cases taking this position and we believe that they state the correct rule." The doctrine thus articulated 16 years ago in *Sicurella* was hardly new. It was long ago established as essential to the administration of criminal justice. In *Stromberg*, the Court reversed a conviction for violation of a California statute containing three separate clauses, finding one of the three clauses constitutionally invalid. As Chief Justice Hughes put the matter, "It is impossible to say under which clause of the statute the conviction was obtained." Thus, "if any of the clauses in question is invalid under the Federal Constitution, the conviction cannot be upheld.

The long established rule of law embodied in these settled precedents thus clearly requires that the judgment before us be reversed. It is so ordered.

Will Congress Bring Back the Draft?[22]

Report of the Friends Committee on National Legislation

Relevant Edited Excerpts

Friends Committee on National Legislation maintains its longstanding opposition to military conscription and compulsory national service. We call upon Congress to redirect the tremendous human and material resources now devoted to war and preparing for war to addressing the root causes of violence, building cooperative, international institutions to peacefully prevent deadly conflicts, and to advancing human security in all its dimensions.

Further, it is time to end the economic draft that is now underway, which draws so many youths from our poorest communities into military service in search of educational and economic opportunities. Our country can and should do better at providing equal opportunities for all of our youth to fulfill their human potential without being forced into military service due to economic necessity.

Finally, we recognize the importance of service to our communities, and we encourage all to serve. But it must be voluntary and an expression of individual conscience —not compelled by the state. Compulsory national service would threaten our basic liberty and undermine the very principle of voluntary service to community.

Friends Committee on National Legislation advocates for an end to compulsory registration for Selective Service, for an end to all civil and criminal sanctions (such as denying federal education grants or drivers licenses to those who do not register for the draft), and for the repeal of the Selective Service Act.

For Your Consideration

The Selective Service System defines conscientious objector in narrow terms. A more inclusive definition would capture those who object to serving in particular wars rather than all wars. What does the Constitution require in relation to conscientious objection? If one opposes all war generally, but remains willing to serve in defense of American soil, but not overseas in defense of American "interests," in conflicts like the one in Iraq, is there an equal protection issue if government honors the former and rejects the latter?

Opposition to military conscription reached its height in this nation during the Vietnam War. There is no denying that the draft is politically unpopular. There has also been a general increase in Americans opposed to War. For example, according to a CBS News Poll, in early December 2006, 75% of Americans in one poll disapproved of the way President George W. Bush is handling the conflict in Iraq.

CBS News Poll Dec. 8–10, 2006.
N = 922adults nationwide. MoE±3 (for all adults). RV = registered voters.

"Do you approve or disapprove of the way George W.Bush is handling the situation with Iraq?

	Approve %	Disapprove %	Unsure %
ALL adults	21	75	4
Republicans	47	47	6
Democrats	5	95	0
Independents	17	77	6

A majority of citizens polled question whether we should have ever gone there to begin with, and 70% report that they have little confidence in his ability to make decision concerning our troops.[23]

On May 8, 2007, eleven Republican members of Congress pleaded with President Bush for seventy-five minutes, to change course in Iraq. Led by Reps. Mark Kirk (R-IL) and

Charlie Dent (R-PA), the meeting included Defense Secretary Robert Gates, Secretary of State Condoleezza Rice, Karl Rove, and Tony Snow. One congressman said that his "district is prepared for defeat." Begging for candor and honesty, he frankly admitted: "The word about the war and its progress cannot come from the White House or even you, Mr. President. There is no longer any credibility. It has to come from Gen. Petraeus."[24]

U.S. Armed Forces have now adopted a military policy called Stop Loss, which prevents soldiers from leaving military service after their contract has expired.[25] Often referred to as a back-door draft, the policy is an involuntary extension of military service under which members are effectively and legally reassigned.

Does reassignment under stop-loss violate a soldier's rights to due process of law?

Question: What is the similarity between the policy that bans partial birth abortion and the military's stop loss policy?

In April 2007, the U.S. Supreme Court in *Gonzales v. Carhart*, upheld the Partial-Birth Abortion Ban Act of 2003; ruling that it did not impose an undue burden on the due process right of women to obtain an abortion.

Congressional findings at the time of passage included the following:

> A moral, medical, and ethical consensus exists that the practice of performing a partial-birth abortion—an abortion in which a physician deliberately and intentionally vaginally delivers a living, unborn child's body until either the entire baby's head is outside the body of the mother, or any part of the baby's trunk past the navel is outside the body of the mother and only the head remains inside the womb, for the purpose of performing an overt act (usually the puncturing of the back of the child's skull and removing the baby's brains) that the person knows will kill the partially delivered infant, performs this act, and then completes delivery of the dead infant—is a gruesome and inhumane procedure that is never medically necessary and should be prohibited.

Opponents of the ban argue that the law allows abortion up to the 24th week of pregnancy. Relevant statutes must consider risks to the health of the mother (determined by the attending physician) as a matter of constitutional right, and this bill does not. Thus, the question is whether the finding that it is "never medically necessary"contrary to women's lived experiences?

Throughout history women have faced the recurring situation of unwanted pregnancy. Of roughly 6 million pregnancies in the U.S. each year, fully half are unintended. Most women in that circumstance choose to have another child; some can't. Of the 3 million unintended, one third will end in termination. One half experienced a contraceptive failure and cannot care for or support a child. Another percentage abort to prevent the birth of a child with birth defects or severe medical problems. Approximately 13,000 pregnancies occur because of rape or incest. Another percentage seek to avoid physical or mental conditions that endanger the health of the woman. The remaining feel certain that they are not fit for the job of parenting. 58% of all abortions are performed in the first 8 weeks; 88% are performed before 13 weeks. Less than 6% of all abortions are done after 16 weeks of pregnancy—almost 50% of abortions after 15 weeks have been delayed by difficulty with affording, finding, or traveling to a specialist. In the eight-year period between 1977 and 2005, women endured 103,757 actual instances of violence and disruption of service at clinics, and triple the number of threats, both personal and political.[26] In all of the sorting, the state, unsurprisingly, has asserted an interest.

Abortion on Demand & Emergency Contraception

Roe v. Wade

410 U.S. 113
January 22, 1973

Facts:

A pregnant single woman (Roe) brought a class action challenging the constitutionality of the Texas criminal abortion laws, which proscribe procuring or attempting an abortion except on medical advice for the purpose of saving the mother's life. A licensed physician (Hallford), who had two State abortion prosecutions pending against him, was permitted to intervene. A childless married couple (the Does), the wife not being pregnant, separately attacked the laws, basing alleged injury on the future possibilities of contraceptive failure, pregnancy, unpreparedness for parenthood, and impairment of the wife's health. A three-judge District Court, which consolidated the actions, held that Roe and Hallford, and members of their classes, had standing to sue and presented justiciable controversies. Ruling that declaratory, though not injunctive, relief was warranted, the court declared the abortion statutes void as vague and overbroadly infringing those plaintiffs' Ninth and Fourteenth Amendment rights. The court ruled the Does' complaint not justiciable.

Texas Law:

> "If any person shall designedly administer to a pregnant woman or knowingly procure to be administered with her consent any drug or medicine, or shall use towards her any violence or means whatever externally or internally applied, and thereby procure an abortion, he shall be confined in the penitentiary not less than two nor more than five years; if it be done without her consent, the punishment shall be doubled. By 'abortion' is meant that the life of the fetus or embryo shall be destroyed in the woman's womb or that a premature birth thereof be caused.

Held:

State criminal abortion laws, like those involved here, that except from criminality only a life-saving procedure on the mother's behalf without regard to the stage of her pregnancy and other interests involved violate the Due Process Clause of the Fourteenth Amendment, which protects against state action the right to privacy, including a woman's qualified right to terminate her pregnancy. Though the State cannot override that right, it has legitimate interests in protecting both the pregnant woman's health and the potentiality of human life, each of which interests grows and reaches a "compelling" point at various stages of the woman's approach to term.

Blackmun, J., delivered the opinion of the Court

We forthwith acknowledge our awareness of the sensitive and emotional nature of the abortion controversy, of the vigorous opposing views, even among physicians, and of the deep and seemingly absolute convictions that the subject inspires. One's philosophy, one's experiences, one's exposure to the raw edges of human existence, one's religious training, one's attitudes toward life and family and their values, and the moral standards one establishes and seeks to observe, are all likely to influence and to color one's thinking and conclusions about abortion.

In addition, population growth, pollution, poverty, and racial overtones tend to complicate and not to simplify the problem. Our task, of course, is to resolve the issue by constitutional measurement, free of emotion and of predilection. We seek earnestly to do this, and, because we do, we have inquired into, and in this opinion place some emphasis upon, medical and medical-legal history and what that history reveals about man's attitudes toward the abortion procedure over the centuries. We bear in mind, too, Mr. Justice Holmes' admonition in his *Lochner* dissent: [The Constitution] is made for people of fundamentally differing views, and the accident of our finding certain opinions natural and familiar or novel and even shocking ought not to conclude our judgment upon the question whether statutes embodying them conflict with the Constitution of the United States."

Roe alleged that she was unmarried and pregnant; that she wished to terminate her pregnancy by an abortion "performed by a competent, licensed physician, under safe, clinical conditions"; that she was unable to get a "legal" abortion in Texas because her life did not appear to be threatened by the continuation of her pregnancy; and that she could not afford to travel to another jurisdiction in order to secure a legal abortion under safe conditions. She claimed that the Texas statutes were unconstitutionally vague and that they abridged her right of personal privacy, protected by the First, Fourth, Fifth, Ninth, and Fourteenth Amendments. By an amendment to her complaint Roe purported to sue "on behalf of herself and all other women" similarly situated.

James Hubert Hallford, a licensed physician, described conditions of patients who came to him seeking abortions, and he claimed that for many cases he, as a physician, was unable to determine whether they fell within or outside the exception. As a consequence, the statutes were vague and uncertain, in violation of the Fourteenth Amendment, and that they violated his own and his patients' rights to privacy in the doctor-patient relationship and his own right to practice medicine, rights he claimed were guaranteed by the First, Fourth, Fifth, Ninth, and Fourteenth Amendments.

On the merits, the District Court held that the "fundamental right of single women and married persons to choose whether to have children is protected by the Ninth Amendment, through the Fourteenth Amendment," and that the Texas criminal abortion statutes were void on their face because they were both unconstitutionally vague and constituted an overbroad infringement of the plaintiffs' Ninth Amendment rights. The principal thrust of appellant's attack on the Texas statutes is that they improperly invade a right, said to be possessed by the pregnant woman, to choose to terminate her pregnancy. Appellant would discover this right in the concept of personal "liberty" embodied in the Fourteenth Amendment's Due Process Clause; or in personal, marital, familial, and sexual privacy said to be protected by the Bill of Rights or its penumbras.

(a) For the stage prior to approximately the end of the first trimester, the abortion decision and its effectuation must be left to the medical judgment of the pregnant woman's attending physician.

b) For the stage subsequent to approximately the end of the first trimester, the State, in promoting its interest in the health of the mother, may, if it chooses, regulate the abortion procedure in ways that are reasonably related to maternal health.

(c) For the stage subsequent to viability the State, in promoting its interest in the potentiality of human life, may, if it chooses, regulate, and even proscribe, abortion except where necessary, in appropriate medical judgment, for the preservation of the life or health of the mother.

Morning-After Pill Study Contradicts Claim by Foes: Easy Access Did Not Lead to Riskier Behavior[27]

By Marc Kaufman

Providing women with easy access to the emergency contraceptive Plan B did not lead them to engage in more risky sexual behavior, a study of more than 2,000 California women has concluded. The study did find that women given a supply to keep at home were more than 1 1/2 times as likely to use the drug after unprotected sex as those who had to pick it up at a clinic or pharmacy. The findings led the study authors to conclude that easy access to Plan B, also called the morning-after pill, could reduce the number of unwanted pregnancies while posing no apparent risk to women. The study contradicts a key claim made by opponents of easier access to Plan B at a time when the Food and Drug Administration is preparing to decide on a second application to allow nonprescription sales of the drug.

The FDA turned down the initial application last May, saying there was not enough information on how easy access would affect the sexual behavior of young teenagers. "Our findings were that women don't change their sexual behavior when the drug is easily available, but rather that they're more likely to use it if access is easier," said lead author Tina R. Raine of the Center for Reproductive Health Research and Policy at the University of California at San Francisco.

The study looked at the experiences of 2,117 San Francisco-area women ages 15 to 24 who were randomly put into one of three groups—one was given the drug to take home, the second could pick it up without a prescription at a clinic, and the third could get it without a prescription at a pharmacy. The study found that about the same percentage of each group had unprotected sex over a six-month period, that incidence of sexually transmitted disease was equal, and that about the same percentage became pregnant. Nonetheless, about 37 percent of women in the group given Plan B to take home used it at least once during the six months, compared with 21 percent in the clinic-access group and 24 percent in the pharmacy-access group.

Plan B consists of the synthetic progestin levonorgestrel and is most effective when used within 24 hours of an unprotected sexual encounter. While the FDA has approved it only for prescription use, six states have passed laws that allow pharmacists to dispense the drug without a prescription after a discussion with the woman.

The California study was conducted to answer critics. If it could be established at the outset that approval of the drug might cause teens to take greater risks, is that considered a compelling reason to withhold the drug? Would the advocates of abstinence and other safety measures have additional opportunities to stem the tide of promiscuity? Simply banning the drug would mean that a large group of women who are not teens would also be denied access to the contraception. Is there an equal protection argument to be made on their behalf or on behalf of everyone capable of becoming pregnant? According to Catherine MacKinnon:

> After childbirth, women tend to be the ones who are primarily responsible for the intimate care of offspring—their own and those of others. Social custom, pressure, exclusion from well-paying jobs, the structure of the marketplace, and lack of adequate daycare have exploited women's commitment to and caring for children and relegated women to this pursuit which is not even considered an occupation but an expression of the X chromosome.[28]
>
> It is women who are caught, to varying degrees, between the reproductive consequences of sexual use and aggression on the one side and the economic and other consequences of the sex role allocations of labor in the market and family on the other. As a result of these conditions, women are prevented from having children they do want and forced to have children they do not want and cannot want because they are not in a position responsibly to care for them because they are women.[29]

The following ***Hypothetical Bill*** provides a unique opportunity to examine the constitutional issues at stake.

> NEWS RELEASE
>
> SENATOR BARNES FROM TEXAS
>
> INTRODUCES A NEW BILL, WHICH IS EXPECTED TO PASS QUICKLY THROUGH BOTH HOUSES OF CONGRESS:
>
> Preamble
>
> Our laws afford constitutional protection to personal decisions related to marriage, procreation, contraception, family and child rearing because these matters involve the most intimate and personal choices a person may make in a lifetime, choices so central to personal dignity and autonomy that they ARE the liberty protected by the Fourteenth Amendment.
>
> At the heart of liberty is the right to define one's own concept of existence, the meaning of the universe, and the mystery of human life. Beliefs about these matters could not define the attributes of personhood were they formed under compulsion of the State or Federal Government.
>
> The sensitive and emotional nature of the abortion controversy: vigorous opposing views and the deep and absolute convictions that the subject inspires on both sides, leads this Congress to acknowledge that regardless of individual philosophy, religion, attitude toward family, or imperatives of profound moral obligation, the constitutional issues related to abortion rest upon recognition of the need to balance the liberty interest of the individual woman, with the states interest in the general welfare.
>
> We deem the following proposal adequate to address the concerns of those who believe that the trimester framework established in *Roe v. Wade,* and later modified toward the undue burden standard of *Planned Parenthood v. Casey,* inadequately resolves our current dilemma.
>
> Treating the fetus as body part is inadequate as a matter of law; the fetus is more like a parasite than a body part.[30] The fetus does not exist to serve the woman, their physical relation is expected to end and always does. Women have constitutional rights of personhood that must be acknowledged and respected at all times. There is no unitary interest between the fetus and pregnant woman once the

woman decides to terminate the pregnancy, thus there is no logical basis for treating the woman as the decisionmaker for the unit.

Bill

Federal funding will become available beginning November 10, 2008, in order to effectuate the following programs for women wishing to terminate an unwanted pregnancy during weeks 5–36.

During the first four weeks, in which it is difficult to establish if conception has occurred, and when Plan B Contraceptive (aka the "morning after" pill) which is designed to prevent pregnancy is widely available, the government has no legitimate interest in matters agreed upon between a woman and her physician.

During weeks 5–12 of a pregnancy, where conception has occurred and a woman wishes to terminate the pregnancy, she shall be admitted to a special medical facility for the purpose of removing the embryo, and placing it into the body of a surrogate mother who desires pregnancy and child birth, and selected according to the standards set forth by the National Adoption, Fertility and Transplant Board.

During weeks 13–36 of a pregnancy, where conception has occurred and a woman wishes to terminate the pregnancy, she shall be admitted to a special medical facility for the purpose of removing the fetus, and placing it into a special life sustaining incubator (used for what are commonly referred to as test tube babies), at which time it will become a ward of the state, until such time as the child may survive without special incubation and suitable adoptive parents are selected according to the standards set forth by the National Adoption, Fertility and Transplant Board.

For Your Consideration

A legislative aide has forwarded the bill to your firm for identification of the social and constitutional issues that may arise.

Is the bill likely to survive constitutional scrutiny?

Reasoning from the Body: A Historical Perspective on Abortion Regulation and Questions of Equal Protection[31]

Reva Siegal

Relevant Edited Excerpts

Reprinted with permission

The State's Regulatory Interest in Abortion procedures

Medical paradigms govern *Roe's* analysis of the state's interest in regulating [a woman's decision to terminate a pregnancy]. *Roe* relies so heavily upon medical science that medical analysis displaces social analysis of whether restricting women's access to abortion is a legitimate exercise of state power.

The pregnant woman cannot be isolated in her privacy. She carries an embryo and, later, a fetus, if one accepts the medical definitions of the developing young in the human uterus. The situation therefore is inherently different from [all other privacy precedents].

When the Court considers the pregnant woman from a physiological standpoint, it assumes that the existence of the embryo/ fetus is sufficient to explain and justify the state's interest in regulating abortion.

The court does not address the possibility that public interest in restricting abortion might be shaped by social judgments about the pregnant woman herself. As in its equal protection jurisprudence, the Court reasons from the premise that the physical reality of pregnancy can objectively substantiate public regulatory judgments concerning the pregnant woman.

Roe holds that the state has an interest in potential life which becomes compelling at the point of viability. It defines this regulatory interest, without reference to the sorts of constitutional considerations that normally attend the use of state power against a citizen. In the Court's reasoning, facts concerning the physiological development of the unborn provide "logical and biological justifications" both limiting and legitimating state action directed against the pregnant woman. *Roe* analyzes the state's interest in potential life as a benign exercise of state power for the protection of the unborn, rather than a coercive exercise of state power against pregnant women, as if the state's interest in protecting potential life scarcely pertained to the pregnant woman herself.

To the extent that *Roe* relied upon physiological reasoning to define the state's interest in potential life, it unleashed a legal discourse of indeterminate content and scope—one legitimating boundless regulation of women's reproductive lives should the Court abandon the trimester framework that presently constrains it. In recognizing the state's interest in potential life, the Court ignored a simple social fact that should be of critical constitutional significance: When a state invokes an interest in potential life to justify fetal-protective regulation, the proposed use of public power concerns not merely the unborn, but women as well.

If one accepts the medical definitions of the developing young in the human uterus" as a sufficient, objective, and authoritative framework for evaluating the state's regulatory interest in abortion—as *Roe* did—state action compelling women to perform the work of motherhood can be justified without ever acknowledging that the state is enforcing a gender status role.

In part, this is because analyzing abortion restrictions within physiological paradigms obscures its social logic, but also, and as importantly, it is because physiological reasons for regulating women's conduct are already laden with socio-political import.

For Your Consideration

Death with dignity for the terminally ill, capital punishment, military drafts, and abortion regulations all highlight the tension surrounding the exercise of State authority that limits individual autonomy, violates equal protection, or unduly limits freedom of conscious choice.

If the founding principles were designed to guard life, liberty, and the pursuit of happiness, then why do the most salient matters of life and death elevate decision-making authority of the state over that of the individual?

Part Two

Unitary Families, Alternative Families & the Limits of Personal Liberty

The harms of discrimination include not only the easily identified disadvantages of the victims (such as exclusion from housing and jobs) and the stigma imposed by the dominant culture but also the advantages given to those who are not its victims. The white, male, heterosexual societal norm is privileged in such a way that its privilege is rendered invisible.[1]

Trina Grillo and Stephanie Wildman

Chapter Five

Construing Sovereign Rights of Unitary Families

Doctrines related to familial privacy are useful for examining state power to govern for the general welfare in light of the guarantees of liberty found in the Fourteenth Amendment. Woodhull would describe that power in terms of it origins: "[I]t must be remembered that it is the sphere of government to perform the duties which are required of it by the people, and that it has, in itself, no rights to exercise. These belong exclusively to the people whom it represents."[2]

We are at a significant crossroad in the development of legal and cultural boundaries in relation to privacy. Ordered liberty flourishes under rules that require states to justify intrusion into matters related to education, marriage, and procreation. Controversy arises most often when law elevates the rights of unitary families over unwed parents and those living in non-traditional households. These issues are cutting edge insofar as their meaningful resolution requires a break with customs steeped in Judeo-Christian doctrines.

This chapter explores the foundations of the social order deemed indespensible to civil liberties. We study case law to demonstrate how key elements of the Court's philosophy ushered in rapidly evolving doctrines where the deep roots of history and tradition do not shield state laws that invade privacy and proscribe free choice.

The Realm of Personal Liberty

Meyer v. State of Nebraska[3]

June 4, 1923

Issue: Criminal conviction for violating Nebraska statute against teaching foreign languages to children in schools.

Facts: Nebraska, like other states passed a law whose object:

> Was to create an enlightened American citizenship in sympathy with the principles and ideals of this country, and to prevent children reared in America from being trained and educated in foreign languages and foreign ideals before they have had an opportunity to learn the English language and observe American ideals. It is a well-known fact that the language first learned by a child remains his mother tongue and the language of his heart. The purpose of the statute is to insure that the English language shall be the mother tongue and

> the language of the heart of the children reared in this country who will eventually become the citizens of this country.

Held:

The liberty guaranteed under the Fourteenth Amendment does not merely guarantee freedom from bodily restraint but also the right of the individual to contract, to engage in any of the common occupations of life, to acquire useful knowledge, to marry, establish a home and bring up children, to worship God according to the dictates of his own conscience, and generally to enjoy those privileges long recognized at common law as essential to the orderly pursuit of happiness by free men. The established doctrine is that liberty under the Fourteenth Amendment may not be interfered with, under the guise of protecting the public interest, by legislative action that is arbitrary or without reasonable relation to some purpose within the competency of the State to effect. Determination by the legislature of what constitutes proper exercise of police power is not final or conclusive but is subject to supervision by the courts.

State law forbidding, under penalty, the teaching in any private, denominational, parochial or public school, of any modern language, other than English, to any child who has not attained and successfully passed the eighth grade, invades the liberty guaranteed by the Fourteenth Amendment and exceeds the power of the State. Reversed.

Pierce v. Society of the Sisters[4]

Decided June 1, 1925

Appeals from the District Court of the United States for the District of Oregon.

Justice McREYNOLDS delivered the opinion.

> The Compulsory Education Act was adopted November 7, 1922:
>
> The challenged act, effective September 1, 1926, requires every parent, guardian, or other person having control or charge or custody of a child between 8 and 16 years to send him to a public school for the period of time a public school shall be held during the current year in the district where the child resides. Failure to do so was declared a misdemeanor.

The Society of Sisters is an Oregon corporation, organized in 1880, with power to care for orphans, educate and instruct the youth, establish and maintain academies or schools, and acquire necessary real and personal property. It has long devoted its property and effort to the secular and religious education and care of children, and has acquired the valuable good will of many parents and guardians. It conducts interdependent primary and high schools and junior colleges, and maintains orphanages for the custody and control of children between 8 and 16. In its primary schools many children between those ages are taught the subjects usually pursued in Oregon public schools during the first eight years, and include systematic religious instruction and moral training according to the tenets of the Roman Catholic Church. It owns valuable buildings, especially constructed and equipped for school purposes. The business is remunerative—the annual income from primary schools exceeds $30,000—and the successful conduct of this requires long time contracts with teachers and parents.

The Compulsory Education Act of 1922 has already caused the withdrawal from its schools of children who would otherwise continue, and their income has steadily declined.

Hill Military Academy is a private corporation organized in 1908 under the laws of Oregon, engaged in owning, operating, and conducting for profit an elementary, college preparatory, and military training school for boys between the ages of 5 and 21 years at an annual cost of $800 per student. The elementary department is divided into eight grades, as in the public schools; the college preparatory department has four grades, similar to those of the public high schools; the courses of study conform to the requirements of the state board of education. Military instruction and training are also given, under the supervision of an army officer. It owns considerable real and personal property, some useful only for school purposes. In order to conduct its affairs, long time contracts must be made for supplies, equipment, teachers, and pupils.

Appellants, law officers of the state and county, have publicly announced that the Act of November 7, 1922, is valid and have declared their intention to enforce it. By reason of the statute and threat of enforcement appellee's business is being destroyed and its property depreciated; parents and guardians are refusing to make contracts for the future instruction of their sons, and some are being withdrawn.

No question is raised concerning the power of the state reasonably to regulate all schools, to inspect, supervise and examine them, their teachers and pupils; to require that all children of proper age attend some school, that teachers shall be of good moral character and patriotic disposition, that certain studies plainly essential to good citizenship must be taught, and that nothing be taught which is manifestly inimical to the public welfare.

The inevitable practical result of enforcing the act under consideration would be destruction of appellees' primary schools, and perhaps all other private primary schools for normal children within the state of Oregon. Appellees are engaged in a kind of undertaking not inherently harmful, but long regarded as useful and meritorious. Certainly there is nothing in the present records to indicate that they have failed to discharge their obligations to patrons, students, or the state. And there are no peculiar circumstances or present emergencies which demand extraordinary measures relative to primary education.

Under the ruling in *Meyer v. Nebraska*, we think it entirely plain that the Act of 1922 unreasonably interferes with the liberty of parents and guardians to direct the upbringing and education of children under their control. As often heretofore pointed out, rights guaranteed by the Constitution may not be abridged by legislation which has no reasonable relation to some purpose within the competency of the state. The fundamental theory of liberty upon which all governments in this Union repose excludes any general power of the state to standardize its children by forcing them to accept instruction from public teachers only. The child is not the mere creature of the state; those who nurture him and direct his destiny have the right, coupled with the high duty, to recognize and prepare him for additional obligations.

The suits were not premature. The injury to appellees was present and very real, not a mere possibility in the remote future. If no relief had been possible prior to the effective date of the act, the injury would have become irreparable. Prevention of impending injury by unlawful action is a well-recognized function of courts of equity. The decrees below enjoining appellant from enforcing the law are affirmed.

Skinner v. State of Oklahoma[5]

June 1, 1942

Issue: Forced sterilization of a class of convicted felons, excluding those convicted of white-collar crimes.

Facts: Petitioner was convicted in 1926 of the crime of stealing chickens and was sentenced to the Oklahoma State Reformatory. In 1929 he was convicted of robbery with a firearm. In 1934 he was convicted again of robbery with firearms and was sentenced to the penitentiary. He was confined there in 1935 when the Act was passed.

Oklahoma's Habitual Criminal Sterilization Act.

> Defines an 'habitual criminal' as a person who, having been convicted two or more times for crimes 'amounting to felonies involving moral turpitude' either in an Oklahoma court or in a court of any other State, is thereafter convicted of such a felony in Oklahoma and is sentenced to a term of imprisonment in an Oklahoma penal institution.

Institution by the Attorney General of a proceeding against such a person in the Oklahoma courts for a judgment that such person shall be rendered sexually sterile, with notice and opportunity to be heard, and the right to a trial by jury.

The issues triable in such a proceeding are narrow and confined.

If the court or jury finds that the defendant is an 'habitual criminal' and that he 'may be rendered sexually sterile without detriment to his or her general health', then the court 'shall render judgment to the effect that said defendant be rendered sexually sterile, by the operation of vasectomy in case of a male, and of salpingectomy in case of a female.

In 1936 the Attorney General instituted proceedings against Jack Skinner. Petitioner in his answer challenged the Act as unconstitutional by reason of the Fourteenth Amendment. A jury trial was had. The court instructed the jury that the crimes of which petitioner had been convicted were felonies involving moral turpitude and that the only question for the jury was whether the operation of vasectomy could be performed on petitioner without detriment to his general health. The jury found that it could be. A judgment directing that the operation of vasectomy be performed on petitioner was affirmed by the Supreme Court of Oklahoma by a five to four decision.

Mr. Justice DOUGLAS delivered the opinion of the U.S. Supreme Court.

This case touches a sensitive and important area of human rights. Oklahoma deprives certain individuals of a right which is basic to the perpetuation of a race—the right to have offspring.

Oklahoma has decreed the enforcement of its law against petitioner, overruling his claim that it violated the Fourteenth Amendment. Because that decision raised grave and substantial constitutional questions, we granted the petition for certiorari. Several objections to the constitutionality of the Act have been pressed upon us.

It is urged that the Act cannot be sustained as an exercise of the police power in view of scientific authorities on the question of inheritability of criminal traits

It is argued that due process is lacking because the defendant is given no opportunity to be heard on the issue as to whether he is the probable potential parent of socially undesirable offspring.

It is also suggested that the Act is penal in character and that the sterilization provided for is cruel and unusual punishment and violative of the Fourteenth Amendment.

We pass those points without intimating an opinion on them, for there is a feature of the Act which clearly condemns it. That is its failure to meet the requirements of the Equal Protection Clause of the Fourteenth Amendment.

Only one other provision of the Act is material here and that is which provides that 'offenses arising out of the violation of the prohibitory laws, revenue acts, embezzlement, or political offenses, shall not come or be considered within the terms of this Act.'

We do not stop to point out all of the inequalities in this Act. A few examples will suffice. In Oklahoma grand larceny is a felony. Larceny is grand larceny when the property taken exceeds $20 in value. Embezzlement is punishable 'in the manner prescribed for feloniously stealing property of the value of that embezzled.' Hence he who embezzles property worth more than $20 is guilty of a felony. A clerk who appropriates over $20 from his employer's till and a stranger who steals the same amount are thus both guilty of felonies. If the latter repeats his act and is convicted three times, he may be sterilized. But the clerk is not subject to the pains and penalties of the Act no matter how large his embezzlements nor how frequent his convictions.

The instant legislation runs afoul of the Equal Protection Clause. We are dealing here with legislation which involves one of the basic civil rights of man. Marriage and procreation are fundamental to the very existence and survival of the race. The power to sterilize, if exercised, may have subtle, far reaching and devastating effects. In evil or reckless hands it can cause races or types which are inimical to the dominant group to wither and disappear. There is no redemption for the individual whom the law touches. Any experiment which the State conducts is to his irreparable injury. He is forever deprived of a basic liberty. We mention these matters not to re-examine the scope of the police power of the States. We advert to them merely in emphasis of our view that strict scrutiny of the classification which a State makes in a sterilization law is essential, lest unwittingly or otherwise invidious discriminations are made against groups or types of individuals in violation of the constitutional guaranty of just and equal laws. The guaranty of 'equal protection of the laws is a pledge of the protection of equal laws.'

When the law lays an unequal hand on those who have committed intrinsically the same quality of offense and sterilizes one and not the other, it has made as an invidious a discrimination as if it had selected a particular race or nationality for oppressive treatment.

We have not the slightest basis for inferring that the lines drawn by the state have any significance in eugenics, or that the inheritability of criminal traits follows the neat legal distinctions which the law has marked between those two offenses. In terms of fines and imprisonment the crimes of larceny and embezzlement rate the same under the Oklahoma code. Only when it comes to sterilization are the pains and penalties of the law different. The Equal Protection Clause would indeed be a formula of empty words if such conspicuously artificial lines could determine who might be sterilized.

Reversed.

Loving v. Commonwealth of Virginia[6]

June 12, 1967

Issue: Anti-miscegenation laws that only punished couples where one partner was white.

Facts: In June 1958, two residents of Virginia, Mildred Jeter, a Negro woman, and Richard Loving, a White man, were married in the District of Columbia. Shortly after their marriage, the Lovings returned to Virginia and established their marital abode in Caroline County. At the October Term, 1958, of the Circuit Court of Caroline County, a grand jury issued an indictment charging the Lovings with violating Virginia's ban on interracial marriages. On January 6, 1959, the Lovings pleaded guilty to the charge and were sentenced to one year in jail; however, the trial judge suspended the sentence for a period of 25 years on the condition that the Lovings leave the State and not return to Virginia together for 25 years. He stated in an opinion that:

Almighty God created the races white, black, yellow, malay and red, and he placed them on separate continents. And but for the interference with his arrangement there would be no cause for such marriages. The fact that he separated the races shows that he did not intend for the races to mix.

After their conviction, the Lovings took up residence in the District of Columbia. On November 6, 1963, they filed a motion in the state trial court to vacate the judgment and set aside the sentence on the ground that the statutes which they had violated were repugnant to the Fourteenth Amendment.

Proceeding on motion to vacate criminal sentences for violating state ban on interracial marriages, the Circuit Court denied their motion. The Court of Appeals affirmed their convictions, under an earlier state decision, *Naim v. Naim* (1955) which concluded that the State has a legitimate purpose in "preserve[ing] the racial integrity of its citizens, prevent[ing] the corruption of blood, a mongrel breed of citizens, and the obliteration of racial pride."

Mr. Chief Justice WARREN delivered the opinion of the Court.

This case presents a constitutional question never addressed by this Court:

Whether a statutory scheme adopted by the State of Virginia to prevent marriages between Whites and other persons violates the Equal Protection and Due Process Clauses of the Fourteenth Amendment?

The two statutes under which appellants were convicted and sentenced are part of a comprehensive statutory scheme aimed at prohibiting and punishing interracial marriages. The Lovings were convicted of violating § 20—58 of the Virginia Code: Leaving The State to Evade The Law.

If any White person and colored person shall go out of this State, for the purpose of being married, and with the intention of returning, and be married out of it, and afterwards return to and reside in it, cohabiting as man and wife, they shall be punished as provided in §20—59, and the marriage shall be governed by the same law as if it had been solemnized in this State. The fact of their cohabitation here as man and wife shall be evidence of their marriage.

Section 20—59, Punishment for marriage, defines the penalty for miscegenation:

> If any White person intermarry with a colored person, or any colored person intermarry with a White person, he shall be guilty of a felony and shall be punished by confinement in the penitentiary for not less than one nor more than five years.

Other central provisions in the statutory scheme automatically voids all marriages between a White person and a colored person without any judicial proceeding.

Sections 20–54 & 1–14 respectively define White persons and colored persons and Indians for purposes of the statutory prohibitions.

Section 20—57 of the Virginia Code provides:

> Marriages void without decree. All marriages between a White person and a colored person shall be absolutely void without any decree of divorce or other legal process.

Section 20—54 of the Virginia Code, Intermarriage prohibited, provides:

> It shall hereafter be unlawful for any White person in this State to marry any save a White person, or a person with no other admixture of blood than White and American Indian.
>
> For the purpose of this chapter, the term "White person" shall apply only to such person as has no trace whatever of any blood other than Caucasian; but persons who have one-sixteenth or less of the blood of the American Indian and have no other non-Caucasian blood shall be deemed to be White persons. All laws heretofore passed and now in effect regarding the intermarriage of White and colored persons shall apply to marriages prohibited by this chapter.

The exception for persons with less than one-sixteenth of the blood of the American Indian is apparently accounted for, in the words of a tract issued by the Registrar of the State Bureau of Vital Statistics, by 'the desire of all to recognize as an integral and honored part of the White race the descendants of John Rolfe and Pocahontas.

Section 1—14 of the Virginia Code provides:

Colored persons and Indians defined.

> Every person in whom there is ascertainable any Negro blood shall be deemed and taken to be a colored person, and every person not a colored person having one fourth or more of American Indian blood shall be deemed an American Indian; except that members of Indian tribes existing in this Commonwealth having one fourth or more of Indian blood and less than one sixteenth of Negro blood shall be deemed tribal Indians.

The Lovings have never disputed in the course of this litigation that Mrs. Loving is a 'colored person' or that Mr. Loving is a 'White person' within the meanings given those terms by the Virginia statutes.

Section 1 of the Fourteenth Amendment of United States Constitution provides:

> All persons born or naturalized in the United States and subject to the jurisdiction thereof, are citizens of the United States and of the State wherein they reside. No State shall make or enforce any law which shall abridge the privileges or immunities of citizens of the United States; nor shall any State deprive any person of life, liberty, or property, without due process of law; nor deny to any person within its jurisdiction the equal protection of the laws.

Virginia is now one of 16 States which prohibit and punish marriages on the basis of racial classifications. Penalties for miscegenation arose as an incident to slavery and have been common in Virginia since the colonial period. The present statutory scheme dates from the adoption of the Racial Integrity Act of 1924, passed during the period of extreme nativism which followed the end of the First World War. The central features of this Act, and current Virginia law, are the absolute prohibition of a White person marrying other than another White person, a prohibition against issuing marriage licenses until the issuing official is satisfied that the applicants' statements as to their race are correct, certificates of racial composition to be kept by both local and state registrars, and the carrying forward of earlier prohibitions against racial intermarriage.

After the initiation of this litigation, Maryland repealed its prohibitions against interracial marriage, leaving Virginia Alabama, Arkansas, Delaware, Florida, Georgia, Kentucky, Louisiana, Mississippi, Missouri, North Carolina, Oklahoma, South Carolina, and Tennessee with their laws in place. Over the past 15 years, 14 States have repealed laws outlawing interracial marriages: Arizona, California, Colorado, Idaho, Indiana, Maryland, Montana, Nebraska, Nevada, North Dakota, Oregon, South Dakota, Utah, and Wyoming. The first state court to recognize that miscegenation statutes violate the Equal Protection Clause was the Supreme Court of California in *Perez v.Sharp*, (1948).

Since marriage has traditionally been subject to state regulation without federal intervention, its regulation should be left to exclusive state control under the Tenth Amendment. While the state court is no doubt correct in asserting that marriage is a social relation subject to the State's police power, *Maynard v. Hill* (1888), the State does not contend in its argument before this Court that its powers to regulate marriage are unlimited notwithstanding the commands of the Fourteenth Amendment. Nor could it do so in light of *Meyer*, and *Skinner*.

Instead, the State argues that the meaning of the Equal Protection Clause, as illuminated by the statements of the Framers, is only that state penal laws containing an interracial element as part of the definition of the offense must apply equally to Whites and Negroes in the sense that members of each race are punished to the same degree. Thus, because its statutes punish equally both the White and the Negro participants in an interracial marriage, these statutes, despite their reliance on racial classifications do not constitute an invidious discrimination based upon race.

The second argument advanced by the State assumes the validity of its equal application theory. The argument is that, if the Equal Protection Clause does not outlaw miscegenation statutes because of their reliance on racial classifications, the question of constitutionality would thus become whether there was any rational basis for a State to treat interracial marriages differently from other marriages.

On this question, the State argues, the scientific evidence is substantially in doubt and, consequently, this Court should defer to the wisdom of the state legislature in adopting its policy of discouraging interracial marriages. Because we reject the notion that the mere equal application of a statute containing racial classifications is enough to remove the classifications from the Fourteenth Amendment's proscription of all invidious racial discriminations, we do not accept the State's contention that these statutes should be upheld if there is any possible basis for concluding that they serve a rational purpose. The mere fact of equal application does not mean that our analysis of these statutes should follow the approach we have taken in cases involving no racial discrimination.

In cases involving distinctions not drawn according to race, the Court has merely asked whether there is any rational foundation for the discriminations, and has deferred to the wisdom of the state legislatures. In the case at bar, however, we deal with statutes containing racial classifications, and the fact of equal application does not immunize the statute from the very heavy burden of justification which the Fourteenth Amendment has traditionally required of state statutes drawn according to race.

The most avid proponents of the post-War Amendments undoubtedly intended them to remove all legal distinctions among all persons born or naturalized in the United States. Their opponents, just as certainly, were antagonistic to both the letter and the spirit of the Amendments and wished them to have the most limited effect.

In one case this Court upheld a conviction under an Alabama statute forbidding adultery or fornication between a White person and a Negro which imposed a greater penalty than that of a statute proscribing similar conduct by members of the same race. The Court reasoned that the statute could not be said to discriminate against Negroes because the punishment for each participant in the offense was the same. However, as recently as the 1964 Term, in rejecting the reasoning of that case, we stated 'Pace represents a limited view of the Equal Protection Clause which has not withstood analysis in the subsequent decisions of this Court.

Equal Protection requires the consideration of whether the classifications drawn by any statute constitute an arbitrary and invidious discrimination. The clear and central purpose of the Fourteenth Amendment was to eliminate all official state sources of invidious racial discrimination in the States. There is patently no legitimate overriding purpose independent of invidious racial discrimination which justifies this classification. The fact that Virginia prohibits only interracial marriages involving White persons demonstrates that [it is a] measure designed to maintain White Supremacy. There can be no doubt that restricting the freedom to marry solely because of racial classifications violates the central meaning of the Equal Protection Clause.

These statutes also deprive the Lovings of liberty without due process of law in violation of the Due Process Clause of the Fourteenth Amendment. The freedom to marry has long been recognized as one of the vital personal rights, essential to the orderly pursuit of happiness by free men. Marriage is one of the 'basic civil rights of man,' fundamental to our very existence and survival.

To deny this fundamental freedom on so unsupportable a basis as the racial classifications embodied in these statutes, classifications so directly subversive of the principle of equality at the heart of the Fourteenth Amendment, is surely to deprive all the State's citizens of liberty without due process of law. The Fourteenth Amendment requires that the freedom of choice to marry not be restricted by invidious racial discriminations.

Under our Constitution, the freedom to marry or not marry, a person of another race resides with the individual and cannot be infringed by the State. These convictions must be reversed. It is so ordered.

Zablocki v. Redhail[7]

Decided Jan. 18, 1978

Issue: State law that conditions eligibility for marriage on status of child support payments.

> Facts: Appellee Redhail is a Wisconsin resident who is unable to enter into a lawful marriage in Wisconsin or elsewhere so long as he maintains his Wisconsin residency. The facts, according to the stipulation filed by the parties in the District Court, are as follows. In January 1972, when appellee was a minor and a high school student, a paternity action was instituted against him in Milwaukee County Court, alleging that he was the father of a baby girl born out of wedlock on July 5, 1971.
>
> After he appeared and admitted that he was the child's father, the court entered an order on May 12, 1972, adjudging appellee the father and ordering him to pay $109 per month as support for the child until she reached 18 years of age. From May 1972 until August 1974, appellee was unemployed and indigent, and consequently was unable to make any support payments. On September 27, 1974, appellee filed an application for a marriage license with appellant Zablocki, the County Clerk of Milwaukee County, and a few days later the application was denied on the sole ground that appellee had not obtained a court order granting him permission to marry, as required by law. Although appellee did not petition a state court thereafter, he would not have been able to satisfy either of the statutory prerequisites for an order granting permission to marry based upon the following stipulated facts.
>
> First, he had not satisfied his support obligations to his illegitimate child, and as of December 1974 there was an arrearage in excess of $3,700.
>
> Second, the child had been a public charge since her birth, receiving benefits under the Aid to Families with Dependent Children program. It is stipulated that the child's benefit payments were such that she would have been a public charge even if appellee had been current in his support payments.
>
> Class action was brought challenging the Wisconsin statute, which provides that:
>
> Any resident having minor issue not in his custody that he is under obligation to support by any court order or judgment may not marry without court approval.
>
> The statute is challenged as violative of the equal protection and Due Process Clauses. Appellants seek declaratory and injunctive relief.
>
> Mr. Justice MARSHALL delivered the opinion of the Court.

At issue in this case is the constitutionality of a Wisconsin statute which specifies that court permission cannot be granted unless the marriage applicant submits proof of compliance with their support obligation and, in addition, demonstrates that the children covered by the support order "are not then and are not likely thereafter to become public charges."

> No marriage license may lawfully be issued in Wisconsin to a person covered by the statute, except upon court order; any marriage entered into without compliance is declared void; and persons acquiring marriage licenses in violation of the law are subject to criminal penalties.

After being denied a marriage license because of his failure to comply with the statute, Redhail brought a class action suit, under 42 U.S.C. §1983, challenging the statute as violative of the Equal Protection and Due Process Clauses of the Fourteenth Amendment, seeking declaratory and injunctive relief. On the merits, the three-judge panel analyzed the Equal Protection claim and concluded that "strict scrutiny" was required because the classification created by the statute infringed upon a fundamental right, in this case: the right to marry. The court then proceeded to evaluate the interests advanced by the State to justify the statute, finding that the classification was not necessary for the achievement of those interests. The court invalidated the statute and enjoined county clerks from enforcing it.

The leading decision of this Court on the right to marry is *Loving v. Virginia*. The Court's opinion could have rested solely on equal protection grounds b/c the statutes discriminated on the basis of race, but the laws also deprived the couple of due process, a fundamental freedom to marry. The Court's language on the latter point bears repeating:

> The freedom to marry has long been recognized as one of the vital personal rights essential to the orderly pursuit of happiness by free men. In *Maynard v. Hill*, the Court characterized marriage as "the most important relation in life," and as "the foundation of the family and of society, without which there would be neither civilization nor progress." In *Meyer*, the Court recognized that the right "to marry, establish a home and bring up children" is a central part of the liberty protected by the Due Process Clause

In *Griswold*, the Court observed:

> We deal with a right of privacy older than the Bill of Rights—older than our political parties, older than our school system. Marriage is a coming together for better or for worse, hopefully enduring, and intimate to the degree of being sacred. It is an association that promotes a way of life, not causes; a harmony in living, not political faiths; a bilateral loyalty, not commercial or social projects. Yet it is an association for as noble a purpose as any involved in our prior decisions.

It is not surprising that the decision to marry has been placed on the same level of importance as decisions relating to procreation, childbirth, child rearing, and family relationships. As the facts of this case illustrate, it would make little sense to recognize a right of privacy with respect to other matters of family life and not with respect to the decision to enter the relationship that is the foundation of the family in our society.

The judgment of the District Court is, accordingly, Affirmed.

Interests of Unwed Fathers & Couples

The Associated Press reported on March 8, 2006, that child support laws were being challenged on equal protection grounds:

> Contending that women have more options than they do in the event of an unintended pregnancy, men's rights activists are mounting a long shot legal campaign aimed at giving them the chance to opt out of financial responsibility for raising a child[8]

Michael H. et al. v. Gerald D.[9]

491 U.S. 110
June 15, 1989

Issue: An unwed father's right to establish paternity when the mother is married to and living with another man (not obviously sterile) at the time of conception.

Facts: In May 1981, Victoria D. was born to Carole D., who was [at the time] married to and resided with, her husband Gerald D. in California. Although Gerald was listed as father on the birth certificate and has always claimed Victoria as his daughter, blood tests showed a 98.07% probability that Michael H., with whom Carole had an affair, was Victoria's father. During Victoria's first three years, she and her mother resided at times with Michael, who held her out as his own, at times with another man named Scott, and at times with Gerald, with whom they have lived since June 1984. In November 1982, Michael filed an action in California Superior Court to establish his paternity and right to visitation. Victoria, through her court-appointed guardian ad litem, filed a cross-complaint asserting that she was entitled to maintain filial relationships with both Michael and Gerald. The court ultimately granted Carole's husband Gerald summary judgment on the ground that there were no triable issues of fact as to paternity.

> Section 2 Cal. Evid. Code @ 621, provides: A child born to a married woman living with her husband, who is neither impotent nor sterile, is presumed to be a child of the marriage.
>
> This presumption may be rebutted only by the husband or wife, and then only in limited circumstances.
>
> Michael filed a filiation action to establish his paternity and right to visitation. The guardian ad litem for Victoria (the child) filed a cross-complaint asserting that if she had more than one de facto father she was entitled to maintain her filial relationship with both. Carole and Gerald reconciled as husband and wife. Gerald intervened in the case, and the California Superior Court granted his motion for summary judgment against Michael and Victoria. The California Court of Appeal affirmed. The California Supreme Court denied discretionary review.
>
> PROCEDURAL POSTURE: Petitioners (Michael as biological father and Victoria his daughter) appealed from the order granting summary judgment in favor of respondent/husband.
>
> JUSTICE SCALIA announced the judgment of the Court:

The instant appeal presents the claim that the presumption of paternity under California law infringes upon the due process rights of a man who wishes to establish his paternity of a child born to the wife of another man, and that the presumption infringes upon the constitutional right of the child to maintain a relationship and visitation with her natural father.

The facts of this case are, we must hope, extraordinary. On May 9, 1976, in Las Vegas, Nevada, Carole D., an international model, and Gerald D., a top executive in a French oil company, were married. The couple established a home in Playa del Rey, California, in which they resided as husband and wife when one or the other was not out of the country on business. In the summer of 1978, Carole became involved in an adulterous affair with a neighbor, Michael H. In September

1980, she conceived a child, Victoria D., who was born on May 11, 1981. Gerald was listed as father on the birth certificate and has always held Victoria out to the world as his daughter. Soon after delivery of the child, however, Carole informed Michael that she believed he might be the father.

In the first three years of her life, Victoria remained always with Carole, but found herself within a variety of quasi-family units. In October 1981, Gerald moved to New York City to pursue his business interests, but Carole chose to remain in California. At the end of that month, Carole and Michael had blood tests of themselves and Victoria, which showed a 98.07% probability that Michael was Victoria's father. In January 1982, Carole visited Michael in St. Thomas, where his primary business interests were based. There, Michael held Victoria out as his child. In March, Carole left Michael and returned to California, where she took up residence with yet another man, Scott K. Later that spring, and again in the summer, Carole and Victoria spent time with Gerald in New York City, as well as on vacation in Europe. In the fall, they returned to Scott in California.

In November 1982, rebuffed in his attempts to visit Victoria, Michael filed a filiation action in California Superior Court to establish his paternity and right to visitation. In March 1983, the court appointed an attorney and guardian ad litem to represent Victoria's interests. Victoria then filed a cross-complaint asserting that if she had more than one psychological or de facto father, she was entitled to maintain her filial relationship, with all of the attendant rights, duties, and obligations, with both. In May 1983, Carole filed a motion for summary judgment. During this period, from March through July 1983, Carole was again living with Gerald in New York. In August, however, she returned to California, became involved once again with Michael, and instructed her attorneys to remove the summary judgment motion from the calendar.

For the ensuing eight months, when Michael was not in St. Thomas he lived with Carole and Victoria in Carole's apartment in Los Angeles and held Victoria out as his daughter. In April 1984, Carole and Michael signed a stipulation that Michael was Victoria's natural father. Carole left Michael the next month, and instructed her attorneys not to file the stipulation. In June 1984, Carole reconciled with Gerald and joined him in New York, where they now live with Victoria and two other children since born into the marriage.

In May 1984, Michael and Victoria, through her guardian ad litem, sought visitation for Michael. To assist in determining whether visitation would be in Victoria's best interests, the Superior Court appointed a psychologist to evaluate Victoria, Gerald, Michael, and Carole. The psychologist recommended that Carole retain sole custody, but that Michael be allowed continued contact with Victoria pursuant to a restricted visitation schedule. The court concurred and ordered limited visitation Michael.

On October 19, 1984, Gerald, who had intervened in the action, moved for summary judgment on the ground that under Cal. Evid. Code there were no triable issues of fact as to Victoria's paternity. This law provides that Victoria is conclusively presumed to be a child of the marriage." The presumption may be rebutted by blood tests, but only if a motion for such tests is made, within two years from the date of the child's birth, either by the husband, or wife—if the natural father has filed an affidavit acknowledging paternity. CEC 621(c) & (d).

On January 28, 1985, having found that affidavits submitted by Carole and Gerald sufficed to demonstrate that the two were cohabiting at conception and birth and that Gerald was neither sterile nor impotent, the Superior Court granted Gerald's motion for summary judgment, rejecting Michael's and Victoria's constitutional challenges. The court also denied motions for continued visitation pending the appeal, although Cal. Civ. Code 4601 provides that a court may, in its discretion, grant "reasonable visitation rights ... to any ... person having an interest in the welfare of the child." Denial was based upon the theory that allowing such visitation would "violate the intention of the Legislature by impugning the integrity of the family unit."

On appeal, Michael asserted, inter alia, that the Superior Court's application of CEC 621 violated both his procedural and substantive due process rights. Victoria also raised a due process challenge to the statute, seeking to preserve her de facto relationship with Michael as well as with Gerald. She also contended that since the statute allows the husband, and to a limited extent the mother but not the child to rebut the presumption of legitimacy, it violates the child's right to equal protection. Victoria also asserted a right to continued visitation with Michael.

The California Court denied permanent visitation rights relying upon an earlier California case, which had held that once an assertion of biological paternity is "determined to be legally impossible," visitation against the wishes of the mother should be denied.

We address first the claims of Michael. At the outset, it is necessary to clarify what he sought and what he was denied. California law, like nature itself, makes no provision for dual fatherhood. Michael was seeking to be declared the father of Victoria. The immediate benefit he evidently sought to obtain from that status was visitation rights. Under California law a parent has statutory right to visitation "unless it is shown that such visitation would be detrimental to the best interests of the child". Moreover, if Michael were successful in being declared the father, other rights would follow—most importantly, the right to be considered as the parent who should have custody. The sum of parental rights with respect to the rearing of a child, include the child's care; the right to the child's services and earnings; the right to direct the child's activities; the right to make decisions regarding the control, education, and health of the child; and the right, as well as the duty, to prepare the child for additional obligations, which include the teaching of moral standards, religious beliefs, and elements of good citizenship." All parental rights, including visitation, were automatically denied by denying Michael status as the father. While Cal. Civ. Code Ann. 4601 places it within the discretionary power of a court to award visitation rights to a non-parent, the Superior Court here, affirmed by the Court of Appeal, held that California law denies visitation, against the wishes of the mother, to a putative father who has been prevented from establishing his paternity.

Michael raises two related challenges to the constitutionality of CEC 621: First, he asserts that requirements of procedural due process prevent the State from terminating his liberty interest in his relationship with his child without affording him an opportunity to demonstrate his paternity in an evidentiary hearing.

We believe this claim derives from a fundamental misconception of the nature of the California statute. According to the California Court of Appeal:

The conclusive presumption is actually a substantive rule of law based upon a determination by the Legislature as a matter of overriding social policy, that given a certain relationship between the husband and wife, the husband is to be held responsible for the child, and that the integrity of the family unit should not be impugned. Of course the conclusive presumption not only expresses the State's substantive policy but also furthers it, excluding inquiries into the child's paternity that would be destructive of family integrity and privacy.

In those circumstances in which California allows a natural father to rebut the presumption of legitimacy of a child born to a married woman, e.g., where the husband is impotent or sterile, or where the husband and wife have not been cohabiting, it is more likely that the husband already knows the child is not his, and thus less likely that the paternity hearing will disrupt an otherwise harmonious and apparently exclusive marital relationship.

In this respect there is no difference between a rule which says that the marital husband shall be irrebuttably presumed to be the father, and a rule which says that the adulterous natural father shall not be recognized as the legal father. Both rules deny someone in Michael's situation a hearing on whether, in the particular circumstances of his case, California's policies would best be served by giving him parental rights. Thus, as many commentators have observed our "irrebuttable presumption" cases must ultimately be analyzed as calling into question not the adequacy of procedures but (like other classifications) the adequacy of the "fit" between the classification and the policy that the classification serves.

Michael contends as a matter of substantive due process that, because he has:

> Established a parental relationship with Victoria, protection of Gerald's and Carole's marital union is an insufficient state interest to support termination of that relationship.

This argument is, of course, predicated on the assertion that Michael has a constitutionally protected liberty interest in his relationship with Victoria.

In an attempt to limit and guide interpretation of the Due Process Clause, we have insisted not merely that the interest denominated as a "liberty" be "fundamental" (a concept that, in isolation, is hard to objectify), but also that it be an interest traditionally protected by our society. Our view of the rationale used to support other cases involving paternity, rest not upon such isolated factors but upon the historic respect—indeed, sanctity would not be too strong a term—traditionally accorded to the relationships that develop within the unitary family.

In *Stanley*, for example, we forbade the destruction of such a family when, upon the death of the mother, the State had sought to remove children from the custody of a father who had lived with and supported them and their mother for 18 years. As Justice Powell stated for the plurality in *Moore v. East Cleveland*: "Our decisions establish that the Constitution protects the sanctity of the family precisely because the institution of the family is deeply rooted in this Nation's history and tradition."

Justice Brennan asserts that only a "pinched conception of the family" would exclude Michael, Carole, and Victoria from protection. We disagree. The family unit accorded traditional respect in our society, which we have referred to as the "unitary family," is typified, of course, by the marital family, but also includes the household of unmarried parents and their children. Perhaps the concept can be expanded even beyond this, but it will bear no resemblance to traditionally respected relationships—and will thus cease to have any constitutional significance—if it is stretched so far as to include the relationship established between a married woman, her lover, and their child, during a 3-month sojourn in St. Thomas, or during a subsequent 8-month period when, if he happened to be in Los Angeles, he stayed with her and the child.

Thus, the legal issue in the present case reduces to whether the relationship between persons in the situation of Michael and Victoria has been treated as a protected family unit under the historic practices of our society, or whether on any other basis it has been accorded special protection. We think it impossible to find that it has. In fact, quite to the contrary, our traditions have protected the marital family (Gerald, Carole, and the child they acknowledge to be theirs) against the sort of claim Michael asserts.

We have never had occasion to decide whether a child has a liberty interest, symmetrical with that of her parent, in maintaining her filial relationship. We need not do so here because, even assuming that such a right exists, Victoria's claim must fail. Victoria's due process challenge is, if anything, weaker than Michael's. Her basic claim is not that California has erred in preventing her from establishing that Michael, not Gerald, should stand as her legal father. Rather, she claims a due process right to maintain filial relationships with both Michael and Gerald. This assertion merits little discussion, for, whatever the merits of the guardian ad litem's belief that such an arrangement can be of great psychological benefit to a child, the claim that a State must recognize multiple fatherhood has no support in the history or traditions of this country. Moreover, even if we were to construe Victoria's argument as forwarding the lesser proposition that, whatever her status vis-a-vis Gerald, she has a liberty interest in maintaining a filial relationship with her natural father, Michael, we find that, at best, her claim is the obverse of Michael's and fails for the same reasons.

Victoria claims in addition that her equal protection rights have been violated because, unlike her mother and presumed father, she had no opportunity to rebut the presumption of her legitimacy. We find this argument wholly without merit. We reject, at the outset, Victoria's suggestion that her equal protection challenge must be assessed under a standard of strict scrutiny because, in denying her the right to maintain a filial relationship with Michael, the State is discriminating against her on the basis of her illegitimacy. Illegitimacy is a legal construct, not a natural trait. Under California law, Victoria is not illegitimate, and she is treated in the same manner as all other legitimate children: she is entitled to maintain a filial relationship with her legal parents.

We apply, therefore, the ordinary "rational relationship" test to Victoria's equal protection challenge. The primary rationale underlying 621's limitation on those who may rebut the presumption of legitimacy is a concern that allowing persons other than the husband or wife to do so may undermine the integrity of the marital union. When the husband or wife contests the legitimacy of their child, the stability of the marriage has already been shaken. In contrast, allowing a claim of illegitimacy to be pressed by the child or, more accurately, by a court-appointed guardian ad litem, may well disrupt an otherwise peaceful union. Since it pursues a legitimate end by rational means, California's decision to treat Victoria differently from her parents is not a denial of equal protection.

The judgment of the California Court of Appeal is Affirmed.

JUSTICE BRENNAN, with whom JUSTICE MARSHALL and JUSTICE BLACKMUN join, dissenting.

Only one other member of the Court fully endorses Justice Scalia's view of the proper method of analyzing questions arising under the Due Process Clause.

Once we recognized that the "liberty" protected by the Due Process Clause of the Fourteenth Amendment encompasses more than freedom from bodily restraint, today's plurality opinion emphasizes, the concept was cut loose from one natural limitation on its meaning. This innovation paved the way, so the plurality hints, for judges to substitute their own preferences for those of elected officials. Dissatisfied with this supposedly unbridled and uncertain state of affairs, the plurality casts about for another limitation on the concept of liberty.

Even if we could agree, moreover, on the content and significance of particular traditions, we still would be forced to identify the point at which a tradition becomes firm enough to be relevant to our definition of liberty and the moment at which it becomes too obsolete to be relevant any longer.

The plurality supplies no objective means by which we might make these determinations. Indeed, as soon as the plurality sees signs that the tradition upon which it bases its decision (the laws denying putative fathers like Michael standing to assert paternity) is crumbling, it shifts ground and says that the case has nothing to do with that tradition, after all. "[W]hat is at issue here," the plurality asserts after canvassing the law on paternity suits, "is not entitlement to a state pronouncement that Victoria was begotten by Michael." But that is precisely what is at issue here, and the plurality's last-minute denial of this fact dramatically illustrates the subjectivity of its own analysis.

It is ironic that an approach so utterly dependent on tradition is so indifferent to our precedents. Citing barely a handful of this Court's numerous decisions defining the scope of the liberty protected by the Due Process Clause to support its reliance on tradition, the plurality acts as though English legal treatises and the American Law Reports always have provided the sole source for our constitutional principles. They have not.

Just as common-law notions no longer define the "property" that the Constitution protects, neither do they circumscribe the "liberty" that it guarantees. On the contrary, "'[l]iberty' and 'property' are broad and majestic terms. They are among the '[g]reat [constitutional] concepts ... purposely left to gather meaning from experience.... [T]hey relate to the whole domain of social and economic fact, and the statesmen who founded this Nation knew too well that only a stagnant society remains unchanged.

It is not that tradition has been irrelevant to our prior decisions. Throughout our decisionmaking in this important area runs the theme that certain interests and practices—freedom from physical restraint, marriage, childbearing, childrearing, and others—form the core of our definition of "liberty." Our solicitude for these interests is partly the result of the fact that the Due Process Clause would seem an empty promise if it did not protect them, and partly the result of the historical and traditional importance of these interests in our society. In deciding cases arising under the Due Process Clause, therefore, we have considered whether the concrete limitation under consideration impermissibly impinges upon one of these more generalized interests.

Today's plurality, however, does not ask whether parenthood is an interest that historically has received our attention and protection; the answer to that question is too clear for dispute. Instead, the plurality asks whether the specific variety of parenthood under consideration—a natural father's relationship with a child whose mother is married to another man—has enjoyed such protection.

If we had looked to tradition with such specificity in past cases, many a decision would have reached a different result. Surely the use of contraceptives by unmarried couples, *Eisenstadt*, or even by married couples, *Griswold*; the freedom from corporal punishment in schools, *Ingraham*; the freedom from an arbitrary transfer from a prison to a psychiatric institution, *Vitek*; and even the right to raise one's natural but illegitimate children, *Stanley*, were not "interest[s] traditionally protected by our society," at the time of their consideration by this Court. If we had asked, therefore, in *Eisenstadt*, *Griswold*, *Ingraham*, *Vitek*, or *Stanley* itself whether the specific interest under consideration had been traditionally protected, the answer would have been a resounding "no." That we did not ask this question in those cases highlights the novelty of the interpretive method that the plurality opinion employs today.

The plurality's interpretive method is more than novel; it is misguided.

The original reasons for the conclusive presumption of paternity are out of place in a world in which blood tests can prove virtually beyond a shadow of a doubt who sired a particular child and in which the fact of illegitimacy no longer plays the burdensome and stigmatizing role it once did. By construing the Fourteenth Amendment to offer shelter only to those interests specifically protected by historical practice, moreover, the plurality ignores the kind of society in which our Constitution exists. We are not an assimilative, homogeneous society, but a facilitative, pluralistic one, in which we must be willing to abide someone else's unfamiliar or even repellent practice because the same tolerant impulse protects our own idiosyncrasies. Even if we can agree, therefore, that "family" and "parenthood" are part of the good life, it is absurd to assume that we can agree on the content of those terms and destructive to pretend that we do. In a community such as ours, "liberty" must include the freedom not to conform. The plurality today squashes this freedom by requiring specific approval from history before protecting anything in the name of liberty.

The document that the plurality construes today is unfamiliar to me. It is not the living charter that I have taken to be our Constitution; it is instead a stagnant, archaic, hidebound document steeped in the prejudices and superstitions of a time long past. This Constitution does not recognize that times change, does not see that sometimes a practice or rule outlives its foundations. I cannot accept an interpretive method that does such violence to the charter that I am bound by oath to uphold.

To describe the issue in this case as whether the relationship existing between Michael and Victoria "has been treated as a protected family unit under the historic practices of our society, or whether on any other basis it has been accorded special protection," is to reinvent the wheel. The better approach—indeed, the one commanded by our prior cases and by common sense—is to ask whether the specific parent-child relationship under consideration is close enough to the interests that we already have protected to be deemed an aspect of "liberty" as well. On the facts before us, therefore, the question is not what "level of generality" should be used to describe the relationship between Michael and Victoria, but whether the relationship under consideration is sufficiently substantial to qualify as a liberty interest under our prior cases.

On four prior occasions, we have considered whether unwed fathers have a constitutionally protected interest in their relationships with their children. Though different in factual and legal circumstances, these cases have produced a unifying theme: although an unwed father's biological link to his child does not, in and of itself, guarantee him a constitutional stake in his relationship with that child, such a link combined with a substantial parent-child relationship will do so. "When an unwed father demonstrates a full commitment to the responsibilities of parenthood by 'com[ing] forward to participate in the rearing of his child,'... his interest in personal contact with his child acquires substantial protection under the Due Process Clause. At that point it may be said that he 'act[s] as a father toward his children."

This commitment is why Mr. Stanley and Mr. Caban won; why Mr. Quilloin and Mr. Lehr lost; and why Michael H. should prevail today. Michael H. is almost certainly Victoria's natural father, has lived with her as her father, has contributed to her support, and has from the beginning sought to strengthen and maintain his relationship with her.

According to its underlying reasoning, the Court rejected Michael H's claim because substantive due process does not require legislation protective of the rights of unwed fathers, if it would disturb the parental rights of a unitary family where a married couple has chosen to raise a child as the husband's offspring although paternity is uncertain. Anna Nicole Smith married Howard Stern in the Bahamas and placed his name on her daughter's birth certificate. The original birth certificate listed the baby as Dannielynn Hope Marshall Stern. Following Anna's death, DNA testing proved that photographer Larry Birkhead is the father of Dannielynn. A new birth certificate was issued in April 2007 for the 7-month-old, who is now Dannielynn Hope Marshall Birkhead. Custody of the little girl was transferred from Howard K. Stern to Larry Birkhead shortly thereafter.[10]

Is the ruling in the Smith case consistent with *Michael H*?

What about the rationale in *Hecht v. Superior Court* elevating testator intent?

The history of denying rights to unwed fathers has a long and interesting trajectory.

> Antimiscegenation laws also kept Blacks outside the family of those favored with rights; and laws restricting the ability of slaveholders to will property or freedom to Blacks suspended them in eternal illegitimacy.... Although the "bad Black mother" is even today a stereotypical way of describing what ails the Black race, the historical reality is that of careless White fatherhood. Blacks are thus, in full culturally imagistic terms, not merely unmothered but badly fathered, abused and disowned by Whites.[11]
>
> Patricia J. Williams, THE ALCHEMY OF RACE AND RIGHTS

The Genetic Tie[12]

Dorothy E. Roberts

An overriding assumption in cases determining a child's legal parentage is that families are created out of biological connections between individuals. Parental rights, however, are not a biological given. Rather, the law historically has interpreted the genetic tie's significance to parenthood in a way that preserves the patriarchal nuclear family. Cases concerning the parental rights of unwed fathers and sperm donors reveal that the law's central objective is to protect the integrity of families founded on heterosexual marriage, while leaving women's autonomous bonds with their children vulnerable.

Denying White Connection to Black Children

Why does the law deny some biological fathers rights to their children? Why does it discount the genetic tie between some men and their offspring? One reason is that the legal requirements for social fatherhood help to preserve the traditional patriarchal family structure. Another purpose might be to invest care of, and responsibility for, children in presumably stable husbands rather than presumably irresponsible unwed fathers. Another explanation arises from the genetic tie's role in the American system of racial slavery.

Uncertainty about paternity has been a universal concern throughout history.

Enforcing female marital fidelity was the only way a man could know that a woman's children were his offspring. Under a racial caste system, female fidelity was doubly important: it guaranteed not only paternity but also racial purity. Since only White women could produce White children, they were responsible for maintaining the purity of the White race. The first laws against interracial fornication and marriage arose from legislators' "particular distaste that White women, who could be producing White children, were producing mulattoes." The law punished with extra severity White women who gave birth to free mulatto children. These children, unlike the racially mixed children of Black women, represented a corruption of the White race.

While the marital presumption (of paternity) was upheld to support White racial purity, it was discarded when White women broke the rule of racial fidelity. Watkins and Wife v. Carlton involved a will contest among three children of a White man, Carlton. Two of his children, Mary and Thomas, challenged their brother William's inheritance on the ground that he was a mulatto and therefore not their father's child. [William] argued that Carlton was [his legal] father since he was married to William's mother.

Rather than uphold the presumption, the Court ordered a new trial so that the jury could consider William's racial appearance and hear expert testimony about the impossibility of "the produce of the White race being other than white." The Court allowed a racial exception to the marital presumption of legitimacy. A dark-skinned child born to a White woman did not benefit from the usual presumption of paternity; he was not deemed to be the son of a White husband.

The law's distinction between social and genetic fatherhood freed White men from social obligations to their Black children. Since a child's legal status followed that of her mother, White men could use Black women's bodies for sexual domination while preserving the racial demarcation necessary for slavery.

> State laws severed or voided every legal link (outside of the master-slave relationship) between White men and their Black children, "just as surely as the law [in the case above] erased the presumed genetic link between a White man and his Black off-spring."

Hollenbaugh v. Carnegie Free Library et al.[13]

December 11, 1978

On petition for Writ of Certiorari to the United States Court of Appeals for the Third Circuit. The petition for writ of certiorari is denied.

Mr. Justice MARSHALL, dissenting.

The Court today lets stand a decision that upholds, after the most minimal scrutiny, an unwarranted governmental intrusion into the privacy of public employees. The ruling below permits a public employer to dictate the sexual conduct and family living arrangements of its employees, without a meaningful showing that these private choices have any relation to job performance. Because I believe this decision departs from our precedents and conflicts with the rulings of other courts I would grant certiorari and set the case for argument.

Mr. Justice BRENNAN would grant certiorari.

Petitioner Rebecca Hollenbaugh served as a librarian and petitioner Fred Philburn as a custodian at the state-maintained Carnegie Free Library in Connellsville, Pa. The two began seeing each other socially, although Mr. Philburn was married at the time. In 1972, Ms. Hollenbaugh learned that she was pregnant with Mr. Philburn's child, and within a month, Mr. Philburn left his wife and moved in with Ms. Hollenbaugh. Due to her pregnancy, Ms. Hollenbaugh sought and was granted a leave of absence by the respondent Board of Trustees from March to September 1973. While petitioners did not conceal their arrangement, neither did they advertise it.

Responding to some complaints from members of the community, the Board of Trustees attempted to dissuade petitioners from continuing to live together. When petitioners refused to alter their arrangement, they were discharged. They subsequently brought this action under U.S.C. § 1983 seeking declaratory and injunctive relief and monetary damages. After a nonjury trial, the District Court found that under the minimum rationality test, petitioners' discharge did not violate the Equal Protection Clause. The court further concluded that petitioners' behavior was not included in the constitutional right to privacy. The Court of Appeals for the Third Circuit affirmed.

I have frequently reiterated my objections to the perpetuation of "the rigid two-tier model [that] still holds sway as the Court's articulated description of the equal protection test." The test that this Court has, in fact, applied has often, I believe, been much more sophisticated. The substantiality of the interests we have required a State to demonstrate in support of a challenged classification has varied with the character of the classification and the importance of the individual interests at stake. Had the courts below undertaken a thoughtful, rather than unreflectively applying the minimum rationality test, the outcome here might well have been different.

Respondents do not claim to have relied on a legislative proscription of particular sexual conduct. The Commonwealth of Pennsylvania repealed its law prohibiting adultery and fornication in 1972. Rather, in the exercise of ad hoc and, it seems, unreviewable discretion, respondents determined to deprive petitioners of their jobs unless "they 'normalized' their relationship through marriage or he moved out.

The District Court found that "the motivating factor behind the discharges of [petitioners] was that they were living together in a state of 'open adultery.' Respondents were unwilling to appear as if they "condoned [petitioners'] extramarital 'affair' and ... the child's birth out of wedlock." Thus, respondents apparently did not object to furtive adultery, but only to petitioners' refusal to hide their relationship. In essence, respondents sought to force a standard of hypocrisy on their employees and fired those who declined to abide by it. In my view, this form of discrimination is particularly invidious.

Such administrative intermeddling with important personal rights merits more than minimal scrutiny. One such right, clearly implicated by petitioners' discharge, is that "of the individual ... to engage in any of the common occupations of life." Perhaps even more vital is "the right to be free, except in very limited circumstances, from unwanted governmental intrusions into one's privacy."

Although we never have demarcated the precise boundaries of this right, we have held that it broadly encompasses "freedom of personal choice in matters of marriage and family life: as it affects pregnancy, marriage, procreation, contraception, family relationships, child rearing and education, abortion, and the right to determine family living arrangements.

Petitioners' rights to pursue an open rather than a clandestine personal relationship and to rear their child together in this environment closely resemble the other aspects of personal privacy to which we have extended constitutional protection. That petitioners' arrangement was unconventional or socially disapproved does not lessen its protected status, in the absence of a judgment that the arrangement so offends social norms as to evoke criminal sanctions.

And certainly, no distinction can be drawn between this case and those cited above in terms of the importance to petitioners of this personal decision. In addition, to impose separate living arrangements as a condition of employment impinges not only on petitioners' associational interests, but also on the interests of their child in having a two-parent home.

Petitioners' choice of living arrangements for themselves and their child is thus sufficiently close to the interests we have previously recognized as fundamental and sufficiently related to the constitutional guarantee of freedom of association that it should not be relegated to the minimum rationality tier of equal protection analysis, a disposition that seems invariably fatal to the assertion of a constitutional right.

Moreover, respondents' actions here may not withstand even the minimal scrutiny of the rational-basis test. In the District Court's view, the test was satisfied because respondents could have legitimately concluded that petitioners' relationship impaired their effectiveness on the job and that failure to discharge them would constitute tacit approval of an illicit relationship.

The court acknowledged, however, that petitioners were "competent employees who had had no significant problems with their employers until the circumstances that gave rise to their discharges." In suggesting that respondents could rationally find petitioner Hollenbaugh unfit to perform her duties, the court observed merely that her job "involved direct and frequent contacts with the community" and that the "community was well aware of [petitioners'] living arrangement." This reasoning reduces to the conclusion that Hollenbaugh was incompetent as a librarian because some members of the community disapproved of her lifestyle. But the District Court never intimated that this disapproval affected the community members' use of the library or that Hollenbaugh's marital status in any way diminished her ability to discharge her duties as a librarian. And the court gave no indication that Philburn's custodial job called for similar contacts with the community or that his performance was affected in any way by his extramarital relationship.

On a record so devoid of evidence in support of petitioners' discharge, the Court of Appeals' holding appears to conflict with decisions of other courts striking down similar attempts by governmental bodies to regulate the private lives of their employees. In the past, Federal Courts have found that a school district rule barring employment of unwed parents was insufficiently related to any legitimate objective to satisfy the requirements of the Equal Protection Clause. A three-judge District Court declared unconstitutional the dismissal of an unmarried, pregnant teacher, finding no compelling interest "which would justify the invasion of [the teacher's] constitutional right of privacy." As was the discharge of postal clerk for living with a woman not his wife. These decisions reflect a considerably greater degree of solicitude for the privacy interests of public employees than was evident in the rulings of the courts below.

I believe that individuals' choices concerning their private lives deserve more than token protection from this Court, regardless of whether we approve of those choices. Accordingly, I dissent from the denial of certiorari.

Eisenstadt v. Baird[14]

405 U.S. 438 (1972)

MR. JUSTICE BRENNAN delivered the opinion of the Court.

Appellee William Baird was convicted at a bench trial in the Massachusetts Superior Court under Massachusetts General Laws Ann., c. 272, 21, first, for exhibiting contraceptive articles in the course of delivering a lecture on contraception to a group of students at Boston University and, second, for giving a young woman a package of Emko vaginal foam at the close of his address.

The Massachusetts Supreme Judicial Court unanimously set aside the conviction for exhibiting contraceptives on the ground that it violated Baird's First Amendment rights, but by a four–to–three vote sustained the conviction for giving away the foam. *Commonwealth v. Baird*, 355 Mass. 746, 247 N. E. 2d 574 (1969).

Massachusetts General Laws Ann., c. 272, 21, under which Baird was convicted, provides a maximum five-year term of imprisonment for "whoever ... gives away ... any drug, medicine, instrument or article whatever [405 U.S. 438, 441] for the prevention of conception," except as authorized in 21A. Under 21A, "[a] registered physician may administer to or prescribe for any married person drugs or articles intended for the prevention of pregnancy or conception. [And a] registered pharmacist actually engaged in the business of pharmacy may furnish such drugs or articles to any married person presenting a prescription from a registered physician." 2 As interpreted by the State Supreme Judicial [405 U.S. 438, 442] Court, these provisions make it a felony for anyone, other than a registered physician or pharmacist acting in accordance with the terms of 21A, to dispense any article with the intention that it be used for the prevention of conception.

The statutory scheme distinguishes among three distinct classes of distributees—first, married persons may obtain contraceptives to prevent pregnancy, but only from doctors or druggists on prescription; second, single persons may not obtain contraceptives from anyone to prevent pregnancy; and, third, married or single persons may obtain contraceptives from anyone to prevent, not pregnancy, but the spread of disease. This construction of state law is, of course, binding on us. E.g., *Groppi v. Wisconsin*, 400 U.S. 505, 507 (1971).

The legislative purposes that the statute is meant to serve are not altogether clear. In *Commonwealth v. Baird*, supra, the Supreme Judicial Court noted only the State's interest in protecting the health of its citizens: "[T]he prohibition in 21," the court declared, "is directly related to" the State's goal of "preventing the distribution of articles designed to prevent conception which may have undesirable, if not dangerous, physical consequences."

In a subsequent decision, *Sturgis v. Attorney General*, the court found "a second and more compelling ground for upholding the statute"—namely, to protect morals through "regulating the private sexual lives of single persons."

The Court of Appeals, for reasons that will appear, did not consider the promotion of health or the protection of morals through the deterrence of fornication to be the legislative aim. Instead, the court concluded that the statutory goal was to limit contraception in and of itself—a purpose that the court held conflicted "with fundamental human rights" under *Griswold v. Connecticut*, 381 U.S. 479 (1965), where this Court struck down Connecticut's prohibition against the use of contraceptives as an unconstitutional infringement of the right of marital privacy.

> We agree that the goals of deterring premarital sex and regulating the distribution of potentially harmful articles cannot reasonably be regarded as legislative aims of 21 and 21A. And we hold that the statute, viewed as a prohibition on contraception per se, violates the rights of single persons under the Equal Protection Clause of the Fourteenth Amendment.

Hugh Carey, etc., et al., Appellants, v. Population Services International et al.[15]

Argued Jan. 10, 1977
Decided June 9, 1977

Action was brought by distributors of contraceptives challenging constitutionality of New York statute which prohibited distribution of contraceptives to anyone under age of 16. Prohibited distribution to anyone over 16 by anyone other than licensed pharmacist and banned advertising and display of contraceptives. The Three-Judge District Court declared the statute unconstitutional in its entirety insofar as it applied to nonprescription contraceptives, and the Supreme Court noted probable jurisdiction.

The Supreme Court, Mr. Justice Brennan, held that:

The right to privacy in connection with decisions affecting procreation extends to minors as well as to adults, and since a State may not impose a blanket prohibition, or even a blanket requirement of parental consent, on the choice of a minor to terminate her pregnancy, *Planned Parenthood of Missouri v. Danforth*, the constitutionality of a blanket prohibition of the distribution of contraceptives to minors is foreclosed.

The argument that sexual activity may be deterred by increasing the hazards attendant on it has been rejected by the Court as a justification for restrictions on the freedom to choose whether to bear or beget a child. *Eisenstadt v. Baird*. Moreover, there is substantial doubt whether limiting access to contraceptives will in fact substantially discourage early sexual behavior. When a State, as here, burdens the exercise of a fundamental right, its attempt to justify that burden as a rational means for the accomplishment of some state policy requires more than the unsupported assertion (appellants here having conceded that there is no evidence that teenage extramarital sexual activity increases in proportion to the availability of contraceptives) that the burden is connected to such a policy.

That under another provision of the statute a minor under 16 may be supplied with a contraceptive by a physician does not save the challenged provision, especially where appellants asserted no medical necessity for imposing a limitation on the distribution of nonprescription contraceptives to minors.

Result: Corporation primarily engaged in mail order retail sale of nonmedical contraceptive devices had standing to challenge statute not only in its own right but also on behalf of potential customers; regulations imposing burden on decision as fundamental as whether to bear or beget a child may be justified only by compelling state interest and must be narrowly drawn to express only those interests; prohibition of distribution of nonmedical contraceptives to persons over 16 except through licensed pharmacist burdened right of individuals to use contraceptives if they so desired and served no compelling state interest and prohibition of any advertisement or display of contraceptives was deemed unconstitutional.

Statutory Rape & Controversial Cases

Michael M. v. Superior Court of Sonoma[16]

March 1981

REHNQUIST, joined by BURGER, STEWART, and POWELL

Issue: Whether California's "statutory rape" law, violates the Equal Protection Clause of the Fourteenth Amendment.

Section 261.5 defines unlawful sexual intercourse as "an act of sexual intercourse accomplished with a female not the wife of the perpetrator, where the female is under the age of 18 years."

The statute thus makes men alone criminally liable for the act of sexual intercourse.

Prior to trial, petitioner sought to set aside the information on both state and federal constitutional grounds, asserting that § 261.5 unlawfully discriminated on the basis of gender. The trial court and the California Court of Appeal denied petitioner's request for relief and petitioner sought review in the Supreme Court of California.

The statute is not unconstitutional as applied to petitioner who, like the girl involved, was under 18 at the time of sexual intercourse, on the asserted ground that the statute presumes in such circumstances that the male is the culpable aggressor. The statute does not rest on such an assumption, but instead is an attempt to prevent illegitimate teenage pregnancy by providing an additional deterrent for men. The age of the man is irrelevant since young men are as capable as older men of inflicting the harm sought to be prevented.

Subjecting the classification to "strict scrutiny," we find that the classification was "supported not by mere social convention but by the immutable physiological fact that it is the female exclusively who can become pregnant." Canvassing "the tragic human costs of illegitimate teenage pregnancies," including the large number of teenage abortions, the increased medical risk associated with teenage pregnancies, and the social consequences of teenage childbearing, the court concluded that the State has a compelling interest in preventing such pregnancies. Because males alone can "physiologically cause the result which the law properly seeks to avoid," the court further held that the gender classification was readily justified as a means of identifying offender and victim. For the reasons stated below, we affirm the judgment of the California Supreme Court.

We have previously declared that a legislature may not "make overbroad generalizations based on sex which are entirely unrelated to any differences between men and women or which demean the ability or social status of the affected class. And yet, this Court has consistently upheld statutes where the gender classification is not invidious, but rather realistically reflects the fact that the sexes are not similarly situated in certain circumstances.

Applying those principles to this case, the fact that the California Legislature criminalized the act of illicit sexual intercourse with a minor female is a sure indication of its intent or purpose to discourage that conduct. The justification for the statute offered by the State, and accepted by the Supreme Court of California, is that the legislature sought to prevent illegitimate teenage pregnancies. That finding, of course, is entitled to great deference.

We are satisfied not only that the prevention of illegitimate pregnancy is at least one of the "purposes" of the statute, but also that the State has a strong interest in preventing such pregnancy. At the risk of stating the obvious, teenage pregnancies, which have increased dramatically over the last two decades, have significant social, medical, and economic consequences for both the mother and her child, and the State. Of particular concern to the State is that approximately half of all teenage pregnancies end in abortion. And of those children who are born, their illegitimacy makes them likely candidates to become wards of the State.

We need not be medical doctors to discern that young men and young women are not similarly situated with respect to the problems and the risks of sexual intercourse. Only women may become pregnant, and they suffer disproportionately the profound physical, emotional, and psychological consequences of sexual activity. The statute at issue here protects women from sexual intercourse at an age when those consequences are particularly severe.

Because virtually all of the significant harmful and inescapably identifiable consequences of teenage pregnancy fall on the young female, a legislature acts well within its authority when it elects to punish only the participant who, by nature, suffers few of the consequences of his conduct. It is hardly unreasonable for a legislature acting to protect minor females to exclude them from punishment. Moreover, the risk of pregnancy itself constitutes a substantial deterrence to young females. No similar natural sanctions deter males. A criminal sanction imposed solely on males thus serves to roughly "equalize" the deterrents on the sexes.

The law stands at a crossroads in fleshing out the justification for, and severity of, punishments in two similar but fundamentally different kinds of legal cases. One can sleep nights without ever fully contemplating whether the law is doing all that it can on questions involving statutory rape, where consensual sexual relations occur between one individual 18 or older and another who is not. One hardly sleeps at all when the issue is one of child molestation, where predatory, coercive or forced sexual abuse is taking place. Sentencing patterns, sex offender reporting requirements, child visitation and custody, and a host of other issues are greatly impacted by this area of law.

The courts seem to grapple with equal protection requirements with respect to gender neutrality when characterizing female victims and perpetrators for purposes of statutory rape law. There are several important questions to contemplate. Can the law rely on irrebuttable presumptions as to when minors are capable of consenting to sex without the use of extensive socio-biological research? Are judges capable of determining when a particular law "simply does not comport with reality?" Is it feasible to eliminate gender classifications altogether, or exclude consensual sexual relations occurring among youth in the same peer group?

We have several theories upon which to explore these obvious questions. There is a deficit of legal scholarship that addresses how widespread criminalization of certain behaviors tends to create more problems for individuals and society. Laws that are unnecessarily intrusive create all manner of social casualties in the name of protecting children.

> The full scope of the liberty guaranteed by the Due Process Clause is not a series of isolated points pricked out in terms of freedom of speech, press, and religion ... and so on. It is a rational continuum which, broadly speaking, includes a freedom from all substantial arbitrary impositions and purposeless restraints, ... and which also recognizes, what a reasonable and sensitive judgment must, that certain interests require particularly careful scrutiny of the state needs asserted to justify their abridgment.[17]

Cases, Controversy & Commentary

Letourneau and Blilie

Consider the following op-ed reports and internet posting detailing certain dynamics of the Letourneau case. The Seattle Times reported the following.[18]

> Mary Kay Letourneau, 35, a schoolteacher, has an affair with a 13-year-old boy, a former student of hers. The affair produces a guilty plea to charges of second-degree child rape. It also produces a baby and, last week, a suspended sentence.
>
> Mark Blilie, 42, a schoolteacher, has an affair with a 15-year-old girl, a former student of his. The affair produces a conviction for third-degree child rape and child molestation and four years in the joint for Blilie. What's wrong with this? I mean, other than the fact that both these people did horrible things, that they abused children and the hopes and trust of entire communities. What's wrong, of course, is the similarity of the situations and the vastly different outcomes. How did this happen? The answers are as simple as human history, and as complicated as the human heart.
>
> But here's a clue. One newspaper account of Letourneau's sentencing hearing contained this passage:
>
>> During the sentencing, the mother of the boy forgave LeTourneau, who appeared in an aquamarine sweater, Black pleated skirt and her hair pinned up

with soft tendrils. She has frequently been described in other news accounts as blond and attractive.

In case you're wondering, the phrase "soft tendrils" did not appear in any of the stories written about Mark Blilie. In fact, there was no physical description of him whatsoever, although judging from a photograph taken on the day of his sentencing, he is a tall, handsome, dark-haired man. The Seattle Times published that photograph with a caption identifying him as "Convicted Child Rapist Mark Blilie."

The caption published with the photograph of Mary Letourneau taken at her sentencing identified her as a "former teacher. I'm not trying to suggest that Blilie should have evaded prison or that Letourneau should be sent there. I frankly don't know. But the circumstances of the two cases are so strikingly similar that you would think their sentences would be as well. Often, in cases like these, the histories of the accused individuals play a crucial role in sentencing. Neither Blilie nor Letourneau had previous criminal histories. The chief difference is Blilie is a man, Letourneau a woman. A fast-developing area of biology is spooling out ingenious Darwinian explanations of human sexual behavior: Men seek multiple sexual partners to increase their chances of reproducing; women seek them to set up a competition among sperm—may the best man win.

Sexual desire, the theorists say, is physical. It is as weird and wonderful and perverse as the world. In some sense, we can't control the desires we have. As a species we're hard-wired for reproduction. It's what we live to do, seeking a sort of serial immortality. Our desires encourage us. I'd bet that 95 people out of a hundred would explain Mark Blilie's actions as a result of nothing more than sexual desire, inadequately constrained. Letourneau has contended throughout her ordeal that her only defense is one from the heart.

The boy was old and wise beyond his years. His own mother calls him an "old soul." Letourneau says she fell in love with him, and although she acknowledges what she did was wrong, she says she loves him still. She says this does not excuse her actions, but might help explain them. Actually, no, it doesn't help explain them. In fact, in some ways it makes them even more confusing and disconcerting. Love, unlike desire, is a human invention. It is almost entirely a creation of culture and is in large part a product of intention.

In some sense, it would be easier to accept Letourneau saying she got carried away by rash and unfortunate desire. To say she loved the boy is to say she wanted to happen what did. It further mystifies everyone but her. We can accept the fact that some people are just plain bad, when they commit crimes. But when good people do bad things and do them on purpose, we are left without our normal, comforting rationalizations. It's very scary because in the end we are left to wonder: What about us?

Joey Buttafuoco & Amy Fisher

The 36-year-old was running an auto body shop on New York's Long Island in 1992 when his 16-year-old lover, Amy Fisher, shot his wife in the face as she answered the door at the couple's home. Fisher was nicknamed the Long Island Lolita and served 7 years in prison for attempted murder. Fisher says she was strung out on the club drug Ecstasy when she shot Mary Jo Buttafuoco.

The Grand Jury handed up an indictment, charging defendant Joseph Buttafuoco with six counts of Rape in the First Degree, 12 counts of Sodomy in the Third Degree and Endangering the Welfare of a Child. He pleaded guilty to one count of statutory rape, was sentenced to six, but served only four months in prison. He has since admitted the affair, but denies the claim that he instructed Amy to shoot his wife.[19]

Guest Feature: D. Hughes on Mary Kay Letourneau[20]

The following is a response to the imprisoning of Mary Kay Letourneau following the revocation of her alternative, community-treatment oriented sentence on February 6, 1998, and partly a general critique of the American criminal justice system by a European.

Dear Editor,

I have been following the Mary Letourneau case since I saw the court TV transmitted on Sky Television some time ago. As a non-American I find it totally incomprehensible that your society appears set on creating as many social casualties as possible. You keep saying "justice is done" in your articles yet I see no signs of "justice" anywhere. All I see is persecution, vengeance and a desire to put the rule of law before any consideration for the damage that you (American society) are doing to so many people. Damage that will cost your society so much time and money attempting to repair.

You are probably thinking, "what business is this of yours?" Well I will answer like this. How did you feel when you heard that a woman in the Middle East was stoned to death for adultery? I would imagine you felt a sense of outrage didn't you? You didn't condone the adultery but considered the punishment outrageous. Right? Well, that's how I see what has gone on with Mary Letourneau. I don't in any way think what she did was very smart, but having lost my first wife through infatuation with a younger man I think I feel some empathy with the situation. I also feel empathy with Steve Letourneau who would probably want to help his wife but knows that her hormones are driving her in a different direction. I've been there. I know.

But that's not all. What Mary Letourneau did is not a crime in Holland—now you see the reasoning behind the analogy with stoning-to-death adulteresses. The age of consent is 12 years. A thirteen-year-old boy can have sex with whomever he wants.

Don't think that we encourage that! BUT in the United States you seem to think that the only way to solve problems is to apply more restrictions and add more laws to the statute book, making it ever more difficult for the average person to know what they may and may not do.

Decriminalization not only reduces the number of people in our jails (the current figures for Holland are 55 per 100,000 people, and in the United States? But if you look at the percentage of teenage pregnancy in Holland it is one tenth of that in the United States. Teenagers found responsible for graffiti don't go to jail, they have to pay the FULL cost of cleaning and restoring the property. And what happens if you don't pay your fines and bills in Holland? The bailiffs come in and claim enough of your property to pay off the debts. Compared with this, imprisonment can seem like a soft option! How much does each prisoner in the United States cost the taxpayer?

So who am I? I am a 50-year-old businessman, happily married with two sons, one 15 and the other 10. You can probably now see why this case took my interest. I lost my first wife through infatuation with a younger man and I have a boy, with my second wife, almost the same age as the one in this case. Last year my elder boy started a serious relationship with a girl. Living in Holland though made my situation very different to the Mary Letourneau situation. I had nothing to fear from the law if he had sex with his girl friend. We didn't encourage it but we didn't oppose it either. We met her parents and they felt just like us. We let them sleep together at our house or her house if they wanted, and we advised them on sex and contraception in a completely open and un-embarrassed way.

Having been through this extremely healthy and positive experience and seen how sensibly and mature these young people behaved, I felt really disturbed by the disastrously negative course the Mary Letourneau case has taken. And what if the girl had been a 34-year-old teacher you are asking yourself? Well, I wouldn't have reacted differently, but I will tell you this with a great deal of confidence, because sexual intercourse is legal, if consent is given, for young people above 12 there is no thrill or excitement or daring associated with it. There is curiosity of course, but my experience of my son and his friends is that they have an extremely sensible outlook to sex.

Had a "Mary Letourneau situation" occurred in Holland I feel sure that it would have fizzled out within months. No daring, no thrill from doing something prohibited, just another relationship. Reality would have hit home fairly quickly and the parties involved would have sorted themselves out without the involvement of any police, lawyers or judges.

Arthur, I am not American but I lived in the United States in 1970, during the Kent State University police brutality and murders. I have represented US companies in Europe ever since then and I have daily contact with Americans by telephone and e-mail. In America you all live under the illusion that you have the freest society in the World. It's not true. Your lives are burdened with a statute book so thick that it is impossible for the ordinary citizen to cope with any encounter with the law. (An American woman I know who is married to a police officer, told me only on my last visit to the States that she was booked recently for driving too slowly.)

You imply in your articles that part of Mary Letourneau's difficulties stem from the fact that she refused therapy. Think about how you felt when you learned that communists in the Soviet Union would send people to mental hospitals for treatment to correct their positive beliefs about capitalism. Could you have written an article stating that Andrei Sakharov and Yelena Bonner were receiving "therapy" in a Gulag because of their anti-communist beliefs? The word "therapy" would have stuck in your throat wouldn't it? The only word you could have used to describe this would have been "brainwashing" wouldn't it? That's how I see the situation with Mary Letourneau and this 14-year-old boy. She knows she loves him, and to deny her feelings for him would be a betrayal of everything she did.

Coming from a country where what she did was not illegal, the word "therapy" sticks in my throat. That she needs help at this time is without doubt but I couldn't tell here that what she did was wrong. Every time I read the reported words of the therapists, "brainwashing" was the only thought that came to my mind. Oh, I didn't tell you, my first wife who became infatuated with a younger man did a doctorate (PhD) in Psychology. I can assure you that female hormones show no respect for either intellectual capacity or academic achievement.

I realize that Mary Letourneau broke your laws. Andrei Sakarov broke Soviet laws. The actions of neither of them broke Dutch law. If you care about your society you should really be asking yourself, "are we criminalizing too much?" Disagreeing with somebody's behavior is not grounds for criminalizing it. A successful and happy society comes from accepting that you don't persecute people just because you don't like what they do. In the United States you spend huge amounts of effort trying to get everybody to conform to a narrow band of ideals and values, rather than accepting that, well, everybody's different. You only have to look at events of the last few weeks in your country. The "right to life" anti-abortion group believe that their cause justifies murdering people. You can't hide from the lunacy in that, can you? Yet it is an example of how far people will go in the United States to try and make other people toe their particular line. The "justice system" goes to the same lengths. A Dieu Karla Tucker. I am not alone in considering this unacceptable. The European Union has asked your Congress to stage future meetings outside Texas because members from every country in Europe find capital punishment abhorrent.

Why should I be bothering to spend my time writing to you? I don't live in the United States and never will. I don't know anybody involved. I have no reason whatsoever to want to get involved. So why? Well first, reflect on this. Mary Letourneau didn't steal anything. She didn't hurt anybody. She made love to a sexually mature male and had his child and your society has sent her to jail for 7 1/2 years. That is not easy to ignore.

From my viewpoint there is a prima facie case for claiming that your system has failed Mary Letourneau, and I don't think that you can honestly deny that. Everything that your system has done has gone wrong and there are a lot of human casualties. Unlike those who die in an aircraft accident, these casualties will be going through a living death for many years.

However, it didn't need to happen, which is why I am writing this. Just as Boeing would send out teams of investigators to find out why an aircraft failed you should be sending out teams of investigators and finding out why your system has failed. I repeat, this didn't need to happen. There are countries in which it wouldn't happen.

You should try and learn from those other countries, for the sake of Steve and Mary Letourneau, for the sake of the unnamed young man, for the sake of the five children, and for the sake of all the other unfortunate people who get stuck in that post-puberty–to–sixteen sexual no-man's land that exists in your society. Statuary rape, increased criminalization, "brainwashing" and as I read in your article today, further prosecution, are not the answer. I hope that you can see that and through your reporting help others become aware of that. I shall continue watching and reading. The Internet has changed the world. Your audience is not just Seattle any more.

Yours sincerely,

David Hughes, Amsterdam

P.S. I find it very interesting that opinions that support Mary Kay Letourneau, made by Americans are often made anonymously. I can think of only one reason for that, they are afraid of becoming part of an American media witch-hunt. Not being an American and not living in a country where sex with a consenting 13-year-old is illegal I have no such fear. It would seem there is more to this Mary Kay Letourneau case than first meets the eye. There is clearly a fear amongst some Americans that sympathy cannot be openly expressed.

Additional comments from Mr. Hughes: Living in a country as small as Holland you are constantly aware of how different the culture is in the neighboring countries, whereas when you live in the United States it is easy to believe that everybody sees the world in just the same way as you and a lot of the time it doesn't.

I would stress that without consent, rape is rape. Here there is no difference. Are twelve-year-olds able to know when to say "no"? You bet they are. Look at Holland's record on teenage pregnancy. It is second to none. There is nobody telling them to say "no". There is no society for virgin girls. There is no advertising campaign. They know that the decision to have sex and the responsibility for the consequences is theirs from puberty onwards.

Are we forcing our children to grow up too soon? No. We are allowing them to grow up in synchronism with their natural sexual development. It is considered quite normal for "children" to be still living with their parents when in their late 20s. If their parents respect their opinions, their freedom and their sexuality from an early age, what reason do they have to want to move out? Boys and girls are given the facts very early and understand there is a lot more fun to be had in life than having a baby.

Ten years ago, Vili Fualaau and Mary Kay Letourneau began an affair that produced two little girls, sent her to jail, resulted in a divorce from her husband, separation from her four older children, and sent the nation into a tail-spin of debate. Recently, the couple celebrated their one-year wedding anniversary, after marrying at a winery last year. They live in three-bedroom beachside house in Normandy Park, Washington. Their daughters were cared for by their paternal grandmother while Letourneau was in prison. They are now living with mom and dad and Letourneau is rebuilding her relationship with her other four children.[21]

Transcript of Larry Elder's Exclusive Interview with Vili Fualaau[22]

LARRY: So how did the relationship start, what happened?

VILI: It all started, well, we were sitting down in a classroom, or in her classroom. And I'm sitting there and I'm on the computer and I'm telling her about this girl I'm in love with. And she's asking me "Well, does she know you're in love with her?" And I say "No." And then she says, "Well, does she love you?" And I said, "I don't know." And she says "Well, is she with someone else?" And I said "Yup." And she said, "Does she love that someone else?" I said "Nope."

LARRY: How did you know that, by the way?

VILI: I didn't know that; that's just what I wanted. And she told me that—we talked about this all the time like when it first started—she tells me that you know she was afraid to know what I was talking about. She had a feeling that I was talking about her which was true. And it started from there.

LARRY: Did you guys begin going somewhere in the school building?

VILI: No. I asked her "When do I get my first kiss?"

LARRY: Wow.

VILI: She says I had to wait 'til I was 18, of age.

LARRY: So Vili, you were sort of the aggressor. And she initially was trying to push you away a little bit.

VILI: Yeah. I mean it's, she tried to, you know ... but I kept forcing her, I mean not forcing her but uh, kind of keep bringing it up again and again.

LARRY: So tell us about the moment, Vili, that you knew that you were going to begin a relationship with her. What happened?

VILI: I didn't really know. To tell you the truth, it just kind of happened.

LARRY: And where would you go?

VILI: Well, we would talk during recess times. All the kids would be out; they would be doing their own thing. And we'll be there just talking to each other about her life, about my life. And that went on for a while. I started to get to know her a lot and about her relationship with her husband. And she started to know a lot about my life and how my home style was. And things started, we started to get to know each other like that and then we eventually started having sex.

LARRY: And when she told you about her now ex-husband, what did she tell you about him—that she wasn't happy?

VILI: Well, she wasn't happy. She was in college and she went over to a party. She was at a party and she knew this guy for a while and they ended up hitting it off. And two weeks later, she finds out that she's pregnant. I don't really remember how that all went. But her parents found out and they told her that she has to get married because of the religion and that it's just, that it's against their religion to have a baby out of wedlock. And so they got married. And through the 11 years she was learning—trying to learn—how to love this guy because she wasn't in love with him. And to get herself away she would try to find happiness through her kids because she wasn't really happy with her husband.

LARRY: Now, do you recall the first time you told her that you loved her?

VILI: I was 13 at the time

LARRY: And did she ever tell you she loved you back?

VILI: Uh huh

LARRY: And did you feel—you know you're 13 years old—did you feel this is going to be something that's going to be fleeting, or did you really think that at some point you guys were going to get together and have a relationship?

VILI: I had a feeling once after our first kiss we were gonna be together in each others' lives for a long time.

LARRY: How did people find out about the affair?

VILI: Well, when she was pregnant, she wrote a letter to me and she was going to bring it over to me, but she forgot it on her bathroom counter. Her husband came home from work and found it and came over to my house and confronted me about it.

LARRY: What was that like? I mean, you're what—13 years old—and a grown man is confronting you over having an affair with his wife? That had to be pretty intense.

VILI: Well, to tell you the truth, I thought he was going to drop me right there and then. But it didn't really work out that way. I had a lot of friends over at my house. He came over, all my friends were asking, "Who is that guy? Who is that guy?" "Oh, that was my teacher's husband." He asked me how many times, or if we were having an affair—he said he already found a letter and this and that so I was in a position to where I couldn't lie. So I just confessed and told him, "Yeah, we are having an affair." He asked me how many times have we had sex. I told him 4 or 5 times even though you know actually I should have said once.

LARRY: I'm sorry, you should have just said once? I don't think it would have mattered, I don't think it would have mattered. (laughter)

VILI: And then he told me if I don't want anyone to find out about it, then to stop calling his house, and stop hanging out with his wife. And I said ok, whatever. And he says ok. Then he leaves and I get a phone call from Mary and she's at her school, she says hello and the next thing I hear, the phone drops. And then she calls me later that night and says that he went down to the school after he left my house and dragged her out of the school in front of the principal and all the other teachers into the car and drove her home. And was just yelling at her about the whole thing.

LARRY: So who called the police? How did she end up being prosecuted?

VILI: I heard his sister-in-law called. I guess he told his sister-in-law and he didn't know what to do. So his sister-in-law said, you know, I guess she probably said something like" This isn't right, you shouldn't have to go through this so I'm gonna call the cops" or something and inform them what's going on.

LARRY: Alright. So she gets prosecuted, she gets convicted. Vili, did it occur to you along the way that however you felt about her, you loved her, she loved you, your relationship in the eyes of the law was a crime, and that she might very well go to prison. Did that occur to you?

VILI: Yeah, it did. I mean, we both knew what we were getting ourselves into, and we know the risk we were taking. Um, I don't know, sometimes you know when you love, everything just, everything around you just doesn't matter. You just got like this force around you. And you forget about a lot of things sometimes. Like you're too caught up in each other. I mean I think a lot of people have had that feeling before and some people lose it, some people still have it.

LARRY: Wow. When you found out she was pregnant, Vili, your reaction was what?

VILI: I'm going to have a lot of responsibilities. I got responsibilities now. And there is nothing I can do about it but to take care of it.

LARRY: She told you that she was pregnant before she told her husband?

VILI: Yeah.

LARRY: Now meanwhile, Vili, your folks, your parents, did they know about this, they know about the affair?

VILI: No they didn't know until the whole thing was exploded all over the media. Until the cops came and told my mother.

LARRY: Alright, so she goes to prison for a couple months, she promises that she'll never do this again, never sees you again, she basically throws herself on the mercy of the court, and she's out of prison after a couple months. And then you guys start up again? Did you have any contact with her when she was in prison the first time, did you write other, did you call her, did she write to you, call you?

VILI: I wrote to her. It's just we had—the state put a no contact order on us so we couldn't get—we couldn't have any contact whatsoever.

LARRY: Not even emails, not even anything.

VILI: No, I did receive some letters from her but it was through someone else—they called, got a hold of me and I got the letters through them. But while she was in there, I did write to her, I wrote a bunch of letters, plenty of letters to her, and I just left them in a box. I would write them out as if I was going to send them to her so I would write it out, and I would put it in an envelope and seal it up and just put it in this box.

LARRY: Now Vili, when she got out of prison, you knew that by having contact with her it was violating the terms of her release and she could go back to jail. What about that? Pretty risky. She goes back to jail, she's gone for 7 years, 7½ years. Vili, at this point, 7½ years, your feelings for her are what, they go up and down?

VILI: Well, while she was behind bars through the 7 years, my feelings were going up and down b/c of the counseling and all the people I was working with. The detectives, counselors, school counselors would tell me she's a sex offender, and she's probably had sex with other students. She totally manipulated you. If she really cared about you she wouldn't have had that kid. And she wouldn't have put me through this and so on so on. It kind of blurred my picture of her, like who I saw back then. So for 7 years, they're telling me, you know, you don't need to wait around for her. I think what would make you happy is if you started dating again. So I started dating. None of my girlfriends worked out. I mean, I guess it just wasn't meant to work out because I didn't really want to be with those girls for the rest of my life.

LARRY: So when she got out the first time, you guys have sex, she gets pregnant a second time, so now you have two daughters.

VILI: Yes.

LARRY: And now that she's out, you have any contact with her now?

VILI: The contact order was lifted on August 6th and ...

LARRY: The no contact order, it was lifted?

VILI: Yes.

LARRY: At whose request?

VILI: My request.

LARRY: I know you wanted the no contact order lifted. Did you have reason to believe that she still had feelings towards you?

VILI: Yes.

LARRY: And why did you feel that way?

VILI: It's, I don't know, you just know sometimes.

LARRY: The day before you met her [when she got out of jail] must have been pretty anxious for you. Couldn't sleep? You haven't seen her in all these years.

VILI: I was up, I figured I slept like an hour. I got up, and the first day we met it wasn't exactly how I expected it, it wasn't exactly how she expected it.

LARRY: Let's back up, there was a phone call first though right?

VILI: Yeah, there was a phone call first.

LARRY: Ok, who called who?

VILI: I called her. I got the phone number from one of my lawyers, and I didn't know what to think. I didn't know if it was a real number or what and they called it and on their answering machine, it says "this is Mary." But from that, I couldn't tell if it was really her or not. And I was supposed to call her at 11:30 that day.

LARRY: Did you think it was some sort of trick?

VILI: Yeah, I was thinking it was a trick, like somebody was a trying to get something, you know sell something to the public, like to record a conversation of mine with her and sell it for some money or something.

LARRY: How did you find out it was legit?

VILI: When I called her, I called her at 11:30 and first thing she said to me was if I called earlier because I tried calling her earlier to have someone else talk to her. I had a friend that was going to talk to her before I did to see if it was really her. And that didn't work out so well so I called her at 11:30 and the first thing she says to me was "Did I call—did I call at five thirty?" And I'm like "No. First of all, how do I know this is you?" And she says, "Can you feel my energy?" And then right away I knew it was her.

LARRY: Was that an expression you guys used?

VILI: Well, no, it's not an expression that we use, it's just the way we talk to each other.

LARRY: Wow. So, Vili, you have two daughters and how old are they?

VILI: 7 and 5.

LARRY: And your mom has custody of both daughters?

VILI: Both.

LARRY: You all live in the same house?

VILI: No.

LARRY: Where do you live?

VILI: I live on my own. Right now, I live with a friend. Through 7 years I was moving from house to house, in and out of jobs. Didn't really get to—I didn't get to finish school.

LARRY: You sort of drifted.

VILI: It was pretty much depressing, sad, miserable, mostly sad.

LARRY: Alright, she's been out now about a month. Have you seen her?

VILI: I've been seeing her everyday.

LARRY: The order has been lifted, you can now see each other, you're an adult, she's obviously an adult, what's next?

VILI: Well, what's next is that we gotta get ourselves financially stable. And we have to work out the family court issues. And then I guess it would be safe to say, well, safe to get married.

LARRY: And your daughters? Are you going to get custody of them from your mom?

VILI: In time I will, in time. Right now, it's a slow process because uh, my mom has this really close relationship with my daughters. She's raised them from when they were just little babies, for 7 years. And they just pretty much became her kids. And I was out looking for jobs. Me and my mom didn't really get along because of the whole thing with me and Mary. It's just the fact that Mary's out now and we're finally together. And we still have the same feelings for each other, times forever. And she's just afraid that when we get married and get custody of the kids back, that she'll never be able to see the kids again. But that's not, that's not gonna happen. And that's nothing I would do to her. Because she's done that for me, taking care of them. And I mean, that just would be cold-blooded for me just to take the kids away from her.

LARRY: This case became very, very, very famous. How does that make you feel?

VILI: I don't know. I've never, I've never been really much of a people person. I'm never really social that much with people—only the people that I'm really close to. Sometimes I'll get, I'll meet new people and I'll start to get close to them. But it's not like how most people, like most of my friends, they go around, you know they—it's very easy for them to talk to new people and this and that. Me, I get shy sometimes talking with people.

LARRY: And, and Vili, have you and Mary Kay been, how can I put this, together? You know what I'm asking? Are, are you, are you intimate?

VILI: We've, we've always ...

LARRY: Well, I mean, since, she's gotten out.

VILI: Oh, since she's out ... yes

LARRY: So, Vili, you mentioned that you want to get married. I assume she said the same thing?

VILI: Yes.

LARRY: Wow. You have a time frame?

VILI: We have a time frame. I can't really say, I can't really pick. We haven't really picked a date yet because we've got so much going on now. But, eventually, we'll find out.

LARRY: Vili, a lot of people were hurt. She has an ex-husband. She has 4 children. How do you feel about that? If, if her ex-husband were here, what would you say to him?

VILI: If they were here? You know I really, I really wouldn't know what to say. I mean, apologies wouldn't really mean anything. I mean, I wouldn't really know what to say or what to do. But I do hope the best for them. You know, that everything goes well for them. And I hope they're getting help with whatever they're doing. And I hope they don't get corrupted with anything negative about this whole outcome with me and Mary.

LARRY: Well, you mentioned that there was friction between you and your mom because of Mary Kay. What does your mom say? Your love for her has been consistent. Her love for you has been consistent. Has she turned around now?

VILI: Um, I don't really know. I mean it's, it's always going to be an awkward picture in everyone's mind. Because of the, you know, way back when and now. And because Mary and my mom are not really that far apart in age. And it's just, it's always gonna be awkward to them. It's not gonna really be that easy for them to accept that in their head. But in their hearts they do accept the both of us being together and they're behind us all the way.

LARRY: Vili, a lot of publicity. Your name is everywhere. Your photo's everywhere. Mary Kay's photo is everywhere. When you guys are in your town and you're walking around, I would imagine a lot of people are looking at you. How does that feel? Do you shut it out?

VILI: No, I mean we're gonna have to accept the public wherever we go. I mean, I think it would be really respectful if people don't like come running up to us, screaming, asking for autographs and things like that. I mean, I'm not a movie star or anything. Our story just became really big.

LARRY: Vili, do you think she should've gone to prison?

VILI: No.

LARRY: What do you think should've happened to her?

VILI: I have no idea. I'm not really good with the legal stuff, so ...

LARRY: I mean, do you think she should've had counseling, or.... ?

VILI: I think they probably should've put her in counseling.

Children under the age of twelve are rarely capable of exercising the level of mature reasoning that would render their consent meaningful for purposes of participating in non-peer sexual activities. A statistically significant percentage of the American teenage and pre-teen population have always been ultra-curious about sex, and more willing to act upon it for various reasons, often with very limited sex education. There is widespread agreement that socially responsible societies embrace public education campaigns designed to assist all of its citizens in making informed choices. This is particularly true of choices made at ages and stages where appreciation of consequences and ability to control impulses may be in short supply. For the young, a broad range of choices carry enormous potential for life-altering change. Issues of knowing consent are rarely discussed when evaluating statutory rape laws. We customarily relate such policies to the state's interest in curbing teen pregnancy and its impact on the lives of young women. However, meaningful critique of statutory rape law has to be an ongoing effort designed to bridge gaps in ways that clarify rather than confuse societal interests relating to legitimate criminal justice goals in the area of child sexual abuse.

For Your Consideration

Statutory Frameworks, Social Reality & Legal Fiction

The law of statutory rape transforms consensual sexual relations, possibly between two people who love one another, into a crime for which one person is sent to jail. The laws of marital/acquaintance rape convert what we universally accept to be sexual battery into an affirmative defense because the victim is familiar. It makes sense to examine how laws distribute the burden of proof in marital and pre-marital rape cases. Statutory rape avoids dealing with consent by removing it from the equation. Exemptions for marital rape avoid consent by presuming that it exists, analogous to the proposed change for procuring organs to harvest for transplant. The legal question is whether such laws provide women with equal protection and with the requisite privileges and immunities of citizenship.

In the early '80s the Supreme Court upheld a California law punishing men for the "act of sexual intercourse accomplished with a female under eighteen who is not the wife of the perpetrator." Criminal convictions and the subsequent sex offender registration resulting from such laws *disconnect penalties from traditional requirements of criminal intent*. Similarly, the jurisdictions that offer exemption from prosecution for marital rape effectively separate penalty from intent when consent is presumed due to the parties marital tie. Thus, under the old California law, a seventeen year-old female is legally capable of consenting to marry a thirty-four-year-old male, incapable of withdrawing consent to sexual intercourse during the marriage, and unable to consent to an intimate sexual relationship with the same man either before or after the marriage has ended, as long as she is 17.

In *Michael H.*, Victoria was born in May of 1981. Blood tests were conducted in October, roughly 5 months later, confirming that he was her biological father. She lived in his home with her mother and came to know him as her father. He filed a petition to establish his right to visitation in November of 1982, approximately one year after his paternity was confirmed. This is the rationale used by a concurring justice to deny that petition:

> Under the circumstances of the case before us, Michael was given a fair opportunity to show that he is Victoria's natural father, that he had developed a relationship with her, and that her interests would be served by granting him visitation rights. On the other hand, the record also shows that after its rather shaky start, the marriage between Carole and Gerald developed a stability that now provides Victoria with a loving and harmonious family home. In the circumstances of this case, I find nothing fundamentally unfair about the exercise of a judge's discretion that, in the end, allows the mother to decide whether her child's best interests would be served by allowing the natural father visitation privileges. Because I am convinced that the trial judge had the authority under state law both to hear Michael's plea for visitation rights and to grant him such rights if Victoria's best interests so warranted, I am satisfied that the California statutory scheme is consistent with the Due Process Clause of the Fourteenth Amendment.[23]

Compare and contrast the rationale behind dissenting statements in *Zablocki,* where the Court rejected a Wisconsin statute authorizing possible denial of marriage licenses for all parties with delinquent child support payments.

> I do not agree with the Court that there is a "right to marry" in the constitutional sense. That right, or more accurately that privilege, is … one to be defined and limited by state law. A State may not only "significantly interfere with decisions to enter into marital relationship," but may in many circumstances absolutely prohibit it. Surely, for example, a State may legitimately say that no one can marry his or her sibling, that no one can marry who is not at least 14 years old, that no one can marry without first passing an examination for venereal disease, or that no one can marry who has a living husband or wife. But, just as surely, in regulating

> the intimate human relationship of marriage, there is a limit beyond which a State may not constitutionally go.[24]

If an individual can legally marry with parental consent at age 14, are there any arguments that favor the decision to place Letourneau in jail for seven years, force her to register as a sex offender, and only have supervised visitation with her four children from her first marriage?

New York Times columnist William Safire, wrote a humorous article called *The Polyandry Solution*, where he observed that the "old nuclear family: husband, wife, two kids, has plunged from one in two to one in four" U.S. families. Factor in science where improvement in nutrition, genetics, cures for most diseases, and where women outlive men, widowhood is increasingly a part of geezerhood." He asks what this combination of events and social trends tell political economists? According to Safire, the most sensible, least costly solution to the long-term loneliness of unchosen singlehood could be the legalization of polyandry—the marriage of a woman with more than one man. "One woman, in the security of being doubly beloved and beneficiaried, can surely provide life-extending companionship to two men. And when one husband passes on, either to his Maker or to some gold-digging bimbo, the long-lived polyandrist would still have the remaining man for mutual comfort and support."[25]

Chapter Six

Post-Modern Notions of Love Without Limits

Evolving Theories of Social Freedom

Ordered Liberty in a Democracy

The Constitution was made for people of fundamentally differing views, and the accident of our finding certain opinions natural and familiar or novel and even shocking ought not to conclude our judgment upon the question whether statutes embodying them conflict with the Constitution of the United States.

Lochner v. New York, 198 U.S. 45 (1905)

Due process has not been reduced to any formula; its content cannot be determined by reference to any code. The best that can be said is that through the course of this Court's decisions it has represented the balance that our Nation, built upon postulates of respect for the liberty of the individual, has struck between that liberty and the demands of organized society.

Moore v. City of East Cleveland, Ohio, 431 U.S. 494 (1977)

The makers of our Constitution undertook to secure conditions favorable to the pursuit of happiness. They recognized the significance of man's spiritual nature, of his feelings and of his intellect. They knew that only a part of the pain, pleasure and satisfactions of life are to be found in material things. They sought to protect Americans in their beliefs, their thoughts, their emotions and their sensations. They conferred, as against the Government, the right to be let alone—the most comprehensive of rights and the right most valued by civilized men. To protect that right, every unjustifiable intrusion by the Government upon the privacy of the individual, whatever the means employed, must be deemed a violation of the Fourth Amendment.

Olmstead v. U.S., 277 U.S. 438 (1928)

A report for the Law Commission of Canada questions the role of the state in the regulation of personal adult relationships. It questions whether governments can rely on conjugal relationships to accomplish important state objectives, when doing so promotes certain kinds of close personal relationships while excluding others. Thus the Commission proposes re-evaluation of the ways in which personal adult relationships are regulated.[1]

Women's History Guide[2]

By Jone Johnson Lewis

In the 1960s and 1970s, free love came to imply a sexually active lifestyle with many casual sex partners and little or no commitment, but in the 19th and early 20th century, the meaning of free love was very different.

When Victoria Woodhull ran for President of the United States on the Free Love platform, she was assumed to be promoting promiscuity. But that was not her intent—for she and others believed they were promoting a different and better sexual morality.

Many thinkers in the 19th century looked at the reality of marriage and its effects on women, and concluded that marriage was not much different from slavery or prostitution. Marriage equaled economic enslavement. Married women had no rights to property, could not divorce, and had few rights to custody of their children if they did.

A pioneer named Fanny Wright inspired by the communitarianism of the "Owenites" established the community of Nashoba. Modeled after John Humphrey Noyes, who promoted throughout the Oneida Community a kind of Free Love that opposed marriage and instead used "spiritual affinity" as the bond of union. Noyes adapted his ideas from Josiah Warren and Dr. and Mrs. T. L. Nichols.

Ms. Wright encouraged free sexual relationships within the community, opposed marriage and promoted sexual fulfillment and knowledge. Owenites taught that sex could be a positive experience, and was not just for procreation but for individual fulfillment and the natural fulfillment of the love of partners for each other. They also advocated for "voluntary motherhood"—the choice of motherhood as well as marriage.

A century later, those who preached sexual liberation and sexual freedom adopted the term "free love," and those who opposed casual sex embraced the term as prima facie evidence of the immorality of its practitioners.

Condemnation of the immorality of the practice and underlying ideal have long been a feature of public debate. Excerpts from a late-19th century undercover investigation of the Movement illustrates the sentiment of the time. A prominent daily news organization published the following.

> We have for sometime been aware of the existence in this City of a body of persons united in a secret society for the purpose, not merely of discussing those principles of extreme social lawlessness known by the general term of Individual Sovereignty, and of confirming themselves in such principles, but also of carrying them into practice, especially in the sexual relations. As soon as this fact came to our knowledge, we did not fail, of course, in the discharge of our duty to the public, to set on foot an investigation for the purpose of ascertaining the truth with regard to such a society, in order to bring the same to the tribunal of public opinion.

Free-Love in New-York. Individual Sovereignty Realized.[3] Principles and Practice of the Free-Lovers

New-York Daily Tribune, 1855

[Relevant Edited Excerpts]

HISTORY OF THE FREE-LOVE SOCIETY

This society calls itself the Progressive Union Club/ League and has grown out of an organization devised by certain social theorists. It meets on Monday and Thursday evenings of each week, over Taylor's upper saloon, 555 Broadway. There are 500–600 members, with an average attendance of 150; though the attendance has been much larger than usual since the affair has gained some general notoriety. There were 300 present at the last meeting. At these semi-weekly meetings, the members of the Club and the strangers whom they introduce walk, talk, waltz, sing, flirt and endeavor to enjoy themselves as best they may—each selecting his or her associate according to attraction and affinities, and always with a due regard to Individual Sovereignty.

Although the exercises, topics, and amusements indulged in take a wide range, the main idea which draws and holds together this motley part is Free Love, or Passional Attraction, as some of them prefer to call it. They repudiate the present system of marriage, deny the right of society or the state to interfere in any way with the subject any further than it may rightfully interfere with any civil contract, and contend that marriage may be a limited or life partnership, at the option of the man and woman who are the sole and rightful judges of the time and manner of its beginning and termination. One of their favorite dogmas is that a woman has the right to choose the father of her own child. This theory, has, we understand, been reduced to practice to a considerable extent in this city.

One young man, whose name we withhold, had considerable difficulty in converting his wife to the new theory, but finally succeeded, and was rather crestfallen when he discovered, a few months later, that his wife was "attracted" in another direction than to himself. He took the matter philosophically, however, and, by the infallible law of passional attraction, finally discovered his true partner in the person of another man's wife; and the four, re-mated are now said to be living lovingly under the same roof.

Another case is that of a woman of fine talents and accomplishments, and rather pretty withal, who actually believes in the new theory, and whose worser half not being the right one, selected the father of her child, a short time since, in the person of a respectable young married gentleman, and is now living on very short commons in an attic, where she is very much unnoticed by the fraternity of Free-Lovers and Leaguers. Instead of sustaining her as they ought, if they are in earnest, the leading and more respectable portion of them, at least, shrug their shoulders and say they are sorry this lady took the course she did; they think it was very unwise and premature; that society is not quite ready for the reception and experimental illustration of their ideas, while they go on preaching the theory which they condemn this zealous advocate for reducing to practice. The father of her child, who is said to be abundantly able to support her, declines doing so on the plea that such assistance would not leave the lady free, but put her in bonds, etc. It is due to her to say that she is very heroic; and in reply to a letter of condolence was quite indignant at expressions of pity and sympathy for her condition. She understands, she says, very well what she is about. She knew beforehand what she was taking upon herself. This was the way by which society was to be reformed and purified, and she was willing—nay, even proud—to bear her full share of the burden and disgrace, if the world chose to call it so, attending such reformation.

The following is one of the official bulletins issued by Mr. Stephen Pearl Andrews in his capacity of Chief of the League:

The League is an organized body, with its headquarters in New-York, its ramifications in the different towns and cities of the United States, and with a capacity of extension to all the countries of the world, its existence marks an epoch in the progress of liberality and thought. The elevation of its purposes transcends the petty ambitions of ordinary political parties as much as its universal toleration and breadth exceed the narrowing and belittling conditions of religious fanaticism and sect.

The League embraces men and women of all nations and creeds, whose religion is devotion to humanity and truth, without inquiring whether their conceptions are embodied in abstract principles or in personal forms. In the contemplation of the League all truth is equally divine truth, whether existing in the discoveries of science or in the revelations of a prophet; the interests of all rational beings, in all spheres, are the interests of each; and every healthy human aspiration is a guiding indication of the divine will.

At the same time no conformity of opinion is enforced, even in the construction put upon these principles, and still less in the form of their expression. They will be accepted by each individual mind only so far as their truth becomes obvious to it, and put in such forms of utterance as shall suit best each individual conception. Apart from the most external particulars relating to organization—such as the terms of admission, for example—no concurrence in action will be obligatory, beyond such as shall result naturally from attraction....

The League, although it has its political side, is not an American party, as defined by the accident of birth or by lines drawn across the surface of the globe. It is only American by its devotion to American ideas, and devoted to them only so far as they are right. It includes and admits people of all nationalities and opinions. It has among its members doctors and students of divinity, Christians of various denominations, Jews, infidels and atheists; and is equally open to the reception of Mohammedans and Pagans. It is probably the first society ever organized upon principles broad enough to include and to harmonize all those conflicting universities of men.

[WE] seek to discover those general truths which affect the spiritual nature of man and his relations to the central source of wisdom and love in the universe, upon which all thinking men can coincide, and to remove all superstition from the human mind by separating the true from the false in every creed and every shade of human opinion; to find, in fact, either a basis of unity or of legitimate diversity in matters of faith which will tend to the fullest recognition of the central Christian ideas—Love, and the actual brotherhood of the race.

There is a charm and attraction for the human mind in the sense of privacy.

While intolerance and persecutions of one kind or another are rife in the world for any freedom of opinion or conduct, which it is the right of another to entertain and pursue, secrecy furnishes a just and necessary protection against an impertinent and prying curiosity into the affairs of others. Society needs an escape from the repressive influences of sect, and of an ignorant and bigoted public opinion—some refuge where every man shall feel free to utter his truest and most intimate convictions upon all subjects, with the assurance that he is not "casting pearls before swine, who will turn again and rend him." It is the strong alone who can dispense with such protection. Hence, a defense for the weak is the next advantage secured.

Every human being has a right to his own privacy, among the prerogatives of life, liberty and the pursuit of happiness—a right which is constantly liable to be invaded in the prevalent ignorance of rights, and a right which men vindicate every day, with a jealous and vigilant respect for their own individuality, in the private and business relations of life. No limit can be put upon the exercise of that right by reference to the number of persons assembled in one place or taken into the secret. Hence, a valuable and important right of humanity is asserted and maintained.

Finally, there is a tendency on the part of all to attribute an undue weight, or to refuse the due weight, to opinions, arguments or measures, on the ground of personality. An abstract principle is equally true, whether discovered by a good or a bad man, American, Englishman or Turk. By secrecy in relation to the origin of views, this natural prejudice is forestalled and prevented. Hence, finally, by secrecy, the greatest practical degree of impartiality is reached.

The league is not the idea of a day, and is not, it is confidently believed, destined to an ephemeral existence. It is the natural confluence, at the right time, of the reformatory currents of thought which have been swelling during the last fifty years in the nations of Christendom, by the adoption of the only principle of consociation broad enough to accommodate the diversities, and to conciliate the good will and arouse the enthusiastic cooperation of all classes of men. The principles of its organization have been cautiously and profoundly studied during a long period of time. It embodies at present, in the extent of its organization, in its aggregate of numbers, of wealth, of social position, of education, of thought, and of the plain common sense of the masses of the people, an assemblage of elements which insures its rapid and permanent growth, and renders it, even already, in no mean sense, a notable power in the earth.

Free Love Grows Up

Free love might sound like a euphemism for group sex, but to Boston's Polyamory community, it's just like marriage—only bigger[4]

Alicia Potter

On a crooked street in Somerville is a purple house that no doubt raises eyebrows every few Thursdays. That's when it becomes a meeting site for Love Without Bounds, a local organization for young believers in free love.

On a recent evening, members of the group arrive in boisterous trios and hand-holding twosomes. They greet each other with deep, lingering embraces—no air kisses here—before plunking onto pillows or curling up together in corners. If ever a crowd spelled "orgy," it's this one.

But two hours pass, and the gathering fails to erupt into any sort of carnal acrobatics. At least the conversation is provocative, but again, not in the way you might think.

Sex is cheap," says a black-clad man, to nods of agreement. "I want relationships."

It feels like a big book club, with slightly different topics of conversation. The members talk about how to ask someone out if you're married. How to fend off jealousy if you're living with your lover and his lover. How to deal with a world of pairs when you're part of a trio. In short, they talk about what it's like to be polyamorous.

Polyamory is the philosophy and practice of loving more than one person at a time. It's different from polygamy—the practice of taking more than one wife—in that polyamory is legal, has nothing to do with Mormonism, and spans a whole range of commitment levels besides marriage. The possibilities are endless; as one 32-year-old man, married, with a child and a lover, puts it, "You don't have to end a relationship to start a new one."

Some polyamorists share a household with two or more common-law spouses; others have one "primary" partner, often a legal spouse, and one or more secondary relationships beyond that. There are triads and Vs. (See "Poly Lingo," right.) The only requirement is that all involved agree on the ground rules.

Polyamorists will point out that the practice has been around for much, if not all, of human history; in the Book of Genesis, for instance, Sarah lets Abraham beget children with her maid Hagar. Our own culture is steadfastly monogamous, but statistics hint that humans and monogamy can be an uneasy marriage: 25 to 60 percent of American men commit adultery, as do 15 to 40 percent of women. Half of all marriages end in divorce. Fourteen percent of all weddings include someone who's tying the knot for the third time.

For the people in this purple house, monogamy isn't a goal; it's a point of departure. And sex, while an important part of the equation, isn't the point.

The point is to find an alternative to monogamy that's less restrictive, but just as stable. The Love Without Bounds members talk about commitment and communication and responsibility with the sort of earnestness that we associate with a couples-therapy session. And, as impossible as it may sound, they are hoping for mainstream recognition.

Boston may be just the place to find it. The area is already home to an active bisexual community, which intersects with the polyamory scene; it's also the birthplace of Family Tree, one of the nation's oldest polyamory support groups, founded in 1975 and still flourishing.

For now, though, the quest for recognition isn't primarily political. It's personal. "Coming out" is a hot topic among the 25 Love Without Bounds members crowded into this tiny living room.

I can say I'm bisexual and everyone knows what that is," says Lisa, 26, who asked that only her first name be used. "People may not like it ... but I don't have to spend 20 minutes defining it. One day, I'd just like to say, 'Hi, I'm poly.' "

Poly lesson number one: the proper response to such an introduction is not "That's the same thing as swinging, right?"

Swinging is impersonal sex," says Deborah M. Anapol of San Rafael, California, author of Polyamory: The New Love Without Limits (Intinet Resource Center, 1997). "And while I'm not judging that, I don't consider it polyamory, because it doesn't focus on the relationship."

In fact, ask people why they became involved with polyamory and you won't hear much about spouse-swapping or other libidinal adventures (though, yes, threesomes and foursomes do occur). More likely, you'll hear love stories. Complex love stories.

There are two people who I think are really special, who I want to spend a lot of time with," says a 32-year-old man who's involved with two women. "It's wonderful to have a way to do that."

Sean Sullivan, 26, agrees. A slight man who looks a little like Jesus, he's been involved for four and a half years with Tamara, a bespectacled redhead whom he met as a freshman at Amherst College. That same year, three of his friends entered into a polyamorous relationship, a triad made up of two women and one man. Their closeness intrigued him: currently, he's involved with one of the women, while Tamara has recently started dating a second man. Soon, Sullivan hopes to house all the relationships under one roof.

There doesn't seem to be a "typical" poly relationship. Triads and Vs are popular among the polys I spoke to, with a long-distance lover here or there. Foursomes—say, a relationship with two married couples—are reportedly the hardest to pull off: first, both spouses must find a couple they like that much, and second, the intensity is difficult to balance (the husband may be smitten with the other woman more than his wife is smitten with the other man, for example). In the poly world, four really can be a crowd. But when the relationships work, whether with three or four or (in Sullivan's case) six, there's a payoff.

"Poly can be a marriage plus more," says Sullivan. "It can be a lifelong partnership [in which] people live together, help raise children together, grow old together. All of the things people speak of when they speak of family values apply even more to polyamory."

Idealistic? Sure. But perhaps no more so than the talk of heart-eyed romantics bent on finding "the One." Data show, too, that Sullivan's vision isn't all that deluded: Arline M. Rubin, of Brooklyn College, has conducted a 20-year study of polyamorous couples and has found that their relationships last just as long as supposedly monogamous ones. Among Family Tree's 75 members are polyamorous grandparents who enjoy not only 40 year-old marriages but also secondary relationships spanning 15 years.

Such commitment is possible, polys say, because their lifestyle diffuses a lot of relationship pressures. Banish the concept of "my one and only," and you lift the burden of meeting all of a lover's emotional and intellectual needs. In essence, polys are free to choose their paramours as most of us choose our friends: as complements to different sides of their personalities. One lover may share a spiritual outlook, another an ironic sense of humor, another a passion for horror movies.

Says Sullivan: "It allows for stronger emotional bonds than I'd have otherwise. I think if I was in a single relationship there would probably be aspects of myself that I wouldn't really be able to share with just one person. Additional relationships mean there's more of myself I can express."

He scratches his thick beard and shrugs. "There's just more companionship."

Sullivan first encountered polyamory as many others do: through science fiction. The summer before college, he read Fallway, by Paula Johnson, a novel in which six humans are raised in an alien world where group marriage is the norm. Something clicked.

I realized that felt very, very comfortable to me," Sullivan recalls. "It portrayed a group of people in a serious, committed relationship, similar to what a relationship would ordinarily be, but with more people, more personalities, more interests, and more dynamics possible. And that just stuck in my mind as something that felt right to me in a way that other [traditional] relationships didn't."

Early poly primers were books such as the 1970s bestseller Open Marriage, by George and Nena O'Neill. But it's science-fiction: Robert Heinlein's classic Stranger in a Strange Land (1961) and Robert Rimmer's, The Harrad Experiment (1966), that polys credit with sustaining polyamory beyond the Aquarian Age. Both novels uphold multiple commitments as the love life of the future.

As a result, the poly subculture—which at this point eludes accurate population figures—doesn't look quite like what you might expect. Sure, there are some polys who could have driven the last van out of Woodstock. Most, however, are cerebral and articulate—more geeky than granola. An uncanny number of polys I met work in high tech, as well as in "helping professions" such as health care (which, according to Anapol, attract people who connect with others easily).

The preponderance of techies is no coincidence. At least in the Boston area, polyamorists tend to build communities via the Internet. The year-old Love Without Bounds started when two polys put up a Web page and sent out e-mails encouraging attendance at a new poly support group.

Poly dating, as you can imagine, doesn't usually start out with a couple of drinks at the Wonder Bar ("Yeah, that's my husband over there, but he wouldn't mind if we got together. No, really, he wouldn't mind...."). Polys meet at poly parties, at polyamorist gatherings like Love Without Bounds meetings, and at other events that attract a poly crowd, such as science-fiction conventions. (Polyamorists also overlap with a few other subcultures: pagans, goths, nudists.) They meet through online personal ads and through ads in the poly magazine Loving More, which recently sponsored a conference that featured relationship-building workshops and social events in New York. Many entertain long-distance relationships with a lover, as the Boston poly scene can get pretty small pretty fast. "It gets a little incestuous around here," admits Lisa, with a laugh.

Recent events should help to widen the local circle. In April, 900 people attended the Fifth International Conference on Bisexuality—at which the workshops on polyamory were among the most popular. Likewise, in the last month, the poly-Boston e-mail list, which keeps polys informed of parties and events, spun off a second list to publicize poly activities in the Southeastern Massachusetts and Providence area.

Polys I spoke to insist that even without panel discussions or Heinlein novels or jobs in computer programming, they'd still be polyamorous. They talk about "relationship orientation"—a propensity for handling multiple commitments that varies from person to person, like the spectrum of sexual orientation. Some people are monogamous; most are in the middle; some are hard-wired polyamorous.

"For me it's not a question of loving polyamory," says Alan Wexelblat, 36, who in 18 years of dating has always had poly relationships. "It's who I am. Even if I were only in one relationship and following monogamous rules, that doesn't change me, just like a bisexual person can be in a relationship with any one person and yet still be identified as bisexual."

It's an interesting idea, especially given the inability of many people to stay reliably within the constraints of monogamy: could it be that those cheating louts are polyamorous but just don't know it?

Likely so, says anthropologist Helen Fisher, author of Anatomy of Love: A Natural History of Mating, Marriage, and Why We Stray (W.W. Norton, 1992). But they're not the only ones: we're all potentially polyamorous.

You would think that more people would be [practicing] polyamory, because, evolutionarily, we're built to have multiple relationships," she says. "We're built to fool around."

Anthropologists now believe that, at the most, 2 percent of all species are completely faithful sexually (among them the Nile crocodile, the American toad, the dung beetle, and some desert wood lice). In her book, Fisher points out that anthropological studies of 853 human societies showed only 16 percent practicing monogamy as we typically define it. And, as we know, even monogamy doesn't guarantee fidelity; in many of the monogamous cultures, researchers discovered covert or tolerated affairs.

Fisher has an explanation for our longings: she says that our brain circuitry has evolved so that the chemical reactions associated with different kinds of love—attachment, infatuation, lust—function independently of one another. In other words, we can find comfort with an old lover, flirt with a cute coworker, and fantasize about that beautiful stranger on the TV—all in the course of an hour.

However," Fisher cautions, "we're not built to share. We get jealous. That puts the human animal in a pickle."

Polyamorists, she says, have found a way out. "They're honestly dealing with the fact that we're not built to be faithful," she explains. "They accept that inevitability and channel it in ways that minimize pain and maximize joy. They attempt paradise."

This paradise, though, can be very unfamiliar territory. Take this scene, for example: Rob Mohns, 25, nuzzles his girlfriend Aileen, 22, while two feet away, knitting a scarf, is his fiancée, 26-year-old Megan O'Neal. As Mohns and his new love practically roll off the couch, O'Neal's face is serene.

"I don't usually get jealous," says O'Neal. "And when I do, it takes me by surprise. It's kind of good, because it usually means that something in this situation isn't working for me, that I need to figure out what it is and go talk to the person."

Spend some time with polyamorists and you realize that communication is what keeps their relationships alive. Polys talk about everything: who they want to go out with, what they do on their dates, how their relationships are progressing.

Poly commitments give new meaning to "the Rules." To the average monogamist, some of these relationship statutes might seem mind-boggling: as a polyamorist, for example, you might negotiate whether or not your lover can sleep with another in your bed. Other rules are kind of silly: one man's girlfriend asked that he accompany only her to first-run movies. Safe sex—condoms, dental dams—is a given; a long-time Family Tree member reports that in nearly 25 years, there has been only one sexually-transmitted-disease scare, and that was a false alarm. But many guidelines are simple and practical: no surprises, no keeping secrets with secondary lovers, and no cheating, which in this context means you don't get involved with someone new without apprising the others.

No, we're not running around doing whatever we damn well please," says Aileen. "We have to talk about things and be open. If we don't, it's disastrous." In that respect, monogamy and polyamory have a lot in common.

In another respect—public acceptance—they have very little in common. However widely practiced polyamory is in other societies, Helen Fisher doesn't think our own culture will ever embrace the idea of Rob and Aileen and Megan.

Americans, says Fisher, are "wedded to the notion of lifelong pair bonding and fidelity. We'll see more divorce and adultery rather than an attempt to channel our urges in an honest way. The majority of Americans will not endorse polyamory—ever."

Our culture, Fisher says, won't try what it doesn't know. Though she believes marrying for life will become rarer and rarer as we live longer, monogamy itself won't likely come into question. In other words, our allegiance to the idea of commitment will far outlast the commitments themselves.

In his book Monogamy (Pantheon, 1996), a collection of thoughts on the subject, British author Adam Phillips puts it this way: "Our belief in the couple—in good couplings—is a measure of our sense of hope." No matter how high the divorce rate spikes, the Sunday paper promises to abound with beaming brides and grooms. Monogamy is like religion, says Phillips: it's a leap of faith we're happy to take.

Polyamory, by contrast, just seems to make people feel uncomfortable, threatened, and maybe even a little guilty. When I mentioned to a friend—a friend with a history of overlapping relationships—that many of us have brushed with polyamory, whether by dating multiple people or by just cheating outright, she replied: "Not me."

And for those who have endured the pain of infidelity, the reaction to the idea of polyamory can be virulent. One polyamorous woman tells of being accosted by a divorcée whose husband had strayed: "She was very condemning and accusatory. She said [polyamory] is wrong, that she'd been really hurt by someone who slept with someone else. I thought, Hey, I didn't sleep with your husband, ma'am!"

Then there's that little problem of sex. No matter how many safety guidelines people obey, society still tsk-tsks at multiple partners as a manifestation of promiscuity and ambivalence about commitment. Katherine Reeder, a Cambridge therapist, admits that she'd question a couple with outside relationships: "I don't think it's necessarily pathological, but [multiple relationships] still break a bond and prevent the deepest possible connection. I'd try to show [the couple] there's a deeper meaning of love."

This type of talk riles polys like Rob Mohns. "People just don't get that it's not about lack of commitment," he says. "It's ironic considering what our culture does accept. Serial monogamy—one [relationship] after another after another—that's okay. Cheating, while it's not nice and you don't want to get caught, is tacitly accepted because it's the norm. But being seriously involved with [two women]? Now, that's not okay!"

Despite such reactions, polyamorists see hope. Brett Hill, editor of Loving More magazine, compares the poly movement now to the gay movement 25 years ago, when many Americans were just learning that friends, coworkers, and other "normal" people were gay.

One of the reasons I've chosen to be out," says Alan Wexelblat, who's a PhD candidate at the MIT Media Lab, "is because ... I am an example, whether I like it or not, of who poly people are and how they behave." One day soon, says Hill, you may learn that your cubicle-mate has not only a fiancé but a boyfriend, too.

But it might not be that simple. Gay relationships are becoming more accepted partly because they're proving stable and committed—that is, they can be just as monogamous as straight relationships. As a result, in spite of the furor over Heather Has Two Mommies, a lot of Americans are proving able to cope with the conceptual leap from the traditional definition of the nuclear family—a man and a woman—to a family structure that revolves around two men or two women. But two men and one woman? That's another story.

[Polyamory] is just weirder," says Teddy, 23, who's monogamous. "I just wasn't raised seeing that type of relationship. At least with gay and straight marriages, everyone's on the same wavelength."

Wexelblat refuses to buy it. "I think the [relationship] configuration is less important than the answers to such questions as: Is it a committed relationship? Do they share accommodations? Do they share financial responsibilities? Are they working on raising kids together?

Those are things that are really important issues for the poly community," he continues, "and to the extent that the gay-rights movement makes headway on those issues, they make headway for us." The polyamory movement does show signs of advancing into the public consciousness. Both MTV and ABC's 20/20 are preparing segments on polyamory to air later this fall, and a couple of documentaries are in the works. Meanwhile, political initiatives to change zoning laws (some towns won't let more than two unrelated people live together) and partner benefits are inching along.

Most promising for polys is that some report they have come out to coworkers and family with little controversy; they even feel comfortable decorating their desks with, yes, pictures of both their primary partner and their lovers. And that will continue, says Wexelblat. "Even if the country as a whole enters into a collective denial and says, 'No, there are no poly people, we refuse to acknowledge your existence,' that doesn't prevent us from existing," he explains. "It doesn't prevent more people from discovering who they are and how they want to live."

Wexelblat—who'll be married next spring, with his lover of eight years in attendance—shakes his head: "You might as well shovel sand against the tide."

Polyamory, Polygamy & Multi-Parent Families

Excerpts from Models of Open Relationships

Kathy Labriola[5]

Edited Relevant Excerpts
Reprinted with permission

INTRODUCTION

Heterosexual, monogamous marriage is sanctioned by society, religion, and the law as the most valued /acceptable form of sexual relating. As a result, most people have not been exposed to other ways of life. In fact, we are so heavily socialized to believe in the ideals of monogamy and marriage, that many people cannot even imagine any other option. In fact, many successful models do exist. This is an overview of the three main types of non-monogamous relationships, including variations on those models and the pros and cons of each. These models have been adapted and customized to fit individual lifestyles, which provides limitless possibilities for accommodating specific emotional and psychological needs.

THE PRIMARY/SECONDARY MODEL

This is the most commonly practiced style of open relating for couples. This model is popular because it is so similar to the western marriage tradition, which brings the full force of church and state to protect the interests and primacy of the couple. For most married or co-habiting couples, it is not such a stretch to have a few outside relationships as long as they know that the primary commitment is to the marriage. They can still be married, have children, live together, be socially acceptable, and "live a normal life", keeping their outside relationships secret from friends and family. It doesn't require making any radical changes in your lifestyle or worldview. One major benefit for many couples is that they feel secure that they won't be abandoned, because their spouse has agreed that outside relationships will be secondary. This is simpler and easier to organize logistically than other forms of open relationships. If there is any conflict over time, loyalty or commitment, the spouse always gets priority.

In this model, the couple is primary, and any other relationships revolve around the couple. Couples of any and all sexual orientations allow each spouse/partner to have outside sexual relationships, either casual or long-term. These outside relationships are secondary. If any conflict develops, the primary relationship takes precedence. The couple usually lives together, shares finances, spends weekends, holidays, and vacations together. It is most frequently practiced by married people or other couples in long-term relationships. The couple makes the rules; secondary lovers have little power over decisions and are not allowed to negotiate for what they want.

There are several variations of the primary/secondary model:

One or both partners have a long or short-term romantic liaison with others. Couples who swing attend sex parties, meet through personals ads or through various activities and networks. Some couples only have sex with other couples, others engage in three-way sex, only have sex with their partner present or absent, one partner freely allows the other to have recreational sex as long as there is no emotional involvement.

The outside lovers usually do not live with them, spend much less time together, have very little voice in decisions and rule-making, and must arrange scheduling around the demands of the primary relationship. Some couples have rules that each spouse has veto power over any new lovers that his or her spouse may choose. In other words, if a woman is interested in a relationship with a new man, her husband has the power to veto that relationship before it starts, for any reason. Other couples allow each person to sleep with whomever they choose, but make rules about how much time they can spend with their other lovers, whether they can spend the night away from home, whether they can spend any weekend time with them, and other restrictions on these trists.

Other partnerships are primary/secondary in form but have a hybrid quality, a modern twist on the traditional married man with a mistress on the side who knows him as well or better than his wife. Traditionally, the outside partner was never acknowledged in public or private. Today's open relationships feature candor, honesty, acknowledgement and a degree of study before the secondary relationship even begins.

As with traditional couplings, a major drawback of this model is that outside relationships are not so simple or easy to predict or control. Having a sexual relationship with someone else often leads to emotional involvement. Falling in love has been known to cause a crisis in the primary relationship and even divorce. For some people, initiating an outside sexual relationship is opening a door to many possibilities; one is that a secondary relationship will grow into something else that does not fit neatly into the confines of the model.

Many people who become "secondary" lovers become resentful of being subjugated to the couple, and begin to issue ultimatums. For this model to be successful, couples must be very convinced that their relationship is strong enough to weather these ups and downs. Conversely, some couples who start with this model decide eventually to shift to some form of the Multiple Primary Partnering models to allow secondary relationships the opportunity for growth and development equal to the primary relationship.

MULTIPLE PRIMARY PARTNER MODEL

There are many variations on this model; the key factor is that all such relationships involve three or more people in a primary relationship in which all members are equal partners. Instead of a couple having priority and control, each partner has equal power to negotiate for what they want in the relationship, in terms of time, commitment, living situation, financial arrangements, sex, and other issues.

Polyfidelity features a closed family unit with 3 or more adults. This is a "group marriage" model, essentially the same as being married—except you're married to two or more people. Usually consisting of three to six adults, all partners live together, share finances, children, and household responsibilities. Depending on the sexual orientation of the members, all adults in the family are sexual partners. For instance, if all members are heterosexual, all the women have sexual relationships with all the men. If the women are bisexual, they may have sexual relationships with the women as well as the men, and so on. However, this is a closed system, and sex is only allowed between family members, there are no outside sexual relations. Some families are open to taking on new partners if all members agree, the new partner then becomes an equal member of the family. Polyfidelity became famous during the '70s and '80s by the Kerista commune in San Francisco. The most common form of this model is a triad of two women and one man, or two men and one woman. Recently, a number of polyfidelitous families have formed with two heterosexual couples who live together as a foursome.

Jane and Tom and Mary and Bill all live together as a polyfidelitous family, and they have three children. They pool their incomes and make house payments, buy food, and provide for the children collectively, sharing child rearing and household responsibilities.

PROS AND CONS OF POLYFIDELITY

Polyfidelity can be a richly rewarding experience, creating an extended family and intentional community. Pooling resources is economical and ecological, and can reduce the stress of child rearing by spreading the work and the responsibility among several adults rather than just one or two parents. However, polyfidelity requires a very high level of compatibility and affinity between all partners. Everyone must agree on where to live, what to cook for dinner, how clean the house should be, how much money to spend and on what, whether to have children and how to raise them. Most people find it difficult enough to locate one partner they can successfully live with for the "long haul", much less two, three, four or more. And living together as a group decreases privacy and autonomy, often leading to interpersonal conflicts and stress. Living in a group requires excellent interpersonal skills, clear communication, assertiveness, co-operation, and flexibility in order to accommodate everyone's needs. Picking compatible partners and being accommodating are both key to success.

MULTIPLE PRIMARY PARTNERS—OPEN MODEL

This model is very different from polyfidelity in that all partners are given much more autonomy and flexibility in developing any relationships they choose and defining those relationships on their own terms. In the primary/secondary model the couple is the center of power, in closed polyfidelity the group makes decisions together. In the Multiple Primary Partners Open Model, the individual is the basic unit and is empowered to make his or her own rules and decisions. Partners may choose to live together, alone or with one or more partners that best suits their needs. This model is open, in that each partner has the right to choose other lovers at any time without the approval of any other partner. Each relationship evolves independently of each partners' other relationships, with rules and level of commitment to be negotiated and (re-negotiated) by the individuals. No one expects to veto a potential partner or "pull rank" and insist on being number one.

PROS AND CONS OF THE OPEN MODEL

There is much more fluidity in this approach, as relationships are allowed to evolve over time with very few rules to direct or restrict their direction or level of commitment. However, it is also much less predictable and may cause anxiety for people who like more structure and prefer a clear hierarchy.

Because all partners are considered equal, each partner can negotiate for what they want. However, all this "processing" requires time, effort, and excellent communication skills. And some people find the potential for conflicting loyalties to be too threatening. For instance, which partner will spend holidays or vacations with you? Will they both go, will they alternate each year, will you spend part of each holiday or vacation with each one? If one partner is going through a crisis, can they demand more of your time and commitment? If you are experiencing problems in one relationship or feel more drawn toward another partner, what behavior is appropriate? Weighing your own needs and the desires of each partner can be very stressful and confusing. Some people find this model requires too much thinking, problem-solving and "going with the flow", and prefer a more rigid structure such as the primary-secondary model or the polyfidelity model.

MULTIPLE NON-PRIMARY RELATIONSHIPS

While the first two models stress commitment and primary relationships, some people prefer to remain essentially single but participate in more than one relationship. They are not looking for a committed relationship. For them, non-monogamy offers the intimacy, love, and sexual satisfaction of involvement in relationships without the constraints of a primary relationship. This model works best for people who have a serious, all-consuming commitment to something other than relationships; people who are very busy with their work, their art, raising children alone, or political involvements. Usually they prefer relationships with people who, like themselves, want less commitment, or people who already have a primary relationship and are looking for a "secondary" relationship. People involved in this model usually don't make a lot of rules about their relationships, and retain a very high degree of personal freedom and autonomy. They usually live alone and make relationships a relatively low priority in their lives.

PROS AND CONS ON NON-PRIMARY MODEL

For this model to be successful, it is crucial to carefully choose partners who will be satisfied with a less committed relationship, and to communicate that clearly to potential partners. This model often works great as long as all parties are too busy or too committed elsewhere to want a primary relationship. However, conflict can arise when circumstances change and one person has more time or develop a desire for a primary relationship. For instance, when Maria finishes her Ph.D., or when Jacob gets a promotion and no longer has to travel for his job, or a married lover gets divorced—they may suddenly demand more time and commitment or even demand a monogamous relationship. Such a change often proves fatal to the existing relationship. However, sometimes people see such a challenge as an opportunity for growth and are able to change their relationship to accommodate everyone's needs.

CONCLUSION

There are many different types of open relationships. For "relationship junkies," there is no one-size-fits-all. There are relationships that are suitable for every age and stage of an individual's life. The models would fit your needs at 25 may be very different at age 50. Outside of age and stage considerations, a lot depends on the individual and how much security they require in a relationship? As if it were guaranteed. Can the need to feel that you're "Number One" or the "One and Only" ever really be satisfied in today's society? What is the optimal level privacy and personal freedom needed to feel comfortable in life? Are individuals truly free to contemplate whether they are happiest living alone, with another person, or with a group? What pushes your psychological buttons? How much time and energy do you have to devote to relationships? What are your expectations of love? To be happy in relationships of any kind you must first know who you are, what

> you want and why you want it. To be happy in an open relationship you have to understand all these things and a sense of what would most likely work for you. Secondly, you must be able to articulately communicate what you want to potential partners in an honest and clear way. And last, but certainly not least, it is crucial to pick partners who want the same type of relationship and are comfortable with your chosen way of life. Excellent interpersonal and communications skills go a long way towards achieving these goals, along with a willingness to negotiate to satisfy the needs of those to whom you are committed.

Dr. Geri D. Weitzman wrote an article entitled ***What Psychology Professionals Should Know About Polyamory Individuals***, which she presented at the 8th Annual Diversity Conference on Albany, New York, March 1999. She summarized the findings of several scientific studies as follows.

> In 1976, Knapp administered a battery of standardized psychological assessment measures to a sample of polyamorous couples. No significant differences were found between the couples in her sample and the general population norms. "That is, neither group was particularly neurotic, immature, promiscuous, maladjusted, pathological, or sexually inadequate ... The response patterns suggested a modal type of individual in a sexually open marriage who was individualistic, an academic achiever, creative, nonconforming, stimulated by complexity and chaos, inventive, relatively unconventional and indifferent to what others said, concerned about his/her own personal values and ethical systems, and willing to take risks to explore possibilities."[6]

We now know that the liberty embodied in the Fourteenth Amendment extends to the choice of whether to live a poly lifestyle. How do we know when a state regulation that hinders that freedom crosses an unacceptable boundary?

Scholar Elizabeth Emens, in her article ***Monogamy's Law: Compulsory Monogamy and Polygamous Existence***, describes a Tennessee court's removal of a 3-year-old from the custody of her mother, April Divilbiss. Divilbiss lived with her husband and another man and appeared on TV describing the possibility of bringing another woman into their relationship. The case is interesting due to the rapid removal upon intervention of paternal grandparents of a non-marital child. The US Supreme Court has given primary decisionmaking authority concerning visitation and other pertinent matters to custodial parents while denying grandparents standing to sue altogether.

Consider the equal protection issues that may have arisen for individuals like April Divilbiss, if her case had come up just two year later, in light of the Supreme Court's rational in the following case.

Troxel v. Granville[7]

June 5, 2000

Justice O'Connor announced the judgment of the Court and delivered an opinion, in which The Chief Justice, Justice Ginsburg, and Justice Breyer join.

> Section 26.10.160(3) of the Revised Code of Washington permits "[a]ny person" to petition a superior court for visitation rights "at any time," and authorizes that court to grant such visitation rights whenever "visitation may serve the best inter-

est of the child." Petitioners Jenifer and Gary Troxel petitioned a Washington Superior Court for the right to visit their grandchildren, Isabelle and Natalie Troxel. Respondent Tommie Granville, the mother of Isabelle and Natalie, opposed the petition. The case ultimately reached the Washington Supreme Court, which held that §26.10.160(3) unconstitutionally interferes with the fundamental right of parents to rear their children.

Tommie Granville and Brad Troxel shared a relationship that ended in June 1991. The two never married, but they had two daughters, Isabelle and Natalie. Jenifer and Gary Troxel are Brad's parents, and thus the paternal grandparents of Isabelle and Natalie. After Tommie and Brad separated in 1991, Brad lived with his parents and regularly brought his daughters to his parents' home for weekend visitation. Brad committed suicide in May 1993. Although the Troxels at first continued to see Isabelle and Natalie on a regular basis after their son's death, Tommie Granville informed the Troxels in October 1993 that she wished to limit their visitation with her daughters to one short visit per month.

In December 1993, the Troxels commenced the present action by filing, in the Washington Superior Court for Skagit County, a petition to obtain visitation rights with Isabelle and Natalie. The Troxels filed their petition under two Washington statutes. Only the latter statute is at issue in this case. Section 26.10.160(3) provides: "Any person may petition the court for visitation rights at any time including, but not limited to, custody proceedings. The court may order visitation rights for any person when visitation may serve the best interest of the child whether or not there has been any change of circumstances." At trial, the Troxels requested two weekends of overnight visitation per month and two weeks of visitation each summer. Granville did not oppose visitation altogether, but instead asked the court to order one day of visitation per month with no overnight stay. In 1995, the Superior Court issued an oral ruling and entered a visitation decree ordering visitation one weekend per month, one week during the summer, and four hours on both of the petitioning grandparents' birthdays.

Granville appealed, during which time she married Kelly Wynn. Before addressing the merits of Granville's appeal, the Washington Court of Appeals remanded the case to the Superior Court for entry of written findings of fact and conclusions of law. On remand, the Superior Court found that visitation was in Isabelle and Natalie's best interests:

"The Petitioners [the Troxels] are part of a large, central, loving family, all located in this area, and the Petitioners can provide opportunities for the children in the areas of cousins and music. " ... The court took into consideration all factors regarding the best interest of the children and considered all the testimony before it. The children would be benefitted from spending quality time with the Petitioners, provided that that time is balanced with time with the childrens' [sic] nuclear family. The court finds that the childrens' [sic] best interests are served by spending time with their mother and stepfather's other six children." Approximately nine months after the Superior Court entered its order on remand, Granville's husband formally adopted Isabelle and Natalie.

The Washington Court of Appeals reversed the lower court's visitation order and dismissed the Troxels' petition for visitation, holding that nonparents lack standing to seek visitation under §26.10.160(3) unless a custody action is pending. In the Court of Appeals' view, that limitation on nonparental visitation actions was "consistent with the constitutional restrictions on state interference with parents' fundamental liberty interest in the care, custody, and management of their children." Having resolved the case on the statutory ground, however, the Court of Appeals did not expressly pass on Granville's constitutional challenge to the visitation statute.

The Washington Supreme Court granted the Troxels' petition for review and, after consolidating their case with two other visitation cases, affirmed. The court disagreed with the Court of Appeals' decision on the statutory issue and found that the plain language of §26.10.160(3) gave the Troxels standing to seek visitation, irrespective of whether a custody action was pending. The Washington Supreme Court nevertheless agreed with the Court of Appeals' ultimate conclusion that the Troxels could not obtain visitation of Isabelle and Natalie pursuant to §26.10.160(3). The court rested its decision on the Federal Constitution, holding that §26.10.160(3) unconstitutionally infringes on the fundamental right of parents to rear their children. In the court's view, there were at least two problems with the nonparental visitation statute. First, according to the Washington Supreme Court, the Constitution permits a State to interfere with the right of parents to rear their children only to prevent harm or potential harm to a child. Section 26.10.160(3) fails that standard because it requires no threshold showing of harm. Second, by allowing " 'any person' to petition for forced visitation of a child at 'any time' with the only requirement being that the visitation serve the best interest of the child," the Washington visitation statute sweeps too broadly. "It is not within the province of the state to make significant decisions concerning the custody of children merely because it could make a 'better' decision." The Washington Supreme Court held that "[p]arents have a right to limit visitation of their children with third persons," and that between parents and judges, "the parents should be the ones to choose whether to expose their children to certain people or ideas." Four justices dissented from the Washington Supreme Court's holding on the constitutionality of the statute.

We granted certiorari, 527 U.S. 1069 (1999), and *now affirm the judgment.*

The March 20, 2006 issue of Newsweek Magazine featured the following article, entitled ***Polygamists, Unite!***[8]

> Marlyne Hammon knows what it's like to feel hated and hunted. In 1953, when she was an infant, her father—along with dozens of other men in her tiny community of Short Creek, Ariz.—was arrested and sent to jail on charges of polygamy. She, her mother and siblings were forcibly exiled from the community and sent to live with a family in a nearby city. Her father was released after a week, but because the family feared further prosecution, they lived apart and corresponded in secret for the next six years. "Our community had this idea that we should live our lives quietly to avoid trouble," she says. "We were taught not to make a big ruckus."
>
> Not anymore. Hammon, who's involved in a polygamous relationship, is a founding member of the Centennial Park Action Committee, a group that lobbies for decriminalization of the practice. She's among a new wave of polygamy activists emerging in the wake of the gay-marriage movement—just as a federal lawsuit challenging anti-polygamy laws makes its way through the courts and a new show about polygamy debuts on HBO. "Polygamy rights is the next civil-rights battle," says Mark Henkel, who, as founder of the Christian evangelical polygamy organization TruthBearer.org, is at the forefront of the movement. His argument: if Heather can have two mommies, she should also be able to have two mommies and a daddy. Henkel and Hammon have been joined by other activist groups like Principle Voices, a Utah-based group run by wives from polygamous marriages. Activists point to Canada, where, in January, a report commissioned by the Justice Department recommended decriminalizing polygamy.
>
> There's a sound legal argument for making the controversial practice legal, says Brian Barnard, the lawyer for a Utah couple, identified in court documents only

> as G. Lee Cooke and D. Cooke, who filed suit after being denied a marriage license for an additional wife. Though the case was struck down by a federal court last year, it's now being considered by the Tenth Circuit Court of Appeals, and Barnard plans to use the same argument—that *Lawrence v. Texas*, the 2003 sodomy case in which the U.S. Supreme Court ruled that individuals have "the full right to engage in private conduct without government intervention," should also apply to polygamous relationships.
>
> Almost always, when the legalization of polygamy is brought up, it's used to make a case against gay marriage. Most notably, Sen. Rick Santorum of Pennsylvania told the Associated Press in 2003 that legalizing gay sex would pave the way for legalized bigamy, polygamy and incest. This "slippery slope" argument angers some gay-rights activists who see the issues as being completely separate. "I frankly would not love to see an article [about polygamy advocacy] in NEWSWEEK because this is the connection that our opponents make, and we feel it's a specious one," says Carisa Cunningham, director of public affairs for Gay and Lesbian Advocates and Defenders. Polygamy activists aren't thrilled with the association, either. Though they closely watch the gay-marriage battle, they are generally religious and conservative—and, like Henkel and Hammon, believe that homosexual behavior is a sin.
>
> Polygamy is a lifestyle choice for a relative handful of Americans. Experts estimate that there are between 30,000 and 50,000 polygamists in the United States who practice a form of Mormonism, though the Church of Jesus Christ of Latter-day Saints, most commonly associated with the term "Mormon," banned the practice in 1890. There's also a growing number of evangelical Christian and Muslim polygamists—some experts say they may even exceed the number who describe themselves as Mormon.
>
> Polygamy rights, not surprisingly, get little support beyond those who are actually polygamists. A May 2005 Gallup poll found that 92 percent of Americans oppose the practice, which is illegal in all 50 states. But the tiny movement may get its biggest boost from an unexpected source: HBO. This week the network debuted a new drama, "Big Love," which offers a sympathetic look at a polygamous family. "We value this as our way of life," says Hammon. "We've got to have a voice in this." Polygamists are finally speaking up—but will anyone listen?

This debate promises to be around for some time. Social scientific research is needed to assess problems relating to state failure to adequately protect young women and children from coercion and children from sexual abuse. Traditional notions of privacy left many vulnerable to physical, sexual and emotional abuse. See, for example, a 1998 article in the New York Times, entitled ***Utah Struggles With A Revival of Polygamy***:[9]

> What has fueled the issue of polygamy statewide as well as nationally is the case of a 16-year-old girl who stumbled into a remote gas station in northern Utah this summer. Covered with fresh bruises on her legs, arms and buttocks, authorities said the girl had run seven miles through the night, fleeing her father's belt and the future he had ordained for her: marriage to her uncle, and life as his 15th wife.
>
> The teen-ager's 911 call has resulted in a charge against her father, John Daniel Kingston, a leader of a wealthy but secretive polygamous clan based in a Salt Lake suburb. Rowenna Erickson, a Tapestry member who left the clan in 1991, said that incest, child marriage and birth defects were becoming more frequent in the clan, which numbers about 1,500 people.

> Although Ms. Erickson said the value of the clan's ranches and companies totaled more than $150 million, she asserted that women and children in the group often lived in poverty, earning minimum wages from business and receiving food stamps.

An unfortunate consequence of the polygamy debate is the scant attention it gives to issues relating to the best interest of the children in these families.

Hollywood does nothing to pick up the slack. In 2006, HBO began a new series that it advertises as follows:

> Think having three wives is a dream come true? Meet Bill Henrickson, a modern-day Utah polygamist who lives in suburban Salt Lake City with his three wives, seven children, and a mounting avalanche of debt and demands. The owner of a growing chain of home improvement stores, Bill struggles to balance the financial and emotional needs of Barb, Nicki and Margene, who live in separate, adjacent houses and take turns sharing their husband each night. While managing the household finances together and routinely sharing "family home nights," they try to keep simmering jealousies in check and their arrangement a secret—polygamy is illegal in Utah and banned by the mainstream Mormon Church. Adding to Bill's woes are a series of crises affecting his parents, who live on a fundamentalist compound in rural Utah, and his ruthless father-in-law, Roman, the powerful head of the polygamist commune where his parents live. Bold, funny and wholly original, Big Love explores the evolving institution of marriage through a typical atypical family.[10]

The London Free Press recently published a story that also deals with multiple parenting. The trend of debating these questions as a matter of law ad infinitim is that all eyes are fixated upon questions of marriage and defining family for their potential impact on what is essentially a debate about monogamy.

3-Parent Family Stirs Debate

By Jennifer O'Brien[11]

> The court ruling recognizing a dad and two moms wins praise and prompts warnings.
>
> Gay rights groups celebrated a landmark court ruling yesterday, while family values groups said the decision to give a London boy two moms is an attack on the traditional family.
>
> The boy's father, who sees his five-year-old son regularly, was "thrilled" but didn't want to comment until he had spoken with the boy's mothers, who are on vacation with the son, said Alf Mamo, lawyer for the father.
>
> "After three years of being in the court system, he's happy to have his son's reality recognized," Mamo said. "The decision respects the dignity of the non-biological mother, which she deserves as a full participating parent in the family."
>
> Gay rights organization Egale Canada says the ruling by the Ontario Court of Appeal recognizes the reality of lesbian couples who are already raising children with the father's involvement.
>
> But supporters of traditional marriage and family values warned the decision offered a "watered down" interpretation of family and could open up the possibility

of multiple parents, perhaps as many as six, for a child—and unforeseen legal headaches if those relationships fail.

"Something that is a social policy decision certainly shouldn't be decided by one courtroom," said Dave Quist, head of the Institute of Marriage and Family Canada.

The government should "hit the pause button" on legislation involving three-parent families as well as same-sex marriage, in-vitro fertilization and stem cell research, to give a commission time to evaluate such issues, he said.

"This will certainly impact everyone in Ontario if it is not appealed."

Locally, the 400-member traditional family values group Citizen Impact also hopes for an appeal.

"It is a situation with lots of ramification and it should have been decided in Parliament," said Jack Baribeau of Citizen Impact.

Citizen Impact has opposed the move to grant mom status to the boy's non-biological parent since 2003 when the case was first heard in a London courtroom.

At that time, Judge David Aston dismissed the application from the same-sex couple on the grounds he didn't have the jurisdiction to make the declaration sought.

The appeal court found recent rulings that have "moved toward a broader discretion, under the impact of changing social conditions and the weight of opinion."

Baribeau said the court was "stepping beyond (its) boundaries."

"I'm not saying individual situations can't be OK. It's just not what's best, as an ideal, and the laws need to reflect what's best," he said.

Former London MP Pat O'Brien, who left the Liberal party over the same-sex marriage issue, said he was disappointed by the ruling.

"Words like mother, father, marriage—could they become meaningless?" he asked.

O'Brien, who is retired but works as a consultant in hopes of getting the government to reverse the same-sex marriage legislation, said the court went beyond its jurisdiction.

But Mamo disagreed.

"The court was able to find a solution in the situation where they acknowledge the legislation does not contemplate the circumstances," he said. "The reason we have a charter is to hold values of individuals as being higher than politics. These decisions are too important to be left to the whims of any particular party or consideration of the cabinet of the day."

He scoffed at the suggestion such a ruling could lead to confusion with multiple-parent families.

"Wouldn't that be wonderful if we see people lined up wanting those responsibilities that a parent has? I really don't see that happening, though."

Related concerns mirror the early debate on open adoption versus non-disclosure of identities. The January 2005 issue of Medical News Today published the following article in its fertility segment.

Parents' attitudes to sperm donation—still some concerns about being open[12]

Two studies to be published in Europe's leading reproductive medicine journal, Human Reproduction, provide a generally optimistic picture about attitudes towards the increasing trend in society to be more open about the use of sperm donors. However, they indicate that not all parents are comfortable with the new openness, there are still many unknowns about attitudes and further research and public education will be needed.

It became compulsory last June in the Netherlands for all sperm donors to be identified. The Fertility Center at Leiden University Hospital has run a double-track system since 1994 allowing couples to choose either an anonymous or an identifiable donor whose details would be available to children when they are 16. This has enabled researchers led by Dr Anne Brewaeys of the university's medical center to compare the reasons for the different choices and provide some insight into the potential impact of the new legislation.

In the UK from April ('05) all children conceived via donors will be entitled to have identifying information when they are 18. In a study led by Dr Emma Lycett of the Family and Child Psychology Research Centre of London's City University, researchers compared the emotions and experiences of parents who favoured openness with their children with those who were not keen on disclosure.

The Netherlands Study

The Dutch study involved 105 couples seeking a sperm donor for their first child. Sixty-one percent were heterosexuals and 39% were lesbian couples. All received counselling before treatment (which did not include upfront advice about the choice of donor) and data were collected on reasons for their choice. Sixty-three per cent of heterosexual couples and all but one of the lesbian couples chose identifiable donors.

"Motives for choosing an identifiable donor were the same for heterosexual and lesbian couples," said Dr Brewaeys. "The majority pointed to the right of the child to know its genetic origins. Although most parents did not want to be involved with the donor they decided it was not for them to block the child's access to donor information. Access to the donor's medical records was an important factor and some couples were also influenced by the fact that the majority of DI children in the future would have access to information because of the forthcoming legislation."

Dr Brewaeys said that for the lesbian couples, the absence of a male infertile partner spared them the stigma of infertility and their children would be informed early in their lives about their origins.

Among heterosexual couples, those opting for anonymous donors had a different profile from those wanting an identifiable donor. They were more likely to have a low socioeconomic status, difficulties coping with male infertility and an attitude of secrecy to the child. Only 12% had considered adoption. By contrast, among those opting for identifiable donors, the majority were better educated and better off financially, the men dealt better with their fertility problems and secrecy towards the child was not an option. About half had previously considered adoption or a known donor.

"The associations between donor choices, education level and infertility distress were intriguing," said Dr Brewaeys. "We believe these are strongly influenced by the sociocultural environment, with those choosing anonymity living more often in a context where other family values prevail. Male infertility and non genetic parenthood remains more of a taboo whereas childlessness is less accepted. Such values may have influenced the high levels of distress about infertility seen in most of the men and the wish not to tell the children about their genetic origins. However, the design of our study does not allow for firm conclusions: we need more sophisticated measures to disentangle the complex relationships that play a part."

She said that the findings, while they could not be generalised to the whole population, suggested that lesbian couples and more privileged heterosexual parents should fare well under the new laws, but couples wanting anonymous donation appeared more vulnerable. "It's essential that we make available pre-treatment counselling focused on individual motives and attitudes and that we continue the counselling after the birth. We also need to develop education campaigns to prevent further stigmatisation of male infertility, as increased tolerance may influence parents' openness. We also need large-scale follow-up studies investigating DI parents' and children's choices and concerns."

The UK study

UK researchers interviewed 46 families from a London clinic who had a 4 to 8-year old child conceived through DI. They found that 39% were inclined to openness and 61% were not. Thirteen per cent had already told their child, 26% intended to in the future, 43% had decided against telling their child and 17% were still uncertain.

They divided the parents into two groups—disclosers being those who had told their child or intended to and non-disclosers being those who were definitely not telling their child or were uncertain.

The two most important reasons the disclosers gave for telling their child were that they favoured openness to avoid accidental discovery and because they wanted to be honest. Almost half also said they believed the child had a right to know their genetic origins. The reaction of the children who had already been told (six couples whose children were aged between 3 and 5) was generally one either of curiosity or disinterest.

The two main reasons for the non-disclosers not to tell their child were that the parents felt there was no reason to tell, or to protect one or more family members, including the feelings of the child itself. Nearly 30% also felt that openness might affect the relationship between the father and child. Some feared the child might reject them with some fathers being concerned they would be rejected in favour of the biological father.

The researchers found that families with two or more siblings were less inclined to be open, possibly because a decision had been made when the first child was born and the climate was less inclined toward openness, and the parents wanted to remain consistent even if their own views had changed. Couples who had been together longer may also have made their decision long before the birth of the child when attitudes were more inclined to secrecy.

Dr Lycett said that although the sample of parents could not be considered representative of DI parents as a whole, the findings suggested a marked proportion of parents recognised the importance of sharing DI information with their child.

"It will be interesting to know what proportion of those parents who intend to tell the child actually follow through," said Dr Lycett. "An earlier European study of parents in this age group found that fewer than 10% had told their child by the time they reached early adolescence, which shows that intention is not necessarily followed by practice. However, in our most recent study of DI children born since the new millennium 46% of parents said that they intended to disclose the donor conception to the child, suggesting a change in attitudes to openness in recent years."

She said the findings will have practical implications for clinics in the provision of counselling before and after a child's birth, particularly for parents who were unsure about how and when to tell children and the impact and reactions they may face.

"The new legislation could mean a greater proportion of parents will be encouraged to be open, as has been the case in Sweden since anonymity was barred, but it remains to be seen how the new laws will affect parental attitudes towards disclosure in the future."

It is always interesting to compare US law with those in Canada and within the European Union where individual rights appear to intersect with concern for family rights and the well-being of children. Thus far, we've compared Dutch law concerning statutory rape, UK practices and attitudes toward family nudity, Canadian attitudes toward three parent families, and report on attitudes across the European Union on artificial insemination and the rights of parents/donors and children born into these circumstances. The shape of family life is changing around the globe with far more predictability than we hear about in the popular press. The question remains, how long will it be before the United States catches up with other democractic cultures in facing its history of repression and criminalization of all manner of social behavor?

Chapter Seven

Sexual Offenses: Consent Implied & Denied under Criminal Statutes

Legislating for the general welfare: protecting public health, safety, welfare, and morals, has long been a province of state government. A significant effort is underway to make sense of our legal history around matters of consent, including statutory definitions, rationale behind laws defining capacity to give or withdraw consent, and severity of punishments that attach to the breach of certain moral codes. Applications of statutory schemes related to sex-offender registration and cases like Mary Kay LeTourneau's provide predictable examples of poorly drafted laws that are unlikely to meet legitimate criminal justice goals. Issues relating to gender bias in sentencing of actual rape, statutory rape, and statutory mitigation of criminal culpability in acquaintance and marital rape cases have revealed deficiencies among researchers and legislatures alike. The question for serious students of constitutional jurisprudence is how to define the state interest in regulating certain kinds of conduct while insuring that judicial application of law is consistent with the mandates of equal protection.

Women under the age of fifteen routinely married and bore children throughout world history. In recent years, the exploitation of young women is now before world commissions charged with looking into human rights violations. Examining widespread sociological changes that have altered worldviews of child development in the modern age is a fascinating project. The history is grounded in the quest for human rights on behalf of women and children. Our examination of moral and criminal penalties for sexual abuse, exploitation and taboo relations begins with the incorporation of presumed consent in early marital rights theory and practice.

Evolution of Marital (Acquaintance) Rape Law

The Early Role of Consent in Conjugal Rights Theory

Regulating degrees of autonomy and consent in intimate relations has long fallen under the auspices of the Church. As religious tenets influenced non-secular law, American women seeking full citizenship rights initiated debate over the relationship between privacy, autonomy and reproductive rights nearly two centuries ago. Women still question unproven claims of legitimacy when examining laws and policies that favor men, and maintain undue control over women's choices, bodies and lives. Those who question most persistently bear the new Scarlet letter; "R." The new derogatory label is Radical. The first battle was waged over women's right to reject coerced sexual relations, linking it to the right to choose the timing and frequency of childbirth. The government continues to legislate around issues that affect women's reproductive choice in concert with the church. This interplay between church and state was most powerful during the period in civil law when men owned women. By the mid-1800s, the subject of husbands' conjugal rights entered the public debate. Predictably, then and now, the major exculpatory thread turns on the issue of consent.

Contest and Consent[1]

Jill Elaine Hasday

Edited Relevant Excerpts

Reprinted with permission

If the modern opponents and defenders of the marital rape exemption agree on any question, it is that their dispute is a new one. The contemporary debate over the exemption operates on the assumption that the law's treatment of marital rape first became controversial in the late twentieth century.

Supporters of the exemption frequently assert that women never saw the need to challenge a husband's conjugal rights until approximately twenty-five years ago. The drafters of the American Law Institute's Model Penal Code, who offer the most sophisticated contemporary defense of the exemption, explain that the rule—"so long an accepted feature of the law of rape"—has only "recently come under attack." Judges similarly note that "until 1977 there was no serious challenge to the spousal exemption," or observe that "[u] ntil the late 1970s there was no real examination of" the subject whatsoever.

And yet we know that a husband's conjugal rights became the focus of public controversy almost immediately after the first organized woman's rights movement coalesced in 1848.

Over the course of the next half-century, politically active women waged a vigorous, public, and extraordinarily frank campaign against a man's right to forced sex in marriage. This nineteenth-century debate over marital rape constitutes a powerful historical record that deserves to be examined in its own right. It also provides a useful framework from which to assess and understand the course of the modern debate over the exemption.

Public discussion and legal decision making about marital rape have proceeded without knowledge of this historical struggle. To some extent, this is because existing historical scholarship has not assimilated into the popular or legal consciousness. Instead, the fight for woman's control over her husband's sexual access is seen as a chapter in the history of birth control or a moral campaign to rationalize sexual desire. It is not seen as part of women's fight for liberty.

Leading nineteenth-century orators argued—in public, vociferously, and systematically—that economic and political equality, including even the vote, would prove hollow, if women did not win the right to set the terms of marital intercourse. Indeed, a woman's lack of control over her person was the key foundation of her subordination. This claim was acutely gender-specific, grounded in the argument that women needed to control the terms of marital intercourse in order to regulate the portion of their lives they would have to devote to raising children. Convinced that women's subordination was ultimately rooted in the structure of marital relations, women demanded both the right to refuse and viable socioeconomic alternatives to submission.

Soon after, mainstream prescriptive authors began to offer extended analyses of the harm that marital rape inflicted.

This prescriptive literature, however, did not challenge a husband's legal right to control marital intercourse. It marshaled, instead, an array of moral, physiological, and strategic arguments designed to convince husbands to voluntarily cede discretion over sex to their wives, promising that the concession would serve the interests of husbands as well as wives. In the hands of the popular prescriptive literature, the demand for enforceable rights to protect women from subordination to their husbands was recast into a series of suggested strategies for marital mutuality, to be pursued in a husband's interest as he saw fit.

Ultimately, the law of marital rape changed only incrementally in the nineteenth century, and only in the context of divorce. As an episode of law reform, the course of the nineteenth-century campaign against marital rape illuminates a deep cultural resistance to altering this aspect of the law, at a time when other aspects of married women's legal status were beginning to evolve.

States willing to augment the property rights of married women in the middle of the nineteenth century, or to ratify woman suffrage in the early twentieth century, were emphatically unwilling to subject husbands to prosecution for marital rape. At least in this arena where sexual and reproductive relations were so directly implicated, authoritative legal sources proved staunchly opposed to the notion of incorporating into the law a vision of marriage as a potentially disharmonious, abusive, even dangerous site of human interaction, in which wives might need and deserve legal rights against their husbands.

The marital rape exemption has undergone more adjustment in the late twentieth century than in the nineteenth. The only change in the law's treatment of marital rape in the nineteenth-century consisted of marginal alterations in the terms on which divorce was available.

The dominant consensual vision of the history of marital rape helps explain why this modern argument from aligned interests has been so powerful. When one starts with the assumption that women have long accepted the marital rape exemption without protest, the proposition that the exemption continues to operate to the mutual benefit of husbands and wives is more likely to seem plausible and even intuitively convincing.

It is hardly surprising that modern defenders of the exemption have been so inclined to assume and assert that the historical survival of a husband's conjugal privileges was uncontested; we have a tremendous cultural need to understand marital relations as consensual and harmonious, notwithstanding the contrary evidence we confront about the nature of some unions. The modern defense of the marital rape exemption is one of the most obvious, if odd, manifestations of that phenomenon. Never do we hear more about the joys of marital love, trust, and intimacy in a contemporary legal context than when courts, lawmakers, and commentators justify the preservation of a husband's legal right to rape his wife.

There is a highly relevant difference between the environment in which the first organized woman's rights movement campaigned against marital rape and present social and legal conditions, however, which suggests that the future course of the modern campaign against marital rape need not run parallel to that of its nineteenth-century predecessor. In the nineteenth century, the harm that a husband's right to marital rape inflicted upon wives was freely and explicitly acknowledged as a social matter. In an era still committed to a wide variety of legal structures subordinating women to men, that acknowledgment was not enough to convince mainstream writers or authoritative legal sources that the creation of legal rights protecting women against their husbands was an appropriate remedy. The modern defense of the marital rape exemption, in contrast, obscures and denies the harm that the rule inflicts upon women.

This has been a crucial tactic because the injury that marital rape causes is far harder to defend, and the absence of legal remediation far harder to justify, in a nation now explicitly committed to women's legal equality. The historical record of struggle over marital rape helps reveal this harm, making concrete what the marital rape exemption's contemporary champions have concealed. In the process, this history provides a foundation upon which the campaign against marital rape can build.

The Law of Marriage in the Nineteenth Century

In the nineteenth century, authoritative legal sources agreed that the rights and obligations of husbands and wives were most appropriately understood, explained, and regulated through the organizing rubric of a status/contract distinction. This distinction classified legal rules into two oppositional categories: status rules (like the marital rape exemption), which fixed marital rights and obligations in the law and made them unalterable by private agreement, and contract rules, which permitted husbands and wives, or couples contemplating marriage, to structure their own legal relationship if they preferred not to rely on the default rules set by the state. Both types of rules governed the marital relation, mainly at alternate parts of its life cycle.

> James Schouler's family law treatise elaborated, "the laws of nature and divine revelation" jointly designated the husband as "the head of the family." "It [was] for the wife to love, honor, and obey; it [was] for the husband to love, cherish, and protect."

The implications of this understanding of the legal relationship between husband and wife can be found throughout nineteenth-century jurisprudence. Most notably for present purposes:

1. A husband enjoyed substantial rights to his wife's person.

2. The common law gave husbands the authority to chastise, or correct, their wives, as long as the corporal punishment did not cause permanent injury. Courts and commentators had formally renounced this right by the latter half of the nineteenth century. But legal authorities continued, nonetheless, to treat wife beating more favorably than other instances of assault and battery and remained extremely reluctant to enforce criminal or civil penalties for marital violence.

3. A husband could also, with only modest limitations, legally restrict his wife's movements in the nineteenth century—could conclusively determine

where the couple would live, could physically restrain his wife to prevent her from leaving that household, and could retrieve her if she did stray, particularly if she had left to go to another man.

4. In recognition of the legal control that husbands exercised over their wives, common law courts in the nineteenth century presumed that married women acted under the coercion of their husbands and accordingly excused them from liability for a wide range of crimes if committed in their husbands' presence. This presumption excluded only the most serious offenses, like treason, murder, and robbery, and crimes understood to be the particular province of women, like keeping a brothel.

The marital rape exemption had deep roots in this legal regime. It was understood, explained, and defended in the context of rules that conclusively inferred consent from the initial agreement to marry and coverture that allowed husbands to exercise complete control over their wives.

There was not the slightest suggestion in nineteenth-century case law and treatises that a husband could be prosecuted for raping his wife. Rape laws stated what a " 'male person'" could not do to " 'any woman, other than his wife.'" Legal writers took pains to emphasize that "[a] man cannot be guilty of a rape upon his own wife," that "a husband does not become guilty of rape by forcing his wife to his own embraces," that rape "may be committed by any male of the age of fourteen or over, not the husband of the female." This clear prohibition on prosecution had its intended effect.

The notable contrast between wives' categorical exemption from rape statutes and the protection against rape (nominally) accorded to other highly vulnerable classes of women also helps illustrate the exemption's deep roots in nineteenth-century law. It was a well-established proposition in nineteenth- century treatises that prostitutes and concubines fell within the purview of rape statutes, even if actual conviction was unlikely since the defendant could present evidence of the victim's occupation to the jury. Legal writers explained that the concern of rape laws centered, not on the status of the victim, but on the fact that the act in question was "against the will of the female on whom it is committed."

Matthew Hale's argument for the marital rape exemption resonated deeply with the coverture principles that shaped the content of most marital status rules in the nineteenth century. His explanation of "mutual matrimonial consent and contract" of husband and wife, evidenced by their agreement to marry. Hale presented a couple's mutual decision to marry as grounds for subjecting wives and husbands to very different obligations and rights. Both a wife and her husband agreed to marry, but where this agreement gave the husband a right of sexual access to his wife, it bestowed an obligation on the wife to submit.

When nineteenth-century cases and treatises considered the marital rape exemption, cited Hale's consent theory. However, they spent just as much time, or more, articulating what I call a "third-party caveat" to the marital rape exemption, also derived from Hale and also meant to legitimate a wife's subordination to her husband. This caveat stated that the marital rape exemption was a personal privilege. It only covered acts that a husband personally committed on his wife; it did not reach cases in which a husband had allowed, or forced, another man to rape his wife. Why were so many pages devoted to stating this limit on the marital rape exemption? The effort indicates, first, what was and was not understood to be contestable. Cases and treatises touching upon the marital rape exemption in the nineteenth century would often cite Hale's irretractible consent theory, but would generally do little else to confirm the existence and soundness of the ban on prosecuting a husband for raping his wife.

The lack of standard forms of support, like case citations, in discussions of the marital rape exemption indicated its status as an understood baseline. In contrast, judges and lawyers clearly felt that they had to do more to explain and justify the third-party caveat, perhaps because the caveat functioned to limit a husband's control over his wife's person. Even though every case and treatise that considered the issue endorsed the caveat, the rule had to be defended rather than just stated.

More fundamentally, though, the emphasis on the third-party caveat reinforced the point that the marital rape exemption drew the line between legal and illegal intercourse so that it depended solely on whether a woman was married to her sexual partner, and not on her consent. All sex outside of marriage, whether consensual or not, was illicit by definition and formally criminalized in fornication and adultery statutes. The marital rape exemption reflected and extended this dichotomy by making marital intercourse legal by definition. The third-party caveat helped to further underscore this demarcation by stressing that the marital rape exemption did not cover any sex outside of marriage, even if accomplished at a husband's command.

Structuring the legality of sex so that it turned exclusively on whether a woman was married to her sexual partner was crucially important because it obscured how the marital rape exemption made a wife's position resemble that of a prostitute. The comparison, which nineteenth-century feminists would press aggressively, appears to have made the exemption's defenders anxious as far back as Hale. Prostitutes were generally thought to be socially degraded in ways that wives were not. But no overwhelming logic presented itself in this context to explain the difference in the work performed. After all, a husband had a duty to support his wife at common law, and the exemption gave him a legal right to take sex in return. If a wife had extramarital relations (against her husband's wishes), the common law permitted the husband to collect civil damages from the other man, financially compensating him for "the invasion of his exclusive right to marital intercourse with his wife."

Rather than attempt to substantively distinguish the terms on which wives and prostitutes provided sexual services, authoritative legal sources, with the help of the third-party caveat, separated the two sets of women by reference to whether or not they were married to the men who had sex with them.

Consider two of the cases that reached a state supreme court. While there is no evidence to suggest that these cases were representative of prosecutions under the third-party caveat, they are instances in which a nineteenth-century court had serious occasion to discuss, and explain, why a husband could be convicted as an accomplice to a rape committed on his wife.

The Supreme Court of Michigan decided *People v. Chapman*, the earlier of the two cases, in 1886. Under a statute rendering all persons who had aided, assisted, or abetted in the commission of a crime liable to punishment as principals, Jeremiah Chapman had been tried and convicted in the rape of his wife, Maggie Chapman. The testimony of Mrs. Chapman and of the actual perpetrator of the offense, James Reagan, indicated that Mr. Chapman had entered into an arrangement with Reagan, whereby Mr. Chapman promised to pay Reagan twenty-five dollars in return for Reagan's agreement to seduce Mrs. Chapman so that her husband could catch the couple in bed and use that evidence to obtain a divorce for adultery. Mrs. Chapman, however, resisted Reagan's advances, and he proceeded to rape her. As Reagan knew, Mr. Chapman was in an adjoining room at the time, watching and listening to all of this through a hole he had bored through the intervening wall. But Mr. Chapman did nothing to stop the rape. Only after it was over, did he burst into the room, declaring "'Now I have caught you.'" Three days later, Mr. Chapman filed a bill for divorce, alleging that his wife had committed adultery with Reagan.

He lost, and on appeal, Mr. Chapman argued that his actions were too tangential to make him an accomplice. The opinion stressed that Mrs. Chapman, a married woman, had been subjected to extramarital intercourse, sex the judges took to be illicit and demeaning by definition. Jeremiah Chapman had then compounded his crime by falsely accusing his wife of adultery, subjecting her to the stigma of extramarital intercourse once more. In the court's words:

A husband who could barter with another for the despoiling of his wife's virtue, and stand by to witness it.... , and remains passive and silent while such object was obtained by violence, and then use such permitted and encouraged rape to divorce her from him, and by this, and perjury added, publish her to the world as an adulteress, is morally guilty of as foul a crime as can be named in the calendar.

State v. Dowell, decided four years later in the Supreme Court of North Carolina, also enforced the third-party caveat. The court describe the case as: "[t]he White husband of a White wife, under menace of death to both parties in case of refusal, and supporting his threat by a loaded gun held over the parties, [had] constrain[ed] a colored man to undertake, and his wife to submit to, an attempted sexual connection." The Illicit intercourse turned on whether the woman was married to her sexual partner, rather than on the woman's consent. The fact that Dowell had attempted to force a Black man to rape his wife certainly underscored the illicit nature of the intercourse at issue, but did not change the basic framework in which the court understood the problem:

The defendant strangely insists that he is not guilty because he is the husband of the prosecutrix; and he relies as a defense upon the marital relation, the duties and obligations of which he has, by all the laws of God and man, so brutally violated. In our opinion, in respect to this offense, he stands upon the same footing as a stranger, and his guilt is to be determined in that light alone ... It is true that a husband may enforce sexual connection; and, in the exercise of this marital right, it is held that he cannot be guilty of the offense of rape. But it is too plain for argument that this privilege is a personal one, only. Hence if ... the husband aids and abets another to ravish his wife, he may be convicted as if he were a stranger. The principle is thus tersely expressed by Sir Matthew Hale: "For, though in marriage she hath given up her body to her husband, she is not to be by him prostituted to another."

Authoritative legal sources in the nineteenth century agreed that a husband could not, and should not, be prosecuted for raping his wife.

Marital Rape Exemption's Effect on the Lived Experience in the 19th Century

The feminist campaign against marital rape did not simply treat a husband's right to control the terms of marital intercourse as an apt symbol of women's legal subjugation. In response, popular prescriptive literature began to delineate the harm of marital rape by focusing exclusively on the actual practice. These marriage manuals and health guides did not seek to change the legal rule granting husbands conjugal rights, but sought to ameliorate the functional effect of the exemption by convincing husbands to voluntarily cede control of marital intercourse to their wives.

Feminists and prescriptive writers engaged in a frank and voluminous dialogue about marital intercourse and marital rape in the latter half of the nineteenth century, but the social scientists of their era shied away from the subject. The studies of women's sexual experiences in marriage that do exist, however, suggest a widespread desire among women to control the terms of marital intercourse, a widespread recognition that they did not have the right to exercise this control, and a widespread experience of harm caused by unwanted sex in marriage.

Katharine Bement Davis's "Factors in the Sex Life of Twenty-Two Hundred Women (1929), is the most systematic and rigorous examination of women's experience of sex in marriage during this approximate period. Davis, a social scientist and penologist, sent ten thousand letters to selected wives, asking them if they would be willing to answer and anonymously return a questionnaire about their sexual experiences. Her questionnaire was very thorough, and she ultimately received completed answers from 1073 married women. Davis's study is not ideal for a number of reasons, including its concentration on women somewhat younger than the contemporaries of the first woman's rights movement and its narrow focus on the middle class and the elite. But notwithstanding its shortcomings, the study offers valuable information about the nature of actual sexual practices in the approximate era in which the first organized woman's rights movement challenged a husband's conjugal rights. Her report presents a fascinating window into women's lives.

The women Davis surveyed repeatedly made clear that they had entered into marriage with the expectation that their husbands had the right to control the terms of marital intercourse, although they were hardly enthusiastic about that husbandly prerogative. When asked whether they had been "'adequately prepared by instruction for the sex side of marriage, a number of women reported that their mothers had explicitly conveyed this information about the nature of marriage to them. As one wife in this cohort explained, ''My mother taught me what to expect. The necessity of yielding to her husband's demands had been a great cross in her own life.' Davis's questioning about whether the women had been "'attracted or repelled by the way in which married sex relations came into [their] experience"' generated even more revealing responses. Nearly a quarter (223) of the first thousand women to respond "replied 'neither."'

Of these, 173 said that they "took it as a matter of fact"—something that every married woman had to go through with, regardless of her feelings. The other 50 qualified the "neither" with the following adjectives: Amused, 1; astonished, 8; bewildered, 3; disappointed, 7; frightened, 8; indifferent, 8; indignant, 1; interested, 5; relieved (that it was no worse), 1; resigned, 3; shocked, 1; sorry, 1; stunned, 1; submissive, 2.

Davis's work also suggests that women's marital happiness in this period importantly turned on how a husband chose to wield his authority over marital intercourse—whether a husband actually exercised his admitted rights or restrained himself voluntarily. Women "attracted" by their first experiences of marital intercourse were significantly more likely to report that their subsequent married life had been happy as well. In explaining what in their early sexual experiences had appealed to them, these women stressed "[o]ver and over again.... the unselfishness, consideration, and self- control of the husband." In contrast, women who had been "repelled" by their introduction to marital intercourse—a group that included almost one quarter (237) of the first thousand women in the study—emphasized "[j]ust the opposite qualities.... The wife ignorant, unprepared, shocked at the strength of her husband's passion; the husband unable to realize this, inconsiderate, uncontrolled; a long period of adjustment—and if this fails, unhappiness for both."

Dr. Clelia Duel Mosher's earlier, if significantly smaller and less systematic, survey of married women's sexual lives accords with Davis's findings. The Mosher study was notably less rigorous than Davis's work. It consists of unprocessed data about just forty-five married women. Dr. Mosher, a physician and professor at Stanford University, did not attempt to analyze her findings or to publish her study. That said, Mosher's work provides useful information about an era somewhat earlier than the period that Davis analyzed. Indeed, Mosher's study, conducted between 1892 and 1920, is the earliest known survey of women's sexual practices in the United States. Seventy percent of the women that Mosher questioned were born before 1870. Seventeen of the forty-five women were born before the Civil War.

Mosher's subjects repeatedly explained that they wished to limit marital intercourse to those occasions when it was agreed to by wife and husband alike. When asked what they thought "would be an ideal habit" of sex in marriage, these women stressed mutuality again and again. "[E]verything to be absolutely mutual," they typically responded. "When desired by both." "No habit at all, but the most sensitive regard of each member of the couple for the personal feeling and desires and health of the other." "The marital relation when mutual," they explained, "begets a certain bond of love and sympathy that is certainly peculiar only to those happily mated."

The married women who responded to the questionnaires that Davis and Mosher distributed made clear that unwanted sex in marriage had caused them real harm and that criminal law categorically refused to entertain claims based on forced sex in marriage, especially when combined with the legal and socioeconomic obstacles to securing a divorce based on marital rape (which will be discussed below). As a practical matter, the marital rape exemption limited a woman's options if she sought to avoid marital rape. As a normative matter, the exemption added the law's sanction to husbandly claims of marital authority. The marital rape exemption was not just a theoretical question for the law books and the legal treatises. It affected how women lived their married lives.

Leading activists identified a husband's conjugal rights as the crucial constitutive element of women's subordination. They called for both an enforceable right to refuse a husband's sexual demands and realistic socioeconomic alternatives to submission. The record of this struggle dramatically expands our understanding of the history of marital rape, and also provides important new insights into the goals, progress, and efficacy of the first organized woman's rights movement, which historians now frequently describe as overwhelmingly dominated by the battle for suffrage. The advocates of "free love," who operated on the leftward fringe of organized feminism in the nineteenth century, articulated the arguments of the woman's rights movement in a more radical voice.

Very soon after the organized woman's rights movement mobilized against a husband's conjugal rights, mainstream authors began to describe and denounce the harm that marital rape inflicted on wives. This prescriptive literature, though, did not contest a husband's legal right to determine the terms of marital intercourse. Instead, it called on husbands to voluntarily refrain from exercising their legal prerogatives, on the ground that such restraint would benefit them as much as their wives. Where women demanded a structure of rights to free women from subordination in marriage, the prescriptive literature turned the concern over marital rape into a call for voluntary strategies to enhance marital happiness and harmony, to be pursued to the extent that they served a husband's interests.

Nineteenth-century Americans were reluctant to speak openly about sex, and the leaders of organized feminism were well aware of the social sanctions for sexual frankness. But their commitment to establishing a woman's right of self-possession as the foundation of her equality led feminists to offer a systematic and thorough critique of marital rape in language wholly understandable to contemporary audiences.

The nineteenth-century woman's rights movement contested a husband's right to determine the terms of marital intercourse vociferously and profoundly. Indeed, this campaign constitutes an important chapter in the history of organized feminism in the nineteenth century, one that sheds new light on the nature and dimensions of that movement.

Nineteenth-century feminists certainly did rely on arguments grounded in classic liberalism, which was the dominant philosophical tradition of the era and well suited to the suffrage demand. Indeed, the Declaration of Sentiments adopted at Seneca Falls was explicitly modeled on the Declaration of Independence. These feminists began with liberalism's dedication to freedom and autonomy, but took it in radically new directions.

In defining what the right to one's own person meant, articulate feminists did not focus on gender-neutral rights to the public sphere or freedom from coercion by the state. They were concerned about married women who submitted to their husbands' sexual demands as the result of force, or threats, or because they lacked palatable alternatives. The woman's rights movement sought to establish a wife's right of refusal and to remake women's social and economic possibilities to create realistic alternatives to marriage.

In making these claims, feminists recognized that some of the most important barriers to female self-possession were located within the structure of marriage, as well as the behavior of individual husbands.

They also objected to the tenuous circumstances under which many never-married, separated, and divorced women lived, subject to both explicit employment discrimination that left women with few ways to support themselves outside of marriage and the social stigma associated with living outside a husband's household. Indeed, feminists called unwanted marital intercourse, where the wife had acquiesced because of her economic and social dependence on her husband, legalized prostitution.

Their argument for self- ownership was not based on a theory of bodily inviolateness that would apply to man and woman like. Rather, it looked to women's exclusive responsibility for raising children. Nineteenth-century feminists did not celebrate the norm assigning women all of the work of childcare. Nonetheless, they took it to be such a profound social expectation that they reasoned within it, contending that women needed to have control over marital intercourse so that they could regulate the amount of their lives they devoted to motherhood.

In the last quarter of the nineteenth century, some courts found legally cognizable cruelty where a husband had subjected his wife to excessive sexual demands and those demands had endangered her health. Allowing these women to divorce their husbands was, it should be noted, a liberalization. Indeed, the decisions were part of a larger liberalization of divorce law in postbellum America, a period in which the number of divorces granted to women claiming cruelty escalated dramatically. These successful divorce suits for sexual cruelty suggest that the critique of marital rape articulated, in different forms, by feminists and popular prescriptive writers was influencing social understandings about appropriate marital behavior, at least in arenas otherwise receptive to change.

Reform of the criminal exemption has also been fragmentary. A majority of states still retain some form of the rule exempting marital rape from prosecution. Some states require a couple to be separated and some extend the exemption to cover unmarried cohabitants. Some only recognize rape if it involves physical force and/or serious physical harm. Some provide vastly reduced penalties, or create special procedural requirements for marital rape prosecutions. Almost all of this law, moreover, is the product of political advocacy and legislative action, rather than constitutional adjudication, so that the nature and continued path of change is insecure.

Lisa Eskow's article, entitled ***The Ultimate Weapon: Demythologizing Spousal Rape Reconceptualizing Its Prosecution***,[2] demonstrates that the law is now properly classifying marital rape as rape, but only under the rubric of domestic violence. It's long over due in the field of legitimate recognition given our current stage of cultural evolution.

Edited Relevant Excerpts
Reprinted with permission

Domestic sexual violence remains an elusive concept. While the marital home no longer provides an impenetrable sanctuary for batterers, the marital bedroom stands as a questionable arena for state intervention. Sex has always been perceived as an integral component of "domestic bliss," both for procreative and romantic reasons. For some, sex is the quintessence of privacy rights, triggering the Fourteenth Amendment's guarantee of freedom from state intrusion. Legal responses to sexual violence often shift within a domestic context, suggesting that forced marital sex is something other than rape. Long perceived as a crime of sexual passion, rape is now widely regarded as an act of violence and is prosecuted as such. Rape within marriage, however, falls into a gray area of the American criminal justice system. It has always been presumed that men should have unlimited sexual access to their wives.

By 1994, twenty-four states had abolished any form of marital rape exemption—either through legislative reform or judicial interpretation of existing statutes. Nevertheless, at least thirteen states still offer preferential or disparate treatment to perpetrators of spousal sexual assault. Several states have actually extended their exemptions to include non-married, cohabiting couples. For example, cohabitation is an affirmative defense to rape in Connecticut, regardless of the legal status of the relationship between the victim and the defendant.

> Connecticut General Statutes § 53a-67.
>
> Affirmative Defenses in Rape Cases
>
> (b) In any prosecution for an offense under this part [with limited exceptions] it shall be an affirmative defense that the defendant and the alleged victim were, at the time of the alleged offense, living together by mutual consent in a relationship of cohabitation, regardless of the legal status of their relationship.
>
> In Delaware, a "voluntary social companion" exemption impedes prosecution of men who engage in non-consensual sex with "a victim who is in the defendant's company on the occasion of the offense as a result of the victim's exercise of rational intellect and free will, without trick, coercion or duress" and who has engaged in consensual sex with the defendant within the past year. Such expansions of the marital rape exemption into other forms of domestic and social relationships reveal the persistent legal and cultural obstacles to securing women's sexual autonomy, not only in marriage, but also in society generally.
>
> Husbands' acts of physical and sexual violence escalate when their wives attempt to leave the marriage. These "separation assaults," as Martha Mahoney terms them, reflect the abusive husband's "quest for control." In Finkelhor and Yllo's study, one-quarter of divorced or separated women reported a past incident of forced marital sex. Over two-thirds were raped shortly after ending a previous separation or when making plans to leave. These findings prompted Finkelhor and Yllo to conclude that "[a] wife's leaving or threatening to leave her marriage frequently provokes a marital rape."
>
> Wives' economic dependency on their husbands may fuel both physically and sexually abusive marriages. Russell identifies a pervasive "notion that the male breadwinner should be the beneficiary of some special immunity because of his family's economic dependence on him." In her study, 90 percent of wives who stayed with their husbands following a rape depended on the husband for money, whereas only 24 percent of those who left faced this financial constraint. Russell also makes the striking observation that 100 percent of those women who were the sole providers for their households at the time of the rape left their husbands following the act. Economic independence, apparently, gave these women not only the financial means, but also the emotional and psychological capacity, to break free from an abusive marriage cycle.
>
> Statements and images endorsing marital rape pervade not only press reports, but also popular culture. Cultural myths about the importance of facilitating conjugal relations are reinforced through gender hierarchies, and rape statutes reflect suspicion of women's credibility and motives by instituting reporting and fresh-complaint requirements and by demanding corroboration or demonstrated force in order to classify a forced sexual encounter as rape in certain situations.

Reva Siegel suggests that facts about women's bodies have long served to justify regulations enforcing judgments about women's roles.[3] That these judgments persist is evident in varying degrees by the state of legal reasoning and its influence on public opinion. For example, bodily integrity and credibility occupied center stage in the formation of rules on acquaintance-rape, solidifying "a norm that animates the rape law more generally, the defense of "mistaken belief in consent" defines whether a rape occurred from the perspective of the accused rapist, not from the perspective of the victim or even based on a social standard of unacceptable force or of mutuality."[4]

Notions of consent have evolved around changes in familial status, as the subordinate role of women has been attacked in meaningful ways. Given our longstanding preoccupation with the ideal of marital privacy, responsibility for crossing boundaries of kinship is difficult to resolve outside the reach of the law. For example, methods for determining when incest has occurred, lack of public education about the consequences of quasi-incestual relations, and insufficient guidelines around family nudity has altered public perception, affected the nature of parental rights and extended the reach of criminal law. Consider the following case, noting the potential for a very different legal response if the [original] primary couple had married.

Incest, Recovered Memories & Child Sexual Abuse

Woody Allen v. Mia Farrow[5]

May 1994

This case is an appeal from a judgment of the Supreme Court entered July 13, 1993, which denied Allen's request for custody of three minor children.

OPINION

In this special proceeding commenced by petitioner to obtain custody of, or increased visitation with, the infant children Moses, Dylan and Satchel, we are called upon to review the decision awarding custody of the three children to the respondent Farrow, and which also denied the petitioner's requests regarding visitation. Upon such review we conclude, for the reasons set forth below, that the determination of the court was in accordance with the best interests of these children, and accordingly, we affirm.

The petitioner and the respondent have brought themselves to this unhappy juncture primarily as a result of two recent events. These are: Mr. Allen's affair with Soon-Yi Previn (Mia Farrow's adopted daughter) and the alleged sexual abuse of daughter Dylan O'Sullivan Farrow by Mr. Allen.

While the parties had difficulties which grew during Ms. Farrow's pregnancy with Satchel, it was the discovery of the relationship between Mr. Allen and Ms. Previn that intensified Ms. Farrow's concerns about Mr. Allen's behavior toward Dylan, and resulted in the retention of counsel by both parties. While various aspects of this matter remain unclear, it is evident that each party assigns the blame for the current state of affairs to the other.

The parties' respective arguments are very clear. The petitioner (Allen) maintains that he was forced to commence this proceeding in order to preserve his parental rights to the three infant children, because the respondent commenced and continues to engage in a campaign to alienate him from his children and to ultimately defeat his legal rights to them. The petitioner contends, alia, that the respondent seeks to accomplish her goals primarily through manipulation of the children's perceptions of him. He wishes to obtain custody, ostensibly to counteract the detrimental psychological effects the respondent's actions have had on his children, and to provide them with a more stable atmosphere in which to develop. Mr. Allen specifically denies the allegations that he sexually abused Dylan and characterizes them as part of Ms. Farrow's extreme overreaction to his admitted relationship with Ms. Previn.

The respondent (Farrow) maintains that the petitioner has shown no genuine parental interest in, nor any regard for, the children's welfare and that any interest he has shown has been inappropriate and even harmful. Respondent cites the fact that the petitioner has commenced and maintained an intimate sexual relationship with her daughter Soon-Yi Previn, which he has refused to curtail, despite the obvious ill effects it has had on all of the children and the especially profound effect it has had on Moses. It is also contended that petitioner has at best, an inappropriately intense interest in, and at worst, an abusive relationship with, the parties' daughter Dylan. Further, the respondent maintains that petitioner's contact with the parties' biological son, Satchel, is harmful to the child in that petitioner represents an emotional threat and has on at least one occasion threatened physical harm. Respondent contends that the petitioner's only motive in commencing this proceeding was to retaliate against the allegations of child sexual abuse made against him by Ms. Farrow.

Certain salient facts concerning both Mr. Allen's and Ms. Farrow's relationships to their children and to each other are not disputed. Review of these facts in an objective manner and the conclusions that flow from them, demonstrate that the determination of the Court as to both custody and visitation is amply supported by the record.

From the inception of Mr. Allen's relationship with Ms. Farrow in 1980, until a few months after the adoption of Dylan O'Sullivan Farrow on June 11, 1985, Mr. Allen wanted nothing to do with Ms. Farrow's children. Although Mr. Allen and Ms. Farrow attempted for approximately six months to have a child of their own, Mr. Allen did so apparently only after Ms. Farrow promised to assume full responsibility for the child. Following the adoption however, Mr. Allen became interested in developing a relationship with the newly adopted Dylan. While previously he rarely spent time in the respondent's apartment, after the adoption of Dylan he went to the respondent's Manhattan apartment more often, visited Ms. Farrow's Connecticut home and even accompanied the Farrow family on vacations to Europe. Allen also developed a relationship with Moses Farrow, who had been adopted by the respondent in 1980 and was seven years old at the time of Dylan's adoption. However, Allen remained distant from Farrow's other six children.

In 1986 Ms. Farrow expressed a desire to adopt another child. Mr. Allen, while not enthusiastic at the prospect of the adoption of Dylan in 1985, was much more amenable to the idea in 1986. Before the adoption could be completed Ms. Farrow became pregnant with the parties' son Satchel. While the petitioner testified that he was happy at the idea of becoming a father, the record supports the finding that Mr. Allen showed little or no interest in the pregnancy. It is not disputed that Ms. Farrow began to withdraw from Mr. Allen during the pregnancy and that afterwards she did not wish Satchel to become attached to Mr. Allen.

According to Mr. Allen, Ms. Farrow became inordinately attached to the newborn Satchel to the exclusion of the other children. He viewed this as especially harmful to Dylan and began spending more time with her, ostensibly to make up for the lack of attention shown her by Ms. Farrow after the birth of Satchel. Mr. Allen maintains that his interest in and affection for Dylan always has been paternal in nature and never sexual. The various psychiatric experts who testified or otherwise provided reports did not conclude that Allen's behavior toward Dylan prior to August of 1992 was explicitly sexual in nature. However, the clear consensus was that his interest in Dylan was abnormally intense in that he made inordinate demands on her time and focused on her to the exclusion of Satchel and Moses even when they were present.

The record demonstrates that Ms. Farrow expressed concern to Allen about his relationship with Dylan, and that Allen expressed his concern to Ms. Farrow about her relationship with Satchel. In 1990 both Dylan and Satchel were evaluated by clinical psychologists. Dr. Coates began treatment of Satchel in 1990. In April of 1991 Dylan was referred to Dr. Schultz, a clinical psychologist specializing in the treatment of young children with serious emotional problems.

In 1990 at about the same time that the parties were growing distant from each other and expressing their concerns about the other's relationship with their youngest children, Mr. Allen began acknowledging Farrow's daughter Soon-Yi Previn. Previously he treated Ms. Previn in the same way he treated Ms. Farrow's other children from her prior marriage, rarely even speaking to them.

In September of 1991, Ms. Previn began to attend Drew College in New Jersey. In December 1991, two events coincided. Mr. Allen's adoptions of Dylan and Moses were finalized and Mr. Allen began his sexual relationship with their sister Soon-Yi Previn.

In January of 1992, Mr. Allen took the photographs of Ms. Previn, which were discovered on the mantelpiece in his apartment by Ms. Farrow and were introduced into evidence at the IAS proceeding. Mr. Allen in his trial testimony stated that he took the photos at Ms. Previn's suggestion and that he considered them erotic and not pornographic. We have viewed the photographs and do not share Mr. Allen's characterization of them. We find the fact that Mr. Allen took them at a time when he was formally assuming a legal responsibility for two of Ms. Previn's siblings to be totally unacceptable.

The distinction Mr. Allen makes between Ms. Farrow's other children and Dylan, Satchel and Moses is lost on this Court. The children themselves do not draw the same distinction that Mr. Allen does. This is sadly demonstrated by the profound effect his relationship with Ms. Previn has had on the entire family. Allen's testimony that the photographs of Ms. Previn "were taken, as I said before, between two consenting adults wanting to do this" demonstrates a chosen ignorance of his and Ms. Previn's relationships to Ms. Farrow, his three children and Ms. Previn's other siblings. His continuation of the relationship, viewed in the best possible light, shows a distinct absence of judgment. It demonstrates to this Court Mr. Allen's tendency to place inappropriate emphasis on his own wants and needs and to minimize and even ignore those of his children. At the very minimum, it demonstrates an absence of any parenting skills.

We recognize Mr. Allen's acknowledgment of the pain his relationship with Ms. Previn has caused the family. We also note his testimony that he tried to insulate the rest of the family from the "dispute" that resulted, and tried to "deescalate the situation" by attempting to "placate" Ms. Farrow. It is true that Ms. Farrow's failure to conceal her feelings from the rest of the family and the acting out of her feelings of betrayal and anger toward Mr. Allen enhanced the effect of the situation on the rest of her family. We note though that the reasons for her behavior, however prolonged and extreme, are clearly visible in the record. On the other hand the record contains no acceptable explanation for Allen's commencement of the sexual relationship with Ms. Previn at the time he was adopting Moses and Satchel, or for the continuation of that relationship at the time he was supposedly experiencing the joys of fatherhood.

While the petitioner's testimony regarding his attempts to de-escalate the dispute and to insulate the family from it, displays a measure of concern for his three children, it is clear that he should have realized the inevitable consequences of his actions well before his relationship with Ms. Previn became intimate. Allen's various inconsistent statements to Farrow of his intentions regarding Ms. Previn and his attempt to have Dr. Schultz explain the relationship to Dylan in such a manner as to exonerate himself from any wrong doing, make it difficult for this Court to find that his expressed concern for the welfare of the family is genuine.

Allen maintains that Farrow's allegations concerning the sexual abuse of Dylan were fabricated by her: as a result of her rage over his relationship with Ms. Previn, and as part of her continued plan to alienate him from his children. However, our review of the record militates against a finding that Ms. Farrow fabricated the allegations without any basis.

Unlike the court at IAS, we do not consider the conclusions reached by Doctors Coates and Schultz and by the Yale-New Haven team, to be totally unpersuasive. While the tendency of Dylan to withdraw into a fantasy and the inconsistencies in her account of the events of August 4, 1992, noted particularly by the Yale-New Haven team, must be taken into account in the evaluation of these serious allegations, the testimony given at trial by the individuals caring for the children that day, the videotape of Dylan made by Ms. Farrow the following day and the accounts of Dylan's behavior toward Mr. Allen both before and after the alleged instance of abuse, suggest that the abuse did occur. While the evidence in support of the allegations remains inconclusive, it is clear that the investigation of the charges in and of itself could not have left Dylan unaffected.

Any determination of issues of child custody or visitation must serve the best interests of the child, and best promote the child's welfare. The existence of a prior arrangement of custody agreed upon by the parties should be given weighty but not absolute priority in the absence of extraordinary circumstances. Such priority is afforded in the belief that stability in a child's life is in the child's best interests. The court, however is not bound by the existence of a prior agreement and has the discretion to order changes in custody as well as other modifications when the totality of circumstances warrants its doing so in the best interests of the child. Primary among those circumstances is the quality of the home environment and the parental guidance the custodial parent provides for the child. It has long been recognized that it is often in the child's best interests to continue to live with his or her siblings. "While this, too, is not an absolute, the stability and companionship to be gained from keeping the children together is an important factor for the court to consider".

With respect to Satchel, the IAS Court denied the petitioner's request for unsupervised visitation. While the court stated that it was not concerned for Satchel's physical safety, it was concerned by Mr. Allen's "demonstrated inability to understand the impact that his words and deeds have upon the emotional well being of the children". We agree. The record supports the conclusion that Mr. Allen may, if unsupervised, influence Satchel inappropriately, and disregard the impact exposure to Mr. Allen's relationship with Satchel's sister, Ms. Previn, would have on the child. His failure to understand the effect of such exposure upon Satchel as well as upon his other children is evidenced by his statement on direct examination in which he stated: "If you ask me personally, I would say the children, the children adore Soon Yi, they adore me, they would be delighted, if you asked me this personally, I would say they would be delighted and have fun with us, being taken places with us. But, I don't want to give you my amateur opinion on that. That's how I feel. And I know it counts for very little."

The record indicates that Ms. Previn when not at college spends most of her time with Mr. Allen. Contact between Ms. Previn and her siblings in the context of the relationship with Mr. Allen would be virtually unavoidable even if Mr. Allen chose to insulate his children from the relationship. Expert medical testimony indicated that it would be harmful for Ms. Previn not to be reintegrated into the family. However, the inquiry here concerns the best interests of Dylan, Moses and Satchel. Their best interests would clearly be served by contact with their sister Soon-Yi, personally and not in Mr. Allen's presence. Seeing both Ms. Previn and Mr. Allen together in the unsupervised context envisioned by Mr. Allen would, at this early stage, certainly be detrimental to the best interests of the children.

Therefore, we hold that in view of the totality of the circumstances, the best interests of these children would be served by remaining together in the custody of Ms. Farrow, with the parties abiding by the visitation schedule established by the trial court whose decision is affirmed in all respects.

Incest Defined in Two State Statutes

Georgia § 16-6-22. Incest

(a) A person commits the offense of incest when he engages in sexual intercourse with a person to whom he knows he is related either by blood or by marriage as follows:

(1) Father and daughter or stepdaughter;

(2) Mother and son or stepson;

(3) Brother and sister of the whole blood or of the half blood;

(4) Grandparent and grandchild;

(5) Aunt and nephew; or

(6) Uncle and niece.

(b) A person convicted of the offense of incest shall be punished by imprisonment for not less than one nor more than 20 years.

Delaware § 766. Incest; class A misdemeanor

(a) A person is guilty of incest if the person engages in sexual intercourse with another person with whom the person has one of the following relationships:

A male and his child, parent, brother, sister, grandchild, niece, nephew.

A male and his father's sister or brother, his mother's sister or brother.

A male and his father's wife.

A male and his wife's child.

A male and the child of his wife's son or daughter.

A female & her parent, child, brother, sister, grandchild, niece, nephew.

A female & her father's sister or brother, her mother's sister or brother.

A female and her mother's husband.

A female and her husband's child.

A female and the child of her husband's son or daughter.

(b) The relationships referred to herein include blood relationships without regard to legitimacy and relationships by adoption. Incest is a class A misdemeanor and is an offense within the original jurisdiction of the Family Court.

For Your Consideration

Had Woody Allen been married to Mia Farrow at the time he began the affair with her daughter, he would have been guilty of incest under both statutes. Child protection advocates generally work to close loopholes that fail to address child sexual abuse. Original incest laws were designed to prevent intermarriage among relatives within a certain degree of kinship on eugenic grounds. Progress in social development theory resulted in pressures toward legal reform that joined the goals of protecting young children and maintenance of familial harmony. Note that the Allen case lacked both a biological link for eugenic purposes and a minor presumed incapable of granting meaningful consent.

Assuming that he had been married to Farrow at the time of the affair, upon what basis could the state justify invoking criminal penalty? How plausible is the assumption that the Court's ruling and opinion regarding custody of Previn's siblings reflect the fact that Allen would have been guilty of incest had he been married to Farrow at the time?

> The New York Daily News printed an article with the catchy headlines*: **WOODY SHOWS OFF NEW BABY***[6]
>
>> Woody, Soon-Yi and baby made three yesterday. Woody Allen and Soon-Yi Previn looked every bit the proud parents as they pushed a 5-month-old baby girl in a pram in the spring sunshine.
>>
>> Allen's public relations firm would neither confirm nor deny an adoption. But Previn has not appeared pregnant in photographs. Allen, who swept Previn away for a wedding in Venice in December 1997, has mused to pals in recent months about starting a family, a friend said.
>>
>> Allen sued Farrow for custody of their three children and Farrow counter sued, charging that Allen had molested 7-year-old Dylan.... After a brutal court fight, Farrow won custody of the three kids and later changed [the children's names] Allen can have only supervised visits with the children.
>>
>> Frank Maco, the Connecticut prosecutor who nearly charged Allen with molesting Dylan in 1992 during the custody fight, shied away from commenting yesterday on the famous film maker's fitness as a dad. Since no charges were

filed, Allen who had vehemently denied the allegation would face no legal hurdles to adoption, Maco said.

Family Nudity

Consider the following family issue and whether it relates to questions of parental fitness/judgment.

Letter to the Editor[7]

Question:

My wife thinks there's nothing wrong with taking a bath naked with our two boys, even though they are now 1 and 3. Frankly, this makes me uncomfortable. I say it's time she covered up in front of our children, but she thinks I'm being a prude. How can we resolve this difference without arguing about it anymore?

Answer:

You'd probably never see this question in a European magazine, muses sex therapist Dennis Sugrue, PhD, clinical associate professor of psychiatry at the University of Michigan Medical School and coauthor of Sex Matters for Women. Despite our culture's constant barrage of sexy media images, "here in the United States, we get pretty uptight when it comes to baring it all," he observes.

"Yet, the truth is that nudity in the home, when handled in a respectful, matter-of-fact way, is perfectly natural and certainly not harmful." In fact, research suggests that children who have seen their parents nude do not grow up to be emotionally scarred, but instead are more likely to be accepting of their own bodies and comfortable with their own sexuality.

If your wife is fine being naked around your sons, they won't think anything of it, other than showing some natural curiosity about body differences. ("Hey, why do only boys have penises?") Nudity is not the same thing as sexuality. However, if you're uncomfortable about her nudity, your sons will pick up on that, and may start feeling shame or increased curiosity.

Use this issue as a springboard for clarifying your values and how you and your wife will teach them to your children. What is it about your wife's nudity in front of the kids that bothers you most? For instance, if seeing her naked makes you lusty, then of course you'll feel weird having those feelings around your children. Alternatively, why does she feel so relaxed about it? Sharing your own most formative sexual experiences—both good and bad—will help you both think things through.

Ideally, these discussions should lead to a compromise you're both comfortable with. For instance, you might agree that it's fine for her to bathe with the boys only when you're not present. But if you still think the practice is wrong across the board, stand up for your opinion. It certainly won't harm the boys for your wife not to take baths with them, and maybe this is just one of those times where she'll have to compromise for the sake of your comfort.

Use a sense of humor when you express your views, rather than being judgmental or shaming, and your wife will probably be less argumentative, and more gracious, about staying out of the family tub.

Holly Robinson lives with her husband and five kids outside of Boston.

For Your Consideration

Outside the messiness of divorce where matters of trust, credibility, and all types of accusations have been known to surface (perhaps for the first time), is it appropriate to discuss a societal response or baseline around questions of family nudity?

Is this issue properly classified as one of nudity, sexual repression, or social fixation upon impropriety and perversion?

What kinds of useful social scientific data might we access by interviewing individuals concerning their early childhood experiences, exposure and experimentation?

What We Remember—Recovered Memories of Incest

A recent case dealing with a father's challenge to his daughter's recovered memories of sex abuse generated close scrutiny and debate about the professional responsibilities of therapists who work with survivors of sexual abuse. Stephanie Ramona, the mother of a young woman with bulimia, was placed in one of the most difficult spots that one can imagine. She had enjoyed a 25-year marriage with Gary Ramona, who now stood accused by their daughter of molesting her from a very young age.[8]

Dr. Allen Dyer delivered the Keynote address: ***Current Controversies Ethical Issues in the Current Debate About Recovered Memory***[9] at a conference on Childhood Sexual Abuse and Memories. There he outlined, two implications in locating ethics at the center of the controversy.

1) We must be concerned with the ethical behavior of mental health professionals.
2) We must wonder also about the values of our society, and why this controversy is emerging at this time in the way it is.

He goes on to note that the word "abuse" has been abused as a professional matter:

> It is worth noting that "abuse" has become a code word to communicate experiences that are too shameful to be spoken about directly. It is also worth noting that rarely is the word "incest" spoken. Even my dictionary is circuitous in its definition. It defines incest as "the crime of cohabitation between persons related within the degrees wherein marriage is prohibited by law." It is much more than that. Incest is not just cohabitation; it is sex in the family.

He also addresses the recent increase and phenomenon of recovered memory therapy:

> One of my patients reported during the first month of her hospitalization that she had been physically and sexually abused by her grandfather during childhood. (The fact that I refer to the first month of hospitalization tells you that this occurred a few years ago.) She had been referred to the university medical center for evaluation of intractable headaches. She was found to be depressed,

and one of the striking things about her presentation was that she had no vocabulary for anger, which she considered to be "un-Christian". I have treated this woman for a number of years and always understood this to be an example of the "recovery of the repressed" memories. Recently I asked her for clarification, and she told me that she had forgotten about her childhood abuse during the years that she was first married and raising her family, but after her children began to leave home, she developed physical symptoms and began to remember her childhood experiences at the hand of her grandfather. I was the first person she told about these experiences, but she remembered them before she entered the hospital. Interestingly it was not the abuse that was particularly difficult for her to deal with. It was the separation. Her children leaving home reminded her of the pain of her mother's abandonment.

I mention this case because it raises questions about the nature of memory about which we will hear more in later presentations. Although repression is a concept with some utility, it is subject to misunderstanding. I think Michael Polanyi's concept of focal and subsidiary awareness may be more accurate. We could say that my patient was only subsidiarily aware of her past experiences while she focused on raising her own children, but when they left home both the abuse by her grandfather and then the abandonment by her mother came to her focal awareness.

Good enough therapy creates an environment in which it is safe to remember and disclose memories, thoughts, feelings, and fantasies to another human being. It creates an environment in which learning can occur. One can and should hope to learn how one came to be the way one is and how one might choose to be different. Doing therapy is a bit like walking a tightrope whether one is the therapist or the person in therapy. It is a delicate balance.

With regard to memories of childhood sexual abuse, that balance has been usefully identified as the balance between belief and suggestion (Brenneis, 1994). "On the one hand, the therapist's belief that one can reconstruct early traumatic experience creates fertile ground for overt and covert suggestion, which in conjunction with an anxious patient seeking affiliation, may lead to the production of false memories. On the other hand, the therapist's belief in the likelihood of repressed abuse and that it can be reconstructed may constitute a necessary precondition for the emergence of valid memories." The good enough therapist must be willing to believe, but be skeptical, not gullible. Yet she or he must be capable of doubting, but in an empathic way, which does not invalidate the patient's or client's experience. Then with empathic attention to the material that is presented the therapist must help the patient understand whether the material presented is recovered memories or unconscious fantasies. That process takes time; it is not infallible; there are no short cuts. The therapist must know her patient well and she must know herself well.

For Your Consideration

Edward Greer wrote an article titled: ***Tales of Sexual Panic in the Legal Academy,***[10] which levels the same charges against legal scholars that clinical psychologists have faced. Evaluate his arguments on the merits.

> The bulk of instances of private sexualized crimes committed by men against girls and boys, of which incest is a paradigmatic example, cannot be redressed by the legal system because, even if reported, they cannot be proven in a court of law. Many who acknowledge that real limitation on the efficacy of the legal system seek other kinds of social reforms to ameliorate this difficulty. Adult women report that they were victims of incest committed by their father decades earlier.
>
> If a woman did not complain earlier because she repressed the traumatic event, but does so now having recently retrieved the memory in the course of psychotherapy, there is a need to guard against merely presuming her claim is true, and shifting the burden upon the accused to prove that it is not (as some have advocated).
>
> We generally have continuous memories of catastrophes which befell us as children. Therapy offers adult survivors a badly needed chance to remedy that gap in their personal development caused by their fathers' inappropriate domination and control.
>
> In less than a decade, incest went from the most taboo and shameful of personal and family secrets to one that permeated the media. In families characterized by verbal, emotional and/or physical maltreatment, sexual awareness is rarely healthy. Destructive familial themes of poor boundaries, sadism, dominance, cloying seduction and possessiveness, narcissistic exploitation of children, invasiveness etc., permeate the interpersonal dialectics of family sexuality even when incestuous contact does not actually occur. At times, children sense their parents' barely successful struggle to control incestuous urges; such children suffer preconscious anxiety that incest is imminent.
>
> As a practical matter, it is problematic to sort out the subset in which incest actually occurs from the instances in which "preconscious anxiety that incest is imminent" is evoked in children with parents who clearly struggle to control incestuous urges.
>
> The latter group is doubtless considerably larger than the former. For every girl who has been involved in an incestuous relationship, considerably more have grown up in covertly incestuous families....
>
> According to one feminist: The definition of sexual abuse and harassment expanded like a deep breath, and women who had long been silent charged that "depending on how we process the abuse, how our psyche copes, a few kisses can be as traumatic and damaging as outright rape and are just as abusive."
>
> Ordinarily when we think of resolving a social problem, we think of eliminating its cause, not simply mitigating its harm.

Many would argue that the covertly incestuous family does not require legal intervention, and therefore rightfully falls outside the purview of the law. The reality is that most parents lack the training and skill to calmly discuss birth control options with their teens, yet we do hold them accountable for early erotic involvement and control of family sexual culture.

According to Dr. Floyd Martinson, the work of University of New Hampshire Psychologist David Finkelhor distinguishes three dimensions of family sexuality that are the most likely determinants of whether a home becomes incestuous.[11]

> First, families may prompt positive or negative attitudes in their children toward sexuality. In sex-positive families, children receive accurate information

about sex and are given positive attitudes about their bodies and shown physical affection, while in sex-negative families sex is fraught with anxiety and taboos.[12]

The second dimension concerns how sexualized the family interaction becomes. In highly sexualized families, members use one another as sexual objects, while low sexualized families discourage sexual activity inside the family.[13]

The third dimension involves personal boundaries. Clear boundaries imply respect for the privacy of each member of the family, with a clear differentiation of sex roles between adults and children. With poor personal boundaries, family members intrude on one another, and adult sexual behavior is not clearly distinguished from child sexual behavior.[14]

Greer generally characterizes incest as unprovable in court when the charges stem from memories recovered during psychotherapy. The case below demonstrates how typical challenges to recovered memories arise. It is indeed controversial to summarily conclude that criminal law is an ineffective response to the sexual molestation of children within families, due to evidentiary issues and other socio-psychological dynamics of abuse.

Deborah Johnson, Plaintiff, v. William Leo Johnson and Josephine Johnson, Defendants[15]

Oct. 7, 1988

Relevant Edited Excerpts

On May 6, 1988, Defendants moved to dismiss arguing that the complaint was barred by a two-year statute of limitations. For the reasons set forth below, Defendants' motion for summary judgment is denied.

PLUNKETT, District Judge.

Plaintiff Deborah Johnson is a citizen and resident of the State of California. Her parents-defendants are citizens of Illinois. Her complaint alleges that "from the time she was approximately three years old until she was approximately twelve or thirteen years old (1958 through 1968), while all parties were residing first in Indiana and then in Ohio, her father-defendant William Leo Johnson did intentionally and repeatedly sexually molest and abuse her.

Plaintiff also alleges that she "suppressed all memories of the sexual abuse and was blamelessly ignorant of the causal connection between father-defendant's acts and the injuries she suffered until on or about March 16, 1987, when in the course of psychotherapy, Plaintiff was able to begin to remember, perceive and understand the nature and scope of her injuries and their causal connection to father-defendant's earlier acts. She alleges that the suppression of these memories was a self-protecting measure which "prevented her from knowing, recognizing and understanding the nature of her injuries and the fact of their causal relationship to her father's ... sexual abuse."

Ms. Johnson alleges that her parents "had a duty to protect her ... and prevent acts of physical, sexual and psychological abuse directed at her as a child. She contends that her mother-defendant Josephine Johnson knew or should have known that her husband, William Leo Johnson, the plaintiff's father, was repeatedly abusing their infant daughter, but she did nothing to protect Plaintiff from its effects. Failure to protect and keep her safe from abuse was a breach of her duty and proximate cause of her daughter's injuries....

Facts

Plaintiff alleges that she was subject to abuse from three years of age to approximately twelve or thirteen years old. Plaintiff was thirty-two years old in 1987.

Plaintiff's therapist, Elizabeth E. Raymer, also filed an affidavit in this case. Ms. Raymer states that she has been treating Plaintiff from approximately January 1987 through the present. Ms. Raymer's diagnosis of Plaintiff "is Multiple Personality Disorder, based upon observation of Ms. Johnson, [her] understanding of the disease, [and her] consultation with other mental health care practitioners in this field and [her] research and reading of scholarly articles in this field...." Ms. Raymer states that because of Plaintiff's "psychiatric disturbance ... [Plaintiff] was unable to remember the sexual abuse by her father until on or about March 16, 1987, when in the course of therapy ... she was able to trust another individual enough to allow suppressed memories and personalities or personality fragments to surface."

Defendants claim that Illinois' two-year personal injury statute of limitations applies to this case. Defendants concede that the Illinois tolling statute for minors could be utilized by Plaintiff. Defendants assert, however, that Plaintiff's cause of action is clearly time barred since it was brought in 1988 when Plaintiff was over 30 years of age. Plaintiff argues that the discovery rule should be applied in this case to toll the beginning of the statute of limitation period until Plaintiff knew she was injured.

Illinois courts have not as yet addressed the issue of whether the discovery rule should apply to toll the statute of limitations beyond the two-year statutory toll period for minors so as to allow adults to bring claims of incest against their abusers.

In fact, this is a relatively new phenomenon and few courts have addressed the issue directly. The cases which have been brought to date have fallen into two categories:

(1) those where the Plaintiff claimed she knew about the sexual assaults at or before majority, but that she was unaware that other physical and psychological problems were caused by the prior sexual abuse;

(2) cases such as this one, where the Plaintiff claims due to the trauma of the experience she had no recollection or knowledge of the sexual abuse until shortly before she filed suit.

Courts in California and Montana have decided that the discovery rule does not apply to type 1 cases where the Plaintiff was aware of the sexual abuse but unaware of the causal connection between the sexual abuse and her physical/psychological problems.

In *Hammer*, a Wisconsin court held "as a matter of law, that a cause of action for incestuous abuse will not accrue until the victim discovers, or in the exercise of reasonable diligence should have discovered, the fact and cause of the injury. In reaching this result, the court balanced plaintiff's and defendant's interests and decided that " 'the injustice of barring meritorious claims before the claimant knows of the injury outweighs the threat of stale or fraudulent actions.'

The "underlying purpose of statutes of limitations, ... is to 'require the prosecution of a right of action within a reasonable time to prevent the loss or impair-

> ment of available evidence and to discourage delay in the bringing of claims. The literal application of a statute of limitations, however, "takes no cognizance of the situation in which the plaintiff is unable to discover, regardless of his diligence, that he has been injured until after the limitations period has passed and suit is forever barred. In order to mitigate this harshness, the courts have by judicial interpretation formulated the so-called discovery rule.
>
> In determining whether the discovery rule should apply, the Illinois Supreme Court has used a case-by-case approach. While the Illinois courts do talk of problems of proof being important in this balancing process.
>
> In a wrongful death case, the court found that it would be a "cruel hoax to deny a widow and 4 minor children an opportunity to test their case on the merits because the widow failed to decipher ... [a] medical term within the requisite period of time.
>
> We find that the Illinois courts would allow the discovery rule to be utilized in this situation. Incest is a crime in Illinois. It is also a major social problem. "It has been estimated that as much as one third of the population has experienced some form of child sexual abuse, much of which occurs within the family.
>
> When incest occurs among family members, it has been estimated that 75 percent [of the cases] involve incest between father and daughter.
>
> Because there is a genuine dispute of fact in this case as to when the Plaintiff knew or should have known of her injury and its wrongful cause, Defendants' motion for summary judgment is denied.

For Your Consideration

Johnson is about standing to sue. Our Constitution requires close scrutiny of rules that bar suits before a plaintiff has had a reasonable opportunity to assert a claim. Given the research that demonstrates how survivors of different forms of sexual abuse are severely damaged in their interpersonal relations, far beyond the requirements of adjusting to the "experience of stolen innocence," how should we define justice for its victims? If their worldview is altered in ways that make discovery and recovery a long and difficult process, does that necessarily require a broader view of issues related to standing, including the tolling of statutes of limitations and other procedural norms to reach legitimate criminal justice goals? Greer's assessment of recovered-memory evidence lacks the vital research necessary to determine that law is inadequate for dealing with incest. Even if we were to accept his assertion that public debate is skewed, because it enables lynch-mobs to form around trials with fantasy-induced tales of abuse passing for testimony, that might not readily distinguish it from certain other criminal cases. Criminal law reform is surely the next frontier. Supposing that some proponents of evidentiary reform are driven by larger, sloppier agendas does not relieve Greer of the responsibility for introducing an appropriate framework for restructuring debate around this critical social issue. Otherwise, the entire debate would shift toward a laissez faire approach that leaves our children languishing in the black-hole of legal rhetoric and indifference. Interdisciplinary forces are needed to reconcile conflicting socio-legal principles and attending psychoanalytic theories so as to address indifference and sloppiness to the extent (if any) that either impacts sexual abuse and battery laws. Nowhere is this more evident than in those recent Supreme Court rulings that serve to weaken former categorical prohibitions related to child pornography.

Child Protection, Technology & the First Amendment

Sustained efforts on the part of therapists, law enforcement officials, and social workers trained to deal with the victims and perpetrators of child sexual abuse and their families are undermined by incongruent socio-legal influences. We have a culture that glorifies and sexualizes youth. We celebrate five-year-old beauty queens, thirteen-year-old fashion models, black spandex and leopard print clothes with faux fur for eight-year-olds, overtly sexualized music accompanied by raw and graphic videos to bolster sales, and a Supreme Court that has difficulty dealing with tremendous clashes in the area of First Amendment jurisprudence in relation to child pornography. Child pornography leads to child sexual abuse. Technological advances have produced nearly instantaneous worldwide distribution of porn, reversing the gains made by law enforcement in earlier decades toward combating distribution and circulation of this and other harmful kinds of pornographic materials.[16] Claims by fringe groups using the slogan "sex before eight or it's too late" has created an uproar that is unlikely to generate meaningful debate around the need for laws that adequately distinguish mutual affectionate coupling where one or more parties is at least twelve years old, from the predatory actions of those with perverse afflictions and/or sexual addictions to children and child pornography.[17] Consumption of child pornography is on the rise. Millions of images are delivered to hundreds of thousands of consumers every year through use of the Internet alone. State legislatures are being called upon to deal directly with the problem while resisting the media drama and partisan political somersaults that have led to bad law and science. Legal categories must accommodate actual consent to sexual activity so as to increase public awareness of distinctions between criminal and moral culpability.

During the past fifteen years, three events have generated a large body of interest in the sexual experiences/exploitation of adolescent boys. The first is the emergence of fringe organizations like the North American Man-Boy Love Association (NAMBLA), which promote adult-child sex between males as harmless in most cases. Then, the Catholic Church descended into turmoil when it was revealed that known pedophile priests were moved from parish to parish, under orders of some of the most influential men in the Archdioceses. Drawing attention away from the priests, media attention mysteriously turned to world-renowned pop artist Michael Jackson, who conveniently became the poster-boy of deviance amid accusations of child molestation. Finally, the Supreme Court upheld a decision by the Boy Scouts to expel a high-ranking openly gay troop leader,[18] bringing into public debate long-held (if unspoken) assumptions about connections between homosexuality and pedophilia.

Former congressman Mark Foley chaired the House Caucus on Missing and Exploited Children, and introduced legislation targeting sexual predators. According to his attorney, Foley was molested by a priest between the ages of 13 and 15. The Florida Republican was forced to resign on September 29, 2006, amid questions over e-mails he wrote to a former page, asking the boy what he liked to do and requesting a photograph. Foley's attorney characterized him as a gay man, who never had sexual contact with a minor; thus any assertion that Foley is a pedophile is "categorically false." Foley checked into a center for a 30-day treatment of alcoholism and mental issues. The lawyer's announcement came shortly after ABC News published correspondences submitted by former pages, demonstrating that Foley had Internet sex with a former page before going to a vote on the House floor in 2003.

Top GOP leaders issued a joint statement calling Foley's alleged actions "an obscene breach of trust. [Foley's] immediate resignation must now be followed by the full weight of the criminal justice system."

President Bush told reporters that he was disgusted by the revelations and disappointed that Foley would violate the trust of the citizens who placed him in office."

Rep. John Shimkus, chairman of the House Page Board, acknowledged knowing about the exchanges. The conservative newspaper, Washington Times, published editorials calling for House Speaker Dennis Hastert's resignation for mishandling the incident, saying he was either negligent or "deliberately looked the other way." The FBI, Florida Department of Law Enforcement, and the House Ethics Committee are investigating Foley's conduct—and whether there was any attempt to cover it up.[19]

There is no statutory rape equivalent for consensual relations involving male teens and adults. The twenty-year-old man who has consensual sex with a fourteen-year-old girl is guilty of statutory rape under most state laws. The twenty-year-old man who has sex with a fourteen-year-old boy is guilty of sexual molestation. Examining the language and dynamics of the law and social scientific research on these issues presents a greater challenge than the early gender-equality cases comparing difference in the treatment of women and men in statutory rape cases.

Rarely a day goes by when parents are not warned about internet predators, whose methods of seduction are broadcast during arrests pursuant to covert sting operations. Even scenes of surveillance at the U.S.-Mexican Border are meant to assure us that law enforcement is doing all it can to make the streets safer for our children.

According to MSNBC's Dateline, Predators are scouring the Internet, targeting children for sex:

> It's a national problem that Dateline has helped uncover. We got such an overwhelming response from our last investigation—some 15,000 emails from parents, grandparents, teachers and law enforcement—telling us to "keep up the good work," and "keep the issue alive." On Wednesday night, April 26, Dateline is back with the fourth undercover investigation. This time, we traveled to small town America. Even far from the big cities and suburbs, vulnerable young teens are not far from danger. A warning: some of what you're about to read is explicit.[20]

Altogether we have fallen into a sort of mass hysteria that leaves parents on perpetual alert and children afraid to even acknowledge those whom they do not know. Viewed in historical context these elements of social interaction are hardly surprising. However, we legitimately expect more of law and science, which are wholly subsidized by taxpayers for the public good.

There is no question but that these issues are multi-layered and complex and as such, require two things: 1) the most responsible concerted efforts to create a path for meaningful redress of harm, and 2) recognition when no harm is present. Those conducting research on these topics are subject to unusual pressures to conform to a certain orthodoxy and adopt a standard set of assumptions at the outset, as if the research itself was a response to the harm that child predators inflict. Merely reaching a non-traditional scientific result provokes questions of bias and hidden agendas among researchers and their critics.

Results from a scientific study of research related to the sexual abuse of children, published in the American Psychological Association journal Psychological Bulletin, in 1998, provides one of the clearest recent examples. The study is titled "*A Meta-Analytic Examination of Assumed Properties of Child Sexual Abuse (CSA) Using College Samples,*" by psychologists Bruce Rind, Philip Tromovitch and Robert Bauserman.[21] The downside of their experience with this publication is reflected in their introductory remarks about the project during an international presentation of the research.

Rind, Tromovitch and Bauserman Introduction

> In America, starting in the mid-1970s, mental health care professionals, politicians, law enforcement personnel, the media, and the lay public began paying considerable attention to child sexual abuse, which we'll often refer to in this talk as "CSA" for short. Eventually, this concern spread to other countries around the world, including Holland. Much of the attention paid to CSA has focused on its possible effects on psychological adjustment. The media, the popular press, and the professional literature have all generally portrayed CSA as a particularly traumatic experience, as a "special destroyer of adult mental health." For example, in the top journal in America for clinical psychology, the authors of a recent article asserted that "child sexual abuse is a traumatic event for which there may be few peers," by which they are essentially saying that virtually nothing could be worse for a young person than to have this experience. Some in the mental health field have even attempted to explain much or all of adult psychopathology as a consequence of CSA.
>
> The common view that has emerged over the past two decades is that CSA has certain basic properties:
>
> 1. it causes harm,
> 2. which occurs on a pervasive basis,
> 3. is usually intense, and
> 4. is equally negative for both boys and girls.
>
> In this view, these properties hold whether we're talking about patients in therapy (that is, clinical samples), or people not in therapy (that is, nonclinical samples). Our research over the past few years has focused on examining these assumed basic properties of CSA. The question that we have asked, and that we will attempt to answer in this presentation, is:
>
> > For people who have experienced CSA, does the experience cause intense psychological harm on a widespread basis for both genders?
>
> Before we describe our research, it is important to discuss terminology. The term child sexual abuse has been used in the psychological literature to describe virtually all sexual interactions between children or adolescents and significantly older persons, as well as between same-age children or adolescents when coercion is involved. The indiscriminate use of this term and related terms such as victim and perpetrator has been criticized by various researchers because of concerns about scientific validity. As one researcher noted, researchers have often failed to distinguish between "abuse" as harm done to a

> child or adolescent and "abuse" as a violation of social norms, which is a problem because it cannot be assumed that violations of social norms lead to harm. As another researcher observed, our society has tended to equate "wrongfulness" with harmfulness in sexual matters, but harmfulness cannot be inferred from wrongfulness. Still another researcher argued that the indiscriminate use of terms suggesting force, coercion, and harm reflects and maintains the belief that these interactions are always harmful, which interferes with objectively appraising them. In earlier research, we demonstrated experimentally that people who read scientific reports of nonnegative sexual interactions between adolescents and adults are biased by the use of negatively-loaded terms such as child sexual abuse.
>
> Problems of scientific validity of the term child sexual abuse are perhaps most apparent when contrasting cases such as the repeated rape of a 5-year-old girl by her father, which undoubtedly produces serious harm, and the willing sexual involvement of a mature 15-year-old adolescent boy with an unrelated adult, which, although violating social norms, may have no implications for harm. By classifying these two very dissimilar events into the single category of child sexual abuse, a scientifically valid understanding of each is threatened.
>
> With these caveats in mind regarding the shortcomings of the term child sexual abuse, we will nevertheless continue to use it in our talk because it is so pervasively used by the authors of the studies we examined. We will, however, return to a discussion of the validity of this term later in our presentation after we have presented our data and analyses. Having said that, based on typical current use of the term CSA, it will be defined as a sexual interaction involving either physical contact or no contact (for example, exhibitionism) between either a child or adolescent and someone substantially older, or between two peers who are children or adolescents when coercion is employed.

Here is the reported response following full publications of their results.

> March 23, 1999—in response to the criticism, the APA declared in a press statement that "the sexual abuse of children is wrong and harmful to its victims" and that "the findings of a research project within an APA journal is in no way an endorsement."
>
> June 9, 1999—the president of the APA, Raymond Fowler, announced in an open letter to Representative Tom DeLay that there was to be an independent review of the controversial study.
>
> July 12, 1999—the United States House of Representatives passed a resolution condemning the study, declaring that child-adult sex could be nothing but "abusive and destructive." The resolution was passed unanimously in the Senate.
>
> September 15, 1999—the American Association for the Advancement of Science (AAAS), whom the politically pressured APA had asked for an independent review of the article, refused to do so as a response to coercive political efforts, and as a matter of professional responsibility saying:
>
>> We see no reason to second-guess the process of peer review used by the APA journal in its decision to publish the article in question. While not without its imperfections, peer review is well established as a standard mechanism for maintaining the flow of scientific information that scientists can refer to, cri-

tique or build on. After examining all the materials available to the committee, we saw no clear evidence of improper application of methodology or other questionable practices on the part of the article's authors.

The Committee also wishes to express its grave concerns with the politicization of the debate over the article's methods and findings. In reviewing the set of background materials available to us, we found it deeply disconcerting that so many of the comments made by those in the political arena and in the media indicate a lack of understanding of the analysis presented by the authors or misrepresented the article's findings.

All citizens, especially those in a position of public trust, have a responsibility to be accurate about the evidence that informs their public statements. We see little indication of that from the most vocal on this matter, behavior that the Committee finds very distressing.

For Your Consideration

As long as well-established, mainstream research directors come under political fire for questioning standards employed in defining social problems and for undertaking important critiques of the rarely questioned orthodoxy, we leave ourselves open to the misinformation that comes with pseudoscience (see story below). Leaving important questions of research open to those with aggressive political agendas threatens public confidence in fairness of law and distorts important policy debates.

Pseudo-scientific Research of Child Porn?

Federal Judge Howard Turrentine denied Attorney Lawrence Stanley's request for the return of 225 pornographic magazines that he claimed were used in a study with the Institute for the Advanced Study of Human Sexuality in San Francisco. Acquitted of child pornography charges in 1989, Stanley is a board member of the North American Man-Boy Love Association, and the editor of the newsletter Uncommon Desires, which is dedicated to "eroticizing sex between men and young girls."

How might a court fashion a set of standards for determining what would constitute legitimate academic research that serves the public interest?

Man-Boy Love Lawyer Wanted in Girl Abuse[22]

Relevant Edited Excerpts

Lawrence Stanley, a Manhattan lawyer, serves as defense counsel for the North American Man-Boy Love Association, and publishes a newsletter featuring nude girls that calls itself "the voice of a politically conscious girl-love underground." Three NAMBLA members were charged with fraudulently forming a nonprofit corporation to secretly raise funds for NAMBLA and promote decriminalization of consensual sex between men and boys. The New York Supreme Court ruled that NAMBLA members were lobbying for the legal right to such conduct. The opinion stated that lobbying as "an activity aimed at changing public attitudes is an exercise of free speech."

This position is supported by the American Civil Liberties Union.

ACLU to Defend Boy-Sex Group Lawsuit Stems from Murder of 10-Year-Old[23]

The ACLU is representing NAMBLA in a suit filed by the family of 10-year-old murder victim Jeffrey Curley. In October 1997, Jeffrey was lured into a car by two college-age men he knew from his neighborhood. He was killed when he resisted one of the men's sexual advances. The fifth-grader's body was found a few days later, floating in a river in a tub of cement. Salvatore Sicari and Charles Jaynes were convicted of the murder and received long prison sentences. The Curleys were awarded $328 million in a civil suit. Jaynes was a member of NAMBLA, and the Curley family filed a $1 million wrongful-death suit against NAMBLA and seven of its leaders. The lawsuit argues that the defendants' advocacy of pedophilia played a role in Jeffrey's murder. A key piece of evidence is a diary that Jaynes kept after joining NAMBLA, in which he wrote about being influenced by materials on NAMBLA's Web site and subsequent obsession with having sex with young male children.

The ACLU Foundation of Massachusetts released a statement defending its decision to take the case:

> We believe NAMBLA has been sued for its advocacy, not of crimes, but for a change in the laws and in society's attitudes about sexual relationships between adults and minors.
>
> Regardless of whether people agree with or abhor NAMBLA's views, holding the organization responsible for crimes committed by others who read their materials would gravely endanger our important First Amendment rights.
>
> There was nothing in those [NAMBLA] publications or Web site which advocated or incited the commission of any illegal acts, including murder or rape.

For Your Consideration

The widespread allegation is that NAMBLA members both participate in and advocate the rape of children by educating men about how to locate young victims, gain their trust, and avoid law enforcement officials. During the early days of the Internet, an adult survivor of sexual abuse warned the Senate Judiciary Committee about the role that America Online (AOL) played in spreading child pornography across national borders. In July 1995, Barry J. Crimmins testified as follows:

> There is a major crime wave taking place on America's computers. The proliferation of child pornography trafficking has created an anonymous "Pedophile Superstore." As a result, the de facto decriminalization of child pornography is taking place. The demand for child pornography is also a demand for innocent children to be abused. Child pornography is not protected speech. It is crime evidence. (AOL) has become an integral link in a network of child pornography traffickers. It cannot claim that it is not aware of this.

I am here to tell the American people that not only are their children unsafe on AOL, their children are unsafe because of it.[24]

Murder, Attempted Murder & Animal Rights

In the post-postmodern world, the nature of sexual relations and individual proclivities have merged with rights rhetoric so as to support plausible arguments that the choice of one's partner or partners is a matter of civil right, and sexual practices intrinsic to those relations an exercise of civil liberty. The dilemma for legal scholars and legislatures (beyond naked power plays) is articulating which set of empirical data—sociological, biological, psychological, etc.—to use in support of constitutional limits given the noninterventionist-slant of free choice theory. The legal quandary is most pronounced when dissecting arguments pertaining to those who would engage non-human mammals as intimate companions or life partners.[25]

The general stance of policy makers and those who shape constitutional debate is fairly concrete. One scholar aptly portrays prevailing attitudes around the need to debate the constitutional question:

> One opponent declared, "he would only go so far as to state that such "relationships" are so far a field from relationships between human beings that they are inapplicable and inappropriate in rational discussions of romantic, intimate, or committed human relationships. Th[is] author will not substantively address such references further as doing so would give such references undeserved validity."[26]

Other opponents only go as far as placing it alongside the laundry list of practices that have been universally condemned from the beginning of time, and routinely referred to as illicit sexual practices or depraved and perverse tendencies.

A recent incident involving the Maine Legislature, and criminal cases involving an attempted murder in one state and the death of a woman in another, have raised a series of legal questions. Reconciling the rationale behind relevant laws deemed necessary for the protection of animals, from so many others that offer them no protection at all is no small task. Critiques of philosopher Peter Singer's commentary on the book DEAREST PET, called ***Heavy Petting***, coupled with these high-profile cases, have brought this and similar questions of sexual taboo out of the shadows in a growing number of states. There is little doubt that advocates on one side of the debate are formulating a strategy in anticipation of the "perfect test-case."

Parkman Zoophile Objects to Bestiality Legislation[27]

Emmet Meara

Relevant Edited Excerpts

> AUGUSTA, MAINE—In what surely must rank as one of the most bizarre moments in State House history, Phillip Buble, 44, of Parkman defended his sexual love for his dog for more than 30 minutes before the squirming members of the Legislature's Criminal Justice Committee on Monday.

Buble opposed a bill that would have made it a felony to abuse an animal physically or sexually. Maine has no such law today.

Buble proudly and emotionally defended what he termed the religion and philosophy of zoophiles or zoosexuals, who have sexual love for animals. Although committee members tried to interrupt Buble several times, he proceeded to read a lengthy statement defending the practice. "Zoos" or people who have sex with animals, are born with a true love for animals and have a lifelong commitment to their care, he told the committee. He said he and his dog, Lady Buble, "live together as a married couple. In the eyes of God we are truly married." Animals can initiate sexual relations and can give consent or withhold it, just as humans can. If it is legal for two animals to have sexual relationships, it should be legal for a human to have sex with an animal, dismissing the proposed law as an attempt "to force morality on a minority. It will be a disservice to zoo couples and would keep zoo couples from coming out of the closet and drive us deeper underground. This helps no one and would force me out of state."

Buble has been a guest on regional radio shows after his father was jailed for beating him. His father, Frank Buble, 71, of Parkman, was jailed for beating his son with a crowbar in frustration over the younger man's continued sexual relations with the dog. The son told the committee that it was the dog that stopped the father "from slaughtering me while I was sleeping." He broke down in tears as he told the story.

"Zoos" are not animal abusers and do far less damage to them than people who eat animal flesh, hunt animals, or allow medical experiments that torture animals, Buble said. The dog he called his "significant other" was kept in a car during testimony.

The bill to criminalize bestiality, LD 1283, was sponsored by Sen. Lloyd P. LaFountain III, D-Biddeford, who said the measure was sparked by "troubling stories which are too perverse to share."

Maine, like 24 other states, should protect animals with cruelty and bestiality control laws, he said. The bestiality law was previously on the books and was removed by mistake, officials said. State officials reported six cases of animal sexual abuse last year involving dogs, horses and cows.

Despite the prevalence of the sexual abuse of animals, a practice supported by an Internet communications network, "no one wants to talk about it," said Deborah Clark of the National Federation of Humane Societies. She told the committee stories of cats destroyed by internal organ damage and of dogs and cows damaged by human sexual abuse, all for "the gratification of perverted souls."

University of Southern Maine professor Pierce Beirne, who has studied bestiality, compared the practice to child abuse where power and lack of consent are the issues. The state has a duty to protect its animals from further harm, he said.

Don Harper, the director of the state Animal Control Association, said Maine had six documented cases and several undocumented reports on bestiality last year. He said that a national study reported that 40 percent of those involved in sexually motivated homicides admitted to previous sexual abuse of animals. In a Missouri study, 50 percent of sexual offenders admitted to having previous sexual intercourse with an animal. Harper said one "zoo" Internet site has 200 links and claims 46,000 visits a day.

For Your Consideration

During class discussion, one student observed how well the case demonstrates that we live in a world where even the smaller female animals need protection from human male sexual abuse.

Zoophilia Might Be Called a Lifestyle[28]

Relevant Edited Excerpts

According to Andrea Beetz Ph.D., author of Love, Violence, and Sexuality in Relationships between Humans and Animals, separate from those whose interest is curiosity, pornography, or sexual novelty, are those for whom zoophilia might be called a lifestyle. A commonly reported starting age is at around 9–11, and this seems consistent for both males and females. Those who discover an interest at an older age often trace it back to nascent form during this period or earlier. Lifestyle zoophiles often share some or all of the following common traits:

- Some form of social individualism. This can be either inhibitive (e.g., shyness) or empowering (e.g., independence of thought). Zoophiles tend not to be people who unquestioningly follow a peer group.
- An emotional respect for animals. Examples of human emotion towards animals in everyday society are common, such as pet memorials. In some cases this will become akin to a partnership, or become sexual.
- Belief that animals and humans are not so different in many ways, similar to the way that homosexuals feel the gender gap is not a major issue.
- A sense that humans can be deceptive and manipulative, and that animals do not have these traits and are less complex socially.
- A "romantic" nature, the desire to have a bond for life.
- Above average awareness of feelings. Causal factors are unclear. They may be close to animals because they empathize well, or have developed empathic skills because of intimate closeness with animals.
- Loneliness, insofar as others of like kind are hard to find.
- An open view on sexuality. Sex is commonly seen as "just part of life." Zoophiles easily accept bisexuality/ homosexuality, but not abuse.
- A higher proportion than average of zoophiles appear to be engaged in supportive work for animal welfare, conservation organizations, and so on.
- That the ideal life would be an animal as lifelong mate, and a human as a companion (with or without the possibility of sexual relationship).

Lifestyle zoophiles experience a high degree of stigma, resulting from an inability to be open or accepted in their relationships. This is not usually religious oriented, but they have difficulty with the loss of loved ones in a world that dismisses animals as secondary species. Animals and humans differ in sexuality. For most animals, sex carries less importance, is burdened with fewer social and conceptual barriers, and is more an immediate than a conceptual experience. Zoophiles may or may not have human partners. In some cases the human partner or family is aware of animal partners. As human partnerships are seen as socially desirable and there is social pressure to be in them, both male and female zoophiles often marry and keep their other lifestyle private.

Laws governing treatment of animals vary according to their intended purpose. Regulations are found for use and control of animals in: farming/ food service, amusement, transportation, entertainment, fur coats and accessories, non-luxury clothing, hunting for sport and medical experiments. Animal rights advocates argue for reconciliation of these areas with laws governing companion-pets. Evidence of regulatory hypocrisy in this area proliferates with each new layer of discussion. We clearly have no prevailing or overarching philosophy concerning the rights of animals in this country. Zoophilia, on the other hand, most certainly takes companion-pet theory to a whole new level.

"O.K., who else has experienced the best-friend relationship as inadequate?"

For Your Consideration

How would you explain why the liberty interest embodied in the Fourteenth Amendment does not extend the right to be left alone to zoophiles? Or, if it does, would that necessitate creation of legal distinctions between romantic love for animals and their sexual abuse?

Rules prohibiting use of animals for sexual gratification have, in statutory form, been listed next to mutilation, necrophilia, murder, rape, sado-masochism, torture, pedophilia, and incest. However, it has most often been associated with cannibalism. One early Arkansas statute made it a crime only if committed with an animal of the same sex. According to biblical tenets it is a crime punishable by death.[29] In fact, the very first juvenile to be put to death in the United States was a 16-year-old convicted of bestiality, living in New Haven, Connecticut, in the 1600s.

The arguments for and against are relatively clear. In academia, repulsion strains the impetus toward a "rational debate" on the issue. Very few scholars even mention the subject. Lay people are reluctant to acknowledge the range of fears that arise in contemplating activities so far beyond what is generally accepted as normal human behavior. Doomsayers warn of the frightening consequences of traveling down certain deplorable paths (just google bestiality), while proponents casually remark that they have lived this way for years (just google zoophiles). This is indeed the cutting edge, and the Constitution requires that it all be sorted out: the state's interest, the constitutional limits, the governing rationale, equal protection for all citizens, and protection for other species. One issue that was never raised in discussion of the case in Maine is that the elder Buble ultimately served only nine months in jail. So short a sentence for attempted murder sends a powerful message about which lives are important.

Shag the Dog[30]

By William Saletan

Relevant Edited Excerpts

> The love that dare not bark its name is now a front-page topic, raised at White House news conferences and in state legislatures, thanks largely to philosopher Peter Singer. In an essay titled "Heavy Petting," Singer asks: What's wrong with fondling Fido? The essay, coupled with two scandals involving sex with dogs—one confirmed in Maine and the other alleged by investigators in California—has elicited cries of outrage and disgust. But the outcry has been largely thoughtless.
>
> It's easy to say that becoming more than friendly with man's best friend is wrong. What's hard is backing up that statement with a principle, and reconciling that principle with laws about meat-eating and other issues related to sexual orientation.
>
> Singer's essay tackles a series of objections. The first is that it's unnatural. "If nature had wanted you to mate with your pet you'd be able to procreate together." Singer points out, however, that we've come to tolerate other non-procreative practices that include use of contraception, masturbation, oral gratification, and homosexuality.
>
> So why the taboo? According to Singer, it's because we think we're intrinsically and categorically superior to other species. This is the dogma that Singer really wants to penetrate. "We are animals," he writes. "This does not make sex across the species barrier normal, or natural, whatever those much-misused words may mean, but it does imply that it ceases to be an offence to our status and dignity as human beings." The answer matters, because the principle that makes sex with animals immoral—whatever that principle is—must apply to other issues as well.
>
> One journal derides Singer for condoning puppy love while his animal rights buddies demand "intolerable paperwork" from researchers who use animals in lab experiments. But if rules about what's done to animals by their owners are important,

why not make rules about what's done to them in labs? You could just as easily ask those of us who eat meat why, if it's wrong to rape animals, it's OK to kill them.

Zoophiles," as they prefer to be called—borrow the language of gay liberation. "I'm the first out-of-the-closet 'zoo' to be attacked because of my sexual orientation," Philip Buble, a zoophile, told the Bangor Daily News four months ago. Buble says the "relationship" between man and beast "can develop to be a sexual one." Testifying before a Maine legislative committee, Buble accused proponents of a ban on animal sexual abuse of trying "to force morality on a minority. It will be a disservice to zoo couples and would keep zoo couples from coming out of the closet and drive us deeper underground." Commenting on DEAREST PET, the book that inspired Singer's essay, other zoophiles articulate an "alternative sexual lifestyle" defined by "loving relationships with their animal lovers."

Then there's the case of the killer dogs in San Francisco. Last week, Marjorie Knoller and her husband, Robert Noel, were collared on manslaughter charges because two dogs in their care mauled to death their neighbor, Diane Whipple. Knoller and Noel, who are lawyers, claim they were taking care of the dogs on behalf of Paul "Cornfed" Schneider, a client whom they have adopted as their son while he serves a life sentence for attempted murder. According to a prison guard's affidavit, documents found in Schneider's possession include a photo of a male dog's genitals, "numerous photos of Knoller posing nude with fighting dog drawings," and a letter from the couple that discusses "sexual activity between Noel, Knoller and the dog" that subsequently killed Whipple. When the first vague report of the photos surfaced, Noel told the San Francisco Chronicle, "I'm not going to confirm it or deny it," adding, "There used to be a time when guy-on-guy or woman-on-woman relationships were looked at as unnatural acts. What concern is it to anybody if there is or isn't a personal relationship?"

Are we championing monogamy? Fidelity? Commitment? Effort? One article suggests as much: "[A] fundamental reason for prohibiting sex with animals is the human desire to join sex [with love] and our recognition of the complexity of that joining, the care with which it must be nurtured and disciplined, the ease with which it is disrupted and led astray."

Strange as it may seem, however, it's hard to prove that Philip Buble doesn't nurture and discipline his love for the canine companion he calls "Lady Buble." He's a one-dog man. A month ago, when Buble's father was sentenced to jail for attacking him with a crowbar—in part out of disgust with Buble's "lifestyle"—Buble sent a formal request to the judge. "I'd like my significant other to attend by my side if possible as she was present in the house during the attack, though not an eyewitness to it, thank goodness," Buble wrote. "I've been informed your personal permission is needed given that my wife is not human." In his legislative testimony a week ago, Buble declared that he and Lady "live together as a married couple. In the eyes of God we are truly married."

Let's try another criterion. How about harm? Many animal rights activists say this is what's wrong with human-animal copulation, as opposed to gay sex. Singer points out that some sex acts between humans and animals "don't seem to do harm to animals." Is Buble harming the dog for whose emotional well-being he expressed such concern in his letter to the judge? Good luck proving it. In last week's testimony, Buble said zoophiles are born to care for animals. He denied that their physical interaction with their pets includes abuse. And he added that

> zoophiles do far less harm to animals than hunters, meat-eaters, and medical experiments do. It's hard to argue with that.
>
> How about consent? When someone has sex with an animal, he foists himself on a creature that has the mental and emotional capacity of a child. Thus, it is no more capable than a child of giving meaningful consent.... [I]f you have had sex with someone who is constitutionally incapable of giving anything that might constitute meaningful consent, you have committed rape. At the very least you have taken advantage of a creature over which you exercise considerable power.
>
> Now we're onto something. The evidence that consent is morally essential—and that animals don't really give it—comes from zoophiles themselves. DEAREST PET reportedly suggests that many artistic images of male animals penetrating women are fantasies projected by men. The usual scenario, according to more reliable records cited in the book, is a man penetrating an animal for his own satisfaction. Buble would persuade people that his pet consents to their putative marriage. His letter to the judge included, next to his signature, a paw print purporting to represent the signature of "Lady Buble." Readers of the letter recognized that the paw print had been drawn by hand, and a reader discerned another discrediting detail: "I also noticed in the picture of Buble and his Lady that the MRS. wears a choke collar. A willing participant indeed."
>
> If you say that sex is permissible only if both parties consent to it, this still leaves you with the problem of explaining why it's OK to kill and eat animals.

Further Consideration

What might be some of the discernible practical consequences of equating animals with humans and providing legal protection on par with ordinary citizens? Consider the ramifications of those instances where we already do.

According to the Associated Press, one of the defendants in a lawsuit filed by a convicted drug dealer is a dog named Andi. The dog is used by the narcotics squad of the Athens County Sheriff's Department and has a badge. Andi is the first non-human defendant to be represented by County Prosecutor C. David Warren. The "German shepherd was informed that he's being sued, sort of. With a paw print, the dog "signed" the paper indicating he had been formally served with the complaint."[31]

By legal artifice, less than 150 years ago, particular members of the human species were treated exactly like animals. Like animal law today, the regulatory apparatus inflicted and allowed all manner of cruelty when directed at slaves, former-slaves and their offspring. The sexual abuse and breeding of slave girls on large southern plantations is but one example of negotiated boundaries around private space and property rights.[32] Sexual exploitation of women owned in chattel slavery, counted as 3/5ths of a person for purposes of taxation, was never criminalized and rarely condemned. Bi-racial children were openly referred to as a mongrel breed and sold in the market like Yorkshire Terriers today. They were sold on the theory that they were less than human with only fleeting experiences with feelings such as pain, fear, and affection. Thus, the precept of inferiority accompanied by theories of low-level intelligence, was used to justify what many willingly accepted as a mere fact of life. Indeed, there was no lack of encouragement from the top. In the words of the Chief Justice of the U.S. Supreme Court in *Dred Scott v. Sanford*:

> They have for more than a century been regarded as beings of an inferior order, and altogether unfit to associate with the White race, either in social or political relations, and so far inferior that they had no rights which the White man was bound to respect, and they were justly and lawfully reduced to slavery for their own benefit, bought and sold and traded as an ordinary article of merchandise and traffic, whenever a profit could be made by it.[33]

It was only when free and educated Blacks gained public attention that the discussion of group relations and shared governance seriously surfaced.

Part Three

Claiming Individual Rights under a System of Group Privileges & Immunities

Our traditional rational approach has always been to define, learn, and interact by categorization, always thinking in terms of categorical opposites. These categories are only rough maps for our comprehension, artificial separations that allow us to break the world into understandable pieces. Left unchecked, a category will lose its status as a malleable tool and become an indisputable truth, leading us to mistake the map for the territory. We have defined ourselves, as a society and as individuals, in terms of race for so long that we have forgotten race only has meaning in our own eyes. Race is neither based on a biological component nor on some inherent moral or character trait. Race is based on nothing outside of our own sociohistorical worldview: "race is an indeterminate social construct that is continually reinvented and manipulated to maintain domination and enhance White privilege." Western culture used the concept of race to justify slavery, thereby color-coding the dominant-subservient categorization: dominant became White, and Black became oppressed. The United States was founded during a time that racial distinctions were axiomatic and the underlying assumption has affected the country ever since.[1]

Kathleen R. Sandy

Chapter Eight

The Racial Divide & American Identity

Exploration of the nature of individual rights in the United States and State government exercise of regulatory powers returns us to the nation's founding. One can only comprehend the nature of individual rights by considering the relationship between group rights and the constitutional amendments that gave rise to the modern expansion of equal protection, substantive due process, and fundamental social freedom. The question of valuation and respect is, to a large degree, integral to an understanding of group rights. [M]ajority group cultures are viewed as universal, and this has a profound impact upon collective perception around which groups are "equal" and worthy of full participation of all the benefits of citizenship."[2] While this chapter discusses the invention of racial categories in the starkest terms, it is less about racism as experienced by many ethnic groups throughout U.S. history, and more about the role of the law in first establishing group rights in a democracy, then attempting to transition to a system of equal distribution of privileges and immunities among citizens.

The Nation's Legacy of Group Rights [& Wrongs]

The U.S. Constitution was adopted in 1787 to unify the nation. As illustrated in the Commentary on the style and artistry of the Declaration of Independence, the preamble invoked equally compelling language. WE THE PEOPLE come together to perfect the union, establish justice, insure tranquility, provide a common defense, and secure the blessings of liberty. The latter is set apart from the Declaration, insofar as the right of property in slaves was distinctly and expressly affirmed in the Constitution prior to passage of the Thirteenth Amendment nearly a century later. Until the Fourteenth Amendment, Blacks were counted as three-fifths of a person for purposes of apportionment. The Constitution banned any prohibition on the importation of slaves before 1808, barred every amendment that would affect their importation, and required the return of slaves who escaped. Jefferson said of slavery in the United States in 1802: "Indeed I tremble for my country when I reflect that God is just, and that his justice cannot sleep forever."[3]

Slavery was vigorously debated and opposed by abolitionists as violative of natural law and Christian principles. Fear of slave revolts loomed large with news of insurrections abroad. At home, there was growing disdain for the southern aristocracy that emerged from the immense wealth of slaveholding dynasties. Abolitionists pressed forward on the grounds that the slave trade and the process of capture and deportation was so inhumane that it created sadists among several generations of slave-owners and overseers. Slave narratives written by Frederick Douglass chronicled the lives of slaves: captivity, plantation life, and his own escape to freedom.[4] His articles were published and widely circulated throughout the North. Like other writers, he portrayed the slave master as the villain, and refused to depict Blacks as brainless, docile, contented buffoons. Abolitionist writing focused upon slave tendencies toward the long-suffering, co-dependent and apologetic characteristics required of devout Christians, which earned them the "good slave" label. Abolitionists are credited with creating literary space for a more realistic portrayal of free and educated Blacks, and framing a much broader dialog for debating the legislative process of dehumanization.

From the 1830s until 1870, abolitionists argued for immediate emancipation. Theirs was part of a broad-based political opposition to slavery's expansion. They were present during the revolution, but became more militant in their crusade during the 1830s. Their activities were greeted with hostile responses in the South and fear in the North. Violent mobs burned mailbags containing abolitionist literature and the House of Representatives passed a "gag rule" that banned consideration of antislavery petitions.[5] However, the 1837 murder of abolitionist editor Elijah Lovejoy brought many converts to their cause. They stressed the obvious deleterious effects by demonstrating how the institution of slavery had corrupted all of society. As a result, abolitionists called for a revolutionary change in America's spiritual values and exercised a notable influence in major religious organizations.[6] As schisms developed between the Methodists and Baptists, they established a number of abolitionist-led free churches.

The state of affairs was dismal. The nation was divided; slave populations were reaching significant proportions in the North as well as South. Significant rebellions were reported from overseas. Widespread conversion of slaves to Christianity subverted the original rationale for enslaving Africans. The struggle to manage free Blacks and develop meaningful classification of the children of bi-racial couples forced Whites to think about Blacks more systematically than ever. By declaring themselves free and independent White America was forced to account for those whom they enslaved and crippled. The result was intense speculation about the nature of the African under the guise of natural science. The well-worn ideological building blocks were used to construct a theory of Black inferiority that disallows a co-equal existence unto this very day.

According to Jeffrey B. Perry, it was all by design.[7] He describes the process in his evaluation of the work of the late Theodore W. Allen.

> In "The Invention of the White Race" Allen focused on Virginia, as the first and pattern-setting continental colony. He emphasized that "When the first Africans arrived in Virginia there were no White people there." He found "no instance of the official use of the word 'white' as a token of social status before its appearance in a Virginia law passed in 1691."
>
> Seventeenth century conditions for African-American and European-American laborers and bond-servants were very similar. Under such conditions solidarity among the laboring classes reached a peak during Bacon's Rebellion where the capitol (Jamestown) was burned; two thousand rebels forced the governor to flee across the Chesapeake Bay and controlled 6/7 of Virginia's land; and, in the latter stages of the struggle, "foure hundred English and Negroes in Arms" demanded their freedom from bondage.

To Allen, the social control problems highlighted by Bacon's Rebellion "demonstrated beyond question the lack of a sufficient intermediate stratum to stand between the ruling plantation elite and the mass of European-American and African-American laboring people, free and bond."

In the period after Bacon's Rebellion the White race was invented as "a bourgeois social control formation in response to [such] laboring class unrest."

Systematic ruling class policies, extended privileges to European laborers and bond-servants and imposed and extended harsher disabilities and blocked normal class mobility for African-Americans.

Out of the clear blue, Blacks were stripped of their long-held right to vote in Virginia. The Governor explained in 1735 that the Virginia Assembly had decided upon this curtailment of the franchise in order "to fix a perpetual Brand upon Free Negros & Mulattos."

The hallmark of racial oppression in its colonial origins and as it has persisted in subsequent historical contexts, is the reduction of all members of the oppressed group to one undifferentiated social status, beneath that of any member of the oppressor group."

The key to understanding racial oppression is the social control buffer—that group in society, which helps to control the poor for the rich. Under racial oppression in Virginia, any persons of discernible non-European ancestry in colonial Virginia after Bacon's Rebellion were denied a role in the social control buffer group, the bulk of which was made up of working-class "Whites."

In the Caribbean, "Mulattos" were included in the social control group and were promoted into middle-class status. The difference "was rooted in the objective fact that in the West Indies there were too few laboring-class Europeans to act as overseers.

Shades of Freedom

Leon Higginbotham Jr.

The Most Enduring Precept[8]

Chief Justice Roger Brooke Taney's opinion in the Dred Scott case did not reflect a unique perception about African Americans in that era. In 1857, it represented the views of the vast majority of Whites in American society. Even in 1996, it might be argued that the belief that African Americans are of an "inferior order" is an idea some find difficult to abandon.

When the majority of White Americans consider the history of this nation, they are apt to conclude that the blood of the Civil War washed clean the sins of slavery and that the marches of the civil rights movement erased the remaining vestiges of segregation and racial oppression. Others not given to excessive historical introspection believe—almost equally sincerely—that they personally have nothing whatever to do with slavery, segregation, or racial oppression because neither they nor as far as they know—their ancestors ever enslaved anyone, ever burned a cross in the night in front of anyone's house, or ever denied anyone a seat at the front of a bus. And so, between the self-absolving denial of the latter group and the self congratulation—which is a deeper form of self-absolution—of the former, it becomes nearly impossible to have an honest discussion about what used to be called "the Negro Problem."

Alexis de Tocqueville once observed that, as in the lives of individuals, the circumstances of the birth of nations deeply affect their developments. At this nation's birth—if the Declaration of Independence and the Constitution are to be taken seriously—there was a theoretical commitment to principles of human freedom and equality. But another equally significant circumstance—as evidenced by the genocide of Native Americans and the enslavement of African Americans—was its dedication to the doctrine of White supremacy.

That doctrine, much as it contradicted the theoretical principles of the Declaration of Independence and the Preamble of the Constitution, deeply and unalterably affected how America has developed as a nation. It gained us the land on which Native Americans and Mexicans used to live; it produced prosperity for the generations who directly and indirectly profited from the free labor of slaves; it resulted in generations of American apartheid; it allowed us to pretend that we were truly a White European nation; it saddled us with what W.E.B. DuBois called "the problem of the color-line." The doctrine of White supremacy and its corollary precept of Black inferiority made us who we were a very long time ago and inevitably still are today.

During oral argument before the Supreme Court in *Brown v. Board of Education*, Attorney Thurgood Marshall, who later became the nation's first Black justice of the high Court, posed the following challenge:

> [T]he only way that this Court can decide this case in opposition to our position is to find that for some reason Negroes are inferior to all other human beings."

The Court ruled that the intentional segregation of African-American children in public schools violated the Equal Protection Clause of the United States Constitution:

> To separate them [African-American children] from others of similar age and qualifications solely because of their race generates a feeling of inferiority as to their status in the community that may affect their hearts and minds in a way unlikely ever to be undone.

Therein lies the paradox of law. Thurgood Marshall and all of the justices knew perfectly well that Thomas Jefferson and Roger Brookes Taney openly declared that Blacks were inferior to Whites. Upon their word, and through government sanction, public schools remain largely segregated to this day. Constitutional law then accommodates even as it challenges unspoken understandings and convenient myths surrounding the practical outcome of doctrines that support "equality under law."

The truth is that our nation was founded explicitly, prospered implicitly, and still often lives uneasily on the precept of Black inferiority and White superiority. That precept legitimized slavery, justified segregation long after slavery was abolished, and remains an essential element of American identity.

The dominance of the precept of inferiority hinges upon its fundamental difference from all the other precepts. Other precepts define or enforce tangible rights, for e.g., master over slaves. Once the law abolished slavery, the original precept of human property ceased to exist. Its existence was tied to law. By contrast, the precept of inferiority did not define any specific right or obligation. "Inferiority" spoke to the state of the mind and the logic of the heart. It posed as an article of faith that the other in the midst are not quite altogether human.

Overt racism in the public sphere is far less tolerated, but still we cannot say that we have reached a time when the belief that African Americans are inferior has disappeared without a trace from the American heart. That is why inferiority remains the most enduring, and perhaps most important, precept.

The Object of Hate

During colonial times, ruling class of English colonists had "difficulties in fostering a sense of community in colonies populated by Portuguese, Spanish, French, Turks, Dutch, Blacks, and Indians." For example, cases reported between 1640 and 1669 in Virginia reveal that White indentured servants, along with African-American slaves, had rebelled against the English colonists by running away and stealing from their masters. In addition to facing rebellion by Whites and African Americans, the English colonies also had to withstand attacks from the Native American population that the colonists were doing their best to subjugate. "Indians and Whites conducted guerrilla raids against each other's settlements with ever increasing ruthlessness."

Faced with rebellion from within and attacks from without, the colonists needed to foster a common identity in order to quell the restless stirrings of their own less-happy members, who had no desire to serve their masters indefinitely, and in order to repel the not-unjustified attacks of the Native Americans, who had no intention of being subjugated quietly. The colonists discovered soon enough that nothing makes better friends of former enemies than a new common enemy. Give a people someone to hate and fear and they will have a reason to live with one another. To say this is not to indulge in any form of romantic despair. It is simply to admit that, even though love and its object may be what redeem our spirit in the next world, hate and its object seem to drive us in this world to conquer the land, build the bridges, raise the armies, and fight the common enemy. For the White colonists, the common object of fear and hate became the others [mainly] Africans in their midst.

Excerpt from the Trail of Tears Association

The Story[9]

The discovery of the New World by European explorers caused endless problems for American Indians, whose homelands were gradually taken from them and whose cultures were dramatically altered, and in some cases destroyed, by the invasion. The first contact between southeastern American Indians and Europeans was the expedition of Hernando de Soto in 1540. De Soto took captives for use as slave labor, while others were abused because the Europeans deemed them savages. Epidemic diseases brought by the Europeans spread through the Indian villages, decimating native populations. Over the next two centuries White settlers arrived, native cultures responded to pressures to adopt the foreign ways, leading to the deterioration of their own culture. During the colonial period Indian tribes often became embroiled in European colonial wars. If they were on the losing side, they frequently had to give up parts of their homelands.

> After the American Revolution the Indians faced another set of problems. Even though it took time for the new government to establish a policy for dealing with the Indians, the precedent had been set during the colonial period. The insatiable desire of White settlers for lands occupied by Indian people inevitably led to the formulation of a general policy of removing the unwanted inhabitants.
>
> National policy to move Indians west of the Mississippi River developed after the Louisiana Territory was purchased from the French in 1803. Whites moving onto these lands pressed the U.S. government to do something about the Indian presence. In 1825 the U.S. government formally adopted a removal policy, which was carried out extensively in the 1830s by Presidents Andrew Jackson and Martin Van Buren. The result was particularly overwhelming for the Indians of the southeastern United States—primarily the Cherokees, Chickasaws, Choctaws, Creeks, and Seminoles.
>
> By late July 1838, with the exception of the Oconaluftee Citizen Indians, the fugitives hiding in the mountains, and some scattered families, virtually all other Cherokees remaining in the East were in the internment camps.

In the South, following the passage of the 1850 Fugitive Slave Law, abolitionists protected Blacks who were subject to capture by using the Underground Railroad. At the height of the debate over slavery, Abraham Lincoln gave an impassioned State of the Nation speech in which he warned that: "A house divided against itself cannot stand," this nation cannot endure half slave and half free.[10] In 1857, the Supreme Court announced its decision in *Dred Scott v. Sanford*, holding that (1) No slave or their descendants can ever be a citizen of any state; (2) Congress cannot exclude slavery from the territories; and (3) the fact that masters travel and bring slaves into a free state does not make the slave free without a state law to the contrary.

Chief Justice Roger Brooks Taney wrote the *Scott* opinion. Taney has been the quintessential fall guy for breaking the racial code of silence. He produced what Pierre Schlag would call the moment of vertigo, when he boldly declared (like a juridical bullhorn) that there was absolutely no contradiction between the Court's view of race and the U.S. Constitution:

> Blacks were not and not intended to be citizens and therefore can claim none of the rights and privileges guaranteed by the constitution. They are a subordinate and inferior class of beings, who have been subjugated by the dominant race whether slave or free and remain that way with no rights except those who hold power choose to grant them. They have for more than a century been regarded as beings of an inferior order, and altogether unfit to associate with the White race, either in social or political relations, and so far inferior that they had no rights which the White man was bound to respect, and they were justly and lawfully reduced to slavery for their own benefit, bought and sold and traded as an ordinary article of merchandise and traffic, whenever a profit could be made by it. This opinion of Blacks was fixed and universal in the minds of the civilized portion of the White race, men in every grade and position in society daily and habitually acted upon it in their private pursuits, as well as in matters of public concern, without doubting for a moment the correctness of this opinion. Accordingly, those of African race were regarded as an article of property, and held and bought and sold in every one of the 13 colonies. The men who framed the declaration were great, high in literary accomplishments in honor and incapable of asserting principles so utterly and flagrantly inconsistent with the principles they were asserting. The language of the

> Declaration could not be supposed in any part of the civilized world to embrace the Negro race. The Constitution recognizes the right of property of the master in a slave and makes no distinction between that kind of property and any other.
>
> These statements (perhaps more so than the decision) sparked a firestorm of criticism near the eve of the Civil War. It is rightfully chronicled as part of the transition from the old way of life to the "new." The standing joke is that these declarations have earned him the distinction of being the Chief Justice who penned the most frequently overturned Supreme Court decision in history. Now thoroughly repudiated, the full-text of the decision is often omitted in constitutional law books.

On January 1, 1863, Abraham Lincoln issued the Emancipation Proclamation. The Thirteenth Amendment was ratified in 1865, prohibiting slavery and involuntary servitude, except as punishment for commission of a crime.

Three days later, Black Codes were introduced throughout the South, ushering in what we now characterize as the Jim Crow Era. The salient feature of the codes was the transparent revision of the former slave codes by simply replacing the word slave with the word servant, leaving nearly all else exactly as it was before.

Officially, Jim Crow was a minstrel character. The entire minstrel era was hailed by Samuel Clemens—also known as Mark Twain—as the greatest of all time. Minstrel consisted of entertaining Whites with images of Black stupidity. The then-illiterate and debased condition of Black America became something to laugh about rather than repent for, virtually overnight.[11] Jim Crow Laws, also called Black Codes, on the other hand, codified official policies of separate but equal, conveniently justified by their debased conditions. Widespread coercive practices led to involuntary servitude and demands for conformity without civil or political recourse.

Even those who remained relatively indifferent to the plight of the Negro conceded that the ultimate effect (if not purpose) of the Black Codes was involuntary servitude. Almost every act, word or gesture of the Negro not consonant with good taste, good manners and good morals (as defined by Whites) was made a crime or misdemeanor for which he was first fined by the magistrates and then consigned to a condition of servitude, often for life, until he could pay the fine.[12]

The Civil Rights Act of 1866 was designed to address the inequalities imposed by the Black Codes. It granted citizenship to all born in the U.S. and enumerated the privileges and immunities of citizenship: to make and enforce contracts, sue in court, be a party in a law suit, give evidence, inherit property, purchase, lease, sell, hold and convey land, enjoy full & equal benefits of all laws passed for the security of person and property, and to be subjected to like pains, penalties and punishments for every infraction.

Critics charged that Congress lacked the power to grant citizenship. When the Constitution was amended for the fourteenth time, it declared that all who were born or naturalized would enjoy full citizenship rights that included due process, equal protection, and the privileges and immunities afforded every other citizen.

The Freedman's Bureau established a guardianship over former slaves to ensure their safety. Southerners hated it, Northerners with no exposure to southern culture worried that it was too paternalistic. Black schools and churches worked with the Bureau to settle a hefty number of newly freed slaves who had been subjected to a lifetime of abuse, even as the former slave-holders instituted a new reign of terror. 1865 to 1920 was a period of intense conflict, when laws were inadequate and professional law enforcement virtually nonexistent. The result was an era of Ku Klux Klan terror throughout the South. Carl Schurz writes:

> Some planters held back their former slaves on their plantations by brute force. Armed bands of White men patrolled the country roads to drive back the Negroes wandering about. Dead bodies of murdered Negroes were found on and near the highways and by-paths. Gruesome reports came from the hospitals—reports of colored men and women whose ears had been cut off, whose skulls had been broken, whose bodies had been slashed by knives or lacerated with scourges (whipped).[13]

The world was racist, violent, and extremely predictable. Poor Whites lived in some of the worst conditions; they were unable to participate politically and had limited opportunities for improving their conditions. Slavery had provided two very important pillars of an emerging capitalistic society: wealth that made independence possible, and an ideological basis to resolve conflict between the propertied and unpropertied Whites. The only property that poor Whites owned was their Whiteness, providing incentive for them to identify with the ruling class on the basis of race. Support of slavery was given in exchange for a larger role in the political process. The long fight for universal male suffrage was assured largely after the opponents and advocates agreed on the major goal of keeping Blacks from voting. From the admission of Maine in 1819 until the end of the Civil War, every new state restricted the right to vote to Whites in their constitutions.

Thaddeus Stevens advocated arming former slaves and seizing the property of rebellion leaders.[14] He advocated a plan of confiscation and redistribution. He opposed readmitting southern states back into the union until securing the right to vote for free Blacks. Otherwise, southerners would only give the right to vote to those whom they could control. The Confiscation Plan would have only resulted in a distribution of 10% of existing prime property. A mere 10% would have provided each slave family with 40 acres and a mule.

The most controversial question of the day was whether newly freed Blacks should be given the right to vote. It was a sobering thought nationwide. A famous abolitionist who opposed slavery on moral grounds is widely quoted as stating "according to the laws of development and progress, it is not practicable to take the slave down from the auction blocks and deliver them to the ballot box."[15] All who supported Negro enfranchisement seemed to agree that a base-level education requirement was necessary for effective use of the right to vote, although no such requirement was demanded from Whites. Others feared that Blacks would be coerced at the polls by slaveholders or be unable to distinguish between the Democrat and Republican parties.

Republicans were forced to give Blacks the right to vote because they were no longer counted as three-fifths of a person, which increased the number of representatives from the South. Only when the Fifteenth Amendment was passed, extending suffrage to Black males, did the Abolitionist Society declare its mission complete. A tightly contested presidential race produced the Tilden-Hayes Compromise which conditioned withdrawal of federal troops from the South, allowing Hayes to ascend to the presidency to break the tie vote. Known as the Compromise of 1877, it marked a unique social revolution.[16] When the nation's commitment to formal equality permanently ended, there were corresponding shifts in science, literature, journalism, history, and religion that persist to this day to justify that decision.

Ultimately, the desire to form a single nation and define the parameters of national citizenship required consensus as to the privileges and immunities that belong to those born or naturalized in the U.S. Clear delineation of civil and political rights became necessary as Congress attempted to reform the basic principles of ownership established during slavery while retaining all the benefits. Constitutional law in much of its form and substance has culminated in a series of attempts to transform what should have started out as a contractual or employment relationship between the races (and/or sexes), but was instead made a property right at the nation's founding, back into a contractual or employment relationship.

Now that you understand what was done, it's well worth contemplating how. The Jim Crow Era describes a social phenomenon prescribed by law and cemented by popular culture. Jim Crow the minstrel character was created in the 1830s by Thomas D. Rice and modeled after an elderly crippled Black slave who sang and shuffled. Rice's performance of Jump Jim Crow in blackface was widely acclaimed throughout the United States and England. Thus emerged a new weapon in the fight over imagery in popular culture:

> The good slave or servant was the apologist for the former genteel White confederacy. Never overtly sexual, often referred to as uncle, Tom, or Remus and the female corollary was the mammy, the overweight maid, cook and nanny responsible for the comfort of the southern White household. With no life of her own, she was imbued with practical wisdom and took an inordinately intense interest in the welfare of the White family and children that she cared for.

Black Americans holding a different vision of what it meant to be free and independent, began to lose ground in the court of public opinion on the question of innocence. Blacks were first portrayed as evil in literature distributed by the Ku Klux Klan, whose advertisements warned about their so-called bestial and cunning nature making them prone to thievery and rape. The counter-image to the Black mammy was Jezebel, the Black female whore—incapable of being tamed or raped, without morals or values.[17]

The 1915 film Birth of a Nation, cited as a milestone in the history of American motion pictures, transformed a novel into vivid visual images that captured the uncles, mammies, buffoons, and mulatto mistresses, claiming to illustrate the circumstances that southern families were reduced to after the Civil War. The opening depicts benevolent masters served by loyal slaves who contentedly pick cotton, perform chores, and aim to please. By the end of the war the tranquil social order had degenerated into lawlessness. The newly emancipated are depicted as roaming the streets terrorizing Whites. Anarchic hordes take over the polls, disenfranchise White voters, and seize control of Congress. Black legislators were portrayed as contemptible fools, swigging whiskey from a bottle, gnawing on fried chicken legs, holding their first legislative session with their shoes off and feet up on the desk. According to the film, emancipation was destructive of the public as well as private sphere, where communities fell prey to ruin, devastation, pillage, and rape. In the climactic scene, a former slave is shown pursuing a young White woman until she leaps to her death from a pedestal-like perch at the edge of a cliff. It was a dramatic and victorious ride to the rescue by the Ku Klux Klan that finally restores civilization.

Thus, the world's very first motion picture film packed movie houses in the North for twelve months, and in the South for fifteen years. A special screening was held at the White House for the president and attended by the entire Supreme Court. President Woodrow Wilson described the film as "like writing history with lightning," stating that one of his regrets was that "the film was so horribly true."[18] To this day, the movie remains one of the highest-grossing box office hits in the history of Hollywood.

There was nothing that educated Blacks, abolitionists, and anti-racists could do to counteract the film's impact. In the aftermath, the Klan gained enormous power in the postwar South. Organized by former commanders, soldiers, leaders of the Confederacy, and local churchmen, they used a combination of mystical talk, white sheets, and domestic terrorism. Through lynching, beating, burning, and other forms of guerrilla warfare, they successfully intimidated Blacks and their White liberal comrades. Theirs, according to Lerone Bennet, was "the boldest and most ruthless political operation in American history." They reduced Blacks to political impotence:

> By stealth and murder, by economic intimidation, political assassinations, and use of unprecedented terror: the braining of the baby in its mother's arms, the slaying of the husband at his wife's feet, the raping of the wife before the husband's eyes, by fear.[19]

In response, Congress passed the Ku Klux Klan Act of 1871. The law provided the following:

> Punishment for conspiracies to overthrow by force any arm of the government; or obstruct justice in the enforcement of civil rights legislation in any court; or threaten the right to vote; state government involved in direct conspiracy or mere acquiescence were subject to control of the militia by order of the President; seizure of state authority constituted a rebellion, giving the President authority to suspend the privilege of the writ of habeas corpus; Klansmen were prohibited from jury service; potential jurors were required to swear under oath that they had never taken part in Klan activity; individuals with knowledge of a conspiracy and power to prevent who failed to intervene were liable for damages and joined as a co-defendants.

The Civil Rights Act of 1875 provided that:

> All persons within the jurisdiction of the United States shall be entitled to the full and equal enjoyment of the accommodations, advantages, facilities and privileges of inns, public conveyances on land or water, theaters, and other places of public amusement, subject only to the conditions and limitations established by law, and applicable alike to citizens of every race and color, regardless of any previous condition of servitude.

The Act sought to accomplish what was not actually achieved until Title II of the Civil Rights Act of 1964 was passed nearly a century later. The 1875 Act accorded equal access to places of public accommodations and was immediately challenged in court. It was struck down by the Supreme Court as an attempt at social rights legislation that the Court deemed to be beyond the scope of congressional power. The Court determined that denial of public accommodations could not be considered a badge or incident of slavery, since it did not involve compulsory service, restraint of movement, prohibition on property ownership, inability to sue or be a witness against a White, or harsher punishment for the same crime. The Court declared *these* to be the Civil Rights of free men.

Justice Harlan's Famous Dissenting Opinion

According to Justice Harlan, the separate-but-equal doctrine must be analyzed in light of the previous relationship between the federal government and the institution of slavery. He notes that the Constitution provided for slavery and secured the right of the slaveholder against any who would free a slave, and the Court prohibited any interference with that right by state governments:

> When a State argued that it retained the right to determine the status of all person within its jurisdictions, this Court declared that Congressional legislation was valid to enforce the master's right. We authorized federal marshals, posses, and

> ordinary citizens to keep Black enslaved. In Dred Scott we declared that the plaintiff, who was born to former slaves who were free at the time of his birth, could not claim the rights of citizenship.[20]

Harlan went on to declare that we were now in a new era: Congress had outlawed slavery via the Thirteenth Amendment in absolute terms. The same Congress, with its passage of the Civil Rights Act of 1866, sought to address the Black Codes and provide wholesale immunity from and protection against all racial discrimination. Harlan speaks plainly of the kind of freedom envisioned by the Thirteenth Amendment. He asserts that there can be no doubt that hotels, theatres, and railroads are established under state authority for public use. To allow any of these quasi-public entities to discriminate is a badge of servitude that can be remedied by federal legislation. Justice Harlan's most astute observation centers on the permanence of racial caste in the United States:

> Congress, with the sanction of this court, passed the most stringent laws—operating directly and primarily upon states and their officers and agents, as well as upon individuals —in vindication of slavery and the right of the master, I submit to you now that the national legislature may with out transcending the limits of the Constitution do for human liberty and the fundamental rights of American citizenship what it did with the sanction of this court for the protection of slavery and the rights of masters in their fugitive slaves.[21]

A week later, during a protest of the decision in Washington, Frederick Douglass described the majority's ruling as a shocking display of moral weakness in high places. He characterized it as an international embarrassment that Blacks fought wars and paid taxes, but still could not secure basic human rights. The laws that did pass were either struck by the Court or simply not enforced. Douglass condemned the motives of ruling class Whites: In the years before the Thirteenth Amendment "you protected the law of church and state to uphold the letter and the spirit of slave laws, exacting a pound of flesh and then some against every infraction. Riding with a Negro did not constitute social equality when she was a slave. The efforts to humiliate the colored people of this country has led to a circumstance where a railroad conductor in South Carolina or Mississippi has more power than the national government."[22]

At the turn of the century, lynching became the dominant tool for managing race relations.[23] What began as extreme violence against Blacks was eventually applied to Whites. When one young Black man flirted with a young White girl and she received his attentions with a smile instead of reporting him, a mob came to lynch him. His father greeted them with a shotgun, allowing the son to escape. The group then gang-raped the girl "to teach her a lesson." According to Dr. Lisa Cardyn, such behavior was part of a growing national trend, where White men imagined themselves as upholders of the race. Their vigilantism was about the right of self-protection and repulsion of so-called unlawful incursions upon life, liberty, and property.

> [White supremacy left many white men believing] they were in danger of being overtaken by an odious force, their lives and identities forever compromised, submerged in a sea of blackness. Heightening their anxiety was the collective nightmare shared by growing numbers of white men who envisioned their women raped, their land despoiled, their manhood threatened by the depredations of freedmen, a figment of the racial imaginary that appeared no less horrifying for being completely unreal.[24]

In 1921, North Tulsa was a very prosperous Black community. Its financial district was referred to as the Black Wall Street. Black residents owned land and operated their own businesses, schools, and banks. When Dick Roland, the Black owner of a shoeshine stand, took an elevator to the top floor of a building to use the colored-only restroom he stepped on the toe of a White female operator, who reportedly screamed just as the door was closing. Roland was arrested the next day on charges of rape. Soon rumors swirled that he would be lynched. White rioters set fire to everything owned by Blacks. Bundles of dynamite were dropped from an airplane and destroyed the entire district. Four-hundred Black residents were interned on fairgrounds in cattle and hog pens. Tulsa authorities led the nation to believe that they would rebuild the district. They later approved a plan to allow railroad tracks and a station to run straight through the district, effectively precluding them from rebuilding the community.[25]

In 1923, Rosewood, Florida, was ravaged by a violent mob that killed dozens of Black residents. It all started when a twenty-two-year-old White woman was having an affair with a White man who left bruises and marks on her body, which she could only explain to her husband by claiming that a Black intruder assaulted her while he was away. The local sheriff led the attack, which lasted six days. A group of White men burned down the town. No one was ever convicted of the murders and state officials simply removed the town from the state map. In 1993, exactly seventy years later, the Florida legislature held a memorial for those who died, reimbursed the Black families for their loss of property, and placed the town back on the map.[26] The opening ceremony began as follows:

> People came from all around to take part in the manhunt. They were people with a thirst for blood. The remaining survivors of Rosewood are still tortured with the lingering image of a parent or grandparent being lynched, or shot, of the family home being burned to the ground, of crawling through the woods in the dead of night and hiding from an armed and crazed mob, of being hated and attacked for nothing more than their skin color.[27]

Four thousand seven hundred and sixty-three Black lynchings were recorded in the early 1900s. This figure excludes hangings when the death penalty was imposed after a hasty trial, secret proceedings, and those that occurred in the backwoods that were later covered-up following threats to introduce federal anti-lynching legislation in the late 1930s. Lynch mobs routinely formed after an all-White jury acquitted a Black man for a crime.[28]

Lynchings were public events, advertised in advance, and often held in public squares, near official buildings. There were forty-three public lynchings of Mexican Americans in New Mexico. Alongside the lynching, there was the ritual of burning at the stake, mutilation, and riddling bodies with bullets. Spectators were allowed to take home an ear or a finger; a Georgia man's knuckles were on display in the local grocery store after he was lynched. During the Rosewood massacre, a Black man was lynched and castrated and his body was hung in front of the home of another Black described as one of Rosewood's most confident Black men. There was no need to utilize the highly public display of lynching for mere criminal acts; it was as often deployed as retribution for economic competition, or aimed at political and intellectual antagonists. A White editor of the nearby paper said that following the massacre, victim's penises, testicles, fingers and toes were kept in mason jars for show.[29] She received death threats for printing what she saw and providing interviews to Northerners. Lynch mobs were formed to displace conventional legal processes. This system of lawlessness from roughly 1870 to 1955 reflects a social consensus that permitted lynching to thrive without punishment as a symbolic expression of the social contract that supports our legal system.

In the 1890s, Ida B. Wells was the editor and half-owner of the Memphis Free Speech Press. When economic competitors lynched three Black businessmen, she wrote a passionate editorial that launched a historic public crusade against lynching. She was almost lynched herself for writing the editorial. She continued to report and editorialize around the lynchings as they took place. Her commentary included both the alleged and the actual reasons for the lynchings. Mocking the imagery of The Birth of a Nation and other Klan literature, she declared:

> Nobody in this country believes the old threadbare lie that Negro men rape white women. If Southern White men are not careful, they will over-reach themselves and public sentiment will have a reaction. A conclusion will then be reached which will be very damaging to the moral reputation of their women.[30]

A White newspaper reprinted her statement and issued this warning:

> Those who are attempting to make the lynching of individuals of their race a means for arousing the worst passion of their kind are playing with a dangerous sentiment. The fact that a Black scoundrel is allowed to live and utter such loathsome and repulsive calumnies is a volume of evidence as to the wonderful patience of Southern Whites. But we have had enough. There are some things that the Southern White man will not tolerate and the obscene intimations of the foregoing have brought the writer to very outmost limit of public patience, we hope we have said enough.[31]

Nazis, Race & International Public Relations

Our involvement in the Second World War was a direct repudiation of Nazi theory. By the end of WWII, the nation faced a public relations dilemma. Black troops were needed for yet another war, but this time the contrast between our policies and practices garnered international attention. In Europe, Black soldiers were treated the same as the others. Upon their return, the decorated soldiers who risked their lives defending principles that this nation had not yet begun to practice could not find employment. President Truman formed a Bi-racial Commission on Civil Rights, whose primary recommendation was the elimination of segregation. Another task force assembled to look into higher education and reached the same conclusion. Integration of the Army at the end of WWII led to similar policies integrating all of the armed services and opening available jobs to all qualified personnel regardless of race.[32] In 1948, Truman issued an Executive Order requiring fair employment practices in all federal service.

President Eisenhower appointed a Commission to oversee the elimination of discrimination in industries filling government contracts.[33] Thus began some movement in publicly owned housing developments. However, despite the 1948 Supreme Court decision outlawing racially restrictive covenants in the sale of private homes, angry mobs continued to burn down the homes of Blacks who tried to live in certain neighborhoods.[34] Blacks migrated North where fair employment legislation was being introduced at the state level. The District of Columbia became the first area to fully enforce the Civil Rights Act of 1875. Blacks were freely admitted to hotels, theaters, restaurants, parks, and other places of public accommodation. When the president announced that he expected the district to become a model of equality for the nation to emulate, Whites moved to Maryland & Virginia.

The Civil Rights Movement flourished in the late 1950s and 60s largely because the South was still a hot-bed of terrorism. It was simply not a punishable crime to kill a Negro or a civil rights worker in the South. In Louisiana, the Klan marched through the Black section of town behind a sheriff's patrol car in the mid 1960s. The National Association for the Advancement of Colored People [NAACP] continued the fight for racial egalitarianism begun by the abolitionists in 1909. The organization became the bane of existence for southern leadership, and a natural target for anti-Black legislation. Strategies included attempts to have it classified as a subversive organization, and the widespread imposition of severe economic reprisals for Blacks who became involved in Civil Rights.[35] Federal Troops were required to uphold court-ordered desegregation in the high schools.[36] When the national organization opened offices in a southern state, the official machinery went into operation. In the famous case of *NAACP v. Alabama*, the state demanded a list of all NAACP members, which was refused. The U.S. Supreme Court found that the state wanted the list for the purpose of exposing NAACP members to community reprisals, such as loss of employment, calling or denial of bank loans, mortgage foreclosures, and violence by the KKK. The court found an interplay between governmental and private action: "only after the initial exertion of state power represented by the production order, did the private action take hold."[37] In the United States, a caste system created and maintained through violence was held out to the world as part of an inherent division of divinely appointed racial talents.

It was this contradiction of meaning, betrayal of citizenship, and breach of faith that led Dr. Martin Luther King, Jr., to conclude the following:

> Writing in Life [magazine], William Faulkner, Nobel prize-winning author from Mississippi, recently urged the NAACP to "stop now for a moment." That is to say, he encouraged Negroes to accept injustice, exploitation and indignity for a while longer. It is hardly a moral act to encourage others patiently to accept injustice which he himself does not endure.[38]

Modern writers have written volumes about the American dilemma:

> A. Leon Higginbotham, Jr.:
>
> By the latter part of the seventeenth century, the colonists would have in place a sort of "social and color ladder," occupied at the top rungs by propertied Whites, in the middle by the poor and servant Whites, and at the bottom rungs by Native Americans and African-American slaves. Through the operation of this social and color ladder, the ruling class of Whites was assured the loyalty of the poor and servant Whites, upon whose loyalty the fate of the colony depended, without the ruling class having to share its wealth and power with the servant class. For the poor and servant Whites, the rewards for their loyalty were the somewhat illusory promise that they too could ascend to the top rungs of the ladder occupied by the propertied Whites, and, much more important, the eternal guarantee that they could never fall to the lower rungs occupied by the Native Americans, or to the lowest rungs occupied by the African Americans. Throughout the eighteenth and nineteenth centuries until 1865, the social and color ladder was reinforced by slaveholders, legislators, and judges who articulated and perfected the rationale of Black inferiority and White superiority. As South Carolina Senator James Henry Hammond ruminated in 1861:
>
>> In all social systems there must be a class to do the menial duties, to per form the drudgery of life. That is, a class requiring but a low order of intellect and but little skill. Its requisites are vigor, docility, fidelity. Such a class

> you must have, or you would not have that other class which leads progress, civilization, and refinement. It constitutes the very mudsill of society and of political government. Fortunately for the South, she has found a race adapted to that purpose at her hand. A race inferior to her own, but eminently qualified in temper, in vigor, in docility, in capacity to stand the climate, to answer all her purposes. We use them for our purpose, and we call them slaves.[39]

Derrick Bell:

> Black people are the magical faces at the bottom of society's well. Even the poorest Whites, those who must live their lives only a few levels above, gain their self-esteem by gazing down on us. Surely, they must know that their deliverance depends on letting down their ropes. Only by working together is escape possible. Over time, many reach out, but most simply watch, mesmerized into maintaining their unspoken commitment to keeping us where we are, at whatever cost to them or to us.[40]

Ralph Ellison:

> Since the beginning of this nation, White Americans have suffered from a deep inner uncertainty as to who they really are. One of the ways that has been used to simplify the answer has been to seize upon the presence of Black Americans and use them as a marker, a symbol of limits, a metaphor for the "outsider." Many Whites could look at the social position of Blacks and feel that color formed an easy and reliable gauge for determining who is American.[41]

The rationale for the precept of inferiority that endures in the American mind:

This is how the story goes …

> Blacks, for reasons of physiology, culture, behavior and even religion, were something less than fully human and were therefore inferior to Whites. As such, Blacks could be enslaved by Whites, not only because of the economic benefits that the raw physical attributes of Blacks would bring Whites in their efforts to turn the primitive American land into a civilized nation, but also because of the moral benefits that dominance by Whites would bring Blacks in soothing their heathen instincts. If, however, the civilizing restraints of slavery were to be removed and they were free, then Blacks have to be segregated from Whites because, left entirely to their own devices, free Blacks would tend to corrupt the moral virtue and physical purity of White society, and because the two races, one a blessed fulfillment of divine destiny, the other a cursed accident of blind evolution, could not possibly live together peacefully in society without the beneficent controlling hand of the superior race upon the inferior one.[42]

Apartheid in the Courthouses

Segregated Spectator Seating[43]
A. Leon Higginbotham, Jr.

In American courtrooms there has never been any formal segregation among White ethnic groups. Protestants have not been segregated from Catholics, or

Jews from Gentiles. Or those White persons whose ancestors were born, as an example, in England, France, Germany, Italy, Sweden from any other European nation. There has never been any segregation in the courtroom on the basis of national origin. Thus, one must identify the evolution of these racial segregation policies and how the courts justified this different treatment for African Americans.

In 1948—the same year the Nationalist Party came into power in South Africa to initiate apartheid—the Mississippi Supreme Court, in *Murray v. State*, was asked to reverse the murder conviction of an African-American man tried in a courtroom that segregated African-American spectators, allowing them to sit only in the balcony. The court's language reveals the long tradition and implicit approval of courthouse racial segregation: "It is asserted that the seating arrangement, suggested pursuant to a custom whose immemorial usage and sanction has made routine, resulted in a concentration in the balcony of those of the same race as the defendant." The court's language not only implicitly approved of that "routine" tradition, but its decision permitted its continuance:

> Assuming that this seating arrangement was insisted upon and deemed prejudicial to such as were piqued thereby—as to which there is no showing—such reactions may not be magnified into a fancied denial of constitutional rights and thereupon made assignable to the defendant.

The court affirmed the conviction. In 1963, fifteen years after the Murray case, when the success of the civil rights movement had sensitized the country to the derogatory meaning of segregation, the Supreme Court finally recognized, in Johnson that race-segregated seating in courts constituted a denial of equal protection.

Ford T. Johnson, Jr., an African American, was seated in a section of the Richmond Traffic Court reserved for Whites, and when requested by the bailiff to move, refused to do so. The judge then summoned the petitioner to the bench and instructed him to be seated in the right-hand section of the courtroom, the section reserved for African Americans. The petitioner moved back in front of the counsel table and remained standing with his arms folded, stating that he would not comply with the judge's order. Upon refusing to obey the judge's further direction to be seated, he was arrested for contempt. At no time did Johnson behave in a boisterous or abusive manner, and there was no disorder in the courtroom.

The state, in its brief to the Supreme Court, conceded that seating space in the Richmond Traffic Court "is assigned on the basis of racial designation, the seats on one side of the aisle being for use of Negro citizens and the seats on the other side being for the use of White citizens." The Supreme Court reversed the conviction, noting:

> It is clear from the totality of circumstances, and particularly the fact that the petitioner was peaceably seated in the section reserved for Whites before being summoned to the bench, that the arrest and conviction rested entirely on the refusal to comply with the segregated seating requirements imposed in this particular courtroom. Such a conviction cannot stand, for it is no longer open to question that a State may not constitutionally require segregation of public facilities. State-compelled segregation in a court of justice is a manifest violation of the State's duty to deny no one the equal protection of its laws.

The ultimate insight that race-segregated seating in courtrooms denied a spectator "equal" protection doubtless rested on what Professor Lawrence has characterized as the central insight of Brown: that equal protection doctrine includes the right to be free from social ostracism and its stigmatizing effect on the "hearts and minds" of African-American adult citizens as well as on African-American children.

What of the nature and scope of damage to the hearts, minds, social and economic well-being of Whites? Perry describes it as the culmination of Allen's life work:

> In 1996, on radio station WBAI in New York, Allen discussed the subject of "American Exceptionalism" and the much-vaunted "immunity" of the United States to proletarian class-consciousness and its effects. His explanation for the relatively low level of class consciousness was that social control in the United States was guaranteed, not primarily by the class privileges of a petit bourgeoisie, but by the white-skin privileges of laboring class Whites; that the ruling class co-opts European-American workers into the buffer social control system against the interests of the working class to which they belong; and that the "White race" by its all-class form, conceals the operation of the ruling class social control system by providing it with a majoritarian "democratic" façade.[44]

Race-Conscious Policies & Practices

John Doe, a minor, by his mother and next friend, Jane Doe, Plaintiff-Appellant, v. Kamehameha Schools/Bernice Pauahi Bishop Estate, et al., Defendants-Appellees[45]

AMICUS BRIEF OF THE JAPANESE AMERICAN CITIZENS LEAGUE OF HAWAI'I-HONOLULU CHAPTER, CENTRO LEGAL DE LA RAZA, AND THE EQUAL JUSTICE SOCIETY IN SUPPORT OF DEFENDANTS-APPELLEES' PETITION FOR REHEARING EN BANC

ARGUMENTS

KAMEHAMEHA SCHOOLS' ADMISSIONS POLICY DOES NOT VIOLATE CIVIL RIGHTS; RATHER, IT SERVES TO RESTORE TO NATIVE HAWAIIANS THAT WHICH 19TH AND 20TH CENTURY "WESTERN INFLUENCE" NEARLY DESTROYED: HAWAIIAN EDUCATION, CULTURE AND A MEASURE OF SELF-GOVERNANCE.

As non-Hawaiian civil rights organizations, amici JACL-Hawai'i, Centro Legal de la Raza, and the Equal Justice Society write to say that the Kamehameha Schools admissions policy favoring Hawaiian children does not transgress civil rights. We have seen the harsh reality of racism and have fought hard for equal justice under law. African-Americans suffered slavery, segregation and present-day discrimination in jobs and housing. Asian-Americans and Latinos faced racialized immigration exclusion, alien land and anti-miscegenation laws, the internment and current treatment as perpetual foreigners. We have experienced the pain of civil rights violations. And we can say that the Kamehameha Schools admissions policy is not about unfair treatment based on race.

Doe's suit is not, as some suggest, about trying to end a program comparable to Jim Crow segregation in the South. Rather, the suit is about an effort to break apart a successful educational program by Hawaiians for Hawaiians that aims to repair the continuing harms of the 19th and 20th century "influx of Western civilization." *Doe v. Kamehameha Sch.*, 295 F. Supp. 2d 1141, 1147 (D. Hawai'i 2003).

The Kamehameha Schools were created in 1883, fifteen years before the United States annexed Hawai'i, by the private trust of Princess Bernice Pauahi Bishop, the last descendant of Hawai'i's first king. Pauahi Bishop created the trust to uplift Hawaiian children through education because the forces of Westernization had nearly decimated the Hawaiian people (a population drop from 400,000 to 45,000) and foreshadowed the American takeover of the Hawaiian government. Pauahi Bishop sought not to exclude others by labeling them inferior or unworthy (a classic civil rights violation) but rather to rebuild her own people (an act of restoration and self-determination). Pauahi Bishop's grasp of the urgency of changing circumstances proved prescient. In 1893, the U.S. assisted in the illegal overthrow of the sovereign Hawaiian nation. American military and plantation owners lobbied hard for annexation, alternatively characterizing indigenous Hawaiians as uncivilized or childlike—in either case, in need of American control.

With a military base at Pearl Harbor and a hot commodity (sugar) at stake, the U.S. annexed Hawai'i in 1898 and not only took control of the provisional government, but also took all former Hawaiian government and royal lands. The beloved former queen was imprisoned for "treason." Hawaiian language was barred from the schools. Plantations diverted water from agrarian Hawaiian communities. More Hawaiians were separated from the land, severing cultural, economic and spiritual connections.

This form of American "westernization" hastened the near-demise of indigenous Hawaiians. Indeed, Congress held hearings on the "Rehabilitation and Colonization of Hawaiians," recommending the Hawaiian Homes Commission Act of 1921 as restorative justice for a "dying race."

Hawaiians in their homeland still bear the worst socioeconomic indicators of all Hawai'i's people—the highest rates of illness, prison incarceration and homelessness, and the lowest rates of higher education and family income.

An apology is warranted for the U.S.'s active role in the "conspiracy" to illegally overthrow the internationally-recognized Hawaiian government and for the ensuing "devastation" of the Hawaiian people.

The Kamehameha Schools admissions policy thus is not about violating civil rights, denigrating one group as inferior to justify better treatment of another. As Judge Kay highlighted in finding a "legitimate nondiscriminatory reason" for the Schools' policy, the School is about a private self-determining effort of restoration for Hawaii's first people.

> IN ASSESSING AN INDIGENOUS GROUP'S ATTEMPTS TO RESTORE A MEASURE OF SELF-GOVERNANCE AND CULTURE THROUGH EDUCATION IN THE FACE OF OVERWHELMING "WESTERN INFLUENCE," THE

COURT'S INQUIRY INTO "LEGITIMATE NONDISCRIMINATORY REASONS" MUST INCORPORATE THE CONTEXT OF COLONIZATION AND ITS RESULTING "DEVASTATION" OF THE NATIVE PEOPLE.

For these reasons, international human rights principles of self-determination and restoration for indigenous peoples illuminate the "remedial legitimacy" of the Kamehameha Schools admissions policy. Even if those principles apply only indirectly, the panel majority erred in its mode of remedial analysis in assessing the Kamehameha Schools admissions policy according to unduly narrow affirmative action precepts. Rehearing is warranted for that crucial reason.

Under §1981, "the defendant must come forward with a legitimate nondiscriminatory reason justifying" its policy. What constitutes a "legitimate nondiscriminatory reason" depends upon context, and the majority adopted the wrong mode of contextual analysis. If an affirmative action diversity program addresses "racial imbalance" in private employment then the narrow Weber-Johnson analysis of "racial exclusion," relied on by the panel, is apt. See slip op. at 1849–50 (describing legal framework under *United Steelworkers of Am. v. Weber*, 443 U.S. 193 (1979) and *Johnson v. Transportation Agency*, 480 U.S. 616 (1987)). But, as Judge Kay below recognized, strict application of Weber-Johnson's private employment remedy criteria is starkly inappropriate for assessing an indigenous group's attempts to repair through self-education the "devastation" and continuing harms of accelerating "Western Influence," or colonialism—which in 1898 included worldwide U.S. territorial acquisitions of not only Hawai'i but also the Philippines, Puerto Rico and Guam.

In assessing whether an indigenous group's response to the Congressionally acknowledged "devastation" constitutes a "legitimate nondiscriminatory reason," the Court cannot tightly limit its inquiry, as the panel did, to whether a challenged program effectively excludes other groups. Slip op. at 8950–51. Instead the Court must ask if the indigenous program's use of race or ancestry is "legitimate" in that it does not denigrate other racial groups (treating them as racially inferior or uncivilized) and, most important, is crafted as a restorative response to colonialism's devastation.

That very inquiry lies at the heart of *Morton v. Mancari*, 417 U.S. 535 (1974), in which the Supreme Court found a Native American blood preference to be a "political" restorative measure (even though race was involved) and therefore legitimate. The fact that the indigenous hiring practice there excluded other racial groups was not determinative. Indeed, race/ancestry had to be an integral factor in the political restoration process because race/ancestry had been key originally in the U.S.'s justification for the confiscation of land, the creation of guardian-ward reservations, and the destruction of culture and self-governance (the savage and uncivilized natives had to be conquered and then watched over).

Although Mancari addressed a constitutional challenge, its foundational inquiry into legitimate reasons is directly relevant here. The majority in this case, however, in its narrow assessment of "legitimate reasons," entirely omitted this analysis. Justices Stevens and Ginsburg have acknowledged the import of this analysis in assessing Native Hawaiian programs.

Scholars worldwide also acknowledge its salience. International scholar, Albert Memmi, a Tunisian Jew and resister of French colonialism, incisively describes colonization as political "aggression" (taking land and resources and controlling indigenous populations) that is often partially justified through "race." Since the aggressor portrays itself as civilized and law-abiding, it needs a mechanism for justifying to its people and the world its bald political take-over of another country and its people.

For Memmi, "racism" in this setting is not simple ignorance or skin color prejudice. Rather, it is characterizing people as "different," less worthy or less human "others" (threatening, uncivilized, inferior) to make political "aggression" for economic or military reasons appear necessary. Given this reality, indigenous political efforts to rectify the devastation of colonization must address race or ancestry as part of the restoration process. This is the jurisprudential foundation for the Supreme Court's *Mancari* decision—regardless of whether the indigenous group is formally recognized as a "political" minority.

Memmi describes four steps in the use of race for politically justifying colonization:

1) Stressing the real or imaginary differences between the racist and its victim;
2) Assigning values to those differences, to the advantage of the racist and the detriment of its victim;
3) Trying to make them absolutes by generalizing from them and claiming that they are final; and
4) Justifying any present or possible aggression or privilege.

It is reflected in Justices Stevens and Ginsburg's observations about the validity of government-supported Hawaiian programs. It is starkly missing, however, from the majority's analysis in this case. Judge Kay correctly determined that the narrow Weber-Johnson mode of analysis for employment affirmative action under §1981 changes substantially when the court is assessing the admissions policy of a private school established by and for the education of an indigenous people to "rectify socioeconomic and educational disadvantages resulting from the influx of western civilization."

In finding "legitimate reasons" for Kamehameha Schools' admissions policy, Judge Kay employed the appropriate mode of analysis: assessing the "unique historical" context of western influence on "Hawaii and Native Hawaiians[,]" including "congressional recognition of the United States' wrongful involvement in the end of the Hawaiian Monarchy and the need to improve educational opportunities for Native Hawaiians[.]" Id. at 1166.

Mancari referred to formally recognized "Indian tribes" as "political" minorities. 417 U.S. at 554. An indigenous group's lack of formal government recognition, however, does not undercut the import of Mancari's foundation for assessing "legitimate" reasons under §1981. See also Kamehameha Sch., slip op. at 8963–67 (Graber, J., dissenting) (citing many Congressional remedial acts based on special relationship between the U.S. and Hawaiians even without formal recognition).

Hawai'i's multiracial populace supports Kamehameha Schools because restorative justice for Hawai'i's indigenous peoples benefits all.

Amici respectfully request that the Court grant the petition.

DATED: August 30, 2005

Residential Segregation and White Privilege[46]

Martha R. Mahoney

Racial segregation was systematically promoted during the 1930s, 1940s, and 1950s by federal programs like the Home Owners Loan Corporation (HOLC), which made loans to homeowners, and the Federal Housing Authority (FHA), which insured private sector loans. These programs refused to lend money to Blacks. They also actively promoted systems of restrictive racial covenants. The greatest impact of these federal agencies in structuring the market, however, lay in the ranking system—the origins of redlining—that the government used to rank communities in their eligibility for federally financed or federally insured loans.

Using these guidelines, the HOLC and FHA actually refused to lend money or underwrite loans for Whites if Whites moved to areas where people of color lived. Private lenders adopted policies in line with federal guidelines. These programs reduced housing opportunities for Blacks. But they also went considerably further in the process of socially constructing whiteness and blackness in urban areas.

If the preference for whiteness is addressed at all, it is raised in examining whether the use of racial steering or quotas to prevent White flight is permissible. The construction of this White preference for whiteness is not examined at all. Racism is treated as a natural and unexamined force.

Lending policies of the HOLC, FHA, and private banks in the years of postwar suburban expansion actively discouraged such communities by forging a requirement that the neighborhood be uniformly White before investments would be made or insured.

Maintaining a development as all-White protected White buyers' ability to finance homes, and at the same time the developers' ability to sell them. It is difficult to overestimate the importance of this lesson—that whiteness equaled attractiveness, safeness, and financial security—in the postwar world. Suburban development came to mean White development, and Whites came to see suburbs as naturally white. The enforcement of whiteness, therefore, prevented the sort of incremental desegregatory developments that might have changed the way suburbia itself was seen by Whites.

The federal requirement of segregation in home financing placed a stamp of approval on private discrimination as well. Both real estate brokers and private lenders followed suit. Once racialized community development was institutionalized as federal policy, any private sector actor who went against the segregated norm would have compromised buyers and their neighbors. Both the ability of the current owners to sell to buyers with federally funded or insured mortgages on resale of the property, and the mortgage insurability of nearby properties, rested on maintaining whiteness in suburbia. Not only were White people socially reluctant to live near Black people, but they were also economically rewarded for living near each other. The incentives, enforcement mechanisms, and preferences for maintaining whiteness were systemic, not merely individual.

The Kerner Commission on Civil Disorders, inquiring into the causes of the racial riots of the late 1960s, did not find Whites moving to the suburbs primarily to avoid Blacks. The "more basic" reason for White migration to the suburbs was the "rising mobility and affluence of middle-class families."

The suburbs had better schools, living conditions, and affordable housing. But all those qualities of ease and comfort were associated with whiteness, and in turn these qualities increasingly defined whiteness. Jobs moved to the suburbs following the White work force and attracting more White workers.

Government-sponsored segregation helped inscribe in American culture the equation of "good neighborhoods" with White ones. In the process, of course, they made all ethnic groups that had access to these neighborhoods "white"—something that had at one historical moment or another been uncertain in terms of the social construction of some groups (such as Jews, Greeks, and Italians) who had been defined as "other." The close correlation between employment opportunity and residential segregation meant that "black" was increasingly linked with "inner-city" and "unemployed or unemployable" in White consciousness; whiteness was identified with "employed or employable," stability and self-sufficiency. Residential segregation was both product and cause of racial constructions that tended to promote further preferences for Whites and further exclusion for Blacks. White neighborhoods increasingly seem to be suitable sites for investment, while Black neighborhoods seem unsuitable.

I have heard many anecdotal reports indicating that, in applying for office jobs, well-qualified Black applicants who put inner-city home addresses on applications or resumes had greater difficulty getting hired than the same individuals did if they used suburban home addresses. Recently, two sociologists were able to uncover employer attitudes by asking employers who would make good employees. The employers frankly revealed their biases, listing race and inner-city residence as explicit parts of their consideration of applicants. Employers freely generalized about race and ethnicity, expressing negative opinions about people of color—especially African-Americans—and positive ideas about Whites. For example, they believed that Whites had a better work ethic than Blacks. Employers' concepts of race and employability were nuanced by ideas about class, mostly signaled by the way employees dressed and spoke.

Space was also important: "inner-city" was equated with "black, poor, uneducated, unskilled, lacking in values, crime, gangs, drugs, and unstable families." "Suburb" meant "white, middle-class, educated, skilled, and stable families." Public school attendance was less favorable than private school, and residence in public housing was also seen as a signal of status. Class and space distinctions among Black applicants for employers, with inner-city Blacks associated with lower classes and with undesirable characteristics as workers. It makes sense, therefore, that Blacks who live in White areas are to some extent identified by greater access to whiteness. And indeed, a recent study showed that Blacks in suburbs did better at finding jobs than Blacks in inner cities. The link between residential segregation and poverty therefore depends on the social construction of race. In particular, the social construction of Whites as employed and employable will continue to attract employers and attract development, as well as discourage the employment of Blacks. The problems that residential segregation bring distance, inconvenience, lower tax base, more concentrated poverty, continue to be reproduced because of their role in reinforcing and reproducing the very idea of race.

Dismantling the Master's House[47]

John Calmore

Relevant Edited Excerpts
Reprinted with Permission

One of the nation's leading scholars on fair housing, Robert Schwemm, suggested that "it may be that one 'Bill Cosby Show' can accomplish as much encouragement of residential integration as scores of Title VIII lawsuits."

Although the legal system may influence preferences, in many contexts it is likely to be of only marginal importance. Racial attitudes may be one of these contexts. It is possible that someone like Bill Cosby will do more for fair housing than will all the lawyers in this room put together. The Bill Cosby Show was a highly popular television series. And by gosh, Bill Cosby's family is just like every other family, except, of course, that the family members are funnier and have more interesting things happen to them.

Schwemm and Ellickson present the "Huxtable Family Syndrome" (HFS), as an idea with vast ramifications for the quest for Black integration. HFS implies that integration would be easier if more Blacks presented themselves like the Huxtables—"an ordinary family" that was "just like every other family" and who would be "dynamite neighbors." To comport with the requirements of HFS, a Black family could have five attractive children, but the parents would both have to be professionals, physicians or attorneys. This "ordinary family" would consist of highly educated, affluent professionals who personified traditional family values.

Initially, the Schwemm-Ellickson view bothered me because it takes what was actually the portrayal of an extraordinary Black family to be merely ordinary in terms of White acceptance. To be on equal footing with an ordinary White family, the Black family would have to be as atypical as the Huxtables. White supremacy is at work here. Less than 2% of the Black population has obtained what is mostly greeted as a false passport.

Success through use of a "false passport," occurs when credentials are discounted because gained through affirmative action, and seen as "trespassing" on White property interests. This is a form of sociological and cultural "passing." Asians and Pacific Islanders can pass ethnically as "model minorities." African Americans pass sociologically and culturally with the right history of socialization, credentials, affluent income, and proper ZIP code.

Even with this individual package, though, integration for the group is problematic for four primary reasons: (1) its anchor is assimilation, (2) its progress is gradual, (3) its tokenistic, and (4) worst of all, it supports and reinforce White dominance and hegemony.

In cultural passing, the intersection of race and class loom large. Choosing to assimilate consists of accepting that only a few will be able to make it pass the gate, being a token and pretending that White dominance is natural has always automatically assured higher economic returns as well as greater economic, political, and social security in the long run."

Passing has a price, and the associated costs are often hidden from public expression and view. Sociologist F. James Davis notes that those who pass biologically sacrifice loyalty to the Black community in order to secure economic opportunities and societal status. White on the outside, but Black on the inside, those who pass biologically experience difficult adjustments and ambiguous identities. Sociological passing has the same costs.

While I realize that the concept of status passing is not perfectly analogous to the biological phenomenon, the family resemblance is sufficient to point to some of the relational and operational difficulties associated with integration. In actuality, I have experienced and observed that status passing more resembles the marginalized, distressing, and contradictory experiences of the light-skinned mulatto, part Black and part white. Here, passing often is imperfect, resulting in a placement between two worlds. It may provoke a number of reactions. Davis summarizes the various ways of trying to cope with the problems of mulatto marginality, and these observations also describe status passing quite well:

1 They may become preoccupied with expressing strong hatred of all Whites, an aggressive pattern that often seems to suggest ambivalent feelings about oneself and the Black community.

2 They may accept the Black identity but worry about color discrimination and conflict within the Black community and hope that color difference can be minimized....

3 They may make a conscious commitment to the Black identity, to embrace the symbols of blackness, and to work hard to prove their pride in being black.

4 They may become strongly committed to reducing discrimination by the White community against all Blacks ...

5 They may accept and make use of the marginal status position, adopting a marginal identity rather than a Black identity, perceiving and dealing objectively with the Black and White communities both while not being fully a part of either, and often being a liaison person between the two.

6 They may suppress the dilemma and reject any kind of racial identity, focusing instead on a professional identity or some absorbing role ...

7 They may decide to pass as white, experiencing all the stress and risks involved in assuming a White identity. Sometimes a person will switch from one mode of adjustment to another, and sometimes adopt more than one style at a time.

Davis' summary provides significant insight into the problems integration warriors experience. It helps as well to explain why a significant number of Blacks, regardless of class position, are profoundly alienated from the very mainstream of society upon which they rely in order to access opportunity, material gain, and status. It also helps to explain why so many Blacks remain ambivalent and conflicted about both the normative weight and instrumental prospects of an integrated future. There is, in short, a fundamental problem with the costs of admission to the White world.

During his Keynote address at a prominent university, Richard Delgado noted the following:

> [It is important] to get beyond colorblind orthodoxy and other received wisdoms and ask searching questions about race, hierarchy, and knowledge. In addressing whiteness, we plan to discuss White transparency and privilege, and the way inattention to this facet of social organization can easily damage the chances of students and communities of color.[48]

Derrick Bell has been making such observations for years. For example, in 1979 he noted:

> At least five "mainstream" law reviews have published symposia or workshop paper on minority admissions issues. All papers published on the issue were by White scholars.[49]

The Id, the Ego, and Equal Protection: Reckoning with Unconscious Racism[50]

By Charles R. Lawrence III

Edited Relevant Excerpts
Republished with Permission

This article reconsiders the doctrine of discriminatory purpose that was established by the 1976 decision, *Washington v. Davis*. This now well-established doctrine requires plaintiffs challenging the constitutionality of a facially neutral law to prove a racially discriminatory purpose on the part of those responsible for the law's enactment or administration.

Davis has spawned a considerable body of literature treating its merits and failings. Minorities and civil rights advocates have been virtually unanimous in condemning *Davis* and its progeny. They have been joined by a significant number of constitutional scholars who have been equally disapproving, if more restrained, in assessing its damage to the cause of equal opportunity. These critics advance two principal arguments. The first is that a motive-centered doctrine of racial discrimination places a very heavy, and often impossible, burden of persuasion on the wrong side of the dispute. Improper motives are easy to hide. And because behavior results from the interaction of a multitude of motives, governmental officials will always be able to argue that racially neutral considerations prompted their actions. Moreover, where several decisionmakers are involved, proof of racially discriminatory motivation is even more difficult.

The second objection to the *Davis* doctrine is more fundamental. It argues that the injury of racial inequality exists irrespective of the decisionmakers' motives. Does the Black child in a segregated school experience less stigma and humiliation because the local school board did not consciously set out to harm her? Are Blacks less prisoners of the ghetto because the decision that excludes them from an all-White neighborhood was made with property values and not race in mind? Those who make this second objection reason that the facts of racial inequality are the real problem. They urge that racially disproportionate harm should trigger heightened judicial scrutiny without consideration of motive.

Supporters of the intent requirement are equally adamant in asserting the doctrine's propriety. They echo the four main arguments that the Court itself set forth in *Davis*:

1 A standard that would subject all governmental action with a racially disproportionate impact to strict judicial scrutiny would cost too much; such a standard, the Court argues, would substantially limit legitimate legislative decisionmaking and would endanger the validity of a 'whole range of existing tax, welfare, public service, regulatory and licensing statutes

2 A disproportionate impact standard would make innocent people bear the costs of remedying a harm in which they played no part;

3 An impact test would be inconsistent with equal protection values, because the judicial decisionmaker would have to explicitly consider race;

4 It would be inappropriate for the judiciary to choose to remedy the racially disproportionate impact of otherwise neutral governmental actions at the expense of other legitimate social interests.

The problems posed by a disproportionate impact standard do not seem insurmountable.

Furthermore, I wish to suggest another way to think about racial discrimination, a way that more accurately describes both its origins and the nature of the injury it inflicts.

Much of one's inability to know racial discrimination when one sees it results from a failure to recognize that racism is both a crime and a disease. This failure is compounded by a reluctance to admit that the illness of racism infects almost everyone.

Acknowledging and understanding the malignancy are prerequisites to the discovery of an appropriate cure. But the diagnosis is difficult, because our own contamination with the very illness for which a cure is sought impairs our comprehension of the disorder.

Scholarly and judicial efforts to explain the constitutional significance of disproportionate impact and governmental motive in cases alleging racial discrimination treat these two categories as mutually exclusive. That is, while disproportionate impact may be evidence of racially discriminatory motive, whether impact or motive is the appropriate focus is normally posed in the alternative: Should racially disproportionate impact, standing alone, trigger a heightened level of judicial scrutiny? Or, should the judiciary apply a deferential standard to legislative and administrative decisions absent proof that the decisionmakers intended a racial consequence? Put another way, the Court thinks of facially neutral actions as either intentionally and unconstitutionally or unintentionally and constitutionally discriminatory. This is a false dichotomy.

Traditional notions of intent do not reflect the fact that decisions about racial matters are influenced in large part by factors that can be characterized as neither intentional—in the sense that certain outcomes are self-consciously sought—nor unintentional—in the sense that the outcomes are random, fortuitous, and uninfluenced by the decisionmaker's beliefs, desires, and wishes.

Americans share a common historical and cultural heritage in which racism has played and still plays a dominant role. Because of this shared experience, we also inevitably share many ideas, attitudes, and beliefs that attach significance to an individual's race and induce negative feelings and opinions about nonWhites. To the extent that this cultural belief system has influenced all of us, we are all racists. At the same time, most of us are unaware of our racism. We do not recognize the ways in which our cultural experience has influenced our beliefs about race or the occasions on which those beliefs affect our actions. In other words, a large part of the behavior that produces racial discrimination is influenced by unconscious racial motivation.

There are two explanations for the unconscious nature of our racially discriminatory beliefs and ideas. First, Freudian theory states that the human mind defends itself against the discomfort of guilt by denying or refusing to recognize those ideas, wishes, and beliefs that conflict with what the individual has learned is good or right. While our historical experience has made racism an integral part of our culture, our society has more recently embraced an ideal that rejects racism as immoral. When an individual experiences conflict between racist ideas and the societal ethic that condemns those ideas, the mind excludes his racism from consciousness.

Second, the theory of cognitive psychology states that the culture—including, for example, the media and an individual's parents, peers, and authority figures—transmits certain beliefs and preferences. Because these beliefs are so much a part of the culture, they are not experienced as explicit lessons. Instead, they seem part of the individual's rational ordering of her perceptions of the world. The individual is unaware, for example, that the ubiquitous presence of a cultural stereotype has influenced her perception that Blacks are lazy or unintelligent. Because racism is so deeply ingrained in our culture, it is likely to be transmitted by tacit understandings: Even if a child is not told that Blacks are inferior, he learns that lesson by observing the behavior of others. These tacit understandings, because they have never been articulated, are less likely to be experienced at a conscious level.

In short, requiring proof of conscious or intentional motivation as a prerequisite to constitutional recognition that a decision is race-dependent ignores much of what we understand about how the human mind works. It also disregards both the irrationality of racism and the profound effect American race relations has had on the individual and collective unconscious.

It may often be appropriate for the legal system to disregard the influence of the unconscious on individual or collective behavior. But where the goal is the eradication of invidious racial discrimination, the law must recognize racism's primary source. The Equal Protection Clause requires the elimination of governmental decisions that take race into account without good and important reasons. Therefore, equal protection doctrine must find a way to come to grips with unconscious racism.

I. 'THY SPEECH MAKETH THEE MANIFEST': A PRIMER ON THE UNCONSCIOUS & RACE

We have found—that is we have been obliged to assume—that very powerful mental processes or ideas exist which can produce all the effects in mental life that ordinary ideas do (including effects that can in their turn become conscious as ideas), though they themselves do not become conscious.

A. Racism: A Public Health Problem

Not every student of the human mind has agreed with Sigmund Freud's description of the unconscious, but few today would quarrel with the assertion that there is an unconscious—that there are mental processes of which we have no awareness that affect our actions and the ideas of which we are aware. There is a considerable, and by now well respected, body of knowledge and empirical research concerning the workings of the human psyche and the unconscious.

Common sense tells us that we all act unwittingly on occasion. We have experienced slips of the tongue and said things we fully intended not to say, and we have had dreams in which we experienced such feeling as fear, desire, and anger that we did not know we had.

But the body of law and legal theory that governs the application of the Equal Protection Clause to cases of alleged racial discrimination should not blind itself to what we know about the unconscious. Racism is in large part a product of the unconscious. It is a set of beliefs whereby we irrationally attach significance to something called race. I do not mean to imply that racism does not have its origins in the rational and premeditated acts of those who sought and seek property and power. But racism in America is much more complex than either the conscious conspiracy of a power elite or the simple delusion of a few ignorant bigots. It is a part of our common historical experience and, therefore, a part of our culture. It arises from the assumptions we have learned to make about the world, ourselves, and others as well as from the patterns of our fundamental social activities.

Richard Wasserstrom has described the significance of race in our culture by contrasting our culture with a hypothetical one where race is an unimportant characteristic: 'In such a culture, race would be largely if not exclusively a matter of superficial physiology; a matter, we might say, simply of the way one looked,' much like eye color. But race does not function in our culture as does eye color, which is an irrelevant category, an unimportant cultural fact. Few of us can recall the color of our best friend's eyes, but when we pass a complete stranger on the street, we will remember his race. We attach significance to race even when we are not aware that we are doing so.

Racism is irrational in the sense that we are not fully aware of the meanings we attach to race or why we have made race significant. It is also arguably dysfunctional to the extent that its irrationality prevents the optimal use of human resources. In this light it seems an appropriate candidate for study and/or treatment by the psychoanalyst as well as for exclusion from law, the discipline that attempts to govern or influence the actions of rational people. But unlike other forms of irrational and dysfunctional behavior, which we think of as deviant or abnormal, racism is 'normal.' It is a malady that we all share, because we have all been scarred by a common history. Racism's universality renders it normal.

Racism's ubiquity underscores the importance of incorporating our knowledge of the unconscious into the legal theory of equal protection. The law has traditionally used psychological theory to define abnormality in order to exclude the irrational from the law's protection or sanction. But where the law's purpose is to eradicate racial discrimination, it must recognize that racism is both irrational and normal. We must understand that our entire culture is afflicted, and we must take cognizance of psychological theory in order to frame a legal theory that can address that affliction.

B. Psychoanalytic Theory: An Explanation of Racism's Irrationality

Several observations about the nature of racial prejudice give credence both to the theory of repression and to the suggestion that racial antagonism finds its source in the unconscious. For example, when we say that racism is irrational, we mean that when people are asked to explain the basis of their racial antagonism they either express an instinctive, unexplained distaste at the thought of associating with the out-group as equals or they cite reasons that are not based on established fact and are often contradicted by personal experience. In one study on racial prejudice, F. L. Hartley included in his survey three fictitious groups he called the Dariens, the Praneans, and the Wallonians. A large portion of respondents who expressed a dislike for Blacks and Jews also disliked these nonexistent groups and advocated restrictive measures against them.

In psychoanalytic terms, this irrational behavior indicates poor 'reality-testing.' When people of normal intelligence behave in a way that rejects what they experience as real, it requires some explanation. Psychoanalytic theory assumes that inadequacy in reality-testing fulfills a psychological function, usually the preservation of an attitude basic to the individual's makeup. If adequate reality-testing threatens to undermine such functionally significant attitude, it is avoided. In such cases, the dislike of out-groups is based on rationalization—that is, on socially acceptable pseudo reasons that serve to disguise the function that the antagonism serves for the individual.

An examination of the beliefs that racially prejudiced people have about out- groups demonstrates their use of other mechanisms observed by both Freudian and non-Freudian behavioralists. For example, studies have found that racists hold two types of stereotyped beliefs: They believe the out-group is dirty, lazy, oversexed, and without control of their instincts (a typical accusation against Blacks), or they believe the out-group is pushy, ambitious, conniving, and in control of business, money, and industry (a typical accusation against Jews). These two types of accusation correspond to two of the most common types of neurotic conflict: that which arises when an individual cannot master his instinctive drives in a way that fits into rational and socially approved patterns of behavior, and that which arises when an individual cannot live up to the aspirations and standards of his own conscience. Thus, the stereotypical view of Blacks implies that their Id, the instinctive part of their psyche, dominates their Ego, the rationally oriented part. The stereotype of the Jew, on the other hand, accuses him of having an overdeveloped Ego. In this way, the racially prejudiced person projects his own conflict into the form of racial stereotypes.

The preoccupation among racially prejudiced people with sexual matters in race relations provides further evidence of this relationship between the unconscious and racism. Taboos against interracial sexual relations, myths concerning the sexual prowess of Blacks, and obsessions with racial purity coexist irrationally with a tendency to break these taboos. Again, psychoanalytic theory provides insights: According to Freud, one's sexual identity plays a crucial role in the unending effort to come to terms with oneself. Thus, the prominence of racism's sexual component supports the theory that racial antagonism grows in large part out of an unstable sense of identity.

Thus far we have considered the role the unconscious plays in creating overtly racist attitudes. But how is the unconscious involved when racial prejudice is less apparent—when racial bias is hidden from the prejudiced individual as well as from others? Increasingly, as our culture has rejected racism as immoral and unproductive, this hidden prejudice has become the more prevalent form of racism. The individual's Ego must adapt to a cultural order that views overtly racist attitudes and behavior as unsophisticated, uninformed, and immoral. It must repress or disguise racist ideas when they seek expression.

Joel Kovel refers to the resulting personality type as the 'aversive racist' and contrasts this type with the 'dominative racist,' the true bigot who openly seeks to keep Blacks in a subordinate position and will resort to force to do so. The aversive racist believes in White superiority, but her conscience seeks to repudiate this belief or, at least, to prevent her from acting on it. She often resolves this inner conflict by not acting at all. She tries to avoid the issue by ignoring the existence of Blacks, avoiding contract with them, or at most being polite, correct, and cold whenever she must deal with them. Aversive racists range from individuals who lapse into demonstrative racism when threatened—as when Blacks get 'too close'—to those who consider themselves liberals and, despite their sense of aversion to Blacks (of which they are often unaware), do their best within the confines of the existing societal structure to ameliorate Blacks' condition.

There is considerably less research and literature concerning the aversive racist than there is concerning the self-conscious racist. This is hardly surprising. Our culture has only recently rejected the morality of White supremacy; the repression of racist ideas is a relatively new phenomenon. It is also a more difficult phenomenon to discern and observe than is self-conscious racism. The researcher's subjects no longer readily admit their membership in the group to be studied. Also, those who would observe and document unconscious racism are not themselves immune from its blight.

The content of the social categories to which people are assigned is generated over a long period of time within a culture and transmitted to individual members of society by a process cognitivists call 'assimilation.' Assimilation entails learning and internalizing preferences and evaluations. Individuals learn cultural attitudes and beliefs about race very early in life, at a time when it is difficult to separate the perceptions of one's teacher (usually a parent) from one's own. In other words, one learns about race at a time when one is highly sensitive to the social contexts in which one lives.

Piaget, in his work on the development of moral judgment in children, described the transition from the stage when children judge pronouncements by their source rather than their content to the stage when children begin to cooperate with equals and to take the role of the other. This ability to see the same data from more than one point of view is the basis of intellectual and moral development. According to Piaget, this transition cannot take place when a child is exposed to only one source of information. These pre-transition conditions, when the child remains in awe of the source of truth, tend to be precisely the conditions under which children learn socially sanctioned truths about race. Lessons learned at this early developmental stage are not questioned: They are learned as facts rather than as points of view.

Furthermore, because children learn lessons about race at this early stage, most of the lessons are tacit rather than explicit. Children learn not so much through an intellectual understanding of what their parents tell them about race as through an emotional identification with who their parents are and what they see and feel their parents do. Small children will adopt their parents' beliefs because they experience them as their own. If we do learn lessons about race in this way, we are not likely to be aware that the lessons have even taken place. If we are unaware that we have been taught to be afraid of Blacks or to think of them as lazy or stupid, then we may not be conscious of our internalization of those feelings and beliefs.

All of these processes, most of which occur outside the actor's consciousness, are mutually reinforcing. Furthermore, there is little in our environment to counteract them; indeed, our culture often supports and rewards individuals for making hostile misjudgments that exaggerate the differences between themselves and members of a racial out-group. Cultural prejudice also removes the possibility of checking judgments against outside reality, further inhibiting the chance that the holder of a prejudiced belief will perceive his mistake and correct it. Thus, through personal and cultural experience the individual comes to associate characteristics such as 'intelligence,' 'laziness,' 'honesty,' or 'dirtiness' with classifications of people. In ambiguous social situations, it will always be easier to find evidence supporting an individual's assumed group characteristics than to find contradictory evidence. Furthermore, whenever one is confronted with the need to interpret the behavior of members of a particular group en masse, there will be little opportunity to observe behavior that conflicts with the group's assumed characteristics.

Case studies have demonstrated that an individual who holds stereotyped beliefs about a 'target' will remember and interpret past events in the target's life history in ways that bolster and support his stereotyped beliefs and will perceive the target's actual behavior as reconfirming and validating the stereotyped beliefs. While the individual may be aware of the selectively perceived facts that support his categorization or simplified understanding, he will not be aware of the process that has caused him to deselect the facts that do not conform with his rationalization. Thus, racially prejudiced behavior that is actually the product of learned cultural preferences is experienced as a reflection of rational deduction from objective observation, which is nonprejudicial behavior. The decisionmaker who is unaware of the selective perception that has produced her stereotype will not view it as a stereotype. She will believe that her actions are motivated not by racial prejudice but by her attraction or aversion to the attributes she has 'observed' in the groups she has favored or disfavored.

D. Unconscious Racism in Everyday Life

Whatever our preferred theoretical analysis, there is considerable commonsense evidence from our everyday experience to confirm that we all harbor prejudiced attitudes that are kept from our consciousness.

When, for example, a well-known sports broadcaster is carried away by the excitement of a brilliant play by an Afro-American professional football player and refers to the player as a 'little monkey' during a nationally televised broadcast, we have witnessed the prototypical parapraxes, or unintentional slip of the tongue. This sportscaster views himself as progressive on issues of race. Many of his most important professional associates are black, and he would no doubt profess that more than a few are close friends. After the incident, he initially claimed no memory of it and then, when confronted with videotaped evidence, apologized and said that no racial slur was intended. There is no reason to doubt the sincerity of his assertion. Why would he intentionally risk antagonizing his audience and damaging his reputation and career? But his inadvertent slip of the tongue was not random. It is evidence of the continuing presence of a derogatory racial stereotype that he has repressed from consciousness and that has momentarily slipped past his Ego's censors.

Likewise, when Nancy Reagan appeared before a public gathering of then-presidential-candidate Ronald Reagan's political supporters and said that she wished he could be there to 'see all these beautiful White people,' one can hardly imagine that it was her self-conscious intent to proclaim publicly her preference for the company of Caucasians.

Incidents of this kind are not uncommon, even if only the miscues of the powerful and famous are likely to come to the attention of the press. But because the unconscious also influences selective perceptions, Whites are unlikely to hear many of the inadvertent racial slights that are made daily in their presence.

Another manifestation of unconscious racism is akin to the slip of the tongue. One might call it a slip of the mind: While one says what one intends, one fails to grasp the racist implications of one's benignly motivated words or behavior. For example, in the late 1950s and early 1960s, when integration and assimilation were unquestioned ideals among those who consciously rejected the ideology of racism, White liberals often expressed their acceptance of and friendship with Blacks by telling them that they 'did not think of them as Negroes.' Their conscious intent was complimentary. The speaker was saying, 'I think of you as normal human beings, just like me.' But he was not conscious of the underlying implication of his words. What did this mean about most Negroes? Were they not normal human beings? If the White liberal were asked if this was his inference, he would doubtless have protested that his words were being misconstrued and that he only intended to state that he did not think of anyone in racial terms. But to say that one does not think of a Negro as a Negro is to say that one thinks of him as something else. The statement is made in the context of the real world, and implicit in it is a comparison to some norm. In this case the norm is whiteness. The White liberal's unconscious thought, his slip of the mind, is, 'I think of you as different from other Negroes, as more like White people.'

One indication of the nonneutrality of the statement, 'I don't think of you as a Negro,' when spoken as a compliment by a White is the incongruity of the response, 'I don't think of you as white.' This could also be a complimentary remark coming from a black, conveying the fact that she does not think of her friend in the usual negative terms she associates with whiteness. But this statement does not make sense coming from an individual who would accept as complimentary a statement characterizing her as unlike other Negroes. If anything, the response only makes sense as a lighthearted but cautionary retort. It conveys the following message: 'I understand that your conscious intent was benign. But let me tell you something, friend. I think being Black is just fine. If anything, our friendship is possible because you are unlike most White folks.'

Of course, the statements of both these interlocutors are ethnocentric. But it is the White who has made the slip of the mind. He was unmindful of the ethnocentric premise upon which his 'compliment' was based. He would find it painful to know that it is a premise in which he believes. His Black friend's ethnocentrism is self-conscious and self-affirming. She is well aware of the impact of her reply. It is a defensive parry against the dominant society's racism.

A crucial factor in the process that produces unconscious racism is the tacitly transmitted cultural stereotype. If an individual has never known a Black doctor or lawyer or is exposed to Blacks only through a mass media where they are portrayed in the stereotyped roles of comedian, criminal, musician, or athlete, he is likely to deduce that Blacks as a group are naturally inclined toward certain behavior and unfit for certain roles. But the lesson is not explicit: It is learned, internalized, and used without an awareness of its source. Thus, an individual may select a White job applicant over an equally qualified Black and honestly believe that this decision was based on observed intangibles unrelated to race. The employer perceives the White candidate as 'more articulate,' 'more collegial,' 'more thoughtful,' or 'more charismatic.' He is unaware of the learned stereotype that influenced his decision. Moreover, he has probably also learned an explicit lesson of which he is very much aware: Good, law-abiding people do not judge others on the basis of race. Even the most thorough investigation of conscious motive will not uncover the race-based stereotype that has influenced his decision.

This same process operates in the case of more far-reaching policy decisions that come to judicial attention because of their discriminatory impact. For example, when an employer or academic administrator discovers that a written examination rejects Blacks at a disproportionate rate, she can draw several possible conclusions: that Blacks are less qualified than others; that the test is an inaccurate measure of ability; or that the testers have chosen the wrong skills or attributes to measure. When decisionmakers reach the first conclusion, a predisposition to select those data that conform with a racial stereotype may well have influenced them. Because this stereotype has been tacitly transmitted and unconsciously learned, they will be unaware of its influence on their decision.

If the purpose of the law's search for racial animus or discriminatory intent is to identify a morally culpable perpetrator, the existing intent requirement fails to achieve that purpose. There will be no evidence of self-conscious racism where the actors have internalized the relatively new American cultural morality which holds racism wrong or have learned racist attitudes and beliefs through tacit rather than explicit lessons. The actor himself will be unaware that his actions, or the racially neutral feelings and ideas that accompany them, have racist origins.

Of course, one can argue that the law should govern only consciously motivated actions—that societal sanctions can do no more than attempt to require that the individual's Ego act as society's agent in censoring out those unconscious drives that society has defined as immoral. Under this view, the law can sanction a defective Ego that has not fully internalized current societal morality and has, therefore, allowed illegal racist wishes to reach consciousness and fruition in an illegal act. But the law should not hold an individual responsible for wishes that never reach consciousness, even if they also come to fruition in discriminatory acts.

The problem is that this argument does not tell us why the law should hold the individual responsible for racial injury that results from one form of Ego disguise but not the other. I believe the law should be equally concerned when the mind's censor successfully disguises a socially repugnant wish like racism if that motive produces behavior that has a discriminatory result as injurious as if it flowed from a consciously held motive.

Washington v. Davis.

(F) Two unsuccessful Black candidates for positions in the District of Columbia Metropolitan Police Department alleged that some of the Department's hiring practices—particularly 'Test 21,' a written test that Blacks failed at a rate roughly four times that of Whites—discriminated against Blacks and violated the guarantee of equal protection implicit in the Fifth Amendment's Due Process Clause. 'Test 21,' which was used throughout the federal civil service, was designed to test verbal ability, vocabulary, reading, and comprehension. While the Court found that the test was a useful indicator of success in police training school, there was no proof that either the test scores or the school's examination scores predicted job performance or measured success in job-related training.

What evidence might the plaintiffs have presented to establish that the government's action in this case had racial meaning? Unlike segregated housing, we do not ordinarily associate the use of civil service exams with race. But an action that has no racial meaning in one context may have significant racial meaning in another. We have seen that human behavior must be examined in context, as it may well derive its meaning from the specific historical and cultural milieu in which it takes place. Despite the race-neutral origins of civil service exams as a generic entity, one has an intuitive sense that their use in this case has racial connotations—that this case is more like the Memphis wall than it is like an increased bus fare or a regressive tax. It is important to pay heed to one's intuitions at this juncture.

At this point, it is helpful to consider the setting in which 'Test 21' was employed. Can one identify the contextual elements that have attracted the attention of our intuition? Are there elements not present in other civil service cases, elements that speak in terms of race? The most obvious racial element is the exam's racially disproportionate impact. One can argue that the government's action racially stigmatizes because Blacks fail the exam in larger numbers than Whites. But not every case of racially disparate impact has racial meaning. An increased bus fare may burden a larger percentage of Blacks than Whites, but we do not think of the fare increase as a direct stigmatization of Blacks. It does not convey a message of racial inferiority. Thus, if the governmental action in *Davis* conveys a racial message, it must derive that meaning from something other than, or in addition to, its racial impact. Like the traffic barrier in *Memphis v. Greene*, there must be something in the particulars of its historical and cultural context that causes us to interpret this action—at least intuitively—in racial terms.

I suggest that there are two such elements. The first involves the nature of the work or activity from which Blacks have been excluded: the job of police officer in a predominantly but not entirely Black community. The second relates to the reason given for their exclusion: that they failed to demonstrate sufficient proficiency in verbal and written language skills.

It is significant that the challenged action in *Davis* excluded Blacks from working as police officers and not as mail carriers or bus drivers. The occupation of police officer has symbolic meaning within our culture. Police officers represent the law as well as enforce it. They are armed and have discretionary authority to use violence. They are charged with protecting the lives and property of some individuals within society and controlling the violent and unlawful behavior of others.

If history—the accumulated meaningful behavior of our culture—has taught us to attach significance to race in considering these elements of the job of police officer—authority, control, protection, and sanctioned violence—then an action that determines the racial composition of a police force also has racial meaning.

Furthermore, throughout American history police forces have had a different relationship to Black communities than to White communities. In White communities, the police officer is viewed as a public servant. His job is to protect the lives and property of those in the community where he works. But the job of the law enforcement officer in Black communities has been to control the communities' inhabitants and to protect the lives and property of Whites who perceive Blacks as the primary potential source of violence and crime.

For Blacks, those entrusted with law enforcement and the firepower that gives them authority have always been servants of the White men in power who exploit Blacks economically and demean them socially. Slaves were forbidden to bear arms and a White police force of overseers and sheriffs' posses enforced the master's law. With the abolition of slavery, the use of organized, socially sanctioned violence against Blacks increased, and the authority of the sheriff's office was often indistinguishable from that of the Ku Klux Klan. As recently as 1967, there were nearly a dozen major American cities where Blacks accounted for over 25 percent of the population that were patrolled by police forces with only a token minority representation. It is not surprising that many Black communities continue to view the police as an occupying army.

The fact that police officers are authority figures to White as well as Black citizens is also significant in determining the cultural meaning of excluding large numbers of Blacks from the D.C. police force. To the extent that our culture attaches specific meaning to the assignment of racial groups to certain occupational and hierarchical roles, behavior that maintains those role assignments will have racial meaning. For example, Whites are accustomed to seeing Blacks as servants performing menial tasks. Thus, Whites are generally neither surprised nor threatened when they see Black porters, maids, and janitors. This is not simply a reflection of the fact that many Blacks have performed these jobs. It is also indicative of a historical and culturally ingrained system of beliefs that leads us to think of Blacks as suited to these jobs, to associate the jobs with Blacks.

By contrast, Whites are not accustomed to seeing Blacks in positions of authority or power. Black managers, Black professors, and Black doctors are confronted with reactions ranging from disbelief to resistance to concern about their competence. The historical exclusion of Blacks from these jobs has been rationalized by a belief in their unsuitability for these roles. What is at issue here is not just occupational stereotypes born out of habit. These stereotypes manifest a larger and more complex ideology that has legitimized the white-over-Black authority relationship. Stereotypes are cultural symbols. They constitute our contemporary interpretation of past and present meaningful behavior.

The argument in defense of all-male police forces provides a useful analogue for understanding our less readily apparent attitudes about authority and race. In suits alleging discrimination against women in the selection of patrol officers, police department defendants have argued that women would not make good officers because the job requires an individual who can command respect from the man on the street. Men, they have argued, would not take orders from women, and, therefore, women would be less effective patrol persons. In other words, the departments' discriminatory hiring practices have been defended as a necessary adaptation to the sexist beliefs and practices of the culture.

Whites would be less likely to verbalize the same argument regarding Blacks, but the fact remains that many individuals in our culture continue to resist and resent taking orders from Blacks. If the court were convinced that the absence or presence of substantial numbers of Black police officers on the D.C. force would be interpreted as the maintenance or disestablishment of culturally instilled beliefs about the need to control Blacks and the appropriate roles for Blacks and Whites in authority relationships, then the Civil Service Commission's decision to rely on 'Test 21' would have racial meaning.

Throughout American history, a cultural myth that describes Blacks as an inherently inferior race has justified their economic and social subjugation. At first, the myth found verification in religious doctrine. By the mid-nineteenth century, the dogma of biblical scripture and verse was supplemented by the pseudoscience of biologists and social scientists who found fodder for the myth in craniometry, eugenics, and cultural anthropology. With the introduction of the I.Q. test in the early twentieth century, the psychometricians assumed primary authorship of this Homeric tale of God and nature's differential distribution of intellectual talent among the races. They provided the theory and numbers to prove the veracity of the myth, and the people's bards—the press, popular literature, and the theater—transformed the racism of pseudoscience into a folklore that shaped the nation's consciousness.

Plaintiffs trying *Davis* under the test proposed in this article would present evidence detailing both the history and the contemporary manifestations of this myth. They would seek to convince the court that most people in our culture believe that the average White person is inherently smarter than the average Black person and that Whites will interpret the racially selective impact of 'Test 21' as a confirmation of that belief. If the culture gives the governmental action this kind of racial meaning, the action constitutes a direct racial stigmatization. Like the segregated beach and the Memphis wall, it conveys a message that has its origins in a pervasive and mutually reinforcing pattern of racially stigmatizing actions, and it adds one more stigmatizing action to that pattern. Presumably, the decisionmakers who chose to use 'Test 21' were aware of that message and were influenced by it, whether consciously or unconsciously.

Confederate Flags on Southern State Capitols[51]

James Forman

Edited Relevant Excerpts

Reprinted with permission

On April 9, 1865, General Robert E. Lee conceded, "[T]here is nothing left for me to do but go and see General Grant." The Confederate Army surrendered, and

Dixie, the Confederate battle flag, ceased to fly. But only temporarily. In 1956, for the first time in nearly a century, Georgia resurrected the Confederate symbol by changing its state flag in symbolic opposition to *Brown v. Board of Education*. South Carolina followed suit six years later, hoisting the flag above its state capitol. The following year, Alabama revived Dixie, with Governor George Wallace raising the flag as part of his "Segregation Forever" campaign. *Brown* is still the law of the land, yet Dixie remains entrenched.

Last year, in *NAACP v. Hunt*, the Eleventh Circuit rejected the National Association for the Advancement of Colored People's (NAACP) claim that the Constitution of the United States and federal statutes mandate the removal of the flag from the Alabama state capitol. Central to the court's conclusion was the notion that the *Hunt* plaintiffs' problem involved neither the flag nor the law, but their "own emotions." Moreover, the court held that "there is no unequal application of the state policy; all citizens are exposed to the flag. Citizens of all races are offended by its position." In sum, the court told the plaintiffs to turn elsewhere for relief, because "the federal judiciary is not empowered to make decisions based on social sensitivity."

This Note takes issue with the *Hunt* court. It proceeds in two parts. Part I argues that the Alabama government's flying of the rebel flag violates the Equal Protection Clause of the Fourteenth Amendment because the flag was raised with the intent to discriminate against blacks. Part II argues that flying the flag violates the First Amendment because it is a form of racist government speech that chills the speech rights of blacks.

Throughout, the argument will focus on the harms the Confederate flag presents, the appropriate legal remedies, and the *Hunt* court's misunderstanding of those harms and remedies. The most fundamental errors in *Hunt's* analysis of the First and Fourteenth Amendment claims stemmed from the court's reliance, however unconscious, on a number of thoroughly repudiated constitutional tenets. Accordingly, this Note will both argue that removing the Confederate flag is constitutionally required and demonstrate that leftover jurisprudential tendencies continue to serve as barriers to a meaningful conception of the First and Fourteenth Amendments.

I. THE FOURTEENTH AMENDMENT

A. The Hunter and Arlington Heights Intent Standards

The Equal Protection Clause of the Fourteenth Amendment provides that no state may "deny to any person within its jurisdiction the equal protection of the laws." In *Washington v. Davis*, the Supreme Court ruled that establishing an equal protection violation requires a showing of discriminatory intent; evidence of discriminatory impact alone does not suffice. The Court reaffirmed this holding in *Hunter v. Underwood*, when it stated, quoting its opinion in *Village of Arlington Heights v. Metropolitan Housing Development Corp.*, that "'official action will not be held unconstitutional solely because it results in a racially disproportionate impact.... Proof of racially discriminatory intent or purpose is required to show a violation of the Equal Protection Clause.'" Determining the existence of discriminatory intent is hardly an easy task. The Supreme Court has, however, provided guidelines by which courts can analyze discriminatory intent claims. Were a court to follow these guidelines faithfully, it would not permit Dixie to remain above the Southern States' capitols.

> A plaintiff challenging government policy under the Equal Protection Clause bears the burden of demonstrating, by a preponderance of the evidence, that racial discrimination was a substantial or motivating factor in the adoption of the policy. Since determining the "motivation behind official action is often a problematic undertaking," courts must look to the context in which actions were taken in order to evaluate the discriminatory intent claim. Accordingly, "determining whether invidious discriminatory purpose was a motivating factor demands a sensitive inquiry into such circumstantial and direct evidence of intent as may be available." Such an inquiry might include: (1) evidence of disparate impact; (2) "the historical background of the decision ... particularly if it reveals a series of official actions taken for invidious purposes"; (3) "the specific sequence of events leading up to the challenged decision"; and (4) legislative or administrative history, especially contemporaneous statements of decisionmakers about their reasons.
>
> Under this discriminatory intent standard, there can be little doubt that racial discrimination was a motivating factor in the Southern States' decisions to hoist Confederate flags. Examining the "sequence of events" in Alabama, for example, shows that the Confederate flag was raised as a symbol of white defiance to court-ordered integration. According to Montgomery newsman Robert Ingram, who testified in *Hunt*:
>
> > [O]n Thursday, April 25, 1963, Montgomery braced for a meeting between the late Robert F. Kennedy, then U.S. Attorney General, and Alabama's new Governor George C. Wallace[.] [The] Governor had already announced his plan to 'stand in the door' at the University of Alabama to block admission of two Black students and Kennedy came in a futile effort to talk Wallace out of his stand[.] Two acts of defiance unfolded that day: (1) a group of ladies placed a floral wreath over the Jefferson Davis gold star, their way of making certain that the sacred spot was not touched by Kennedy's feet, and (2) shortly after 7:00 a.m. capitol guards hoisted the Confederate Battle flag. The flag, Ingram concluded, "has flown ever since."

Many read the U.S. Constitution as prohibiting the flying of the flag under these circumstances. The flag was used as a form of racist government speech that chills the speech rights of Blacks, and a violation of the Equal Protection Clause of the Fourteenth Amendment which provides that no state may "deny to any person within its jurisdiction the equal protection of the laws."

In *Washington v. Davis*, the Supreme Court ruled that wherever there is a showing of discriminatory intent, there is a constitutional violation. Evidence of discriminatory impact alone does not suffice. Official action will not be held unconstitutional solely because it results in a racially disproportionate result, such as finding a town with a Black population of 59% but a Black community college enrollment of only 2.7%. Proving discriminatory intent is quite difficult. Plaintiffs challenging government policy under the Equal Protection Clause bear the burden of demonstrating that racial discrimination was a motivating factor in the adoption of the policy. Official action is viewed in light of circumstantial and direct evidence, which includes a showing of disparate impact, along with the specific sequence of events leading up to the decision, and contemporaneous statements of decision makers are all part of the equation.

Under this standard, there can be little doubt that racial discrimination was a motivating factor in the Southern States' decisions to hoist Confederate flags. In every state the flag was raised as a symbol of White defiance to court-ordered integration. In addition to standing in the doorway of the University of Alabama to protest the admission of Black students, George Wallace ordered National Guardsmen to surround the Birmingham public schools. That same year, he sent the National Guard into battle against Birmingham Blacks protesting segregation. The U.S. Supreme Court in 1989 denied plaintiffs' equal protection claim, despite this history, stating that Black *feelings* about the flag were not matters properly before the court.

Many believe that in the years following this decision, a Black-led economic boycott against southern resorts such as those found on Myrtle Beach and Hilton Head, South Carolina, finally prompted removal of this enduring symbol of Black subordination.[52]

> Higginbotham wrote that his book SHADES OF FREEDOM was mostly a record of the past.[53] He went on to say that:
>
> > Perhaps it is also in some way a lesson for our own time. Between 1989 and 1991, the collapse of Communism in Eastern Europe and the break-up of the former Soviet Union brought about a rapid and public resurgence of anti-Semitism in Russia. All sorts of deceptive arguments, from the supposed inordinate wealth of the Jews, to their mythical religious depravity, were used to explain the shambles in which the country found itself. Once again Jews became the common object of hate around which other Russians tried to rebuild a common identity that had withered under Communism, and that had now all but died with the fall of the Soviet state. Thousands of Jews left Russia during that period because life there for them was unbearable.[54]
> >
> > The night before she was to leave Russia with her family, a Jewish woman wrote an anonymous letter to a Moscow weekly. She warned Russians not to suppose that the moral and economic devastation wrought upon their society by so many years of totalitarian government could ever be erased simply by expelling Jews from the country. Russia, she predicted, would not find peace and redemption by hating Jews because "[h]atred that rages in souls and suddenly loses its immediate object does not disappear without a trace."[55]
> >
> > The precept of Black inferiority is the hate that raged in the American soul through over 240 years of slavery and nearly ninety years of segregation. Once slavery was abolished, and once the more oppressive forms of segregation were eliminated, many Whites' hate still had not lost its immediate object. The ashes of that hate have, over the course of so many generations, accumulated at the bottom of our memory. There they lie uneasily, like a heavy secret which Whites can never quite confess which Blacks can never quite forgive, and which, for both Blacks and Whites, forestalls until a distant day any hope of peace and redemption.[56]

Reflecting on the American experience, Professor Charles Lawrence has developed a theory of racism that embodies the systemic imputation of stigma onto African Americans through the courts and through extralegal actions. As he explains, racism is part of the common cultural heritage of all Americans. "Racism is a group of assumptions about the world and its inhabitants that are expressed, often unconsciously, in a "mutually reinforcing and pervasive pattern of stigmatizing actions that cumulate to compose an injurious whole that is greater than the sum of its parts."[57]

> These assumptions are based on notions, explicit or implicit, of [the other in their midsts] as dirty, lazy, oversexed, in poor control of their ids, and otherwise less than fully human. Indeed, such assumptions give rise to behavior, such as

the establishment of race-segregated housing and bathrooms that dramatize White stereotypes of African Americans as impure, contaminating, or untouchable. Similarly, the use of devices that reduce the number of African-American policemen or that challenge the competency of African-American professors and managers reinforces a cultural message that Whites should be in positions of authority over African Americans. While, as Lawrence's article demonstrates, these cultural messages can be decoded, they are often tacit, or even unconscious.[58]

Chapter Nine

Sexual Orientation, Gender Identity & DNA

> Western culture assumes that sex, gender, and sexual orientation are fused and that they essentially, necessarily, and naturally relate to one another.[1]

> Racial, economic and other kinds of equality are instrumentally necessary for the abolition of gender.... As long as any stable hierarchies exist, democracy is threatened, and democracy is needed for the proper authorization of social goals—particularly the radical social goal of abolishing gender. Individuals cannot be expected to pay the personal costs of conforming to social expectations if they have no voice in the determination of those expectations, and if they cannot realize the benefits of the social arrangement.[2]

In societies prone to caste, and most are, the impetus to validate one set of behaviors, lives and lifestyles over others is unrelenting. The push to justify what are primarily religious objections by establishing a moral theory of social contract in conjunction with laws that constrain human choice is an ongoing process. Customary rhetoric of obligation and necessity founded upon divine mandates, tradition, and science as primary sources of authority has skewed and confused more than it has clarified the requirements of a constitutional democracy.

Stanley Kurtz, an affiliate of the Hoover Institute, believes that the road to polyamory is paved with acceptance of gay marriage and that both undermine the nuclear family.[3] The public good for which the state asserts an interest when regulating intimate relations is often couched in terms of the future of the family. Such debates provide a subtext for unspoken concerns about the future of our democracy, economy and/or status as a world power. Without a concrete sense of how Kurtz views the role of family, it remains unclear why his research ignores the merit of myriad studies detailing public initiatives that serve to stabilize youngsters' lives without regard to or perhaps in spite of the structure or functionality of their family life. Instead, he calls attention to what he describes as "the media's reflexive labeling of doubts about gay marriage as homophobia," such that he finds it nearly impossible to debate the social effects of marriage reform. From a constitutional perspective, the issue of gay marriage is well worth examining even if you don't happen to view life-long marriage as a great societal anchor. As we noted in the Divilbiss case, in Chapter Six, these debates influence the judicial orientation on how sexual preferences and practices impact fitness to parent minor children. Kurtz is absolutely correct about one thing: "The Supreme Court's ringing affirmation of sexual liberty in *Lawrence v. Texas* makes the entire debate unavoidable."[4]

Sexual liberty is a new and relatively odd characterization of the facts of a case that deals with consensual sodomy. Such practices have long been viewed as a civil liberty among consenting adults; hardly anyone can remember the last time a heterosexual couple was charged with sodomy, married or not. The Lawrence Court has merely, and rightfully, upheld the privacy rights of all Americans through meaningful application of the equal protection doctrine. The history of regulating sexual practices corresponds to the tenets of Judeo-Christian philosophy of nature and autonomy. As Victoria Woodhull observed early on, among the welcomed effects of religious liberty is the impetus toward a more coherent debate about marriage and familial obligations in this and other cultures.

Kurtz' liberty assessment is an interesting point of departure from the homophobia versus public good debate, that leads us toward questions of whose interests are served most and best as we criminalize, decriminalize, normalize, and pathologize certain human behaviors. Equal protection issues have re-surfaced for gay men in the criminal context with the proliferation of sex offender registration laws. Hardly any of the policy debates include discussions of the symbolic functions of the law alongside its capacity for practical delivery of equal protection.

The primary inquiry related to homosexuality has centered on the nature versus nurture debate. Once the original claims of mental defect were proven false, the question of whether there is a gay gene to indicate homosexual preface surfaced as scientists sought to understand all facets of sexual orientation.[5] The genetic testing of intersexed persons pursuant to studies on transgender qualities has fueled the question.[6] Ethical dilemmas concerning the collection, storage and use of DNA samples abound.[7] Some argue that we all have equal capacity for bi-sexuality, and only socialization and cultural adaptation accounts for the large majority who identify themselves as heterosexual.[8] These debates continue apace while the constitutional dilemma narrows down to the same issues of substantive due process presented in previous chapters: What is the state's interest in regulating intimate choices, particularly to the extent that it attempts to proscribe an individual's choice of partner(s)?

Transexuality, Intersexuality & Bisexuality

Operations of Legal Rhetoric[9]

By Susan Etta Keller

Edited Relevant Excerpts

Reprinted with permission

A transsexual is someone who undergoes or contemplates undergoing anatomical and hormonal modifications in order to live in and be recognized as a different gender than the one attributed at birth. An individual transsexual's gender presentation may be so coherent that at any particular moment it draws no attention. However, the life history of any transsexual involves a shifting and a doubleness of gender attribution over time, which challenges cultural understandings of the ease and naturalness of the gender attribution process.

Legal opinions, as a genre, rarely draw attention. But they should, and for similar reasons. Individual legal opinions in a particular doctrinal area may appear to offer coherent and unified explanations of their decisions. However, they also offer a shifting and a doubleness of the rhetoric used to justify outcomes, both in the conflicts apparent in the aggregate and in the incoherencies in any particular opinion. The phenomenon of transsexuality provides writers of judicial opinions with the sort of controversy that renders these qualities of legal texts particularly visible.

An increasing number of transgender theorists and activists urge that claims about and images of transsexual identity undergo a shift in perspective. By moving the experience of surgical operations to the conceptual foreground, these theorists hope to reveal more fully the complex mechanisms of gender at work in the lives and histories of transsexuals. I seek a similar foregrounding of the rhetorical operations in judicial opinions in order to reveal the more complex mechanisms of decisionmaking. Just as an embrace by transsexuals of their personal histories might have significant implications for an understanding of gender, so might an embrace within legal decisionmaking of the repudiated, the excluded, the crisis-generating features that appear to mar the smooth consistency of opinions alter our understanding of judging. In this Article, I emphasize the rhetorical operations of decisions in which judges contemplate the identity claims of transsexuals in order to offer insights into the condition of both judging and gender, as well as the connection between the two.

The phenomenon of transsexuality may offer controversy for two contradictory reasons. This conflict is illustrated by the celebrated case of Renee Richards, a male to female transsexual who won the right to play in the women's division of the U.S. Open Tennis Tournament. At the same time, the phenomenon of transsexuality also offers an opportunity for people of very diverse viewpoints to identify with the struggles of individual transsexuals. The following thought exercise may suggest how. Imagine you have gone to the doctor with some troubling symptoms and are told:

> You have a rare condition. Without further medical intervention you will transform biologically over the next three months into the other gender. Biologically means hormonally and anatomically, internally and externally. However, there are steps that can be taken to forestall this change. These treatments involve major surgery, and can be painful and costly. Your insurance may or may not cover them. Furthermore, you may find the results unsatisfactory; we will never be able to restore you to the way you look and feel today. You may not have the same degree of sexual function you have had in the past or would have in your new gender without the intervention. However, we can ensure that your physical appearance will allow others, whether strangers or intimates, to attribute to you your old gender. Which choice would you make?

Defining Male and Female: Intersexuality and the Collision Between Law and Biology[10]

Julie A. Greenberg

Edited Relevant Excerpts
Reprinted with permission

I. Introduction

"He was a boy, became a girl, and then a boy again." This provocative headline sounds like it should have appeared in a supermarket tabloid. This headline actually appeared in the Los Angeles Times and cited a critical study that had just been reported in the Archives of Pediatric & Adolescent Medicine.

For many decades, the medical and psychological communities have attempted to resolve the issue of how one's sex (whether an individual is a male or female) should be determined for medical purposes. Until recently, however, legal authorities generally have been blind to the need to define the terms "male" and "female" for legal purposes. The law typically has operated under the assumption that the terms "male" and "female" are fixed and unambiguous despite medical literature demonstrating that these assumptions are not true.

Although the law generally presumes these terms are unambiguous, courts and administrative agencies have been forced to determine an individual's legal sex under some limited circumstances. These cases typically have involved transsexuals—individuals whose biological sex does not conform with their self-identified sex.

The law has largely ignored other medical conditions in which an individual's sex may be ambiguous. Recent medical literature indicates that approximately one to four percent of the world's population may be intersexed and have either ambiguous or noncongruent sex features. Thus, the manner in which the law defines "male," "female," and "sex" will have a profound impact on at least 2.7 million persons in the United States. If, as some experts believe, the number of intersexed people is four percent, approximately ten million people in the United States will be affected.

Medical experts recognize that many factors contribute to the determination of an individual's sex. According to medical professionals, the typical criteria of sex include:

1. Genetic or chromosomal sex—XY or XX;

2. Gonadal sex (reproductive sex glands)—testes or ovaries;

3. Internal morphologic sex (determined after three months gestation)—

seminal vesicles/prostrate or vagina/uterus/fallopian tubes;

4. External morphologic sex (genitalia)—penis/scrotum or clitoris/labia;

5. Hormonal sex—androgens or estrogens;

6. Phenotypic sex (secondary sexual features)—facial and chest hair or breasts;

7. Assigned sex and gender of rearing; and

8. Sexual identity.

For most people, these factors are all congruent, and one's status as a man or woman is uncontroversial. For intersexuals, some of these factors may be incongruent, or an ambiguity within a factor may exist.

The assumption is that there are two separate roads, one leading from XY chromosomes at conception to manhood, the other from XX chromosomes at conception to womanhood. The fact is that there are not two roads, but one road with a number of forks that turn in the male or female direction. Most of us turn in the same direction at each fork.

The bodies of the millions of intersexed people have taken a combination of male and female forks and have followed the road less traveled. These individuals have noncongruent sexual attributes. For these individuals, the law must determine which of the eight sexual factors will determine their sex and whether any one factor should be dispositive for all legal purposes.

"We don't believe in pressuring the children. When the time is right, they'll choose the appropriate gender."

Marjorie H. Rowland v. Mad River Local School District[11]

February 25, 1985

On petition for writ of certiorari to the United States Court of Appeals for the Sixth Circuit. The petition for a writ of certiorari is denied.

Justice BRENNAN, with whom Justice MARSHALL joins, dissenting.

This case raises important constitutional questions regarding the rights of public employees to maintain and express their private sexual preferences.

> In December 1974, petitioner was suspended from her non-tenured position as a high school guidance counselor. In April1975, the respondent School District acting through its School Board decided not to renew petitioner's contract.

Because determination of the appropriate constitutional analysis to apply in such a case continues to puzzle lower courts and because this Court has never addressed the issues presented, I would grant certiorari and set this case for oral argument.

A jury later made unchallenged findings :

That petitioner was suspended and not rehired solely because she was bisexual and had told her secretary and some fellow teachers that she was bisexual, and not for "any other reason."

That petitioner's mention of her bisexuality did not "in any way interfere with the proper performance of [her or other school staff members'] duties or with the regular operation of the school generally."

That petitioner had suffered damages as a result of the decisions to suspend and not rehire her in the form of personal humiliation, mental anguish, and lost earnings.

The trial judge ruled that these findings supported petitioner's claims for violation of her constitutional right to free speech and to equal protection of the laws under the Fourteenth Amendment. He therefore entered a judgment for damages for petitioner.

The Court of Appeals for the Sixth Circuit reversed. The court first ruled that the decision to discharge petitioner based on her workplace statements was unobjectionable under the First Amendment because petitioner's speech was not about "a matter of public concern."

While accepting the jury's finding that petitioner's mention of her bisexuality had not interfered "in any way" with the "regular operation of the school," the court concluded that it was constitutionally permissible to dismiss petitioner "for talking about it."

Second, the court held that no equal protection claim could possibly have been made out, because there was presented "no evidence of how other employees with different sexual preferences were treated." Without citation to any precedent, the court characterized the judgment for petitioner in the absence of such comparative evidence as "plain error."

This ruling overturned the jury's clear finding to the contrary that when the school Principal and Superintendent had suspended petitioner and recommended to the School Board that she not be rehired, they had "treated [petitioner] differently than similarly situated employees, because she was homosexual/bisexual."

The Court of Appeals also criticized the trial judge for "ignor[ing]" an additional finding that petitioner had not properly performed her job on one occasion when she had identified two homosexual students that she was counseling to her secretary.

Of course, because the jury had determined that the one incident of poor performance was not a motivating factor in the decision to fire petitioner, it was entirely correct for the trial judge not to consider the incident in entering judgment for petitioner (plaintiff must show that constitutionally protected conduct was "motivating factor" in hiring decision, and that school board would not have reached same decision absent that conduct).

This case starkly presents issues of individual constitutional rights that have "swirled nationwide for many years." Petitioner did not lose her job because she disrupted the school environment or failed to perform her job. She was discharged merely because she is bisexual and revealed this fact to acquaintances at her workplace. These facts are rendered completely unambiguous by the jury's findings. Yet after a jury and the trial court who heard and evaluated the evidence rendered verdicts for petitioner, the court below reversed based on a crabbed reading of our precedents and unexplained disregard of the jury and judge's factual findings. Because they are so patently erroneous, these maneuvers suggest only a desire to evade the central question: may a State dismiss a public employee based on her bisexual status alone? I respectfully dissent from the Court's decision not to give its plenary attention to this issue.

That petitioner was discharged for her nondisruptive mention of her sexual preferences raises a substantial claim under the First Amendment. "For at least 15 years, it has been settled that a State cannot condition public employment on a basis that infringes the employee's constitutionally protected interest in freedom of expression." Nevertheless, *Connick* held that if "employee expression cannot be fairly considered as relating to any matter of political, social, or other concern to the community," disciplinary measures taken in response to such expression cannot be challenged under the First Amendment "absent the most unusual circumstances."

The court below ruled that *Connick* requires the conclusion that a bisexual public employee constitutionally may be dismissed for "talking about it." This conclusion does not result inevitably from *Connick*, and may be questioned on at least two grounds: first, because petitioner's speech did indeed "touch upon" a matter of public concern, and second, because speech even if characterized as private is entitled to constitutional protection when it does not in any way interfere with the employer's business.

We have unanimously held that "a teacher's exercise of his right to speak on issues of public importance may not furnish the basis for his dismissal from public employment." Our subsequent decisions demonstrate that decisions not to rehire nontenured public employees may be challenged under the *Pickering* First Amendment rationale.

Connick recognized that some issues are "inherently of public concern," citing "racial discrimination" as one example. I think it impossible not to note that a similar public debate is currently ongoing regarding the rights of homosexuals. The fact of petitioner's bisexuality, once spoken, necessarily and ineluctably involved her in that debate. Speech that "touches upon" this explosive issue is no less deserving of constitutional attention than speech relating to more widely condemned forms of discrimination.

Apart from the First Amendment, we have held that "[a] State cannot exclude a person from ... any ... occupation ... for reasons that contravene the Due Process or Equal Protection Clause of the Fourteenth Amendment." In applying the Equal Protection Clause, "we have treated as presumptively invidious those classifications that disadvantage a 'suspect class,' or that impinge upon the exercise of a 'fundamental right. The Equal Protection Clause protects against arbitrary and irrational classifications, and against invidious discrimination stemming from prejudice and hostility". Under this rubric, discrimination against homosexuals or bisexuals based solely on their sexual preference raises significant constitutional questions under both prongs of our settled equal protection analysis.

First, homosexuals constitute a significant and insular minority of this country's population. Because of the immediate and severe opprobrium often manifested against homosexuals once identified publicly, members of this group are particularly powerless to pursue their rights openly in the political arena. Homosexuals have historically been the object of pernicious and sustained hostility, and it is fair to say that discrimination against homosexuals is "likely ... to reflect deep-seated prejudice rather than ... rationality." State action against members of a group based on status has been subjected to strict, or at least heightened, scrutiny by this Court.

Judge Edwards' dissent cited evidence indicating that homosexuals may constitute from 8–15% of the average population. Marmor, Homosexual Behavior: Modern Reappraisal concluded that nonheterosexual preference, like minority race status, "evoke[s] deeply felt prejudices and fears on the part of many people." Second, discrimination based on sexual preference has been found by many courts to infringe various fundamental constitutional rights, such as the rights to privacy or freedom of expression. Infringement of such rights found to be "explicitly or implicitly guaranteed by the Constitution," requires the State to demonstrate some compelling interest to survive strict judicial scrutiny. I have previously noted that a multitude of our precedents supports the view that public employees maintain, no less than all other citizens, a fundamental constitutional right to make "private choices involving family life and personal autonomy.

Whether constitutional rights are infringed in sexual preference cases, and whether some compelling state interest can be advanced to permit their infringement, are important questions that this Court has never addressed, and which have left the lower courts in some disarray. See, e.g., *Gay Alliance of Students v. Matthews* (refusal to allow homosexual student group equal access to state university facilities invalidated because infringement of First Amendment rights to expression and association not supported by any "substantial governmental interest"); *benShalom v. Secretary of the Army* (regulation requiring discharge based on homosexual "tendencies, desire, or interest, but ... without overt homosexual acts" held unconstitutional as violative of First and Ninth Amendment rights and right to privacy), *New York v. Onofre*, (criminal statute prohibiting private homosexual conduct found to infringe constitutional rights to privacy and equal protection under compelling state interest" test), also *Rich v. Secretary of the Army* (noting "significant split of authority as to whether some private consensual homosexual behavior may have constitutional protection" but finding military's "compelling interest" in regulating homosexual conduct sufficient to uphold discharge based on false denial of homosexuality); (naval discharge for homosexual conduct upheld as "rationally related" to permissible goals of the military; no constitutional right of privacy implicated).

In this case, the School District has not even attempted to posit some legitimate interest that was advanced by terminating petitioner for her nondisruptive mention of her sexual preference. The School District had a full and fair opportunity to persuade a jury that petitioner's bisexuality or her mention of it interfered with some aspect of school administration, but the jury found to the contrary.

Finally, even if adverse state action based on homosexual conduct were held valid under application of traditional equal protection principles, such approval would not answer the question, posed here, whether the mere nondisruptive expression of homosexual preference can pass muster even under a minimal rationality standard as the basis for discharge from public employment. This record plainly demonstrates that petitioner did not proselytize regarding her bisexuality, but rather that it became known simply in the course of her normal workday conversations. The School agreed to submit the issue of disruption to the jury, and the jury found that knowledge of petitioner's non-heterosexual status did not interfere with operations "in any way." I have serious doubt in light of that finding whether the result below can be upheld under any standard of equal protection review.

Petitioner's first mention of her bisexuality at school apparently came in response to friendly but repeated questions from her secretary as to why petitioner seemed in a particularly "good mood" one day. When petitioner eventually responded that she was in love with a woman, the secretary apparently was upset by the unexpected answer, and reported it to petitioner's Principal. On another occasion, petitioner was confronted by an angry mother who wanted to know why petitioner was counseling her to accept her son's expressed homosexuality when such conduct was "against the Bible." Petitioner did not inform the mother of her own preferences, but did inform her Vice Principal, because she was "uneasy" that if the mother complained her own "job would be at stake."

Finally, petitioner mentioned her bisexuality to some of her fellow teachers, first simply in the course of her friendships with them and later to enlist their support when it became clear that she would be disciplined for her bisexuality. This evidence indicates that petitioner's "speech" perhaps is better evaluated as no more than a natural consequence of her sexual orientation, in the same way that coworkers generally know whom their fellow employees are dating or to whom they are married. Under this view, petitioner's First Amendment and equal protection claims may be seen to converge, because it is realistically impossible to separate her spoken statements from her status. The suggestion below that it was error not to separate the claims precisely for the jury's benefit, and reliance on that suggestion to avoid discussion of the merits of petitioner's claim again simply exposes the Court of Appeals' reluctance to confront forthrightly the difficult issues posed by petitioner's case. The jury's role was to find the facts, which it did in detail. It is the court's proper role to analyze, not avoid, those facts in light of the applicable legal principles.

The issues in this case are clearly presented. By reversing the jury's verdict, the Court of Appeals necessarily held that adverse state action taken against a public employee based solely on his or her expressed sexual preference is constitutional.

Nothing in our precedents requires that result; indeed, we have never addressed the topic. Because petitioner's case raises serious and unsettled constitutional questions relating to this issue of national importance, an issue that cannot any longer be ignored.

I respectfully dissent from the decision to deny this petition for a writ of certiorari.

Discrimination Based on Sexual Orientation

Roy Romer v. Richard G. Evans et al.[12]

May 1996

Facts: After various Colorado municipalities passed ordinances banning discrimination based on sexual orientation in housing, employment, education, public accommodations, health and welfare services, and other transactions and activities, Colorado voters adopted by statewide referendum "Amendment 2" to the State Constitution:

> No Protected Status Based on Homosexual, Lesbian or Bisexual Orientation. Neither the State of Colorado, through any of its branches or departments, nor any of its agencies, political subdivisions, municipalities or school districts, shall enact, adopt or enforce any statute, regulation, ordinance or policy whereby homosexual, lesbian or bisexual orientation, conduct, practices or relationships shall constitute or otherwise be the basis of or entitle any person or class of persons to have or claim any minority status, quota preferences, protected status or claim of discrimination. This Section of the Constitution shall be in all respects self-executing.

Respondents, who include aggrieved homosexuals and municipalities, commenced this litigation in state court against petitioner state parties to declare Amendment 2 invalid and enjoin its enforcement.

The trial court's grant of a preliminary injunction was sustained by the Colorado Supreme Court, which held that Amendment 2 was subject to strict scrutiny under the Equal Protection Clause of the Fourteenth Amendment because it infringed the fundamental right of gays and lesbians to participate in the political process.

On remand, the trial court found that the Amendment failed to satisfy strict scrutiny. It enjoined Amendment 2's enforcement, and the State Supreme Court affirmed.

Held: Amendment 2 violates the Equal Protection Clause.

On grant of certiorari, petitioners appealed decision of Supreme Court of Colorado that held that a state constitutional amendment that was adopted by statewide referendum was subject to strict scrutiny under U.S. Const. Amend. XIV because it infringed the fundamental rights of gays and lesbians to participate in political process.

JUDGES: KENNEDY, J., delivered the opinion of the Court, in which STEVENS, O'CONNOR, SOUTER, GINSBURG, and BREYER, JJ., joined. SCALIA, J., filed a dissenting opinion, in which REHNQUIST, C. J., and THOMAS, J., joined.

If the constitutional conception of "equal protection of the laws" means anything, it must at the very least mean that a bare desire to harm a politically unpopular group cannot constitute a legitimate governmental interest. By requiring that a classification bear a rational relationship to an independent and legitimate legislative end, courts ensure that classifications are not drawn for the purpose of disadvantaging the group burdened by the law. Even in the ordinary equal protection case calling for the most deferential of standards, a court insists on knowing the relation between the classification adopted and the object to be attained. The search for the link between classification and objective gives substance to the Equal Protection Clause; it provides guidance and discipline for the legislature, which is entitled to know what sorts of laws it can pass; and it marks the limits of judicial authority.

In the ordinary case, a law will be sustained if it can be said to advance a legitimate government interest, even if the law seems unwise or works to the disadvantage of a particular group, or if the rationale for it seems tenuous. The State's principal argument that Amendment 2 puts gays and lesbians in the same position as all other persons by denying them special rights is rejected as implausible. The extent of the change in legal status effected by this law is evident from the authoritative construction of Colorado's Supreme Court:

The amendment's immediate effect is to repeal all existing statutes, regulations, ordinances, and policies of state and local entities barring discrimination based on sexual orientation, and that its ultimate effect is to prohibit any governmental entity from adopting similar, or more protective, measures in the future absent state constitutional amendment—and from a review of the terms, structure, and operation of the ordinances that would be repealed and prohibited by Amendment 2. Even if, as the State contends, homosexuals can find protection in laws and policies of general application, Amendment 2 goes well beyond merely depriving them of special rights. It imposes a broad disability upon those persons alone, forbidding them, but no others, to seek specific legal protection from injuries caused by discrimination in a wide range of public and private transactions.

Sweeping and comprehensive is the change in legal status effected by this law. So much is evident from the ordinances the Colorado Supreme Court declared would be void by operation of Amendment 2. Homosexuals, by state decree, are put in a solitary class with respect to transactions and relations in both the private and governmental spheres. The amendment withdraws from homosexuals, but no others, specific legal protection from the injuries caused by discrimination, and it forbids reinstatement of these laws and policies.

The primary rationale the State offers for Amendment 2 is respect for other citizens' freedom of association, and in particular the liberties of landlords or employers who have personal or religious objections to homosexuality.

Central both to the idea of the rule of law and to our guarantee of equal protection is the principle that government and each of its parts remain open on impartial terms to all who seek its assistance. Equal protection is not achieved through indiscriminate imposition of inequalities. Respect for this principle explains why laws singling out a certain class of citizens for disfavored legal status or general hardships are rare. A law declaring that in general it shall be more difficult for one group of citizens than for all others to seek aid from the government is itself a denial of equal protection. The U.S. Constitution neither knows nor tolerates classes among citizens. Those words are understood to state a commitment to the law's neutrality where the rights of persons are at stake. The Equal Protection Clause, U.S. Const. Amend. XIV, enforces this principle.

In order to reconcile the Fourteenth Amendment's promise that no person shall be denied equal protection with the practical reality that most legislation classifies for one purpose or another, the Court has stated that it will uphold a law that neither burdens a fundamental right nor targets a suspect class so long as the legislative classification bears a rational relation to some independent and legitimate legislative end. Amendment 2 fails, indeed defies, even this conventional inquiry:

> First, the amendment is at once too narrow and too broad, identifying persons by a single trait and then denying them the possibility of protection across the board. This disqualification of a class of persons from the right to obtain specific protection from the law is unprecedented and is itself a denial of equal protection in the most literal sense.
>
> Second, the sheer breadth of Amendment 2, which makes a general announcement that gays and lesbians shall not have any particular protections from the law, is so far removed from the reasons offered for it, i. E., respect for other citizens' freedom of association, particularly landlords or employers who have personal or religious objections to homosexuality, and the State's interest in conserving resources to fight discrimination against other groups, that the

> amendment cannot be explained by reference to those reasons; the amendment raises the inevitable inference that it is born of animosity toward the class that it affects. Amendment 2 cannot be said to be directed to an identifiable legitimate purpose or discrete objective.

One century ago, the first Justice Harlan admonished this Court that the Constitution "neither knows nor tolerates classes among citizens." Unheeded then, those words now are understood to state a commitment to the law's neutrality where the rights of persons are at stake. It is not within our constitutional tradition to enact laws of this sort. Laws singling out a certain class of citizens for disfavored legal status or general hardships are rare. The Equal Protection Clause enforces this principle and today requires us to hold invalid a provision of Colorado's Constitution.

It is a status-based classification of persons undertaken for its own sake, something the Equal Protection Clause does not permit.

A second and related point is that laws of the kind now before us raise the inevitable inference that the disadvantage imposed is born of animosity toward gays, lesbians and bi-sexuals: Even laws enacted for broad and ambitious purposes often can be explained by reference to legitimate public policies which justify the incidental disadvantages they impose on certain persons. Amendment 2, however, in making a general announcement that gays and lesbians shall not have any particular protections from the law, inflicts on them immediate, continuing, and real injuries that outrun and belie any legitimate justifications that may be claimed for it.

We must conclude that Amendment 2 classifies homosexuals not to further a proper legislative end but to make them unequal to everyone else. This Colorado cannot do.

A State cannot so deem a class of persons a stranger to its laws. Amendment 2 violates the Equal Protection Clause, and the judgment of the Supreme Court of Colorado is affirmed.

It is so ordered.

Bowers v. Hardwick et al.[13]

June 1986

On certiorari, Georgia challenged a decision from the Eleventh Circuit, that held that Ga. Code Ann. @ 16-6-2 unconstitutionally violated respondent's fundamental rights under the Due Process Clause by criminalizing consensual sodomy. Georgia Code Ann. @ 16-6-2 (1984) provides:

> (a) A person commits the offense of sodomy when he performs or submits to any sexual act involving the sex organs of one person and the mouth or anus of another....
>
> (b) A person convicted of the offense of sodomy shall be punished by imprisonment for not less than one or more than 20 years....

John and Mary Doe (a heterosexual married couple) were also plaintiffs in the action. They alleged that they wished to engage in sexual activity proscribed by @ 16-6-2 in the privacy of their home, App. 3, and that they had been "chilled and deterred" from engaging in such activity by both the existence of the statute and Hardwick's arrest. The District Court held, however, that because they had neither sustained, nor were in immediate danger of sustaining, any direct injury from the enforcement of the statute, they did not have proper standing to maintain the action. The Court of Appeals affirmed the District Court's judgment dismissing the Doe's claim for lack of standing, and the Doe's do not challenge that holding in this Court.

> Facts: Hardwick (a gay man) was charged with committing sodomy with an adult male in the bedroom of his home. When the district attorney decided not to present the matter to the grand jury unless further evidence developed, Hardwick brought suit in federal district court, challenging the constitutionality of the statute.
>
> Procedural Envelope: The district court dismissed respondent's suit for failure to state a claim. On appeal, relying on U.S. Supreme Court decisions in *Griswold v. Connecticut*, 381 U.S. 479 (1965); *Eisenstadt v. Baird*, 405 U.S. 438 (1972); *Stanley v. Georgia*, 394 U.S. 557 (1969); and *Roe v. Wade*, 410 U.S. 113 (1973), the Eleventh Circuit Court of Appeals went on to hold that the Georgia statute violated respondent's fundamental rights because his homosexual activity is a private and intimate association that is beyond the reach of state regulation by reason of the Ninth Amendment and the Due Process Clause of the Fourteenth Amendment. The Circuit Court concluded that in order to prevail, the state would have to prove that the statute is supported by a compelling interest and is the most narrowly drawn means of achieving that end.
>
> On certiorari, the U.S. Supreme Court reversed, holding that the state statute against sodomy was constitutional, as the Due Process Clause of Fourteenth Amendment did not create a fundamental right for homosexuals to engage in consensual sodomy, even in the privacy of respondent's home.

In a 5–4 opinion written by Justice White, joined by Burger, Powell, Rehnquist and O'Connor the Court held:

The rights qualifying for heightened judicial protection includes those fundamental liberties that are implicit in the concept of ordered liberty, such that neither liberty nor justice would exist if they were sacrificed ... they are deeply rooted in this Nation's history and tradition.

> (a) The Constitution does not confer a fundamental right upon homosexuals to engage in sodomy. None of the fundamental rights announced in this Court's prior cases involving family relationships, marriage, or procreation bear any resemblance to the right asserted in this case. And any claim that those cases stand for the proposition that any kind of private sexual conduct between consenting adults is constitutionally insulated from state proscription is unsupportable.
>
> (b) Against a background in which many States have criminalized sodomy and still do, to claim that a right to engage in such conduct is "deeply rooted in this Nation's history and tradition" or "implicit in the concept of ordered liberty" is, at best, facetious.
>
> (c) There should be great resistance to expanding the reach of the Due Process Clauses to cover new fundamental rights. Otherwise, the Judiciary necessarily would take upon itself further authority to govern the country without constitutional authority. The claimed right in this case falls far short of overcoming this resistance.

(d) The fact that homosexual conduct occurs in the privacy of the home does not affect the result.

(e) Sodomy laws should not be invalidated on the asserted basis that majority belief that sodomy is immoral is an inadequate rationale to support the laws.

(f) We express no opinion on the constitutionality of the Georgia statute as applied to other acts of sodomy.

Statements from the Justices:

Justice White:

The issue presented is whether the Federal Constitution confers a fundamental right upon homosexuals to engage in sodomy and hence invalidates the laws of the many States that still make such conduct illegal and have done so for a very long time.

The reach of the line of cases cited in alleged support of Hardwick was sketched in *Carey v. Population Services International*, *Pierce v. Society of Sisters*, and *Meyer v. Nebraska*, as dealing with child rearing and education; *Prince v. Massachusetts*, with family relationships; *Skinner v. Oklahoma*, with procreation; *Loving v. Virginia*, with marriage; *Griswold v. Connecticut*, and *Eisenstadt v. Baird*, with contraception; and *Roe v. Wade*, with abortion. The latter three cases were interpreted as construing the Due Process Clause of the Fourteenth Amendment to confer a fundamental individual right to decide whether or not to beget or bear a child.

Accepting the decisions in these cases and the above description of them, we think it evident that none of the rights announced in those cases bears any resemblance to the claimed constitutional right of homosexuals to engage in acts of sodomy that is asserted in this case. No connection between family, marriage, or procreation on the one hand and homosexual activity on the other has been demonstrated, either by the Court of Appeals or by respondent. Moreover, any claim that these cases nevertheless stand for the proposition that any kind of private sexual conduct between consenting adults is constitutionally insulated from state proscription is unsupportable ...

Sodomy was a criminal offense at common law and was forbidden by the laws of the original 13 States when they ratified the Bill of Rights. In 1868, when the Fourteenth Amendment was ratified, all but 5 of the 37 States in the Union had criminal sodomy laws. In fact, until 1961, all 50 States outlawed sodomy, and today, 24 states and the District of Columbia continue to provide criminal penalties for sodomy performed in private and between consenting adults.

If the [Constitution were protective of] voluntary sexual conduct between consenting adults, it would be difficult, except by fiat, to limit the claimed right to homosexual conduct while leaving exposed to prosecution adultery, incest, and other sexual crimes even though they are committed in the home. We are unwilling to start down that road.

Respondent asserts that there must be a rational basis for the law and that there is none in this case other than the presumed belief of a majority of the electorate in Georgia that homosexual sodomy is immoral and unacceptable. This is said to be an inadequate rationale to support the law. The law, however, is constantly based on notions of morality, and if all laws representing essentially moral choices are to be invalidated under the Due Process Clause, the courts will be very busy indeed.

CHIEF JUSTICE BURGER, concurring.

I write separately to underscore my view that: the proscriptions against sodomy have very "ancient roots." Decisions of individuals relating to homosexual conduct have been subject to state intervention throughout the history of Western civilization. Condemnation of those practices is firmly rooted in Judeo-Christian moral and ethical standards. Homosexual sodomy was a capital crime under Roman law.

Blackstone described "the infamous crime against nature" as an offense of "deeper malignity" than rape, a heinous act "the very mention of which is a disgrace to human nature," and "a crime not fit to be named." To hold that the act of homosexual sodomy is somehow protected as a fundamental right would be to cast aside millennia of moral teaching.

JUSTICE POWELL, concurring.

I agree with the Court that there is no fundamental right—i. e., no substantive right under the Due Process Clause—such as that claimed by respondent Hardwick, and found to exist by the Court of Appeals. This is not to suggest, however, that respondent may not be protected by the Eighth Amendment of the Constitution. The Georgia statute at issue in this case, Ga. Code Ann. @ 16-6-2 (1984), authorizes a court to imprison a person for up to 20 years for a single private, consensual act of sodomy. In my view, a prison sentence for such conduct—certainly a sentence of long duration—would create a serious Eighth Amendment issue.

Under the Georgia statute a single act of sodomy, even in the private setting of a home, is a felony comparable in terms of the possible sentence imposed to serious felonies such as aggravated battery, first-degree arson, and robbery.

The history of nonenforcement suggests the moribund character today of laws criminalizing this type of private, consensual conduct. Some 26 States have repealed similar statutes. But the constitutional validity of the Georgia statute was put in issue by respondents, and for the reasons stated by the Court, I cannot say that conduct condemned for hundreds of years has now become a fundamental right.

JUSTICE BLACKMUN, with whom JUSTICE BRENNAN, JUSTICE MARSHALL, and JUSTICE STEVENS join, dissenting.

This case is no more about "a fundamental right to engage in homosexual sodomy," as the Court purports to declare, than *Stanley v. Georgia* was about a fundamental right to watch obscene movies. Rather, this case is about "the most comprehensive of rights and the right most valued by civilized men," namely, "the right to be let alone."

It is revolting to have no better reason for a rule of law than that so it was laid down in the time of Henry IV. It is still more revolting if the grounds upon which it was laid down have vanished long since, and the rule simply persists from blind imitation of the past."

The fundamental right to privacy, if it means anything, it means that, before Georgia can prosecute its citizens for making choices about the most intimate aspects of their lives, it must do more than assert that the choice they have made is an "'abominable crime not fit to be named among Christians.

The Court's almost obsessive focus on homosexual activity is particularly hard to justify in light of the broad language Georgia has used. Unlike the Court, the Georgia Legislature has not proceeded on the assumption that homosexuals are so different from other citizens that their lives may be controlled in a way that would not be tolerated if it limited the choices of those other citizens.

The sex or status of the persons who engage in the act is irrelevant as a matter Georgia law. In fact, to the extent I can discern a legislative purpose for Georgia's 1968 enactment of @ 16-6-2, that purpose seems to have been to broaden the coverage of the law to reach heterosexual as well as homosexual activity.

Michael Hardwick's standing may rest in significant part on Georgia's apparent willingness to enforce against homosexuals a law it seems not to have any desire to enforce against heterosexuals. His claim that @ 16-6-2 involves an unconstitutional intrusion into his privacy and his right of intimate association does not depend in any way on his sexual orientation.

Until 1968, Georgia defined sodomy as "the carnal knowledge and connection against the order of nature, by man with man, or in the same unnatural manner with woman." In *Thompson v. Aldredge*, (1939), the Georgia Supreme Court held that the law did not prohibit lesbian activity. And in *Riley v. Garrett*, 1963), the Georgia Supreme Court held that the law did not prohibit heterosexual cunnilingus.

Hardwick's complaint expressly invoked the Ninth Amendment, and he relied heavily before this Court on *Griswold*, which identifies that amendment as one of the specific constitutional provisions giving "life and substance" to our understanding of privacy.

I need not reach either the Eighth Amendment or the Equal Protection Clause issues because I believe that Hardwick has stated a cognizable claim that @ 16-6-2 interferes with constitutionally protected interests in privacy and freedom of intimate association. But neither the Eighth Amendment nor the Equal Protection Clause is so clearly irrelevant that a claim resting on either provision should be peremptorily dismissed. The Court's cramped reading of the issue before it makes for a short opinion, but it does little to make for a persuasive one.

Despite historical views of homosexuality, it is no longer viewed by mental health professionals as a "disease" or disorder. Neither is it simply a matter of deliberate personal election. Homosexual orientation may well form part of the very fiber of an individual's personality. Consequently, the Eighth Amendment may pose a constitutional barrier to sending an individual to prison for acting on that attraction regardless of the circumstances. An individual's ability to make constitutionally protected "decisions concerning sexual relations," (*Carey v. Population Serv. Int'l*), is rendered empty indeed if he or she is given no real choice but a life without any physical intimacy.

With respect to the Equal Protection Clause's applicability to @ 16-6-2, I note that Georgia's exclusive stress before this Court on its interest in prosecuting homosexual activity despite the gender-neutral terms of the statute may raise serious questions of discriminatory enforcement, questions that cannot be disposed of before this Court on a motion to dismiss.

Our cases long have recognized that the Constitution embodies a promise that a certain private sphere of individual liberty will be kept largely beyond the reach of government." (*Thornburgh*).

In construing the right to privacy, the Court has proceeded along two somewhat distinct, albeit complementary, lines. First, it has recognized a privacy interest with reference to certain decisions that are properly for the individual to make. Second, it has recognized a privacy interest with reference to certain places without regard for the particular activities in which the individuals who occupy them are engaged.

While it is true that these cases may be characterized by their connection to protection of the family, we protect those rights not because they contribute, in some direct and material way, to the general public welfare, but because they form so central a part of an individual's life.

[The] concept of privacy embodies the moral fact that a person belongs to himself and not others nor to society as a whole. And so we protect the decision whether to marry precisely because marriage "is an association that promotes a way of life, not causes; a harmony in living, not political faiths; a bilateral loyalty, not commercial or social projects." (*Griswold*)

We protect the decision whether to have a child because parenthood alters so dramatically an individual's self-definition, not because of demographic considerations or the Bible's command to be fruitful and multiply.

And we protect the family because it contributes so powerfully to the happiness of individuals, not because of a preference for stereotypical households. The "ability independently to define one's identity that is central to any concept of liberty" cannot truly be exercised in a vacuum; we all depend on the "emotional enrichment from close ties with others."

Only the most willful blindness could obscure the fact that sexual intimacy is "a sensitive, key relationship of human existence, central to family life, community welfare, and the development of human personality."

The fact that individuals define themselves in a significant way through their intimate sexual relationships with others suggests, in a Nation as diverse as ours, that there may be many "right" ways of conducting those relationships, and that much of the richness of a relationship will come from the freedom an individual has to choose the form and nature of these intensely personal bonds.

The makers of our Constitution undertook to secure conditions favorable to the pursuit of happiness. They recognized the significance of man's spiritual nature, of his feelings and of his intellect. They knew that only a part of the pain, pleasure and satisfactions of life are to be found in material things.

They sought to protect Americans in their beliefs, their thoughts, their emotions and their sensations.

Although I do not think it necessary to decide today issues that are not even remotely before us, it does seem to me that a court could find simple, analytically sound distinctions between certain private, consensual sexual conduct, on the one hand, and adultery and incest (the only two vaguely specific "sexual crimes" to which the majority points, on the other. For example, marriage, in addition to its spiritual aspects, is a civil contract that entitles the contracting parties to a variety of governmentally provided benefits. A State might define the contractual commitment necessary to become eligible for these benefits to include a commitment of fidelity and then punish individuals for breaching that contract. Moreover, a State might conclude that adultery is likely to injure third persons, in particular, spouses and children of persons who engage in extramarital affairs. With respect to incest, a court might well agree with respondent that the nature of familial relationships renders true consent to incestuous activity sufficiently problematical that a blanket prohibition of such activity is warranted. Notably, the Court makes no effort to explain why it has chosen to group private, consensual homosexual activity with adultery and incest rather than with private, consensual heterosexual activity by unmarried persons or, indeed, with oral or anal sex within marriage.

The parallel between Loving and this case is almost uncanny. There, too, the State relied on a religious justification for its law: that "Almighty God created the races white, black, yellow, malay and red, and he placed them on separate continents.... The fact that he separated the races shows that he did not intend for the races to mix"), with Brief for Petitioner 20–21 (relying on the Old and New Testaments and the writings of St. Thomas Aquinas to show that "traditional Judeo-Christian values proscribe such conduct"). There, too, defenders of the challenged statute relied heavily on the fact that when the Fourteenth Amendment was ratified, most of the States had similar prohibitions Yet the Court held, not only that the invidious racism of Virginia's law violated the Equal Protection Clause, but also that the law deprived the Lovings of due process by denying them the "freedom of choice to marry" that had "long been recognized as one of the vital personal rights essential to the orderly pursuit of happiness by free men."

The assertion that "traditional Judeo-Christian values proscribe" the conduct involved, cannot provide an adequate justification for the statute. That certain, but by no means all, religious groups condemn the behavior at issue gives the State no license to impose their judgments on the entire citizenry. The legitimacy of secular legislation depends instead on whether the State can advance some justification for its law beyond its conformity to religious doctrine.

Justice Stevens

Society has every right to encourage its individual members to follow particular traditions in expressing affection for one another and in gratifying their personal desires. It, of course, may prohibit an individual from imposing his will on another to satisfy his own selfish interests. It also may prevent an individual from interfering with, or violating, a legally sanctioned and protected relationship, such as marriage. And it may explain the relative advantages and disadvantages of different forms of intimate expression. But when individual married couples are isolated from observation by others, the way in which they voluntarily choose to conduct their intimate relations is a matter for them—not the State—to decide.

The essential "liberty" that animated the development of the law in cases like *Griswold*, *Eisenstadt*, and *Carey* surely embraces the right to engage in nonreproductive, sexual conduct that others may consider offensive or immoral.

Although the meaning of the principle that "all men are created equal" is not always clear, it surely must mean that every free citizen has the same interest in "liberty" that the members of the majority share. From the standpoint of the individual, the homosexual and the heterosexual have the same interest in deciding how he will live his own life, and, more narrowly, how he will conduct himself in his personal and voluntary associations with his companions. State intrusion into the private conduct of either is equally burdensome.

Early Impact of Sexual Predator Registration Laws

Megan's Laws[14]

Robert L. Jacobson

Relevant Edited Excerpts
Reprinted with Permission

In the 1990s, sexual predator registration laws have blossomed across the nation. After prodding from Congress and from public pressure, every state has enacted a "Megan's Law," a statute that requires certain sex offenders to register with law enforcement agencies and potentially be the subject of public notification.

Before 1990, only a handful of states had enacted sex offender registration statutes; of those states that had enacted registration statutes, some, like California, enforced their statutes halfheartedly.

This indifference changed quickly in the 1990s: after several released sex offenders attacked children in high-profile crimes, states responded by rushing to enact registration programs. Washington enacted the first modern sex offender registration statute in 1990 after a convicted rapist mutilated and raped a young boy; the statute was the first in the nation to authorize police to notify community residents when a released offender moved into the neighborhood.

Several states followed Washington's embrace of community notification. After seven-year-old Megan Kanka was murdered by a released child molester who lived across the street from her, the New Jersey legislature rushed to enact its namesake Megan's Law as an emergency measure, bypassing the assembly's normal committee process and public hearings. When New York legislators passed a comparable statute, the legislators demonstrated their retributive intent, characterizing released sex offenders as "depraved," "animals," and the "human equivalent of toxic waste." Likewise, the California legislature amended its statute in 1994 to allow community notification, and state officials rushed to bring the registration list up to date.

Congress responded to the public outcry over these crimes by enacting, in 1994, the Jacob Wetterling Crimes Against Children and Sexually Violent Offender Registration Act, a statute that requires each state to enact its own sex offender registration program or lose ten percent of its federal crime fighting grants. Responding to this congressional mandate and public momentum, every state had enacted its own sex offender registration act by early 1996, most containing provisions for community notification.

Although states may enact more-stringent requirements for their registration programs, the Jacob Wetterling Act establishes certain minimum standards. To comply, states must require persons who are convicted either of sexual crimes against minors or of sexually violent offenses, like rape, to provide fingerprints and report their home address to a state law enforcement agency. States also must enact programs to notify the community of dangerous offenders.

Notably, the Jacob Wetterling Act does not require registration of those convicted of nonviolent sexual offenses, such as indecent exposure, consensual sodomy, or statutory rape; the federal agency guidelines for the Act note specifically that requiring registration for consensual sodomy "would not further the Act's objectives." Congress expanded the Act in 1996 by directing the FBI to establish a national database of reported sexual offenders. Since the FBI relies on states to identify sex offenders for the national database, the database could magnify the problem of overinclusive state registration statutes by including within the database those convicted of minor sex offenses.

Within these minimum standards, states have broad discretion to require registration for other crimes. Each state's registration statute contains a list defining which offenses impose automatic registration. In addition to the crimes required by the Jacob Wetterling Act, many states impose registration for convictions of other serious sexual crimes, such as sexual battery, incest, and trafficking in child pornography, and several states authorize judicial discretion to impose registration for other crimes committed "as a result of sexual compulsion or for purposes of sexual gratification."

Sex offender registration laws are most pernicious when they apply retroactively to old convictions. Although not required by the Jacob Wetterling Act, most states apply their programs retroactively, either to persons under criminal supervision at the time of the statute's enactment or to any living person ever convicted of the specified offenses.

Reinforcing Old Patterns of Anti-Gay Police Harassment

Although the statutes are nominally designed to protect the public from dangerous sexual offenders, many of them have returned full circle to their roots of California's anti-gay harassment. Several of the states require registration for consensual sodomy, purposefully branding gay men and lesbians as sex criminals. Many more states have unintentionally added to the harassment by requiring registration for minor crimes that are often enforced disproportionately against gay men. Even still, more states compound the problem by making their statutes retroactive and requiring registration for convictions from decades before; a time when police harassment of gay men was particularly severe.

Michael was a distinguished Korean War veteran, twenty-three years old and only sixteen days away from an honorable discharge. His arrest one night in 1956, for having sex with another man in a San Diego "lover's lane," however, changed that. He was convicted of the felony crime of "sexual perversion," sentenced to five years of probation, fined, and given an undesirable military discharge. As he walked through a gauntlet of Navy officers who ripped the medals off his chest, he probably assumed that his troubles with the law were, at least, now behind him.

Michael's actions, however, took on unexpected significance nearly forty years later. In 1995, at the age of sixty-one, a letter from the Los Angeles Police Department ordered him to register with the state as a convicted sex offender. After a two-year struggle with hundreds of attorneys' hours spent on his case, Michael finally was allowed to clear his name from the registry.

States differ on how long registration must last. Under the Jacob Wetterling Act, individuals must register with their state annually for at least ten years for first-time sexual offenses and for their lifetime after second offenses. Many states impose longer registration periods for first-time offenders, including lifetime registration, regardless of the nature of the crime or the individual's evaluated risk of recidivism.

Significantly, a 1996 amendment to the Jacob Wetterling Act requires states to adopt some form of community notification by disclosing "relevant information that is necessary to protect the public" about released offenders. However, since the amendment lacks guidelines about how states should implement their programs, their procedures vary widely. Some simply make all information about released sexual offenders available "to any person upon request," while others impose duties on police to warn the public about certain released offenders. Louisiana's statute provides the most aggressive community notification: sex offenders personally must mail notification of their conviction to every neighbor within a three-block radius of their home, and a judge may require them to provide additional notice like "signs, handbills, bumper stickers, or clothing labeled to that effect." Generally, however, states attempt to limit community notification to the more dangerous offenders. Some simply require the police to exercise discretion about when to notify communities, while others create administrative agencies to evaluate offenders' criminal records, assign appropriate risk designations, and notify the community accordingly.

On May 14, 2007, law enforcement officers from eight states asked MySpace.com on to turn over the names of registered sex offenders who use the social networking Website. Why? Media reported nearly 100 criminal incidents across the country involving adults who used MySpace to prey or attempt to prey on children." MySpace reportedly partnered with Sentinel Tech to build a sex offender database that shows that thousands of known sex offenders are confirmed members. Attorney General Roy Cooper has presented legislation to the North Carolina General Assembly that would make it a felony for registered sex offenders to use social networking sites.[15]

What is the likely impact of such legislation on the issues identified in Jacobson's article?

Boy Scouts v. Dale

June 2000

REHNQUIST delivered the opinion of the Court.[16]

Petitioners are the Boy Scouts of America and the Monmouth Council, a division of the Boy Scouts of America (collectively, Boy Scouts). The Boy Scouts is a private, not-for-profit organization engaged in instilling its system of values in young people. The Boy Scouts asserts that homosexual conduct is inconsistent with the values it seeks to instill. Respondent is James Dale, a former Eagle Scout whose adult membership in the Boy Scouts was revoked when the Boy Scouts learned that he is an avowed homosexual and gay rights activist. The New Jersey Supreme Court held that New Jersey's public accommodations law requires that the Boy Scouts admit Dale. This case presents the question whether applying New

Jersey's public accommodations law in this way violates the Boy Scouts' First Amendment right of expressive association.

James Dale entered scouting in 1978 at the age of eight by joining Monmouth Council's Cub Scout Pack 142. Dale became a Boy Scout in 1981 and remained a Scout until he turned 18. By all accounts, Dale was an exemplary Scout. In 1988, he achieved the rank of Eagle Scout, one of Scouting's highest honors.

Dale applied for adult membership in the Boy Scouts in 1989. The Boy Scouts approved his application for the position of assistant scoutmaster of Troop 73. Around the same time, Dale left home to attend Rutgers University. After arriving at Rutgers, Dale first acknowledged to himself and others that he is gay. He quickly became involved with, and eventually became the co-president of, the Rutgers University Lesbian/Gay Alliance. In 1990, Dale attended a seminar addressing the psychological and health needs of lesbian and gay teenagers. A newspaper covering the event interviewed Dale about his advocacy of homosexual teenagers' need for gay role models. In early July 1990, the newspaper published the interview and Dale's photograph over a caption identifying him as the co-president of the Lesbian/Gay Alliance.

Later that month, Dale received a letter from Monmouth Council Executive James Kay revoking his adult membership. Dale wrote to Kay requesting the reason for Monmouth Council's decision. Kay responded by letter that the Boy Scouts "specifically forbid membership to homosexuals."

In 1992, Dale filed a complaint against the Boy Scouts in the New Jersey Superior Court. The complaint alleged that the Boy Scouts had violated New Jersey's public accommodations statute and its common law by revoking Dale's membership based solely on his sexual orientation. New Jersey's public accommodations statute prohibits, among other things, discrimination on the basis of sexual orientation in places of public accommodation.

The New Jersey Superior Court's Chancery Division granted summary judgment in favor of the Boy Scouts. The court held that New Jersey's public accommodations law was inapplicable because the Boy Scouts was not a place of public accommodation, and that, alternatively, the Boy Scouts is a distinctly private group exempted from coverage under New Jersey's law. The court rejected Dale's common-law claim holding that New Jersey's policy is embodied in the public accommodations law. The court also concluded that the Boy Scouts' position in respect of active homosexuality was clear and held that the First Amendment freedom of expressive association prevented the government from forcing the Boy Scouts to accept Dale as an adult leader.

The New Jersey Superior Court's Appellate Division affirmed the dismissal of Dale's common-law claim, but otherwise reversed and remanded for further proceedings.

It held that New Jersey's public accommodations law applied to the Boy Scouts and that the Boy Scouts violated it. The Appellate Division rejected the Boy Scouts' federal constitutional claims.

The New Jersey Supreme Court affirmed the judgment of the Appellate Division. It held that the Boy Scouts was a place of public accommodation subject to the public accommodations law, that the organization was not exempt from the law under any of its express exceptions, and that the Boy Scouts violated the law by revoking Dale' s membership based on his avowed homosexuality. After considering the state-law issues, the court addressed the Boy Scouts' claims that application of the public accommodations law in this case violated its federal constitutional rights "'to enter into and maintain ... intimate or private relationships ... [and] to associate for the purpose of engaging in protected speech.'"

With respect to the right to intimate association, the court concluded that the Boy Scouts' large size, non-selectivity, inclusive rather than exclusive purpose, and practice of inviting or allowing nonmembers to attend meetings, establish that the organization is not 'sufficiently personal or private to warrant constitutional protection' under the freedom of intimate association.'"

With respect to the right of expressive association, the court "agreed that Boy Scouts expresses a belief in moral values and uses its activities to encourage the moral development of its members." But the court concluded that it was "not persuaded ... that a shared goal of Boy Scout members is to associate in order to preserve the view that homosexuality is immoral."

Accordingly, the court held "that Dale's membership does not violate the Boy Scouts' right of expressive association because his inclusion would not 'affect in any significant way [the Boy Scouts'] existing members' ability to carry out their various purposes.'" The court also determined that New Jersey has a compelling interest in eliminating "the destructive consequences of discrimination from our society," and that its public accommodations law abridges no more speech than is necessary to accomplish its purpose. Finally, the court addressed the Boy Scouts' reliance on *Hurley v. Irish-American Gay, Lesbian and Bisexual Group of Boston, Inc.*, in support of its claimed First Amendment right to exclude Dale. The court determined that Hurley did not require deciding the case in favor of the Boy Scouts because "the reinstatement of Dale does not compel Boy Scouts to express any message."

We granted the Boy Scouts' petition for certiorari to determine whether the application of New Jersey's public accommodations law violated the First Amendment.

In *Roberts v. United States Jaycees*, we observed that "implicit in the right to engage in activities protected by the First Amendment" is "a corresponding right to associate with others in pursuit of a wide variety of political, social, economic, educational, religious, and cultural ends." This right is crucial in preventing the majority from imposing its views on groups that would rather express other, perhaps unpopular, ideas. See ibid. (stating that protection of the right to expressive association is "especially important in preserving political and cultural diversity and in shielding dissident expression from suppression by the majority"). Government actions that may unconstitutionally burden this freedom may take many forms, one of which is "intrusion into the internal structure or affairs of an association" like a "regulation that forces the group to accept members it does not desire." Forcing a group to accept certain members may impair the ability of the group to express those views, and only those views, that it intends to express. Thus, "[f]reedom of association ... plainly presupposes a freedom not to associate." Ibid.

The forced inclusion of an unwanted person in a group infringes the group's freedom of expressive association if the presence of that person affects in a significant way the group's ability to advocate public or private viewpoints. But the freedom of expressive association, like many freedoms, is not absolute. We have held that the freedom could be overridden "by regulations adopted to serve compelling state interests, unrelated to the suppression of ideas, that cannot be achieved through means significantly less restrictive of associational freedoms.

To determine whether a group is protected by the First Amendment's expressive associational right, we must determine whether the group engages in "expressive association." The First Amendment's protection of expressive association is not reserved for advocacy groups. But to come within its ambit, a group must engage in some form of expression, whether it is public or private.

The general mission of the Boy Scouts is clear: "To instill values in young people." Ibid. The Boy Scouts seeks to instill these values by having its adult leaders spend time with the youth members, instructing and engaging them in activities like camping, archery, and fishing. During the time spent with the youth members, the scoutmasters and assistant scoutmasters inculcate them with the Boy Scouts' values—both expressly and by example. It seems indisputable that an association that seeks to transmit such a system of values engages in expressive activity.

Given that the Boy Scouts engages in expressive activity, we must determine whether the forced inclusion of Dale as an assistant scoutmaster would significantly affect the Boy Scouts' ability to advocate public or private viewpoints. This inquiry necessarily requires us first to explore, to a limited extent, the nature of the Boy Scouts' view of homosexuality.

The values the Boy Scouts seeks to instill are "based on" those listed in the Scout Oath and Law..The Boy Scouts explains that the Scout Oath and Law provide "a positive moral code for living; they are a list of 'do's' rather than 'don'ts.The Boy Scouts asserts that homosexual conduct is inconsistent with the values embodied in the Scout Oath and Law, particularly with the values represented by the terms "morally straight" and "clean."

The Scout Oath and Law do not expressly mention sexuality or sexual orientation. And the terms "morally straight" and "clean" are by no means self-defining. Different people would attribute to those terms very different meanings. For example, some people may believe that engaging in homosexual conduct is not at odds with being "morally straight" and clean." And others may believe that engaging in homosexual conduct is contrary to being "morally straight" and "clean." The Boy Scouts says it falls within the latter category.

The Boy Scouts asserts that it "teaches that homosexual conduct is not morally straight," and that it does "not want to promote homosexual conduct as a legitimate form of behavior," We accept the Boy Scouts' assertion. We need not inquire further to determine the nature of the Boy Scouts' expression with respect to homosexuality. But because the record before us contains written evidence of the Boy Scouts' viewpoint, we look to it as instructive, if only on the question of the sincerity of the professed beliefs.

A 1978 position statement to the Boy Scouts' Executive Committee, signed by Downing B. Jenks, the President of the Boy Scouts, and Harvey L. Price, the Chief Scout Executive, expresses the Boy Scouts' official position with regard to "homosexuality and Scouting":

> "Q. May an individual who openly declares himself to be a homosexual be a volunteer Scout leader?
>
> "A. No. The Boy Scouts of America is a private, membership organization and leadership therein is a privilege and not a right. We do not believe that homo-

> sexuality and leadership in Scouting are appropriate. We will continue to select only those who in our judgment meet our standards and qualifications for leadership."

Thus, at least as of 1978—the year James Dale entered Scouting—the official position of the Boy Scouts was that avowed homosexuals were not to be Scout leaders.

A position statement promulgated by the Boy Scouts in 1991 (after Dale's membership was revoked but before this litigation was filed) also supports its current view:

> "We believe that homosexual conduct is inconsistent with the requirement in the Scout Oath that a Scout be morally straight and in the Scout Law that a Scout be clean in word and deed, and that homosexuals do not provide a desirable role model for Scouts."

This position statement was redrafted numerous times but its core message remained consistent. For example, a 1993 position statement, the most recent in the record, reads, in part:

> The Boy Scouts of America has always reflected the expectations that Scouting families have had for the organization. We do not believe that homosexuals provide a role model consistent with these expectations. Accordingly, we do not allow for the registration of avowed homosexuals as members or as leaders of the BSA.

The Boy Scouts publicly expressed its views with respect to homosexual conduct by its assertions in prior litigation. For example, throughout a California case with similar facts filed in the early 1980s, the Boy Scouts consistently asserted the same position with respect to homosexuality that it asserts today. We cannot doubt that the Boy Scouts sincerely holds this view.

Dale was the co-president of a gay and lesbian organization at college and remains a gay rights activist. Dale's presence in the Boy Scouts would, at the very least, force the organization to send a message, both to the youth members and the world, that the Boy Scouts accepts homosexual conduct as a legitimate form of behavior.

The First Amendment simply does not require that every member of a group agree on every issue in order for the group's policy to be "expressive association." The Boy Scouts takes an official position with respect to homosexual conduct, and that is sufficient for First Amendment purposes. In this same vein, Dale makes much of the claim that the Boy Scouts does not revoke the membership of heterosexual Scout leaders that openly disagree with the Boy Scouts' policy on sexual orientation. But if this is true, it is irrelevant.

The presence of an avowed homosexual and gay rights activist in an assistant scoutmaster's uniform sends a distinctly different message from the presence of a heterosexual assistant scoutmaster who is on record as disagreeing with Boy Scouts policy. The Boy Scouts has a First Amendment right to choose to send one message but not the other. The fact that the organization does not trumpet its views from the housetop, or that it tolerates dissent within its ranks, does not mean that its views receive no First Amendment protection.

Having determined that the Boy Scouts is an expressive association and that the forced inclusion of Dale would significantly affect its expression, we inquire whether the application of New Jersey's public accommodations law to require that the Boy Scouts accept Dale as an assistant scoutmaster runs afoul of the Scouts' freedom of expressive association. We conclude that it does.

DISSENT: JUSTICE STEVENS, with whom JUSTICE SOUTER, JUSTICE GINSBURG and JUSTICE BREYER join, dissenting.

New Jersey "prides itself on judging each individual by his or her merits" and on being "in the vanguard in the fight to eradicate the cancer of unlawful discrimination of all types from our society."

Since 1945, it has had a law against discrimination. The law broadly protects the opportunity of all persons to obtain the advantages and privileges "of any place of public accommodation.

The New Jersey Supreme Court's construction of the statutory definition of a "place of public accommodation" has given its statute a more expansive coverage than most similar state statutes. And as amended in 1991, the law prohibits discrimination on the basis of nine different traits including an individual's "sexual orientation."

In its "exercise of this high power" today, the Court does not accord this "courageous State" the respect that is its due. The majority holds that New Jersey's law violates BSA's right to associate and its right to free speech. But that law does not "impose any serious burdens" on BSA's "collective effort on behalf of [its] shared goals. Nor does it force BSA to communicate any message that it does not wish to endorse. New Jersey's law, therefore, abridges no constitutional right of the Boy Scouts.

James Dale joined BSA as a Cub Scout in 1978, when he was eight years old. Three years later he became a Boy Scout, and he remained a member until his 18th birthday. Along the way, he earned 25 merit badges, was admitted into the prestigious Order of the Arrow, and was awarded the rank of Eagle Scout—an honor given to only three percent of all Scouts. In 1989, BSA approved his application to be an Assistant Scoutmaster.

On July 19, 1990, after more than 12 years of active and honored participation, the Boys Scouts sent Dale a letter advising him of the revocation of his membership. The letter stated that membership in BSA "is a privilege" that may be denied "whenever there is a concern that an individual may not meet the high standards of membership which the BSA seeks to provide for American youth..Expressing surprise at his sudden expulsion, Dale sent a letter requesting an explanation of the decision. In response, BSA sent him a second letter stating that the grounds for the decision "are the standards for leadership established by the Boy Scouts of America, which specifically forbid membership to homosexuals." At that time, BSA had publicly expressed no such standard.

In this case, Boy Scouts of America contends that it teaches the young boys who are Scouts that homosexuality is immoral. Consequently, it argues, it would violate its right to associate to force it to admit homosexuals as members, as doing so would be at odds with its own shared goals and values. This contention, quite plainly, requires us to look at what, exactly, are the values that BSA actually teaches.

BSA's mission statement reads as follows: "It is the mission of the Boy Scouts of America to serve others by helping to instill values in young people and, in other ways, to prepare them to make ethical choices over their lifetime in achieving their full potential.

Its federal charter declares its purpose is "to promote, through organization, and cooperation with other agencies, the ability of boys to do things for themselves and others, to train them in scout craft, and to teach them patriotism, courage, self-reliance, and kindred values, using the methods which were in common use by Boy Scouts on June 15, 1916.

BSA describes itself as having a "representative membership," which it defines as "boy membership [that] reflects proportionately the characteristics of the boy population of its service area." In particular, the group emphasizes that "neither the charter nor the bylaws of the Boy Scouts of America permits the exclusion of any boy.... To meet these responsibilities we have made a commitment that our membership shall be representative of all the population in every community, district, and council."

To bolster its claim that its shared goals include teaching that homosexuality is wrong, BSA directs our attention to two terms appearing in the Scout Oath and Law. The first is the phrase "morally straight," which appears in the Oath ("On my honor I will do my best ... To keep myself ... morally straight"); the second term is the word "clean," which appears in a list of 12 characteristics together comprising the Scout Law.

The Boy Scout Handbook defines "morally straight," as such:

> To be a person of strong character, guide your life with honesty, purity, and justice. Respect and defend the rights of all people. Your relationships with others should be honest and open. Be clean in your speech and actions, and faithful in your religious beliefs. The values you follow as a Scout will help you become virtuous and self-reliant."

The Scoutmaster Handbook emphasizes these points about being "morally straight":

> In any consideration of moral fitness, a key word has to be 'courage.' A boy's courage to do what his head and his heart tell him is right. And the courage to refuse to do what his heart and his head say is wrong. Moral fitness, like emotional fitness, will clearly present opportunities for wise guidance by an alert Scoutmaster."

As for the term "clean," the Boy Scout Handbook offers the following:

> A Scout is CLEAN. A Scout keeps his body and mind fit and clean. He chooses the company of those who live by these same ideals. He helps keep his home and community clean.
>
> You never need to be ashamed of dirt that will wash off. If you play hard and work hard you can't help getting dirty. But when the game is over or the work is done, that kind of dirt disappears with soap and water.
>
> There's another kind of dirt that won't come off by washing. It is the kind that shows up in foul language and harmful thoughts.
>
> Swear words, profanity, and dirty stories are weapons that ridicule other people and hurt their feelings. The same is true of racial slurs and jokes making fun of ethnic groups or people with physical or mental limitations. A Scout knows there is no kindness or honor in such mean-spirited behavior. He avoids it in his own words and deeds. He defends those who are targets of insults." Moreover:
>
> Most people keep themselves clean outside. But how about the inside? Do we try to keep our minds and our language clean? I think that's even more important than keeping the outside clean.

> A Scout, of course, should be clean inside and out. Water, soap, and a toothbrush take care of the outside. Only your determination will keep the inside clean. You can do it by following the Scout Law and the example of people you respect—your parents, your teachers, your clergyman, or a good buddy who is trying to do the same thing."

It is plain as the light of day that neither one of these principles—"morally straight" and "clean"—says the slightest thing about homosexuality. Indeed, neither term in the Boy Scouts' Law and Oath expresses any position whatsoever on sexual matters.

BSA's published guidance on that topic underscores this point. Scouts, for example, are directed to receive their sex education at home or in school, but not from the organization: "Your parents or guardian or a sex education teacher should give you the facts about sex that you must know." Boy Scout Handbook. To be sure, Scouts are not forbidden from asking their Scoutmaster about issues of a sexual nature, but Scoutmasters are, literally, the last person Scouts are encouraged to ask: "If you have questions about growing up, about relationships, sex, or making good decisions.

More specifically, BSA has set forth a number of rules for Scoutmasters when these types of issues come up:

"You may have boys asking you for information or advice about sexual matters ...

"How should you handle such matters?

> "Rule number 1: You do not undertake to instruct Scouts, in any formalized manner, in the subject of sex and family life. The reasons are that it is not construed to be Scouting's proper area, and that you are probably not well qualified to do this.
>
> "Rule number 2: If Scouts come to you to ask questions or to seek advice, you would give it within your competence. A boy who appears to be asking about sexual intercourse, however, may really only be worried about his pimples, so it is well to find out just what information is needed.
>
> "Rule number 3: You should refer boys with sexual problems to persons better qualified than you [are] to handle them. If the boy has a spiritual leader or a doctor who can deal with them, he should go there. If such persons are not available, you may just have to do the best you can. But don't try to play a highly professional role. And at the other extreme, avoid passing the buck." Scoutmaster Handbook.

In light of BSA's self-proclaimed ecumenism, furthermore, it is even more difficult to discern any shared goals or common moral stance on homosexuality. Insofar as religious matters are concerned, BSA's bylaws state that it is "absolutely nonsectarian in its attitude toward ... religious training."

The BSA does not define what constitutes duty to God or the practice of religion. This is the responsibility of parents and religious leaders." In fact, many diverse religious organizations sponsor local Boy Scouts. Because a number of religious groups do not view homosexuality as immoral or wrong and reject discrimination against homosexuals, it is exceedingly difficult to believe that BSA nonetheless adopts a single particular religious or moral philosophy when it comes to sexual orientation. This is especially so in light of the fact that Scouts are advised to seek guidance on sexual matters from their religious leaders (and Scoutmasters are told to refer Scouts to them); BSA surely is aware that some religions do not teach that homosexuality is wrong.

In 1991, BSA issued two statements both stating: "We believe that homosexual conduct is inconsistent with the requirement in the Scout Oath that a Scout be morally straight and in the Scout Law that a Scout be clean in word and deed, and that homosexuals do not provide a desirable role model for Scouts." A third statement issued in 1992 was substantially the same. By 1993, however, the policy had changed: "BSA Position

The Boy Scouts of America has always reflected the expectations that Scouting families have had for the organization.

> "We do not believe that homosexuals provide a role model consistent with these expectations. "Accordingly, we do not allow for the registration of avowed homosexuals as members or as leaders of the BSA."

Aside from the fact that these statements were all issued after Dale's membership was revoked, there are four important points relevant to them. First, while the 1991 and 1992 statements tried to tie BSA's exclusionary policy to the meaning of the Scout Oath and Law, the 1993 statement abandoned that effort. Rather, BSA's 1993 homosexual exclusion policy was based on its view that including gays would be contrary to "the expectations that Scouting families have had for the organization."

Instead of linking its policy to its central tenets or shared goals—to teach certain definitions of what it means to be "morally straight" and "clean"—BSA chose instead to justify its policy on the "expectation" that its members preferred to exclude homosexuals. The 1993 policy statement, in other words, was not based on any expressive activity or on any moral view about homosexuality. It was simply an exclusionary membership policy, similar to those we have held insufficient in the past.

Second, even during the brief period in 1991 and 1992, when BSA tried to connect its exclusion of homosexuals to its definition of terms found in the Oath and Law, there is no evidence that Scouts were actually taught anything about homosexuality's alleged inconsistency with those principles. Beyond the single sentence in these policy statements, there is no indication of any shared goal of teaching that homosexuality is incompatible with being "morally straight" and "clean." Neither BSA's mission statement nor its official membership policy was altered; no Boy Scout or Scoutmaster Handbook was amended to reflect the policy statement; no lessons were imparted to Scouts; no change was made to BSA's policy on limiting discussion of sexual matters; and no effort was made to restrict acceptable religious affiliations to those that condemn homosexuality. In short, there is no evidence that this view was part of any collective effort to foster beliefs about homosexuality.

Indeed, the record in evidence is to the contrary. "I never heard and am not aware of any discussion about homosexuality that occurred during any Scouting meeting or function.... Prior to September 1991, I never heard any mention whatsoever of homosexuality during any Scouting function") (affidavit of former Boy Scout whose young children were Scouts, and was himself an Assistant Scoutmaster and Merit Badge Counselor).

Third, BSA never took any clear and unequivocal position on homosexuality. Though the 1991 and 1992 policies state one interpretation of "morally straight" and "clean," the group's published definitions appearing in the Boy Scout and Scoutmaster Handbooks take quite another view. And BSA's broad religious tolerance combined with its declaration that sexual matters are not its "proper area" renders its views on the issue equivocal at best and incoherent at worst. We have never held, however, that a group can throw together any mixture of contradictory positions and then invoke the right to associate to defend any one of those views. At a minimum, a group seeking to prevail over an antidiscrimination law must adhere to a clear and unequivocal view.

New Jersey's law prohibits discrimination on the basis of sexual orientation. And when Dale was expelled from the Boy Scouts, BSA said it did so because of his sexual orientation, not because of his sexual conduct.

To prevail on a claim of expressive association in the face of a State's antidiscrimination law:

> It is not enough simply to engage in some kind of expressive activity.
>
> It is not enough to adopt an openly avowed exclusionary membership policy.
>
> It is not sufficient merely to articulate some connection between the group's expressive activities and its exclusionary policy.
>
> Rather, we asked whether upholding the anti-discrimination law at issue "imposed any serious burdens" on the group's "collective effort on behalf of [its] shared goals."

The only apparent explanation for the majority's holding, then, is that homosexuals are simply so different from the rest of society that their presence alone—unlike any other individual's—should be singled out for special First Amendment treatment. Under the majority's reasoning, an openly gay male is irreversibly affixed with the label "homosexual." That label, even though unseen, communicates a message that permits his exclusion wherever he goes. His openness is the sole and sufficient justification for his ostracism. Though unintended, reliance on such a justification is tantamount to a constitutionally prescribed symbol of inferiority. As counsel for the Boy Scouts remarked:

> Dale "put a banner around his neck when he ... got himself into the newspaper.... He created a reputation.... He can't take that banner off. He put it on himself and, indeed, he has continued to put it on himself."

Over the years, BSA has generously welcomed over 87 million young Americans into its ranks. In 1992 over one million adults were active BSA members. The notion that an organization of that size and enormous prestige implicitly endorses the views that each of those adults may express in a non-Scouting context is simply mind boggling. Indeed, in this case there is no evidence that the young Scouts in Dale's troop, or members of their families, were even aware of his sexual orientation, either before or after his public statements at Rutgers University.

It is equally farfetched to assert that Dale's open declaration of his homosexuality, reported in a local newspaper, will effectively force BSA to send a message to anyone simply because it allows Dale to be an Assistant Scoutmaster. For an Olympic gold medal winner or a Wimbledon tennis champion, being "openly gay" perhaps communicates a message—for example, that openness about one's sexual orientation is more virtuous than concealment; that a homosexual person can be a capable and virtuous person who should be judged like anyone else; and that homosexuality is not immoral—but it certainly does not follow that they necessarily send a message on behalf of the organizations that sponsor the activities in which they excel. The fact that such persons participate in these organizations is not usually construed to convey a message on behalf of those organizations any more than does the inclusion of women, African-Amcricans, rcligious minorities, or any other discrete group. Surely the organizations are not forced by antidiscrimination laws to take any position on the legitimacy of any individual's private beliefs or private conduct.

Unfavorable opinions about homosexuals "have ancient roots." *Bowers v. Hardwick*, 478 U.S. 186, 192, 92 L. Ed. 2d 140, 106 S. Ct. 2841 (1986). Like equally atavistic opinions about certain racial groups, those roots have been nourished by sectarian doctrine: Habit, rather than analysis, makes it seem acceptable and natural to distinguish between male and female, alien and citizen, legitimate and illegitimate; for too much of our history there was the same inertia in distinguishing between Black and white"). Over the years, however, interaction with real people, rather than mere adherence to traditional ways of thinking about members of unfamiliar classes, have modified those opinions.

Lawrence v. Texas

2003

Responding to a report involving weapons at Petitioner's home, Houston police entered Lawrence's apartment and saw him engaging in a private, consensual sexual act with another adult man. Both were arrested and convicted of deviate sexual intercourse in violation of a Texas statute forbidding two persons of the same sex to engage in certain intimate sexual conduct. The ultimate question is whether Bowers is controlling and, if so, on what grounds?

Justice Kennedy delivered the opinion of the Court.[17]

Liberty protects the person from unwarranted government intrusions into a dwelling or other private places. In our tradition the State is not omnipresent in the home. And there are other spheres of our lives and existence, outside the home, where the State should not be a dominant presence. Freedom extends beyond spatial bounds. Liberty presumes an autonomy of self that includes freedom of thought, belief, expression, and certain intimate conduct. The instant case involves liberty of the person both in its spatial and more transcendent dimensions.

The question before the Court is the validity of a Texas statute making it a crime for two persons of the same sex to engage in certain intimate sexual conduct.

In Houston, Texas, officers of the Harris County Police Department were dispatched to a private residence in response to a reported weapons disturbance. They entered an apartment where one of the petitioners, John Geddes Lawrence, resided. The right of the police to enter does not seem to have been questioned. The officers observed Lawrence and another man, Tyron Garner, engaging in a sexual act. The two petitioners were arrested, held in custody over night, and charged and convicted before a Justice of the Peace.

The complaints described their crime as "deviate sexual intercourse, namely anal sex, with a member of the same sex (man)." App. to Pet. for Cert. 127a, 139a. The applicable state law is Tex. Penal Code Ann. §21.06(a) (2003). It provides: "A person commits an offense if he engages in deviate sexual intercourse with another individual of the same sex." The statute defines "deviate sexual intercourse" as follows:

"(A) any contact between any part of the genitals of one person and the mouth or anus of another person; or

"(B) the penetration of the genitals or the anus of another person with an object." § 21.01(1).

The petitioners exercised their right to a trial de novo in Harris County Criminal Court. They challenged the statute as a violation of the Equal Protection Clause of the Fourteenth Amendment and of a like provision of the Texas Constitution. Tex. Const., Art. 1, § 3a. Those contentions were rejected. The petitioners, having entered a plea of nolo contendere, were each fined $ 200 and assessed court costs of $ 141.25. App. to Pet. for Cert. 107a–110a.

The Court of Appeals for the Texas Fourteenth District considered the petitioners' federal constitutional arguments under both the Equal Protection and Due Process Clauses of the Fourteenth Amendment. After hearing the case en banc the court, in a divided opinion, rejected the constitutional arguments and affirmed the convictions. The majority opinion indicates that the Court of Appeals considered our decision in *Bowers* to be controlling on the federal due process aspect of the case. *Bowers* then being authoritative, this was proper.

We granted certiorai to consider three questions:

"1. Whether Petitioners' criminal convictions under the Texas "Homosexual Conduct" law—which criminalizes sexual intimacy by same-sex couples, but not identical behavior by different-sex couples—violate the Fourteenth Amendment guarantee of equal protection of laws?

"2. Whether Petitioners' criminal convictions for adult consensual sexual intimacy in the home violate their vital interests in liberty and privacy protected by the Due Process Clause of the Fourteenth Amendment?

"3. Whether *Bowers* should be overruled?"

The petitioners were adults at the time of the alleged offense. Their conduct was in private and consensual.

We conclude the case should be resolved by determining whether the petitioners were free as adults to engage in the private conduct in the exercise of their liberty under the Due Process Clause of the Fourteenth Amendment to the Constitution. For this inquiry we deem it necessary to reconsider the Court's holding in *Bowers*.

There are broad statements of the substantive reach of liberty under the Due Process Clause in earlier cases, including *Pierce* and *Meyer* but the most pertinent beginning point is our decision in *Griswold*.

In *Griswold* the Court invalidated a state law prohibiting the use of drugs or devices of contraception and counseling or aiding and abetting the use of contraceptives. The Court described the protected interest as a right to privacy and placed emphasis on the marriage relation and the protected space of the marital bedroom.

After *Griswold* it was established that the right to make certain decisions regarding sexual conduct extends beyond the marital relationship. In *Eisenstadt* the Court invalidated a law prohibiting the distribution of contraceptives to unmarried persons. The case was decided under the Equal Protection Clause,;

but with respect to unmarried persons, the Court went on to state the fundamental proposition that the law impaired the exercise of their personal rights, ibid. It quoted from the statement of the Court of Appeals finding the law to be in conflict with fundamental human rights, and it followed with this statement of its own:

> "It is true that in *Griswold* the right of privacy in question inhered in the marital relationship ... the right of privacy means anything, it is the right of the individual, married or single, to be free from unwarranted governmental intrusion into matters so fundamentally affecting a person as the decision whether to bear or beget a child."

The opinions in *Griswold* and *Eisenstadt* were part of the background for the decision in *Roe*. As is well known, the case involved a challenge to the Texas law prohibiting abortions, but the laws of other States were affected as well. Although the Court held the woman's rights were not absolute, her right to elect an abortion did have real and substantial protection as an exercise of her liberty under the Due Process Clause. The Court cited cases that protect spatial freedom and cases that go well beyond it. *Roe* recognized the right of a woman to make certain fundamental decisions affecting her destiny and confirmed once more that the protection of liberty under the Due Process Clause has a substantive dimension of fundamental significance in defining the rights of the person.

In *Carey* the Court confronted a New York law forbidding sale or distribution of contraceptive devices to persons under 16 years of age. Although there was no single opinion for the Court, the law was invalidated. Both *Eisenstadt* and *Carey*, as well as the holding and rationale in *Roe*, confirmed that the reasoning of *Griswold* could not be confined to the protection of rights of married adults. This was the state of the law with respect to some of the most relevant cases when the Court considered *Bowers v. Hardwick*. The facts in *Bowers* had some similarities to the instant case. A police officer, whose right to enter seems not to have been in question, observed Hardwick, in his own bedroom, engaging in intimate sexual conduct with another adult male. The conduct was in violation of a Georgia statute making it a criminal offense to engage in sodomy. One difference between the two cases is that the Georgia statute prohibited the conduct whether or not the participants were of the same sex, while the Texas statute, as we have seen, applies only to participants of the same sex. Hardwick was not prosecuted, but he brought an action in federal court to declare the state statute invalid. He alleged he was a practicing homosexual and that the criminal prohibition violated rights guaranteed to him by the Constitution. The Court, in an opinion by Justice White, sustained the Georgia law. Chief Justice Burger and Justice Powell joined the opinion of the Court and filed separate, concurring opinions. Four Justices dissented.

The Court began its substantive discussion in *Bowers* as follows: "The issue presented is whether the Federal Constitution confers a fundamental right upon homosexuals to engage in sodomy and hence invalidates the laws of the many States that still make such conduct illegal and have done so for a very long time."

That statement, we now conclude, discloses the Court's own failure to appreciate the extent of the liberty at stake. To say that the issue in *Bowers* was simply the right to engage in certain sexual conduct demeans the claim the individual put forward, just as it would demean a married couple were it to be said marriage is simply about the right to have sexual intercourse. The laws involved in *Bowers* and here are, to be sure, statutes that purport to do no more than prohibit a particular sexual act. Their penalties and purposes, though, have more far-reaching consequences, touching upon the most private human conduct, sexual behavior, and in the most private of places, the home. The statutes do seek to control a personal relationship that, whether or not entitled to formal recognition in the law, is within the liberty of persons to choose without being punished as criminals.

This, as a general rule, should counsel against attempts by the State, or a court, to define the meaning of the relationship or to set its boundaries absent injury to a person or abuse of an institution the law protects. It suffices for us to acknowledge that adults may choose to enter upon this relationship in the confines of their homes and their own private lives and still retain their dignity as free persons. When sexuality finds overt expression in intimate conduct with another person, the conduct can be but one element in a personal bond that is more enduring. The liberty protected by the Constitution allows homosexual persons the right to make this choice.

Having misapprehended the claim of liberty there presented to it, and thus stating the claim to be whether there is a fundamental right to engage in consensual sodomy, the *Bowers* Court said: "Proscriptions against that conduct have ancient roots." In academic writings, and in many of the scholarly amicus briefs filed to assist the Court in this case, there are fundamental criticisms of the historical premises relied upon by the majority and concurring opinions in *Bowers*. Brief for Cato Institute as Amicus Curiae 16–17; Brief for American Civil Liberties Union et al. as Amici Curiae 15–21; Brief for Professors of History et al. as Amici. We need not enter this debate in the attempt to reach a definitive historical judgment, but the following considerations counsel against adopting the definitive conclusions upon which *Bowers* placed such reliance.

At the outset it should be noted that there is no longstanding history in this country of laws directed at homosexual conduct as a distinct matter. Beginning in colonial times there were prohibitions of sodomy derived from the English criminal laws passed in the first instance by the Reformation Parliament of 1533. The English prohibition was understood to include relations between men and women as well as relations between men and men. Nineteenth-century commentators similarly read American sodomy, buggery, and crime-against-nature statutes as criminalizing certain relations between men and women and between men and men. The absence of legal prohibitions focusing on homosexual conduct may be explained in part by noting that according to some scholars the concept of the homosexual as a distinct category of person did not emerge until the late 19th century. See, e.g., J. Katz, THE INVENTION OF HETEROSEXUALITY, "The modern terms homosexuality and heterosexuality do not apply to an era that had not yet articulated these distinctions." Thus early American sodomy laws were not directed at homosexuals as such but instead sought to prohibit nonprocreative sexual activity more generally. This does not suggest approval of homosexual conduct. It does tend to show that this particular form of conduct was not thought of as a separate category from like conduct between heterosexual persons.

Laws prohibiting sodomy do not seem to have been enforced against consenting adults acting in private. A substantial number of sodomy prosecutions and convictions for which there are surviving records were for predatory acts against those who could not or did not consent, as in the case of a minor or the victim of an assault. As to these, one purpose for the prohibitions was to ensure there would be no lack of coverage if a predator committed a sexual assault that did not constitute rape as defined by the criminal law. Thus the model sodomy indictments presented in a 19th-century treatise, see 2 Chitty, supra, at 49, addressed the predatory acts of an adult man against a minor girl or minor boy. Instead of targeting relations between consenting adults in private, 19th-century sodomy prosecutions typically involved relations between men and minor girls or minor boys, relations between adults involving force, relations between adults implicating disparity in status, or relations between men and animals.

To the extent that there were any prosecutions for the acts in question, 19th-century evidence rules imposed a burden that would make a conviction more difficult to obtain even taking into account the problems always inherent in prosecuting consensual acts committed in private. Under then-prevailing standards, a man could not be convicted of sodomy based upon testimony of a consenting partner, because the partner was considered an accomplice. A partner's testimony, however, was admissible if he or she had not consented to the act or was a minor, and therefore incapable of consent. The rule may explain in part the infrequency of these prosecutions. In all events that infrequency makes it difficult to say that society approved of a rigorous and systematic punishment of the consensual acts committed in private and by adults. The longstanding criminal prohibition of homosexual sodomy upon which the *Bowers* decision placed such reliance is as consistent with a general condemnation of nonprocreative sex as it is with an established tradition of prosecuting acts because of their homosexual character.

The policy of punishing consenting adults for private acts was not much discussed in the early legal literature. We can infer that one reason for this was the very private nature of the conduct. Despite the absence of prosecutions, there may have been periods in which there was public criticism of homosexuals as such and an insistence that the criminal laws be enforced to discourage their practices. But far from possessing "ancient roots," American laws targeting same-sex couples did not develop until the last third of the 20th century. The reported decisions concerning the prosecution of consensual, homosexual sodomy between adults for the years 1880–1995 are not always clear in the details, but a significant number involved conduct in a public place. See Brief for American Civil Liberties Union et al. as Amici Curiae 14–15, and n 18.

It was not until the 1970s that any States singled out same-sex relations for criminal prosecution, and only nine States have done so. The historical grounds relied upon in *Bowers* are more complex than the majority opinion and the concurring opinion by Chief Justice Burger indicate. Their historical premises are not without doubt and, at the very least, are overstated.

It must be acknowledged, of course, that the Court in *Bowers* was making the broader point that for centuries there have been powerful voices to condemn homosexual conduct as immoral. The condemnation has been shaped by religious beliefs, conceptions of right and acceptable behavior, and respect for the traditional family. For many persons these are not trivial concerns but profound and deep convictions accepted as ethical and moral principles to which they aspire and which thus determine the course of their lives. These considerations do not answer the question before us, however. The issue is whether the majority may use the power of the State to enforce these views on the whole society through operation of the criminal law. "Our obligation is to define the liberty of all, not to mandate our own moral code."

Chief Justice Burger joined the opinion for the Court in *Bowers* and further explained his views as follows: "Decisions of individuals relating to homosexual conduct have been subject to state intervention throughout the history of Western civilization. Condemnation of those practices is firmly rooted in Judeo-Christian moral and ethical standards." As with Justice White's assumptions about history, scholarship casts some doubt on the sweeping nature of the statement by Chief Justice Burger as it pertains to private homosexual conduct between consenting adults. In all events we think that our laws and traditions in the past half-century are of most relevance here. These references show an emerging awareness that liberty gives substantial protection to adult persons in deciding how to conduct their private lives in matters pertaining to sex. "History and tradition are the starting point but not in all cases the ending point of the substantive due process inquiry."

This emerging recognition should have been apparent when *Bowers* was decided. In 1955 the American Law Institute promulgated the Model Penal Code and made clear that it did not recommend or provide for "criminal penalties for consensual sexual relations conducted in private." It justified its decision on three grounds: (1) The prohibitions undermined respect for the law by penalizing conduct many people engaged in; (2) the statutes regulated private conduct not harmful to others; and (3) the laws were arbitrarily enforced and thus invited the danger of blackmail.

In *Bowers* the Court referred to the fact that before 1961 all 50 States had outlawed sodomy, and that at the time of the Court's decision 24 States and the District of Columbia had sodomy laws. Justice Powell pointed out that these prohibitions often were being ignored, however. Georgia, for instance, had not sought to enforce its law for decades. ("The history of nonenforcement suggests the moribund character today of laws criminalizing this type of private, consensual conduct").

The sweeping references by Chief Justice Burger to the history of Western civilization and to Judeo-Christian moral and ethical standards did not take account of other authorities pointing in an opposite direction. A committee advising the British Parliament recommended in 1957 repeal of laws punishing homosexual conduct. The Wolfenden Report: Report of the Committee on Homosexual Offenses and Prostitution (1963). Parliament enacted the substance of those recommendations 10 years later. Sexual Offences Act 1967, § 1.

Of even more importance, almost five years before *Bowers* was decided the European Court of Human Rights considered a case with parallels to Bowers and to today's case. An adult male resident in Northern Ireland alleged he was a practicing homosexual who desired to engage in consensual homosexual conduct. The laws of Northern Ireland forbade him that right. He alleged that he had been questioned, his home had been searched, and he feared criminal prosecution. The court held that the laws proscribing the conduct were invalid under the European Convention on Human Rights. Dudgeon . Authoritative in all countries that are members of the Council of Europe (21 nations then, 45 nations now), the decision is at odds with the premise in *Bowers* that the claim put forward was insubstantial in our Western civilization.

In our own constitutional system, the deficiencies in *Bowers* became even more apparent in the years following its announcement. The 25 States with laws prohibiting the relevant conduct referenced in the *Bowers* decision are reduced now to 13, of which 4 enforce their laws only against homosexual conduct. In those States where sodomy is still proscribed, whether for same-sex or heterosexual conduct, there is a pattern of nonenforcement with respect to consenting adults acting in private. The State of Texas admitted in 1994 that as of that date it had not prosecuted anyone under those circumstances, *State v. Morales.*

Two principal cases decided after *Bowers* cast its holding into even more doubt. In *Casey*, the Court reaffirmed the substantive force of the liberty protected by the Due Process Clause. The *Casey* decision again confirmed that our laws and tradition afford constitutional protection to personal decisions relating to marriage, procreation, contraception, family relationships, child rearing, and education. Id. In explaining the respect the Constitution demands for the autonomy of the person in making these choices, we stated as follows:

> These matters, involving the most intimate and personal choices a person may make in a lifetime, choices central to personal dignity and autonomy, are central to the liberty protected by the Fourteenth Amendment. At the heart of liberty is the right to define one's own concept of existence, of meaning, of the universe, and of the mystery of human life. Beliefs about these matters could not define the attributes of personhood were they formed under compulsion of the State." Ibid.

Persons in a homosexual relationship may seek autonomy for these purposes, just as heterosexual persons do. The decision in *Bowers* would deny them this right.

The second post-*Bowers* case of principal relevance is *Romer*. There the Court struck down class-based legislation directed at homosexuals as a violation of the Equal Protection Clause. *Romer* invalidated an amendment to Colorado's constitution which named as a solitary class persons who were homosexuals, lesbians, or bisexual either by "orientation, conduct, practices or relationships," (internal quotation marks omitted), and deprived them of protection under state antidiscrimination laws. We concluded that the provision was "born of animosity toward the class of persons affected" and further that it had no rational relation to a legitimate governmental purpose.

As an alternative argument in this case, counsel for the petitioners and some amici contend that *Romer* provides the basis for declaring the Texas statute invalid under the Equal Protection Clause. That is a tenable argument, but we conclude the instant case requires us to address whether *Bowers* itself has continuing validity. Were we to hold the statute invalid under the Equal Protection Clause some might question whether a prohibition would be valid if drawn differently, say, to prohibit the conduct both between same-sex and different-sex participants.

Equality of treatment and the due process right to demand respect for conduct protected by the substantive guarantee of liberty are linked in important respects, and a decision on the latter point advances both interests. If protected conduct is made criminal and the law which does so remains unexamined for its substantive validity, its stigma might remain even if it were not enforceable as drawn for equal protection reasons. When homosexual conduct is made criminal by the law of the State, that declaration in and of itself is an invitation to subject homosexual persons to discrimination both in the public and in the private spheres. The central holding of *Bowers* has been brought in question by this case, and it should be addressed. Its continuance as precedent demeans the lives of homosexual persons.

The stigma this criminal statute imposes, moreover, is not trivial. The offense, to be sure, is but a class C misdemeanor, a minor offense in the Texas legal system. Still, it remains a criminal offense with all that imports for the dignity of the persons charged. The petitioners will bear on their record the history of their criminal convictions. Just this Term we rejected various challenges to state laws requiring the registration of sex offenders. We are advised that if Texas convicted an adult for private, consensual homosexual conduct under the statute here in question the convicted person would come within the registration laws of at least four States were he or she to be subject to their jurisdiction. This underscores the consequential nature of the punishment and the state-sponsored condemnation attendant to the criminal prohibition. Furthermore, the Texas criminal conviction carries with it the other collateral consequences always following a conviction, such as notations on job application forms, to mention but one example.

The foundations of *Bowers* have sustained serious erosion from our recent decisions in *Casey* and *Romer*. When our precedent has been thus weakened, criticism from other sources is of greater significance. In the United States criticism of *Bowers* has been substantial and continuing, disapproving of its reasoning in all respects, not just as to its historical assumptions. See, e.g., C. Fried, Order and Law: Arguing the Reagan Revolution—A Firsthand Account 81–84 (1991); R. Posner, Sex and Reason 341–350 (1992). The courts of five different States have declined to follow it in interpreting provisions in their own state constitutions parallel to the Due Process Clause of the Fourteenth Amendment.

To the extent *Bowers* relied on values we share with a wider civilization, it should be noted that the reasoning and holding in *Bowers* have been rejected elsewhere. The European Court of Human Rights has followed not *Bowers* but its own decision in. Other nations, too, have taken action consistent with an affirmation of the protected right of homosexual adults to engage in intimate, consensual conduct. See Brief for Mary Robinson et al. as Amici Curiae 11–12. The right the petitioners seek in this case has been accepted as an integral part of human freedom in many other countries. There has been no showing that in this country the governmental interest in circumscribing personal choice is somehow more legitimate or urgent.

In *Casey* we noted that when a Court is asked to overrule a precedent recognizing a constitutional liberty interest, individual or societal reliance on the existence of that liberty cautions with particular strength against reversing course. ("Liberty finds no refuge in a jurisprudence of doubt").

The holding in *Bowers*, however, has not induced detrimental reliance comparable to some instances where recognized individual rights are involved. Indeed, there has been no individual or societal reliance on *Bowers* of the sort that could counsel against overturning its holding once there are compelling reasons to do so. *Bowers* itself causes uncertainty, for the precedents before and after its issuance contradict its central holding.

The rationale of *Bowers* does not withstand careful analysis. In his dissenting opinion in *Bowers* Justice Stevens came to these conclusions:

> Our prior cases make two propositions abundantly clear. First, the fact that the governing majority in a State has traditionally viewed a particular practice as immoral is not a sufficient reason for upholding a law prohibiting the practice; neither history nor tradition could save a law prohibiting miscegenation from

constitutional attack. Second, individual decisions by married persons, concerning the intimacies of their physical relationship, even when not intended to produce offspring, are a form of "liberty" protected by the Due Process Clause of the Fourteenth Amendment. Moreover, this protection extends to intimate choices by unmarried as well as married persons."

Justice Stevens' analysis, in our view, should have been controlling in *Bowers* and should control here. *Bowers* was not correct when it was decided, and it is not correct today. It ought not to remain binding precedent, and now is overruled.

The present case does not involve minors. It does not involve persons who might be injured or coerced or who are situated in relationships where consent might not easily be refused. It does not involve public conduct or prostitution. It does not involve whether the government must give formal recognition to any relationship that homosexual persons seek to enter. The case does involve two adults who, with full and mutual consent from each other, engaged in sexual practices common to a homosexual lifestyle. The petitioners are entitled to respect for their private lives. The State cannot demean their existence or control their destiny by making their private sexual conduct a crime. Their right to liberty under the Due Process gives them the full right to engage in their conduct without intervention of the government. "It is a promise of the Constitution that there is a realm of personal liberty which the government may not enter." The Texas statute furthers no legitimate state interest which can justify its intrusion into the personal and private life of the individual.

Had those who drew and ratified the Due Process Clauses of the Fifth Amendment or the Fourteenth Amendment known the components of liberty in its manifold possibilities, they might have been more specific. They did not presume to have this insight. They knew times can blind us to certain truths and later generations can see that laws once thought necessary and proper in fact serve only to oppress. As the Constitution endures, persons in every generation can invoke its principles in their own search for greater freedom.

The judgment of the Court of Appeals for the Texas Fourteenth District is reversed, and the case is remanded for further proceedings not inconsistent with this opinion.

It is so ordered.

Revisiting Marriage As a Fundamental Right

Baehr v. Lewin[18]

May 1993

Facts: On or about December 17, 1990, Baehr/Dancel, Rodrigues/Pregil, and Lagon/Melilio (the applicant couples) filed applications for marriage licenses with the DOH, pursuant to HRS @ 572-6 (1992). The DOH denied the applicant couples' marriage license applications solely on the ground that the applicant couples were of the same sex

HRS @ 572-1 provides: Requisites of valid marriage contract. In order to make valid the marriage contract, it shall be necessary that:

(1) The respective parties do not stand in relation to each other of ancestor and descendant of any degree whatsoever, brother and sister of the half as well as to the whole blood, uncle and niece, aunt and nephew, whether the relationship is legitimate or illegitimate;

(2) Each of the parties at the time of contracting the marriage is at least sixteen years of age; provided that with the written approval of the family court of the circuit court within which the minor resides, it shall be lawful for a person under the age of sixteen years, but in no event under the age of fifteen years, to marry, subject to section 572-2 [relating to consent of parent or guardian];

(3) The man does not at the time have any lawful wife living and that the woman does not at the time have any lawful husband living;

(4) Consent of neither party to the marriage has been obtained by force, duress, or fraud;

(5) Neither of the parties is a person afflicted with any loathsome disease concealed from, and unknown to, the other party;

(6) It shall in no case be lawful for any person to marry in the State without a license for that purpose duly obtained from the agent appointed to grant marriage licenses; and

(7) The marriage ceremony be performed in the State by a person or society with a valid license to solemnize marriages and the man and woman to be married and the person performing the marriage ceremony be all physically present at the same place and time for the marriage ceremony.

It is now well established that a right to personal privacy, or a guarantee of certain areas or zones of privacy, is implicit in the United States Constitution.

Article I, section 6 of the Hawaii Constitution expressly states that "[t]he right of the people to privacy is recognized and shall not be infringed without the showing of a compelling state interest." The privacy concept embodied in this constitutional principle is to be treated as a fundamental right.

It is not surprising that the decision to marry has been placed on the same level of importance as decisions relating to procreation, childbirth, child rearing, and family relationships. As the facts of this case illustrate, it would make little sense to recognize a right of privacy with respect to other matters of family life and not with respect to the decision to enter the relationship that is the foundation of the family in our society.

At a minimum, article I, section 6 of the Hawaii Constitution encompasses all of the fundamental rights expressly recognized as being subsumed within the privacy protections of the United States Constitution. When article I, section 6 of the Hawaii Constitution was being adopted, the 1978 Hawaii Constitutional Convention, acting as a committee of the whole, clearly articulated the rationale for its adoption: By amending the Constitution to include a separate and distinct privacy right, it is the intent of your Committee to insure that matters of privacy are treated as a fundamental right for purposes of constitutional analysis.

The power to regulate marriage is a sovereign function reserved exclusively to the respective states. By its very nature, the power to regulate the marriage contract includes the power to determine the requisites of a valid marriage contract and to control the qualifications of the contracting parties, the forms and procedures necessary to solemnize the marriage, the duties and obligations it creates, its effect upon property and other rights, and the grounds for marital dissolution. In other words, marriage is a state-conferred legal status, the existence of which gives rise to rights and benefits reserved exclusively to that particular relationship.

Marriage is a partnership to which both partners bring their financial resources as well as their individual energies and efforts. Notwithstanding the state's acknowledged stewardship over the institution of marriage, the extent of permissible state regulation of the right of access to the marital relationship is subject to constitutional limitations or constraints.

By its plain language, article I, section 5 of the Hawaii Constitution prohibits state-sanctioned discrimination against any person in the exercise of his or her civil rights on the basis of sex: No person shall be deprived of life, liberty or property without due process of law, nor be denied the equal protection of the laws, nor be denied the enjoyment of the person's civil rights or be discriminated against in the exercise thereof because of race, religion, sex or ancestry.

On its face, Hawaii Revised Statutes (HRS) @ 572-1 (1985) restricts the marital relation to a male and a female. Accordingly, on its face and as applied, HRS @ 572-1 denies same-sex couples access to the marital status and its concomitant rights and benefits.

It is the state's regulation of access to the status of married persons, on the basis of the applicants' sex, that gives rise to the question whether the applicant couples have been denied the equal protection of the laws in violation of article I, section 5 of the Hawaii Constitution.

"Strict scrutiny" analysis is applied to laws classifying on the basis of suspect categories or impinging upon fundamental rights expressly or impliedly granted by the constitution, in which case the laws are presumed to be unconstitutional unless the state shows compelling state interests which justify such classifications and that the laws are narrowly drawn to avoid unnecessary abridgments of constitutional rights.

Where suspect classifications or fundamental rights are not at issue, the appellate courts of this state have traditionally employed the rational basis test. Under the rational basis test, the inquiry is whether a statute furthers a legitimate state interest.

Sex is a "suspect category" for purposes of equal protection analysis under article I, section 5 of the Hawaii Constitution; HRS @ 572-1 is therefore subject to the "strict scrutiny" test.

Homosexual" and "same-sex" marriages are not synonymous; by the same token, a "heterosexual" same-sex marriage is, in theory, not oxymoronic. A "homosexual" person is defined as "[o]ne sexually attracted to another of the same sex." Taber's Cyclopedic Medical Dictionary 839 (16th ed. 1989).

"Homosexuality" is "sexual desire or behavior directed toward a person or persons of one's own sex." Webster's Encyclopedic Unabridged Dictionary of the English Language 680 (1989). Conversely, "heterosexuality" is "[s]exual attraction for one of the opposite sex," Taber's Cyclopedic Medical Dictionary at 827, or "sexual feeling or behavior directed toward a person or persons of the opposite sex." Webster's Encyclopedic Unabridged Dictionary of the English Language at 667. Parties to "a union between a man and a woman" may or may not be homosexuals. Parties to a same-sex marriage could theoretically be either homosexuals or heterosexuals.

Lewin is correct that the plaintiffs' complaint does not allege that the plaintiffs, or any of them, are homosexuals. Thus it is Lewin, who, by virtue of his motion for judgment on the pleadings, has sought to place the question of homosexuality in issue.

HRS @ 572-1 is presumed to be unconstitutional unless it can be shown that the statute's sex-based classification is justified by compelling state interests and that it is narrowly drawn to avoid unnecessary abridgments of constitutional rights.

The plaintiffs-appellants appeal the circuit court's order granting the motion of the defendant that resulted in the dismissal of plaintiffs' action with prejudice for failure to state a claim upon which relief can be granted.

For example, the circuit court "found" that:

(1) HRS @ 572-1 "does not infringe upon a person's individuality or lifestyle decisions, and none of the plaintiffs has provided testimony to the contrary".

(2) HRS @ 572-1 "does not ... restrict [or] burden ... the exercise of the right to engage in a homosexual lifestyle"

(3) Hawaii has exhibited a "history of tolerance for all peoples and their cultures".

(4) "the plaintiffs have failed to show that they have been ostracized or oppressed in Hawaii and have opted instead to rely on a general statement of historic problems encountered by homosexuals which may not be relevant to Hawaii"

(5) "homosexuals in Hawaii have not been relegated to a position of 'political powerlessness.'... [T]here is no evidence that homosexuals and the homosexual legislative agenda have failed to gain legislative support in Hawaii"

(6) the "[p]laintiffs have failed to show that homosexuals constitute a suspect class for equal protection analysis under the Hawaii State Constitution

(7) "the issue of whether homosexuality constitutes an immutable trait has generated much dispute in the relevant scientific community"

(8) HRS @ 572-1 "is obviously designed to promote the general welfare interests of the community by sanctioning traditional man-woman family units and procreation

We disagree that "questions of whether heterosexuality, homosexuality, bisexuality, and asexuality are 'biologically fated' are relevant questions of fact. This preoccupation seems simply to restate the immaterial question whether sexual orientation is an "immutable trait." A complaint should not be dismissed for failure to state a claim unless it appears beyond doubt that the plaintiff can prove no set of facts in support of his or her claim that would entitle the plaintiff to relief. The duty of the appellate court is therefore to view the plaintiff's complaint in a light most favorable to him or her in order to determine whether the allegations contained therein could warrant relief under any alternative theory. For this reason, in reviewing an order dismissing the plaintiff's complaint for failure to state a claim, the appellate court's consideration is strictly limited to the allegations of the complaint, which must be deemed to be true.

For purposes of Lewin's motion, it is our duty to view the factual allegations of the plaintiffs' complaint in a light most favorable to them and because it does not appear beyond doubt that the plaintiffs cannot prove any set of facts in support of their claim that would entitle them to the relief they seek, we hold that the circuit court erroneously dismissed the plaintiffs' complaint.

CONCLUSION

Because, for the reasons stated in this opinion, the circuit court erroneously granted Lewin's motion for judgment on the pleadings and dismissed the plaintiffs' complaint, we vacate the circuit court's order and judgment and remand this matter for further proceedings consistent with this opinion. On remand, in accordance with the "strict scrutiny" standard, the burden will rest on Lewin to overcome the presumption that HRS @ 572-1 is unconstitutional by demonstrating that it furthers compelling state interests and is narrowly drawn to avoid unnecessary abridgments of constitutional rights.

Accordingly, we vacate the circuit court's order and judgment and remand this matter to the circuit court for further proceedings consistent with this opinion.

Appendices by concurring Judge:

In March 1993, the Cox News Service reported in relevant part as follows:

> The issue of whether people become homosexuals because of "nature or nurture" is one of the most controversial subjects scientists have confronted in recent years. Until the middle 1980s, the prevailing view among most scientists was that homosexual "tendencies" were mostly the result of upbringing. Later, researchers at the Salk Institute in San Diego found anatomical differences between homosexual and heterosexual men in parts of the brain noted for differences between men and women. Theories gravitate to the role of male sex hormones.

The Honolulu Advertiser, March 12, 1993, at A-24, col. 1.

> It is natural, therefore, that just as parents have the inclination and right to wish to influence the development of a child's character, they have the inclination and right to try to influence a child's sexual orientation. Gay advocates argue, however, that such influence is an illusion. Sexual orientation, they claim, is biologically fated and thus entirely impervious to environmental influence.

The Honolulu Advertiser, May 2, 1993, at B-2, cols. 3, 4 and 5.

> If heterosexuality, homosexuality, bisexuality, and asexuality are " biologically fated then the word "sex" also includes those differences. Therefore, the questions whether heterosexuality, homosexuality, bisexuality, and asexuality are "biologically fated" are relevant questions of fact which must be determined before the issue presented in this case can be answered. If the answers are yes, then each person's "sex" includes both the "biologically fated" male-female difference and the "biologically fated" sexual orientation difference, and the Hawaii Constitution probably bars the State from discriminating against the sexual orientation difference by permitting opposite-sex Hawaii Civil Law Marriages and not permitting same-sex Hawaii Civil Law Marriages. If the answers are no, then each person's "sex" does not include the sexual orientation difference, and the Hawaii Constitution may permit the State to encourage heterosexuality and discourage homosexuality, bisexuality, and asexuality by permitting opposite-sex Hawaii Civil Law Marriages and not permitting same-sex Hawaii Civil Law Marriages.

Defense of Marriage Act

In determining the meaning of any Act of Congress, or of any ruling, regulation, or interpretation of the various administrative bureaus and agencies of the United States, the word "marriage" means only a legal union between one man and one woman as husband and wife, and the word "spouse" refers only to a person of the opposite sex who is a husband or a wife.[19]

Goodridge et al. v. Department of Public Health[20]

November 2003

Present: Marshall, C.J., Greaney, Ireland, Spina, Cowin, Sosman, & Cordy, J.J.

MARSHALL, C.J.

Marriage is a vital social institution. The exclusive commitment of two individuals to each other nurtures love and mutual support; it brings stability to our society. For those who choose to marry, and for their children, marriage provides an abundance of legal, financial, and social benefits. In return it imposes weighty legal, financial, and social obligations. The question before us is whether, consistent with the Massachusetts Constitution, the Commonwealth may deny the protections, benefits, and obligations conferred by civil marriage to two individuals of the same sex who wish to marry. We conclude that it may not. The Massachusetts Constitution affirms the dignity and equality of all individuals. It forbids the creation of second-class citizens. In reaching our conclusion we have given full deference to the arguments made by the Commonwealth. But it has failed to identify any constitutionally adequate reason for denying civil marriage to same-sex couples.

We are mindful that our decision marks a change in the history of our marriage law. Many people hold deep-seated religious, moral, and ethical convictions that marriage should be limited to the union of one man and one woman, and that homosexual conduct is immoral. Many hold equally strong religious, moral, and ethical convictions that same-sex couples are entitled to be married, and that homosexual persons should be treated no differently than their heterosexual neighbors. Neither view answers the question before us. Our concern is with the Massachusetts Constitution as a charter of governance for every person properly within its reach. "Our obligation is to define the liberty of all, not to mandate our own moral code."

Whether the Commonwealth may use its formidable regulatory authority to bar same-sex couples from civil marriage is a question not previously addressed by a Massachusetts appellate court. It is a question the United States Supreme Court left open as a matter of Federal law in Lawrence, where it was not an issue. There, the Court affirmed that the core concept of common human dignity protected by the Fourteenth Amendment to the United States Constitution precludes government intrusion into the deeply personal realms of consensual adult expressions of intimacy and one's choice of an intimate partner. The Court also reaffirmed the central role that decisions whether to marry or have children bear in shaping one's identity. The Massachusetts Constitution is, if anything, more protective of individual liberty and equality than the Federal Constitution; it may demand broader protection for fundamental rights; and it is less tolerant of government intrusion into the protected spheres of private life.

Barred access to the protections, benefits, and obligations of civil marriage, a person who enters into an intimate, exclusive union with another of the same sex is arbitrarily deprived of membership in one of our community's most rewarding and cherished institutions. That exclusion is incompatible with the constitutional principles of respect for individual autonomy and equality under law.

The plaintiffs are fourteen individuals from five Massachusetts counties. As of April 11, 2001, the date they filed their complaint, the plaintiffs Gloria Bailey, sixty years old, and Linda Davies, fifty-five years old, had been in a committed relationship for thirty years; the plaintiffs Maureen Brodoff, forty-nine years old, and Ellen Wade, fifty-two years old, had been in a committed relationship for twenty years and lived with their twelve year old daughter; the plaintiffs Hillary Goodridge, forty-four years old, and Julie Goodridge, forty-three years old, had been in a committed relationship for thirteen years and lived with their five year old daughter; the plaintiffs Gary Chalmers, thirty-five years old, and Richard Linnell, thirty-seven years old, had been in a committed relationship for thirteen years and lived with their eight year old daughter and Richard's mother; the plaintiffs Heidi Norton, thirty-six years old, and Gina Smith, thirty-six years old, had been in a committed relationship for eleven years and lived with their two sons, ages five years and one year; the plaintiffs Michael Horgan, forty-one years old, and David Balmelli, forty-one years old, had been in a committed relationship for seven years; and the plaintiffs David Wilson, fifty-seven years old, and Robert Compton, fifty-one years old, had been in a committed relationship for four years and had cared for David's mother in their home after a serious illness until she died.

The plaintiffs include business executives, lawyers, an investment banker, educators, therapists, and a computer engineer. Many are active in church, community, and school groups. They have employed such legal means as are available to them—for example, joint adoption, powers of attorney, and joint ownership of real property—to secure aspects of their relationships. Each plaintiff attests a desire to marry his or her partner in order to affirm publicly their commitment to each other and to secure the legal protections and benefits afforded to married couples and their children.

The Department of Public Health (department) is charged by statute with safeguarding public health. Among its responsibilities, the department oversees the registry of vital records and statistics (registry), which "enforce[s] all laws" relative to the issuance of marriage licenses and the keeping of marriage records, and which promulgates policies and procedures for the issuance of marriage licenses by city and town clerks and registers. The registry is headed by a registrar of vital records and statistics (registrar), appointed by the Commissioner of Public Health (commissioner) with the approval of the public health council and supervised by the commissioner.

In March and April 2001, each of the plaintiff couples attempted to obtain a marriage license from a city or town clerk's office. As required under G.L. c. 207, they completed notices of intention to marry on forms provided by the registry, and presented these forms to a Massachusetts town or city clerk, together with the required health forms and marriage license fees. In each case, the clerk either refused to accept the notice of intention to marry or denied a marriage license to the couple on the ground that Massachusetts does not recognize same-sex marriage. Because obtaining a marriage license is a necessary prerequisite to civil marriage in Massachusetts, denying marriage licenses to the plaintiffs was tantamount to denying them access to civil marriage itself, with its appurtenant social and legal protections, benefits, and obligations.

On April 11, 2001, the plaintiffs filed suit in the Superior Court against the department and the commissioner seeking a judgment that "the exclusion of the [p]laintiff couples and other qualified same-sex couples from access to marriage licenses, and the legal and social status of civil marriage, as well as the protections, benefits and obligations of marriage, violates Massachusetts law." The plaintiffs alleged violation of the laws of the Commonwealth, including but not limited to their rights under arts. 1, 6, 7, 10, 12, and 16, and Part II, c. 1, § 1, art. 4, of the Massachusetts Constitution.]

The department, represented by the Attorney General, admitted to a policy and practice of denying marriage licenses to same-sex couples. It denied that its actions violated any law or that the plaintiffs were entitled to relief. The parties filed cross motions for summary judgment.

A Superior Court judge ruled for the department. In a memorandum of decision and order dated May 7, 2002, he dismissed the plaintiffs' claim that the marriage statutes should be construed to permit marriage between persons of the same sex, holding that the plain wording of G.L. c. 207, as well as the wording of other marriage statutes, precluded that interpretation. Turning to the constitutional claims, he held that the marriage exclusion does not offend the liberty, freedom, equality, or due process provisions of the Massachusetts Constitution, and that the Massachusetts Declaration of Rights does not guarantee "the fundamental right to marry a person of the same sex." He concluded that prohibiting same-sex marriage rationally furthers the Legislature's legitimate interest in safeguarding the "primary purpose" of marriage, "procreation." The Legislature may rationally limit marriage to opposite-sex couples, he concluded, because those couples are "theoretically ... capable of procreation," they do not rely on "inherently more cumbersome" noncoital means of reproduction, and they are more likely than same-sex couples to have children, or more children.

After the complaint was dismissed and summary judgment entered for the defendants, the plaintiffs appealed. Both parties requested direct appellate review, which we granted.

Although the plaintiffs refer in passing to "the marriage statutes," they focus, quite properly, on G.L. c. 207, the marriage licensing statute, which controls entry into civil marriage. As a preliminary matter, we summarize the provisions of that law.

General Laws c. 207 is both a gatekeeping and a public records statute. It sets minimum qualifications for obtaining a marriage license and directs city and town clerks, the registrar, and the department to keep and maintain certain "vital records" of civil marriages. The gatekeeping provisions of G.L. c. 207 are minimal. They forbid marriage of individuals within certain degrees of consanguinity, §§ 1 and 2, and polygamous marriages. They prohibit marriage if one of the parties has communicable syphilis, and restrict the circumstances in which a person under eighteen years of age may marry. The statute requires that civil marriage be solemnized only by those so authorized.

The record-keeping provisions of the law are more extensive. Marriage applicants file standard information forms and a medical certificate in any Massachusetts city or town clerk's office and tender a filing fee. The clerk issues the marriage license, and when the marriage is solemnized, the individual authorized to solemnize the marriage adds additional information to the form and returns it (or a copy) to the clerk's office (marriage certificate) The clerk sends a copy of the information to the registrar, and that information becomes a public record.

In short, for all the joy and solemnity that normally attend a marriage, governing entrance to marriage, is a licensing law. The plaintiffs argue that because nothing in that licensing law specifically prohibits marriages between persons of the same sex, we may interpret the statute to permit "qualified same sex couples" to obtain marriage licenses, thereby avoiding the question whether the law is constitutional. This claim lacks merit.

The Federal Marriage Amendment: To Protect the Sanctity of Marriage or Destroy Constitutional Democracy[21]

Joan Schaffner

Edited Relevant Excerpts
Reprinted with permission

State Experimentation

States have experimented with the definition of marriage over the years, demonstrating the usefulness of such experimentation. The most obvious parallel to the same-sex marriage debate is the history of anti-miscegenation statutes in this country. Long ago citizens began challenging state anti-miscegenation laws, which outlawed the marriage between individuals of different races. In 1852, Maine became one of the first states to uphold the constitutionality of an anti-miscegenation statute and declare interracial marriages null and void. It was not until 1948 that California became the first state to declare its anti-miscegenation statute unconstitutional. During the next twenty years, cases were brought in other states challenging similar anti-miscegenation statutes and several successfully invalidated them. However, it was not until 1967, when the U.S. Supreme Court held in *Loving v. Virginia* that no state could deny two people a marriage license merely because they were of different races. The Court held that this denial violated federal constitutional principles of liberty and equality. *Loving* thus set a new federal floor for individual rights throughout the nation. Interestingly, these events never would have transpired had the proposed anti-miscegenation amendment been ratified.

A similar history with regard to same-sex marriage is developing in our lifetime. The very first challenge to state marriage laws that deprived same-sex couples of a right to marry was brought in Minnesota. In 1971, the Minnesota Supreme Court dismissed the challenge and the U.S. Supreme Court declined to hear the appeal. For many years, same-sex couples challenged similar statutes in other states and lost.

However, in 1993, the Supreme Court of Hawaii held that denying same-sex couples a right to marry amounted to sex-based discrimination and violated the Equal

Rights Amendment of the Hawaii Constitution unless the state could justify the discriminatory treatment. On remand, the Hawaii trial judge found that the state failed to justify the discriminatory treatment and held the state statute violated the equal rights of same-sex partners. The case was appealed to the Supreme Court of Hawaii for a second time and, while on appeal, the state legislature passed two laws: (1) a Reciprocal Beneficiaries Act—granting couples ineligible to marry, certain basic benefits, and (2) a proposed constitutional amendment stating that the Hawaii legislature shall have the power to reserve marriage for opposite-sex couples. In 1998, the citizens of Hawaii approved the state constitutional amendment.

Meanwhile, same-sex couples in the state of Vermont were challenging the Vermont marriage laws, which denied same-sex couples marriage licenses. The challengers argued that the Vermont marriage laws violated the Common Benefits Clause of the Vermont Constitution. In 1999, the Vermont Supreme Court agreed and held that same-sex couples in Vermont are entitled to the same benefits and protections afforded by Vermont law to married opposite-sex partners. The Court did not find that the denial of a marriage license violated the constitution but rather the denial of the benefits associated with a marriage license did. The court instructed the Vermont legislature to craft an appropriate means for granting the same marital benefits to same-sex couples as enjoyed by opposite-sex couples. In April 2000, the Vermont Legislature created civil unions for such couples.

The *Goodridge* decision of the Massachusetts Supreme Court in November, 2003 is the most recent attempt by a state appellate court to expand the rights of same-sex couples. That court held that same-sex couples have a right to marry (not just a right to benefits), and that any separate but equal solution would be unconstitutional under the Massachusetts Constitution. In other words, the court held that a civil union recognizing same-sex couples and granting identical benefits is not constitutionally adequate in Massachusetts. The court directed the Massachusetts legislature to begin issuing marriage licenses to same-sex couples on May 17, 2004. The Governor of Massachusetts requested a stay from the Court while the legislature attempted to pass an amendment to the Massachusetts Constitution, but the request was not granted. The first same-sex couples were married in Massachusetts on May 17, 2004. When the federal government attempts to step in and cut-off the debate among the states, by setting a federal ceiling on individual rights nationwide, it destroys a central purpose of our dual state and federal system and, worse, enshrines inequality and prejudice into our Constitution.

B. Protecting States from Activist Sister States

The federal government has an interest in protecting the states from each other. In other words, each state is a separate sovereign, and no state can infringe the sovereignty of the other states. The proponents of the marriage amendment claim there is a legitimate need to amend the federal constitution to protect states from the "activist" judges of other states, like those in Massachusetts. They also argue that to allow individual states to issue marriage licenses to same-sex couples will place all other states in the position of having to recognize those marriages and to grant benefits to the couples in violation of their public policy.

This claim is misleading and unrealistic. The *Goodridge* decision and the marriage licenses granted in Massachusetts affect no other state or the federal government directly. Albeit indirectly, each state's laws affect every other state and the federal government.

The Full Faith and Credit Clause of the Constitution defines the credit that each state must grant to other states' legal acts and protects the states from overreaching sister states. The full faith and credit clause was drafted to reconcile the desire for diversity among the states with mutual respect for differences of opinion. While the clause states that each state must give full faith and credit to the public acts, records, and judicial proceedings of the other states, it is not absolute. The Supreme Court recognizes various exceptions to the generalized requirement of mutual respect, most notably when recognizing a judgment by a sister state that the home state finds fundamentally objectionable. In fact, it was common during the period when the anti-miscegenation statutes were being challenged for states not to recognize interracial marriages granted in other states on the basis that those marriages were odious, against the will of God and public policy, and an attempt by citizens to avoid their home state's restrictive marriage laws. Thus, there is precedent to support the idea that states need not recognize same-sex marriages granted in sister states if they are deemed contrary to that state's public policy.

Moreover, the federal legislature has already acted to protect states from sister states that have decided to permit same-sex marriages. In 1996, after the Hawaii Supreme Court decision on same-sex marriage was announced, the federal government enacted the Defense of Marriage Act ("DOMA") granting the states the power to refuse recognize a same-sex marriage entered into in another state. Many states followed suit and enacted their own statutes refusing to recognize same-sex marriages. These state statutes are designed to support states' claims, under the full faith and credit clause, that recognition of same-sex marriages would violate a fundamental state policy interest.

There are strong arguments that the federal DOMA statute is unconstitutional. The primary argument for challenging DOMA is that the Act "is the antithesis of a full faith and credit measure which lacks sufficient generality and, without adequate justification, encroaches upon an area traditionally reserved for state regulation." In mid-July 2004, the first suit challenging a state's power to refuse recognition of a valid Massachusetts same-sex marriage was filed in Florida. The plaintiffs sought declaratory judgment that Florida's and the federal government's refusal to recognize their Massachusetts marriage license violated their fundamental rights of equal protection and due process, the full faith and credit clause, the Privileges and Immunities Clauses, and the Commerce Clause of the U.S. Constitution. Although the court granted defendants' motion to dismiss, proponents [would be able to] use the possible success of such suits to strengthen their contention that the marriage amendment is necessary. If DOMA is struck down as unconstitutional, it is incapable of protecting states from the acts of sister states. However, even if DOMA were held unconstitutional, the full faith and credit clause arguably allows states to decline to recognize marriages that are against their states' public policy, providing sufficient protection to state sovereignty.

For Your Consideration

Consider the following statements and answer the questions that follow.

Thoughts on marriage as a question of law and public policy, by Robert George[22]

> The kind of defense of traditional marriage envisioned by conservatives, even if thought to be true from a moral viewpoint, is nevertheless unfair as a matter of law. "Law and policy must be neutral with regard to *competing* understandings of marriage and sexual morality."
>
> *On the other hand*
>
> Where a culture "promotes and supports a sound understanding of marriage it cannot allow ideologies and practices that are hostile to it," for that would undermine the institution of marriage in that culture.

Symbolic understanding of law[23]

THE LAW IS A TEACHER

> I. It will teach either that marriage is a reality in which people can choose to participate, but whose contours people cannot make and remake at will (e.g., a one-flesh communion of persons united in a form of life uniquely suitable to the generation, education, and nurturing of children).
>
> OR
>
> II. The law will teach that marriage is a mere convention, which is malleable in such a way that individuals, couples, or, indeed, groups, can choose to make of it whatever suits their desires, interests, or subjective goals.

Many would agree that we are living with the result of law's attempt to teach the first lesson. Do you agree, and how would you describe that result?

What would be the result of law's attempt to teach the second lesson?

The writer posing the question claims that:

> Given the biases of human sexual psychology, we will witness the development of practices and ideologies that truly tend to undermine the sound understanding and practice of marriage, together with the development of pathologies that tend to reinforce the very practices and ideologies that cause them.

If true, would this particular state of affairs be any different from what we are now experiencing as a result of law's attempt to teach lesson number one? How so?

Do you agree that "marriage is the kind of good that can be chosen and meaningfully participated in only by people who have a sound basic understanding of it and choose it with that understanding in mind?" What are the factors contributing to today's rate of divorce and the choice of many not to marry at all?

Chapter Ten

Gendered Roles & Questions of Equality under the Law

Excerpts from Seneca Falls Resolution 1848

The history of mankind is a history repeated injuries and usurpations on the part of man toward woman, having in direct object the establishment of an absolute tyranny over her. To prove this, let facts be submitted to a candid world.

He has compelled her to submit to laws in the formation of which she had no voice.

He has monopolized nearly all the profitable employment and from those she is permitted to follow she receives a scanty remuneration. He closes against her all the avenues to wealth and distinction that he leaves open to himself, permitting her to teach neither theology, medicine nor law.

He has denied her the facilities for obtaining a thorough education all colleges being closed against her.

He has endeavored in every way that he could to destroy her confidence in her own power, to lessen her self-respect, and to make her willing to lead a dependent and abject life.

The applicability of these reigning conceptions of equality, consent, and human need to at least half the population went unquestioned as women—including those owned neither in marriage, or in slavery—were deemed in theory to be participants in the social compact, at the same time that most women in life were not allowed to sign a contract.

Catherine MacKinnon[1]

Noble & Benign Roles

Bradwell v. Illinois[2]

December 1872

Mrs. Myra Bradwell, residing in the State of Illinois, made application to the judges of the Supreme Court of the State for a license to practice law. She accompanied her petition with the usual certificate from an inferior court of her good character, and that on due examination she had been found to possess the requisite qualifications.

And with this affidavit she also filed a paper asserting that, under the foregoing facts, she was entitled to the license prayed for by virtue of the second section of the fourth article of the Constitution of the United States, and of the fourteenth article of amendment of that instrument.

The statute of Illinois on the subject of admissions to the bar, enacts that:

> no person shall be permitted to practice as an attorney or counselor-at-law, or to commence, conduct, or defend any action, suit, or plaint, in which he is not a party concerned, in any court of record within the State, either by using or subscribing his own name or the name of any other person, without having previously obtained a license for that purpose from some two of the justices of the Supreme Court, which license shall constitute the person receiving the same an attorney and counselor-at-law, and shall authorize him to appear in all the courts of record within the State, and there to practice as an attorney and counselor-at-law, according to the laws and customs thereof.

On Mrs. Bradwell's application first coming before the court, the license was refused, and it was stated as a sufficient reason that under the decisions of the Supreme Court of Illinois, the applicant—as a married woman would be bound neither by her express contracts nor by those implied contracts which it is the policy of the law to create between attorney and client.

After the announcement of this decision, Mrs. Bradwell, admitting that she was a married woman—though she expressed her belief that such fact did not appear in the record—filed a printed argument in which her right to admission, notwithstanding that fact, was earnestly and ably maintained. The court thereupon gave an opinion in writing. Extracts are here given:

In many respects it is left to our discretion to establish the rules by which admission to this office shall be determined. But this discretion is not an arbitrary one, and must be held subject to at least two limitations. One is, that the court should establish such terms of admission as will promote the proper administration of justice; the second, that it should not admit any persons or class of persons who are not intended by the legislature to be admitted, even though their exclusion is not expressly required by the statute.

Whether, in the existing social relations between men and women, it would promote the proper administration of justice, and the general well-being of society, to permit women to engage in the trial of cases at the bar, is a question opening a wide field of discussion, upon which it is not necessary for us to enter.

It is sufficient to say that, in our opinion, the other implied limitation upon our power, to which we have above referred, must operate to prevent our admitting women to the office of attorney at law. If we were to admit them, we should be exercising the authority conferred upon us in a manner which, we are fully satisfied, was never contemplated by the legislature.

Female attorneys at law were unknown in England, and a proposition that a woman should enter the courts of Westminster Hall in that capacity, or as a barrister, would have created hardly less astonishment than one that she should ascend the bench of bishops, or be elected to a seat in the House of Commons.

That God designed the sexes to occupy different spheres of action, and that it belonged to men to make, apply, and execute the laws, was regarded as an almost axiomatic truth.

In view of these facts, we are certainly warranted in saying that when the legislature gave to this court the power of granting licenses to practice law, it was with not the slightest expectation that this privilege would be extended to women.

JUDGMENT AFFIRMED.

Concurrence:

As an historical fact, the civil law, as well as nature herself, has always recognized a wide difference in the respective spheres and destinies of man and woman. Man is, or should be, woman's protector and defender.

The natural and proper timidity and delicacy which belongs to the female sex evidently unfits if for many of the occupations of civil life. The constitution of the family organization, which is founded in the divine ordinance, as well as in the nature of things, indicates the domestic sphere as that which properly belongs to the domain and functions of womanhood.

The harmony, not to say identity, of interests and views which belong, or should belong, to the family institution is repugnant to the idea of a woman adopting a distinct and independent career from that of her husband. So firmly fixed was this sentiment in the founders of the common law that it became a maxim of that system of jurisprudence that a woman had no legal existence separate from her husband, who was regarded as her head and representative in the social state.

Notwithstanding some recent modifications of this civil status, many of the special rules of law flowing from and dependent upon this cardinal principle still exist in full force in most States. One of these is, that a married woman is incapable, without her husband's consent, of making contracts which shall be binding on her or him. This very incapacity was one circumstance which the Supreme Court of Illinois deemed important in rendering a married woman incompetent fully to perform the duties and trusts that belong to the office of an attorney and counselor.

It is true that many women are unmarried and not affected by any of the duties, complications, and incapacities arising out of the married state, but these are exceptions to the general rule. The paramount destiny and mission of woman are to fulfill the noble and benign offices of wife and mother. This is the law of the Creator. And the rules of civil society must be adapted to the general constitution of things, and cannot be based upon exceptional cases.

The humane movements of modern society, which have for their object the multiplication of avenues for woman's advancement, and of occupations adapted to her condition and sex, have my heartiest concurrence.

But I am not prepared to say that it is one of her fundamental rights and privileges to be admitted into every office and position, including those which require highly special qualifications and demanding special responsibilities.

In the nature of things it is not every citizen of every age, sex, and condition that is qualified for every calling and position. It is the prerogative of the legislator to prescribe regulations founded on nature, reason, and experience for the due admission of qualified persons to professions and callings demanding special skill and confidence. This fairly belongs to the police power of the State; and, in my opinion, in view of the peculiar characteristics, destiny, and mission of woman, it is within the province of the legislature to ordain what offices, positions, and callings shall be filled and discharged by men, and shall receive the benefit of those energies and responsibilities, and that decision and firmness which are presumed to predominate in the sterner sex.

For these reasons I think that the laws of Illinois now complained of are not obnoxious to the charge of abridging any of the privileges and immunities of citizens of the United States.

Dissent

From many of our cases the conclusion is irresistible, that the profession of the law, like the clerical profession and that of medicine, is an avocation open to every citizen of the United States. And while the legislature may prescribe qualifications for entering upon this pursuit, they cannot, under the guise of fixing qualifications, excluded a class of citizens from admission to the bar. The legislature may say at what age candidates shall be admitted; may elevate or depress the standard of learning required. But a qualification, to which a whole class of citizens never can attain, is not a regulation of admission to the bar, but is, as to such citizens, a prohibition. For instance, a State legislature could not, in enumerating the qualifications, require the candidate to be a White citizen.

This would be the exclusion of all colored citizens, without regard to age, character, or learning.

Yet no sound mind can draw a distinction between such an act and a custom, usage, or law of a State, which denies this privilege to all female citizens, without regard to age, character, or learning.

If the legislature may, under pretense of fixing qualifications, declare that no female citizen shall be permitted to practice law, it may as well declare that no colored citizen shall practice law; for the only provision in the Constitution of the United States which secures to colored male citizens the privilege of admission to the bar, or the pursuit of the other ordinary avocations of life, is the provision that "no State shall make or enforce any law which shall abridge the privileges or immunities of a citizen." And if this provision does protect the colored citizen, then it protects every citizen, Black or white, male or female.

Now, Mrs. Bradwell is a citizen of the United States, and of the State of Illinois, residing therein; she has been judicially ascertained to be of full age, and to possess the requisite character and learning. Still admission to the bar was denied her, not upon the ground that she was not a citizen; not for want of age or qualification; not because the profession of the law is not one of those avocations which are open to every American citizen as matter of right, upon complying with the reasonable regulations prescribed by the legislature; but first upon the ground that inconvenience would result from permitting her to enjoy her legal rights in this, to wit, that her clients might have difficulty in enforcing the contracts they might make with her, as their attorney, because of her being a married woman; and, finally, on the ground of her sex, merely.

Notwithstanding the argument against adopting the Fourteenth Amendment in the full scope of its language, is futile to resist its full and proper operation, now that it has been adopted. But that objection is really without force; for Mrs.

Bradwell, admitted to the bar, becomes an officer of the court, subject to its summary jurisdiction. Any malpractice or unprofessional conduct towards her client would be punishable by fine, imprisonment, or expulsion from the bar, or by all three. Her clients would, therefore, not be compelled to resort to actions at law against her. The objection arising from her coverture was in fact abandoned, in its more full consideration of the case, by the court itself; and the refusal put upon the fact that the statute of Illinois, interpreted by the light of early days, could not have contemplated the admission of any woman, though unmarried, to the bar.

But whatever the statute of Illinois meant, I maintain that the Fourteenth Amendment opens to every citizen of the United States, male or female, Black or white, married or single, the honorable professions as well as the servile employments of life; and that no citizen can be excluded from any one of them. Intelligence, integrity, and honor are the only qualifications that can be prescribed as conditions precedent to an entry upon any honorable pursuit or profitable avocation, and all the privileges and immunities which I vindicate to a colored citizen, I vindicate to our mothers, our sisters, and our daughters. The inequalities of sex will undoubtedly have their influence, and be considered by every client desiring to employ counsel.

There may be cases in which a client's rights can only be rescued by an exercise of the rough qualities possessed by men. There are many causes in which the silver voice of woman would accomplish more than the severity and sternness of man could achieve. Of a bar composed of men and women of equal integrity and learning, women might be more or less frequently retained, as the taste or judgment of clients might dictate. But the broad shield of the Constitution is over them all, and protects each in that measure of success which his or her individual merits may secure.

Minor v. Happersett[3]

1874

The Fourteenth Amendment to the Constitution of the United States, in its first section, thus ordains; All persons born or naturalized in the United States, and subject to the jurisdiction thereof, are citizens of the United States, and of the State wherein they reside. No State shall make or enforce any law, which shall abridge the privileges or immunities of citizens of the United States. Nor shall any State deprive any person of life, liberty, or property, without due process of law; nor deny to any person within its jurisdiction, the equal protection of the laws.

And the Constitution of the State of Missouri thus ordains:

"Every male citizen of the United States shall be entitled to vote."

Under a statute of the State all persons wishing to vote at any election, must previously have been registered in the manner pointed out by the statute, this being a condition precedent to the exercise of the elective franchise.

Facts: In this state of things, on the 15th of October, 1872 (one of the days fixed by law for the registration of voters), Mrs. Virginia Minor, a native born, free, White citizen of the United States, and of the State of Missouri, over the age of twenty-one years, wishing to vote for electors for President and Vice-President of the United States, and for a representative in Congress, and for other officers, at the general election held in November, 1872, applied to one Happersett, the registrar of voters, to register her as a lawful voter, which he refused to do, assigning for cause that she was not a "male citizen of the United States," but a woman. She thereupon sued him in one of the inferior State courts of Missouri, for wilfully refusing to place her name upon the list of registered voters, by which refusal she was deprived of her right to vote.

The Supreme Court affirmed the judgment in favor of defendant registrar who refused to register plaintiff female as a lawful voter.

The Court held that suffrage was not coextensive with citizenship and that the Constitution had not added the right of suffrage to the privileges and immunities of citizenship as they existed at the time the Constitution was adopted.

The word "citizen" is often used to convey the idea of membership in a nation.

In that sense, women, born of citizen parents within the jurisdiction of the United States, have always been considered citizens of the United States, as much so before the adoption of the Fourteenth Amendment to the Constitution as since.

The right of suffrage was not necessarily one of the privileges or immunities of citizenship before the adoption of the Fourteenth Amendment, and that amendment does not add to these privileges and immunities. It simply furnishes additional guaranty for the protection of such as the citizen already had.

At the time of the adoption of that amendment, suffrage was not coextensive with the citizenship of the States; nor was it at the time of the adoption of the Constitution.

Neither the Constitution nor the Fourteenth Amendment made all citizens voters.

A provision in a State constitution which confines the right of voting to "male citizens of the United States," is no violation of the Federal Constitution. In such a State women have no right to vote.

The question is presented in this case, whether, since the adoption of the Fourteenth Amendment, a woman, who is a citizen of the United States and of the State of Missouri, is a voter in that State, notwithstanding the provision of the constitution and laws of the State, which confine the right of suffrage to men alone. We might, perhaps, decide the case upon other grounds, but this question is fairly made. From the opinion we find that it was the only one decided in the court below, and it is the only one which has been argued here. The case was undoubtedly brought to this court for the sole purpose of having that question decided by us, and in view of the evident propriety there is of having it settled, so far as it can be by such a decision, we have concluded to waive all other considerations and proceed at once to its determination.

It is contended that the provisions of the constitution and laws of the State of Missouri which confine the right of suffrage and registration therefore to men, are in violation of the Constitution of the United States, and therefore void. The argument is, that as a woman, born or naturalized in the United States and subject to the jurisdiction thereof, is a citizen of the United States and of the State in which she resides, she has the right of suffrage as one of the privileges and immunities of her citizenship, which the State cannot by its laws or constitution abridge.

There is no doubt that women may be citizens. They are persons, and by the Fourteenth Amendment "all persons born or naturalized in the United States and subject to the jurisdiction thereof" are expressly declared to be "citizens of the United States and of the State wherein they reside." But, in our opinion, it did not need this amendment to give them that position. Before its adoption the Constitution of the United States did not in terms prescribe who should be citizens of the United States or of the several States, yet there were necessarily such citizens without such provision.

There cannot be a nation without a people. The very idea of a political community, such as a nation is, implies an association of persons for the promotion of their general welfare.

Each one of the persons associated becomes a member of the nation formed by the association. He owes it allegiance and is entitled to its protection. Allegiance and protection are, in this connection, reciprocal obligations. The one is a compensation for the other; allegiance for protection and protection for allegiance.

To determine, then, who were citizens of the United States before the adoption of the amendment it is necessary to ascertain what persons originally associated themselves together to form the nation, and what were afterwards admitted to membership.

The Constitution does not, in words, say who shall be natural-born citizens. Resort must be had elsewhere to ascertain that. At common-law, with the nomenclature of which the framers of the Constitution were familiar, it was never doubted that all children born in a country of parents who were its citizens became themselves, upon their birth, citizens also. These were natives, or natural-born citizens, as distinguished from aliens or foreigners. Some authorities go further and include as citizens children born within the jurisdiction without reference to the citizenship of their parents.

As to this class there have been doubts, but never as to the first. For the purposes of this case it is not necessary to solve these doubts. It is sufficient for everything we have now to consider that all children born of citizen parents within the jurisdiction are themselves citizens. The words "all children" are certainly as comprehensive, when used in this connection, as "all persons," and if females are included in the last they must be in the first. That they are included in the last is not denied. In fact the whole argument of the plaintiffs proceeds upon that idea.

Under the power to adopt a uniform system of naturalization Congress, as early as 1790, provided "that any alien, being a free White person," might be admitted as a citizen of the United States, and that the children of such persons so naturalized, dwelling within the United States, being under twenty-one years of age at the time of such naturalization, should also be considered citizens of the United States, and that the children of citizens of the United States that might be born beyond the sea, or out of the limits of the United States, should be considered as natural-born citizens. These provisions thus enacted have, in substance, been retained in all the naturalization laws adopted since. In 1855, however, the last provision was somewhat extended, and all persons theretofore born or thereafter to be born out of the limits of the jurisdiction of the United States, whose fathers were, or should be at the time of their birth, citizens of the United States, were declared to be citizens also.

The amendment did not add to the privileges and immunities of a citizen. It simply furnished an additional guaranty for the protection of such as he already had. No new voters were necessarily made by it. Indirectly it may have had that effect, because it may have increased the number of citizens entitled to suffrage under the constitution and laws of the States, but it operates for this purpose, if at all, through the States and the State laws, and not directly upon the citizen.

The Constitution has not added the right of suffrage to the privileges and immunities of citizenship as they existed at the time it was adopted. This makes it proper to inquire whether suffrage was coextensive with the citizenship of the States at the time of its adoption. If it was, then it may with force be argued that suffrage was one of the rights which belonged to citizenship, and in the enjoyment of which every citizen must be protected. But if it was not, the contrary may with propriety be assumed. In this condition of the law in respect to suffrage in the several States it cannot for a moment be doubted that if it had been intended to make all citizens of the United States voters, the framers of the Constitution would not have left it to implication. So important a change in the condition of citizenship as it actually existed, if intended, would have been expressly declared.

And still again, after the adoption of the Fourteenth Amendment, it was deemed necessary to adopt a fifteenth, as follows: "The right of citizens of the United States to vote shall not be denied or abridged by the United States, or by any State, on account of race, color, or previous condition of servitude." The Fourteenth Amendment had already provided that no State should make or enforce any law which should abridge the privileges or immunities of citizens of the United States. If suffrage was one of these privileges or immunities, why amend the Constitution to prevent its being denied on account of race. Nothing is more evident than that the greater must include the less, and if all were already protected why go through with the form of amending the Constitution to protect a part?

As has been seen, all the citizens of the States were not invested with the right of suffrage. In all, save perhaps New Jersey, this right was only bestowed upon men and not upon all of them. Under these circumstances it is certainly now too late to contend that a government is not republican, within the meaning of this guaranty in the Constitution, because women are not made voters.

The same may be said of the other provisions just quoted. Women were excluded from suffrage in nearly all the States by the express provision of their constitutions and laws. If that had been equivalent to a bill of attainder, certainly its abrogation would not have been left to implication. Nothing less than express language would have been employed to effect so radical a change.

So also of the amendment which declares that no person shall be deprived of life, liberty, or property without due process of law, adopted as it was as early as 1791. If suffrage was intended to be included within its obligations, language better adapted to express that intent would most certainly have been employed. The right of suffrage, when granted, will be protected. He who has it can only be deprived of it by due process of law, but in order to claim protection he must first show that he has the right.

Muller v. Oregon[4]

1908

MR. JUSTICE BREWER delivered the opinion of the court.

On February 19, 1903, the legislature of the State of Oregon passed an act in these words:

Sec. 1 No female (shall) be employed in any mechanical establishment, or factory, or laundry in this State more than ten hours during any one day. The hours of work may be so arranged as to permit the employment of females at any time so that they shall not work more than ten hours during the twenty-four hours of any one day."

Sec. 3 made a violation of the provisions of the prior sections a misdemeanor, subject to a fine of not less than $10 nor more than $25.

On September 18, 1905, an information was filed in the Circuit Court of the State for the county of Multnomah, charging that the defendant "on the 4th day of September, A.D. 1905, in the county of Multnomah and State of Oregon, then and there being the owner of a laundry, known as the Grand Laundry, in the city of Portland, and the employer of females therein, did then and there unlawfully permit and suffer one Joe Haselbock, he, the said Joe Haselbock, then and there being an overseer, superintendent and agent of said Curt Muller, in the said Grand Laundry, to require a female, to wit, one Mrs. E. Gotcher, to work more than ten hours in said laundry on said 4th day of September, A.D. 1905, contrary to the statutes in such cases made and provided, and against the peace and dignity of the State of Oregon."

A trial resulted in a verdict against the defendant, who was sentenced to pay a fine of $10. The Supreme Court of the State affirmed the conviction.

The single question is the constitutionality of the statute under which the defendant was convicted so far as it affects the work of a female in a laundry. That it does not conflict with any provisions of the state constitution is settled by the decision of the Supreme Court of the State.

The contentions of the plaintiff are thus stated in his brief:

Because the statute attempts to prevent persons, sui juris, from making their own contracts, and thus violates the provisions of the Fourteenth Amendment, as follows:

No State shall make or enforce any law which shall abridge the privileges or immunities of citizens of the United States; nor shall any State deprive any person of life, liberty, or property, without due process of law; nor deny to any person within its jurisdiction the equal protection of the laws.'

Because the statute does not apply equally to all persons similarly situated, it is class legislation.

The statute is not a valid exercise of the police power. The kinds of work proscribed are not unlawful, nor are they declared to be immoral or dangerous to the public health; nor can such a law be sustained on the ground that it is designed to protect women on account of their sex. There is no necessary or reasonable connection between the limitation prescribed by the act and the public health, safety or welfare."

It is the law of Oregon that women, whether married or single, have equal contractual and personal rights with men. We may therefore say with perfect confidence that, with these three sections upon the statute book, the wife can deal, not only with her separate property, acquired from whatever source, in the same manner as her husband can with property belonging to him, but that she may make contracts and incur liabilities, and the same may be enforced against her, the same as if she were a femme sole. There is now no residuum of civil disability resting upon her which is not recognized as existing against the husband. The current runs steadily and strongly in the direction of the emancipation of the wife, and the policy, as disclosed by all recent legislation upon the subject in this State, is to place her upon the same footing as if she were a femme sole, not only with respect to her separate property, but as it affects her right to make binding contracts; and the most natural corollary to the situation is that the remedies for the enforcement of liabilities incurred are made coextensive and coequal with such enlarged conditions."

It thus appears that, putting to one side the elective franchise, in the matter of personal and contractual rights they stand on the same plane as the other sex. Their rights in these respects can no more be infringed than the equal rights of their brothers. We held in *Lochner* that a law providing that no laborer shall be required or permitted to work in a bakery more than sixty hours in a week or ten hours in a day was not as to men a legitimate exercise of the police power of the State, but an unreasonable, unnecessary and arbitrary interference with the right and liberty of the individual to contract in relation to his labor, and as such was in conflict with, and void under, the Federal Constitution.

This analysis is invoked by plaintiff as decisive of the question before us. But this assumes that the difference between the sexes does not justify a different rule respecting a restriction of the hours of labor.

Then follow extracts from over ninety reports of committees, bureaus of statistics, commissioners of hygiene, inspectors of factories, both in this country and in Europe, to the effect that long hours of labor are dangerous for women, primarily because of their special physical organization. The matter is discussed in these reports in different aspects, but all agree as to the danger.

It would of course take too much space to give these reports in detail. Following them are extracts from similar reports discussing the general benefits of short hours from an economic aspect of the question. In many of these reports individual instances are given tending to support the general conclusion.

Perhaps the general scope and character of all these reports may be summed up in what an inspector for Hanover says:

The reasons for the reduction of the working day to ten hours—(a) the physical organization of women, (b) her maternal functions, (c) the rearing and education of the children, (d) the maintenance of the home—are all so important and so far reaching that the need for such reduction need hardly be discussed.

It is undoubtedly true, as more than once declared by this court, that the general right to contract in relation to one's business is part of the liberty of the individual, protected by the Fourteenth Amendment to the Federal Constitution; yet it is equally well settled that this liberty is not absolute and extending to all contracts, and that a State may, without conflicting with the provisions of the Fourteenth Amendment, restrict in many respects the individual's power of contract.

That woman's physical structure and the performance of maternal functions place her at a disadvantage in the struggle for subsistence is obvious. This is especially true when the burdens of motherhood are upon her. Even when they are not, by abundant testimony of the medical fraternity continuance for a long time on her feet at work, repeating this from day to day, tends to injurious effects upon the body, and as healthy mothers are essential to vigorous offspring, the physical well-being of woman becomes an object of public interest and care in order to preserve the strength and vigor of the race.

Still again, history discloses the fact that woman has always been dependent upon man. He established his control at the outset by superior physical strength, and this control in various forms, with diminishing intensity, has continued to the present. As minors, though not to the same extent, she has been looked upon in the courts as needing especial care that her rights may be preserved. Education was long denied her, and while now the doors of the school room are opened and her opportunities for acquiring knowledge are great, yet even with that and the consequent increase of capacity for business affairs it is still true that in the struggle for subsistence she is not an equal competitor with her brother. Though limitations upon personal and contractual rights may be removed by legislation, there is that in her disposition and habits of life which will operate against a full assertion of those rights. She will still be where some legislation to protect her seems necessary to secure a real equality of right. Doubtless there are individual exceptions, and there are many respects in which she has an advantage over him; but looking at it from the viewpoint of the effort to maintain an independent position in life, she is not upon an equality.

Differentiated by these matters from the other sex, she is properly placed in a class by herself, and legislation designed for her protection may be sustained, even when like legislation is not necessary for men and could not be sustained. It is impossible to close one's eyes to the fact that she still looks to her brother and depends upon him. Even though all restrictions on political, personal and contractual rights were taken away, and she stood, so far as statutes are concerned, upon an absolutely equal plane with him, it would still be true that she is so constituted that she will rest upon and look to him for protection; that her physical structure and a proper discharge of her maternal functions—having in view not merely her own health, but the well-being of the race—justify legislation to protect her from the greed as well as the passion of man.

The limitations which this statute places upon her contractual powers, upon her right to agree with her employer as to the time she shall labor, are not imposed solely for her benefit, but also largely for the benefit of all. Many words cannot make this plainer. The two sexes differ in structure of body, in the functions to be performed by each, in the amount of physical strength, in the capacity for long-continued labor, particularly when done standing, the influence of vigorous health upon the future well-being of the race, the self-reliance which enables one to assert full rights, and in the capacity to maintain the struggle for subsistence. This difference justifies a difference in legislation and upholds that which is designed to compensate for some of the burdens which rest upon her.

We have not referred in this discussion to the denial of the elective franchise in the State of Oregon, for while it may disclose a lack of political equality in all things with her brother, that is not of itself decisive. The reason runs deeper, and rests in the inherent difference between the two sexes, and in the different functions in life which they perform.

For these reasons, and without questioning in any respect the decision in *Lochner v. New York*, we are of the opinion that it cannot be adjudged that the act in question is in conflict with the Federal Constitution, so far as it respects the work of a female in a laundry, and the judgment of the Supreme Court of Oregon is Affirmed.

Women in the Military

Frontiero v. Richardson[5]

May 1973

A servicewoman's application for increased quarters allowances and medical and dental benefits for her husband as a dependent was denied because she failed to demonstrate that her husband was dependent on her for more than one-half of his support, as required by 37 USCS 401, 403 (quarters allowances) and 10 USCS 1072, 1076 (medical and dental benefits). Thereupon the servicewoman instituted an action in the United States District Court for the Middle District of Alabama, contending that the statutes—which allow a serviceman to claim his wife as a dependent for such benefits without regard to whether she is in fact dependent upon him for any part of her support—unreasonably discriminated on the basis of sex in violation of the Due Process Clause of the Fifth Amendment.

The three-judge District Court upheld the constitutionality of the statutes.

On direct appeal, eight members of the United States Supreme Court reversed.

Military matters fall under the jurisdiction of the federal government.

While the Fifth Amendment contains no Equal Protection Clause, it does forbid discrimination that is so unjustifiable as to be violative of due process.

Classifications based upon sex, like classifications based upon race, alienage, and national origin, are inherently suspect and must therefore be subjected to close judicial scrutiny.

Under traditional equal protection analysis, a legislative classification must be sustained unless it is patently arbitrary and bears no rational relationship to a legitimate governmental interest. A departure from traditional rational basis analysis of statutes with respect to sex-based classifications is justified.

In considering the constitutionality of federal statutes containing classifications based on sex, the conclusion of Congress, as expressed in later enacted statutes, that such classifications are inherently invidious, is not without significance.

Under the applicable standard of strict judicial scrutiny, the statutory scheme whereby a servicewoman may not claim her husband as a dependent for the purposes of obtaining increased quarters allowance (37 USCS 401, 403) and medical and dental benefits (10 USCS 1072, 1076) unless she proves that he is in fact dependent upon her for over one-half of his support, whereas a serviceman is allowed to claim his wife without regard to whether she is dependent upon him for any part of her support, is unconstitutional as constituting an invidious discrimination against servicewomen in violation of the Due Process Clause of the Fifth Amendment, where the only purpose allegedly served by the dissimilar treatment of men and women was mere administrative convenience, saving the government money by conclusively presuming that wives of servicemen were financially dependent upon their husbands while requiring service women to establish dependency in fact, but the government failed to present evidence to show that such differential treatment in fact saved the government money.

[T]here can be no doubt that our Nation has had a long and unfortunate history of sex discrimination. Traditionally, such discrimination was rationalized by an attitude of "romantic paternalism" which, in practical effect, put women, not on a pedestal, but in a cage. Indeed, this paternalistic attitude became so firmly rooted in our national consciousness that, 100 years ago, a distinguished Member of this Court was able to proclaim:

Man is, or should be, woman's protector and defender. The natural and proper timidity and delicacy which belongs to the female sex evidently unfits it for many of the occupations of civil life. The constitution of the family organization, which is founded in the divine ordinance, as well as in the nature of things, indicates the domestic sphere as that which properly belongs to the domain and functions of womanhood. The harmony, not to say identity, of interests and views which belong, or should belong, to the family institution is repugnant to the idea of a woman adopting a distinct and independent career from that of her husband.

The paramount destiny and mission of woman are to fulfill the noble and benign offices of wife and mother. This is the law of the Creator." As a result of notions such as these, our statute books gradually became laden with gross, stereotyped distinctions between the sexes and, indeed, throughout much of the 19th century the position of women in our society was, in many respects, comparable to that of Blacks under the pre-Civil War slave codes. Neither slaves nor women could hold office, serve on juries, or bring suit in their own names, and married women traditionally were denied the legal capacity to hold or convey property or to serve as legal guardians of their own children. And although Black men were guaranteed the right to vote in 1870, women were denied even that right—which is itself "preservative of other basic civil and political rights" until adoption of the Nineteenth Amendment half a century later.

It is true, of course that the position of women in America has improved markedly in recent decades. Nevertheless, it can hardly be doubted that, in part because of the high visibility of the sex characteristic, women still face pervasive, although at times more subtle, discrimination in our educational institutions, in the job market and, perhaps most conspicuously, in the political arena.

Moreover, since sex, like race and national origin, is an immutable characteristic determined solely by the accident of birth, the imposition of special disabilities upon the members of a particular sex because of their sex would seem to violate "the basic concept of our system that legal burdens should bear some relationship to individual responsibility.

What differentiates sex from such non-suspect statuses as intelligence or physical disability, and aligns it with the recognized suspect criteria, is that the sex characteristic frequently bears no relation to ability to perform or contribute to society. As a result, statutory distinctions between the sexes often have the effect of invidiously relegating the entire class of females to inferior legal status without regard to the actual capabilities of its individual members.

We might also note that, over the past decade, Congress has itself manifested an increasing sensitivity to sex-based classifications. In Tit. VII of the Civil Rights Act of 1964, for example, Congress expressly declared that no employer, labor union, or other organization subject to the provisions of the Act shall discriminate against any individual on the basis of "race, color, religion, sex, or national origin." Similarly, the Equal Pay Act of 1963 provides that no employer covered by the Act "shall discriminate ... between employees on the basis of sex." And @ 1 of the Equal Rights Amendment, passed by Congress on March 22, 1972, and submitted to the legislatures of the States for ratification, declares that "equality of rights under the law shall not be denied or abridged by the United States or by any State on account of sex." Thus, Congress itself has concluded that classifications based upon sex are inherently invidious, and this conclusion of a coequal branch of Government is not without significance to the question presently under consideration.

With these considerations in mind, we can only conclude that classifications based upon sex, like classifications based upon race, alienage, or national origin, are inherently suspect, and must therefore be subjected to strict judicial scrutiny. Applying the analysis mandated by that stricter standard of review, it is clear that the statutory scheme now before us is constitutionally invalid.

The Government offers no concrete evidence, however, tending to support its view that such differential treatment in fact saves the Government any money. In order to satisfy the demands of strict judicial scrutiny, the Government must demonstrate, for example, that it is actually cheaper to grant increased benefits with respect to all male members, than it is to determine which male members are in fact entitled to such benefits and to grant increased benefits only to those members whose wives actually meet the dependency requirement. Here, however, there is substantial evidence that, if put to the test, many of the wives of male members would fail to qualify for benefits. And in light of the fact that the dependency determination with respect to the husbands of female members is presently made solely on the basis of affidavits, rather than through the more costly hearing process, the Government's explanation of the statutory scheme is, to say the least, questionable.

Rostker v. Goldberg[6]

1981

JUSTICE REHNQUIST delivered the opinion of the Court.

The question presented is whether the Military Selective Service Act [MSSA] violates the Fifth Amendment to the United States Constitution in authorizing the President to require the registration of males and not females.

Congress is given the power under the Constitution "To raise and support Armies," "To provide and maintain a Navy," and "To make Rules for the Government and Regulation of the land and naval Forces."

Registration provisions serve no other purpose beyond providing a pool for subsequent induction. Registration for the draft was discontinued in 1975. In early 1980, President Carter determined that it was necessary to reactivate the draft registration process. [The immediate impetus for this decision was the Soviet armed invasion of Afghanistan].

Congress agreed that it was necessary to reactivate the registration process, and allocated funds for that purpose.

Although Congress considered the question at great length it declined to amend the MSSA to permit the registration of women.

Article I, section 8 of the Constitution commits exclusively to the Congress the powers to raise and support armies, provide and maintain a Navy, and make rules for Government and regulation of the land and naval forces, and pursuant to these powers it lies within the discretion of the Congress to determine the occasions for expansion of our Armed Forces, and the means best suited to such expansion should it prove necessary."

[The] different treatment of men and women naval officers ... reflects, not archaic and over broad generalizations, but, instead, the demonstrable fact that male and female line officers in the Navy are not similarly situated with respect to opportunities for professional service. Current restrictions on women officers' participation in combat and in most sea duty closed off the same opportunities for promotion as men.

Congress recognized that its decision on registration involved judgments on military needs and operations, and that its decisions were entitled to particular deference: "The Supreme Court's most recent teachings in the field of equal protection cannot be read in isolation from its opinions giving great deference to the judgment of Congress and military commanders in dealing [with] the management of military forces and the requirements of military discipline.

The Court has made it unmistakably clear that even our most fundamental constitutional rights must in some circumstances be modified in the light of military needs, and that Congress' judgment as to what is necessary to preserve our national security is entitled to great deference. While proposals to register women were being rejected in the course of transferring funds to register males, Committees in both Houses which had conducted hearings on the issue were also rejecting the registration of women.

The foregoing clearly establishes that the decision to exempt women from registration was not the " 'accidental by-product of a traditional way of thinking about females firmly in mind.

No major country has women in combat jobs in their standing army. The existence of the combat restrictions clearly indicates the basis for Congress' decision to exempt women from registration. The purpose of registration was to prepare for a draft of combat troops. Since women are excluded from combat, Congress concluded that they would not be needed in the event of a draft, and therefore decided not to register them.

JUSTICE WHITE, with whom JUSTICE BRENNAN joins, dissenting.

Common sense and experience in recent wars, where women volunteers were employed in substantial numbers, belie this view of "reality." It should not be ascribed to Congress, particularly in the face of the testimony of military authorities, hereafter referred to, that there would be a substantial number of positions in the services that could be filled by women both in peacetime and during mobilization, even though they are ineligible for combat.

I would also have little difficulty agreeing to a reversal if all the women who could serve in wartime without adversely affecting combat readiness could predictably be obtained through volunteers. In that event, the equal protection component of the Fifth Amendment would not require the United States to go through, and a large segment of the population to be burdened with, the expensive and essentially useless procedure of registering women. But again I cannot agree with the Court, that Congress concluded or that the legislative record indicates that each of the services could rely on women volunteers to fill all the positions for which they might be eligible in the event of mobilization. On the contrary, the record as I understand it, supports the District Court's finding that the services would have to conscript at least 80,000 persons to fill positions for which combat-ready men would not be required. The consistent position of the Defense Department representatives was that their best estimate of the number of women draftees who could be used productively by the services in the event of a major mobilization would be approximately 80,000 over the first six months.

Of course, the division among us indicates that the record in this respect means different things to different people, and I would be content to vacate the judgment below and remand for further hearings and findings on this crucial issue. Absent that, however, I cannot agree that the record supports the view that all positions for which women would be eligible in wartime could and would be filled by female volunteers.

The Court also submits that because the primary purpose of registration and conscription is to supply combat troops and because the great majority of noncombat positions must be filled by combat-trained men ready to be rotated into combat, the absolute number of positions for which women would be eligible is so small as to be de minimis and of no moment for equal protection purposes, especially in light of the administrative burdens involved in registering all women of suitable age. There is some sense to this; but at least on the record before us, the number of women who could be used in the military without sacrificing combat readiness is not at all small or insubstantial, and administrative convenience has not been sufficient justification for the kind of outright gender-based discrimination involved in registering and conscripting men but no women at all.

As I understand the record, then, in order to secure the personnel it needs during mobilization, the Government cannot rely on volunteers and must register and draft not only to fill combat positions and those noncombat positions that must be filled by combat-trained men, but also to secure the personnel needed for jobs that can be performed by persons ineligible for combat without diminishing military effectiveness. The claim is that in providing for the latter category of positions, Congress is free to register and draft only men. I discern no adequate justification for this kind of discrimination between men and women. Accordingly, with all due respect, I dissent.

United States v. Virginia[7]

1996

Facts: Virginia Military Institute (VMI) is the sole single-sex school among Virginia's public institutions of higher learning. VMI's distinctive mission is to produce "citizen-soldiers," men prepared for leadership in civilian life and in military service. Using an "adversative method" of training not available elsewhere in Virginia, VMI endeavors to instill physical and mental discipline in its cadets and impart to them a strong moral code. Reflecting the high value alumni place on their VMI training, VMI has the largest per-student endowment of all public undergraduate institutions in the Nation. The United States sued Virginia and VMI, alleging that VMI's exclusively male admission policy violated the Fourteenth Amendment's Equal Protection Clause.

The District Court ruled in VMI's favor.

The Fourth Circuit reversed and remanded: ordered Virginia to remedy the constitutional violation. In response, Virginia proposed a parallel program for women: Virginia Women's Institute for Leadership (VWIL), located at Mary Baldwin College, a private liberal arts school for women.

The District Court found that Virginia's proposal satisfied the Constitution's equal protection requirement, and the Fourth Circuit affirmed. The appeals court deferentially reviewed Virginia's plan and determined that provision of single-gender educational options was a legitimate objective. Maintenance of single-sex programs, the court concluded, was essential to that objective. The court recognized, however, that its analysis risked bypassing equal protection scrutiny, so it fashioned an additional test, asking whether VMI and VWIL students would receive "substantively comparable" benefits. Although the Court of Appeals acknowledged that the VWIL degree lacked the historical benefit and prestige of a VMI degree, the court nevertheless found the educational opportunities at the two schools sufficiently comparable.

GINSBURG, J., STEVENS, O'CONNOR, KENNEDY, SOUTER, and BREYER, J.J.,

VMI has notably succeeded in its mission to produce leaders; among its alumni are military generals, Members of Congress, and business executives. The school's alumni overwhelmingly perceive that their VMI training helped them to realize their personal goals. VMI's endowment reflects the loyalty of its graduates. Neither the goal of producing citizen-soldiers nor VMI's implementing methodology is inherently unsuitable to women. And the school's impressive record in producing leaders has made admission desirable to some women. Nevertheless, Virginia has elected to preserve exclusively for men the advantages and opportunities a VMI education affords.

VMI today enrolls about 1,300 men as cadets. Its academic offerings in the liberal arts, sciences, and engineering are also available at other public colleges and universities in Virginia.

But VMI's mission is special. It is the mission of the school to:

> Produce educated and honorable men, prepared for the varied work of civil life, imbued with love of learning, confident in the functions and attitudes of leadership, possessing a high sense of public service, advocates of the American democracy and free enterprise system, and ready as citizen-soldiers to defend their country in time of national peril.

In contrast to the federal service academies, institutions maintained "to prepare cadets for career service in the armed forces," VMI's program "is directed at preparation for both military and civilian life":"[o]nly about 15% of VMI cadets enter career military service.

Their program is "an adversative, or doubting, model of education" which features "[p]hysical rigor, mental stress, absolute equality of treatment, absence of privacy, minute regulation of behavior, and indoctrination in desirable values." As one Commandant of Cadets described it, the adversative method " 'dissects the young student,' " and makes him aware of his " 'limits and capabilities,' " so that he knows " 'how far he can go with his anger, ... how much he can take under stress, ... exactly what he can do when he is physically exhausted.'

VMI cadets live in spartan barracks where surveillance is constant and privacy nonexistent; they wear uniforms, eat together in the mess hall, and regularly participate in drills. Entering students are incessantly exposed to the rat line, "an extreme form of the adversative model," comparable in intensity to Marine Corps boot camp. Tormenting and punishing, the rat line bonds new cadets to their fellow sufferers and, when they have completed the 7-month experience, to their former tormentors.

VMI's "adversative model" is further characterized by a hierarchical "class system" of privileges and responsibilities, a "dyke system" for assigning a senior class mentor to each entering class "rat," and a stringently enforced "honor code," which prescribes that a cadet " 'does not lie, cheat, steal nor tolerate those who do.

VMI attracts some applicants because of its reputation as an extraordinarily challenging military school, and "because its alumni are exceptionally close to the school." "[W]omen have no opportunity anywhere to gain the benefits of [the system of education at VMI]."

In 1990, prompted by a complaint filed with the Attorney General by a female high-school student seeking admission to VMI, the United States sued the Commonwealth of Virginia and VMI, alleging that VMI's exclusively male admission policy violated the Equal Protection Clause of the Fourteenth Amendment. Trial of the action consumed six days and involved an array of expert witnesses on each side.

In the two years preceding the lawsuit, the District Court noted, VMI had received inquiries from 347 women, but had responded to none of them. [S]ome women, at least," the court said, "would want to attend the school if they had the opportunity." The court further recognized that, with recruitment, VMI could "achieve at least 10% female enrollment"—"a sufficient 'critical mass' to provide the female cadets with a positive educational experience." And it was also established that "some women are capable of all of the individual activities required of VMI cadets." In addition, experts agreed that if VMI admitted women, "the VMI ROTC experience would become a better training program from the perspective of the armed forces, because it would provide training in dealing with a mixed-gender army."

The District Court ruled in favor of VMI, however, and rejected the equal protection challenge pressed by the United States. To succeed, the United States must show "at least that the classification serves important governmental objectives and that the discriminatory means employed are substantially related to the achievement of those objectives."

In response to the Fourth Circuit's ruling, Virginia proposed a parallel program for women: Virginia Women's Institute for Leadership (VWIL). The 4-year, state-sponsored undergraduate program would be located at Mary Baldwin College, a private liberal arts school for women, and would be open, initially, to about 25 to 30 students. Although VWIL would share VMI's mission—to produce "citizen-soldiers"—the VWIL program would differ, as does Mary Baldwin College, from VMI in academic offerings, methods of education, and financial resources.

Having determined, deferentially, the legitimacy of Virginia's purpose, the court considered the question of means. Exclusion of "men at Mary Baldwin College and women at VMI," the court said, was essential to Virginia's purpose, for without such exclusion, the Commonwealth could not "accomplish [its] objective of providing single-gender education."

The cross-petitions in this suit present two ultimate issues.

First, does the exclusion of women from VMI's extraordinary opportunities for military training and civilian leadership development, deny to women "capable of all of the individual activities required of VMI cadets," the equal protection of the laws guaranteed by the Fourteenth Amendment?

Second, if VMI's "unique" situation, as Virginia's sole single-sex public institution of higher education—offends the Constitution's equal protection principle, what is the remedial requirement?

Today's skeptical scrutiny of official action denying rights or opportunities based on sex responds to volumes of history. As a plurality of this Court acknowledged a generation ago, "our Nation has had a long and unfortunate history of sex discrimination." Through a century plus three decades and more of that history, women did not count. Not until 1920 did women gain a constitutional right to the franchise. And for a half century thereafter, it remained the prevailing doctrine that government, both federal and state, could withhold from women opportunities accorded men so long as any "basis in reason" could be conceived for the discrimination.

In 1971, for the first time in our Nation's history, this Court ruled in favor of a woman who complained that her State had denied her the equal protection of its laws. Without equating gender classifications, for all purposes, to classifications based on race or national origin, we have carefully inspected official action that closes a door or denies opportunity to women (or to men). Case law evolving since 1971 "reveal[s] a strong presumption that gender classifications are invalid"). To summarize the Court's current directions for cases of official classification based on gender: Focusing on the differential treatment or denial of opportunity for which relief is sought, the reviewing court must determine whether the proffered justification is "exceedingly persuasive." The burden of justification is demanding and it rests entirely on the State.

The heightened review standard our precedent establishes does not make sex a proscribed classification. Supposed "inherent differences" are no longer accepted as a ground for race or national origin classifications. Physical differences between men and women, however, are enduring: "[T]he two sexes are not fungible; a community made up exclusively of one [sex] is different from a community composed of both. Inherent differences" between men and women, we have come to appreciate, remain cause for celebration, but not for denigration of the members of either sex or for artificial constraints on an individual's opportunity. Sex classifications may be used to compensate women "for particular economic disabilities [they have] suffered," to "promot[e] equal employment opportunity, to advance full development of the talent and capacities of our Nation's people. But such classifications may not be used, as they once were, to create or perpetuate the legal, social, and economic inferiority of women.

Virginia's public institutions of higher learning include an incomparable military college, Virginia Military Institute (VMI). The United States maintains that the Constitution's equal protection guarantee precludes Virginia from reserving exclusively to men the unique educational opportunities VMI affords. We agree.

Measuring the record in this case against the review standard just described, we conclude that Virginia has shown no "exceedingly persuasive justification" for excluding all women from the citizen-soldier training afforded by VMI.

We therefore affirm the Fourth Circuit's initial judgment, which held that Virginia had violated the Fourteenth Amendment's Equal Protection Clause. Because the remedy proffered by Virginia—the Mary Baldwin VWIL program—does not cure the constitutional violation, i.e., it does not provide equal opportunity, we reverse the Fourth Circuit's final judgment in this case.

Nuances of Gender Discrimination

The nuances of gender discrimination are subtle and pervasive. Catherine MacKinnon notes that the problem with equality law is that it operates in ways that preclude redress unless sexism plays out like racism. In many ways it does.

According to Vicki Schultz, in ***Reconceptualizing Sexual Harassment***:

> A core element of [sexual] harassment is conduct having the aim or effect of undermining [women's] work competence. Sometimes this conduct assumes a blatant form. [S]upervisors or coworkers openly question a woman's right to hold the job at all: They tell her she is not cut out for the work, inform her that she should be at home with her children, or greet her with a "Men only" sign or equally graphic announcement that she is unwelcome. More typically, the men verbally demean a woman's competence or ability to do the job, the content of the denigration varying with the type of work. Sometimes, it takes the form of belittling a woman's physical prowess, as in firefighting and corrections. Sometimes, it takes the form of disparaging her technical competence, as in the trades, sciences, or medicine. Sometimes, it takes the form of denigrating her intellectual achievement, as in the academy. Sometimes, it takes the form of questioning her capacity for adequate aggressiveness, as in police work or sales. Sometimes, it takes the form of characterizing her as overly aggressive or abrasive, as in law, management, or other elite professions. Sometimes, it takes the form of simply pronouncing her generally incompetent or unproductive. And, all too often, it takes the form of calling her dumb, stupid, or worthless: "You're a woman, what do you know?"
>
> Perhaps even more dangerous than such verbal denigration of women's competence, men can take actions that convert those statements into self-fulfilling prophesies. As the cases already analyzed in this Article reveal, there are diverse methods of subverting a woman's perceived or actual competence; the form of the conduct again varies with the occupational setting. Sometimes, it takes the form of deliberate sabotage of a woman's work performance, such as stealing a policewoman's case files, informing a lab worker that faulty equipment is sound, falsifying medical records to make it appear as though a female surgery resident made an error, or simply assigning her tasks that are impossible to accomplish. Sometimes, it takes the form of denying a woman adequate training, assignments, or other opportunities to learn a job fully, refusing to mentor her, or ostracizing her from the informal networks through which crucial job skills are passed on. Sometimes, it takes the form of evaluating a woman's performance by sexist and differential standards, or requiring her to perform service-oriented tasks that are outside her job description, such as cleaning, serving coffee, or providing secretarial support. Sometimes, it takes the form of denying a woman the privileges and perks needed to succeed on the job, as, for example, withholding from saleswomen or managers the right to deal with clients or the use of a company car, credit card, or office. Sometimes, it takes the form of assigning a woman duties

> below her skill level or extending her forms of "help" that signal she is incompetent to perform the simplest of tasks. Sometimes, it takes the form of gender-neutral acts of physical assault, verbal taunts, or other hazing in order to demoralize a woman psychologically or to threaten or intimidate her physically. And, far too frequently, it even takes the form of discrediting her mental stability or sanity.[8]

Women have been close to 50% of graduating classes in American law schools for decades, yet represent—on average—roughly 15% or less of big firm partners and federal judges. Women are 16% of a 435 member House of Representatives and 16% of the United States Senate. In legal academia, tenure positions are disappearing. Women hold only 25% of those positions, while lower paying, long-term, employment-at-will contracts, and short-term adjunct and legal instructor positions are increasing and *disproportionately* staffed by women.

A routine variety of explanations are offered for women's lack of progress in law and other fields. For example, in 2006, Lawrence H. Summers, the recent former president of Harvard University, explained that the relative dearth of women in the upper ranks of science might be the result of "innate" intellectual deficiencies, particularly in mathematics.[9]

A July 2006 article featured in the Washington Post, *entitled **Male Scientist Writes of Life as Female Scientist Biologist,*** provides an interesting counter perspective.[10]

> Neurobiologist Ben Barres has a unique perspective on former Harvard president Lawrence Summers's assertion that innate differences between the sexes might explain why many fewer women than men reach the highest echelons of science. That's because Barres used to be a woman himself.

Barres, a neurobiologist at Stanford University's Medical Center, was named Barbara at birth. He changed his name to Ben after deciding to undergo sex re-assignment, a process that he completed in 1997. Barres published an article in July 2006, citing institutional bias as the reason for the shortage of women in the sciences.[11] He reports that following his operation, another scientist who was unaware of it was heard to say, "Ben Barres gave a great seminar today, but then his work is much better than his sister's." The scientist assumed that he and Barbara were related.

> As a female undergraduate at MIT, Barres once solved a difficult math problem that stumped many male classmates, only to be told by a professor: "Your boyfriend must have solved it for you."
>
> "By far," Barres wrote, "the main difference I have noticed is that people who don't know I am transgendered treat me with much more respect" than when he was a woman. "I can even complete a whole sentence without being interrupted by a man."
>
> Barres said the switch had given him access to conversations that would have excluded him previously: "I had a conversation with a male surgeon and he told me he had never met a woman surgeon who was as good as a man."
>
> Barres said he has realized from personal experience that many men are unconscious of the privileges that come with being male, which leaves them unable to countenance talk of glass ceilings and discrimination.

New York Times reporter Cornelia Dean wrote an article during the fall of 2006, for the papers science section, entitled ***Institutions Hinder Female Academics, Panel Says.***[12] Headed by Dr. Donna Shalala, a former Secretary of Health and Human Services who is now president of the University of Miami, the panel was convened by the National Academy of Sciences. Its members included Elizabeth Spelke, a professor of psychology at Harvard, Ruth Simmons, the president of Brown University, and Ana Maria Cauce, a psychologist at the University of Washington. The Panel's report, "*Beyond Bias and Barriers: Fulfilling the Potential of Women in Academic Science and Engineering*," was dedicated to electrical engineer Denice Denton, who served on the panel and as chancellor of the University of California, Santa Cruz, before committing suicide in 2006. The report described overwhelming evidence that the real problems are unconscious but pervasive bias, "arbitrary and subjective" evaluation processes, and a work environment in which "anyone lacking the work and family support traditionally provided by a 'wife' is at a serious disadvantage."[13]

> For 30 years, the report says, women have earned at least 30 percent of the nation's doctorates in social and behavioral sciences, and at least 20 percent of the doctorates in life sciences. Yet they appear among full professors in those fields at less than half those levels. Women from minorities are "virtually absent."[14]

Former general counsel of Immigration and Naturalization Service recently testified before the Senate Judiciary Committee seeking *corporate-friendly* immigration policies on behalf of his new employers, a group of Fortune 500 companies from several industries. His job is to make sure Senators understand just how much America's economic vitality is weakening in relation to China, India and Japan.[15] The question raised by the panel discussed above was how is that in the era of global competition the nation could afford such under use of human capital: We have incontrovertible data that women do have the ability to do science and engineering at a very high level "Why aren't they electing these fields when the national need and the opportunities in the fields are so great?"

When high-ranking academics are not offering explanations that center on women's capabilities, they resort to discussions of women's natural tendencies to choose motherhood over career, women are uncompetitive and less productive partly because they take too much time off for their families. Significant studies demonstrate that pressures mount toward a kind of social-darwinism that places a different set of demands upon women that could hardly be characterized as a choice, or trade-off between two desirable ends.[16]

> Studies of women physicians, for example, have shown that although the supply of women physicians has dramatically increased (500% between 1970 and 1985), women physicians continue to choose or to be shunted into particular specialties that are either circumscribed in terms of time demands or have softer, more feminine edges. They tend to take salaried positions while 80% of male physicians are self-employed. Women physicians make about $50,000 less per year than their male colleagues, and are poorly represented in academic posts, especially at the administrative level. Furthermore, when women physicians are compared to male physicians, they are less likely to be married, less likely to have children, less likely to receive help from their spouses for childcare and household responsibilities, less likely to receive academic promotions. They feel significantly more tension between family and career than their male peers and are more likely to change their behavior to accommodate family considerations. Much of this situation has been true throughout the twentieth century, and most women physicians who have had successful careers and families too have generally been extraordinarily privileged and often gifted "superwomen." Those women mounted piecemeal, personal and private solutions to dilemmas which loomed unsolvable to many others who might have also made perfectly satisfactory women doctors, had access to such a career been structured differently. Recent studies of women lawyers and corporate executives have revealed strikingly similar patterns.[17]

Why Do So Few Women Reach the Top of Big Law Firms?[18]

Timothy L. O'Brien
New York Times

Bettina B. Plevan, a 60-year-old specialist in labor and employment law, has spent more than three decades at Proskauer navigating the professional riptides and intellectual cross-currents of firm life on her way to reeling in one of the legal world's most storied and most lucrative prizes: a partnership.

"I decided I wanted to be a partner shortly after I got here—by nature I have a lot of drive, I'm competitive and I have a lot of energy," she says. "For me, being a partner was a way in which my talents and skills could be recognized. And I wanted that recognition."

Ms. Plevan is president of the New York City Bar Association, only the second woman to hold that position since the organization's founding in 1870. She has a job that makes her happy and reflects her sense of herself. She is an accomplished lawyer. She has arrived. She also is an anomaly.

Although the nation's law schools for years have been graduating classes that are almost evenly split between men and women, and although firms are absorbing new associates in numbers that largely reflect that balance, something unusual happens to most women after they begin to climb into the upper tiers of law firms. They disappear.

"What de-motivates them to want to continue working in the law?" Once law school graduation rates were substantially equalized between men and women, that pipeline was supposed to cause partnerships to equalize as well. The pipeline has been gushing for about two decades and partnership disparity remains.

According to Karen M. Lockwood, a partner at Howrey in Washington. "Law firms are way beyond discrimination—this is about advancement and retention. Problems with advancement and retention are grounded in biases, not discrimination.

Large firms are becoming larger, expanding their global reach and practice areas and are focused more tightly on benchmarks such as "billable hours" to assess the performance of individual lawyers. They also compete voraciously for coveted spots in news media reports that ranked them by financial yardsticks such as profit per partner. Those forces gained momentum in the 1990s and continue today. Women entering this environment discovered that men enjoyed some distinct advantages. Women lawyers enjoy less access to the networking and business development opportunities that flourish in largely male playgrounds—think golf courses or football games—or through an invitation for a casual after-work drink with a male boss. "Women aren't being adequately mentored.

Lauren Stiller Rikleen, a 52-year-old partner, details the hurdles facing female lawyers in her recently published book "Ending the Gauntlet: Removing Barriers to Women's Success in the Law." She writes that law firms need to reorganize if they want to encourage and retain women as partners, and that roadblocks—whether they be errant mentoring, opaque networking opportunities, low-grade case assignments or arbitrary male control of key management committees—should all be reviewed. "Law firms like to talk about running the firm like a business and looking at the numbers, but they're running on an institutional model that's about 200 years old."

Ms. Lockwood is also exploring the impact of what she describes as the "maternal wall" on female lawyers. She says that this wall is built on the unstated assumption among male partners that women who return to firms after having children will automatically be less willing to work hard or will be less capable than they were prior to that—resulting in less-choice assignments or less-senior postings.

According to Jane DiRenzo Pigott, "Women self-promote in a different way than men, and because women don't get their success acknowledged in the same way as men who more aggressively self-promote. For her part, Ms. Plevan says she has never been shy about saying, "I want," and that this has served her well in her career. She also said that she and her husband, who is a partner, carefully and jointly managed their family life together as they raised two sons, one of whom required extra attention because of a learning disability. The Plevans engineered this by cutting back on their social calendar, sharing household chores and making sure that at least one parent was home for dinner most nights. "I organized my personal life so I was able to move toward my goals." The Plevans' incomes allowed them to hire household help, and they had relatives nearby to help.

According to "Women in Law," a 2001 study by Catalyst, a New York research firm that tracks women's experiences in a wide range of workplaces, most male lawyers don't see a lack of mentoring and networking opportunities—or commitments to family and personal responsibilities—as significant barriers to women's advancement. Those biases, says Catalyst, are more pronounced in the legal world than in other industries and professions. Ms. Plevan agrees. "As long as firms are male-dominated, it's much less likely that firms will make changes to accept the challenges of work-life balance" she says. "It's not that men aren't receptive to these issues, it's that they're not aware."

"I think the pressures on women from spouses, family, peers, schools and others is huge. I think the real solution is a reassessment of the role that women play in the family," adds Ms. Matthai, who is president of the Los Angeles County Bar Association. "One thing we need is a sense of shared responsibilities for the household and, most importantly, shared responsibilities for taking care of the kids." Ms. Matthai said that conditions for women had improved a good deal over the last 30 years, but added: "We have a long way to go."

For Your Consideration

What changes might you anticipate in a discussion about the glass ceiling for women, if talented professional women opened their own law firms that provided quality childcare and related educational and recreational programs on site to serve their offspring from birth to 18 years of age?

It's time for a closer look at the demands of the market. Market explanations are interesting. Across disciplines, men usually explain studies that prove high levels of bias against professional women as a function of the market. The 18-member panel headed by Dr. Shalala had only one man, who is chancellor of the University of California, Berkeley, yet she notes that the National Academy of Sciences committee that reviewed the report had ten.[19] As final arbiters, combining theories of necessity and evolution effectively closes the debate on sex discrimination. Women who believe their time is better spent finding solutions to women's problems study the market and its overall effect on the quality of family life.

Understanding Domesticity

Cross-Dressing in the Master's Clothes[20]

Kathryn Abrams
109 Yale L.J. 745

A Review of UNBENDING GENDER: WHY FAMILY AND WORK CONFLICT AND WHAT TO DO ABOUT IT. By Joan Williams

The Bonds of Domesticity

Unbending Gender opens with a vivid portrait of the tensions between family and market work.

1. Men are consumed by the demands of their employers, salvaging only brief intervals to connect with their families.

2. Women, who remain the primary caregivers whatever their employment status, move frantically from dissatisfied employers to needy children, exhausting and disappointing themselves in the process. Mothers who devote themselves exclusively to caregiving—and the children who remain in their custody—are predictably impoverished upon divorce.

In Williams's analysis, it is not simply a lack of institutional expedients, such as family leave or flextime. It is domesticity, a complex system of norms and institutional arrangements that keeps men tethered to an increasingly demanding workplace, women professionally marginalized and economically dependent, and children often destitute upon their parents' divorce.

Domesticity is a system in which institutions reflect and perpetuate popular attitudes toward market and family work.

Domesticity is a complex system of gender norms.

Domesticity is an ideology and a practice that:

Positions men as "ideal workers" in the market

Positions women as economically marginalized caregivers in the home

It justifies this arrangement by reference to the innate characteristics of the two sexes and to the incontrovertible needs of corporations and of small children.

The normative assumptions of domesticity,are embodied in three central tenets: Employers are entitled to"ideal workers" who are immunized from family responsibilities; men are expected and entitled to perform as "ideal workers"; and women should have "all the time and love in the world to give" to their children.

A full program for change must address both attitudes and institutions.

These tenets are held in place by at least two supporting assumptions, which make it particularly difficult to glimpse the influence of domesticity or to reach it by structural or attitudinal reforms.

Williams does so by advocating legal changes that would require employers and families to recognize and to accommodate the work done by parents in caring for children.

While the practical, "can do" ethos of the book is invigorating, I remain unconvinced by the Deweyian aspect of Williams's pragmatism: the decision to deploy the norms of domesticity against themselves.

Whether "the master's tools," in the words of the late Audre Lorde, can disassemble "the master's house" is, to my mind, a context-specific question: It depends on the nature of the problem, the flexibility of the tools, and the durability of the house. Dismantling may well require more than rearrangement of the surface features of our work and family structure. One must strike at the attitudes toward:

Masculinity

Femininity

Capitalism

The State

These norms may be too institutionally entrenched for successful resolution by pluralizing options.

The first of these supporting assumptions is "commodification anxiety": a tendency to characterize (women's) familial labors as an expression of love and commitment that corresponds with our reluctance to regard family work as compensable labor. This undervaluing causes, legal actors and family members to underestimate caregivers' contributions to their families material well-being. It is why most women who stay at home end up impoverished upon divorce.

The second support for domesticity is the use of a rhetoric of choice to describe and justify work/family decisions. Motivated by liberal precepts and by psychological mechanisms of denial, men and women tend to see themselves as free agents, acting on their individual preferences in addressing family and work responsibilities.

What this assumption of "choice" obscures is both the constrained character of the alternatives available and the fact that all choices are rigorously conditioned by the normative "force field" created by domesticity. Workers affected by this "force field" make choices consistent with the basic premises, yet they experience and defend those choices as an authentic expression of their individual character. As with "commodification anxiety," this assumption makes it more difficult to see domesticity at work in the structure of market and family labor and to do something about it.

This is not simply a scuffle over maternity leaves or flextime schedules, but a complex, multifaceted system that renders most women professionally marginalized and economically dependent or destitute.

Williams draws the central elements of her portrait:

The assumption that employers are entitled to "ideal workers" free from family responsibilities.

That men are entitled to perform in this way regardless of their familial commitments.

That women, whatever their market labor commitments, should have "all the time and love in the world to give.

The belief that women who select among the slender and socially policed range of options available for accommodating market and family responsibilities are exercising authentic, autonomous choice.

To make matters more interesting, Williams addresses a larger historical discussion of the movement "from status to affect."

Williams describes in evocative detail how explanations emphasizing women's inferiority gave way to those emphasizing their characteristic domestic proclivities in accounting for the distinctive roles of women.

She proposes two kinds of initiatives:

Legal proposals which restructure the workplace to accommodate employees with important parenting responsibilities and redefine family income as the joint property of wage-earners and caregivers, both during marriage and, particularly, upon divorce.

The second initiatives are "discursive" or "talk"-related proposals, which reframe longstanding debates and provide conceptual and relational guidance as to how to proceed.

The path to change lies in pluralizing employers' and parents' options for managing market and family work, rather than directly challenging those choices that currently exist.

She offers a series of anti-discrimination actions aimed at protecting and demarginalizing part-time and flextime work, and she proposes a regime of joint property that would protect primary caregivers and their children upon divorce. Williams elaborates each of these claims in painstaking detail, demonstrating a care and conscientiousness about the nuts and bolts of her proposals that many legal scholars lack. Finally, the substantive vision enacted by Williams's proposals is itself positive: I have no doubt that, were we to wave a wand and enact Williams's legal changes, we would be considerably better off than we are today.

In a theory whose road-readiness is presented as an important virtue, judicial resistance or incomprehension is a more serious drawback in practice.

Even if we assume that courts will embrace these legal innovations, the proper question is not whether these changes will make us better off than we are today. The current structure of market and family work is prejudicial to virtually all parents (albeit in different ways), and many kinds of changes would have at least slight ameliorative effects.

The question, rather, is whether the changes proposed are sufficient to make important inroads on the tenacious, tentacular system of domesticity that Williams exposes.

Her proposals reflect important departures from the current abysmal arrangements, they quite explicitly leave intact many normative premises on which domesticity thrives: the single-minded, unencumbered worker as at least one vision of the ideal employee, and the "commodification anxiety" that renders courts and policymakers reluctant to assign market value to the work performed in the home.

Williams builds on an analysis introduced by feminists such as Vicki Schultz to argue that employers who construct workplaces around male bodies and male norms deny equal employment opportunities to women. To expect an employee to work overtime, to travel on short notice, or to undertake other tasks that require insulation from family needs is to presuppose an employee who is male or who is, at least, inhabiting a masculine gender role.

"Given that nearly ninety percent of women become mothers during their working lives,"that most of them work part-time or exclusively within the home, and that virtually all eschew overtime, to require the attributes of the "ideal worker" for promotion, benefits, or "plum" assignments is to deny the vast majority of women basic employment opportunities. To provide grounding for a prospective legal claim, Williams surveys a range of policies that individual employers have undertaken to accommodate familial responsibilities; she also reviews a sizeable empirical literature that demonstrates that these expedients reduce absenteeism and employee turnover and increase productivity and employee loyalty. She then proposes claims under Title VII and the Equal Pay Act that would establish that a failure to provide these options or to promote those who choose them is employment discrimination.

While men have slowly and incrementally expanded their role in childcare over the past two or three decades, it has been far more difficult to loosen their attachment to "primary provider" status within the family, a role that usually calls for "ideal-worker" performance.

Sociologist Michael Kimmel, for example, observes that some men's widely cited willingness to give up their jobs to spend more time with their children is "more often rhetorical than real; few men would actually switch places with their non-working wives if given the opportunity." This is partly because, within many corporate cultures, "investing more energy into the home is a form of treason" —a view that throws the normative weight of American capitalism into the effort to preserve the link between masculinity and provider status. But even where governmental and corporate cultures have become increasingly accommodating, men may struggle with conceptions of masculinity that have been instilled in a broad range of social settings. Evidence of this tendency is found in studies of paternal leaves in Norway and Sweden, countries that have striven to facilitate men's access to and use of paternity leaves by means of a broad range of governmental regulations. In these contexts, men take less frequent and shorter leaves and engage in different kinds and styles of parenting activities.

More interestingly, some of these fathers attempt to distinguish their parenting activities explicitly from those of mothers by criticizing the mothers' style of parenting or by designating certain activities, most notably housework, as outside the bounds of the paternal caregiving job. While scholars attribute some of these differences, such as those involving frequency or length of paternal leave, to structural features of market work, they see others, such as the explicit abstention from housework, as reflecting an attitudinal struggle over whether serious caregiving activity can be reconciled with dominant understandings of masculinity. Unless the norms that support a link between masculinity and provider status are identified, analyzed, and gradually revised—something that Williams seems reluctant to do—her family-friendly alternatives will remain hothouse flowers, artificially protected by a set of legal supports, but normatively inconsistent with their environment and viewed with suspicion or ambivalence by many employees. The price of Williams's reluctance to challenge bedrock norms of our economic and gender systems may be a limit on her ability to transform the structure of market work.

The present legal approach fails to recognize, Williams argues, that a market wage is in fact earned by two members of a two-parent family: the one who focuses on market work and the one who (employed or not) provides the stream of family services that permits him to function as an ideal worker.

"Have you and Tim picked out a name for the career obstacle yet?"

For Your Consideration

If you could wave a magic wand and provide a permanent solution for women's inequality, what would you do?

How relevant are the following factors?

According to Kathryn Abrams:

> [Self]-definition occurs, first, by becoming aware of the way that one's self, and one's self-conception, are socially constituted. A woman may become aware, for example, that images or attitudes she has regarding her body, her competence to perform certain tasks, or her strength or vulnerability in relation to others, are shaped by norms that describe these matters at least partly as a function of gender. Developing this awareness does not permit her to transcend these socially conditioned visions of self, but it allows her greater room in which to affirm, reinterpret, resist, or partially replace them. When she becomes aware of them not solely as attitudes that she holds, but as norms embedded in social institutions or practices that are transmitted to her and to others, she may begin to compare them with other feelings or intuitions that she has about herself. Though she does not have recourse to some complete, pre-social self that can be uncovered, she may draw on moments of insight that arise from her reflection on her experience, or attitudes she holds that are shaped by other social influences. This process of reflection and comparison, which is facilitated by her awareness of certain self-conceptions as socially shaped, may allow her to identify more strongly with certain images and strive for greater distance from others.[21]

Part Four

Information Privacy & the Role of Lawyers in the 21st Century

Army surveillance, like Army regimentation, is at war with the principles of the First Amendment. Those who already walk submissively will say there is no cause for alarm. But submissiveness is not our heritage. The First Amendment was designed to allow rebellion to remain as our heritage. The Constitution was designed to keep government off the backs of the people. The Bill of Rights was added to keep the precincts of belief and expression, of the press, of political and social activities free from surveillance. The Bill of Rights was designed to keep agents of government and official eavesdroppers away from assemblies of people. The aim was to allow men to be free and independent and to assert their rights against government.

Justice Marshall concurring in *Laird v. Tatum*

Chapter Eleven

Civil Liberties, National Security & USA PATRIOT Act

The following statement was read before casting the only NO vote in the Senate against the USA PATRIOT Act.

> Of course, there is no doubt that if we lived in a police state, it would be easier to catch terrorists. If we lived in a country that allowed the police to search your home at any time for any reason; if we lived in a country that allowed the government to open your mail, eavesdrop on your phone conversation, or intercept your email communication; if we lived in a country that allowed the government to hold people in jail indefinitely based on what they write or think, or based on mere suspicion that they are up to no good, then the government would no doubt discover and arrest more terrorists. But that probably would not be a country in which we would want to live. And that would not be a country for which we could, in good conscience, ask our young people to fight and die. In short, that would not be America. Preserving our freedom is one of the main reasons that we are now engaged in this new war on terrorism. We will lose that war without firing a shot if we sacrifice the liberties of the American people.[1]
>
> Sen. Russell Feingold, Wisconsin

Report from Electronic Privacy Information Center[2]

The Days Following September 11, 2001

The clumsily–titled Uniting and Strengthening America by Providing Appropriate Tools Required to Intercept and Obstruct Terrorism Act of 2001 (USA PATRIOT Act, or *USAPA*) introduced a plethora of legislative changes which significantly increased the surveillance and investigative powers of law enforcement agencies in the United States. The Act did not, however, provide for the system of checks and balances that traditionally safeguards civil liberties in the face of such legislation.

Legislative proposals in response to the terrorist attacks of September 11, 2001 were introduced less than a week after the attacks. President Bush signed the final bill, the USA PATRIOT Act, into law on October 26, 2001. Though the Act made significant amendments to over 15 important statutes, it was introduced with great haste and passed with little debate, and without a House, Senate, or conference report. As a result, it lacks background legislative history that often retrospectively provides necessary statutory interpretation.

The Act was a compromise version of the Anti–Terrorism Act of 2001 (ATA), a far–reaching legislative package intended to strengthen the nation's defense against terrorism. The ATA contained several provisions vastly expanding the authority of law enforcement and intelligence agencies to monitor private communications and access personal information. The final legislation included a few beneficial additions from the Administration's initial proposal: most notably, a so–called sunset provision (which provides that several sections of the act automatically expire after a certain period of time, unless they are explicitly renewed by Congress) on some of the electronic surveillance provisions, and an amendment providing judicial oversight of law enforcement's use of the FBI's Carnivore system.

However, the USA PATRIOT Act retains provisions appreciably expanding government investigative authority, especially with respect to the Internet. Those provisions address issues that are complex and implicate fundamental constitutional protections of individual liberty, including the appropriate procedures for interception of information transmitted over the Internet and other rapidly evolving technologies.

One of the most striking features of the USA PATRIOT Act is the lack of debate surrounding its introduction. Many of the provisions of the Act relating to electronic surveillance were proposed before September 11th, and were subject to much criticism and debate. John Podesta, White House Chief of Staff from 1998—2001, has questioned what has changed since then.

The events of September 11 convinced ... overwhelming majorities in Congress that law enforcement and national security officials need new legal tools to fight terrorism. But we should not forget what gave rise to the original opposition—many aspects of the bill increase the opportunity for law enforcement and the intelligence community to return to an era where they monitored and sometimes harassed individuals who were merely exercising their First Amendment rights. Nothing that occurred on September 11 mandates that we return to such an era.

John Podesta, **USA PATRIOT Act—The Good, the Bad, and the Sunset**[3]

When the legislative proposals were introduced by the Bush administration in the aftermath of September 11th, Attorney General John Ashcroft gave Congress one week in which to pass the bill—without changes. Vermont Democrat Patrick Leahy, chairman of the Senate Judiciary Committee, managed to convince the Justice Department to agree to some changes, and members of the House began to make significant improvements. However, the Attorney General warned that further terrorist acts were imminent, and that Congress could be to blame for such attacks if it failed to pass the bill immediately.

Extensive and hurried negotiation in the Senate resulted in a bipartisan bill, stripped of many of the concessions won by Sen. Leahy. Senator Thomas Daschle, the majority leader, sought unanimous consent to pass the proposal without debate or amendment; Senator Russ Feingold was the only member to object. Minor changes were made in the House, which passed the bill 357 to 66. The Senate and House versions were quickly reconciled, and the Act was signed into law on October 26, 2001.

Overview

The USA PATRIOT Act introduced sweeping changes to U.S. law, including amendments to:

- Wiretap Statute (Title III):

- Electronic Communications Privacy Act
- Computer Fraud and Abuse Act
- Foreign Intelligence Surveillance Act
- Family Education Rights and Privacy Act
- Pen Register and Trap and Trace Statute
- Money Laundering Act
- Immigration and Nationality Act
- Money Laundering Control Act
- Bank Secrecy Act
- Right to Financial Privacy Act
- Fair Credit Reporting Act

Senator Russ Feingold was particularly concerned with the effects the Act might have on the civil liberties of immigrants. Feingold expressed his concern and certainty that the enhanced authority to profile and engage in electronic surveillance would be disproportionately wielded:

Now here is where my caution in the aftermath of the terrorist attacks and my concerns over the reach of the anti–terrorism bill come together. To the extent that the expansive new immigration powers that the bill grants to the Attorney General are subject to abuse, who do we think that is most likely to bear the brunt of the abuse? It won't be immigrants from Ireland. It won't be immigrants from El Salvador or Nicaragua. It won't even be immigrants from Haiti or Africa. It will be immigrants from Arab, Muslim and south Asian countries. In the wake of these terrible events out government has been given vast new powers and they may fall most heavily on a minority of our population who already feel particularly acutely the pain of this disaster.

— Senator Russ Feingold, Statement on the Anti–Terrorism Bill (Oct. 25, 2002)

The implications for online privacy are considerable. For example, the Act increases the ability of law enforcement agencies to authorize installation of pen registers and trap and trace devices (a pen register collects the outgoing phone numbers placed from a specific telephone line; a trap and trace device captures the incoming numbers placed to a specific phone line—a caller–id box is a trap and trace device), and to authorize the installation of such devices to record all computer routing, addressing, and signaling information. The Act also extends the government's ability to gain access to personal financial information and student information without any suspicion of wrongdoing, simply by certifying that the information likely to be obtained is relevant to an ongoing criminal investigation.

Surveillance and Privacy Laws Affected

The USA PATRIOT Act significantly expanded law enforcement authority to surveil and capture communications. There are three major laws that create the framework for the government interception of communications:

- Title III: Requires probable cause, a high legal standard to meet, from a judge for real–time interception of the content of voice and data communications. See EPIC's Wiretapping Page.

- Electronic Communications Privacy Act (ECPA): Governs government access to stored email and other electronic communications. Within ECPA, the Pen Register statute governs real time interception of "numbers dialed or otherwise transmitted on the telephone line to which such device is attached." Although the use of such devices requires a court order, it does not require probable cause: there is no judicial discretion, and the court must authorize the surveillance upon government certification. A government attorney need only certify to the court that the "information likely to be obtained by such installation and use is relevant to an ongoing criminal investigation." Therefore, the Pen Register and Trap and Trace statute lacks many of the privacy protections found in the wiretap statute.
- Foreign Intelligence Surveillance Act (FISA): Authorizes the government to carry out electronic surveillance—against any person, even Americans—in the United States upon obtaining a judicial order based upon probable cause that the target is a foreign power or an agent of a foreign power. FISA, which applies primarily to the government's power in foreign intelligence and counter–intelligence cases, therefore does not offer many of the protections required under the federal wiretap statute.

For Your Consideration

Laws affected by the USA PATRIOT Act represent some of the most significant increases in law enforcement authority in the history of the United States. The government has restricted civil liberties and expanded surveillance ostensibly to protect American interests. According to the Bill of Rights Defense Committee, nationwide figures as of January 14, 2007, demonstrate that 409 local, county, and state resolutions have passed to condemn or opt out of USAPA provisions and similar efforts are underway in 280 additional jurisdictions.[4]

Amitai Etzioni's book, HOW PATRIOTIC IS THE PATRIOT ACT?, discounts the view that the trade–off between freedom and security involves undue pain. Instead he posits Responsive Communitarianism as the solution for brokering a peaceful co–existence between the demands of liberty and social order.[5] Adopting a centrist view in defense of liberty and national security, his search begins with a definition of democracy:

> A polity in which there are regular, institutionalized changes in power, in line with the preferences of the people freely expressed. It entails a whole fabric of institutions: two or more political parties, some measure of checks and balances among the various branches of government, courts that effectively protect individual rights, and a free press.[6]

Constitutional democracies embody a framework of rights that are not subject to majority rule. Noted political theorists often question whether the United States is now at the end of its democratic heyday. Civil libertarians have observed that since September 11, 2001, the government has curtailed most rights, reinterpreted the scope of many others, and seized power in unprecedented ways, all in the name of national security and protection from threats of bio–terrorism. In addition, there has been a concerted increase in efforts to undermine the historic influence of natural social critics. Governmental targeting and retribution for its critics in the media and academia have raised significant questions about the changing political landscape.

Journalist Kristina Borjesson asserts that we are "operating in an extremely toxic–to–truth environment polluted by official secrecy, business interests, government and business alliances, and corrupt public relations campaigns, waged both inside and outside our government."[7]

Etzioni cites the case of Weimar Germany as a key example of how democracies fail. The Weimar Hypothesis is that under certain tangible conditions governmental legitimacy is lost, after which tyranny prevails.[8] Critiques of the Bush Administration suggested in the summer of 2006, that Executive leadership has both failed to meet major public needs, and created grave doubt as to the legitimacy of U.S. policy around the world. According to Dr. Patrick M. Cronin, who served as Assistant Administrator at the U.S. Agency for International Development under President George Bush, and who currently serves as the Director of Studies at the International Institute for Strategic Studies in London: The United States is on a the path of "superpower suicide."[9]

> The global perception of a disregard for ethics and human life costs the United States the currency of international affairs: legitimacy. Compounding bad policy with bad public diplomacy suggests just how far removed Washington is from the reality shared by most of the world.[10]

The Post-9/11 legislative acts that permit roving surveillance, tracing, recording, and FBI surveillance of political and religious organizations, as well as student–exchange profiling are billed as terrorist prevention measures. Military tribunals, arrests of those labeled enemy combatants, indictments for providing "material support for terrorist organizations," and detaining prisons at Guantanamo Bay, in Cuba, are justified as retribution for past crimes against the United States and U.S. interests abroad. President George W. Bush's Military Order No. 1, issued on Nov. 13, 2001, and later revealed in the media, gave him the power to detain anyone who was not a U.S. citizen anywhere in the world, hold them indefinitely, try them in U.S. created military tribunals, and disregard the Geneva Convention, which is designed to protect soldiers' basic human rights and due process in time of war.[11]

There is no doubt that privacy and security are not in balance. The Individual Rights and Civil Liberties of all Americans are directly impacted by several new measures. Widespread monitoring of electronic devices, workplace communication, financial transactions, and the mining of public and private databases for the purpose of creating individual profiles has brought an end to privacy. The concern is whether abuse of these profiles will lead to an end of democracy as well.

Government surveillance of cellular, digital, and internet communication impact rights of privacy, anonymity, and due process of law. Etzioni suggests that four criteria exist for establishing viable public policies for protection of civil liberties from a communitarian perspective. The criteria include: 1) the presence of compelling reasons for government modification of existing legal and ethical standards absent a clear and present danger; 2) meeting real challenges through voluntary means; 3) using the least coercive means possible while simultaneously serving both community and individual interests; and 4) avoiding the unintended side effects of policy and legislation.[12]

Our nation's experience with identifying and defining clear and present danger standards suggests that modification of ethical and legal standards are appropriate whenever they violate fundamental rights. The National Law Journal has named Attorney Martin Garbus the nation's most prominent First Amendment Lawyer, and Garbus appears less concerned with the unintended collateral effects of legislation, than he is with obdurate officials and the rhetoric that enables them to avoid the letter of the law and spirit of liberty for unstated, partisan purposes:

> No president in over 200 years of our history has ever before claimed the "unitary powers" that Bush claims are his. Not President Lincoln during the Civil War, not President Wilson during World War I, not President Roosevelt during World War II, not President Truman during Korea, and not Presidents Johnson and Nixon during Vietnam. The President claims that he has the right to interpret laws "in a manner consistent with the Constitutional authority of the President."
>
> What does "unitary powers" mean? It means that if the President alone decides that the country is faced with what he alone defines to be a critical problem, his authority is unchecked. In other words, he decides where the power lies in the Constitution—he decides the contour of his power. This sounds more like a monarchy, more like authoritarianism than a democracy.
>
> Bush can start his own wars, preemptive or otherwise, is the ultimate interpreter of foreign treaties, he defines enemy combatants as he wishes, he detains prisoners for as long as he wishes, he continues surveillance on foreign intercepts for as long as he wishes, he tortures as he wishes, he can ignore Congressional directives and statutes such as those creating FISA, as well as essential elements of our Constitution. This litany has no end. We cannot now anticipate all the ramifications of the "unitary" president and his claim of "inherent powers," except that it clearly allows him to fully take over the government.[13]

Post-9/11 Privacy in the Workplace

Effect of USA PATRIOT Act on Workplace Privacy—Law[14]

October 1, 2002

Sproule, Clare M.

> Legal protections for employees against surveillance exist, but so, too, do lawful provisions for employers and government agencies to monitor employees' workplace activities—especially in the aftermath of 9/11 and passage of the USA PATRIOT Act.
>
> An often–repeated refrain since the terrorist attacks on the World Trade Center and the Pentagon is "The world has changed since 9/11." One of the biggest changes may be employees' willingness to shift their emphasis from protecting their workplace privacy to increasing their security. Prior to the 9/11 attacks, workplace–privacy initiatives were gaining momentum, driven by pressure from legislators, regulators, and employee lawsuits.
>
> Surveillance activities that were objectionable before 9/11 suddenly became palatable, however, when viewed as a response to security concerns both in the workplace and as part of the United States' "homeland security" initiatives. (1) There is little doubt that privacy will reemerge as a paramount concern once employees begin to feel physically secure. (2) As such, employers who now develop a moni-

toring policy that is responsive to reasonable security issues and also sensitive to their employees' privacy interests, and who communicate the scope and purpose of the monitoring program to their employees, will be in a position to continue their surveillance policies when their workers' focus changes from security back to privacy.

The real loss of privacy in the workplace since 9/11 will most likely not be from increased employer surveillance, however, but rather from the provisions of the USA PATRIOT Act, (3) which eased the restrictions on the government's access to electronic information that employers capture and store. Even though "security concerns" is one of the primary reasons given by employers for monitoring the workplace, (4) the reality is that the security of most workplaces has not changed as a result of the terrorist attacks. (5) The biggest threat to most employees on the job remains work–related violence committed by disgruntled fellow employees or ex–employees. (6) While much of the electronic information gleaned from employers' surveillance activities may not be helpful in preventing workplace violence, the government believes such information may be helpful in preventing future terrorist attacks. One question for employers will be, should they voluntarily cooperate with law–enforcement officials by turning over any such information, or should their employees' privacy interests prevail over the nation's security concerns? (7) In light of the PATRIOT Act, employers may not even be aware of government surveillance of their employees, or may have no choice but to allow the government access to their employees' private communications.

Electronic Monitoring and Surveillance—An Everyday Occurrence

Even before 9/11 electronic monitoring and surveillance was prevalent in the American workplace. Seventy-seven percent of employers responding to an American Management Association survey in January 2001 reported engaging in some form of electronic oversight of their employees. That number was up from the 67 percent who reported doing so just two years earlier. Active monitoring of employees' activities has more than doubled since 1997, with the largest increases being in the number of employers reporting reviewing employee computer files or e-mail messages. Employers responding to the survey reported engaging in some or all of the following forms of monitoring:

* recording and review of telephone conversations;
* storage and review of voice mail messages;
* storage and review of computer files;
* storage and review of e-mail messages;
* monitoring Internet connections;
* video recording of employee job performance;
* telephone use (time spent, numbers called);
* computer use (time logged on, keystroke counts, etc.); and
* video surveillance for security purposes.

Employers gave these five reasons (in order of importance) for monitoring their employees' activities: legal liability, security concerns (protecting corporate assets), legal compliance, productivity measurement, and performance review.

Electronic Devices—Treasure Troves of Information

While employers have been recording and storing electronic information on their employees for their own purposes for years, it is doubtful that many of them ever thought that the government would some day seek access to such information. However, the investigations in the aftermath of 9/11 revealed that electronic monitoring devices that employers already had in place contained valuable information that the government could have used to track down and monitor potential terrorists and their activities. One of the main purposes of the PATRIOT Act is to make it easier for the government to obtain and share such information in the interest of preventing future attacks.

Although the technology used by most employers to monitor their employees has grown more sophisticated over the years, it pales in comparison to the highly sophisticated surveillance devices that government agents have at their disposal. While most employers use video cameras, tape recorders, and computer programs to monitor and record information, the government uses—among other devices—satellites, wiretaps, microphones, beepers, biometric technology, and a controversial software program called "Carnivore" to conduct its surveillance.

Numerous government agencies use state-of-the-art surveillance technology, including the Secret Service; the Central Intelligence Agency; the Federal Bureau of Investigation; the Bureau of Alcohol, Tobacco, and Firearms; the Drug Enforcement Agency; the Internal Revenue Service; the Immigration and Naturalization Service; the Environmental Protection Agency; and the U.S. Postal Service. Distinctions are drawn among the various purposes for which the surveillance is being conducted—whether evidence gathering, general intelligence gathering, or intelligence gathering for national security—and different standards apply to each.

Work tools that spy, too. There are many electronic devices that employers routinely provide to employees for business purposes that employees also use for their personal business, with or without their employer's approval (e.g., PCs, fax machines, cell phones). Such devices record and save a wealth of information that most employers do not routinely monitor or review, and in some cases may not even be aware exists. The government, however, has recognized that electronic devices used by employees may contain information associated with terrorist or criminal activity that could be valuable during an investigation or for intelligence gathering.

Putting aside the invaluable information that can be gleaned from telephone and computer surveillance, other electronic devices can contain important information as well. For instance, wireless telephones may contain the following useful information: numbers called from the cell phone, numbers saved for speed dial, caller ID for incoming calls to the cell phone, and information stored in memory such as names, addresses, phone and pager numbers, PIN numbers, and other access numbers or passwords. Fax machines can contain speed-dial lists, stored copies of incoming and outgoing faxes, and fax-transmission and -receipt logs. Caller-ID and electronic paging devices may contain telephone numbers and other alpha or numeric messages. In addition, "smart cards," plastic cards that are the size of a standard credit card, which are capable of storing monetary value and other data, can yield invaluable information regarding point-of-sale transactions, exchange of value between cardholders or over the Internet, and other data and files similar to that found on a computer.

Personal Use of Business Assets

Many employers permit their employees to use the equipment for personal purposes (e.g., composing and printing letters, surfing the worldwide web). Under those circumstances, an employee's expectation of privacy regarding any personal information that may be stored on the equipment (by design or default) may be different than when the employer has put employees on notice that company-owned equipment may not be used for personal business, and that the employer may monitor the employee's use of that equipment.

Employers should consider adding all of the electronic devices that workers use to their electronic-surveillance and -monitoring policies to avoid any confusion regarding personal use, company use, and surveillance. Employers should also consider their employees' privacy interests before allowing the government unfettered access to such information.

Privacy Protections Limiting Electronic Surveillance in the Workplace

The extent of employees' privacy rights in the workplace may depend on whether they work in the "private" or "public" sector. For instance, the Fourth Amendment's protection against unreasonable searches and seizures in the workplace applies only to public employees. However, private employers that monitor electronic communications in the workplace must be aware that many state constitutions guarantee a right to privacy that parallels the protections of the U.S. Constitution's Fourth and Fourteenth Amendments. They also need to be aware of state statutes and common law that may affect their right to monitor their employees' electronic communications in the workplace. The determining factor in such cases usually turns on whether—under the specific circumstances—the employee had a reasonable expectation of privacy regarding her electronic communications. Unionized private-sector employees may also benefit from additional protections against invasions of their privacy.

Most private-sector employees' electronic communications are also protected under various federal statutes. The Electronic Communications Privacy Act of 1986 ("ECPA") has been interpreted to apply to the monitoring of electronic exchanges, as well as wire and oral communications in the workplace, and prohibits their intentional interception and disclosure. The ECPA defines interception as the acquisition of the contents of any electronic communication "through the use of any electronic, mechanical, or other device." It has been interpreted to prohibit, unless otherwise exempted under the statute, listening to, reading, or copying electronic communications while they are en route to their final destination. This means that using monitoring devices or software that captures oral, wire, or electronic communications while they are in any stage of transmission would be considered interception as that term is defined under Title I.

There are several exceptions that might allow an employer to conduct electronic surveillance of their employers without violating the ECPA. One exception allows a provider of "electronic communication service ... to intercept ... [a] communication in the normal course of his employment while engaged in any activity which is a necessary incident to the rendition of his service or to the protection of the rights or property of the provider of that service." It is generally believed that employers who have their own e-mail system may fall within the definition of a service provider, while there is some question as to whether employers who contract with third parties to provide this service do so.

A second exception allows a network provider to intercept an electronic communication on a device provided to the user (e.g., a PC) that is being used in the ordinary course of accomplishing her job. This is frequently referred to as the "business-use exception" and seems to allow surveillance as long as the employer has a legitimate business purpose for doing so. Prior consent to intercept a communication is a third exception, regardless of whether the interception was made in the ordinary course of business. Section 2511(2) (d) of the ECPA provides that it is not a violation of Title I if the person intercepting the communication is a party to the communication or if one of the parties to the communication has given prior consent to such interception, unless such communication is intercepted for the purpose of committing any criminal or tortuous act.

Title II of the ECPA governs stored communications and imposes liability for a person or entity that gains access to stored communications without authorization, or exceeds authorization to acquire the information from a facility through which electronic communication is provided. There are two main exceptions to Title II that most likely apply in workplace situations. The first is that the rule does not apply to conduct "by the person or entity providing a wire or electronic communications service...." Again, it is likely that employers who have their own e-mail systems may fall within Title II's definition of a service provider. The second exception is for conduct that is authorized by a "user of that service with respect to a communication of or intended for that user." Therefore, an employer can monitor an employee's stored communications if one of the parties to the communication consents to the access.

The most effective way for employers to avoid liability under these statutes and the common law is to promulgate and post an electronic-monitoring and -surveillance policy so that employees are aware that their actions and communications in the workplace are subject to recording and review. According to a recent American Management Association survey, 95 percent of companies that actively monitor their employees' e-mail, Internet, or software use have written policies, compared to 75 percent of firms that do no such monitoring.

Legislation that would require employers to notify their employees if they wished to conduct electronic surveillance of employees' communications was recently proposed. While the Notice of Electronic Monitoring Act was tabled shortly thereafter, that should not deter employers from availing themselves of the many benefits that an electronic-monitoring and -surveillance policy can provide in avoiding liability under certain circumstances.

Scope of Governmental Electronic Surveillance Activity

The government has four basic surveillance mechanisms for people living in the United States: (1) interception orders authorizing the interception of communications; (2) search warrants authorizing the search of physical premises and seizure of tangible evidence like books, videotapes, cell phones, and facsimile machines; (3) "pen register" and "trap-and-trace device" orders (pen-trap orders), which authorize the collection of telephone numbers dialed to and from a particular communications device; and (4) subpoenas compelling the production of tangible things such as records, including electronic records. (34) Each of those mechanisms has its own procedures and standard of proof, which varies depending on whether surveillance is done by domestic law enforcement or foreign intelligence.

(Employers should become familiar with these.) As the government increases its surveillance activities in an effort to identify terrorists and terror networks in the United States, it is increasingly likely that employers may be served with search warrants or subpoenas, or be asked to allow wiretapping of their employees' communication devices to facilitate these efforts.

There are two sources of authority for government wiretapping in the United States: (1) the Federal Wiretap Act ("Title III"), which was adopted in 1968 and which has been amended several times since then, requires a court order issued by a judge who must conclude that there is probable cause to believe that one of the crimes contained in the act has been or is about to be committed; and (2) the Foreign Intelligence Surveillance Act of 1978 ("FISA"), which allows wiretapping of aliens and citizens in the United States based on a finding that there is probable cause to believe that the target is a member of a foreign terrorist group or an agent of a foreign power. For U.S. citizens and permanent resident aliens, FISA requires probable cause to believe that the person is engaged in activities that may involve a criminal violation. Both Title III and FISA allow the government to carry out wiretaps without a court order in emergency situations involving risk of death or serious injury and in national security cases.

Effect of the PATRIOT Act on Workplace Privacy

The PATRIOT Act changed substantially the government's ability to conduct surveillance under Title III and FISA. It made terrorism a predicate act for which a wiretap under Title III can be authorized and lowered the threshold for which surveillance pursuant to FISA is permitted. At the same time, the act lowered the barriers that had been erected between the law-enforcement and national-security agencies, thus allowing for greater sharing of information gained through surveillance, by whatever means. It also makes it easier for law-enforcement officers to obtain surreptitious or so-called "sneak and peek" warrants, which allow them to delay notifying a target that a search or seizure has been conducted.

The PATRIOT Act also amended FISA so that now both statutes permit "roving taps," allowing the government to obtain a court order that does not identify a specific telephone line or e-mail account to be tapped, but instead allows the government to tap "any phone line, cell phone, or Internet account that a suspect uses." This is an important development because in many workplaces employees have access to many different phones and computers, including those of their co-workers.

Clearly, the government would be interested in tapping all of the electronic equipment that is reasonably accessible to a suspected terrorist. In addition, the PATRIOT Act provides explicit legal authorization under Title III and EISA for government surveillance of e-mail and Internet communications, paving the way for increased use by the FBI of its controversial "Carnivore" software. Carnivore gives the FBI access to its target's communications, as well as the communications of non-targets who use the same Internet-service provider. It is likely that these added powers will infringe on the privacy rights of many innocent co-workers and clients. The PATRIOT Act also lowered the standard for the government to be allowed to listen to stored communications such as voicemail and clarified the standard for obtaining stored e-mails. Section 209(1) of the PATRIOT Act deleted "electronic storage of such communication" from the definition of "wire communication" in 18 U.S.C. [section] 2510(1) and added the word "wire" to 18 U.S.C. [section] 2703. The government can now obtain voicemail and other stored communications without an intercept order. Only a search warrant is needed. This is an area where employers may be tempted to "cooperate" with the government and turn over records and stored communications without requiring the law-enforcement officials to obtain a warrant. Careful consideration should be given to all of the issues that are raised by such cooperation before doing so.

Employers: Be Prepared

Physical security has become and will remain a high priority with each new "threat" of terrorism that is issued. The question is, how long will security concerns trump privacy issues if there are no more attacks? When the PATRIOT Act was passed, the horror of 9/11 was still fresh in everyone's mind, so that most people were willing to sacrifice their privacy if it made it more likely that the government could root out terrorists and help prevent future attacks. However, as time passes and the government's surveillance activities become more intrusive, most people are likely to reconsider the equation. Employers already monitor and store a significant amount of information on their employees' activities and communications through electronic surveillance of the workplace. Is it in their best interests to preserve such information, or should the information be destroyed after it has served the employers' purposes? Also, is it their obligation to review such information for suspicious activities by their employees and report those suspicions to the government? They can expect that the government is going to want access to this information if its agents believe that such access is in the nation's security interest. In that event, the privacy of many innocent people will most likely be invaded. Employers should evaluate these issues and discuss with corporate counsel how to address them if they arise. They need to consider whether they should be engaging in more or less electronic surveillance of their employees. Finally, they should put their employees on notice of how they are going to be monitored and how the employer plans to respond to the government's request for such information in their electronic surveillance and monitoring policy.

Effects of Data Mining

According to Jim Harper, privacy is a subjective condition that individuals enjoy when two factors are in place: legal ability to control personal information, and exercise of that control consistent with one's interests and values. Consumers seek privacy on the terms they want it through voluntary exchange. They routinely refuse transactions that don't satisfy them in important ways. The greatest threat to privacy in the private sector is ignorance. If you don't know how information moves in the Information Economy, you can't reject practices that you disapprove of. The actions of educated and aware consumers have traditionally determined what uses of information are acceptable.

Here's an example of how that has changed.

The Bank Secrecy Act requires banks to retain certain records about customers, while denying consumers the power to control personal information that their financial institutions may hold or derive. The BSA prevents banks from offering consumers privacy on the terms they may want it. Its reporting requirements take things quite a bit further. Here, personal information is transferred to a government agency, which is not bound by contract or accountable to any higher authority if it makes new, unanticipated disclosures or uses of data. There may be details in the BSA that I don't know about, but most federal agencies can make new uses of information merely by declaring them in the Federal Register. There are a variety of ways that governments deprive citizens of privacy, and the Bank Secrecy Act has elements of each. First, it is anti-privacy law. It says to consumers and financial institutions: you may not get together and agree to keep financial arrangements private. Second, it is a surveillance program: the government is peering in on people's lives without their consent or participation. Finally, BSA reports go into a public record, and specifically a database. This causes the information to be uniquely persistent, transferable, copyable, and usable. No private sector entity has the power to take privacy from people like the government does. And the government does it with aplomb in the Bank Secrecy Act.[15]

Testimony

United States Senate Committee on the Judiciary
Balancing Privacy and Security:
The Privacy Implications of Government Data Mining Programs
January 10, 2007

The Honorable Robert Barr
Chief Executive Officer, Liberty Strategies, LLC

As a former member of Congress, I have been disappointed to see the Congress shirk its responsibility to the American people and sit silently by while the Constitution is gutted of meaning.

As chairman of Patriots to Restore Checks and Balances, an alliance of individuals and organizations—conservatives and liberals—committed to upholding the Constitution, I have worked with many Republicans and Democrats to do what is right for the American people. I appreciate the opportunity to talk today about the constitutional questions raised by the federal government's data-mining practices.

It is unconscionable that ordinary Americans' jobs and finances—their entire lives—are at risk because they do not know what information the government is collecting about them; or what it is doing with that private information; or who government is sharing the information with. And if that information is wrong, they have no way of knowing about it, no way of seeing it, and no way of correcting it.

Data mining presents many serious threats to the First, Second, Fourth and Fifth Amendments to the Constitution. That is nearly half of the Bill or Rights! Where will this end? With the repeal of the Constitution so that the White House won't have to worry about those inconvenient and troublesome laws any more?

The federal government constantly is taking in huge amounts of information on Americans from many sources; some of these databases are known, some are not; some may be lawful, others not. Every month there is a new revelation. Last week we learned that the administration wants to open our mail at its discretion, in addition to listening to our phone calls and reading our e-mails without court order.

Just weeks earlier the Department of Homeland Security admitted that its Secure Flight program to screen domestic air passengers violated the Privacy Act. Just prior to that, we learned that Customs and Border Patrol was using the Automated Targeting System, designed initially for cargo security, to assign a terror risk score to travelers entering the United States. Anyone in this room who has traveled abroad in recent years is likely in this system. And their records will be kept for 40 years.

States will soon begin to implement the Real ID law, creating a national registry of tens of millions of drivers. Accessible to officials across the nation, this database, currently being finalized for implementation in 2008, is almost certain to contain individuals' fingerprints, photo, Social Security number, immigration status and more (possibly including other biometric data and an RFID chip).

We learned recently the FBI has been using "national security letters" to excess; in one example, using this easy way to demand access to private data, to collect information on nearly 300,000 people who did nothing more suspicious than that they spent the Christmas holiday in Las Vegas. Who knows how many other instances of mass data collection have occurred in the past few years, all in the name of national security? The government is re-analyzing perfectly lawful behavior through unproven data-mining programs and bringing vast numbers of innocent Americans under suspicion.

Adding insult to injury, there is no scientific proof that data-mining to identify terrorists even works. No scientist has ever demonstrated that the government can predict who will commit an act of terror at some future time. Yet, the government spends tens of billions of taxpayers' dollars on data-mining programs each year—collecting, manipulating, retaining and disseminating the most personal and private information on unknowing American citizens and others.

Chilling effects on ordinary Americans necessarily follow. For example, an individual decides to learn Arabic to help their country fight terrorism. They travel to an Arabic speaking nation such as Egypt, which maintains close and cooperative ties with the U.S., to study the language, but when they come home and apply for a job with the federal government, they can't pass the background check because a database, perhaps the Automated Targeting System, shows that they traveled to Egypt. This just isn't right, and it may very well be counter-productive. Data-mining, therefore, has the propensity to make us more vulnerable, not safer.

Data-mining undermines the First Amendment guarantees for freedom of association. Using link-analysis data mining, a person can easily be found guilty by association. This means that anyone who comes into contact—even incidental contact—with a person whose name appears on some list as a terrorist suspect, become a suspect themselves. Once a person is linked to a terrorist, it is virtually impossible to clear his or her name—if they even know they have come under suspicion.

The First Amendment also implies a right to travel and to move freely throughout society. However, when the simple fact of traveling puts people under suspicion, then they may very well curtail or stop traveling for business and other purposes to avoid the hassle of extra scrutiny at the airport or being put on a "watch list."

Concerns about data-mining relate to other of our rights guaranteed by the Bill of Rights. For example, I am deeply concerned about data mining threatening the Second Amendment right to bear arms. Although the government is prohibited by law from creating a national registry of gun owners, it can purchase records from data brokers that in a sense provide this information. This is also a problem under the Real ID Act, which will contain all sorts of data the average applicant for, or holder of, a state drivers license, possibly including information on firearms records. The government will claim it isn't creating a "registry," it is just analyzing data, and they will have circumvented the registry prohibition. Perhaps the nation's farmers who buy nitrate-rich fertilizer will also end up in the data mining programs and come under suspicion without reason.

Data mining is also entirely incompatible with the Fourth Amendment prohibition on unreasonable search and seizure. Our justice system and ability to prosecute suspects is based on crimes that have been committed or planned. It is absurd for the government to use databases to predict individuals' future acts. We do not live in the Hollywood movie scenario depicted in Minority Report, where law enforcement halts "pre-crimes" before they happen, yet the practice of government data-mining, which collects personal information on citizens and other persons often without any suspicion or evidence they have done anything wrong, grows exponentially; a practice undermining the very rights supposed to be protected by the Fourth Amendment.

The Fifth Amendment's Due Process Clause requires that the government tell Americans what personal information is collected about us, how it is being used, and to provide a right to challenge and correct erroneous information that wrongly could be used to deny us our rights and privileges. Yet, none of these shadowy data mining programs provides such a process.

I urge this committee and Congress to consider seriously strict laws to regulate data-mining by government and private industry, and provide oversight concerning their government contracts, so that government agencies are not able to evade federal laws that provide at least some protection against abuse; laws such as the Privacy Act and the Freedom of Information Act. The point here is not to unduly restrict or prohibit the accumulation or analysis of commercially-relevant data for legitimate business purposes. Rather the goal should be to ensure the process possesses a necessary degree of transparency, that it provides essential privacy protection for the consumer, and that such databases are not a tool whereby government can circumvent the law or the requirements of the Bill of Rights.

Funding for the Total Information Awareness system and other discredited programs may have been cut off because of privacy concerns, but other heads of the beast have sprung up in its place with new names. These programs have no greater safeguards for Americans' privacy and should also be ended. Finally, I urge the committee to re-introduce and pass the Personal Data Privacy and Security Act and the Federal Agency Data-Mining Reporting Act in the 110th Congress.

One Nation under Surveillance

For Your Consideration

Media watchdogs echo many of these concerns. The Associated Press reported a story in December 2005 called ***Report of NSA Spying Prompts Call for Probe*:**[16]

> The New York Times reported that during the year following the Sept. 11 attacks, Bush authorized the NSA to monitor the international phone calls and international e-mails of hundreds—perhaps thousands—of people inside the United States. [Before the attacks] the NSA typically limited its domestic surveillance to foreign embassies and missions via court order. The Pentagon said it was reviewing its use of a classified database of information about suspicious people and activity inside the United States after a report by NBC News said the database listed activities of anti-war groups that were not a security threat to Pentagon property or personnel.
>
> The Times said it delayed publication of the report for a year because the White House said it could jeopardize continuing investigations and alert would-be terrorists. The Times said it omitted information from the story that administration officials argued could be useful to terrorists.

What are the weaknesses in the view that if you have nothing to hide, you needn't worry?

A report submitted to President George W. Bush in January 2006, by an American Bar Association Task Force on Domestic Surveillance, responds to revelations about the secret NSA program.[17] A roster of task force members, which includes a former Director of the FBI, former General Counsel of the CIA and former Counsel of the National Security Agency, is available at http://www.abanet.org/op/domsurv.

The report includes six provisions that:

> Call on the President to abide by our constitutional system of checks and balances and respect the roles of Congress and the judiciary in protecting national security consistent with the Constitution.
>
> Oppose any further electronic surveillance in U.S. for foreign intelligence purposes that does not comply with the Foreign Intelligence Surveillance Act and urge the President, if he believes FISA is inadequate, to seek amendment or new legislation.
>
> Urge Congress to affirm that the Authorization for Use of Military Force adopted by Congress in September 2001 did not provide an exception to FISA, saying such an exception must be explicit.
>
> Urge Congress to conduct a comprehensive, thorough investigation of the National Security Agency's domestic surveillance program.
>
> Urge Congress to assure proceedings of that investigation are open to public.
>
> Urge Congress to review and make recommendations regarding intelligence oversight process.

In August 2006, US District Judge Anna Diggs Taylor ruled that the Bush administration's domestic surveillance program is unconstitutional, and ordered the National Security Agency to immediately cease using warrantless wiretaps as violative of free speech and privacy rights.[18]

The Washington Post reported in January 2007 that a bill:

Introduced by Sens. Russell Feingold (D-Wis.) and John E. Sununu (R-N.H.) requires federal agencies to report the development and use of data-analysis technologies to "discover predictive or anomalous patterns indicating criminal or terrorist activity."[19] According to The Chair of the Judiciary Committee:

> The American people have neither the assurance that these massive data banks will make us safer, nor the confidence that their privacy rights will be protected."

Another source warned:

"We cannot rely on this or any other administration to pull back on its own. The executive branch likes information on citizens far too much to voluntarily stop developing ever more and expanded databases."

The ACLU said some programs appear to be a "dragnet on the general population," including a Homeland Security program that "correlates events and people to specific information" and a Defense Intelligence Agency data-mining program to "identify foreign terrorists or U.S. citizens connected to foreign terrorism activities."

Data mining is used by the Health and Human Services Department to monitor food and drug safety. The department is developing a data-mining tool to track and report "adverse incidents" involving food, cosmetics, and dietary supplements.

Homeland Security is developing an "incident data mart," which will "look through incident logs for patterns of events." Incident is defined as "an event involving law enforcement or government agency for which a log was created (e.g. traffic ticket, drug arrest, or firearm possession)." The system will "look at crimes in a particular geographic location, particular types of arrest, or any type of unusual activity."

The GAO report did not include classified programs, and some agencies did not respond to its request for information, including the CIA, National Security Agency, and the Equal Employment Opportunity Commission.

James Dempsey, executive director of the Center for Democracy & Technology, said it is likely that there are data-mining programs not listed in the report.[20]

The West Is Restricting Freedom in Response to Terror[21]

Richard Rorty

Reprinted with permission

The interior ministers of the EU nations have been holding meetings to co-ordinate anti-terrorist measures. If the war involves nuclear weapons, the measures their governments will consider it necessary to impose are likely to bring about the end of many of the socio-political institutions that emerged in Europe and North America in the past two centuries.

If the direct effects of terrorism were all we had to worry about, their thinking goes, there would be no reason to fear that democratic institutions would not survive. After all, equivalent amounts of death and destruction caused by natural disasters would not threaten those institutions. If there were a sudden shift of tectonic plates that caused skyscrapers to collapse all around the Pacific Rim, hundreds of thousands of people would die within minutes. But the emergency powers claimed by governments would be temporary and local. It is only in the US that the Government has proclaimed a permanent state of war, and had that claim taken seriously. In a worst-case scenario, historians will have to explain why the golden age of democracy lasted only about 200 years.

Yet if much less severe damage occurred as a result of terrorism, the officials charged with national security, those who bear the responsibility for preventing further attacks, will probably think it necessary to end the rule of law, as well as the responsiveness of governments to public opinion. Politicians and bureaucrats will strive to outdo one another in proposing outrageous measures. The rage felt when immense suffering is caused by human agency rather than by forces of nature will probably lead the public to accept these measures.

The result would be a cascade of government actions that would, in the course of a few years, bring about a fundamental change in the conditions of social life in the West. The courts would be brushed aside, and the judiciary would lose its independence. Regional military commanders would be given the kind of authority that once belonged to locally elected officials. The media would be coerced into leaving protests against government decisions unreported.

Fear of such developments is, of course, more common among Americans like me than among Europeans. For it is only in the US that the Government has proclaimed a permanent state of war, and had that claim taken seriously by the citizens. Christopher Hitchens has jeeringly said that many American leftists are more afraid of Attorney-General John Ashcroft than they are of Osama bin Laden. I am exactly the sort of person Hitchens has in mind. Ever since the White House rammed the USA PATRIOT Act through Congress, I have spent more time worrying about what my Government will do than about what the terrorists will do.

Such developments would gradually reduce the effectiveness of the various institutions that have made it possible for public opinion to influence the actions of democratic governments. At the end of this process of erosion, democracy would have been replaced by something quite different. This would probably be neither military dictatorship nor Orwellian totalitarianism, but rather a relatively benevolent despotism.

That sort of power structure survived the end of the Soviet Union and is now resolidifying under Vladimir Putin and his fellow KGB alumni. The same structure seems to be taking shape in China and in South-East Asia. In countries run in this way, public opinion does not greatly matter. Elections may still be held, but opposition parties are not allowed to pose any serious threat to the powers that be. Careers are less open to talent, and more dependent on connections with powerful persons. Since the courts and the police review boards are relatively powerless, it is often necessary for shopkeepers to pay protection money to the police, or to criminals tolerated by the police, to stay in business. It is dangerous for citizens to complain about corruption or abuse of power by public officials. High culture is restricted to areas that are irrelevant to politics (as it was in the Soviet Union, and still is in China). No more uncensored media. No more student demonstrations. Not much in the way of civil society. Life for much of the world would not be greatly changed if the dismal scenario I have just outlined were to play out in the West.

In north-east Brazil, as in the villages of equatorial Africa and Central Asia, nobody would notice that the world had changed, that a light had gone out. But in the countries in which the greatest moral progress has been made, that progress would cease. After a few generations, utopian fantasies of an open society might be cherished only by a few readers of old books.

Is there anything the citizens of the West can do to make it less likely that their grandchildren will live under the sort of neo-feudalism I have described? The only thing I can think of that might make a difference is a willingness to challenge the culture of government secrecy. Demands for government openness should start in the areas of nuclear weaponry and of intelligence-gathering—the places where the post-World War II obsession with secrecy began.

As a first step, the citizenry could demand that their governments publish the facts about their stockpiles of weapons of mass destruction. Then they might insist that these governments make public the details of two sets of planned responses: one to the use of such weapons by other governments, and another for their use by criminal gangs such as al-Qaeda. They could also demand that their governments join in efforts to update the laws of war, and to create something like a code of international criminal justice. As many legal scholars have been pointing out since September 11, the laws of war were designed to cover the acts of national governments. Criminal law was intended to deal with acts committed within a nation's borders by its own citizens.

There are plenty of grey areas where neither sort of law applies. In these areas, governments are now pretty much free to do as they please: to parachute hit squads into Third World countries in which terrorists are thought to be holding meetings, to bring about regime change in nations suspected of supporting terrorists, and so on. There is not much point in saying that such actions are against international law: they may prove to be the only way of preventing, for example, nerve gas in the London Underground. Updated laws, openly agreed on by international bodies and adopted, after debate, by national governments, would specify when such actions were legitimate. Such updating would provide a good occasion to draw up new multilateral agreements, and to think about using the United Nations for new purposes.

If Western governments were made to disclose and discuss what they plan to do in various sorts of emergency, it would at least be slightly harder for demagogic leaders to argue that the most recent attack justifies their doing whatever they like. Crises are less likely to produce institutional change, and to have unpredictable results, if they have been foreseen and discussed.

Open discussion of needed changes in international law should be accompanied by a new openness about many other topics. There is no good reason why the governments of France, Britain, the US and Israel should not inform their citizens about the nuclear devices they have in stock. Nor is there any reason not to disclose the full history of the development of chemical and biological weapons. It is time for the public to be shown the texts of the agreements between governments that have made it possible to girdle the globe with more than 700 US military bases. There was little enough reason for refusing to make this sort of information public even when the Cold War was at its height. It is hard to imagine what help its disclosure could give to the terrorists.

The progress humanity made in the 19th and 20th centuries was largely due to the increased role of public opinion in determining government policies. But the lack of public concern about government secrecy has, in the past 60 years, created a new political culture in each of the democracies. In the US and in many EU countries an elite has come to believe it cannot carry out its mission of providing national security if its preparations are carried out in public. The events of September 11 greatly strengthened this conviction. Further attacks are likely to persuade those elites they must destroy democracy in order to save it.

In a worst-case scenario, historians will someday have to explain why the golden age of Western democracy lasted only about 200 years. The saddest pages in their books are likely to be those in which they describe how the citizens of the democracies, by their craven acquiescence in government secrecy, helped bring the disaster on themselves.

"Our intelligence shows that everybody loves us."

SMART Security

In 2005, Congresswoman Lynn Woolsey introduced SMART Security:

Rep. Lynn Woolsey (CA) introduced the Sensible, Multilateral American Response to Terrorism (SMART) Security platform (H.Con. Res. 158). The SMART Security resolution has 50 cosponsors.

Summary of Bill

SMART Security Resolution[22]

I. Prevent future acts of terrorism.

How would SMART Security accomplish this?

Work with the U.N. and NATO to root out terrorist networks.

Strengthen intelligence capabilities aimed at tracking and arresting those involved in terrorism—while still respecting human and civil rights.

Enhance international efforts to cut of financing for terrorist organizations.

II. Stop the spread of weapons of mass destruction.

How would SMART Security accomplish this?

Set an example for the rest of the world by renouncing the development of new nuclear weapons and the testing of nuclear weapons.

Work with the Russian Federation to dismantle nuclear warheads, reduce nuclear stockpiles, and secure nuclear materials in Russia, and replicate this approach in other unstable regions.

Pursue diplomacy, enhanced inspection regimes, and regional security arrangements to reduce proliferation.

Cease the sale and transfer of weapons to regimes involved in human rights abuses and to regions of conflict.

Ensure that highly enriched uranium is stored only in secure locations.

III. Address root causes of terrorism and violent conflict.

How would SMART Security accomplish this?

Increase development aid and debt relief for the world's poorest countries.

Integrate peace-building and conflict prevention initiatives into developmental programs.

Work with the international community to address the growing problem of resource scarcity.

Support programs that promote sustainable development, democracy-building, human rights education, conflict resolution, and educational opportunities for women and girls.

Engage the international community in post-conflict reconstruction and political transition processes.

IV. Shift U.S. Budget Priorities to Meet our security needs.

How would SMART Security accomplish this?

Create a more effective national security strategy focused on multilateralism, nonproliferation, diplomacy, and conflict prevention.

Cease paying for outdated weapons systems that do not address today's security threats.

Reduce dependence on foreign oil by promoting long-term energy security through greater investment in sustainable and renewable alternatives.

Provide adequate peacekeeping, reconstruction, and developmental funding for troubled countries and regions.

V. Pursue alternatives to war.

How would SMART Security accomplish this?

Increase U.S. and international capacities for the prevention of armed conflict, including more effective conflict assessment and early warning systems, multilateral rapid response mechanisms, human rights monitoring, civilian policing, and effective justice systems.

Strengthen U.S. diplomacy and regional institutions to prevent and resolve violent conflict.

Support civil society programs as a critical component in the prevention and resolution of violent conflict.

For Your Consideration

What would it take to reach a measure of tangible success in achieving SMART Security goals?

The following is the preamble for the 2007 Sixth Annual International Conference on an Interfaith Perspective on Globalisation for the Common Good, entitled:

A Non-violent Path to Conflict Resolution and Peacebuilding (Building a World that is Just, Free and Prosperous for All)

Conflict resolution in international affairs is currently undergoing enormous pressures, due in part to the challenges of globalisation and its many cultural, religious and economic contexts. To address this crisis, which has sadly been described as a "Clash of Civilisations", we propose a dialogue among civilisations: an inter-active international symposium to contribute meaningfully to the promotion of a global culture of prevention and non-violent conflict resolution, mediation and negotiation.

Today's world of globalisation is marked by immense wealth and acute poverty. Moreover, total concentration on wealth creation and economic growth—without our knowing how or why—has led to an erosion of moral and spiritual values. It has also resulted in a destructive decline in the institutions that have traditionally promoted and protected these essential human values: the family, religious institutions and community structures. There is a growing a poverty of values such as love, compassion, justice, morality, solidarity, spirituality and faith, alongside an increase of materialism and consumerism in many parts of the world. And when social justice and human rights are routinely denied for the seemingly invisible amongst us, peace remains only a dream.

We believe there is an alternative, based on the moral and spiritual values shared by all the world religions. The mystic tradition in every faith affirms that all of life is sacred. The most powerful way for faith-based and spiritual communities to influence beliefs, norms and institutions is through a prophetic voice and public action. Highly visible faith and interfaith affirmation of the great spiritual truths of peace, justice and the sacredness of the Earth and human life can make a tremendous contribution to the non-violent path of conflict resolution and the creation

> of a world that is just, free and prosperous. Action and service by spiritual and faith communities and groups can provide a vital source of inspiration and energy for the healing of the world.

Given that separation of church and state is a central tenet of constitutional democracy, how effective might the fruits of such a meeting become in a long-term strategy for addressing the issues the organizers have raised?

How do these issues affect individual rights within the United States?

Chapter Twelve

Legal Training & Responsibilities in the New Empire

Yale Law Dean Harold H. Koh spoke of realizing four areas of commitment to make Yale an even greater law school in the 21st century. His letter to alums (in chapter two) cites commitment to the profession, public service, globalization and renewal as key elements of the school's success. Koh's general assessment provides an interesting point of departure from the standard critique of the legal profession by broadening the debate, moving the dialogue from what we have been toward what we can become and still hope to achieve in the 21st century. Evolving dynamics in all four categories promise to transform the future role of lawyers.

There has certainly been no shortage of cataclysmic events to prompt thought-provoking discussions about the role of lawyers both within American society and the broader international community. Some of them include the Catholic church sex-abuse scandal, the Enron scandal, Bush Administration threats to constitutional democracy and to lawyers that defend civil liberties, human rights violations against women around the world, ethnic cleansing abroad, destabilization of political regimes, insecurity arising from the constant threat of war, and the loss of our nation's legitimacy/credibility around the world.

Lawyers for Enron & the Catholic Church

The following is a March 2004 essay by UCLA Professor Stephen Bainbridge, published by Mirror of Justice, a blog dedicated to the development of Catholic legal theory, titled The ***Shameful Role of Lawyers in the Church Sex Abuse Scandal.***[1]

> Last weekend, we here at the University of St. Thomas sponsored a symposium on "Understanding the Intersection of Business and Legal Ethics," in which, among many others, our co-blogger Stephen Bainbridge made an important contribution and all presentations of which will be published in the University of St. Thomas Law Review.
>
> During the course of that event, in which many of the speakers addressed the various scandals arising in the business world—the Savings & Loan crisis of several years ago, Enron, Martha Stewart, etc.—in which lawyers failed in their role as moral counselor, I could not help but be disturbed by the painful parallel with the recent scandals of the American Catholic Church, Inc. Of course, the Catholic Church is not, or at least should not be, a business enterprise. And in-

deed a large part of the priest abuse problem was that the Church often conceived of itself as such. As Ralph McInerny says, some "bishops acted like CEOs rather than shepherds."

Given the nature of the UST symposium, which looked not only to business ethics but also to the ethics of lawyers advising businesses, my more immediate focus was on the behavior of those lawyers retained by the Church either as general counsel or to represent it with respect to lawsuits alleging sexual abuse of minors by priests. Given the nature of this weblog on Catholic Social Thought and the law, the proper role of lawyers as Catholics, that is, people of faith who are in the legal profession, in proper counseling is directly pertinent.

The report of the National Review Board appointed by the bishops issued just a couple of weeks ago. It includes a section titled "Reliance on Attorneys," a title that is meant to indicate not something salutary but rather delineate yet another of the multiple errors made by the bishops. In other words, when the bishops sought the advice of members of our profession, they went astray. Ouch.

Consider the details of the grievous errors outlined in the National Review Board report, which, while levied against the bishops in the first instance, encompass their lawyers as well: Attorneys used "tactics [that] often were inappropriate for the Church, and which tended to compound the effects of the abuse that already had been inflicted." These tactics included defenses that "could be construed as blaming the victim," arguing that the Church had no responsibility for priests by claiming they were "independent contractors," and "in general adopting an overly adversarial approach."

Moreover, the report says that "certain lawyers recommended, and certain bishops insisted, that the victims sign confidentiality agreements, which stifled their ability to discuss their experiences openly and thwarted awareness by the laity of the problem." In addition, lawyers counseled Church leaders not to meet with or apologize to victims, even when the abuse was clearly substantiated. Not only does the report correctly say that this approach undermined the primary pastoral mission of the bishops, but it suggests that it ultimately led to greater legal liability as many victims said they would not have filed suit had someone heard their complaints and apologized.

The report says this problem was caused by "disastrous pastoral decisions" in selecting lawyers based on "friendship [with bishops] and a misguided perception of the lawyers' loyalty to the Church." As a consequence, the lawyers chosen "failed to adapt their tactics to account for the unique role and responsibilities of the Church."

To be sure, as another part of that report states, "[t]he first role of a bishop or any Church leader must be to act as a pastor to the Catholic faithful." Thus, the bishops have primary responsibility here, and cannot avoid that responsibility by alluding to the advice of counsel. Or as the report puts it, "the Church should not hide behind its lawyers." That much is a given.

Nonetheless, is it not sad that counsel from their lawyers is cited as a problem, rather than as one of the means toward a solution? Is it not a scandal to us in the legal profession that, rather than assisting Church leaders in finding a morally superior means of responding to the sex abuse problem, Church lawyers are said to have exacerbated it? Now I am sure there were exceptions to this sorry pattern and perhaps we may hear at some point encouraging stories about individual lawyers who were part of the solution rather than the problem. And perhaps many of these lawyers did in fact provide moral counseling but because of confidentiality expectations have not been able to so reveal it publicly (although the bishops presumably waived any such confidentiality when cooperating with the investigation by the national review board). Nonetheless, it cannot be gainsaid that, on the whole, the involvement of lawyers made this serious problem a greater disaster.

What can we learn from this about our role as lawyers? To begin with, the growing revival in professional responsibility scholarship and education of attention to the foundational role of lawyers as moral as well as legal counselors needs to be heard and emphasized just as much among the Church's lawyers as the rest of profession. One would have thought that the Church's own legal representatives, with the full encouragement of their clients the bishops, would have been at the forefront of the movement to enhance ethical lawyering and moral counseling. Instead, the National Review Board report suggests they were among the last to get the message. How can we help ensure that this never happens again? As the bishops now seek to restore confidence in the Church among the faithful, how can we restore confidence in lawyers of faith as committed to partnership with Church leaders in providing legal advice that serves a greater moral purpose?

A Changing Role for Lawyers in a Post-Enron World?[2]

Rex R. Perschbacher

What does the post-Enron world look like for lawyers? Some believe that lawyers need to become gatekeepers, there to watch over and control corporate officers and directors. Currently lawyers do not have a real gatekeeping role. Unlike auditors, lawyers don't have public duties of care, disclosure, or independence. Instead, lawyers are supposed to be zealously loyal to their clients. Thus they make very poor gatekeepers. But things may change a bit. Let's take a look at lawyers for publicly traded corporations before, during, and after the Enron collapse.

1. Before

What was the corporate lawyer's world before Enron? Prior to Enron's fall, there were some specific ethical rules for lawyers representing corporations. The rules said these lawyers had to be careful to remember that they represented the corporation and not the individuals who make up the corporation. That is very hard to do since it is the individual corporate officers who hire and fire, pay, and talk to the attorneys. The corporation may be a person in the eyes of the law, but to the corporation's lawyer, the corporation is an unlikely friend and confidant. Nevertheless the rules required the corporation's lawyer who learned of illegal or criminal conduct possibly attributable to the corporation, to report it up the chain of corporate command as far as he or she could: to audit committees and the like. So went the rule.

In addition, there is an opposing rule that attorneys all know about—that they are supposed to keep their client's confidences, more or less absolutely. California requires that this be done absolutely. Nationally, the American Bar Association ("ABA") suggests rules that are fuzzier. And in a case of exquisite bad timing, the ABA had before it a chance to amend its Model Rule in August of 2001. In particular, the ABA had the chance to change the rule to allow lawyers to divulge their clients' secrets to prevent the clients from using their lawyer's services to commit a crime or fraud and to allow a lawyer to breach client confidentiality to prevent, mitigate, or rectify a financial loss arising from the client's use of the lawyer's services to commit a fraud. The proposed changes were badly defeated within the ABA's House of Delegates, and one was withdrawn. And so the rules remain very absolute. An attorney may, if she wants, reveal client confidences to prevent an imminent death or the like by her client, but nothing else in the national view.

2. During

What about the lawyers' role in the Enron mess? Lawyers caught a break in the whirlwind of publicity following Enron's bankruptcy filing, probably because what Arthur Anderson did looked so bad. But lawyers were in the Enron mess up to their eyeballs. Specifically, two large firms were involved. Vinson & Elkins, Enron's general counsel, investigated Sharon Watkins's whistle blowing complaints and did not find anything to be worried about. Kirkland & Ellis, a Chicago-based firm representing Enron in setting up many of the entities that moved revenues off to the side, similarly reported they found nothing to be concerned about. In fact, Enron was Vinson & Elkins' biggest client. More lawyers were involved as both Enron and Anderson had lawyers on their staffs. All failed in some way, but lawyers didn't catch all the flak, at least not publicly. Lawyers got a break at least in part because of the *Central Bank v. First Interstate Bank* case, from 1994, that said lawyers are not liable for aiding and abetting in securities fraud just because they advise a corporate client who commits it, if they are not actively involved in creating and manipulating misinformation and are not principal actors in the fraud. This case supports the idea that lawyers involved with Enron are not liable just because they were involved when the fraud went on.

So lawyers got a break. Nevertheless, when everything did go bad in Enron, Milberg Weiss, the firm representing the Regents of the University of California, and you, and me, and our pension funds, sued those two law firms as well. They hope to get around the Central Bank holding. It's yet to be determined whether they'll succeed in doing so. In their 500-page complaint, they devote about 50 pages to attacking the work of the lawyers for Enron.

3. After

Nevertheless, what's happening in the wake of Enron—the last phase of this story? One good thing resulted from it and may yet prove to be very beneficial. The ABA created a Taskforce on Corporate Responsibility that reported a number of changes that it wants to make to the relevant Rules. In particular, the Taskforce wants to tighten up the rule about whom lawyers report things to in order to make it easier for lawyers to report wrongdoing and to expand their reporting to include a wider range of wrongdoing. In particular, the Taskforce has recommended that the ABA go back and change the rules on confidentiality and make changes that would allow lawyers to reveal fraud or other misdeeds of a client in order to prevent great harm to the public. Nevertheless, the hope for all that to be accomplished isn't very great. I wouldn't bet on the ABA revisiting these proposed changes in the attorney-client privilege, and, even if it did, I wouldn't bet on the states quickly adopting the changes to their rules. It's a long arduous process.

But something else is on the horizon that lawyers and corporate officials should be aware of. Congress finally woke up and passed the Sarbanes-Oxley Act of 2002 that made a myriad of reforms, setting up an accounting board and the like. It has some particular relevance for lawyers and may change the way lawyers relate to their clients, to the SEC, and, in the long run, to the public. In particular, for about 50 years the Securities Exchange Commission ("SEC") has had a rule that allows it to suspend or bar professionals from practice for improper professional conduct. The SEC has used this rule against accountants, but has almost never used it against lawyers. It just hasn't enforced it against lawyers—or, very, very rarely. The SEC tends to turn things over to the states. In the wake of Enron, that is unlikely to be the case anymore. In fact, the new law specifically directs that the SEC, not later than 180 days after enactment (which was the end of January), issue rules, in the public interest and for the protection of investors, setting forth minimum standards of professional conduct for attorneys appearing and practicing before the commission in any way, including a requirement that attorneys report evidence of a material violation of securities law, or a breach of fiduciary duty, or similar violation, to the legal counsel, chief executive officer, or the equivalent of the corporation.

So, what could this mean? I think what this could mean is a real invigoration of lawyers' rules at the federal level, something that's never been done there. It may also mean that we might really develop some national controls over attorneys—but different rules, tougher rules that would undo the state monopoly of the regulation of the legal practice that is largely in the hands of the lawyers themselves in determining whether they act rightly or wrongly. That, I think, is an interesting, threatening, and liberating possible future for lawyers and Enron

---

Robert F. Nagel provides a critically realistic assessment of what people don't know about American Lawyers. The following are excerpts of his review of Mark Miller's book, THE HIGH PRIESTS OF AMERICAN POLITICS: THE ROLE OF LAWYERS IN AMERICAN POLITICAL INSTITUTIONS.[3]

> He sets out to study, for example, the extent to which lawyers control decision-making procedures, the vocabulary and methods of debate, and even our legislators' sense of what is possible. He concludes, not surprisingly, that lawyers wield great power.[4]
>
> Even if his conclusion will not exactly stun most Americans, some of Miller's data will convince them that the situation is even worse than they feared. Did you know that in the 1980s lawyers were governors in as many as 66 percent of the states? That 25 of the 41 presidents have been lawyers? Or that of the 18 people in Clinton's cabinet in 1993, 13 were lawyers?
>
> Advertisement
>
> It gets worse. Miller recounts how heavily lawyers are represented in Congress, state legislatures, regulatory agencies, lobbying groups, public interest organizations, influential academic posts, and, of course, the judiciary.
>
> One of Miller's most interesting—and depressing—findings is that lawyers tend to be unrealistic and uncritical in their attitudes towards judges. Lawyers, for example, are more likely than other legislators to believe that judicial interpretations are not political. They are less likely to respond to judicial excesses by trying to limit judges' power. And the most prestigious lawyer-legislators, such as those who sit on the Senate Judiciary Committee, are actually so en-

> tranced by the model of "The Judge" that they talk and act as if they themselves were jurists.
>
> Our system was built on the idea that power cannot be trusted—that ambition must be used to check ambition. To an astonishing extent, this principle has not worked with federal judges, who go merrily on their way enjoying ever more prestige even as they abuse their role. Miller helps us understand why. The legislative branch that is supposed to help check judicial excesses has been infiltrated by the same legalistic vocabulary and value system that fuels judges' behavior. Even more worrisome is Miller's suggestion that this lawyers' ideology now "resides in the minds of Americans": To the extent that we have all become lawyers, there is no one to keep judges in check.
>
> Miller is concerned about a broader danger than the loss of control over the judicial branch. He describes the lawyers' mindset as being too incremental, too nit-picking, and too procedural. This, he argues, legitimates whatever system is in place and reduces our capacity for imaginative, bold changes. But this fear does not fit well with some of Miller's own observations. Were the 25 lawyers who Miller says signed the Declaration of Independence apologists for the status quo? Was Abraham Lincoln so stunted by his legal training that he could not sustain a brave vision or undertake decisive acts?
>
> No. The problem that legalism presents for democracy probably lies elsewhere. Miller gets closer to it when he describes how President Clinton miscalculated on the issue of gays in the military. Miller says Clinton, viewing the question through the eyes of an attorney, saw only a clear constitutional issue and overlooked public opposition. In the same vein, Miller describes lawyer-politicians as "free agents" who tend to operate independently from political parties, interest groups, and even their constituents. It is this—the lawyer's tendency toward intellectual arrogance and myopia—that is the real threat. While legal training has many virtues, it does impart an instinct to argue rather than to discuss, to prevail rather than to coexist, and to confuse the advocate's preferences with "law." The lawyer's vice, in short, is imperiousness, which is a serious flaw in a system that rests on the consent of the governed. But then, most Americans already know this. At least they do when they are not engaged—against the shrill and cynical public debate that has come to dominate our bleak political landscape—in behaving like lawyers themselves.

Government Lawyers in the News

There are many avenues for wielding legal power. Below you'll find the dozen or so recent governmental deployments that have garnered media attention.

Newsweek Web Exclusive[5]

> After months of working below the radar, a huge U.S. legal team hired by the Kingdom of Saudi Arabia has sprung into action and begun a major counteroffensive against a landmark lawsuit seeking $1 trillion in damages on behalf of the victims of the September 11 terror attacks. The Saudi royal family and others have

offered up seven-figure retainers to some of the most politically connected law firms in the country. Baker Botts, still boasts former secretary of State James Baker as one of its senior partners. Its recent alumni include Robert Jordan, the former personal lawyer for President Bush who is now U.S. ambassador to Saudi Arabia. An internal list of other law firms retained in the case reads like a veritable "who's who" of the U.S. legal community.

Boston Globe report[6]

President Bush has consulted a lawyer in case he is called as a witness in the grand jury investigation into who in his administration leaked the identity of covert CIA agent Valerie Plame to a columnist last summer, the White House said yesterday.

CNN[7]

Attorneys with the Bush administration, such as U.S. Justice Department lawyer Paul Clement, are urging the Supreme Court to permit government-sponsored displays of the Ten Commandments.

Wall Street Journal[8]

Readying for a constitutional showdown over gun control, the Bush administration has issued a 109-page memorandum aiming to prove that the Second Amendment grants individuals nearly unrestricted access to firearms.

USA Today[9]

On the birthday of Martin Luther King Jr., Bush announced his opposition to an affirmative action program at the University of Michigan. King was a strong supporter of "compensatory or preferential treatment" for blacks who have been disadvantaged by the combined effects of nearly 250 years of slavery and the Jim Crow century that followed.

Washington Post[10]

Legislation drafted by Justice Department lawyers in 2003 would have provided legal backing for several aspects of the Bush administration's warrantless eavesdropping program. Lawmakers and the public were not aware at the time that President Bush had already issued a secret order allowing the National Security Agency to intercept international calls involving U.S. citizens and legal residents. Some critics of the surveillance program said the draft legislation raises questions about recent administration claims that Bush had clear legal authority to order warrantless domestic spying in late 2001 and [therefore] had no need to go to Congress for explicit approval.

Fox News[11]

Lawyers for the Bush administration and a group of Georgia workers urged the Supreme Court Wednesday to allow a floor-covering manufacturer to be sued for racketeering for allegedly using recruiters to find and hire illegal workers.

PBS[12]

Federal Court denied Justice Department's case noting that the anthrax vaccine has never been approved by the FDA. "Until the vaccine has proven tested in that area, the United States cannot demand that members of the armed forces serve as guinea pigs for experimental drugs."

Washington Post[13]

> Lawyers for President Bush have concluded he can launch an attack on Iraq without new approval from Congress, in part because they say that permission remains in force from the 1991 resolution giving Bush's father authority to wage war in the Persian Gulf, according to administration officials.

Wall Street Journal[14]

> Bush administration lawyers contended last year that the president wasn't bound by laws prohibiting torture and that government agents who might torture prisoners at his direction couldn't be prosecuted by the Justice Department.

NPR[15]

> Tension has been growing between career lawyers and political appointees in the Justice Department's Civil Rights Division. Some career professionals who have left the Civil Rights Division say they left because they were shut out of the decision making process in a way that did not occur under previous administrations.

Newsday[16]

> Reversing the trend of the 1990s, the percentages of black and women attorneys at the Justice Department have declined under Attorney General John Ashcroft, according to the first snapshot of diversity at Justice in two years.

Boston Globe[17]

> President Bush has quietly claimed the authority to disobey more than 750 laws enacted since he took office, asserting that he has the power to set aside any Congressional statute that conflicts with his interpretation of the Constitution.
>
> For example, military rules and regulations, affirmative-action provisions, requirements that Congress be told about immigration services problems, "whistleblower" protections for nuclear regulatory officials, and safeguards against political interference in federally funded research.

Chicago Tribune[18]

> President Bush is bracing for what could be an onslaught of investigations by the new Democratic-led Congress by hiring lawyers to fill key White House posts and preparing to play defense on countless document requests and possible subpoenas.

Testimony of
KAREN J. MATHIS
PRESIDENT OF THE AMERICAN BAR ASSOCIATION
Senate Judiciary Committee
concerning

"The Thompson Memorandum's Effect on the Right to Counsel in Corporate Investigations"

September 12, 2006

I am the President of the American Bar Association (ABA) and a practicing attorney here to testify before you today on behalf of the ABA and its more than

410,000 members on the critical issues surrounding "the Thompson Memorandum's Effect on the Right to Counsel in Corporate Investigations."

The ABA strongly supports preserving the attorney-client privilege and the work product doctrine.

We are concerned about language in the Department of Justice's Thompson Memorandum—and other related federal governmental policies and practices—that have begun to seriously erode these fundamental rights.

We also are concerned about the separate provision in the Thompson Memorandum that erodes employees' constitutional and other legal rights, including the right to effective legal counsel and the right against self-incrimination.

A number of federal governmental agencies—including the Department of Justice and the U.S. Sentencing Commission—have adopted policies in recent years that weaken the attorney-client privilege and work product doctrine in the corporate context by encouraging federal prosecutors to routinely pressure companies and other organizations to waive these legal protections as a condition for receiving credit for cooperation during investigations.

The Department of Justice's privilege waiver policy is set forth in a January 2003 memorandum written by then-Deputy Attorney General Larry Thompson entitled "Principles of Federal Prosecution of Business Organizations." The so-called "Thompson Memorandum" instructs federal prosecutors to consider certain factors in determining whether corporations and other organizations should receive cooperation credit—and hence leniency—during government investigations.

One of the key factors cited in the Thompson Memorandum is the organization's willingness to waive attorney-client and work product protections and provide this confidential information to government investigators. The Thompson Memorandum stated in pertinent part that:

> One factor the prosecutor may weigh in assessing the adequacy of a corporation's cooperation is the completeness of its disclosure including, if necessary, a waiver of the attorney-client and work product protections, both with respect to its internal investigation and with respect to communications between specific officers, directors, and employees and counsel. Such waivers permit the government to obtain statements of possible witnesses, subjects and targets, without having to negotiate individual cooperation or immunity agreements. In addition, they are often critical in enabling the government to evaluate the completeness of a corporation's voluntary disclosure and cooperation. Prosecutors may, therefore, request a waiver in appropriate circumstances. The Department does not, however, consider waiver of a corporation's attorney-client and work product protection an absolute requirement, and prosecutors should consider the willingness of a corporation to waive such protection when necessary to provide timely and complete information as one factor in evaluating the corporation's cooperation.

The American Bar Association is concerned that the Department of Justice's privilege waiver policy has brought about a number of profoundly negative, if unintended, consequences.

From a practical standpoint, companies have no choice but to waive when requested to do so, as the government's threat to label them as "uncooperative" will have a profound effect not just on charging and sentencing decisions, but on each company's public image, stock price, and credit worthiness as well.

The growing trend of government-coerced waiver was confirmed by a recent survey of over 1,200 in-house and outside corporate counsel that was completed by the Association of Corporate Counsel, the National Association of Criminal Defense Lawyers, and the ABA in March 2006.[6] According to the survey, almost 75% of corporate counsel respondents believe that a "culture of waiver" has evolved in which governmental agencies believe that it is reasonable and appropriate for them to expect a company under investigation to broadly waive attorney-client or work product protections. In addition, 52% of in-house respondents and 59% of outside respondents have indicated that there has been a marked increase in waiver requests as a condition of cooperation in recent years. One example of this growing "culture of waiver" came to light last year when then-U.S. Attorney (and current Deputy Attorney General) Paul McNulty met with approximately fifty corporate general counsel to discuss the growing erosion of the attorney-client privilege. The former General Counsel of a now defunct steel company was one of those attending the meeting, and his story follows.

> When Bethlehem Steel was still in existence, a disgruntled former employee told authorities that the company was burying toxic waste at one of its sites in Texas. Fifty federal agents arrived at the company with a search warrant and backhoes and started digging up the yard. No buried drums were ever found, but, in the course of the search, the investigators found evidence of garden variety environmental violations that, in most circumstances, likely would have been pursued as civil violations. Perhaps understandably, the Department of Justice did not want to drop the matter altogether, and decided to pursue a criminal investigation.

At its very first meeting with the General Counsel, the Department of Justice demanded the privileged internal report prepared by outside counsel and sought cooperation from the company in pursuing charges against individual employees. No middle-ground alternative was entertained. Firmly believing that no knowing or intentional violation had occurred, the General Counsel declined the request, and the company prepared its defenses. In the end, the Department did not charge a single individual; the company negotiated a plea and paid a fine.

The Bethlehem Steel example exemplifies a situation where prosecutors—operating under an increasingly expansive interpretation of the Thompson Memorandum—do not wait for a company to volunteer waiver, but rather seek internal investigation reports and privilege waivers even in cases that arguably never should have been prosecuted. When the other general counsels in the room were asked if they had had similar experiences, 75% of the attendees said they had.

* * *

The Department of Justice formally responded to the ABA's May 2 letter on July 18, 2006, and a copy of that letter is attached to this written statement as Appendix B. This response failed to address many of the specific concerns raised by the ABA and simply reasserted the Department's existing policy of coerced waiver.

On September 5, 2006, a group of ten prominent former senior Department of Justice officials from both parties—including three former Attorneys General, three former Deputy Attorneys General, and four former Solicitors General—

submitted a letter to Attorney General Gonzales expressing their opposition to the privilege waiver provisions of the Thompson Memorandum.

This remarkable letter, coming from the very people who ran the Department of Justice a few short years ago, demonstrates just how widespread the concerns over the Department's privilege waiver policy have become. The fact that these individuals previously served as the nation's top law enforcement officials—and were able to convict wrongdoers without demanding the wholesale production of privileged materials—makes their comments even more credible.

In addition to the ABA, the coalition, and former Department of Justice officials, many Congressional leaders have also raised concerns over the privilege waiver provisions in the Department's Thompson Memorandum. On March 7, 2006, the House Judiciary Subcommittee on Crime, Terrorism, and Homeland Security held a hearing on the privilege waiver issue. The Justice Department and several representatives of the coalition appeared and testified, while the ABA submitted a written statement for the record. During the hearing, virtually all of the Subcommittee members from both political parties expressed strong support for preserving the attorney-client privilege and serious concerns regarding the Department's waiver policy.

Although the ABA and the coalition are very encouraged by the Sentencing Commission's recent decision to reconsider and reverse its 2004 privilege waiver amendment to the Federal Sentencing Guidelines, the Department of Justice has declined to modify its privilege waiver policy as stated in the Thompson Memorandum. As a result, many federal prosecutors continue to demand that companies waive their privileges as a condition for receiving cooperation credit.

In addition, in response to the 2005 McCallum Memorandum, local U.S. Attorneys are now in the process of adopting local privilege waiver review procedures, which will likely result in numerous different waiver policies throughout the country.

For these reasons, the ABA urges the Committee, in the course of exercising its oversight authority, to send a strong message to the Department of Justice that the attorney-client privilege and the work product doctrine are fundamental principles of our legal system that must be protected, and that the Thompson Memorandum and other related Department directives to its prosecutors are improperly undermining those fundamental rights. The ABA urges the Committee to encourage the Department to modify the Thompson Memorandum to:

(1) prohibit federal prosecutors from demanding, requesting, or encouraging, directly or indirectly, that companies waive their attorney-client or work product protections during investigations,

(2) specify the types of factual, non-privileged information that prosecutors may request from companies during investigations as a sign of cooperation, and

(3) clarify that any voluntary decision by a company to waive the attorney-client privilege and the work product doctrine shall not be considered when assessing whether the entity provided effective cooperation.

The Department of Justice's policy is inconsistent with the fundamental legal principle that all prospective defendants—including an organization's current and former employees, officers, directors and agents—are presumed to be innocent.

When implementing the directives in the Thompson Memorandum, prosecutors often take the position that certain employees and other agents suspected of wrongdoing are "culpable" long before their guilt has been proven or the company has had an opportunity to complete its own internal investigation. In those cases, the prosecutors often pressure the company to fire the employees in question or refuse to provide them with legal representation or otherwise assist them with their legal defense as a condition for receiving cooperation credit. The Department's policy stands the presumption of innocence principle on its head.

In addition, the policy overturns well-established corporate governance practices by forcing companies to abandon the traditional practice of indemnifying their employees and agents or otherwise assisting them with their legal defense for employment-related conduct until it has been determined that the employee or agent somehow acted improperly.

Second, it should be the prerogative of a company to make an independent decision as to whether an employee should be provided defense or not. The fiduciary duties of the directors in making such decisions are clear, and they are in the best position to decide what is in the best interest of the shareholders.

Third, these provisions of the Thompson Memorandum improperly weaken the entity's ability to help its employees to defend themselves in criminal actions. The Thompson Memorandum seeks to undermine the ability of employees and other personnel to defend themselves, by seeking to prevent companies from sharing records and other relevant information with them and their lawyers.

Fourth, several of these employee-related provisions of the Thompson Memorandum have been declared to be constitutionally suspect by the federal judge presiding over the pending case of U.S. v. Stein.

> When dictators and tyrants seek to destroy the freedoms of men, their first target is the legal profession and through it the rule of law.[19]
>
> Leon Jaworski

Former Prosecutors McKay and Iglesias believe that investigation into the firings of Department of Justice Attorneys could reveal that the dismissal of eight federal prosecutors was ordered by Karl Rove and motivated by an attempt to influence ongoing public-corruption or voter-fraud investigations.[20]

Deputy assistant secretary of defense suggested boycott of detainees' lawyers[21]

In a January 2007 radio interview, Charles "Cully" Stimson, the deputy assistant secretary of defense for the United States stated in a radio interview:

That he found it "shocking" that lawyers at many of the nation's top law firms represent detainees, and went on to list the names of more than a dozen major firms he suggested should be boycotted. "And I think, quite honestly, when corporate CEOs see that those firms are representing the very terrorists who hit their bottom line back in 2001, those CEOs are going to make those law firms choose between representing terrorists or representing reputable firms."

When asked who might be paying the law firms to represent Guantanamo detainees, Stimson hinted at wrongdoing.

> "It's not clear, is it? Some will maintain that they're doing it out of the goodness of their heart—that they're doing it pro bono, and I suspect they are," he said. "Others are receiving monies from who knows where and I'd be curious to have them explain that."

Neal Sonnett, a Miami lawyer and president of the American Judicature Society, a nonpartisan group of judges, lawyers and others stated that Stimson made a "blatant attempt to intimidate lawyers and their firms who are rendering important public service in upholding the rule of law and our democratic ideals.

Stimson also described Guantanamo as "transparent, with visits from more than 2,000 journalists since it opened five years ago, claiming that international outrage over the detention center as "small little protests around the world" that were "drummed up by Amnesty International" and inflated by liberal news media outlets.

FBI agents have documented more than two-dozen incidents of possible mistreatment at Guantanamo. In one, a detainee's head was wrapped in duct tape because he chanted the Quran; in a second, a detainee pulled out his hair after hours in a sweltering room.

In a December court ruling, a federal judge in Washington decried the plight of "some of the unfortunate petitioners who have been detained for many years in the terrible conditions at Guantanamo Bay." The judge criticized a system in which dozens have been held without charges and cut off from the world for lack of English or knowledge about the law, leaving them no choice but to turn to a fellow prisoner with outside connections for legal help. Since the detention center opened, the U.S. military has transferred or released about 380 detainees. Some 395 remain in the prison.

The term "Bush lawyer" is Australian slang for a hick counsellor, ignorant of the law. Thanks to recent decisions of the US Supreme Court and inquiries into torture at Abu Ghraib, it has been given a wider meaning, to denote the lawyers in US Government service who have misunderstood or misrepresented the fundamental rules of human rights in their advice to the President. Their mistakes have been so damaging that the British Attorney-General has taken to tendering his own advice to the White House about Guantanamo Bay—namely to close it.[22]

Geoffrey Robertson

Future Role of Lawyers

For Your Consideration

What do you believe the role of lawyers will be in the new empire?

Consider the following excerpts from an essay by Princeton Professor G. John Ikenberry.

The "E" Word[23]

No one disagrees that U.S. power is extraordinary. It is the character and logic of U.S. domination that is at issue in the debate over empire. The United States is not just a superpower pursuing its interest; it is a producer of world order. Over the decades—with more support than resistance from other nations—it has fashioned a distinctively open and rule-based international order. Its dynamic bundle of oversized capacities, interests, and ideals constitutes an "American project" with unprecedented global reach. For better or worse, other states must come to terms with or work around this protean order.

The United States possesses a near-monopoly on the use of force internationally; on the domestic level, meanwhile, the institutions and behaviors of states are increasingly open to global—that is, American—scrutiny. Since September 11, the Bush administration's assertion of "contingent sovereignty" and the right of preemption have made this transformation abundantly clear. The rise of unipolarity and the simultaneous unbundling of state sovereignty is a new and volatile brew.

But is the resulting political formation an empire? And if so, will the American empire suffer the fate of great empires of the past: ravaging the world with its ambitions and excesses until overextension, miscalculation, and mounting opposition hasten its collapse?

The term "empire" refers to the political control by a dominant country of the domestic and foreign policies of weaker countries. The European colonial empires of the late nineteenth century were the most direct, formal kind. The Soviet "sphere of influence" in Eastern Europe entailed an equally coercive but less direct form of control. The British Empire included both direct colonial rule and "informal empire." If empire is defined loosely, as a hierarchical system of political relationships in which the most powerful state exercises decisive influence, then the United States today indeed qualifies.

If the United States is an empire, however, it is like no other before it. To be sure, it has a long tradition of pursuing crude imperial policies, most notably in Latin America and the Middle East. But for most countries, the U.S.-led order is a negotiated system wherein the United States has sought participation by other states on terms that are mutually agreeable. This is true in three respects. First, the United States has provided public goods—particularly the extension of security and the support for an open trade regime—in exchange for the cooperation of other states. Second, power in the U.S. system is exercised through rules and institutions; power politics still exist, but arbitrary and indiscriminate power is reigned in. Finally, weaker states in the U.S.-led order are given "voice opportunities"—informal access to the policymaking processes of the United States and the intergovernmental institutions that make up the international system. It is these features of the post-1945 international order that have led historians such as Charles Maier to talk about a "consensual empire" and Geir Lundestad to talk about an "empire of invitation." The American order is hierarchical and ultimately sustained by economic and military power, but it is put at the service of an expanding system of democracy and capitalism.

Fundamentally, then, the debate over the new American empire hinges on how extensive and deeply rooted these characteristics are—and whether its assertion of power since September 11 constitutes a fundamental break with this liberal past.

Global Access to Justice

Former United Nation's Secretary-General and Nobel Peace Prize winner Kofi Annan "spoke up for what he believed should be global norms of behavior that all had to do with the rights of the individual,"according to NY Times Magazine writer James Traub, author of ***The Best Intentions: Kofi Annan and the UN in the Era of American World Power.*** [24] "No Secretary-General succeeded in making the UN a place to advance economic rights in the Third World to the degree that he did."

There are international norms, agreed upon my UN member states, to guide the development of good legal representation. No system is perfect, but here we want to focus upon whether these things are possible, at the lowest end of our expectation, and likely given what we know about the probability of political infection and tendencies of human nature.

Basic Principles on the Role of Lawyers

Eighth United Nations Congress on the Prevention of
Crime and the Treatment of Offenders
Havana, 27 August to 7 September 1990[25]

Whereas in the Charter of the United Nations the peoples of the world affirm, inter alia, their determination to establish conditions under which justice can be maintained, and proclaim as one of their purposes the achievement of international cooperation in promoting and encouraging respect for human rights and fundamental freedoms without distinction as to race, sex, language or religion, Whereas the Universal Declaration of Human Rights enshrines the principles of equality before the law, the presumption of innocence, the right to a fair and public hearing by an independent and impartial tribunal, and all the guarantees necessary for the defence of everyone charged with a penal offence,

Whereas the International Covenant on Civil and Political Rights proclaims, in addition, the right to be tried without undue delay and the right to a fair and public hearing by a competent, independent and impartial tribunal established by law,

Whereas the International Covenant on Economic, Social and Cultural Rights recalls the obligation of States under the Charter to promote universal respect for, and observance of, human rights and freedoms,

Whereas the Body of Principles for the Protection of All Persons under Any Form of Detention or Imprisonment provides that a detained person shall be entitled to have the assistance of, and to communicate and consult with, legal counsel,

Whereas the Standard Minimum Rules for the Treatment of Prisoners recommend, in particular, that legal assistance and confidential communication with counsel should be ensured to untried prisoners,

Whereas the Safe guards guaranteeing protection of those facing the death penalty reaffirm the right of everyone suspected or charged with a crime for which capital punishment may be imposed to adequate legal assistance at all stages of the proceedings, in accordance with article 14 of the International Covenant on Civil and Political Rights,

Whereas the Declaration of Basic Principles of Justice for Victims of Crime and Abuse of Power recommends measures to be taken at the international and national levels to improve access to justice and fair treatment, restitution, compensation and assistance for victims of crime,

Whereas adequate protection of the human rights and fundamental freedoms to which all persons are entitled, be they economic, social and cultural, or civil and political, requires that all persons have effective access to legal services provided by an independent legal profession,

Whereas professional associations of lawyers have a vital role to play in upholding professional standards and ethics, protecting their members from persecution and improper restrictions and infringements, providing legal services to all in need of them, and cooperating with governmental and other institutions in furthering the ends of justice and public interest, The Basic Principles on the Role of Lawyers, set forth below, which have been formulated to assist Member States in their task of promoting and ensuring the proper role of lawyers, should be respected and taken into account by Governments within the framework of their national legislation and practice and should be brought to the attention of lawyers as well as other persons, such as judges, prosecutors, members of the executive and the legislature, and the public in general. These principles shall also apply, as appropriate, to persons who exercise the functions of lawyers without having the formal status of lawyers.

Access to lawyers and legal services

1. All persons are entitled to call upon the assistance of a lawyer of their choice to protect and establish their rights and to defend them in all stages of criminal proceedings.

2. Governments shall ensure that efficient procedures and responsive mechanisms for effective and equal access to lawyers are provided for all persons within their territory and subject to their jurisdiction, without distinction of any kind, such as discrimination based on race, colour, ethnic origin, sex, language, religion, political or other opinion, national or social origin, property, birth, economic or other status.

3. Governments shall ensure the provision of sufficient funding and other resources for legal services to the poor and, as necessary, to other disadvantaged

persons. Professional associations of lawyers shall cooperate in the organization and provision of services, facilities and other resources.

4. Governments and professional associations of lawyers shall promote programmes to inform the public about their rights and duties under the law and the important role of lawyers in protecting their fundamental freedoms. Special attention should be given to assisting the poor and other disadvantaged persons so as to enable them to assert their rights and where necessary call upon the assistance of lawyers.

Special safeguards in criminal justice matters

5. Governments shall ensure that all persons are immediately informed by the competent authority of their right to be assisted by a lawyer of their own choice upon arrest or detention or when charged with a criminal offence.

6. Any such persons who do not have a lawyer shall, in all cases in which the interests of justice so require, be entitled to have a lawyer of experience and competence commensurate with the nature of the offence assigned to them in order to provide effective legal assistance, without payment by them if they lack sufficient means to pay for such services.

7. Governments shall further ensure that all persons arrested or detained, with or without criminal charge, shall have prompt access to a lawyer, and in any case not later than forty-eight hours from the time of arrest or detention.

8. All arrested, detained or imprisoned persons shall be provided with adequate opportunities, time and facilities to be visited by and to communicate and consult with a lawyer, without delay, interception or censorship and in full confidentiality. Such consultations may be within sight, but not within the hearing, of law enforcement officials.

Qualifications and training

9. Governments, professional associations of lawyers and educational institutions shall ensure that lawyers have appropriate education and training and be made aware of the ideals and ethical duties of the lawyer and of human rights and fundamental freedoms recognized by national and international law.

10. Governments, professional associations of lawyers and educational institutions shall ensure that there is no discrimination against a person with respect to entry into or continued practice within the legal profession on the grounds of race, colour, sex, ethnic origin, religion, political or other opinion, national or social origin, property, birth, economic or other status, except that a requirement, that a lawyer must be a national of the country concerned, shall not be considered discriminatory.

11. In countries where there exist groups, communities or regions whose needs for legal services are not met, particularly where such groups have distinct cultures, traditions or languages or have been the victims of past discrimination, Governments, professional associations of lawyers and educational institutions should take special measures to provide opportunities for candidates from these groups to enter the legal profession and should ensure that they receive training appropriate to the needs of their groups. Duties and responsibilities

12. Lawyers shall at all times maintain the honour and dignity of their profession as essential agents of the administration of justice.

13. The duties of lawyers towards their clients shall include:

(a) Advising clients as to their legal rights and obligations, and as to the working of the legal system in so far as it is relevant to the legal rights and obligations of the clients;

(b) Assisting clients in every appropriate way, and taking legal action to protect their interests;

(c) Assisting clients before courts, tribunals or administrative authorities, where appropriate.

14. Lawyers, in protecting the rights of their clients and in promoting the cause of justice, shall seek to uphold human rights and fundamental freedoms recognized by national and international law and shall at all times act freely and diligently in accordance with the law and recognized standards and ethics of the legal profession.

15. Lawyers shall always loyally respect the interests of their clients.

Guarantees for the functioning of lawyers

16. Governments shall ensure that lawyers"

(a) are able to perform all of their professional functions without intimidation, hindrance, harassment or improper interference;

(b) are able to travel and to consult with their clients freely both within their own country and abroad; and

(c) shall not suffer, or be threatened with, prosecution or administrative, economic or other sanctions for any action taken in accordance with recognized professional duties, standards and ethics.

17. Where the security of lawyers is threatened as a result of discharging their functions, they shall be adequately safeguarded by the authorities.

18. Lawyers shall not be identified with their clients or their clients' causes as a result of discharging their functions.

19. No court or administrative authority before whom the right to counsel is recognized shall refuse to recognize the right of a lawyer to appear before it for his or her client unless that lawyer has been disqualified in accordance with national law and practice and in conformity with these principles.

20. Lawyers shall enjoy civil and penal immunity for relevant statements made in good faith in written or oral pleadings or in their professional appearances before a court, tribunal or other legal or administrative authority.

21. It is the duty of the competent authorities to ensure lawyers access to appropriate information, files and documents in their possession or control in sufficient time to enable lawyers to provide effective legal assistance to their clients. Such access should be provided at the earliest appropriate time.

22. Governments shall recognize and respect that all communications and consultations between lawyers and their clients within their professional relationship are confidential.

Freedom of expression and association

23. Lawyers like other citizens are entitled to freedom of expression, belief, association and assembly. In particular, they shall have the right to take part in public discussion of matters concerning the law, the administration of justice and the promotion and protection of human rights and to join or form local, national or

international organizations and attend their meetings, without suffering professional restrictions by reason of their lawful action or their membership in a lawful organization. In exercising these rights, lawyers shall always conduct themselves in accordance with the law and the recognized standards and ethics of the legal profession.

Professional associations of lawyers

24. Lawyers shall be entitled to form and join self-governing professional associations to represent their interests, promote their continuing education and training and protect their professional integrity. The executive body of the professional associations shall be elected by its members and shall exercise its functions without external interference.

25. Professional associations of lawyers shall cooperate with Governments to ensure that everyone has effective and equal access to legal services and that lawyers are able, without improper interference, to counsel and assist their clients in accordance with the law and recognized professional standards and ethics.

Disciplinary proceedings

26. Codes of professional conduct for lawyers shall be established by the legal profession through its appropriate organs, or by legislation, in accordance with national law and custom and recognized international standards and norms.

27. Charges or complaints made against lawyers in their professional capacity shall be processed expeditiously and fairly under appropriate procedures. Lawyers shall have the right to a fair hearing, including the right to be assisted by a lawyer of their choice.

28. Disciplinary proceedings against lawyers shall be brought before an impartial disciplinary committee established by the legal profession, before an independent statutory authority, or before a court, and shall be subject to an independent judicial review.

29. All disciplinary proceedings shall be determined in accordance with the code of professional conduct and other recognized standards and ethics of the legal profession and in the light of these principles.

Imagine a Just World

Imagine a world where the majority of the world's legal resources were dedicated to justice and equality rather than conquest and domination. Imagine a world dedicated to Human Rights for Women. Human Rights Watch reports the following.[26]

> Millions of women throughout the world live in conditions of abject deprivation of, and attacks against, their fundamental human rights for no other reason than that they are women.
>
> Combatants and their sympathizers in conflicts, such as those in Sierra Leone, Kosovo, the Democratic Republic of Congo, Afghanistan, and Rwanda, have raped women as a weapon of war with near complete impunity. Men in Pakistan, South Africa, Peru, Russia, and Uzbekistan beat women in the home at astound-

ing rates, while these governments alternatively refuse to intervene to protect women and punish their batterers or do so haphazardly and in ways that make women feel culpable for the violence. As a direct result of inequalities found in their countries of origin, women from Ukraine, Moldova, Nigeria, the Dominican Republic, Burma, and Thailand are bought and sold, trafficked to work in forced prostitution, with insufficient government attention to protect their rights and punish the traffickers. In Guatemala, South Africa, and Mexico, women's ability to enter and remain in the work force is obstructed by private employers who use women's reproductive status to exclude them from work and by discriminatory employment laws or discriminatory enforcement of the law. In the U.S., students discriminate against and attack girls in school who are lesbian, bi-sexual, or transgendered, or do not conform to male standards of female behavior. Women in Morocco, Jordan, Kuwait, and Saudi Arabia face government-sponsored discrimination that renders them unequal before the law—including discriminatory family codes that take away women's legal authority and place it in the hands of male family members—and restricts women's participation in public life.

Abuses against women are relentless, systematic, and widely tolerated, if not explicitly condoned. Violence and discrimination against women are global social epidemics, notwithstanding the very real progress of the international women's human rights movement in identifying, raising awareness about, and challenging impunity for women's human rights violations.

We live in a world in which women do not have basic control over what happens to their bodies. Millions of women and girls are forced to marry and have sex with men they do not desire. Women are unable to depend on the government to protect them from physical violence in the home, with sometimes fatal consequences, including increased risk of HIV/AIDS infection. Women in state custody face sexual assault by their jailers. Women are punished for having sex outside of marriage or with a person of their choosing (rather than of their family's choosing). Husbands and other male family members obstruct or dictate women's access to reproductive health care. Doctors and government officials disproportionately target women from disadvantaged or marginalized communities for coercive family planning policies.

Our duty as activists is to expose and denounce as human rights violations those practices and policies that silence and subordinate women. We reject specific legal, cultural, or religious practices by which women are systematically discriminated against, excluded from political participation and public life, segregated in their daily lives, raped in armed conflict, beaten in their homes, denied equal divorce or inheritance rights, killed for having sex, forced to marry, assaulted for not conforming to gender norms, and sold into forced labor. Arguments that sustain and excuse these human rights abuses—those of cultural norms, "appropriate" rights for women, or western imperialism—barely disguise their true meaning: that women's lives matter less than men's. Cultural relativism, which argues that there are no universal human rights and that rights are culture-specific and culturally determined, is still a formidable and corrosive challenge to women's rights to equality and dignity in all facets of their lives.

The Women's Rights Division of Human Rights Watch fights against the dehumanization and marginalization of women. We promote women's equal rights and human dignity. The realization of women's rights is a global struggle based on universal human rights and the rule of law. It requires all of us to unite in solidarity to end traditions, practices, and laws that harm women. It is a fight for freedom to be fully and completely human and equal without apology or permission. Ultimately, the struggle for women's human rights must be about making women's lives matter everywhere all the time. In practice, this means taking action to stop discrimination and violence against women.

For Your Consideration

Technological advances have prompted investigation into whether information overload tends to breed political inertia. This is an especially relevant question for those who believe in representative democracy and doubt the evidence that suggests that it has reached its functional end. In the face of massive injustice, the tendency to feel overwhelmed evokes longing for a sense of community. The promise of individual rights has been that physical and cultural mobility could enable the selection and perfection of shared community. Some say the promise has been hindered by a rising cult of fear insofar as public dialog is skewed in favor of political extremists leaving scant opportunities for the formation of consensus about the best way to view and respond to social injustice. The journey upon which we imagine ourselves to be is the heart and soul of civic engagement. The lack of ethics and honor embodied in the phrase "you can't fight City Hall" demonstrates that the theory of participatory democracy and the practice bear no resemblance. We need new ways of communicating about and manifesting equality.

How necessary is it to assume that shared cultural norms and edicts will provide the safety and predictability that we desire as we speak of the future and its connection to decisions that we make today? One community set a fine example. The City of Berkeley, California, has a Human Rights Policy and a Peace and Justice Commission.[27]

Section 3.68.030 "Peace and justice" defined.

For the purpose of this chapter, "peace and social justice" shall refer to the goal of creating a world community in which the relations between people are based on equality, respect for human rights, and the abhorrence of exploitation and all forms of oppression. (Ord. 5705-NS § 3, 1986)

Section 3.68.010 Findings.

The council finds as follows:

The intentional destruction of cities in war is the rule and not the exception.

State, national and international governmental bodies have failed to control war and in fact, have in many cases, been responsible for war and the conditions of war.

The wealth that could be spent to help the poor, heal the sick, house the homeless, educate the children, and care for the elderly is now spent on ever more costly weapons of mass destruction.

Peace is not a fictitious tranquil end-state, but the process of solving differences constructively, creatively, and non-violently.

Peace is inseparable from justice.

> The present threat of nuclear or biological holocaust is not peace, but a condition of war against all humanity.
>
> Initiatives are needed to reverse the drift toward war and to remove the causes of war.
>
> Our best protection lies in initiating, devising, and promulgating peaceful and just policy alternatives.
>
> Individual citizens, unless organized, are virtually powerless in confronting and influencing larger governmental bodies.
>
> It is the responsibility of one and all to labor hard for peace and justice within forums of appropriate scale.
>
> The residents of Berkeley have continually demonstrated their concern for peace and justice based on equality among all peoples.
>
> The residents of Berkeley have welcomed to our City those who have been forced into exile, and who have come fleeing torture and death.
>
> The Berkeley City Council, to act successfully in furthering peace and justice, must have wise counsel, accurate research, vigorous analysis, articulate formulation of issues and proposals for action, and thus the establishment of a Peace and Justice Commission is proper. (Ord. 5705 § 1, 1986)

Georgetown University Law Professor Charles Abernathy has devoted his career to the field of civil rights, and his commentary provokes thought on the original question: What is the most effective way to train lawyers to protect civil rights?

> Civil rights is more than constitutional law because statutory considerations play such an important role. Civil Rights is broader than race or sex discrimination, broader of course, in the topical sense, especially with Congress' newer legislation. Focusing on a single topic fails to disclose the similarities that many civil rights topics share, and the pertinent differences which so shape polices and decisions. The topical approach produces students long on policy but short on the skills necessary too implement policy, and if there is anything the civil rights areas needs it is attorneys as skilled as they are committed.[28]

The Association of American Law School's 2006 Annual Meeting featured a workshop: *A Search for Balance in the Whirlwind of Law School.* Santa Clara University Law Professor Stephanie M. Wildman developed a concurrent session entitled Connection to Purpose.[29]

> The topic naturally raises the question, "What purpose?" In my experience of over 30 years as a legal educator in a number of different educational settings, I have seen many students who come to law school because they care about justice. Some ask, as they are graduating, "Where was the class about justice?" So from my current role as Director of the Center for Social Justice and Public Service at Santa Clara University, my connection to purpose is a commitment to social justice.

Democracy and Social Justice: Founding Centers for Social Justice in Law Schools[30]

Stephanie Wildman

Protecting democracy by combating inequality is the task of social justice lawyers.

The practice of democracy mandates inclusion of the diverse populations of this nation into the social order. Social justice lawyers seek to give meaning to democratic ideals in the daily lives of individuals and communities that are marginalized, subordinated, and underrepresented. Social justice lawyering envisions the practice of law both on behalf of and alongside of subordinated peoples, with the efforts and achievements of members of the community a crucial aspect of the work. While lawyers are not the complete solution, lawyers remain a key ingredient needed in social justice work.

Leaders in legal education and the bar have been calling on law schools to make consciousness about social justice pervasive in law schools and accessible to all students, even those who might choose other career paths. As the gatekeepers for the profession, law schools play a critical role in educating students for social justice. Two groups of students attend law school: those who wish to pursue careers in public interest and social justice work and the rest of the student population, who need to understand that access to justice is the province of all lawyers. Legal education need not dissociate students from the aspiration for justice that motivated many of them to choose law as a profession.

In a 1997 article titled, ***Law and The Possibility of Justice***, Verna Sanchez concluded that the professional and ethical tenets related to law teaching that are endorsed by the Association of American Law School have not yet found their way into the general curriculum at our nation's law schools. [31]

Edited Relevant Excerpts
Reprinted with permission

During a commencement speech a graduate explained that a friend asked what she learned during three years in law school. She mentioned torts, contracts, and criminal law. Her friend inquired about the class on justice.

We have all asked: What is justice? Academics are obligated to consider a deeper question: What do we teach about justice and the legal system? What is difficult to explain is how the issue of justice became separated from the study of law. Following three years in law school, hundreds of cases and rules of law, students graduate without ever considering the role of justice. Students learn various methods of legal thought and analysis: brief the case, learn the facts, find the issue, find the holding, isolate the rationale for the decision, apply it to a hypothetical set of facts. Seldom are they invited to think about justice and the law and the relationship between the two.

As lawyers, we are accustomed to seeing the standard, once-a-year article in the ABA Journal (or comparable professional publication) about those lawyers who practice public interest law. The article is usually written in a way that makes it apparent that, overall, these people are aberrant but interesting "specimens." The "idealist" of course, is always juxtaposed against the "pragmatist." In fact, the pragmatist is usually meant to be what an idealist becomes when he or she "grows up." That is, work that carries with it a goal of attaining a common good or betterment of society is a sign of immaturity—a stage, perhaps, to be gotten through until one acquires "good sense" and moves on. But it is the idealist, I contend, who worries most about questions of justice: do we have it, does the law consider or offer it, can we get it, and if so, how?

Some have argued that justice is an elusive, philosophical idea. Even if this is so, society can only benefit by continued debate and discussion about it. We are harmed, within the academy and without, by turning away from, or benignly neglecting the topic. But ours is a society that seems to have moved further and further away from respecting ideas or the life of the mind. Instead, we are fed "sound bites," a meager substitute for genuine intellectual exchange within and among the polity. Abstract concepts and the realm of ideas have been almost completely superseded by "things." The extension of this perspective is that anything can be bought and sold. And we all remember that our own history includes a time when some people were indeed treated only as commodities.

When a society equates liberty with ownership then the right of the individual emerges as paramount to the right of the community. It becomes ever more difficult to try and persuade people of the intrinsic value of a just society when you may not be able to offer tangible proof of the benefits, especially for each individual person. The problems of fairness and equality, for example, cannot be resolved without acknowledgement of the need for a meaningful ethos that balances the needs of the individual and the community in ways that benefit both, thereby, advancing justice.

Conclusion

There are few areas of law that have not been subjected to exacting constitutional analysis. Layers of legal doctrine develop from the Supreme Court's interpretation of single provisions in the Constitution, such as laws defining the parameters of a reasonable search and seizure, guarantees of trial by jury and those actions by the government that constitute cruel and unusual punishment. Other areas are difficult to define because they clash with perceived constitutional mandates. In Tort law, for example, the individual's right to be free from intentional infliction of emotional distress collided head on with protection for freedom of speech and association when a group of neo-Nazis marched through a residential community of Holocaust survivors, boldly displaying the swastika.

The various doctrines and rules of constitutional law impact nearly every area of civil life. This reality does not diminish the special role of civil rights lawyers. Fourteenth Amendment guarantees of Due Process and Equal Protection are the bulwark of anti-discrimination law and the foundation of functioning democracies. The Constitution mandates procedural regularity in the form of written notice of adjudicative/administrative processes, meaningful opportunity to be heard, access to information relied upon by officials in the decision-making process and, in many cases, the opportunity for appeal. Such procedures should be free from bias in the application and execution of governmental authority. When the official rule requires different treatment for individuals in similar circumstances, there is prima facie evidence of discrimination and the law may be deemed unjust. For example, until recently, employers routinely excluded coverage of prescriptive contraceptives for women under their healthcare plans, while including benefits for other preventative medical services, medications, and devices. The exclusionary language did not explicitly reference "birth control pills" or "women's oral contraceptives." Nevertheless, exclusion of "prescription contraceptives" when they are only used by women, and most often to prevent pregnancy, a medical condition that only affects women, has a disparate impact. It disproportionately burdens women's health care rights. When discretionary powers result in the application of a neutrally stated law in a discriminatory manner, courts must look to equal protection doctrine for proper balancing of the states' asserted interests in maintaining a system that routinely and disproportionately burdens an identifiable group. The statistics on the administration of capital punishment in the United States provides a continuing cogent example.

> Verna Sanchez concluded her article excerpted above with a personal commitment that I share:
>
> I believe it is our obligation, as professors, lawyers, and law students, to seek justice when and how we can. We must teach justice, talk about it, write about it, and work for it, so that all of us may come to desire it, recognize the need for it and the benefit derived from it, and therefore possibly make it real, always.[1]

According to Pierre Schlag, a noted scholar on legal reasoning, Sanchez's view is nothing short of revolutionary. In training students to think like lawyers, the pedagogical norm is to strip them of the soulful commitment to anything other than a formal, universal, neutral and impersonal view of the law, and they are taught that is the primary method of judicial reasoning. From this unitary perspective, they begin to embrace legal authorities. Their overriding goal is to understand precedent, demonstrate detached objectivity, and master the art of legal argumentation so that submission into ways of law becomes the passport to its practice.[2] Gaining confidence that one could argue anything all while subscribing to the view that the legal skills of the hired gun is the beauty of the system, does not readily lend itself to the real-world task of achieving equality and justice. We must reach a tipping point where an informed citizenry, disgusted by the spreading casualties, corruption, militarism and diseases, overcomes its fear of retribution and actively enlists the best and brightest among us, including the nation's lawyers, for the task of fighting the dangers of autocratic governance. We could begin by undertaking a candid assessment of the contours of representative democracy and its role in our nation's future.

Notes

Chapter One

1. STEPHEN BREYER, ACTIVE LIBERTY: INTERPRETING OUR DEMOCRATIC CONSTITUTION (2005).

2. Louis Fisher, *Point/Counterpoint: Unchecked Presidential Wars*, 148 U. PA. L. REV. 1637, 1639 (2000).

3. *Id.*

4. *See generally* Polly J. Price, *Precedent and Judicial Power After the Founding*, 42 B.C. L. REV. 81 (2000).

5. BENJAMIN N. CARDOZO, THE NATURE OF THE JUDICIAL PROCESS (1921).

6. Steven G. Gey, *"Under God", the Pledge of Allegiance and Other Constitutional Trivia*, 81 N.C. L. REV. 1865, 1875 (2003).

7. Harry Lee Anstead, *Communities Coming Together on Issues of Human Relations to Achieve Social Justice for Indigenous Peoples*, 10 ST. THOMAS L. REV. 25, 33 (1997).

8. Calder v. Bull, 3 U.S. 386, 387–88 (1798) (Justice Samuel Chase, writing for the majority).

9. George Van Cleve, *Somerset's Case Revisited: Somerset's Case and its Antecedents in Imperial Perspective*, 24 LAW & HIST. REV. 601, 607 (2006).

10. *Focus on the Slave Trade*, BBC NEWS, Sept. 3, 2001, http://news.bbc.co.uk/ 2/hi/africa/ 1523100.stm.

11. *Id.*

12. Eric L. Muller, *Fixing a Hole: How the Criminal Law Can Bolster Reparations Theory*, 47 B.C. L. REV 659, 689 (2006).

13. *See* Pamela D. Bridgewater, *Un/Re/Dis Covering Slave Breeding in Thirteenth Amendment Jurisprudence*, 7 WASH. & LEE R.E.A. L.J. 11 (2001); Darlene C. Goring, *The History of Slave Marriage in the United States*, 39 J. MARSHALL L. REV. 299 (2006).

14. Alfreda Robinson, *Troubling "Settled" Waters: The Opportunity and Peril of African-American Reparations*, 24 B.C. THIRD WORLD L.J. 139 (2004).

15. Michael Byers, *Policing the High Seas: The Proliferation Security Initiative*, 98 A.J.I.L. 526, 534 (2004).

16. Thomas Jefferson, *Declaration on Taking Arms* (Thomas Jefferson's First Draft) (1775) *in* 2 JOURNALS OF THE CONTINENTAL CONGRESS 128, 140, 128–57 (Washington Chauncey Ford ed., 1904).

17. Brian Tierney, *Historical Roots of Modern Rights: Before Locke and After*, 3 AVE MARIA L. REV. 23, 24–25 (2005).

18. JOHN H. FRANKLIN & ALFRED A. MOSS, JR., FROM SLAVERY TO FREEDOM: A HISTORY OF AFRICAN-AMERICANS 71 (7th ed., Knopf 1997).

19. Stephanie Phillips, *Claiming our Foremothers: The Legend of Sally Hemings and the Tasks of Black Feminist Theory*, 8 HASTINGS WOMEN'S L.J. 401, 403–04, 406–17 (1997); Aaron Schwabach, *Perspective: Thomas Jefferson and Sally Hemings*, 21 T. JEFFERSON L. REV. 41 (1999).

20. A. Leon Higginbotham, Jr., In the Matter of Color: Race and the American Legal Process: The Colonial Period 382 (1978).

21. Stephen E. Lucas, *The Stylistic Artistry of the Declaration of Independence*, Prologue, Spring 1990, at 22, 25–43.

22. *Id.*

23. *Id.*

24. *Id.*

25. Kristin E. Kandt, *In The Name of God; An American Story of Feminism, Racism, and Religious Intolerance: The Story of Alma Bridwell White*, 8 Am. U. J. Gender Soc. Pol'y & L. 753 (2000). The text of the resolution can be found at http://www.nps.gov/wori/report1.htm (last visited Jan. 24, 2007).

26. For more on the history of the Pledge of Allegiance, see *The Story of the Pledge of Allegiance*, http://www.flagday.org/Pages/StoryofPledge.html (last visited Jan. 24, 2007). Christian dominance is explored in detail in Joseph R. Duncan, Jr., *Privilege, Invisibility, and Religion: A Critique of the Privilege that Christianity Has Enjoyed in the United States*, 54 Ala. L. Rev. 617, 626 (2003).

27. Victoria C. Woodhull, "And the Truth Shall Make You Free": A Speech on the Principles of Social Freedom (Nov. 20, 1871), *available at* http://memory.loc.gov/cgi-bin/query/S?ammem/nawbib:@field(TITLE+@od1(+And+the+truth+shall+make+you+free+++)).

28. Amanda Frisken, Victoria Woodhull's Sexual Revolution (2004); Mary Gabriel, Notorious Victoria: The Life of Victoria Woodhull Uncensored (1998); Barbara Goldsmith, Other Powers: The Age of Suffrage, Spiritualism, and the Scandalous Victoria Woodhull (1998).

29. http://fair-use.org/passages-from-not-by-law-alone.

30. Martin Luther King, Jr., I Have a Dream (Aug. 28, 1963), *available at* http://www.usconstitution.net/dream.html.

31. Poe v. Ulman, 367 U.S. 497, 522 (1961).

32. *See generally* Paulo Freire, Cultural Action for Freedom (1973); Paulo Freire, Education for Critical Consciousness (1973); Paulo Freire, Pedagogy of the Oppressed (1970).

33. Leonard Atos & Cynthia Deitle, *California's Attempts to Disarm the Black Panthers*, 36 San Diego L. Rev. 947 (1999).

Chapter Two

1. Patricia J. Williams, The Alchemy of Race and Rights 10 (1991).

2. Gerald B. Wetlaufer, *Systems of Belief in Modern American Law: A View from Century's End*, 49 Am. U. L. Rev. 1 (1999).

3. Chris Gus Kanios, *Mediation: A Progressive Model of Dispute Resolution*, The Center for Guerrilla Law, http://www.guerrillalaw.com/mediation.html (last visited Jan. 31, 2007).

4. Independent Courts: How Important Are They? by Ed O'Brien, published in *ABA Commission on Separation of Powers Special Report*, 1997, located at http://www.abanet.org/publiced/resources/indcourtsarticle.html ©1997 by the American Bar Association. Reprinted with permission.

5. http://www.cnn.com/2007/SHOWBIZ/TV/05/04/paris.hilton.ap/index.html, http://www.usmagazine.com/paris_goes_to_court.

6. Richard Michael Fischl , *The Politics of Constraint: It's Conflict All the Way Down*, 22 Cardozo L. Rev. 773, 781 (2001).

7. Louis Menand, The Metaphysical Club: Story of Ideas in America 339 (2001).

8. Stephen Breyer, Active Liberty: Interpreting Our Democratic Constitution (2005).

9. Harvie Wilkinson III, *The Role of Reason in the Rule of Law*, 56 U. Chi. L. Rev. 779 (1989). *See generally* Timothy P. Terrell, *Flatlaw: An Essay on the Dimensions of Legal Reasoning and the Development of Fundamental Normative Principles*, 72 Cal. L. Rev. 288 (1984).

10. David Kairys, *Perspectives on Critical Legal Studies: Law and Politics*, 52 Geo. Wash. L. Rev. 243 (1984).

11. Pierre Schlag, Enchantment of Reason 15 (1998).

12. *Id.* at 19.

13. *Id.* at 37.

14. Aristotle, The Politics of Aristotle 146 (Earnest Baker trans., 1946).

15. Anthony Carty, *Nietzsche and Socrates / Or the Spirit of the Devil and the Law*, 24 Cardozo L. Rev. 621, 628 (2003).

16. I.F. Stone, self-interview, *Stone Breaks the Socrates Story: An Old Muckraker Sheds Fresh Light on the 2,500-Year-Old Mystery and Reveals Some Athenian Political Realities that Plato Did his Best to Hide*, N.Y. Times, Apr. 8, 1979, at 22, *available at* LEXIS, NYT.

17. *Id.*

18. Charles Sykes, The End of Privacy 15 (1999).

19. David D. Garner, *Socratic Misogyny?—Analyzing Feminist Criticisms of Socratic Teaching in Legal Education*, 2000 B.Y.U. L. Rev. 1597 (2000).

20. Harvie Wilkinson III, *The Role of Reason in the Rule of Law*, 56 U. Chi. L. Rev. 779, 797 (1989).

21. Pierre Schlag, *Normativity and the Politics of Form*, 139 U. Pa. L. Rev. 801 (1991).

22. Lucinda M. Finley, *Breaking Women's Silence in Law: The Dilemma of the Gendered Nature of Legal Reasoning*, 64 Notre Dame L. Rev. 886, 888 (1989).

23. *Id.*

24. Statement of Good Practices by Law Professors in the Discharge of their Ethical and Professional Responsibilities, Association of American Law Schools, http://www.aals.org/about_handbook_sgp_eth.php (last visited Jan. 31, 2007).

25. Gerald B. Wetlaufer, *Systems of Belief in Modern American Law: A View from Century's End*, 49 Am. U. L. Rev. 1 (1999).

26. Robin West, *Law, Literature, and the Celebration of Authority*, 83 Nw. U.L. Rev. 977, 1007 (1989).

27. 3 John Adams, Defence of the Constitutions of Government of the United States of America 157–58 (new ed., 1794) (1788).

28. Harold Hongju Koh, *A Letter From Dean Harold Hongju Koh* (June 2004) http://www.law.yale.edu/YLR/pdf/v51–2/Kohletter.pdf.

29. *Preamble*, Section III, Canons of Judicial Conduct for the Commonwealth of Virginia, *available at* http://www.courts.state.va.us/jirc/canons_112398.html.

30. Abner Mikva, Op-ed., *The Wooing of Our Judges*, N.Y. Times, Aug. 28, 2000, at A12, *available at* LEXIS, NYT.

31. Brian Ross, *Supreme Ethics Problem?: What Was Supreme Court Justice Antonin Scalia Doing on Day of Supreme Court Swearing-In?*, ABC News, Jan. 23, 2006, http://abcnews.go.com/Nightline/story?id=1541642.

32. Nancy Benac, *Scalia Begins Third Decade on Court*, Sept. 29, 2006, *available at* http://www.bu.edu/phpbin/news-cms/news/?dept=634&id=40833.

33. *The Nomination of John G. Roberts Jr. to be Chief Justice of the United States: Hearing Before the S. Comm. on the Judiciary*, 109th Cong. (2005) (statement of Judith Resnik, Professor, Yale Law School), *available at* http://judiciary.senate.gov/testimony.cfm?id=1611&wit_id=4630.

34. Douglas T. Kendall & Jason C. Rylander, *Tainted Justice: How Private Judicial Trips Undermine Public Confidence in the Judiciary*, 18 Geo. J. Legal Ethics 65, 67–68 (2004).

35. Pierre Schlag, Enchantment of Reason 20–21 (1998).

36. Daron Acemoglu, *Why Not A Political Coase Theorem? Social Conflict, Commitment, And Politics*, 31 J. Comp. Econ. 620–52 (2003).

Chapter Three

1. Planned Parenthood of Se. Pa. v. Casey, 505 U.S. 833 (1992).

2. *Id.*

3. Griswold v. Connecticut, 381 U.S. 479 (1965).

4. For the full text of the Fourteenth Amendment to U.S. Constitution, see page 13 of this book.

5. Griswold v. Connecticut, 381 U.S. 479 (1965).

6. Revised Unif. Anatomical Gift Act (2006). Approved on July 7–14, 2006, the text of the UAGA 2006 can be found at http://www.law.upenn.edu/bll/ulc/uaga/2006final.htm.

7. *Id.*

8. Linda C. Fentiman, *Organ Donation as National Service*, 27 Suffolk Univ. L. Rev. 1593, 1593–1602, 1604 (1993).

9. In 1977, thirty-seven-year-old Sandra Ilene West, of Beverly Hills, California devised her multi-million dollar estate to her brother-in-law, on the condition that he bury her seated in her baby-blue 1964 Ferrari, wearing her favorite lace nightgown. According to court instructions, West and her automobile were interred in a large box and covered over with two truckloads of cement to discourage vandals. Jesse Dukeminier & Stanley Johanson, Wills, Trusts, and Estates 410 n.19 (5th ed. 1994).

10. *Treatment Keeps Girl Child-sized*, BBC News, Jan. 4, 2007, http://news.bbc.co.uk/2/hi/americas/6229799.stm.

11. *Id.*

12. *Id.*

13. 497 U.S. 261 (1990).

14. Kenneth C. Kirk, *The Alaska Health Care Decisions Act, Analyzed*, 22 Alaska L. Rev. 213 (2005).

15. 521 U.S. 793 (1997).

16. 521 U.S. 702 (1997).

17. 521 U.S. 793 (1997).

18. Or. Rev. Stat. §127 (1995).

19. Charles Lane, *Justices Uphold Oregon Assisted Suicide Law in a Blow to Administration; Ruling Paves Way for Other States to Follow Suit*, Wash. Post, Jan.18, 2006, at A01, *available at* LEXIS, WPOST.

20. Michael Cholbi, *Suicide*, The Stanford Encyclopedia of Philosophy (Edward N. Zalta, ed., Winter 2006 Edition), *available at* <http://plato.stanford.edu/archives/win2006/entries/suicide/>.

Chapter Four

1. Vacco v. Quill, 521 U.S. 793 (1997).

2. Edward Lazarus, Closed Chambers, The Rise, Fall, and Future of the Modern Supreme Court (2005).

3. McCleskey v. Kemp, 481 U.S. 279 (1987).

4. Laura M. Argys & Naci H. Mocan, *Who Shall Live and Who Shall Die? An Analysis of Prisoners on Death Row in the United States*, 33 J. Legal Stud. 255 (2004).

5. Angela J. Davis, Arbitrary Justice: The Power of the American Prosecutor (2007).

6. McGautha v. California, 402 U.S. 183, 205 (1971).

7. Donald S. Connery, *You, Me and The Death Penalty*, Hartford Courant, Jan. 9, 2005, *available at* LEXIS, HTCOUR.

8. *See generally* Robin D. Barnes, *Blue By Day and White By [K]night: Regulating the Political Affiliations of Law Enforcement and Military Personnel*, 81 Iowa L. Rev. 1079 (1996).

9. Donald S. Connery, *You, Me and The Death Penalty*, Hartford Courant, Jan. 9, 2005, *available at* LEXIS, HTCOUR.

10. *Id.*

11. Booth v. Maryland, 482 U.S. 496 (1987).

12. South Carolina v. Gathers, 490 U.S. 805 (1989).

13. *Dignity Denied: New Report Reveals Bias Against Surviving Family Members Who Oppose the Death Penalty*, Murder Victims' Families for Reconciliation (2002) http://talkleft.com/new_archives/000263.html.

14. *Id.*

15. Roper v. Simmons, 543 U.S. 551 (2005).

16. *Id.*

17. *Id.*

18. Donald S. Connery, *You, Me And The Death Penalty*, Hartford Courant, Jan. 9, 2005, *available at* LEXIS, HTCOUR.

19. The European Union is an economic and political union established in 1993 after the ratification of the Maastricht Treaty by members of the European Community. The purpose is to expand the political scope of the European Economic Community, especially in the area of foreign policy, security policy, creation of a central bank, and the adoption of a common currency. For a statement of the European Union's stance on the death penalty, see External Relations, European Commission web page, www.europa.eu.int/comm/external_relations/human_rights/adp/ (last visited Jan. 24, 2007).

20. Administrative Board, United States Catholic Conference, *Statement on Registration and Conscription for Military Service*, Feb. 14, 1980, http://www.usccb.org/sdwp/peace/military.htm.

21. David Chandler, *Conscience and War*, http://www.davidchandler.com/writings/ConscienceAndWar.htm (last visited Jan. 24, 2007).

22. Friends Committee on National Legislation, *Will Congress Bring Back the Draft?: The U.S. Military Is Facing Manpower Shortages Carrying Out Wars in Iraq and Afghanistan and Other Expanding Missions,* Sept. 30, 2004 http://www.fcnl.org/issues/item.php?item_id=1090&issue_id =37. Reprinted by permission of the Friends Committee on National Legislation, a Quaker lobby in the public interest.

23. CNN/Opinion Research Poll, PollingReport.com, Dec. 8–10, 2006, http://www.pollingreport.com/iraq.htm. For this poll, N=922 adults nationwide; MoE Å 3 (for all adults); RV = registered voters.

24. http://thinkprogress.org/.

25. Evan M. Wooten, *Banging on the Backdoor Draft: The Constitutional Validity of Stop-Loss in the Military*, 47 Wm. and Mary L. Rev. 1061 (2005).

26. Elinor Ament, *Constitutional Law Chapter: Anti-Abortion Protesting*, 7 Geo. J. Gender & L. 663 (2006).

27. Marc Kaufman, *Morning After Pill Study Contradicts Claim by Foes Easy Access Did Not Lead to Riskier Behavior*, Wash. Post, Jan. 5, 2005, at A09, *available at* LEXIS, WPOST.

28. Catherine A. MacKinnon, *Reflections on Sex Equality Under the Law*, 100 Yale L.J. 1281, 1312–13 (1991).

29. *Id.*

30. *Id.* at 1314–15.

31. Reva Siegal, *Reasoning from the Body: A Historical Perspective on Abortion Regulation and Questions of Equal Protection*, 44 Stan. L. Rev. 261, 275–277 (1992).

Chapter Five

1. Obscuring the Importance of Race: The Implication of Making Comparisons between Racism and Sexism [or other isms] 1991 Dukee L.J. 397

2. Victoria C. Woodhull, "And the Truth Shall Make You Free": A Speech on the Principles of Social Freedom (Nov. 20, 1871), available at http://memory.loc.gov/cgi-bin/query/S?ammem/naw-bib:@field(TITLE+@od1(+And+the+truth+shall+make+you+free+++)).

3. Meyer v. Nebraska, 262 U.S. 390 (1923).

4. Pierce v. Society of the Sisters of the Holy Names of Jesus and Mary, 268 U.S. 510 (1925).

5. Skinner v. Oklahoma, 316 U.S. 535 (1942).

6. Loving v. Virginia, 388 U.S. 1 (1967).

7. Zablocki v. Redhail, 434 U.S. 374 (1978).

8. David Crary, Men's Rights Group Eyes Child Support Stay, Mar. 8, 2006, http://www.sfgate.com/cgi-bin/article.cgi?file=/news/archive/2006/03/08/national/a131433S11.DTL.

9. Michael H. v. Gerald D., 491 U.S. 110 (1989).

10. http://www.cnn.com/2007/SHOWBIZ/05/01/smith.baby.ap/index.html.

11. Patricia J. Williams, The Alchemy of Race and Rights (1991).

12. Dorothy E. Roberts, The Genetic Tie, 62 U. Chi. L. Rev. 209, 252–60 (1995).

13. Hollenbaugh v. Carnegie Free Library, 439 U.S. 1052 (1978).

14. Einstadt v. Baird, 405 U.S. 438 (1972).

15. Carey v. Population Servs. Int'l, 431 U.S. 678 (1977).

16. Michael M. v. Superior Court of Sonoma, 450 U.S. 464 (1981).

17. Poe v. Ulman, 367 U.S. 497, 542–43 (1961) (Harlan, J., dissenting).

18. Bert H. Hoff, Reporting on Teachers Who Sexually Abuse Students, http://www.menweb.org/mcdermot.htm (describing excerpts of an article written by columnist Terry McDermott, LeTourneau and Blilie—Similar Cases but Different Outcomes, Seattle Times, Nov. 16, 1997, available at LEXIS, SEATTM).

19. Fisher: Ecstasy Made Me Shoot Mary Jo, Apr. 27, 2006, http://wcbs880.com/pages/29801.php?contentType=4&contentId=133681.

20. David J. Hughes, Guest Feature, Letter to the Editor, Seattle Times, February 1998 (permission to reprint granted from the author).

21. Letourneau Marries Former Student, May 21, 2005, http://www.cbsnews.com/stories/2005/05/21/national/main697018.shtml; Alex Tresniowski, One Year Later, People, May 5, 2006, at 90, available at LEXIS, PEOPLE.

22. Larry Elder, Exclusive Interview with Vili Fualaau at age 20, The Larry Elder Show (radio broadcast Sept., 15, 2004).

23. Michael H. v. Gerald D., 491 U.S. 110, 133 (1989) (Stevens, J., concurring).

24. Zablocki v. Redhail, 434 U.S. 374, 393 (1978) (Rehnquist, J., dissenting).

25. William Safire, A Polyandry Solution, N.Y. Times, May 21, 2001, at A17, available at LEXIS, NYT.

Chapter Six

1. Law Commission of Canada, Beyond Conjugality: Recognizing and Supporting Personal Adult Relationships (2001), *available at* http://www.lcc.gc.ca/en/themes/pr/cpra/report. asp.

2. Jone Johnson Lewis, *Women's History*, About.com, http://womenshistory.about.com (last visited Jan. 25, 2007).

3. *Free Love in New-York; Individual Sovereignty Realized; Secret Society of the League; Its Origin, History and Organization; Principles and Practice of the Free-Lovers*, N.Y. Daily Trib., Oct. 16, 1855, *available at* http://www.spirithistory.com/nyleague.html.

4. Alicia Potter, *Free Love Grows Up*, Boston Phoenix, Oct. 15–22, 1998, *available at* http://www.bostonphoenix.com/archive/features/98/10/15/POLYAMORISTS.html.

5. Kathy Labriola, *Models of Open Relationships*, http://www.cat-and-dragon.com/stef/Poly/Labriola/open.html (last visited Jan. 25, 2007).

6. Geri D. Weitzman, *What Psychology Professionals Should Know About Polyamory*, http://www.polyamory.org/~joe/polypaper.htm (last visited Jan. 31, 2007).

7. Troxel v. Granville, 530 U.S. 57 (2000).

8. Elise Soukhoup, *Polygamists, Unite!*, Newsweek, Mar. 20, 2006, *available at* http://www.msnbc.msn.com/id/11786790/site/newsweek/page/2/.

9. James Brooke, *Utah Struggles With a Revival of Polygamy*, N.Y. Times, Aug. 23, 1998, at 12, *available at* LEXIS, NYT.

10. http://www.hbo.com/biglove/about/index.html.

11. Jennifer O'Brien, *3-Parent Family Stirs Debate*, London Free Press, Jan. 4, 2007 http://lfpress.ca/newsstand/News/Local/2007/01/04/3155462-sun.html.

12. *Parents' Attitudes to Sperm Donation—Still Some Concerns About Being Open*, Med. News Today, Jan. 26, 2005, http://www.medicalnewstoday.com/medicalnews.php?newsid=19254.

Chapter Seven

1. Jill Elaine Hasday, *Contest and Consent: A Legal History of Marital Rape*, 88 Calif. L. Rev. 1373, 1375–1417 (2000).

2. Lisa Eskow, *The Ultimate Weapon: Demythologizing Spousal Rape and Reconceptualizing Its Prosecution*, 48 Stan. L. Rev. 677, 678–79, 682–83 (1996).

3. Reva Siegal, *Reasoning from the Body: A Historical Perspective on Abortion Regulation and Questions of Equal Protection*, 44 Stan. L. Rev. 261, 265–69 (1992).

4. Catherine A. MacKinnon, *Reflections on Sex Equality Under the Law*, 100 Yale L.J. 1281, 1304 (1991).

5. Allen v. Farrow, 197 A.D.2d 327 (1994).

6. Dave Goldiner, *Woody Shows off New Baby*, N.Y. Daily News, Apr. 25, 1999, *available at* LEXIS, DLYNWS.

7. Holly Robinson, *Naked Truth on Family Nudity*, Healthykids.com, Dec. 8, 2004, at http://www.healthykids.com/hk/story.jhtml?storyid=/templatedata/hk/story/data/AB122004NakedAroundKids_12082004.xml.

8. Bill Hewitt and Liz Mullen, A Father Fights Back: Gary Ramona Challenges his Daughter's "Recovered" Memories of Abuse, People, May 16, 1994, at 52, available at LEXIS, PEOPLE.

9. Allen Dyer, Keynote Address, Childhood Sexual Abuse and Memories: Current Controversies; Ethical Issues in the Current Debate About Recovered Memory Therapy (Mar. 31, 1995), *available at* http://faculty.etsu.edu/dyer/lectures/KC.TXT.doc.

10. Edward Greer, *Tales of Sexual Panic in the Legal Academy*, 95 Case W. Res. L. Rev. 513, 517–52 (1998).

11. Floyd Martinson, The Sexual Life of Children (1994) (citing David Finkelhor, *Psychological, Cultural and Family Factors in Incest and Family Sexual Abuse*, J. Marriage & Fam. Counseling, Oct. 1978, at 4.

12. *Id.*

13. *Id.*

14. *Id.*

15. Johnson v. Johnson, 701 F. Supp 1363 (1988).

16. Brian G. Slocum, *Virtual Child Pornography: Does It Mean the End of the Child Pornography Exception to the First Amendment?*, 14 Alb. L.J. Sci. & Tech. 637 (2004).

17. Chad R. Fears, *Shifting the Paradigm in Child Pornography Criminalization:* United States v. Maxwell, 1998 B.Y.U. L. Rev. 835, 874 n.7 1998 (2005).

18. Boy Scouts of Am. v. Dale, 530 U.S. 640 (2000).

19. http://www.cnn.com/2006/POLITICS/10/03/foley.scandal/index.html.

20. http://www.msnbc.msn.com/id/12503802/.

21. Bruce Rind, Philip Tromovitch & Robert Bauserman, *A Meta-Analytic Examination of Assumed Properties of Child Sexual Abuse (CSA) Using College Samples*, 124 Psychological Bull. 22–53 (1998).

22. Gene Mustain, *Man-Boy Love Lawyer Wanted in Girl Abuse*, Daily News, Sept. 21, 1995, at 34, *available at* LEXIS, DLYNWS.

23. Cheryl Wetzstein, *ACLU to Defend Boy-Sex Group; Lawsuit Stems from Homosexual Murder of 10-year-old*, Wash. Times, Sept. 1, 2000, at A3, *available at* LEXIS, WTIMES.

24. *Child Pornography on the Internet: Hearing on S. 892 Before the Senate Judiciary Committee*, 104th Cong. (1995) (statement of Barry F. Crimmins), *available at* http://www.cdt.org/speech/cda/950724crimmins.html.

25. Lee Hall, *Interwoven Threads: Some Thoughts on Professor MacKinnon's Essay* Of Mice and Men, 14 UCLA Women's L.J. 163 (2005) (book review).

26. Summer L. Nastich, *Questioning the Marriage Assumptions: The Justifications for "Opposite-Sex Only" Marriage as Support for the Abolition of Marriage*, 21 Law & Ineq. J. 114, 166 n. 171 (2003).

27. Emmet Meara, *Parkman Zoophile Objects to Bestiality Legislation*, Bangor Daily News, Mar. 27, 2001, at A1, *available at* http://www.gibe.com/forum/messages.asp?pref=&topicid=5477&forumid=13.

28. Excerpts from *Zoophilia as a Lifestyle*, *Zoophilia*, Wikipedia at http://en.wikipedia.org/wiki/Zoophilia#Zoophilia_as_a_lifestyle (last visited Jan. 25, 2007).

29. Leviticus 20:15–16 (New International Version).

30. William Saletan, *Shag the Dog*, Slate, Apr. 5, 2001, http://www.slate.com/id/103801.

31. *Barking Up the Wrong Tree? Convict Sues Dog*, MSNBC, Dec. 14, 2005, http://www.msnbc.msn.com/id/10466263/from/RSS/.

32. Harriet A. Jacobs, Incidents in the Life of a Slave Girl 27–36 (L. Maria Child & Jean Fagan Yellin eds., Harvard Univ. Press 1987) (1861).

33. 60 U.S. 393 (1856).

Chapter Eight

1. Kathleen R. Sandy, COMMENTARY: *The Discrimination Inherent in America's Drug War: Hidden Racism Revealed by Examining the Hysteria over Crack*, 54 Ala. L. Rev. 665, 674 (2003).

2. Robin M. Fields, Note: In Search of Democracy: Reconciling Majority Rule, Minority Rights, and Group Rights in South Africa And The United States, 16 B.C. Third World L.J. 65 (1996).

3. Molefi Kete Asante, African American History: A Journey of Liberation 152 (2d ed. 2001).

4. Frederick Douglass, Narrative of the Life of Frederick Douglass, An American Slave (Signet Classic 1997) (1845).

5. Michael Kent Curtis, *Teaching Free Speech from an Incomplete Fossil Record*, 34 Akron L. Rev. 231, 247 (2000).

6. Richard Albert, *Beyond the Conventional Establishment Clause Narrative*, 28 Seattle Univ. L. R. 329 (2005).

7. Jeffrey B. Perry, *In Memoriam: Theodore W. Allen*, at http://clogic.eserver.org/2005/perry.html (last visited Jan. 25, 2007).

8. A. Leon Higginbotham, Jr., Shades of Freedom: Racial Politics and Presumptions of the American Legal Process 7 (1996).

9. *The Story*, Trail of Tears Association, http://www.nationaltota.org/the-story (last visited Jan. 25, 2007).

10. Abraham Lincoln, "House Divided" Speech at Springfield, Illinois, June 16, 1858, *in* 1 ABRAHAM LINCOLN, SPEECHES AND WRITINGS 1832–1858, at 426 (Don E. Fehrenbacher, ed., Library of America ed. 1989).

11. Cheryl I. Harris, *Finding Sojourner's Truth: Race, Gender, and the Institution of Property*, 18 CARDOZO L. REV. 309 (1996).

12. Abel A. Bartley, *The Fourteenth Amendment: The Great Equalizer of the American People*, 36 AKRON L. REV. 473, 479–80 (2003).

13. Carl Schurz, *Can the South Solve the Negro Problem?* (1903), *in* FROM SLAVERY TO FREEDOM: THE AFRICAN-AMERICAN PAMPHLET COLLECTION, 1824–1909, *available at* http://www.loc.gov/index.html.

14. *Thaddeus Stevens: Champion of Freedom*, Pennsylvania Historical Museum Commission, http://www.phmc.state.pa.us/ppet/stevens/page5.asp?secid=31, at 5 (last visited Jan. 25, 2007).

15. William Lloyd Garrison, quoted in C. Vann Woodward, *The Political Legacy of Reconstruction*, 26 J. NEGRO EDUC. 231–40 (1957).

16. John J. Gibbons, 62 N.Y.U. L. REV. 1379 (1987) (reviewing ROBERT J. KACZOROWSKI, THE POLITICS OF JUDICIAL INTERPRETATION: THE FEDERAL COURTS, DEPARTMENT OF JUSTICE AND CIVIL RIGHTS, 1866–1876 (1985)).

17. Lori A. Tribbett-Williams, *Saying Nothing, Talking Loud: Lil' Kim and Foxy Brown, Caricatures of African-American Womanhood*, 10 S. CAL. REV. L. & WOMEN'S STUD. 167 (2000).

18. Christopher A. Bracey, *Louis Brandeis and the Race Question*, 52 ALA. L. REV. 859, 875 (2001).

19. LERONE BENNETT, JR., BEFORE THE MAYFLOWER: A HISTORY OF THE NEGRO IN AMERICA, 1619–1964 (1982).

20. Civil Rights Cases, 109 U.S. 3 (1883) (Harlan, J., dissenting).

21. *Id.* at 53.

22. JAMES M. GREGORY, FREDERICK DOUGLASS, THE ORATOR (1893).

23. SHERRILYN A. IFILL, ON THE COURTHOUSE LAWN: CONFRONTING THE LEGACY OF LYNCHING IN THE TWENTY-FIRST CENTURY (2007).

24. Lisa Cardyn, *Sexualized Racism/Gendered Violence: Outraging the Body Politic in the Reconstruction South*, 100 MICH. L. REV. 675 (2002).

25. J. Ogletree, Jr., *Tulsa Reparations: The Survivors' Story*, 24 B.C. THIRD WORLD L.J. 13, 17–22 (2004).

26. Jeanne Bassett, *House Bill 591: Florida Compensates Rosewood Victims and their Families for a Seventy-one-year-old Injury*, 22 FLA. ST. U.L. REV. 503, 506–08 (1994).

27. Lori Rozsa, *Massacre in a Small Town in 1923*, ATLANTA J. & CONST., Jan. 17, 1993, at M1, *available at* LEXIS, ATLJNL.

28. Taunya Lovell Banks, *Exploring White Resistance to Racial Reconciliation in the United States*, 55 RUTGERS L. REV. 903 (2003).

29. Jon Hanson & Kathleen Hanson,*The Blame Frame: Justifying (Racial) Injustice in America*, 41 Harv. C.R.-C.L. L. REV. 413 n.117 and accompanying text (2006).

30. Emma Coleman Jordan, *A History Lesson: Reparations for What*, 58 N.Y.U. ANN. SURV. AM. L. 557, 564 (2003).

31. *Id.*

32. Ronald Walters, *"The Association Is for the Direct Attack": The Militant Context of the NAACP Challenge to Plessy*, 43 WASHBURN L.J. 329, 345–46 (2004).

33. David L. Rose , *Twenty-Five Years Later: Where Do We Stand on Equal Employment Opportunity Law Enforcement?*, 42 VAND. L. REV. 1121, 1124–25 (1989).

34. A. Leon Higginbotham, Jr., *De Jure Housing Segregation in the United States and South Africa: The Difficult Pursuit For Racial Justice*, 1990 U. ILL. L. REV. 763 (1990).

35. Robin D. Barnes, *The Reality and Ideology of First Amendment Jurisprudence:Giving Aid and Comfort to Racial Terrorists*, *in* Freeing the First Amendment: Critical Perspectives on Freedom of Expression (Robert Jensen & David Allen, eds., 1995).

36. Constance Baker Motley, *The Historical Setting of* Brown *and Its Impact on the Supreme Court's Decision*, 61 Fordham L. Rev. 9 (1992).

37. Robin D. Barnes, *Blue By Day and White By [K]night: Regulating the Political Affiliations of Law Enforcement and Military Personnel*, 81 Iowa L. Rev. 1079, 1089–91 (1996).

38. Martin Luther King, Jr., "Our Struggle" (speech in New York, N.Y. Apr. 1956) *in* 3 The Papers of Martin Luther King, Jr. 236 (1997).

39. A. Leon Higginbotham, Jr., Shades of Freedom: Racial Politics and Presumptions of the American Legal Process 13–14 (1996).

40. Derrick Bell, Faces at the Bottom of The Well: The Permanence of Racism 1 (1992).

41. Ralph Ellison, *What America Would Be Like Without Blacks*, *in* The Collected Essays of Ralph Ellison 582–83 (John F. Callahan ed., 1995).

42. A. Leon Higginbotham, Jr., Shades of Freedom: Racial Politics and Presumptions of the American Legal Process 14 (1996).

43. *Id.* at 132–34.

44. Jeffrey Perry, *In Memoriam: Theodore W. Allen*, at http://clogic.eserver.org/2005/perry.html (last visited Jan. 25, 2007).

45. Doe v. Kamehameha Schools, 441 F.3d 1029 (9th Cir. 2006).

46. Martha A. Mahoney, *Segregation, Whiteness, and Transformation*, 143 U. PA. L. Rev. 1659, 1669–75 (1995).

47. John O. Calmore, *Random Notes of an Integration Warrior*, 81 Minn. L. Rev. 1441, 1445–46, 1450–52 (1997).

48. Richard Delgado and Jean Stefancic, Critical Race Theory and White Privilege: Legal Constructs and Pedagogical Possibilities, Keynote Address at the Critical Connections Conference, Institute of Race and Ethnicity, University of Wisconsin, Madison (Apr. 19, 2002), *available at* http://www.uwm.edu/Dept/IRE/Events/Conferences/CriticalConnections/index.html.

49. Derrick Bell, Bakke, *Minority Admissions, and the Usual Price of Racial Remedies*, 67 Calif. L. Rev. 1 (1979).

50. Charles Lawrence, *The Id, the Ego, and Equal Protection: Reckoning With Unconscious Racism,* 39 Stan. L. Rev. 317, 318–23, 328–44, 369–75 (1987).

51. James Forman, *Driving Dixie Down: Removing the Confederate Flag from Southern State Capitols*, 101 Yale L.J. 505, 505–08 (1991). Reprinted by permission of The Yale Law Journal Company and William S. Hein Company from The Yale Law Journal, Vol. 101, pages 505–526.

52. I. Bennett Capers, *Flags*, 48 How. L.J. 121 (2004).

53. A. Leon Higginbotham, Jr., Shades of Freedom: Racial Politics and Presumptions of the American Legal Process 17 (1996).

54. *Id.*

55. *Id.*

56. *Id.*

57. *Id.* at 129.

58. *Id.* at 129–130.

Chapter Nine

1. Jennifer L. Nye, *The Gender Box*, 13 Berkeley Women's L.J. 226 (1998).

2. Louise M. Antony, *Back to Androgeny: What Bathrooms Can Teach Us About Equality*, 9 J. Contemp. Legal Issues 1 (1998).

3. Stanley Kurtz, *Beyond Gay Marriage*, Wkly. Standard, Aug. 4 / Aug. 11, 2003.

4. *Id.*

5. Dean Hamer & Peter Copeland, The Science of Desire: The Search for the Gay Gene and the Biology of Behavior (1995) (discussing studies suggesting genetic bases for sexual orientation).

6. Katrina C. Rose, *A History of Gender Variance in Pre-20th Century Anglo-American Law*, 14 Tex. J. Women & L. 77 (2004).

7. Andrea De Gorgey, *The Advent of DNA Databanks: Implications for Information Privacy*, 16 Am. J. L. & Med. 381, 383 (1990).

8. Kenji Yoshino, *The Epistemic Contract of Bisexual Erasure*, 52 Stan. L. Rev. 353 (2000).

9. Susan Etta Keller, *Operations of Legal Rhetoric: Examining Transsexual and Judicial Identity*, 34 Harv. C.R.-C. L. L. Rev. 329–31 (1999).

10. 41 Ariz. L. Rev. 265 (1999).

11. Rowland v. Mad River Local Sch. Dist., 470 U.S. 1009 (1985).

12. Romer v. Evans, 517 U.S. 620 (1996).

13. Bowers v. Hardwick, 478 U.S. 186 (1986).

14. Robert L. Jacobson, *Meagan's Laws: Reinforcing Old Patters of Anti-Gay Police Harassment*, 87 Geo L.J. 2431, 2431–32, 2445–49 (1999).

15. http://www.cnn.com/2007/TECH/internet/05/14/myspace.sex.offenders.ap/.

16. Boy Scouts of Am. v. Dale, 530 U.S. 640 (2000).

17. Lawrence v. Texas, 539 U.S. 558 (2003).

18. Baehr v. Lewin, 74 Haw. 530 (1993).

19. Defense of Marriage Act, Pub. L. No. 104–199, 110 Stat. 2419 (1996) (codified at 1 U.S.C. 7 and 28 U.S.C. 1738C (2000)).

20. 798 N.E.2d 941 (Mass. 2003).

21. Joan Schaffner, *The Federal Marriage Amendment: to Protect the Sanctity of Marriage or Destroy Constitutional Democracy?*, 54 Am. U. L. Rev. 1487, 1528–34 (2005).

22. Robert P. George, *What's Sex Got to Do with it? Marriage, Morality, and Rationality*, 49 Am. J. Juris. 63 (2004).

23. *Id.*

Chapter Ten

1. Catherine A. MacKinnon, *Reflections on Sex Equality Under the Law*, 100 Yale L.J. 1281, 1281–84 (1991).

2. Bradwell v. Illinois, 83 U.S. 130 (1872).

3. Minor v. Happersett, 88 U.S. 162 (1874).

4. Muller v. Oregon, 208 U.S. 412 (1908).

5. Frontiero v. Richardson, 411 U.S. 677 (1973).

6. Rostker v. Goldberg, 453 U.S. 57 (1981).

7. United States v. Virginia, 518 U.S. 515 (1996).

8. Vicki Schultz, Reconceptualizing Sexual Harassment, 107 Yale L.J. 1683, 1762-64, 1998.

9. Marcella Bombardieri, *Summers' Remarks on Women Draw Fire*, Boston Globe, Jan. 17, 2005, http://www.boston.com/news/education/higher/articles/2005/01/17/summers_remarks_on_women_draw_fire/.

10. Shankar Vedantam,*Male Scientist Writes of Life as Female Scientist; Biologist Who Underwent Sex Change Describes Biases Against Women*, Wash. Post, July 13, 2006, at A10, *available at* LEXIS, WPOST.

11. *Id.* (referring to Ben A. Barres, *Does Gender Matter?*, 442 NATURE 133 (2006)).

12. Cornelia Dean, *Institutions Hinder Female Academics, Panel Says*, N.Y. TIMES, Sept. 18, 2006, http://www.nytimes.com/2006/09/18/science/19womencnd.html?ex=1316232000&en=4410c9fff5ea2f61&ei=5088&partner=rssnyt&emc=rss.

13. *Id.*

14. *Id.*

15. *U.S. Visa Policy: Competition for International Scholars, Scientists and Skilled Workers: Hearing Before the Subcomm. On Immigration, Border Security and Citizenship of the S. Comm. on the Judiciary*, 109th Cong. (2006) (Statement of Mr. Bo Cooper, Former General Counsel, Immigration and Naturalization Service) *available at* http://judiciary.senate.gov/testimony.cfm?id=1801&wit_id= 5707.

16. WOMEN'S COMMITTEE OF THE AMERICAN STUDIES ASSOCIATION, PERSONAL LIVES AND PROFESSIONAL CAREERS: THE UNEASY BALANCE (2002), *available at* http://www.georgetown.edu/crossroads/AmericanStudiesAssn/newsletter/archive/newsarchive/womcmterep.htm.

17. *Id.*

18. Timothy L. O'Brien, *Why Do So Few Women Reach the Top of Big Law Firms?*, N.Y. Times, Mar. 19, 2006, *available at* LEXIS, NYT. ©2006 by the New York times Co. Reprinted with permission.

19. Cornelia Dean, *Institutions Hinder Female Academics, Panel Says*, N.Y. TIMES, Sept. 18, 2006, http://www.nytimes.com/2006/09/18/science/19womencnd.html?ex=1316232000&en=4410c9fff5ea2f61&ei=5088&partner=rssnyt&emc=rss.

20. Kathryn Abrams, *Cross-Dressing in the Master's Clothes*, 109 YALE L.J. 745, 746, 748–55, 760–62 (2000). Reprinted by permission of The Yale Law Journal Company and William S. Hein Company from The Yale Law Journal, Vol. 109, pages 745–782.

21. Kathryn Abrams, From Automony to Agency: Feminist Perspectives on Self-Direction, 40 Wm and Mary L. Rev. 805, 825-26, 1999.

Chapter Eleven

1. 147 CONG. REC. S11019 (2001) (statement of Sen. Feingold), *available at* http://www.epic.org/privacy/terrorism/usaPATRIOT/feingold.html.

2. Electronic Privacy Information Center, Report, *The USA PATRIOT Act*, http://www.epic.org/privacy/terrorism/usaPATRIOT/default.html (last visited Jan. 28, 2007).

3. *USA PATRIOT Act—The Good, the Bad, and the Sunset*, by John Podesta, published in Human Rights, Volume 29, No. 1, Winter 2002. ©2002 by the American Bar Association. Reprinted with permission.

4. Bill of Rights Defense Committee website, http://www.bordc.org/list.php?sortAlpha=1 (last visited Jan. 26, 2006).

5. AMITAI ETZIONI, HOW PATRIOTIC IS THE PATRIOT ACT? 3 (2004).

6. *Id.* 10–11.

7. KRISTINA BORJESSON, INTO THE BUZZSAW: LEADING JOURNALISTS EXPOSE THE MYTH OF A FREE PRESS 328 (2004).

8. AMITAI ETZIONI, HOW PATRIOTIC IS THE PATRIOT ACT? 12–14 (2004).

9. Patrick M. Cronin, *Stop the Bleeding of American Legitimacy*, June 21, 2006, CARNEGIE ETHICS ONLINE, http://www.cceia.org/resources/ethics_online/5381.html.

10. *Id.*

11. *Detained at Guantanamo; Military Tribunals: The Fairness Test*, CBC NEWS ONLINE, July 11, 2006, http://www.cbc.ca/news/background/guantanamo/military_tribunals.html.

12. AMITAI ETZIONI, HOW PATRIOTIC IS THE PATRIOT ACT? 79–80 (2004).

13. Martin Garbus, *How Close Are We to the End of Democracy?*, HUFFINGTON POST, May 9, 2005, http://www.huffingtonpost.com/martin-garbus/how-close-are-we-to-the-e_b_14171.html.

14. Clare M. Sproule, *The Effect of the USA PATRIOT Act on Workplace Privacy Law*, 43 Cornell Hotel & Rest. Admin. Q. 65–73 (2002). Cornell Hotel and Restaurant Administration Quarterly (Journal Volume Number and Issue Number) pp. 65–73, copyright 20xx by (Copyright Holder), Reprinted by Permission of (Publisher—either Sage Publications, Corwin Press or Pine Force) Inc.

15. Prepared Remarks of Jim Harper, Editor of Privacilla.org, to the Bank Secrecy Act Advisory Group, U.S. Dept. of the Treasury (Oct. 22, 2003), *available at* http://www.privacilla.org/releases/BSAAG_remarks_10-22-03.html.

16. Jennifer Loven, *Report of NSA Spying Prompts Call for Probe*, SFGate.com, Dec. 16, 2005, http://www.sfgate.com/cgi-bin/article.cgi?f=/n/a/2005/12/16/national/w090413S17.DTL.

17. *Majority of Americans Say President Should Not Suspend Constitutional Freedoms Without Court Order or Congressional Authorization, ABA Public Opinion Poll*, ABANews.org, Feb. 10, 2006, http://www.abanet.org/media/releases/news021006.html.

18. Dan Eggen & Dafna Linzer, *Judge Rules Against Wiretaps, NSA Program Called Unconstitutional*, Wash. Post, Aug. 18, 2006, at A01, *available at* http://www.washingtonpost.com/wp-dyn/content/article/2006/08/17/AR2006081700650.html.

19. Ellen Nakashima & Alec Klein, *Daylight Sought For Data Mining, Senators Want Federal Use Disclosed*, Wash. Post, Jan. 11, 2007, at D03, *available at* LEXIS, WPOST.

20. *See* Audrey Hudson, *U.S. Agencies Collect, Examine Personal Data on Americans*, http://www.pushhamburger.com/collecting.htm (last visited Jan. 28, 2006). For the full GAO report, see U.S. Gen. Accounting Office, Data Mining: Government Efforts Cover a Wide Range of Uses (2004), *available at* www.gao.gov/new.items/d04548.pdf.

21. Richard Rorty, *The West is Restricting Freedom in Response to Terror*, TheAge.com.au, Apr. 24, 2006, http://www.theage.com.au/articles/2004/04/26/1082831494716.html.

22. Congresswoman Lynn Woolsey website, *Iraq One Year Later; Terror is Up, Security Down*, Mar. 18, 2004, http://woolsey.house.gov/SMARTheadlines.asp?ARTICLE4898=4906.

Chapter Twelve

1. *The Shameful Role of Lawyers in the Church Sex Abuse Scandal*, Mar. 13, 2004, http://www.mirrorofjustice.com/mirrorofjustice/2004/03/the_shameful_ro.html.

2. Rex R. Perschbacher, *A Changing Role for Lawyers in a Post-Enron World?*, 3 U.C. Davis Bus. L.J. 2 (2002).

3. Mark C. Miller, The High Priests of American Politics: The Role of Lawyers in American Political Institutions (1995). Reprinted with permission from *The Washington Monthly*. Copyright by Washington Monthly Publishing, LLC, 1319 F St. NW, Suite 710, Washington, DC, 2004. (202) 393-5155. Web site: www.washingtonmonthly.com.

4. Robert F. Nagel, Wash. Monthly, 1996, http://www.findarticles.com/p/articles/mi_m1316/is_n5_v28/ai_18285122.

5. Michael Isikoff and Mark Hosenball, *A Legal Counterattack: Saudis hire some of the toniest U.S. law firms to defend them against the landmark $1 trillion lawsuit on behalf of the victims of 9-11*, Newsweek, Apr. 16, 2003, http://www.msnbc.msn.com/id/3067906/.

6. Charlie Savage, *Bush Consults Lawyer on Investigation into CIA Leak*, Boston Globe, June 3, 2004, at A1, *available at* http://www.commondreams.org/headlines04/0603-10.htm.

7. Bill Mears, *Supreme Court Weighs Ten Commandments Cases*, CNN, Mar. 7, 2005, http://www.cnn.com/2005/LAW/03/02/scotus.ten.commandments/index.html.

8. Jess Bravin, *Bush Lawyers Target Gun Control's Legal Rationale*, Wall St. J., Jan. 7, 2005, at A4, *available at* http://users2.wsj.com/lmda/do/checkLogin?mg=wsj-users2&url=http%3A%2F%2Fonline.wsj.com%2Farticle%2FSB110505856950619585.html.

9. DeWayne Wickham, *Coretta Scott King, Bush Forever Linked by Symbolism*, USAToday.com, Feb. 6, 2006, http://www.usatoday.com/news/opinion/columnist/wickham/2006-02-06-king-bush_ x.htm.

10. Dan Eggen, *Bush Lawyers Drafted Bill in 2003 on Surveillance; Plan Would Have Given Legal Backing to Spying*, S.F. Chron., Jan. 28, 2006, at A4, http://www.sfgate.com/cgi-bin/article.cgi?file=/c/a/2006/01/28/MNGAIGV0U51.DTL.

11. *Bush Administration Lawyers Want to Sue Business for Hiring Illegal Workers*, Foxnews.com, Apr. 26, 2006, http://www.foxnews.com/story/0,2933,193243,00.html.

12. Ray Suarez, *Vaccine Ruling*, PBS.org, Dec. 23, 2003, http://www.pbs.org/newshour/bb/military/july-dec03/anthrax_12–23.html.

13. Mike Allen & Juliet Eilperin, *Bush Aides Say Iraq War Needs No Hill Vote; Some See Such Support as Politically Helpful*, Wash. Post, Aug. 26, 2002, at A01, *available at* LEXIS, WPOST.

14. Jess Bravin, *Pentagon Report Set Framework for Use of Torture; Security or Legal Factors Could Trump Restrictions, Memo to Rumsfeld Argued*, Wall St. J., June 7, 2004, at A1, *available at* LEXIS, WSJNL.

15. Ari Shapiro, *Career Lawyers Leaving Justice Department*, NPR.org, Oct. 6, 2005, http://www.npr.org/templates/story/story.php?storyId=4946744.

16. Tom Brune, *Justice Dept.'s Diversity Issues: Records Show Percentages of Female, Black Attorneys Falling*, Newsday, Dec. 23, 2003, *available at* LEXIS, NEWSDY.

17. Charlie Savage, *Bush Challenges Hundreds of Laws*, Boston Globe, Apr. 30, 2006, at A1, *available at* http://www.boston.com/news/nation/articles/2006/04/30/bush_challenges_hundreds_of_laws/.

18. Julie Hirschfeld Davis, *Bracing for Congressional Probes, Bush Hires Lawyers; Democrats Have Vowed More Scrutiny*, Chi. Trib., Dec. 27, 2006, at C5, *available at* http://www.chicagotribune.com/news/nationworld/chi-0612270296dec27,1,4477082.story?coll=chi-newsnationworld-hed.

19. *Law Day 2006: Legal Panelists Debate Balance Of Power*, Libr. of Congress Info. Bull., June 2006, *available at* http://www.loc.gov/loc/lcib/0606/lawday.html.

20. http://www.theittlist.com/.

21. *Pentagon Won't Back Official Who Blasted Gitmo Lawyers*, Jan. 13, 2007, CNN.com, http://www.cnn.com/2007/POLITICS/01/13/pentagon.detainees.ap/index.html?eref=rss_latest.

22. Geoffrey Robertson, *In Thrall to the Bush Lawyers*, TheAge.com.au, Aug. 17, 2006, http://www.theage.com.au/news/opinion/in-thrall-to-the-bush-lawyers/2006/08/16/1155407878903.html.

23. G. John Ikenberry, *Illusions of Empire: Defining the New American Order*, Foreign Aff., Mar./Apr. 2004, *available at* http://www.foreignaffairs.org/20040301fareviewessay83212a/g-john-ikenberry/illusions-of-empire-defining-the-new-american-order.html. Reprinted by permission of FOREIGN AFFAIRS. Copyright 2004 by the Council on Foreign Relations, Inc.

24. *UN: Assessing A Secretary-General's Impact*, Radio Free Eur./Radio Liberty, Dec. 19, 2006, http://www.rferl.org/featuresarticle/2006/12/3f478154-fb0b-41cd-936a-efe8e1acbd78.html.

25. Eighth United Nations Congress on the Prevention of Crime and the Treatment of Offenders, Aug. 27–Sept. 7, 1990, *Basic Principles on the Role of Lawyers*, U.N. Doc. A/CONF.144/28/Rev.1 (1990), at 118.

26. *See* Human Rights Watch, Women's Rights, http://hrw.org/women/ (last visited Jan. 28, 2007).

27. *See* City of Berkeley, California website, http://www.ci.berkeley.ca.us/bmc/Berkeley_Municipal_Code/title_3/68/030.html (last visited Jan. 28, 2006) (defining "peace and justice").

28. Charles F. Abernathy, Civil Rights & Constitutional Litigation, Cases & Materials (2000).

29. Stephanie M. Wildman, Connection to Purpose, AALS Annual Meeting Workshop: A Search for Balance in the Whirlwind of Law School (Jan. 5, 2006), *available at* http://aals.org.cnchost.com/am2006/program/balance/Wildmanoutline.pdf.

30. Stephanie Wildman, *Democracy and Social Justice: Founding Centers for Social Justice in Law Schools*, 55 J. Legal Educ. 252 (2005).

31. Verna C. Sanchez, *Law and the Possibility of Justice*, W. New Eng. L. Rev. 183, 183–84, 188–91 (1997).

Conclusion

1. *Id.* at 191.
2. Pierre Schlag, Enchantment of Reason 126 (1998).

Index

Abernathy, Charles, 370, 388
Abolition, 73–74, 80, 237, 243, 382
Abolitionist Society, 210
Abortion, 20, 60, 87–93, 118, 122, 256, 275, 379, 381
Abrams, Kathryn, 317, 386
Adams, John, 28, 377
Adams, Samuel, 9
Affirmative Action, 221–222, 225, 355
Allen, Theodore W., 204, 382, 384
Allen, Woody, 173, 178
Alito Jr., J. Samuel A., 68
Alternative Families, 95
American Bar Association's Commission on Professionalism, 28
American Fertility Society, 53
American Psychological Association, 188
American Revolution, 7, 9, 208
Americans With Disabilities Act, 65–66
Animal Abuse, 193, 197
Animal Rights, 192, 195–197
Anthony, Susan B., 12
Anti-miscegenation, 102, 219, 289, 291
Anti-Terrorism Act of 2001, 326
Anti-terrorism bills, 325
Apartheid, 206, 217–218
Ashcroft, John, 68, 326, 342, 356
Assisted Suicide, 55, 59–61, 66–69, 75, 378
Association of American Law Schools, 28, 30, 377
Autonomy, 5, 43–72, 91, 93, 150–151, 161, 170, 172, 244, 250, 273, 279, 287

Bacon's Rebellion, 204–205
Bank Secrecy Act, 327, 337, 387
Barr, Robert, 337
Barres, Ben, 313, 386
Bauserman, Robert, 188, 382
Bestiality, 196
Becker, Carl, 10
Bell, Derrick, 217, 227, 384
Benac, Nancy, 32, 377
Bennet, Lerone, 212
Berkeley, 317, 369–370, 384, 388
Big Love, HBO Series, 155-56
Bill of Rights, 20, 43, 71, 89, 107, 256, 323, 328, 337, 339, 386
Bi-racial Commission on Civil Rights, 215
Bisexuality, 144, 194, 244, 248–251, 284–285
Black Codes, 209, 213
Black Panther Party for Self Defense, 17
Black Wall Street, 213
Breyer, Stephen, 3, 23, 69, 375–376
Buren, Martin Van, 208
Bush, George, Gov., 77
Buttafuoco, Joseph, 124

Calmore, John, 225, 384
Canons of Judicial Conduct, 30, 377
Carnivore, 326, 332, 335
Capital Punishment, 61, 73, 75–76, 79–80, 93, 127, 363, 373
Cardozo, Benjamin, 375
Catholic Priests, 350
Chandler, David, 82, 379
Chief Justice, U.S. Supreme Court, 198
Child Pornography, 185–186, 190–191, 262, 381–382
Child Sexual Abuse, 123, 134, 173–174, 178, 183, 185–186, 188–189, 382
Child Support, 87, 105–107, 135, 139, 380
Civil Liberties, 6, 30, 97, 191, 276–277, 325–347, 349

Civil Rights, 5–6, 15, 36, 79, 101, 105, 205, 209, 211–213, 215–216, 218–220, 227, 283, 305, 329, 345, 349, 356, 363–364, 370, 373, 383, 388
Civil Rights Act of 1866, 209, 213
Civil Rights Act of 1875, 212, 215
Civil Rights Act of 1964, 212, 305
Civil War, 44, 169, 205, 209–211, 330
Clemens, Samuel, 209
Cleveland, Ohio, 137
Community Rights Counsel, 31, 40
Compromise of 1877, 210
Compulsory Education Act 1922, 98–99
Confederate Flag, 239–240, 384
Conjugal Rights, 161–162, 168–169
Connery, Donald S., 76, 378–379
Conscientious Objection, 82, 86
Consent, 8, 11, 40, 43–44, 48–50, 56, 67, 70, 88, 120, 125–126, 128, 134–136, 161–162, 165–167, 172–173, 178, 186, 193, 198, 260, 276–277, 281–282, 293, 295, 326, 334, 337, 354, 381
Continental Congress, 7, 9, 375
Contraception, 43, 67, 88, 90–91, 118–120, 126, 196, 256, 274, 279
Corporate Investigations, 356
Critias, 26
Custody, 98, 106, 109–111, 115, 123, 132–133, 138, 152–154, 173–174, 176–178, 273, 317, 368

Data Mining, 70, 336–339, 341, 387
Davis, James F, 225
Dean, Cornelia, 313, 386
Death Row Syndrome, 75
Declaration of Independence, 7–8, 10–11, 15, 170, 203, 206, 354, 376
Declaration of the Causes and Necessity of Taking Up Arms, 7
Delgado, Richard, 226, 384
Democracy, 5, 17, 21, 24, 26, 33, 35, 37, 41, 137, 203, 243, 309, 328–330, 341–342, 344, 347, 349, 354, 362, 369–370, 374, 382, 385–386, 388
Department of Health and Human Services, 47
Desegregation, 216
Dialectical Method, 26–27
Dignity Denied, 78, 379
Discrimination, 15, 20, 78, 95, 101, 104–105, 117, 170, 213, 215, 219, 223, 226–231, 237, 240, 249–253, 264–265, 268, 270, 272, 279, 283, 289, 304–305, 308, 311–313, 315, 317, 320, 364–365, 368, 370, 373, 382
Disparate Impact, 236, 240, 373
Divilbiss, April, 152
DNA, 76–77, 115, 243–292, 385
Domestic Surveillance, 335, 340–341
Domesticity, 317–320
Douglas, 17, 40, 74, 100, 377
DuBois, W.E.B., 206
Due Process, 5, 38, 43, 56–57, 60, 65, 87–89, 100, 102–103, 105–108, 110–113, 115, 123, 135, 137, 203, 209, 236, 244, 249, 254–257, 260, 274–275, 278–281, 283, 288, 291, 297, 300–301, 304, 329, 339, 373
Dyer, Allen, 180, 381

Eighth Amendment, 73, 75, 79, 98, 257–258
Elder, Larry, 128, 380
Electronic Communications Privacy Act, 327–328, 333
Electronic Privacy Information Center, 325
Electronic Monitoring, 22, 329, 331–334, 336
Ellison, Ralph, 217, 384
Emancipation Proclamation, 15, 209
Emens, Elizabeth, 152
Emergency Contraception, 88
Enfranchisement, 13, 210
Enron, 349, 351–353
Equal Justice Society, 219
Equal Pay Act, 305, 320
Equal protection, 5, 38, 43–44, 55, 60, 65–66, 70, 74, 86, 90, 93, 101–107, 110, 112, 117–121, 123, 135, 152, 161, 196, 203, 206, 209, 218–219, 227–231, 236, 239–241, 244, 248–254, 258, 260, 274, 279, 283–284, 291, 297, 301, 304, 307–311, 373, 379, 381, 384
Equal Protection Clause, 60, 66, 74, 101, 104–105, 117, 119–121, 206, 229–230, 236, 239–240, 249, 252–254, 258, 260, 274, 279, 291, 304, 308, 310–311

Eskow, Lisa, 171, 381
Etzioni, Amitai, 328, 386
Exoneration, 76
Expressive Association, 264–267, 272

Family Nudity, 160, 173, 179–180, 381
Fair Housing, 17, 225
Federal Assisted Suicide Funding Restriction Act of 1997, 60
Federal Judicial Center, 32, 36
Federal Wiretap Act, 335
Federalist Society, 32
Feingold, Russ, 326–327
Fentiman, Linda, 46, 378
Forman, James, 238, 384
Fifteenth amendment, 210, 300
Fifth Amendment, 44, 89, 236, 281, 304, 306–307, 339
First Amendment, 44, 65, 67, 89, 119, 186, 191, 239, 248–251, 253, 264–267, 272, 297, 323, 326, 329, 338–339, 381, 384
Free Exercise Clause, 67
Religious Freedom Restoration Act, 67
Fisher, Amy, 124
Foley, Mark Congressman, 186
Foreign Intelligence Surveillance Act, 327–328, 335, 340
Forman, James, 238, 384
Foreign Intelligence Surveillance Act, 327–328, 335, 340
Fourteenth Amendment, 43–44, 57, 59, 65–67, 74, 88–89, 91, 97–98, 100–106, 113–114, 120–121, 135, 152, 171, 195, 203, 239–240, 248–249, 252–253, 255–256, 260, 274, 279–281, 286, 294, 296–298, 300–302, 308, 310–311, 373, 378, 383
Fourth Amendment, 44, 89, 137, 333, 339
Free Love Movement, 138-142
Freedman's Bureau, 209
Freire, Paulo, 17, 376
Friends Committee on National Legislation, 85–86, 379
Fualaau, Vili, 128, 380
Fugitive Slave Law of 1850, 208
Fundamental rights, 1, 3, 5, 28, 43–44, 46, 51, 80, 101, 105, 120–121, 213, 250, 252, 254–255, 275, 282–283, 287–288, 291, 295, 307, 329, 357, 359, 361, 363–365, 367

Gag rule, 204
Gametes, 51, 53
Garbus, Martin, 329, 386
Gay Rights, 156, 263, 267
Gender Discrimination, 252–253, 289, 312
Gender Roles, 163, 295, 303-06
George III, King, 9
George, Robert, 144, 385
Goldberg, Arthur J., 73-75
Goldiner, Dave, 381
Government Surveillance, 328–329, 331–337
Greenberg, Julie, 245
Greer, Edward, 181, 381
Grillo, Trina, 95
Group Sex, 90, 141
Guantanamo, 329, 360–361, 386

Harlan, John Justice, 212-14, 254
Harper, Jim, 336, 387
Hasday, Jill, 162, 381
Hellenic Concepts, 26
Hemmings, Sally, 8
Higginbotham, A. Leon, 216–217, 376, 382–384
Hilton, Paris, 22, 376
Homeland Security, 330, 338, 341, 359
Homophobia, 243–244
Homosexuality, 186, 194, 196, 244, 250–251, 253, 258, 264–272, 276, 283–285
Hughes, David, 127, 380
Human Rights, 8, 15, 29, 39, 53, 77, 80, 82, 100, 120, 136, 161, 163, 213, 221, 275, 278, 280, 329, 345–346, 349, 361, 363–369, 379, 386, 388
Human Rights Watch, 367–368, 388
Ikenberry, John, 361, 388

In-vitro fertilization, 157
Incest, 87, 155, 173, 177–178, 180, 182–185, 195, 256, 259–260, 262, 381
Individual Rights, 1, 5–6, 14, 17, 19, 22, 27, 34, 38, 43, 51, 54, 160, 192, 201,

203, 248, 280, 289–290, 328–329, 347, 363, 369
Inferiority, 198, 204, 206–207, 216–217, 236, 241, 272, 311, 319
Information Economy, 336
Informed Consent, 43, 56, 67
International Slave Trade, 6–7
Intersexuality, 244–245
Involuntary Servitude, 7, 209

Jacob Wetterling Crimes Against Children and Sexually Violent Offender Registration Act, 261
Jacobson, Robert L., 261, 385
Jefferson, Thomas, 7–8, 206, 375
Jim Crow, 209, 211, 220, 355
Johnson, Charles, 14
Judicial Independence, 20–22, 33, 35, 37–39
Judicial Junkets, 32
Justice, 3, 5–6, 9, 12, 16–17, 19, 23, 27–28, 30, 32–41, 43–44, 57, 61, 68–69, 73–79, 83–85, 89, 98, 100, 102, 106, 108, 111–113, 117, 119–120, 125, 127, 134–135, 152, 154, 161, 171, 185, 187, 192, 198, 203, 205–206, 208–209, 212–213, 218–220, 222, 247, 254–257, 260, 268–269, 273, 275, 277–278, 280–281, 294, 300, 306–307, 323, 326, 339, 343, 346, 349, 355–360, 363–367, 369–371, 373–375, 377–378, 383, 388

Kairys, David, 23, 377
Kanios, Gus, 19
Kendall, Douglas, 40, 377
Kaufman, Marc, 90, 379
Keller, Susan E., 244
Kennedy, Robert, 75, 240
Kerner Commission on Civil Disorders, 223
Kimmel, Michael, 320
Kindleberger, Charles, 41
King, Martin Luther, Jr., 15, 216, 355, 376, 384
Koh, Harold Hongju, 30, 377
Ku Klux Klan, 210–212, 237

Lane, Charles, 68, 378
Last Aid Kit, 74
Lawrence, Charles R., 227
Lazarus, Ed, 73
Leahy, Patrick, 326
Legal Theory, 23–24, 178, 192, 230–231, 349, 384
Letourneau, Mary Kay, 123, 125, 127–128, 161
Lewis, Jone J., 138
Lincoln, Abraham, 208–209, 354, 383
Lind, John, 9
Lovejoy, Elijah, 204
Loven, Jennifer, 387
Lucas, Stephen E., 8, 376
Lynching, 212–215, 383

MacKinnon, Catherine, 15, 91, 312, 379, 381, 385
Madison, James, 5
Marital Rape Exemptions, 135
Marriage, 14, 67, 91, 97, 101–102, 104–109, 112–113, 115–118, 135–136, 138–139, 141–145, 148–149, 152, 155–157, 162–164, 166–172, 175, 177, 180, 198, 243–244, 255–256, 259–260, 274–275, 279, 281–283, 286–293, 319, 368, 375, 381–382, 385
Marshall, Thurgood, 36, 206
Mathis, Karen, 356
Meara, Emmet, 192, 382
Megan's Law, 261
Memphis Free Speech Press, 214
Menand, Louis, 23, 376
Military Conscription, 80, 82, 85–86, 379
Military Selective Service Act, 306
Minstrel Shows, 209-211
Mikva, Abner, 31, 209, 211
Monogamy, 142, 145–148, 152, 156, 197
Morning After Pill, 92, 379
Multiple Parent Families, 152-57, 160
Murder Victim's Families for Reconciliation, 78
Mustain, Gene, 382

NAACP, 22, 216, 239
Nagel, Robert, 353, 387
NAMBLA, 186, 190–191
Nation of Islam, 84
National Association for the Advancement of Colored People, 216, 239
National Organ and Tissue Research and Transplantation Board, 50

National Security, 7, 27, 307, 325–347, 355
National Security Agency, 340–341, 355
Native Americans, 206–207, 216
Nazis, 215
Nineteenth Amendment, 5, 305
Ninth Amendment, 44, 88–89, 250, 255, 258
North American Man-Boy Love Association, 186, 190
Notice of Electronic Monitoring Act, 334

O'Brien, Timothy L., 315
O'Brien, Ed, 20, 376
O'Brien, Jennifer, 381
Oklahoma Habitual Criminal Sterilization Act, 100
Open Relationships, 148–149, 151, 194, 269, 381
Ordered Liberty, 43, 97, 137, 255
Oregon Death with Dignity Act, 68, 70
Organ Donation, 45–46, 48–50, 378
Organ Transplantation, 45–47, 49–50

Parentage, 53, 115
Parental Rights, 110–111, 115, 173
Partial Birth Abortion,87
Pedagogy, 376
Pedophilia, 186, 191, 195
Perry, Jeffrey, 204, 382, 384
Perschbacher, Rex, 351, 387
Persistent Vegetative State, 55, 58
Plan B, Emergency Contraception, 90-92
Plato, 26, 377–378
Podesta, John, 326, 386
Police Harassment, 262, 385
Polyamory, 141–148, 152, 243, 381
Polygamy, 142, 148, 154–156, 381
Potter, Alicia, 141, 380
Preamble of the Constitution, 206
Previn, Soon Yi, 173-78
Privacy, 20, 27, 34, 43–44, 88–89, 92, 97, 107, 111, 117–120, 137, 140–141, 150–151, 155, 157, 161, 171, 173, 183, 244, 250, 254–259, 274–275, 282, 309, 323, 325, 327–331, 333, 335–339, 341, 377, 385–387
Psychological Bulletin, 188

Racial Integrity Act of 1924, 104
Race, 7, 17, 19, 100–101, 103–105, 107, 115–116, 140, 199, 201, 204–206, 208–210, 212–213, 215, 217–222, 224–226, 228–238, 250, 283, 300, 303–306, 311, 363–365, 370, 376, 379–380, 383–384
Racism, 76, 203, 207, 219, 222–223, 228–236, 238, 241, 260, 312, 376, 379, 382–384
Rape, 74, 87, 121, 123, 125, 127–128, 134–135, 160–172, 182, 187, 189, 191, 195, 197–198, 211, 214–215, 257, 262, 277, 381
Reason, 7, 22, 25–27, 29, 41, 61, 63, 79, 83, 90, 99–100, 116, 127–128, 131, 149, 157, 159, 189, 197, 206–207, 220–221, 224, 228, 234, 236, 248, 255, 257, 264, 277, 280, 284, 286, 294–295, 303, 311, 313, 325, 339, 342–343, 366–367, 376–377, 389
Recovered Memories of Sexual Abuse, 180-183
Religious Freedom, 12, 15, 67
Reproductive Rights, 34, 73, 161
Resnik, Judith, 33, 40
Right to Die, 43–72, 75
Right to Marry, 6, 107, 135, 165, 282, 288–290
Right to Privacy, 88–89, 107, 117, 120, 137, 141, 250, 255, 257, 259, 274–275, 282, 327, 333
Right to Vote, 5–6, 44, 162, 205, 210, 212, 298, 300, 305
Rind, Bruce, 188, 382
Roberts, John G, 33, 68, 377
Robinson, Holly, 180, 381
Rorty, Richard, 341, 387
Rosewood Florida, 214, 383
Ross, Brian, 377
Ryan, George Gov., 77

Safire, William, 136, 380
Saletan, William, 196, 382
Same Sex Marriage, 281, 286, 288–289
Sanchez, Verna, 371, 373, 388
Sandy, Kathleen, 201
Scalia, J. Antonin, 32-33
Schiavo, Terri Schindler, 58-59, 68

Schlag, Pierre, 25, 27–28, 40, 208, 374, 377, 389
Schultz, Vicki, 312, 320, 385
Schurz, Carl, 210, 383
Semen, Rights In, 53
Seneca Falls Resolution 1848, 293
Sex Discrimination, 305, 311, 317, 364, 370
Sex Offender Registration, 135, 244, 261–262
Sexism, 312, 379
Sexual Harassment, 15, 182, 312, 385
Sexual Orientation, 145, 149, 196–197, 243–292, 385
Sexual Predators, 186–187
Sexuality, 128, 179, 182, 190, 194, 266, 276
Shalala, Donna, 313
Siegal, Reva, 92, 379, 381
Singer, Peter, 192, 196
Slavery, 6–8, 13, 17, 43, 103, 116, 138, 198–199, 201, 203–206, 208–213, 217, 219, 237, 241, 293, 355, 375, 383
SMART Security Resolution, 344
Social Freedom, 12–13, 15, 137, 203, 376, 380
Socrates, 26–27, 70–71, 377
Socratic Method, 26–27
Sodomy, 125, 155, 244, 254–258, 262, 275–279
Stanton, Elizabeth C., 12
Statutory Rape, 121, 123, 125, 134–135, 160–161, 187, 195, 262
Sterilization, 100–101
Stevens, Thaddeus, 210
Stone, I.F., 377
Suffrage, 163, 169–170, 210, 298, 300, 376
Sugar Act in 1764, 7
Suicide, 52, 55, 59–61, 65–72, 75, 153, 314, 329, 378
Sykes, Charles, 27, 377

Taney, Roger Brookes, 206
Terrorism, 34, 212, 216, 325–326, 335–336, 338, 341–342, 344–345, 359, 386
Third Amendment, 44
Thirteenth Amendment, 203, 209, 213, 375
Thompson Memorandum, 356
Trail of Tears, 207, 383
Transgender, 244–245
Transexual, 244
Trial of Socrates, 26
Tromovitch, Philip, 188
Truman, Harry, 215
Tulsa Bombing, 213-14

Unconscious Racism, 229–235, 384
Uniform Anatomical Gift Act(2006), 45
Unitary Family, 110–111, 115
United Nations, 79, 343, 363, 388
United Network for Organ Sharing, 47
Unwed fathers, 107, 114–116
USA PATRIOT Act, 325-28, 330-36

Vacco, Timothy Dr., 59
Vietnam War, 86

Weimar Hypothesis, 329
Weitzman, Geri D, 152, 381
Wildman, Stephanie, 95, 370, 388
Williams, Patricia J, 19, 115, 376, 380
Wilson, Woodrow, 211
Wiretapping, 327, 335
Wolfgang, Marvin, 74
Women in Combat, 307–308
Women's Reproductive choice, 162
Women's Rights, 12, 115, 162, 168–170, 368, 373, 388
Woodhull, Victoria C., 12, 376, 380
Woolsey, Lynn, 344, 387
World Trade Center, 330
World War II, 330

Zones of privacy, 43, 282
Zoophilia, 194–195, 382